murach's ADO.NET 4 database programming with VB 2010

Anne Boehm & Ged Mead

TRAINING & REFERENCE

murach's
ADO.NET 4
database programming with
VB 2010

Anne Boehm & Ged Mead

MIKE MURACH & ASSOCIATES, INC.
1-800-221-5528 • (559) 440-9071 • Fax: (559) 440-0963
murachbooks@murach.com • www.murach.com

Author: Ged Mead
Anne Boehm

Editor: Mike Murach

Cover Design: Zylka Design

Production: Tom Murach

Books for .NET developers

Murach's Visual Basic 2010
Murach's ADO.NET 4 Database Programming with VB 2010
Murach's ASP.NET 4 Web Programming with VB 2010
Murach's C# 2010
Murach's ADO.NET 4 Database Programming with C# 2010
Murach's ASP.NET 4 Web Programming with C# 2010
Murach's SQL Server for Developers
Murach's C++ 2008

Books for web developers

Murach's HTML, XHTML, and CSS
Murach's PHP and MySQL
Murach's JavaScript and DOM Scripting

Books for Java programmers

Murach's Java SE 6
Murach's Java Servlets and JSP (2nd Ed.)
Murach's Oracle SQL and PL/SQL

Please check www.murach.com for details on all our books

Printed in the United States of America

10 9 8 7 6 5 4 3 2 1
ISBN: 978-1-890774-62-2

Contents

Expanded contents

Section 2 How to use data sources and datasets for Rapid Application Development

Chapter 3 How to work with data sources and datasets

Chapter 4 How to work with bound controls and parameterized queries

Introduction

Today, the critical applications in any company are database applications. Those are the applications that store, retrieve, and update the data in a database like Microsoft SQL Server. That's why you can't get far as a programmer unless you know how to write serious database applications.

That, of course, is where this book comes in. Its goal is to show you how to use Visual Studio 2010, ADO.NET 4, and Visual Basic 2010 to develop database applications the way the best professionals develop them. Along the way, you'll also learn how XML, report preparation, LINQ, and the Entity Framework fit into the picture.

Although this book assumes that you already know the essentials of Visual Basic programming, you don't need any database programming experience. But if you do have some experience, you'll move more quickly through this book, and this book will take you to new levels of expertise.

What this book does

To present the database programming skills in a manageable progression, this book is divided into five sections.

- Section 1 explains the background concepts and skills that you need for database programming with ADO.NET 4. If you're new to database programming, this section is essential to getting started right. But if you already have database experience, you can skim this section.
- Section 2 shows you how to use data sources and datasets for prototyping and Rapid Application Development (RAD). These are the skills that will help you quickly develop working versions of database applications so they can be reviewed and enhanced.
- Section 3 shows you how to develop 3-layer applications that use presentation, business, and database classes. This is the approach that professionals use because it applies a logical structure to database applications. You'll also learn how to use object data sources in this section, because they can make this approach to application development even more effective.
- In section 4, you'll learn how to use ASP.NET 4 data controls to develop web applications. That includes controls for both SQL and object data sources as well as controls that present data, like the GridView and DetailsView controls. These controls help you develop database-driven web applications faster and better than ever. And object data sources give you complete control over how the database processing is done.
- Finally, in section 5, you'll learn advanced skills that every ADO.NET programmer should be aware of. These include how to work with XML, how to use the Report Designer to create reports, how to use the ReportViewer control to display reports in both Windows and web applications, how and why to use

LINQ instead of SQL to query a database, and how to use the Entity Framework in combination with LINQ so you can work with objects and let the framework handle the database operations.

Why you'll learn faster and better with this book

Like all our books, this one has features that you won't find in competing books. That's why we believe you'll learn faster and better with our book than with any other. Here are just a few of those features.

- This book explains everything you need to know to develop ADO.NET database applications at a professional level. That sounds simple. But to get all of this information from other sources would take you three or four other books – and you'd still have to figure out how it all worked together!
- At the end of most of the chapters, you'll find exercises that guide you through the development and enhancement of the book applications. This will help ensure that you fully understand the content of each chapter and can apply its skills. Then, if you have any problems with the exercises, you can get back on track by reviewing the book examples, applications, and explanations.
- To show you how all of the pieces of a database application interact, this book presents 23 complete applications that range from the simple to the complex. As we see it, the only way to master database programming is to study the code in applications like these. And yet, you won't find anything like this in other books.
- If you page through this book, you'll see that all of the information is presented in "paired pages." This means that the essential syntax, guidelines, and examples are presented on the right page, and the perspective and deeper explanations are presented on the left page. This helps you learn faster because you can decide what level of detail you need to read for each topic in the book.
- With most competing books, you can waste a lot of time trying to find a snippet of information that you know is in there…somewhere. But with its "paired pages" presentation method and a comprehensive index, this book becomes the ideal on-the-job reference, long after you've used it to master its skills.

Three companion books that will enhance your skills

As you read this book, you may discover that your Visual Basic skills aren't as strong as they ought to be. In that case, we recommend that you get a copy of *Murach's Visual Basic 2010*. It will get you up-to-speed with the language. It will show you how to work with the most useful .NET classes. And it will show you how to use business classes, which is essential when you develop 3-layer database applications.

Another book that we recommend for database programmers is *Murach's SQL Server 2008 for Developers*. To start, this book shows you how to write SQL statements in all their variations so you can code the right SQL statements for your ADO.NET command objects. This often gives you the option of having SQL Server do more of the data handling so your ADO.NET applications can do less. Beyond that, this book shows you how to design and implement databases and how to use advanced features like stored procedures, triggers, and functions.

If you need to learn how to develop web applications with Visual Basic, *Murach's ASP.NET 4 with Visual Basic 2010* is the third companion. By the time you finish the first four chapters, you'll know how to develop and test multi-form web applications. By the time you finish the book, you'll be able to develop commercial web applications at a professional level. And that's especially true if you have the database skills that you'll learn in this book.

What software you need

To develop Windows and web applications with Visual Basic 2010, you can use any of the full editions of Visual Studio 2010, including the Professional Edition, Premium Edition, or Ultimate Edition. All of these come with everything you need to develop the applications presented in this book, including Visual Studio, Microsoft .NET Framework 4, Visual Basic 2010, a built-in web server, and a scaled-back version of SQL Server called SQL Server 2008 Express Edition.

However, if you don't have a retail edition, you can use Visual Basic 2010 Express Edition to develop Windows applications. You can use Visual Web Developer 2010 Express Edition to develop ASP.NET 4 applications. And you can use SQL Server 2008 Express Edition to develop database applications with these editions. Together, these products provide everything you need for developing both Windows and web applications. And all three can be downloaded from Microsoft's web site for free!

If you use Visual Basic 2010 Express Edition with this book, you should be aware that this edition doesn't let you create reports as shown in chapter 16. But apart from that, the Express Edition has only a few minor differences from the retail editions. The good news is that all the other projects in this book can be created with the Express editions, and all the skills you learn and applications you develop with the Express editions will work with any of the full editions of Visual Studio.

How our downloadable files can help you learn

If you go to our web site at www.murach.com, you can download all the files that you need for getting the most from this book. These files include:

- the source code for all of the applications presented in this book

- the source code for the starting points for all of the exercises
- the source code for the solutions to the exercises
- the database and files that are used by the applications and exercises

The code for the book applications is valuable because it lets you run the applications on your own PC, view all of the source code, experiment with the code, and copy and paste any of the source code into your own applications. The exercise starts and solutions are valuable because they let you practice what you've learned and check your solutions against model solutions.

Support materials for trainers and instructors

If you're a corporate trainer or a college instructor who would like to use this book for a course, we offer an Instructor's CD that includes: (1) a complete set of PowerPoint slides that you can use to review and reinforce the content of the book; (2) instructional objectives that describe the skills a student should have upon completion of each chapter; (3) test banks that measure mastery of those skills; (4) the solutions to the exercises in this book (these are also included in the book downloads so your students can access them); (5) projects that the students start from scratch; and (6) solutions to those projects.

To learn more about this Instructor's CD and to find out how to get it, please go to our web site at www.murach.com and click on the Trainers link or the Instructors link. Or, if you prefer, you can call Kelly at 1-800-221-5528 or send an email to kelly@murach.com.

Please let us know how this book works for you

When we published the first edition of this book back in 2003, we wanted to teach you how to become a professional database developer in just a few weeks and also give you a great on-the-job reference. Although the technology has changed since then, our goals remain the same today.

We've also listened to your feedback on the previous editions and have implemented your recommendations. For instance, we've added a section on developing web applications. And we've added a section that presents XML programming, report preparation, LINQ, and the Entity Framework.

Now, if you have any comments about this book, we welcome them and invite you to contact us at murachbooks@murach.com. We thank you for buying this book. We hope you enjoy reading it. And we wish you great success with your database programming.

Anne Boehm, Author

Ged Mead, Author

Section 1

An introduction to ADO.NET programming

Before you can learn the details of developing database applications with ADO.NET 4, you need to understand the background concepts and terms. That's why chapter 1 introduces you to the basics of using relational databases and SQL. Then, chapter 2 introduces you to the ADO.NET classes that you'll use for developing database applications as well as the two basic approaches that you'll use for developing those applications.

1

An introduction to database programming

This chapter introduces you to the basic concepts and terms that apply to database applications. In particular, it explains what a relational database is and how you work with it using SQL, the industry-standard language for accessing data in relational databases.

If you have much experience with database programming, you can just review the figures in this chapter to make sure that you understand everything. Otherwise, this chapter will give you the background that you need for learning how to develop ADO.NET applications.

To illustrate the required concepts and terms, this chapter presents examples that use *Microsoft SQL Server 2008 Express* as the database management system. Please note, however, that any application that you develop with SQL Server Express will also run on any of the professional editions of *Microsoft SQL Server 2008*. Similarly, because SQL is a standard language, the underlying concepts and terms also apply to database management systems like Oracle or MySQL.

An introduction to client/server systems

In case you aren't familiar with client/server systems, this topic introduces you to their essential hardware and software components. Then, the rest of this chapter presents additional information on these components and on how you can use them in database applications.

The hardware components of a client/server system

Figure 1-1 presents the three hardware components of a *client/server system*: the clients, the network, and the server. The *clients* are usually the PCs that are already available on the desktops throughout a company. And the *network* is made up of the cabling, communication lines, network interface cards, hubs, routers, and other components that connect the clients and the server.

The *server*, commonly referred to as a *database server*, is a computer that has enough processor speed, internal memory (RAM), and disk storage to store the files and databases of the system and to provide services to the clients of the system. This computer is often a high-powered PC, but it can also be a midrange system like an IBM iSeries or a Unix system, or even a mainframe system. When a system consists of networks, midrange systems, and mainframe systems, often spread throughout the country or world, it is commonly referred to as an *enterprise system*.

To back up the files of a client/server system, a server usually has a tape drive or some other form of offline storage. It often has one or more printers or specialized devices that can be shared by the users of the system. And it can provide programs or services like email that can be accessed by all the users of the system. In larger networks, however, features such as backup, printing, and email are provided by separate servers. That way, the database server can be dedicated to the task of handling database requests.

In a simple client/server system, the clients and the server are part of a *local area network* (*LAN*). However, two or more LANs that reside at separate geographical locations can be connected as part of a larger network such as a *wide area network* (*WAN*). In addition, individual systems or networks can be connected over the Internet.

A simple client/server system

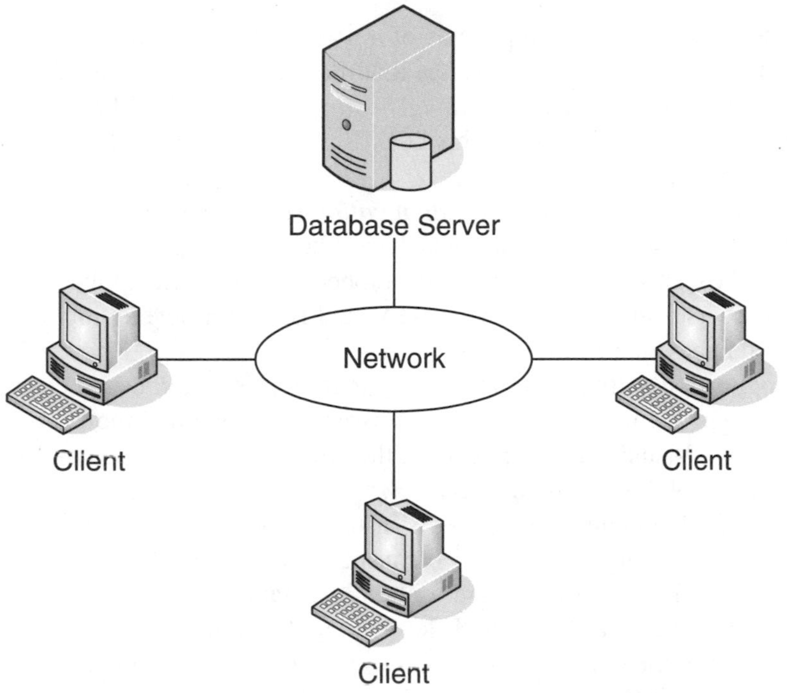

The three hardware components of a client/server system

- The *clients* are the PCs, Macintoshes, or workstations of the system.
- The *server* is a computer that stores the files and databases of the system and provides services to the clients. When it stores databases, it's often referred to as a *database server*.
- The *network* consists of the cabling, communication lines, and other components that connect the clients and the servers of the system.

Client/server system implementations

- In a simple *client/server system* like the one shown above, the server is typically a high-powered PC that communicates with the clients over a *local area network* (*LAN*).
- The server can also be a midrange system, like an IBM iSeries or a Unix system, or it can be a mainframe system. Then, special hardware and software components are required to make it possible for the clients to communicate with the midrange and mainframe systems.
- A client/server system can also consist of one or more PC-based systems, one or more midrange systems, and a mainframe system in dispersed geographical locations. This type of system is commonly referred to as an *enterprise system.*
- Individual systems and LANs can be connected and share data over larger private networks, such as a *wide area network* (*WAN*) or a public network like the Internet.

Figure 1-1 The hardware components of a client/server system

The software components of a client/server system

Figure 1-2 presents the software components of a typical client/server system. In addition to a *network operating system* that manages the functions of the network, the server requires a *database management system* (*DBMS*) like Microsoft SQL Server, Oracle, or MySQL. This DBMS manages the databases that are stored on the server.

In contrast to a server, each client requires *application software* to perform useful work. This can be a purchased software package like a financial accounting package, or it can be custom software that's developed for a specific application. This book, of course, shows you how to use Visual Basic for developing custom software for database applications.

Although the application software is run on the client, it uses data that's stored on the server. To make this communication between the client and the data source possible for a Visual Basic application, the client accesses the database via a *data access API* such as ADO.NET 4.

Once the software for both client and server is installed, the client communicates with the server by passing *SQL queries* (or just *queries*) to the DBMS through the data access API. These queries are written in a standard language called *Structured Query Language* (*SQL*). SQL lets any application communicate with any DBMS. After the client sends a query to the DBMS, the DBMS interprets the query and sends the results back to the client. (In conversation, SQL is pronounced as either *S-Q-L* or *sequel*.)

As you can see in this figure, the processing done by a client/server system is divided between the clients and the server. In this case, the DBMS on the server is processing requests made by the application running on the client. Theoretically, at least, this balances the workload between the clients and the server so the system works more efficiently. In contrast, in a file-handling system, the clients do all of the work because the server is used only to store the files that are used by the clients.

Client software, server software, and the SQL interface

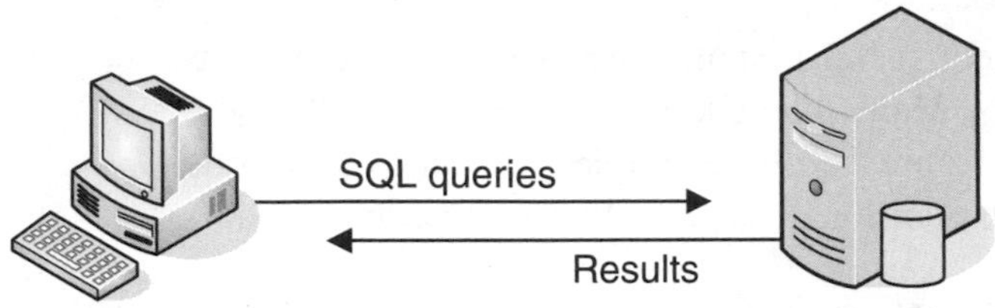

Client
Application software
Data access API

Database Server
Network operating system
Database management system
Database

Server software

- To manage the network, the server runs a *network operating system* such as Windows Server 2008.
- To store and manage the databases of the client/server system, each server requires a *database management system* (*DBMS*) such as Microsoft SQL Server.
- The processing that's done by the DBMS is typically referred to as *back-end processing*, and the database server is referred to as the *back end*.

Client software

- The *application software* does the work that the user wants to do. This type of software can be purchased or developed.
- The *data access API* (*application programming interface*) provides the interface between the application program and the DBMS. The newest data access API is ADO.NET 4, which is a part of Microsoft's .NET Framework.
- The processing that's done by the client software is typically referred to as *front-end processing*, and the client is typically referred to as the *front end*.

The SQL interface

- The application software communicates with the DBMS by sending *SQL queries* through the data access API. When the DBMS receives a query, it provides a service like returning the requested data (the *query results*) to the client.
- *SQL*, which stands for *Structured Query Language*, is the standard language for working with a relational database.

Client/server versus file-handling systems

- In a client/server system, the processing done by an application is typically divided between the client and the server.
- In a file-handling system, all of the processing is done on the clients. Although the clients may access data that's stored in files on the server, none of the processing is done by the server. As a result, a file-handling system isn't a client/server system.

Figure 1-2 The software components of a client/server system

Other client/server system architectures

In its simplest form, a client/server system consists of a single database server and one or more clients. Many client/server systems today, though, include additional servers. In figure 1-3, for example, you can see two client/server systems that include an additional server between the clients and the database server.

The first illustration is for a Windows-based system. With this system, only the user interface for an application runs on the client. The rest of the processing that's done by the application is stored in one or more *classes* on the *application server*. Then, the client sends requests to the application server for processing. If the request involves accessing data in a database, the application server formulates the appropriate query and passes it on to the database server. The results of the query are then sent back to the application server, which processes the results and sends the appropriate response back to the client.

As you can see in this illustration, two types of classes can be stored on an application server. *Business classes* can represent business entities used by an application. For example, an application that accepts invoices for a vendor might use business classes that represent vendors, invoices, and invoice line items. In addition, business classes can implement business rules.

An application server can also be used to store *database classes*. These classes provide the code that's needed to process the database requests, such as retrieving data from the database and storing data in the database. Because these classes work directly with the database, they are sometimes stored on the database server instead of the application server.

Web-based applications use a similar type of architecture, as illustrated by the second example in this figure. In a web application, a *web browser* running on the client is used to send requests to a *web application* running on a *web server* somewhere on the Internet. The web application, in turn, can use *web services* to perform some of its processing. Then, the web application or web service can pass requests for data on to the database server.

Although this figure gives you an idea of how client/server systems can be configured, you should realize that they can be much more complicated than what's shown here. In a Windows-based system, for example, business classes and database classes can be distributed over any number of application servers, and those classes can communicate with databases on any number of database servers. Similarly, the web applications and services in a web-based system can be distributed over numerous web servers that access numerous database servers.

A Windows-based system that uses an application server

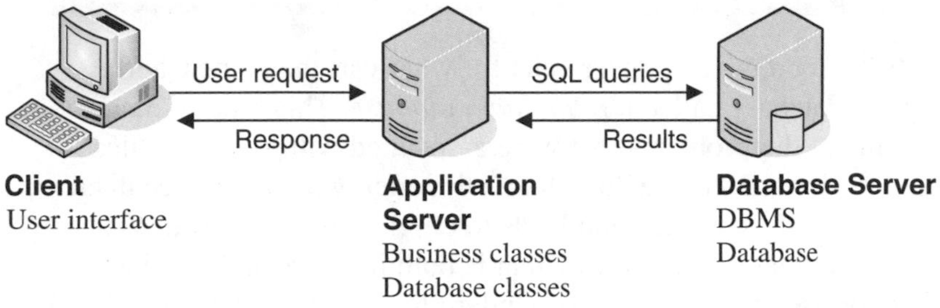

A simple web-based system

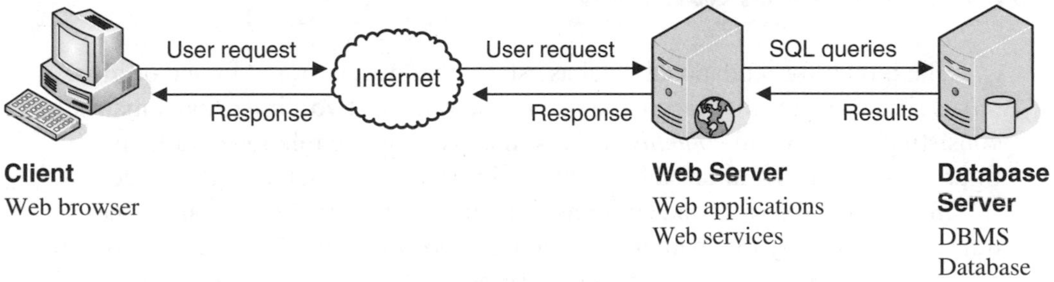

Description

- In addition to a database server and clients, a client/server system can include additional servers, such as *application servers* and *web servers*.
- Application servers are typically used to store *business classes*. Business classes can represent business entities, such as vendors or invoices, or they can implement business rules, such as discount or credit policies.
- An application server can also be used to store *database classes*, which handle all of the application's data processing. These classes can also be stored on the database server.
- Web servers are typically used to store *web applications* and *web services*. Web applications are applications that are designed to run on a web server. Web services are like business components, except that, like web applications, they are designed to run on a web server.
- In a web-based system, a *web browser* running on a client sends a request to a web server over the Internet. Then, the web server processes the request and passes any requests for data on to the database server.
- More complex system architectures can include two or more application servers, web servers, and database servers. This can include technologies such as SharePoint 2010, a business collaboration platform that can be accessed through Internet or intranet connections.

Figure 1-3 Other client/server system architectures

An introduction to relational databases

In 1970, Dr. E. F. Codd developed a model for what was then a new and revolutionary type of database called a *relational database*. This type of database eliminated some of the problems that were associated with standard files and other database designs. By using the relational model, you can reduce data redundancy, which saves disk storage and leads to efficient data retrieval. You can also view and manipulate data in a way that is both intuitive and efficient. Today, relational databases are the de facto standard for database applications.

How a table is organized

The model for a relational database states that data is stored in one or more *tables*. It also states that each table can be viewed as a two-dimensional matrix consisting of *rows* and *columns*. This is illustrated by the relational table in figure 1-4. Each row in this table contains information about a single vendor.

In practice, the rows and columns of a relational database table are sometimes referred to by the more traditional terms, *records* and *fields*. In fact, some software packages use one set of terms, some use the other, and some use a combination.

If a table contains one or more columns that uniquely identify each row in the table, you can define these columns as the *primary key* of the table. For instance, the primary key of the Vendors table in this figure is the VendorID column.

In this example, the primary key consists of a single column. However, a primary key can also consist of two or more columns, in which case it's called a *composite primary key*.

In addition to primary keys, some database management systems let you define additional keys that uniquely identify each row in a table, called *non-primary keys*. In SQL Server, these keys are also called *unique keys*, and they're implemented by defining *unique key constraints* (also known simply as *unique constraints*). The main difference between a unique key and a primary key is that a unique key can be null and a primary key can't. If a unique key consists of more than one column, then only one of the columns can have a null value.

Indexes provide an efficient way to access the rows in a table based on the values in one or more columns. Because applications typically access the rows in a table by referring to their key values, an index is automatically created for each key you define. However, you can define indexes for other columns as well. If, for example, you frequently need to sort the rows in the Vendors table by zip code, you can set up an index for that column. Like a key, an index can include one or more columns.

The Vendors table in a Payables database

Primary key **Columns**

VendorID	Name	Address1	Address2
1	US Postal Service	Attn: Supt. Window Services	PO Box 7005
2	National Information Data Ctr	PO Box 96621	
3	Register of Copyrights	Library Of Congress	101 Independence Ave SE
4	Jobtrak	1990 Westwood Blvd Ste 260	
5	Newbrige Book Clubs	3000 Cindel Drive West	
6	California Chamber Of Commerce	3255 Ramos Cir	
7	Towne Advertiser's Mailing Svcs	Kevin Minder	3441 W Macarthur Blvd
8	BFI Industries	PO Box 9369	
9	Pacific Gas & Electric	PO Box 52001	
10	Robbins Mobile Lock And Key	4669 N. Fresno	
11	Bill Marvin Electric Inc	4583 E Home	
12	City Of Fresno	PO Box 2069	
13	Golden Eagle Insurance Co	PO Box 85826	
14	Expedata Inc	4420 N. First Street, Suite 108	
15	ASC Signs	1528 N Sierra Vista	
16	Internal Revenue Service	PO Box 5000	

Rows

Concepts

- A *relational database* uses *tables* to store and manipulate data. Each table consists of one or more *records*, or *rows*, that contain the data for a single entry. Each row contains one or more *fields*, or *columns*, with each column representing a single item of data.
- Most tables contain a *primary key* that uniquely identifies each row in the table. The primary key often consists of a single column, but it can also consist of two or more columns. If a primary key uses two or more columns, it's called a *composite primary key*.
- In addition to primary keys, some database management systems let you define one or more *non-primary keys*. In SQL Server, these keys are called *unique keys*, and they're implemented using *unique key constraints*. Like a primary key, a non-primary key uniquely identifies each row in the table.
- A table can also be defined with one or more *indexes*. An index provides an efficient way to access data from a table based on the values in specific columns. An index is automatically created for a table's primary and non-primary keys.

Figure 1-4 How a table is organized

How the tables in a database are related

The tables in a relational database can be related to other tables by values in specific columns. The two tables shown in figure 1-5 illustrate this concept. Here, each row in the Vendors table is related to one or more rows in an Invoices table. This is called a *one-to-many relationship*.

Typically, relationships exist between the primary key in one table and the *foreign key* in another table. The foreign key is simply one or more columns in a table that refer to a primary key in another table. In SQL Server, relationships can also exist between a unique key in one table and a foreign key in another table. For simplicity, though, you can assume that the relationships are between primary keys and foreign keys.

One-to-many relationships are the most common type of database relationship. However, two tables can also have a one-to-one or many-to-many relationship. If a table has a *one-to-one relationship* with another table, the data in the two tables could be stored in a single table. Because of that, one-to-one relationships are used infrequently.

In contrast, a *many-to-many relationship* is usually implemented by using an intermediate table, called a *linking table*, that has a one-to-many relationship with the two tables in the many-to-many relationship. In other words, a many-to-many relationship can usually be broken down into two one-to-many relationships.

The relationship between the Vendors and Invoices tables in the database

Primary key

VendorID	Name	Address1	Address2	City
114	Postmaster	Postage Due Technician	1900 E Street	Fresno
115	Roadway Package System, Inc	Dept La 21095		Pasadena
116	State of California	Employment Development Dept	PO Box 826276	Sacramento
117	Suburban Propane	2874 S Cherry Ave		Fresno
118	Unocal	P.O. Box 860070		Pasadena
119	Yesmed, Inc	PO Box 2061		Fresno
120	Dataforms/West	1617 W. Shaw Avenue	Suite F	Fresno
121	Zylka Design	3467 W Shaw Ave #103		Fresno
122	United Parcel Service	P.O. Box 505820		Reno
123	Federal Express Corporation	PO Box 1140	Dept A	Memphis

InvoiceID	VendorID	InvoiceNumber	InvoiceDate	InvoiceTotal
161	123	969287221	6/17/2010	571.2500
162	92	90906D	6/17/2010	265.0000
163	94	390222-03	6/25/2010	395.0000
164	108	527761	7/7/2010	1500.0000
165	114	CBM0153-V-T90...	7/9/2010	185.6000
166	122	989715-213	7/12/2010	223.4500
167	115	300137619	7/14/2010	3277.5700
168	104	PO2/8634	7/15/2010	2445.0000
169	123	970271130	7/20/2010	626.7900
170	94	412840-93	7/30/2010	185.0000
171	123	979265411	8/3/2010	285.0000

Foreign key

Concepts

- The tables in a relational database are related to each other through their key columns. For example, the VendorID column is used to relate the Vendors and Invoices tables above. The VendorID column in the Invoices table is called a *foreign key* because it identifies a related row in the Vendors table.
- Usually, a foreign key corresponds to the primary key in the related table. In SQL Server, however, a foreign key can also correspond to a unique key in the related table.
- When two tables are related via a foreign key, the table with the foreign key is referred to as the *foreign key table* and the table with the primary key is referred to as the *primary key table*.
- The relationships between the tables in a database correspond to the relationships between the entities they represent. The most common type of relationship is a *one-to-many relationship* as illustrated by the Vendors and Invoices table. A table can also have a *one-to-one relationship* or a *many-to-many relationship* with another table.

Figure 1-5 How the tables in a database are related

How to enforce referential integrity

Although the primary keys and foreign keys indicate how the tables in a database are related, those relationships aren't enforced automatically. To enforce relationships, you use *referential integrity* features like the ones described in figure 1-6. Although the features covered here are for SQL Server 2008, most database systems have similar features.

To understand why referential integrity is important, consider what would happen if you deleted a row from the Vendors table and referential integrity wasn't in effect. Then, if the Invoices table contained any rows for that vendor, those rows would be *orphaned*. Similar problems could occur if you inserted a row into the foreign key table or updated a primary key or foreign key value.

To avoid these problems and to maintain the referential integrity of the tables, you can use one of two features: foreign key constraints or triggers. A *foreign key constraint* defines how referential integrity should be enforced when a row in a primary key table is updated or deleted. The most common options are to raise an error if the primary key row has corresponding rows in the foreign key table or to *cascade* the update or delete operation to the foreign key table.

For example, suppose a user attempts to delete a vendor that has invoices in the Invoices table. In that case, the foreign key constraint can be configured to either raise an error or automatically delete the vendor's invoices along with the vendor. Which option is best depends on the requirements of the application.

Triggers are special procedures that can be executed automatically when an insert, update, or delete operation is executed on a table. A trigger can determine whether an operation will violate referential integrity. If so, the trigger can either cancel the operation or perform additional actions to ensure that referential integrity is maintained.

Although most database servers provide for foreign key constraints, triggers, or both, not all databases take advantage of these features. In that case, it's up to the application programmer to enforce referential integrity. For example, before deleting a vendor, your application would have to query the Invoices table to make sure the vendor has no invoices. Whenever you develop an application that modifies database information, you need to find out what the application's referential integrity requirements are, whether those requirements are implemented in the database by constraints or triggers, and which referential integrity requirements must be implemented in the application's code.

The dialog boxes for defining foreign key constraints in SQL Server 2008

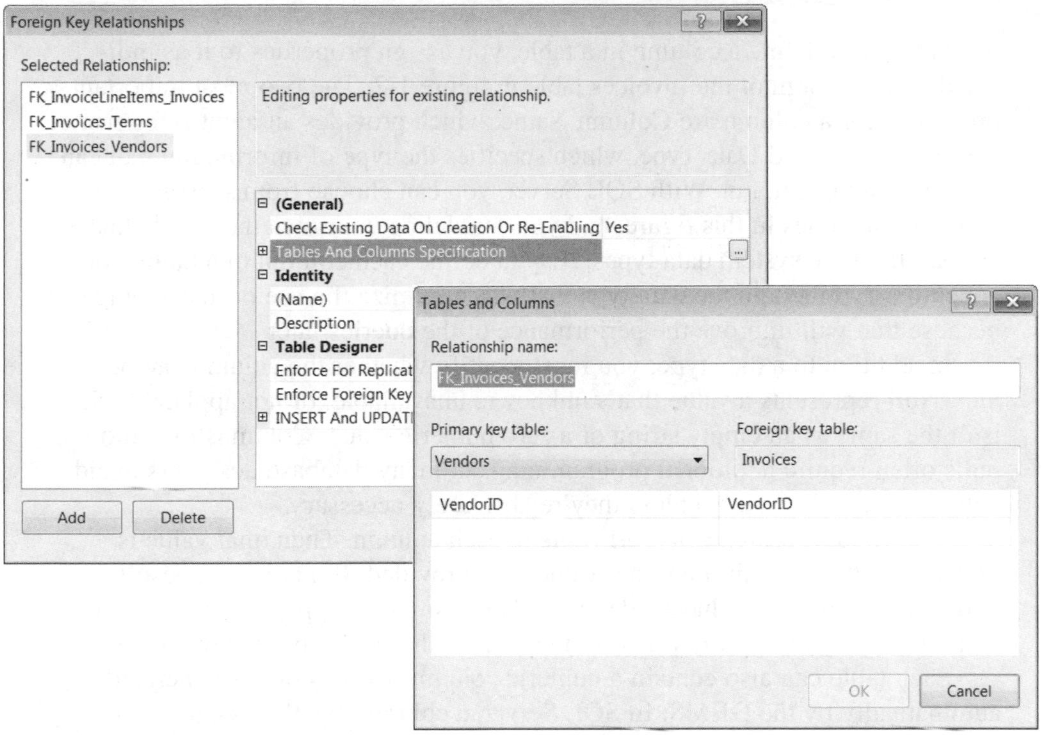

Description

- *Referential integrity* means that the relationships between tables are maintained correctly. That means that the foreign key values in a table with a foreign key must have matching primary key values in the related table.
- In SQL Server 2008, you can enforce referential integrity by using foreign key constraints or triggers.
- A *foreign key constraint* tells SQL Server what to do when a row in a primary key table is updated or deleted and a foreign key table has related rows. The two most common options are to return an error (No Action) or to *cascade* the update or delete operation to all related rows in the foreign key table.
- A *trigger* is a SQL procedure that's defined in the database and executed automatically whenever an insert, update, or delete operation is performed on a table. A trigger can determine if a referential integrity violation has occurred and then handle it accordingly.
- If referential integrity isn't enforced and a row is deleted from the primary key table that has related rows in the foreign key table, the rows in the foreign key table are said to be *orphaned*.

Figure 1-6 How SQL Server enforces referential integrity

How the columns in a table are defined

When you define a column in a table, you assign properties to it as indicated by the design of the Invoices table in figure 1-7. The two most important properties for a column are Column Name, which provides an identifying name for the column, and Data Type, which specifies the type of information that can be stored in the column. With SQL Server, you can choose from *system data types* like the ones in this figure, and you can define your own data types that are based on the system data types. As you define each column in a table, you generally try to assign the data type that will minimize the use of disk storage because that will improve the performance of the queries later.

In addition to a data type, you must identify whether the column can be *null*. Null represents a value that's unknown, unavailable, or not applicable. It isn't the same as an empty string or a zero numeric value. Columns that allow nulls often require additional programming, so many database designers avoid columns that allow nulls unless they're absolutely necessary.

You can also assign a *default value* to each column. Then, that value is assigned to the column if another value isn't provided. If a column doesn't allow nulls and doesn't have a default value, you must supply a value for the column when you add a new row to the table. Otherwise, an error will occur.

Each table can also contain a numeric column whose value is generated automatically by the DBMS. In SQL Server, a column like this is called an *identity column*. Identity columns are often used as the primary key for a table.

A *check constraint* defines the acceptable values for a column. For example, you can define a check constraint for the Invoices table in this figure to make sure that the InvoiceTotal column is greater than zero. A check constraint like this can be defined at the column level because it refers only to the column it constrains. If the check constraint for a column needs to refer to other columns in the table, however, it can be defined at the table level.

After you define the constraints for a database, they're managed by the DBMS. If, for example, a user tries to add a row with data that violates a constraint, the DBMS sends an appropriate error code back to the application without adding the row to the database. The application can then respond to the error code.

An alternative to using constraints is to validate the data that is going to be added to a database before the program tries to add it. That way, the constraints shouldn't be needed and the program should run more efficiently. In many cases, both data validation and constraints are used. That way, the programs run more efficiently if the data validation routines work, but the constraints are there in case the data validation routines don't work or aren't coded.

The Server Explorer design view window for the Invoices table

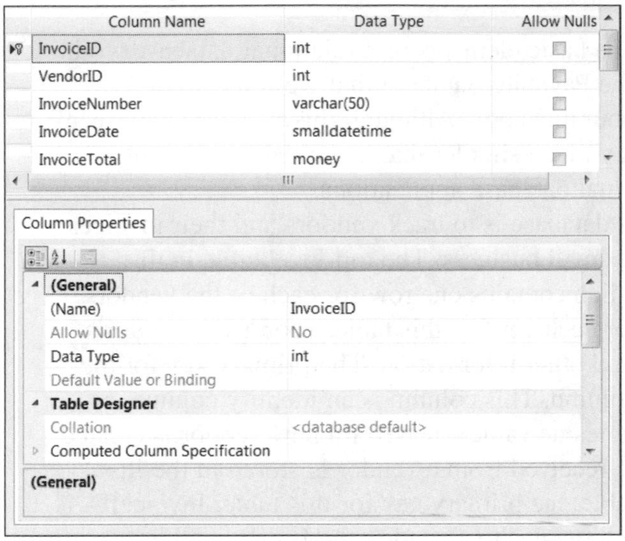

Common SQL Server data types

Type	Description
bit	A value of 1 or 0 that represents a True or False value.
char, varchar, text	Any combination of letters, symbols, and numbers.
date, time, datetime, smalldatetime	Alphanumeric data that represents a date, a time, or both a date and time. Various formats are acceptable.
decimal, numeric	Numeric data that is accurate to the least significant digit. The data can contain an integer and a fractional portion.
float, real	Floating-point values that contain an approximation of a decimal value.
bigint, int, smallint, tinyint	Numeric data that contains only an integer portion.
money, smallmoney	Monetary values that are accurate to four decimal places.

Description

- The *data type* that's assigned to a column determines the type of information that can be stored in the column. Depending on the data type, the column definition can also include its length, precision, and scale.
- Each column definition also indicates whether or not the column can contain *null values*. A null value indicates that the value of the column is not known.
- A column can be defined with a *default value*. Then, that value is used for the column if another value isn't provided when a row is added to the table.
- A column can also be defined as an *identity column*. An identity column is a numeric column whose value is generated automatically when a row is added to the table.
- To restrict the values that a column can hold, you define *check constraints*. Check constraints can be defined at either the column level or the table level.

Figure 1-7 How the columns in a table are defined

The design of the Payables database

Now that you've seen how the basic elements of a relational database work, figure 1-8 shows the design of the Payables database that we'll use in the programming examples throughout this book. Although this database may seem complicated, its design is actually much simpler than most databases you'll encounter when you work on actual database applications.

The purpose of the Payables database is to track vendors and their invoices for the payables department of a small business. The top-level table in this database is the Vendors table, which contains one row for each of the vendors the company purchases from. For each vendor, this table records the vendor's name, address, phone number, and other information. The primary key for the Vendors table is the VendorID column. This column is an identity column, so SQL Server automatically generates its value whenever a new vendor is created.

Information for each invoice received from a vendor is stored in the Invoices table. Like the Vendors table, the primary key for this table, InvoiceID, is an identity column. To relate each invoice to a vendor, the Invoices table includes a VendorID column. A foreign key constraint is used to enforce this relationship. That way, an invoice can't be added for a vendor that doesn't exist, and vendors with outstanding invoices can't be deleted.

The InvoiceLineItems table contains the line item details for each invoice. The primary key for this table is a combination of the InvoiceID and InvoiceSequence columns. The InvoiceID column relates each line item to an invoice, and a foreign key constraint that cascades updates and deletes from the Invoices table is defined to enforce this relationship. The InvoiceSequence column gives each line item a unique primary key value. Note, however, that this column is not an identity column. As a result, the application programs that create line items must calculate appropriate values for this column.

The other three tables in the Payables database—States, Terms, and GLAccounts—provide reference information for the Vendors, Invoices, and InvoiceLineItems tables. The States table has a row for each state in the U.S. The primary key for this table is StateCode. Each Vendor has a State column that relates the vendor to a row in the States table.

The Terms table records invoice terms, such as "Net Due 10 Days" or "Net Due 90 Days." The primary key of this table is TermsID, which is an identity column. Each invoice also has a TermsID column that relates the invoice to a row in the Terms table. In addition, each Vendor has a DefaultTermsID column that provides the default terms for new invoices for that vendor.

Finally, the GLAccounts table provides general-ledger account information for the Payables database. The primary key of this table is AccountNo. Each line item also includes an AccountNo column that specifies which account the purchase should be charged to, and each Vendor has a DefaulAccountNo column that provides a default account number for new invoices. The foreign key constraints that enforce the relationships between the GLAccounts table and the Vendors and InvoiceLineItems tables are defined so that updates are cascaded to those tables. That way, if an account number changes, that change is reflected in the related vendors and line items.

The tables that make up the Payables database

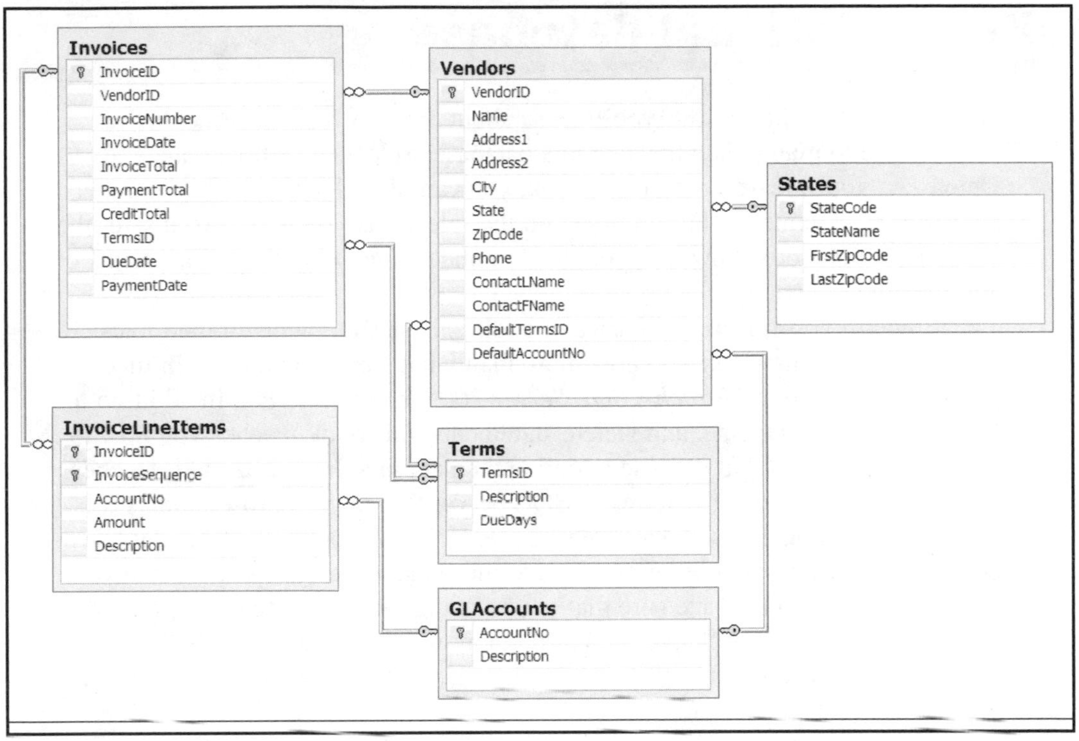

Description

- The Vendors table contains one row for each vendor. Its primary key is VendorID, which is an identity column that's generated automatically by SQL Server whenever a new vendor is added.
- The Invoices table contains one row for each invoice. Its primary key is InvoiceID, which is an identity column that's generated automatically whenever a new invoice is added. VendorID is a foreign key that relates each invoice to a vendor. TermsID is a foreign key that relates each invoice to a row in the Terms table.
- The InvoiceLineItems table contains one row for each line item of each invoice. Its primary key is a combination of InvoiceID and InvoiceSequence. InvoiceID is also a foreign key that relates the line item to an invoice.
- States, Terms, and GLAccounts are simple reference tables that are related to the Vendors, Invoices, and InvoiceLineItems tables by foreign keys.
- The relationships between the tables in this diagram appear as links, where the endpoints indicate the type of relationship. A key indicates the "one" side of a relationship, and the infinity symbol (∞) indicates the "many" side.

Figure 1-8 The design of the Payables database

How to use SQL to work with a relational database

In the topics that follow, you'll learn about the four SQL statements that you can use to manipulate the data in a database: Select, Insert, Update, and Delete. As you'll learn later in this book, you can often let Visual Studio generate the SQL statements for you based on the selections you make. To master the material in this book, however, you need to understand what these statements do and how they're coded.

Although you'll learn the basics of coding these statements in the topics that follow, you may want to know more than what's presented here. In that case, we recommend *Murach's SQL Server 2008 for Developers*. In addition to the Select, Insert, Update, and Delete statements, this book teaches you how to code the statements that you use to define the data in a database, and it teaches you how to use the other features of SQL Server that the top professionals use.

Although SQL is a standard language, each DBMS is likely to have its own *SQL dialect*, which includes extensions to the standard language. So when you use SQL, you need to make sure that you're using the dialect that's supported by your DBMS. In this chapter and throughout this book, all of the SQL examples are for Microsoft SQL Server's dialect, which is called *Transact-SQL*.

How to query a single table

Figure 1-9 shows how to use a Select statement to query a single table in a database. In the syntax summary, you can see that the Select clause names the columns to be retrieved and the From clause names the table that contains the columns. You can also code a Where clause that gives criteria for the rows to be selected. And you can code an Order By clause that names one or more columns that the results should be sorted by and indicates whether each column should be sorted in ascending or descending sequence.

If you study the Select statement below the syntax summary, you can see how this works. Here, the Select statement retrieves columns from the Invoices table. It selects a row only if the row has a balance due that's greater than zero. And it sorts the returned rows by invoice date in ascending sequence (the default).

Please note in this Select statement that the last column in the query, BalanceDue, is calculated by subtracting PaymentTotal and CreditTotal from InvoiceTotal. In other words, a column by the name of BalanceDue doesn't actually exist in the database. This type of column is called a *calculated column*, and it exists only in the results of the query.

This figure also shows the *result table*, or *result set*, that's returned by the Select statement. A result set is a logical table that's created temporarily within the database. When an application requests data from a database, it receives a result set.

Simplified syntax of the Select statement

```
 SELECT column-1 [, column-2]...
 FROM table-1
[WHERE selection-criteria]
[ORDER BY column-1 [ASC|DESC] [, column-2 [ASC|DESC]]...]
```

A Select statement that retrieves and sorts selected columns and rows from the Invoices table

```
SELECT InvoiceNumber, InvoiceDate, InvoiceTotal,
    PaymentTotal, CreditTotal,
    InvoiceTotal - PaymentTotal - CreditTotal AS BalanceDue
FROM Invoices
WHERE InvoiceTotal - PaymentTotal - CreditTotal > 0
ORDER BY InvoiceDate
```

The result set defined by the Select statement

	InvoiceNumber	InvoiceDate	InvoiceTotal	PaymentTotal	CreditTotal	BalanceDue
1	362101	2010-09-28	25.32	0.00	0.00	25.32
2	992609-278	2010-10-05	328.05	0.00	0.00	328.05
3	836772	2010-10-06	559.00	0.00	0.00	559.00
4	320256328	2010-10-08	1778.44	0.00	0.00	1778.44
5	370933	2010-10-19	36.00	0.00	0.00	36.00
6	9996474	2010-11-02	503.20	0.00	100.00	403.20
7	984343173	2010-11-09	143.78	0.00	0.00	143.78
8	993376-631	2010-11-12	98.50	0.00	0.00	98.50
9	320838622	2010-11-16	2854.68	0.00	0.00	2854.68

Concepts

- The result of a Select statement is a *result table*, or *result set*, like the one shown above. A result set is a logical set of rows that consists of all of the columns and rows requested by the Select statement.
- The Select clause lists the columns to be included in the result set. This list can include *calculated columns* that are calculated from other columns in the table and columns that use SQL Server *functions*.
- The From clause names the table that the data will be retrieved from.
- The Where clause provides a condition that specifies which rows should be retrieved. To retrieve all rows from a table, omit the Where clause.
- The Order By clause lists the columns that the results are sorted by and indicates whether each column is sorted in ascending or descending sequence.
- To select all of the columns in a table, you can code an asterisk (*) in place of the column names. For example, this statement will select all of the columns from the Invoices table:

  ```
  Select * From Invoices
  ```

Figure 1-9 How to query a single table

How to join data from two or more tables

Figure 1-10 presents the syntax of the Select statement for retrieving data from two tables. This type of operation is called a *join* because the data from the two tables is joined together into a single result set. For example, the Select statement in this figure joins data from the Invoices and Vendors table into a single result set.

An *inner join* is the most common type of join. When you use an inner join, rows from the two tables in the join are included in the result set only if their related columns match. These matching columns are specified in the From clause of the Select statement. In the Select statement in this figure, for example, rows from the Invoices and Vendors tables are included only if the value of the VendorID column in the Vendors table matches the value of the VendorID column in one or more rows in the Invoices table. If there aren't any invoices for a particular vendor, that vendor won't be included in the result set.

Although this figure shows how to join data from two tables, you should know that you can extend this syntax to join data from additional tables. If, for example, you want to include data from the InvoiceLineItems table in the results shown in this figure, you can code the From clause of the Select statement like this:

```
From Vendors
    Join Invoices
        On Vendors.VendorID = Invoices.VendorID
    Join InvoiceLineItems
        On Invoices.InvoiceID = InvoiceLineItems.InvoiceID
```

Then, in the column list of the Select statement, you can include any of the columns in the InvoiceLineItems table.

The syntax of the Select statement for joining two tables

```
 SELECT column-list
 FROM table-1
     [INNER] JOIN table-2
     ON table-1.column-1 {=|<|>|<=|>=|<>} table-2.column-2
[WHERE selection-criteria]
[ORDER BY column-list]
```

A Select statement that joins data from the Vendors and Invoices tables

```
SELECT Name, InvoiceNumber, InvoiceDate, InvoiceTotal
FROM Vendors JOIN Invoices
    ON Vendors.VendorID = Invoices.VendorID
WHERE InvoiceTotal >= 500
ORDER BY Name, InvoiceTotal DESC
```

The result set defined by the Select statement

	Name	InvoiceNumber	InvoiceDate	InvoiceTotal
54	United Parcel Service	989699-682	2010-06-11 00:00:00	958.76
55	US Postal Service	77239A	2010-02-12 00:00:00	628.50
56	Venture Communications Int'l	ADC/23/2010	2010-01-14 00:00:00	655.00
57	Wakefield Co	97-1138A	2010-03-01 00:00:00	625.00
58	Wang Laboratories, Inc.	MABO1489	2009-10-21 00:00:00	936.93
59	Wang Laboratories, Inc.	MABO1490	2010-02-18 00:00:00	550.00
60	Wang Laboratories, Inc.	MABO1491	2010-06-01 00:00:00	550.00
61	Wang Laboratories, Inc.	MABO1492	2010-09-14 00:00:00	550.00
62	Wells Fargo Bank	I77271-O01	2009-08-26 00:00:00	662.00
63	Yesmed, Inc	21763	2010-09-14 00:00:00	5124.56
64	Yesmed, Inc	10843	2009-09-11 00:00:00	4901.26
65	Zylka Design	97/522	2009-10-28 00:00:00	1962.13
66	Zylka Design	97/222	2009-11-25 00:00:00	1000.46

Concepts

- A *join* lets you combine data from two or more tables into a single result set.
- The most common type of join is an *inner join*. This type of join returns rows from both tables only if their related columns match.

Figure 1-10 How to join data from two or more tables

How to add, update, and delete data in a table

Figure 1-11 presents the basic syntax of the SQL Insert, Update, and Delete statements. You use the Insert statement to insert one or more rows into a table. As you can see, the syntax of this statement is different depending on whether you're adding a single row or selected rows.

To add a single row to a table, you specify the name of the table you want to add the row to, the names of the columns you're supplying data for, and the values for those columns. The example in this figure adds a row to the Terms table. Because the value of the TermsID column is generated automatically, though, it's not included in the Insert statement. If you're going to supply values for all the columns in a table, you can omit the column names, but then you must be sure to specify the values in the same order as the columns appear in the table.

Note that you typically use single quotes to identify strings. For example, the string for the Description column is enclosed in single quotes. However, if a string value contains a single quote, you'll need to replace the single quote with two single quotes.

To add selected rows to a table, you include a Select statement within the Insert statement. Then, the Select statement retrieves data from one or more tables based on the conditions you specify, and the Insert statement adds rows with that data to another table. In the example in this figure, the Select statement selects all the columns from the rows in the Invoices table that have been paid in full and inserts them into a table named InvoiceArchive.

To change the values of one or more columns in a table, you use the Update statement. On this statement, you specify the name of the table you want to update, the names of the columns you want to change and expressions that indicate how you want to change them, and a condition that identifies the rows you want to change. In the example in this figure, the Update statement changes the TermsID value to 4 for each row in the Invoices table that has a TermsID value of 1.

To delete rows from a table, you use the Delete statement. On this statement, you specify the table you want to delete rows from and a condition that indicates the rows you want to delete. The Delete statement in this figure deletes all the rows from the Invoices table that have been paid in full.

How to add a single row

The syntax of the Insert statement for adding a single row

```
INSERT [INTO] table-name [(column-list)]
    VALUES (value-list)
```

A statement that adds a single row to a table

```
INSERT INTO Terms (Description, DueDays)
    VALUES ('Net due 90 days', 90)
```

How to add selected rows

The syntax of the Insert statement for adding selected rows

```
INSERT [INTO] table-name [(column-list)]
    Select-statement
```

A statement that adds selected rows from one table to another table

```
INSERT INTO InvoiceArchive
    SELECT * FROM Invoices
    WHERE InvoiceTotal - PaymentTotal - CreditTotal = 0
```

How to update rows

The syntax of the Update statement

```
UPDATE table-name
    SET column-1 = expression-1 [, column-2 = expression-2]...
    [WHERE selection-criteria]
```

A statement that changes the value of the TermsID column for selected rows

```
UPDATE Invoices
    SET TermsID = 4
    WHERE TermsID = 1
```

How to delete rows

The syntax of the Delete statement

```
DELETE [FROM] table-name
    [WHERE selection-criteria]
```

A statement that deletes all paid invoices

```
DELETE FROM Invoices
    WHERE InvoiceTotal - PaymentTotal - CreditTotal = 0
```

Description

- You can use the Insert statement to insert a single row or selected rows into a database table.
- You can use the Update statement to change the values of one or more columns in one or more rows of a database table.
- You can use the Delete statement to delete one or more rows from a database table.

Figure 1-11 How to add, update, and delete data in a table

How to work with other database objects and functions

In addition to the tables you've already learned about, relational databases can contain other database objects like views, stored procedures, and triggers. You can also use functions to work with the data in a database. In the topics that follow, you'll be introduced to these objects and functions.

How to work with views

A *view* is a predefined query that's stored in a database. To create a view, you use the Create View statement as shown in figure 1-12. This statement causes the Select statement you specify to be stored with the database. In this case, the Create View statement creates a view named VendorsMin that retrieves three columns from the Vendors table.

To access a view, you issue a Select statement that refers to the view. This causes a *virtual table*—a temporary table that's created on the server—to be created from the Select statement in the view. Then, the Select statement that referred to the view is executed on this virtual table to create the result set.

Although views can be quite useful, they require some additional overhead. That's because every time an application refers to a view, the view has to be created from scratch. If that's a problem, an alternative is to use stored procedures.

A Create View statement for a view named VendorsMin

```
CREATE VIEW VendorsMin AS
    SELECT Name, State, Phone
    FROM Vendors
```

A Select statement that uses the VendorsMin view

```
SELECT * FROM VendorsMin
WHERE State = 'CA'
ORDER BY Name
```

The virtual table that's created when the Select statement that uses the view is executed

Name	State	Phone
US Postal Service	WI	8005551205
National Information Data Ctr	DC	3015558950
Register of Copyrights	DC	2027078800
Jobtrak	CA	8005558725
Newbrige Book Clubs	DC	8005559980
California Chamber Of Commerce	CA	9165556670
Towne Advertiser's Mailing Svcs	CA	*NULL*
BFI Industries	CA	5595551551
Pacific Gas & Electric	CA	8005556081

The result set that's created from the view

	Name	State	Phone
1	Abbey Office Furnishings	CA	5595558300
2	American Express	CA	8005553344
3	ASC Signs	CA	NULL
4	Aztek Label	CA	7145559000
5	Bertelsmann Industry Svcs. Inc	CA	8055550584
6	BFI Industries	CA	5595551551
7	Bill Jones	CA	NULL
8	Bill Marvin Electric Inc	CA	5595555106
9	Blanchard & Johnson Associates	CA	2145553647

Description

- A *view* consists of a Select statement that's stored with the database. Because views are stored as part of the database, they can be managed independently of the applications that use them.
- When you refer to a view, a *virtual table* is created on the server that represents the view. Then, the result set is extracted from this virtual table. For this reason, a view is also called a *viewed table*.
- Views can be used to restrict the data that a user is allowed to access or to present data in a form that's easy for the user to understand. In some databases, users may be allowed to access data only through views.

Figure 1-12 How to work with views

How to work with stored procedures and triggers

A *stored procedure* is a set of one or more SQL statements that are stored together in a database. To create a stored procedure, you use the Create Procedure statement as shown in figure 1-13. Here, the stored procedure contains a single Select statement. To use the stored procedure, you send a request for it to be executed.

When the server receives the request, it executes the stored procedure. If the stored procedure contains a Select statement like the one in this figure, the result set is sent back to the calling program. If the stored procedure contains Insert, Update, or Delete statements, the appropriate processing is performed.

Notice that the stored procedure in this figure accepts an *input parameter* named @State from the calling program. The value of this parameter is then substituted for the parameter in the Where clause so only vendors in the specified state are included in the result set.

When it's done with its processing, a stored procedure can also pass *output parameters* back to the calling program, which you can learn more about in figure 7-1 of chapter 7. In addition, stored procedures can include *control-of-flow language* that determines the processing that's done based on specific conditions.

A *trigger* is a special type of stored procedure that's executed automatically when an insert, update, or delete operation is performed on a table. Triggers are used most often to validate data before a row is added or updated, but they can also be used to maintain the relationships between tables. Although you don't work with triggers directly from an application program, you need to know what triggers exist for the tables in a database and what operations they perform. That way, you'll know what processing an application needs to do before it updates the table.

A Create Procedure statement for a procedure named spVendorsByState

```
CREATE PROCEDURE spVendorsByState @State char AS
    SELECT Name, State, Phone
    FROM Vendors
    WHERE State = @State
    ORDER BY Name
```

The result set that's created when the stored procedure is executed with the @State variable set to 'CA'

	Name	State	Phone
1	Abbey Office Furnishings	CA	5595558300
2	American Express	CA	8005553344
3	ASC Signs	CA	NULL
4	Aztek Label	CA	7145559000
5	Bertelsmann Industry Svcs. Inc	CA	8055550584
6	BFI Industries	CA	5595551551
7	Bill Jones	CA	NULL
8	Bill Marvin Electric Inc	CA	5595555106
9	Blanchard & Johnson Associates	CA	2145553647

Concepts

- A *stored procedure* consists of one or more SQL statements that have been compiled and stored with the database. A stored procedure can be started by application code on the client.
- Stored procedures can improve database performance because the SQL statements in each procedure are only compiled and optimized the first time they're executed. In contrast, SQL statements that are sent from a client to the server have to be compiled and optimized every time they're executed.
- In addition to Select statements, a stored procedure can contain other SQL statements such as Insert, Update, and Delete statements. It can also contain *control-of-flow language*, which lets you perform conditional processing within the stored procedure.
- A *trigger* is a special type of procedure that's executed when rows are inserted, updated, or deleted from a table. Triggers are typically used to check the validity of the data in a row that's being updated or added to a table.

Figure 1-13 How to work with stored procedures and triggers

How to work with functions

Figure 1-14 introduces you to three types of *functions* that you can use when you code SQL statements. Here, each table lists just a few of the functions that are available in each category. But please note that all functions return a single value.

To illustrate, the first coding example in this figure is a Select statement that uses three *scalar functions*. These are functions that can operate on the data in a single row. Here, the GETDATE function is used to get the current date, which is displayed in the first column of the result set. Then, the GETDATE function is used as a parameter for the DATEDIFF function, which returns the number of days between the date in the InvoiceDate column and the current date.

In contrast, the second coding example is a SELECT statement that uses two *aggregate functions*. These are functions that can operate on the data in two or more rows. In this case, the COUNT function returns the number of rows selected by the query, and the SUM function returns the sum of the values in the InvoiceTotal column of the selected rows.

The third table in this figure presents two of the *system functions* that are available with SQL Server, and each database management system has its own system functions. In this table, both functions return the last value that was generated for an identity column. As you may remember from figure 1-7, an identity column is a numeric column whose value is generated automatically when a row is added to a table. As a result, you can use one of these functions to find out what the generated number is after you add a row to a table.

Besides these three types of functions, you can create *user-defined functions* that are stored with the database. These functions are most often written and used by SQL programmers within the stored procedures and triggers that they write. Although user-defined functions can also be used by application programmers, there are no examples of their use in this book.

Some of the SQL Server scalar functions

Function name	Description
`LTRIM(string)`	Returns the string with any leading spaces removed.
`LEFT(string,length)`	Returns the specified number of characters from the beginning of the string.
`GETDATE()`	Returns the current system date and time.
`DATEDIFF(datepart,startdate,enddate)`	Returns the number of datepart units between the specified start and end dates.

Some of the SQL Server aggregate functions

Function name	Description
`AVG([ALL|DISTINCT] expression)`	The average of the non-null values in the expression.
`SUM([ALL|DISTINCT] expression)`	The total of the non-null values in the expression.
`COUNT(*)`	The number of rows selected by the query.

Some of the SQL Server system functions

Function name	Description
`@@IDENTITY`	Returns the last value generated for an identity column on the server. Returns Null if no identity value was generated.
`IDENT_CURRENT('tablename')`	Returns the last identity value that was generated for a specified table.

A Select statement that includes three scalar functions

```
SELECT InvoiceDate, GETDATE() AS 'Today''s Date',
    DATEDIFF(day, InvoiceDate, GETDATE()) AS Age
FROM Invoices
```

	InvoiceDate	Today's Date	Age
177	2010-09-14	2010-11-24 14:48:17.020	71
178	2010-09-17	2010-11-24 14:48:17.020	68
179	2010-09-20	2010-11-24 14:48:17.020	65

A Select statement that includes two aggregate functions

```
SELECT COUNT(*) AS NumberOfInvoices, SUM(InvoiceTotal) AS
    TotalInvoiceAmount
FROM Invoices
WHERE InvoiceDate > '2010-10-01'
```

	NumberOfInvoices	TotalInvoiceAmount
1	9	7245.00

Description

- A *function* performs an operation and returns a single value. A *scalar function* operates on one or more values in a single row and returns a single value. An *aggregate function* operates on values in two or more rows and returns a summarizing value. And a *system function* returns information about SQL Server values, objects, and settings.

Figure 1-14 How to work with functions

Perspective

In this chapter, you've learned the basic concepts and terms that relate to client/server programming, relational databases, and SQL. Although you don't need to be an expert in database design or SQL programming to develop database applications with Visual Basic, you at least need to be familiar with those concepts and terms. There's a lot more to learn, though, and for that we recommend *Murach's SQL Server 2008 for Developers*.

Terms

SQL Server 2008 Express
SQL Server 2008
client/server system
client
server
network
database server
enterprise system
local area network (LAN)
wide area network (WAN)
network operating system
database management system (DBMS)
back-end processing
back end
application software
data access API
application programming interface (API)
front-end processing
front end
SQL query
query
Structured Query Language (SQL)
query results
application server
business class
database class
web browser
web application
web server
web service
relational database
table
record
row
field
column
primary key
composite primary key
non-primary key
unique key
unique key constraint
index
foreign key
foreign key table
primary key table
one-to-many relationship
one-to-one relationship
many-to-many relationship
linking table
referential integrity
foreign key constraint
cascade update
cascade delete
trigger
orphaned row
data type
system data type
null value
default value
identity column
check constraint
SQL dialect
Transact-SQL
result table
result set
calculated column
join
inner join
view
virtual table
viewed table
stored procedure
input parameter
output parameter
control-of-flow language
function
scalar function
aggregate function
system function
user-defined function

2

An introduction to ADO.NET 4

ADO.NET consists of a set of classes defined by the .NET Framework that you can use to access the data in a database. The current version of ADO.NET is ADO.NET 4, and that's the version you'll learn about in this book.

This chapter introduces you to the primary ADO.NET classes that you'll use as you develop database applications with Visual Basic. This chapter also introduces you to the two basic ways that you can develop database applications with ADO.NET. If you've used ADO.NET 3.5, you'll see that the classes that are included in ADO.NET 4 and the basic features Visual Studio 2010 provides for developing database applications have changed very little.

An overview of ADO.NET

ADO.NET (*ActiveX Data Objects .NET*) is the primary data access API for the .NET Framework. It provides the classes that you use as you develop database applications with Visual Basic as well as the other .NET languages. In the topics that follow, you'll learn the two basic ways that you can use the ADO.NET classes for accessing and updating the data in a database.

How to use ADO.NET with datasets

One way to develop database applications with ADO.NET is to use datasets. With this approach, your application gets data from a database and stores it in a *dataset* that is kept in cache memory on disk. Then, your application can add, update, or delete rows in the dataset, and it can later save those changes from the dataset to the database.

When you use this approach, your application uses the ADO.NET objects shown in figure 2-1. To load data into a *data table* within a dataset, you use a *data adapter*. Its main function is to manage the flow of data between a dataset and a database. To do that, it uses *commands* that define the SQL statements to be issued. The command for retrieving data, for example, typically defines a Select statement. Then, the command connects to the database using a *connection* and passes the Select statement to the database. After the Select statement is executed, the result set it produces is sent back to the data adapter, which stores the results in the data table.

To update the data in a database, the data adapter determines which rows in the data table have been inserted, updated, or deleted. Then, it uses commands that define Insert, Update, and Delete statements for the data table to update the associated rows in the database. Like the command that retrieves data from the database, the commands that update the database use a connection to connect to the database and perform the requested operation.

Note that the data in a dataset is independent of the database that the data was retrieved from. In fact, the connection to the database is typically closed after the data is retrieved from the database. Then, the connection is opened again when it's needed. Because of that, the application must work with the copy of the data that's stored in the dataset. The architecture that's used to implement this type of data processing is referred to as a *disconnected data architecture*.

Although this approach is more complicated than a connected architecture, it has several advantages. One advantage is that using a disconnected data architecture can improve system performance due to the use of fewer system resources for maintaining connections. Another advantage is that it makes ADO.NET compatible with ASP.NET web applications, which are inherently disconnected.

Basic ADO.NET objects

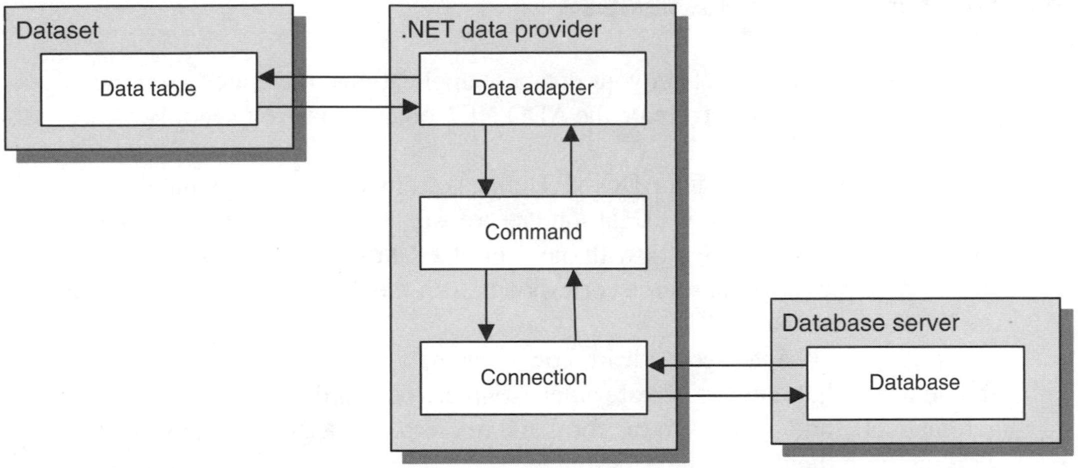

Description

- A *.NET data provider* provides the classes that let you create the objects that you use to retrieve data from a database and to store data in a database.
- One way to work with a database when you use ADO.NET is to retrieve data from a database into a dataset and to store data from the dataset to the database.
- A *dataset* contains one or more *data tables* that store the data retrieved from the database. Then, the application can work with the data in the data tables, and it can insert, update, and delete rows in the data tables.
- To retrieve data from a database and store it in a data table, a *data adapter* object issues a Select statement that's stored in a *command* object. Next, the command object uses a *connection* object to connect to the database and retrieve the data. Then, the data is passed back to the data adapter, which stores the data in the dataset.
- To update the data in a database based on the data in a data table, the data adapter object issues an Insert, Update, or Delete statement that's stored in a command object. Then, the command object uses a connection to connect to the database and update the data.
- When you use a data adapter to work with the data in a database, the data provider remains connected to the database only long enough to retrieve or update the specified data. Then, it disconnects from the database and the application works with the data via the dataset object. This is referred to as a *disconnected data architecture*.
- The disconnected data architecture offers improved system performance due to the use of fewer system resources for maintaining connections.

Figure 2-1 How to use ADO.NET with datasets

Two ways to create the ADO.NET objects for working with datasets

When you use datasets in your database applications, there are two basic techniques you can use to create the ADO.NET objects that you need. Both are illustrated in figure 2-2.

First, you can create the ADO.NET objects from a *data source* that's shown in the *Data Sources window*. Data sources are a feature of .NET 4 that makes it easy to create forms that work with the data in a data source such as a database. In this example, the data source corresponds with the data in the Terms table in the Payables database.

In the next chapter, you'll learn how to create a data source. For now, you should know that once you create a data source, you can drag it onto a form to automatically add controls to the form and to create the ADO.NET objects for working with the data in the data source.

In this figure, for example, you can see the controls and objects that are generated when you drag the Terms table onto the form. Here, a DataGridView control has been added to the form to display the terms in the Terms table, and a toolbar has been added that lets you work with this data.

In addition, five objects have been added to the *Component Designer tray* below the form. Three of these are ADO.NET objects. The first one, named PayablesDataSet, defines the dataset for the form. Then, an object named TermsTableAdapter defines the table adapter for the Terms table. A *table adapter* is an object that's generated by the designer. It includes a data adapter, a connection object, and one or more command objects. In essence, then, it combines the three classes of a .NET data provider that you saw in the previous figure. You'll learn more about table adapters in the next chapter. Finally, an object named TableAdapterManager makes sure that if two or more related tables are updated by the controls on the form, referential integrity is maintained.

The other two objects in the Component Designer tray are used to bind the controls on the form to the data source. The first object, named TermsBindingSource, identifies the Terms table as the data source for the controls. The second object, named TermsBindingNavigator, defines the toolbar that's displayed across the top of the form.

Although you don't usually need to change the properties of the objects in the Component Designer tray, you should know that you can do that using the same technique you use to change the properties of a control on a form. That is, you just select an object to display its properties in the Properties window and then work with them from there.

The second technique for creating ADO.NET objects is to write the code yourself. In this figure, for example, you can see the code that creates four objects: a connection, a command named selectCommand that contains a Select statement, a data adapter named termsDataAdapter, and a dataset named termsDataSet. Because you're most likely to use data sources to work with datasets, I won't present this coding technique in this book.

Using the Data Sources window to create ADO.NET objects

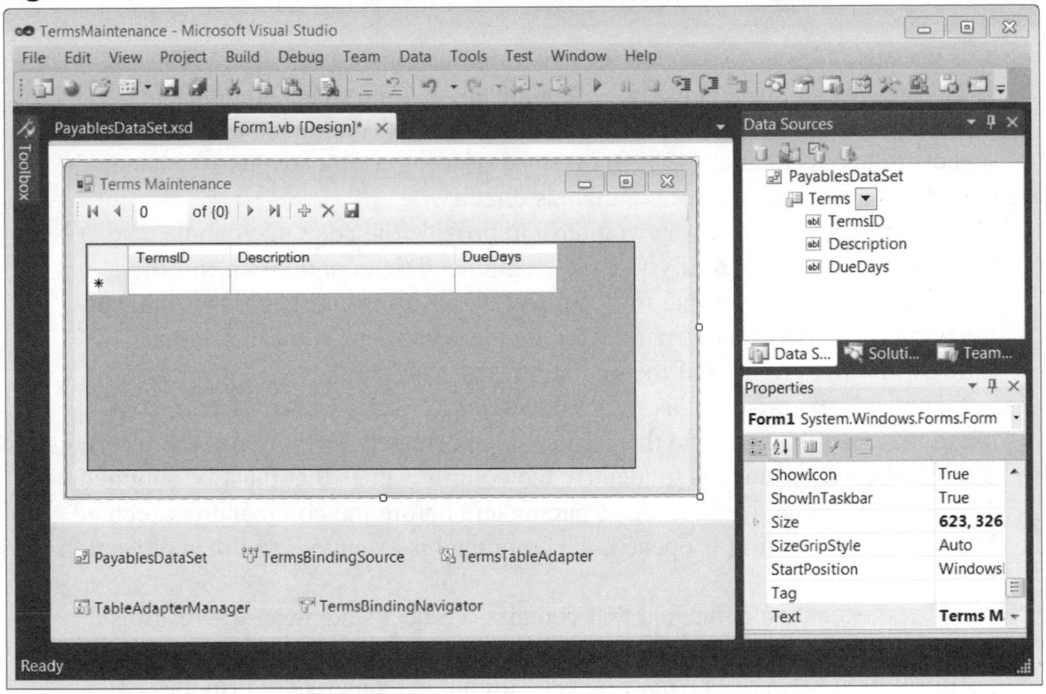

Visual Basic code that creates ADO.NET objects

```
Dim connectionString As String =
    "Data Source=localhost\SqlExpress;Initial Catalog=Payables;" &
    "Integrated Security=True"
Dim connection As New SqlConnection(connectionString)

Dim selectStatement As String = "SELECT * FROM Terms"
Dim selectCommand As New SqlCommand(selectStatement, connection)

Dim termsDataAdapter As New SqlDataAdapter(selectCommand)

Dim termsDataSet As New DataSet
```

Description

- You can use the *Data Sources window* in Visual Studio to create a *data source*. Then, you can drag the data source onto the form to automatically generate a table adapter object and a dataset object.
- A *table adapter* is like a data adapter, but it has a built-in connection object, and it can contain more than one query. You'll learn how to work with table adapters in chapter 3.
- To create ADO.NET objects in code, you write declarations that identify the class each object is created from.

Figure 2-2 Two ways to create the ADO.NET objects for working with datasets

How to use ADO.NET without using datasets

The second way to develop database applications using ADO.NET is to work with the database directly, without using datasets. This approach is illustrated in figure 2-3. As you can see, you still use command and connection objects to access the database. But instead of using a data adapter to execute the commands, you execute the commands directly.

When you work this way, you have to provide the code that handles the result of each command. If you issue a command that contains an Insert, Update, or Delete statement, for example, the result is an integer that indicates the number of rows that were affected by the operation. You can use that information to determine if the operation was successful.

The code example in this figure illustrates how this works. Here, a command that inserts a row into the Terms table is created. In this case, the Insert statement uses parameters to identify the column values that must be supplied. Then, values are assigned to these parameters before the command is executed. Finally, the connection is opened, the command is executed, and the connection is closed.

If you execute a command that contains a Select statement, the result is a result set that contains the rows you requested. To read through the rows in the result set, you use a *data reader* object. Although a data reader provides an efficient way of reading the rows in a result set, you can't use it to modify those rows. In addition, it only lets you read rows in a forward direction, so once you read the next row, the previous row is unavailable. Because of that, you typically use a data reader either to retrieve rows that are displayed in a control such as a combo box, or to retrieve and work with a single database row at a time.

ADO.NET components for accessing a database directly

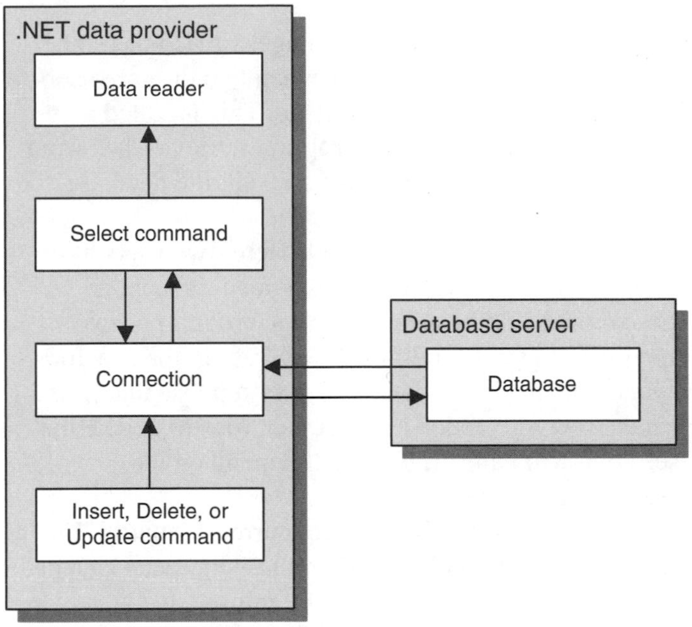

Code that creates and executes a command that inserts a row

```
Dim insertStatement As String =
    "INSERT Terms (Description, DueDays) " &
    "VALUES (@Description, @DueDays)"
Dim insertCommand As New SqlCommand(insertStatement, connection)
insertCommand.Parameters.AddWithValue("@Description", terms.Description)
insertCommand.Parameters.AddWithValue("@DueDays", terms.DueDays)
connection.Open()
Dim count As Integer = insertCommand.ExecuteNonQuery
connection.Close()
```

Description

- Instead of executing the commands associated with a data adapter to manage the flow of data between a dataset and a database, you can execute those commands directly. When you do that, you create and work with the ADO.NET objects through code.
- To retrieve data from a database, you execute a command object that contains a Select statement. Then, the command object uses a connection to connect to the database and retrieve the data. You can then read the results one row at a time using a *data reader* object.
- To insert, update, or delete data in a database, you execute a command object that contains an Insert, Update, or Delete statement. Then, the command object uses a connection to connect to the database and update the data. You can then check the value that's returned to determine if the operation was successful.

Figure 2-3 How to use ADO.NET without using datasets

Concurrency and the disconnected data architecture

Although the disconnected data architecture has advantages, it also has some disadvantages. One of those is the conflict that can occur when two or more users retrieve and then try to update data in the same row of a table. This is called a *concurrency* problem. This is possible because once a program retrieves data from a database, the connection to that database is dropped. As a result, the database management system can't manage the update process.

To illustrate, consider the situation shown in figure 2-4. Here, two users have retrieved the Vendors table from a database, so a copy of the Vendors table is stored on each user's PC. These users could be using the same program or two different programs. Now, suppose that user 1 modifies the address in the row for vendor 123 and updates the Vendors table in the database. And suppose that user 2 modifies the phone number in the row for vendor 123 and then tries to update the Vendors table in the database. What will happen? That will depend on the *concurrency control* that's used by the programs.

When you use ADO.NET, you have two choices for concurrency control. First, you can use *optimistic concurrency*, which checks whether a row has been changed since it was retrieved. If it has, the update or deletion will be refused and a *concurrency exception* will be thrown. Then, the program should handle the error. For example, it could display an error message that tells the user that the row could not be updated and then retrieve the updated row so the user can make the change again.

In contrast, the *"last in wins"* technique works the way its name implies. Since no checking is done with this technique, the row that's updated by the last user overwrites any changes made to the row by a previous user. For the example above, the row updated by user 2 will overwrite changes made by user 1, which means that the phone number will be right but the address will be wrong. Since errors like this corrupt the data in a database, optimistic concurrency is used by most programs, which means that your programs have to handle the concurrency exceptions that are thrown.

If you know that concurrency will be a problem, you can use a couple of programming techniques to limit concurrency exceptions. If a program uses a dataset, one technique is to update the database frequently so other programs can retrieve the current data. The program should also refresh its dataset frequently so it contains the recent changes made by other programs.

Another way to avoid concurrency exceptions is to retrieve and work with just one row at a time. That way, it's less likely that two programs will update the same row at the same time. In contrast, if two programs retrieve the same table, they will of course retrieve the same rows. Then, if they both update the same row in the table, even though it may not be at the same time, a concurrency exception will occur when they try to update the database.

Of course, you will understand and appreciate this more as you learn how to develop your own database applications. As you develop them, though, keep in mind that most applications are multi-user applications. That's why you have to be aware of concurrency problems.

Two users who are working with copies of the same data

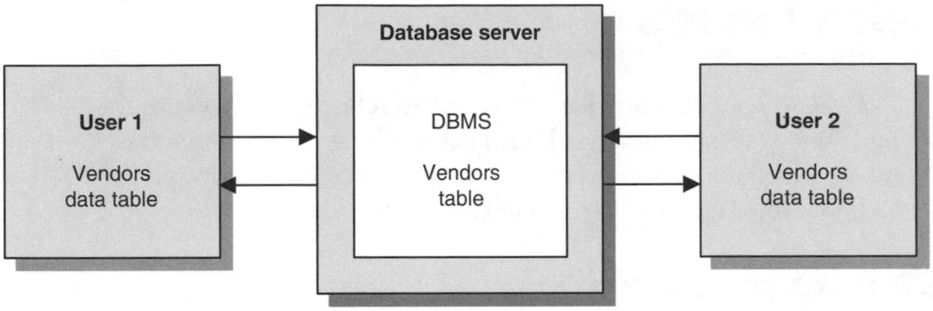

What happens when two users try to update the same row

- When two or more users retrieve the data in the same row of a database table at the same time, it is called *concurrency*. Because ADO.NET uses a disconnected data architecture, the database management system can't prevent this from happening.
- If two users try to update the same row in a database table at the same time, the second user's changes could overwrite the changes made by the first user. Whether or not that happens, though, depends on the *concurrency control* that the programs use.
- By default, ADO.NET uses *optimistic concurrency*. This means that the program checks to see whether the database row that's going to be updated or deleted has been changed since it was retrieved. If it has, a *concurrency exception* occurs and the update or deletion is refused. Then, the program should handle the exception.
- If optimistic concurrency isn't in effect, the program doesn't check to see whether a row has been changed before an update or deletion takes place. Instead, the operation proceeds without throwing an exception. This is referred to as "*last in wins*" because the last update overwrites any previous update. And this leads to errors in the database.

How to avoid concurrency errors

- For many applications, concurrency errors rarely occur. As a result, optimistic concurrency is adequate because the users will rarely have to resubmit an update or deletion that is refused.
- If concurrency is likely to be a problem, a program that uses a dataset can be designed so it updates the database and refreshes the dataset frequently. That way, concurrency errors are less likely to occur.
- Another way to avoid concurrency errors is to design a program so it retrieves and updates just one row at a time. That way, there's less chance that two users will retrieve and update the same row at the same time.

Figure 2-4 Concurrency and the disconnected data architecture

The ADO.NET data providers and their classes

The *.NET data providers* provide the ADO.NET classes that you use for connecting to and working directly with a database. That's why these classes are sometimes called the *connected classes*. In the topics that follow, you'll learn more about the data providers and the classes that they provide.

The .NET data providers

All .NET data providers include the core classes for creating the four types of objects listed in the first table in figure 2-5. You've already learned the basic functions of these classes, and you'll learn more about these classes throughout this book.

The second table in this figure lists the three data providers that come with the .NET Framework 4. The SQL Server data provider is designed to provide efficient access to a Microsoft SQL Server database. The OLE DB data provider is a generic data provider that can access any database that supports the industry standard OLE DB interface. And the ODBC provider lets you access any database that can work with ODBC, another industry standard database interface. Although you can use the OLE DB data provider to access a SQL Server database, you shouldn't do that unless you plan on migrating the data to another database since the SQL Server data provider is optimized for accessing SQL Server data.

Besides the providers that come with the .NET Framework, several database vendors have developed .NET data providers that are optimized for use with their databases. For example, .NET data providers are available for the popular MySQL and Sybase databases as well as for a variety of other databases. Before you develop an application using the OLE DB provider, then, you should check with your database vendor to see if a specialized .NET data provider is available.

The third table in this figure lists the names of the classes you use to create objects using the SQL Server, OLE DB, and ODBC providers. Notice that these classes use prefixes ("Sql," "OleDb," and "Odbc") to indicate which provider each class belongs to.

When you develop a Visual Basic application that uses ADO.NET, you'll want to add an Imports statement for the namespace that contains the data provider classes at the beginning of each source file that uses those classes. That way, you won't have to qualify the references to these classes. These namespaces are listed in the second table in this figure.

Now that you're familiar with the core classes of the three .NET data providers that come with the .NET Framework, the next four topics describe the classes of the SQL Server data provider in more detail. You should realize, though, that the information presented in these topics applies to the classes of the other data providers as well.

.NET data provider core objects

Object	Description
Connection	Establishes a connection to a database.
Command	Represents an individual SQL statement or stored procedure that can be executed against the database.
Data reader	Provides read-only, forward-only access to the data in a database.
Data adapter	Provides the link between the command and connection objects and a dataset object.

Data providers included with the .NET framework

Provider	Namespace	Description
SQL Server	System.Data.SqlClient	Lets you access SQL Server databases.
OLE DB	System.Data.OleDb	Lets you access any database that supports OLE DB.
ODBC	System.Data.Odbc	Lets you access any database that supports ODBC.

Class names for the data providers

Object	SQL Server	OLE DB	ODBC
Connection	SqlConnection	OleDbConnection	OdbcConnection
Command	SqlCommand	OleDbCommand	OdbcCommand
Data reader	SqlDataReader	OleDbDataReader	OdbcDataReader
Data adapter	SqlDataAdapter	OleDbDataAdapter	OdbcDataAdapter

An Imports statement for the SQL Server data provider namespace

```
Imports System.Data.SqlClient
```

Description

- The *.NET data providers* provide the ADO.NET classes that are responsible for working dircctly with a database. In addition to the core classes shown above, classes are provided for other functions such as passing parameters to commands and working with transactions.
- To use a .NET data provider in an application, you should add an Imports statement for the appropriate namespace at the beginning of the source file. Otherwise, you'll have to qualify each class you refer to with the SqlClient, OleDb, Odbc, or OracleClient namespace since these namespaces aren't included as references by default.
- Other .NET data providers are available to provide efficient access to non-Microsoft databases such as MySQL, Sybase, PostgreSQL, and IBM DB2.
- All of the ADO.NET objects are implemented by classes in the System.Data namespace of the .NET Framework. However, the specific classes used to implement the connection, command, data reader, and data adapter objects depend on the .NET data provider you use.

Figure 2-5 The .NET data providers

The SqlConnection class

Before you can access the data in a database, you have to create a connection object that defines the connection to the database. To do that, you use the SqlConnection class presented in figure 2-6.

The most important property of the SqlConnection class is ConnectionString. A *connection string* is a text string that provides the information necessary to establish a connection to a database. That means it includes information such as the name of the database you want to access and the database server that contains it. It can also contain authentication information such as a user ID and password.

The two methods of the SqlConnection class shown in this figure let you open and close the connection. In general, you should leave a connection open only while data is being retrieved or updated. That's why when you use a data adapter, the connection is opened and closed for you. In that case, you don't need to use the Open and Close methods.

The SqlCommand class

To execute a SQL statement against a SQL Server database, you create a SqlCommand object that contains the statement. Figure 2-6 presents the SqlCommand class you use to create this object. Notice that the Connection property of this class associates the command with a SqlConnection object, and the CommandText property contains the SQL statement to be executed.

The CommandType property indicates how the command object should interpret the value of the CommandText property. Instead of specifying a SQL statement for the CommandText property, for example, you can specify the name of a stored procedure. If you specify a SQL statement, you set the value of the CommandType property to CommandType.Text. If you specify the name of a stored procedure, you set it to CommandType.StoredProcedure.

Earlier in this chapter, you learned that you can use a data adapter to execute command objects. In addition, you can execute a command object directly using one of the three Execute methods shown in this figure. If the command contains a Select statement, for example, you can execute it using either ExecuteReader or ExecuteScalar. If you use ExecuteReader, the results are returned as a DataReader object. If you use ExecuteScalar, only the value in the first column and row of the query results is returned. You're most likely to use this method with a Select statement that returns a single summary value or the value of an identity column for a row that was just inserted into the database.

If the command contains an Insert, Update, or Delete statement, you'll use the ExecuteNonQuery method to execute it. This method returns an integer value that indicates the number of rows that were affected by the command. For example, if the command deletes a single row, the ExecuteNonQuery method returns 1.

Common properties and methods of the SqlConnection class

Property	Description
ConnectionString	Contains information that lets you connect to a SQL Server database. The connection string includes information such as the name of the server, the name of the database, and login information.
Method	**Description**
Open	Opens a connection to a database.
Close	Closes a connection to a database.

Common properties and methods of the SqlCommand class

Property	Description
Connection	The SqlConnection object that's used by the command to connect to the database.
CommandText	The text of the SQL command or the name of a stored procedure.
CommandType	A constant in the CommandType enumeration that indicates whether the CommandText property contains a SQL statement (Text) or the name of a stored procedure (StoredProcedure).
Parameters	The collection of parameters used by the command.
Method	**Description**
ExecuteReader	Executes a query and returns the result as a SqlDataReader object.
ExecuteNonQuery	Executes the command and returns an integer representing the number of rows affected.
ExecuteScalar	Executes a query and returns the first column of the first row returned by the query.

Description

- Each command object is associated with a connection object through the command's Connection property. When a command is executed, the information in the ConnectionString property of the connection object is used to connect to the database.
- When you use a data adapter to work with a database, the connection is opened and closed automatically. If that's not what you want, you can use the Open and Close methods of the connection object to open and close the connection.
- You can use the three Execute methods of a command object to execute the SQL statement it contains. You can also execute the SQL statement in a command object using methods of the data adapter. See figure 2-7 for more information.

Figure 2-6 The SqlConnection and SqlCommand classes

The SqlDataAdapter class

As you have learned, the job of a data adapter is to provide a link between a database and a dataset. The four properties of the SqlDataAdapter class listed in figure 2-7, for example, identify the four SQL commands that the data adapter uses to transfer data from the database to the dataset and vice versa. The SelectCommand property identifies the command object that's used to retrieve data from the database. And the DeleteCommand, InsertCommand, and UpdateCommand properties identify the commands that are used to update the database based on changes made to the data in the dataset.

To execute the command identified by the SelectCommand property and place the data that's retrieved in a dataset, you use the Fill method. Then, the application can work with the data in the dataset without affecting the data in the database. If the application makes changes to the data in the dataset, it can use the data adapter's Update method to execute the commands identified by the DeleteCommand, InsertCommand, and UpdateCommand properties and post the changes back to the database.

The SqlDataReader class

A data reader provides an efficient way to read the rows in a result set returned by a database query. In fact, when you use a data adapter to retrieve data, the data adapter uses a data reader to read through the rows in the result set and store them in a dataset.

A data reader is similar to other types of readers you may have encountered in the .NET Framework, such as a TextReader, a StreamReader, or an XmlReader. Like these other readers, a data reader lets you read rows but not modify them. In other words, a data reader is read-only. In addition, it only lets you read rows in a forward direction. Once you read the next row, the previous row is unavailable.

Figure 2-7 lists the most important properties and methods of the SqlDataReader class. You use the Read method to read the next row of data in the result set. In most cases, you'll code the Read method in a loop that reads and processes rows until the end of the data reader is reached.

To access a column of data from the current row of a data reader, you use the Item property. To identify the column, you can use either its index value like this:

```
drVendors.Item(0)
```

or its name like this:

```
drVendors.Item("Name")
```

Since Item is the default property, you can also omit it like this:

```
drVendors("Name")
```

Common properties and methods of the SqlDataAdapter class

Property	Description
SelectCommand	A SqlCommand object representing the Select statement or stored procedure used to query the database.
DeleteCommand	A SqlCommand object representing the Delete statement or stored procedure used to delete a row from the database.
InsertCommand	A SqlCommand object representing the Insert statement or stored procedure used to add a row to the database.
UpdateCommand	A SqlCommand object representing the Update statement or stored procedure used to update a row in the database.
Method	**Description**
Fill	Executes the command identified by the SelectCommand property and loads the result into a dataset object.
Update	Executes the commands identified by the DeleteCommand, InsertCommand, and UpdateCommand properties for each row in the dataset that was deleted, added, or updated.

Common properties and methods of the SqlDataReader class

Property	Description
Item	Accesses the column with the specified index or name from the current row.
FieldCount	The number of columns in the current row.
Method	**Description**
Read	Reads the next row. Returns True if there are more rows. Otherwise, returns False.
Close	Closes the data reader.

Description

- When the Fill method of a data adapter is used to retrieve data from a database, the data adapter uses a data reader to load the results into a dataset. If you don't use a dataset, you can work with a data reader directly.
- A data reader provides read-only, forward-only access to the data in a database. Because it doesn't require the overhead of a dataset, it's more efficient than using a data adapter. However, it can't be used to update data. To do that, you have to use other techniques.

Figure 2-7 The SqlDataAdapter and SqlDataReader classes

ADO.NET datasets

Unlike the .NET data providers that provide the connected classes for accessing the data in a database, an ADO.NET dataset provides the *disconnected classes* for working with the data in a database. In the next two topics, you'll learn how a dataset is organized, and you'll get an overview of the classes you use to define dataset objects.

How a dataset is organized

Figure 2-8 illustrates the basic organization of an ADO.NET dataset. The first thing you should notice in this figure is that a dataset is structured much like a relational database. It can contain one or more tables, and each table can contain one or more columns and rows. In addition, each table can contain one or more constraints that can define a unique key within the table or a foreign key of another table in the dataset. If a dataset contains two or more tables, the dataset can also define the relationships between those tables.

Although a dataset is structured much like a relational database, it's important to realize that each table in a dataset corresponds to the result set that's returned from a Select statement, not necessarily to an actual table in a database. For example, a Select statement may join data from several tables in a database to produce a single result set. In this case, the table in the dataset would represent data from each of the tables involved in the join.

You should also know that each group of objects in the diagram in this figure is stored in a collection. All of the columns in a table, for example, are stored in a collection of columns, and all of the rows are stored in a collection of rows. You'll learn more about these collections in the next figure and in later chapters.

The basic dataset object hierarchy

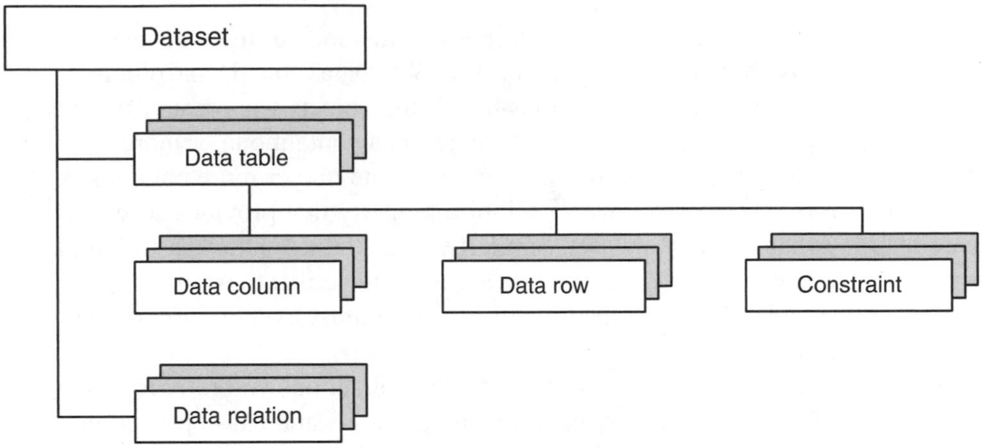

Description

- A dataset object consists of a hierarchy of one or more data table and *data relation* objects.
- A data table object consists of one or more *data column* objects and one or more *data row* objects. The data column objects define the data in each column of the table, including its name, data type, and so on, and the data row objects contain the data for each row in the table.
- A data table can also contain one or more *constraint* objects that are used to maintain the integrity of the data in the table. A unique key constraint ensures that the values in a column, such as the primary key column, are unique. And a foreign key constraint determines how the rows in one table are affected when corresponding rows in a related table are updated or deleted.
- The data relation objects define how the tables in the dataset are related. They are used to manage constraints and to simplify the navigation between related tables.
- All of the objects in a dataset are stored in collections. For example, the data table objects are stored in a data table collection, and the data row objects are stored in a data row collection. You can refer to these collections through the properties of the containing objects.

Figure 2-8 How a dataset is organized

The dataset classes

Figure 2-9 presents some of the properties and methods of the four main classes that you use to work with a dataset: DataSet, DataTable, DataColumn, and DataRow. As you saw in the previous figure, the objects you create from these classes form a hierarchy where each dataset can contain one or more tables and each table can contain one or more rows and one or more columns.

Because of that, a dataset contains a Tables property that provides access to the collection of tables in the dataset. Similarly, a data table contains a Columns property and a Rows property that provide access to the collections of columns and rows in the table. These are the properties you're most likely to use as you work with these objects.

Although they're not shown in this figure, the collections you refer to through the Tables property of a dataset and the Columns and Rows properties of a data table have properties and methods of their own. For instance, each collection has a Count property that you can use to determine how many items are in the collection. To get the number of tables in a dataset named payablesDataSet, for example, you can use code like this:

```
payablesDataSet.Tables.Count()
```

To access a specific item in a collection, you use the Item property. On that property, you specify the index value or name of the item you want to access. To access the Vendors table in payablesDataSet, for example, you can use code like this:

```
payablesDataSet.Tables.Item("Vendors")
```

Since Item is the default property of the collection class, however, you typically omit it like this:

```
payablesDataSet.Tables("Vendors")
```

The code in this figure shows how you can use a For Each...Next statement to loop through the items in a collection. Here, the statement loops through the rows in the Vendors table. To do that, it uses a variable that's declared as a DataRow object. Then, the For Each...Next statement uses this variable to retrieve the value of the Name column in each row. You can use similar code to loop through the columns in a table or the tables in a dataset.

Common properties of the DataSet class

Property	Description
DataSetName	The name of the dataset.
Tables	A collection of the DataTable objects contained in the dataset.
Relations	A collection of the DataRelation objects contained in the dataset.

Common properties and methods of the DataTable class

Property	Description
TableName	The name of the table.
Columns	A collection of the DataColumn objects contained in the data table.
Rows	A collection of the DataRow objects contained in the data table.
Constraints	A collection of the Constraint objects contained in the data table.
Method	**Description**
NewRow	Creates a new row in the table.

Common properties of the DataColumn class

Property	Description
ColumnName	The name of the column.
AllowDBNull	Indicates whether the column allows null values.
AutoIncrement	Indicates whether the column is an auto-increment column, which is similar to an identity column in SQL Server.

Common properties and methods of the DataRow class

Property	Description
Item	Accesses the specified column of the row.
Method	**Description**
Delete	Deletes a row.
IsNull	Indicates whether the specified column in the row contains a null value.

Code that refers to the rows collection in the tables collection of a dataset

```
Dim message As String
For Each dr As DataRow In vendorsDataSet.Tables("Vendors").Rows
    message &= dr.Item("Name").ToString & vbCrLf
Next
MessageBox.Show(message)
```

Description

- You'll use the properties and methods of the dataset classes most often when you work with ADO.NET objects through code.
- Each collection of objects has properties and methods that you can use to work with the collection.

Figure 2-9 The DataSet, DataTable, DataColumn, and DataRow classes

How ADO.NET applications are structured

As you saw earlier in this chapter, you can use two basic techniques to retrieve and work with the data in a database. With the first technique, you use a data adapter (or a table adapter that contains a data adapter) to retrieve the data and store it in a dataset and to update the database with changes made to the dataset. With the second technique, you work with the database by executing command objects directly, and you work with result sets using a data reader. In the next two topics, you'll see how the structures of applications that use these two techniques differ.

How an application that uses datasets is structured

When you develop an application that uses datasets, it typically consists of the two layers shown in figure 2-10. The first layer, called the *presentation layer*, consists of the form classes that display the user interface, plus the dataset classes used by the application. When you use a data source as shown in figure 2-2, for example, the application includes a dataset class that defines the tables and columns in the data source. Then, you can use the objects that are created when you drag the data source to a form for working with the data in the dataset that's created.

The second layer, called the *database layer*, always includes the database itself. In addition, this layer can include database classes that provide the data access required by the application. These classes typically include methods that connect to the database and retrieve, insert, add, and delete information from the database. Then, the presentation layer can call these methods to access the database, leaving the details of database access to the database classes.

Please note, however, that you can't use database classes when you develop an application by using a data source. That's because the table adapter object that you use to work with the database is generated for you when you drag a data source to a form. As a result, all of the code in an application like this is typically stored in the presentation layer.

The primary benefit of using data sources and datasets is rapid application development. This is especially useful for developing small, relatively simple applications and for prototyping larger applications. As an application gets more complicated, though, so does the use of data sources and datasets. So at some point, it often makes sense to use a three-layer architecture with business classes as shown in the next figure.

In case you aren't familiar with the term *prototyping*, it refers to quickly developing a working model of an application that can be reviewed by the intended users. Then, the users can point out what's wrong with the prototype or what they want changed, and the prototype can be changed accordingly. When the users agree that the prototype does or will do everything that they want, the application can be completely rewritten, often with a three-layer architecture.

The standard architecture of an application that uses datasets

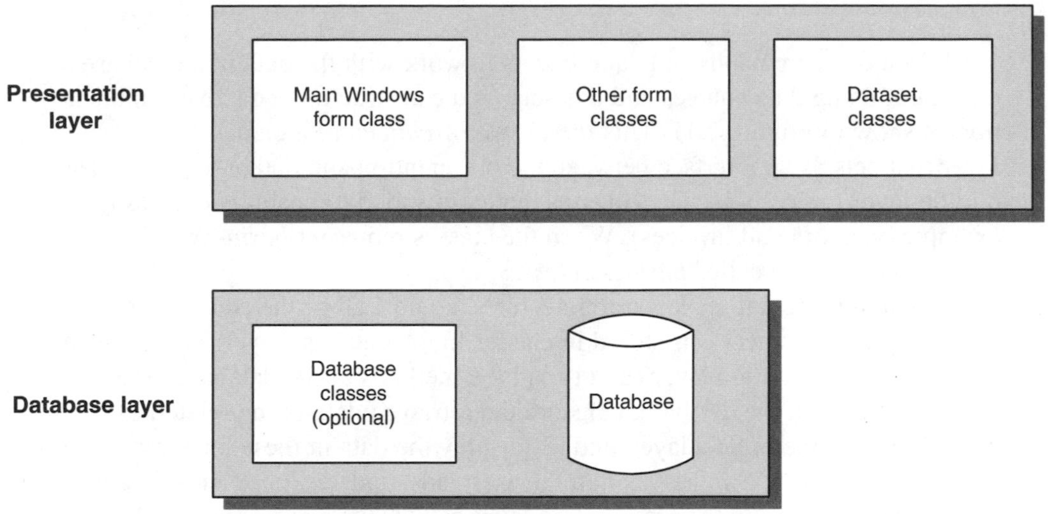

Description

- When you use a dataset to store the data that's retrieved from a database, the application is typically separated into two layers: the presentation layer and the database layer.
- The *presentation layer* consists of the forms that provide the application's user interface. In addition, this layer contains the dataset classes that define the data that the forms can use.
- The *database layer* consists of the database itself, and it can also include database classes that provide the methods for retrieving and updating the database for the application.
- If you create ADO.NET objects using a data source, you won't be able to use database classes in the database layer. If you create ADO.NET objects through code, you will be able to use database classes in the database layer, although that isn't a common practice.
- You can also store the dataset classes in a layer between the presentation layer and the database layer. Since data sources and datasets are typically used for rapid application development, however, this isn't a common technique.

Figure 2-10 How an application that uses datasets is structured

How an application that uses business classes is structured

If you use commands and data readers to work with the data in a database instead of using data sources and datasets, you can structure a database application as shown in figure 2-11. This *three-layer architecture* includes a *middle layer* that acts as an interface between the presentation and database layers. The middle layer typically includes classes that correspond to business entities (for example, vendors and invoices). When the classes represent *business objects*, they are commonly called *business classes*.

When you use a three-layer architecture like this, all of the code that's related to database access is stored in classes in the database layer. Then, a form class in the presentation layer can (1) call the methods of the database classes to retrieve data from the database, (2) store the retrieved data in the related business objects in the middle layer, and (3) display the data in these business objects on the form. Similarly, when the user adds, updates, or deletes data in a form, the form class in the presentation layer can (1) change the data in the related business objects, and (2) call the methods of a database class to save the changes to the database.

Although this approach to application development may seem complicated, using an architecture like this has some distinct advantages. First, it is usually easier to debug and maintain a three-layer application because you have complete control over the code. In contrast, you are forced to rely on a large amount of generated code when you use data sources and datasets.

Second, a three-layer architecture allows classes to be shared among applications. In particular, the classes that make up the database and middle layers can be placed in *class libraries* that can be used by more than one application.

Third, a three-layer architecture allows application development to be spread among members of a development team. For instance, one group of developers can work on the database layer, another group on the middle layer, and a third group on the presentation layer.

Fourth, you can run different layers of an application on different servers to improve performance. In that case, a three-layer architecture is often referred to as a *three-tier architecture*. But often, these terms are used interchangeably without implying how the layers are implemented in terms of hardware.

Finally, using a three-layer architecture makes it possible to use object data sources. As you will see in chapter 9, object data sources let you use database classes to get the data you need for an application, store that data in business objects, and still get some of the benefits that are associated with the use of data sources.

The architecture of an application that uses business classes

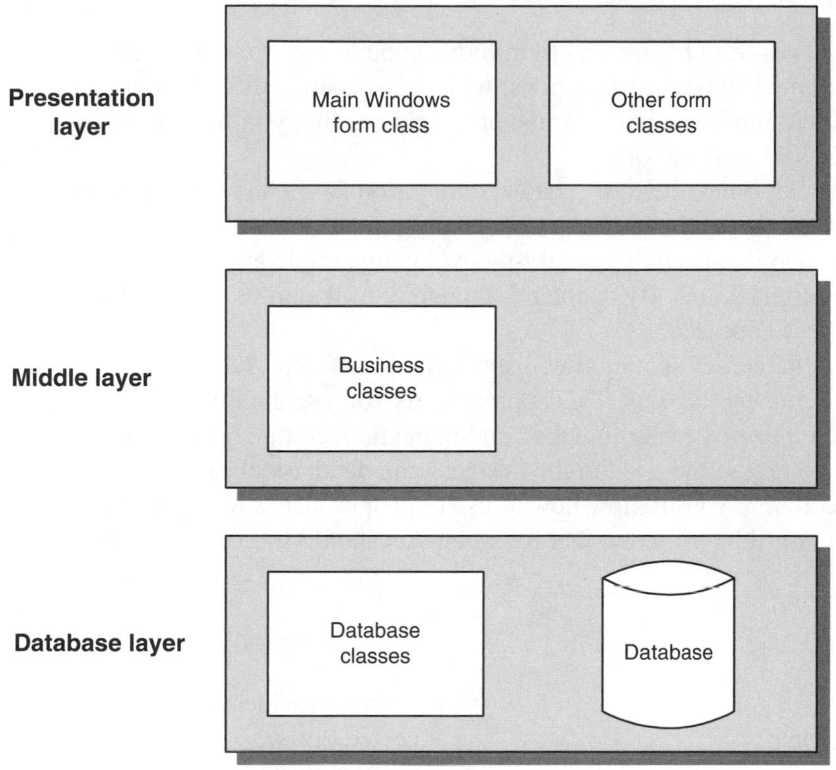

Description

- To simplify development and maintenance, many applications that use business classes use a *three-layer architecture* that includes a middle layer.
- The classes in the *middle layer*, sometimes called the *business rules layer*, act as an interface between the classes in the presentation and database layers. These classes can represent business entities, such as vendors or invoices, or they can implement business rules, such as discount or credit policies.
- When the classes in the middle layer represent business entities, the classes can be referred to as *business classes*, and the objects that are created from these classes can be referred to as *business objects*.
- When you use business classes, you don't use datasets. Instead, you use commands and data readers to work directly with the database, and the data you retrieve from the database is stored in business objects.
- Often, the classes that make up the database layer and the middle layer are implemented in *class libraries* that can be shared among applications.

Figure 2-11 How an application that uses business classes is structured

Perspective

One of the goals of this chapter was to introduce you to the two basic ways that you can develop ADO.NET applications: with datasets and without datasets. The other goal was to introduce you to some of the classes that you'll be using as you develop ADO.NET applications.

With that as background, the three chapters in section 2 will show you how to build significant database applications by using data sources and datasets. As you will see, this approach is especially useful for developing simple applications or prototyping larger applications. By chapter 5, though, you'll start to see some of the limitations of this approach.

Then, the five chapters in section 3 will show you how to build database applications without using datasets. This approach lets you use the three-layer architecture, which makes it easier to debug and maintain a complicated application and also lets you reuse the code in the business and database classes. By the time you finish section 3, you'll know how to use both approaches to application development, and you'll have a good feel for when you should use each approach.

Terms

ADO.NET
ActiveX Data Objects
dataset
data table
data adapter
command
connection
disconnected data architecture
data source
Data Sources window
Component Designer tray
table adapter
data reader
concurrency
concurrency control
optimistic concurrency
concurrency exception
"last in wins"
.NET data provider
connected classes
connection string
disconnected class
data relation
data column
data row
constraint
presentation layer
database layer
prototyping
three-layer architecture
middle layer
business rules layer
business class
business object
class library
three-tier architecture

Section 2

How to use data sources and datasets for Rapid Application Development

Now that you're familiar with the basic concepts and terms related to database programming, you're ready to learn the details of developing database applications. In this section, you'll learn how to use Visual Studio's data sources feature that you were introduced to in chapter 2. This is the quickest and easiest way to develop database applications.

In chapter 3, you'll learn the basic skills for working with data sources and datasets. Then, in chapter 4, you'll learn some additional skills for working with bound controls, and you'll learn one way to create queries that use parameters. Finally, in chapter 5, you'll learn how to use the Dataset Designer to work with the schema for a dataset. When you complete this section, you'll be able to develop significant database applications on your own.

3

How to work with data sources and datasets

In this chapter, you'll learn how to use data sources and datasets to develop database applications. This makes it easier than ever to generate Windows forms that work with the data that's in the data sources. And this is especially useful for developing simple applications or prototyping larger applications.

How to create a data source

As its name implies, a *data source* specifies the source of the data for an application. Since most applications get their data from a database, the figures that follow show how to create a data source that gets data from a database.

How to use the Data Sources window

The data sources that are available to a project are listed in the Data Sources window as shown in figure 3-1. Here, the second screen shows a data source for the Terms table that's available from the Payables database that's described in figure 1-8 of chapter 1. As you can see, this data source includes three columns from the Terms table named TermsID, Description, and DueDays.

If no data sources are available to a project, the Data Sources window will display an Add New Data Source link as shown in the first screen. Then, you can click on this link to start the Data Source Configuration Wizard described in figures 3-2 through 3-6. This wizard lets you add a new data source to the project. When you're done, you can drag the data source onto a form to create bound controls as described later in this chapter.

An empty Data Sources window

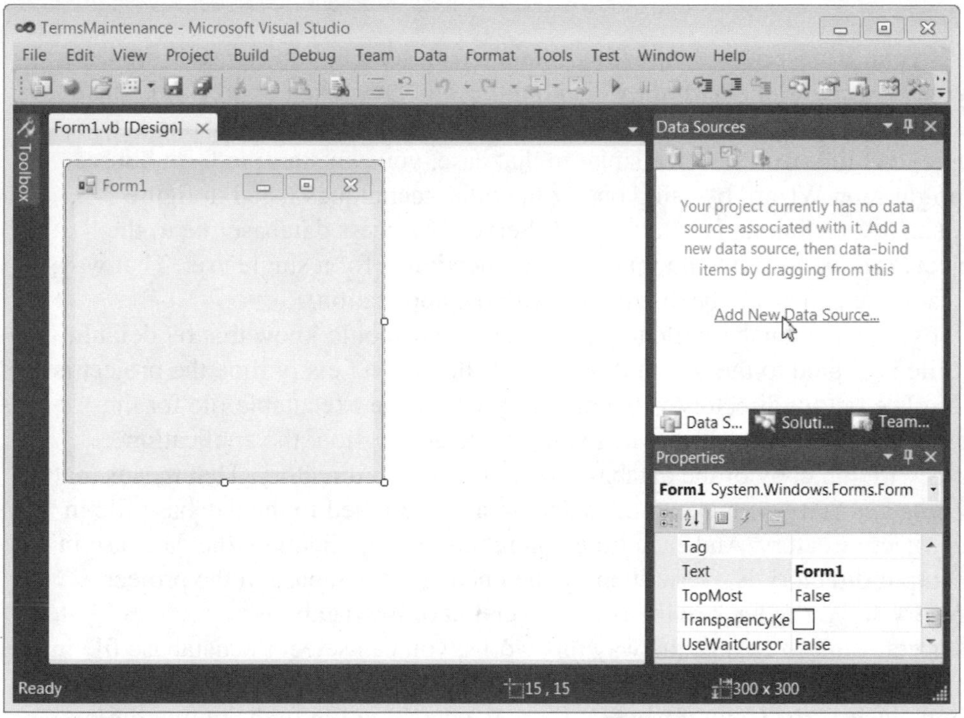

A Data Sources window after a data source has been added

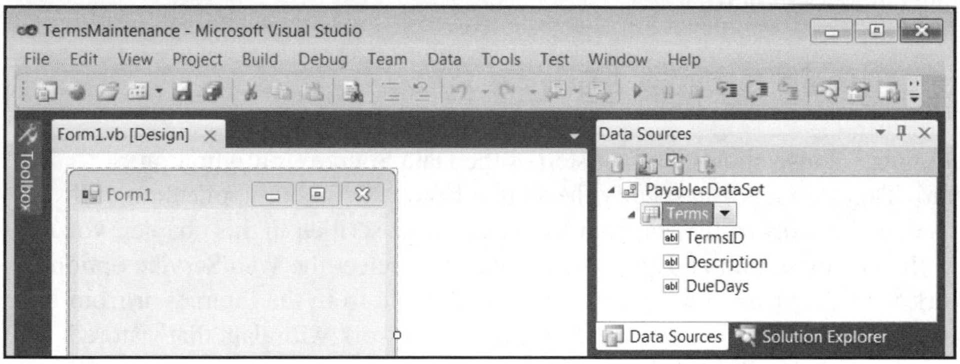

Description

- A *data source* shows all the tables and columns in the dataset that are available to your application.
- You can display the Data Sources window by clicking on the Data Sources tab that's usually grouped with the Solution Explorer at the right edge of the Visual Studio window or by selecting the Show Data Sources command from the Data menu.
- To create a data source, you can click the Add New Data Source link. Then, you can drag the data source onto a form to create controls that are bound to the data source.

Figure 3-1 How to use the Data Sources window

How to start the Data Source Configuration Wizard

If your project doesn't already contain a data source, you can start the Data Source Configuration Wizard by clicking the Add New Data Source link that's shown in the previous figure. However, if your project already contains a data source, this link won't be available. In that case, you can start the Data Source Configuration Wizard by using one of the other techniques listed in figure 3-2.

The last technique is to add a SQL Server or Access database file to the project. You may want to do that if the application is for a single user. That way, the database can easily be distributed with the application.

If you add a database file to your project, you should know that by default, that file is copied to the output directory for the project every time the project is built. (The output directory is the directory where the executable file for the application is stored.) Then, when you run the application, the application works with the copy of the database file in the output directory. That means that any changes that you make to the database aren't applied to the database file in the project directory. And each time you rebuild the application, the database in the output directory is overwritten by the unchanged database in the project directory so you're back to the original version of the database.

If you want to change the way this works, you can select the database file in the Solution Explorer and change its "Copy to Output Directory" property from "Copy always" to "Copy if newer." Then, the database file in the output directory won't be overwritten unless the database file in the project directory contains more current data.

How to choose a data source type

Figure 3-2 also shows the first step of the Data Source Configuration Wizard. This step lets you specify the source from which your application will get its data. To work with data from a database as described in this chapter, you select the Database option. However, you can also select the Web Service option to work with data from a web service that's available from the Internet or from an intranet. Or, you can select the Object option to work with data that's stored in a business object. This option lets you take advantage of the objects that are available from the middle layer of an application as described in chapter 9. Finally, the SharePoint option lets you link to a SharePoint site and access data that's available there.

The first step of the Data Source Configuration Wizard

Four ways to start the Data Source Configuration Wizard

- Click on the Add New Data Source link that's available from the Data Sources window when a project doesn't contain any data sources.
- Click on the Add New Data Source button at the top of the Data Sources window.
- Select the Add New Data Source command from Visual Studio's Data menu.
- Add a SQL Server (.mdf) or Access (.mdb) data file to the project using the Project→Add→Existing Item command. Then, the wizard will skip to the step shown in figure 3-6 that lets you choose the database objects you want to include.

How to choose a data source type

- To get your data from a database, select the Database option. This option lets you create applications like the ones described in this chapter.
- To get your data from a web service, select the Web Service option. This option lets you browse the web to select a web service that will supply data to your application.
- To get your data from a business object, select the Object option. This option lets you create applications like the ones described in chapter 9. You can also use this option with applications that use LINQ to SQL or the Entity Framework as described in chapters 17 and 18.
- To get your data from a SharePoint site, select the SharePoint option. This option lets you connect to a SharePoint site and choose the SharePoint objects that you want to use in your application. This option is not available in the Express Editions of Visual Studio 2010.

Note

- Before you start this procedure, you need to install your database server software on your own PC or on a network server, and you need to attach your database to it. For more information, please refer to appendix A.

Figure 3-2 How to start the Data Source Configuration Wizard and choose a data source type

How to choose a database model for a data source

The second step of the Data Source Configuration Wizard, shown in the first example in figure 3-3, gives you the choice of two database models. The first choice is the traditional data model, in which a dataset is added to the project. That's the model that is used in most of this book. The alternative is the Entity Data Model, a newer approach that lets you create objects directly from the fields of the underlying database. You'll learn how to use that model in chapter 18.

How to choose the connection for a data source

The third step of the Data Source Configuration Wizard is shown in the second example in this figure. It lets you choose the data connection you want to use to connect to the database. If you've previously defined a data connection, you can choose that connection from the drop-down list. To be sure you use the right connection, you can click the button with the plus sign on it to display the connection string.

If the connection you want to use hasn't already been defined, you can click the New Connection button. Then, you can use the dialog boxes shown in the next figure to create the connection.

Before I go on, you should know that once you create a connection using the Data Source Configuration Wizard, it's available to any other project you create. To see a list of the existing connections, you can open the Server Explorer window (View→Server Explorer) and then expand the Data Connections node. You can also use the Server Explorer to create data connections without creating a data source.

The second step of the Data Source Configuration Wizard

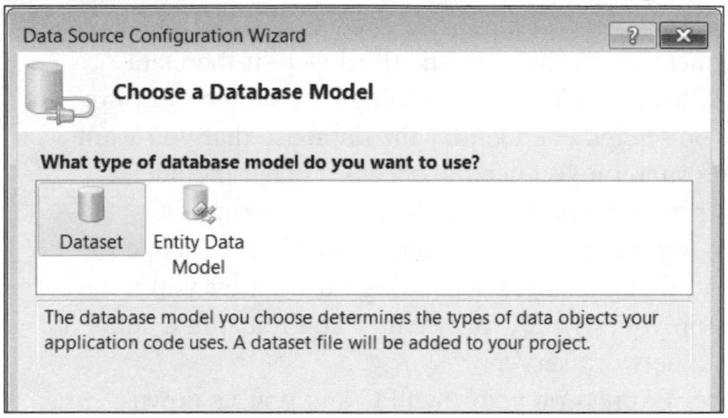

The third step of the Data Source Configuration Wizard

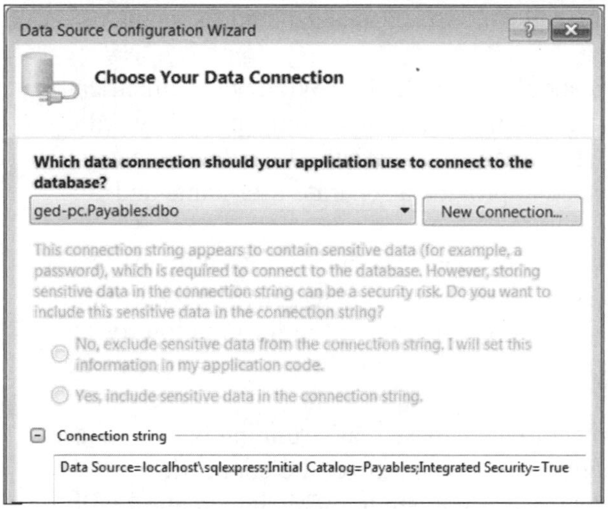

Description

- When you click the Next button in the first step of the Data Source Configuration Wizard, the Choose a Database Model dialog box is displayed. Here, you can choose Dataset for the standard data model or Entity Data Model for the model that uses the Entity Framework.
- When you click the Next button in the Choose a Database Model step, the Choose Your Data Connection dialog box is displayed. Then, if you've already established a connection to the database you want to use, you can choose that connection. Otherwise, you can click the New Connection button to display the Add Connection dialog box shown in the next figure.
- To see the connection string for an existing connection, click the button with the plus sign on it in the Choose Your Data Connection box. To see the detail, you may need to adjust the height of the form.

Figure 3-3 How to choose the connection for a data source

How to create a connection to a database

If you click the New Connection button from the third step of the Data Source Configuration Wizard, the Add Connection dialog box shown in figure 3-4 is displayed. This dialog box helps you identify the database that you want to access and provides the information you need to access it. That includes specifying the name of the server that contains the database, entering the information that's required to log on to the server, and specifying the name of the database. How you do that, though, varies depending on whether you're running SQL Server Express on your own PC or whether you're using a database server that's running on a network server.

If you're using SQL Server Express on your own PC and you've downloaded and installed it as described in appendix A, you can use the localhost keyword to specify that the database server is running on the same PC as the application. This keyword should be followed by a backslash and the name of the database server: SqlExpress.

For the logon information, you should select the Use Windows Authentication option. Then, SQL Server Express will use the login name and password that you use to log in to Windows as the name and password for the database server too. As a result, you won't need to provide a separate user name and password in this dialog box.

Last, you enter or select the name of the database that you want to connect to. In this figure, for example, the connection is for the Payables database that's used throughout this book. When you're done supplying the information for the connection, you can click the Test Connection button to be sure that the connection works.

In contrast, if you need to connect to a database that's running on a database server that's available through a network, you need to get the connection information from the network or database administrator. This information will include the name of the database server, logon information, and the name of the database. Once you establish a connection to the database, you can use that connection for all of the other applications that use that database.

By default, Visual Studio assumes you want to access a SQL Server database as shown here. This works for SQL Server 7, 2000, 2005, and 2008 databases including SQL Server Express databases. If you want to access a different type of database, though, you can click the Change button to display the Change Data Source dialog box. Then, you can select the data source and data provider you want to use to access that data source. If you want to access an Oracle database, for example, you can select the Oracle Database item in the Data Source list. Then, you can choose the data provider for Oracle or the data provider for OLE DB from the Data Provider drop-down list.

The Add Connection and Change Data Source dialog boxes

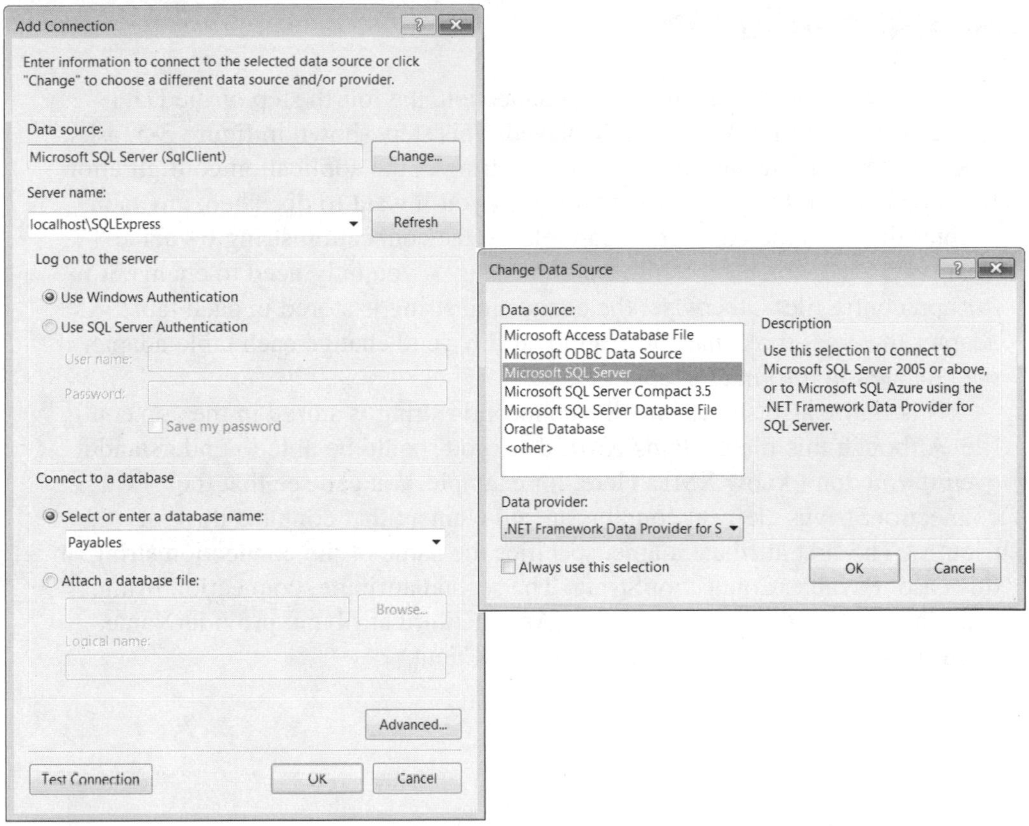

Description

- By default, a connection uses the SQL Server data provider. If that's not what you want, you can click the Change button in the Add Connection dialog box to display the Change Data Source dialog box. Then, you can choose the data source and data provider you want to use.
- To create a connection, specify the name of the server that contains the database, enter the information that's required to log on to the server, and specify the name of the database you want to connect to.
- To be sure that the connection is configured properly, you can click the Test Connection button in the Add Connection dialog box.

Express Edition differences

- The Change Data Source dialog box provides only three options: Microsoft Access Database File, Microsoft SQL Server Compact 3.5, and Microsoft SQL Server Database File. The default is Microsoft SQL Server Compact 3.5, which probably isn't what you want.
- The Add Connection dialog box is simpler, and it includes a Database File Name text box that you use to specify the database. To do that, you click the Browse button to the right of the text box and use the resulting dialog box to point to the data file for the database.

Figure 3-4 How to create a connection to a database

How to save a connection string in the app.config file

After you select or create a data connection, the fourth step of the Data Source Configuration Wizard is displayed. This step, shown in figure 3-5, asks whether you want to save the connection string in the application configuration file (app.config). In most cases, that's what you'll want to do. Then, any table adapter that uses the connection can refer to the connection string by name. That way, if the connection information changes, you only need to change it in the app.config file. Otherwise, the connection string is stored in each table adapter that uses the connection, and you'll have to change each table adapter if the connection information changes.

This figure also shows how the connection string is stored in the app.config file. Although this file contains XML data, you should be able to understand it even if you don't know XML. Here, for example, you can see that the connectionStrings element contains an add element that contains three attributes. The first attribute, name, specifies the name of the connection string, in this case, PayablesConnectionString. The second attribute, connectionString, contains the actual connection string. And the third attribute, providerName, identifies the data provider, in this case, SqlClient.

The next step of the Data Source Configuration Wizard

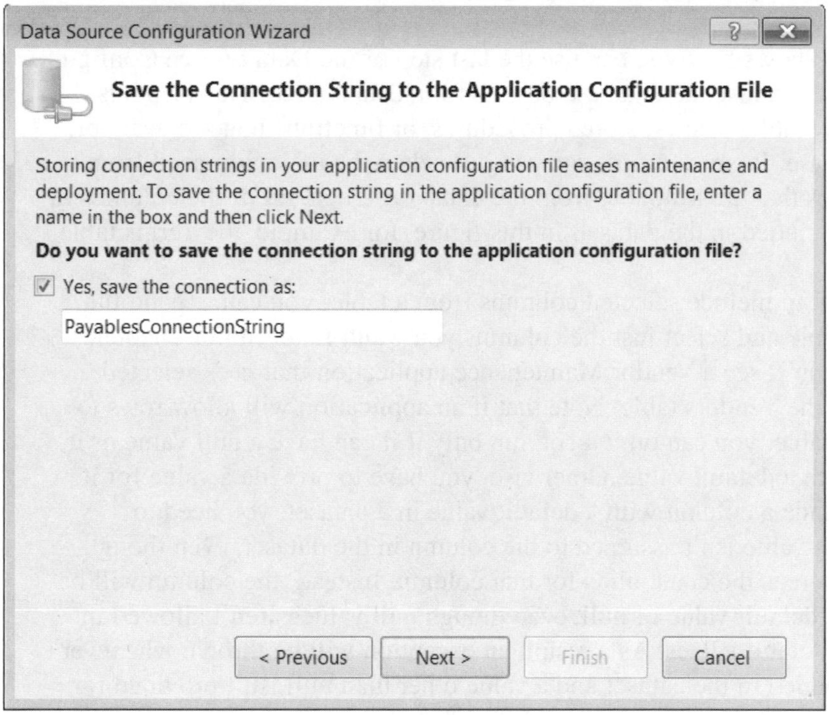

The information that's stored in the app.config file

```
<connectionStrings>
    <add name="TermsMaintenance.My.MySettings.PayablesConnectionString"
        connectionString="Data Source=localhost\sqlexpress;
                          Initial Catalog=Payables;
                          Integrated Security=True"
        providerName="System.Data.SqlClient" />
</connectionStrings>
```

Description

- By default, the connection string is saved in the application configuration file (app.config). If that's not what you want, you can remove the check mark from the Yes option in the third step of the Data Source Configuration Wizard shown above.
- If you don't save the connection string in the app.config file, the string is specified for the connection of each table adapter you create from the data source. Because of that, we recommend you always save the connection string in the app.config file. Then, only the name of the connection string is stored in the connection for each table adapter.
- You can also enter the name you want to use for the connection string in this dialog box. By default, the connection string is given a name that consists of the database name appended with "ConnectionString".

Figure 3-5 How to save a connection string in the app.config file

How to choose database objects for a data source

Figure 3-6 shows how you can use the last step of the Data Source Configuration Wizard to choose the database objects for a data source. This step lets you choose any tables, views, stored procedures, or functions that are available from the database. In some cases, you can just select the table you need from the list of tables that are available from the database. Then, all of the columns in the table are included in the dataset. In this figure, for example, the Terms table is selected.

If you want to include selected columns from a table, you can expand the node for the table and select just the columns you want. Later in this chapter, for example, you'll see a Vendor Maintenance application that uses selected columns from the Vendors table. Note that if an application will allow rows to be added to a table, you can omit a column only if it can have a null value or if it's defined with a default value. Otherwise, you have to provide a value for it.

If you include a column with a default value in a dataset, you need to realize that this value isn't assigned to the column in the dataset, even though the dataset enforces the constraints for that column. Instead, the column will be defined with a default value of null, even though null values aren't allowed in columns with default values. As a result, an exception will be thrown whenever a new row is added to the dataset and a value other than null isn't provided for that column.

This means that either the user or the application must provide an acceptable value for the column. One way to do that is to provide a way for the user to enter a value for the column. Another way is to use the Dataset Designer to set the DefaultValue property for this column as described in this figure. You'll learn more about working with the Dataset Designer later in this chapter.

In a larger project, you might want to include several tables in the dataset. Then, the dataset will maintain the relationships between those tables whenever that's appropriate. Or, you might want to use views, stored procedures, or functions to work with the data in the database. If you have experience working with these database objects, you shouldn't have any trouble understanding how this works. Otherwise, you can refer to *Murach's SQL Server 2008 for Developers* for more information.

This step of the wizard also lets you select whether you want to store any of the data in a local database cache. If you select this option, another wizard step is displayed that lets you choose which tables you want to store in the cache and how you want the data in each table to be synchronized with the data in the database. Then, when you complete the wizard, a local database is added to your application. This database is then used to populate the associated tables in the dataset. After that, the local database is updated only if the data in the database on the server changes.

A local database cache can be useful if the data in the database changes infrequently. To use this feature, however, you have to add code that starts the synchronization process. For more information on how to do that, please refer to the Visual Studio documentation.

The last step of the Data Source Configuration Wizard

Description

- In the last step of the Data Source Configuration Wizard, you can choose the database objects that you want to include in the dataset for your project.
- In this step, you can choose from any tables, views, stored procedures, or functions that are available from the database. In addition, you can expand the node for any table, view, stored procedure, or function and choose just the columns you want to include in the data source.
- You can also enter the name you want to use for the dataset in this dialog box. By default, the name is the name of the database appended with "DataSet".
- If you select the Enable Local Database Caching option, another wizard step is displayed that lets you choose which tables you want to cache and how you want those tables synchronized with the tables in the database. For more information, see the Visual Studio documentation.

How to work with columns that have default values

- If a column in a database has a default value, that value isn't included in the column definition in the dataset. Because of that, you may want to omit columns with default values from the dataset unless they're needed by the application. Then, when a row is added to the table, the default value is taken from the database.
- If you include a column that's defined with a default value, you must provide a value for that column whenever a row is added to the dataset. One way to do that is to let the user enter a value. Another way is to display the Dataset Designer as described in figure 3-16, click on the column, and use the Properties window to set the DefaultValue property.

Figure 3-6 How to choose database objects for a data source

The schema file created by the Data Source Configuration Wizard

After you complete the Data Source Configuration Wizard, the new data source is displayed in the Data Sources window you saw in figure 3-1. In addition to this data source, Visual Studio generates a file that contains the *schema* for the dataset class. This file defines the structure of the dataset, including the tables it contains, the columns that are included in each table, the data types of each column, and the constraints that are defined for each table.

This schema file is listed in the Solution Explorer window and is given the name you specified for the dataset in the last step of the Data Source Configuration Wizard with a file extension of *xsd*. In figure 3-7, for example, you can see the schema file named PayablesDataSet.xsd. As you'll learn later in this chapter, you can view a graphic representation of this schema by double-clicking on this file.

Beneath the schema file, the Solution Explorer displays the file that contains the generated code for the dataset class. In this figure, this code is stored in the PayablesDataSet.Designer.vb file. When you create bound controls from the data source as shown in this chapter, the code in this class is used to define the dataset object that the controls are bound to. Although you may want to view this code to see how it works, you shouldn't change it. If you do, the dataset may not work correctly.

By the way, you should know that a dataset that's created from a dataset class like the one shown here is called a *typed dataset*. The code in the dataset class makes it possible for you to refer to the tables, rows, and columns in the typed dataset using the simplified syntax you'll see in this chapter and the next chapter.

A project with a dataset defined by a data source

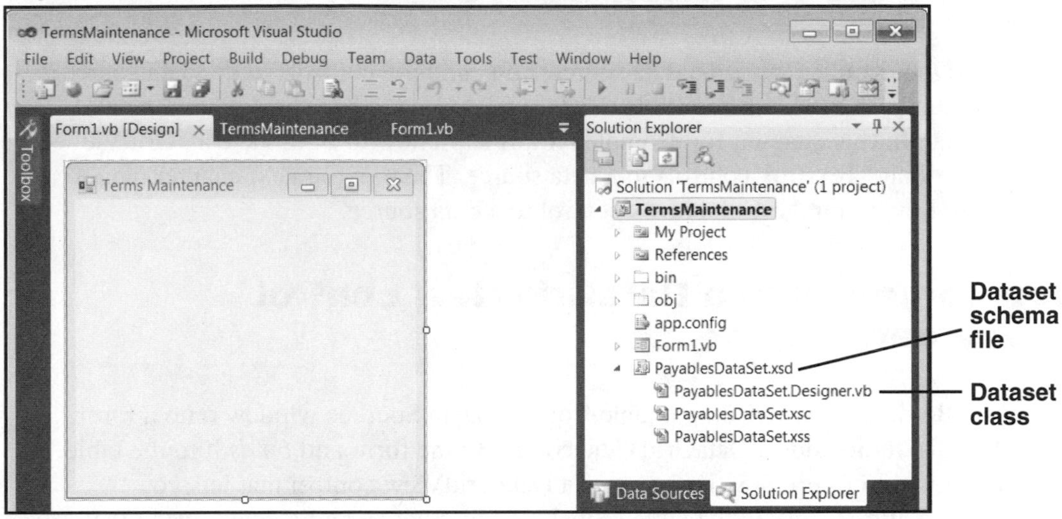

Description

- After you create a data source, it's displayed in the Data Sources window. Then, you can use it to create bound controls as shown in this chapter.
- Visual Studio also generates a file that contains the *schema* for the dataset defined by the data source. This file appears in the Solution Explorer and has a file extension of *xsd*. It defines the structure of the dataset, including the tables it contains, the columns in each table, the data types of each column, and the constraints for each table.
- Subordinate to the schema file is a file that contains the generated code for the dataset class. Visual Studio uses this class to create a dataset object when you add the data source to a form.

Notes

- The schema that's generated for a dataset also includes classes that define the table adapter and table adapter manager classes that provide for working with the database. You'll learn about the objects created from these classes in the next figure.
- To see the files that are subordinate to the schema file, click the Show All Files button at the top of the Solution Explorer. Then, expand the node for the schema file.

Figure 3-7 The schema file created by the Data Source Configuration Wizard

How to use a data source

Once you've created a data source, you can bind controls to the data source and then use the bound controls to add, update, and delete the data in the data source. In this chapter, for example, you'll learn how to bind the DataGridView control and TextBox controls to a data source. Then, in the next chapter, you'll learn how to bind a ComboBox control to a data source.

How to generate a DataGridView control from a data source

By default, if you drag a table from the Data Sources window onto a form, Visual Studio adds a DataGridView control to the form and *binds* it to the table as shown in figure 3-8. This creates a DataGridView control that lets you browse all the rows in the table as well as add, update, and delete rows in the table. To provide this functionality, Visual Studio adds a toolbar to the top of the form that provides navigation buttons along with Add, Delete, and Save buttons.

To bind a DataGridView control to a table, Visual Studio uses a technique called *complex data binding*. This just means that the *bound control* is bound to more than one data element. The DataGridView control in this figure, for example, is bound to all the rows and columns in the Terms table.

When you generate a DataGridView control from a data source, Visual Studio also adds five additional objects to the Component Designer tray at the bottom of the Form Designer. First, the DataSet object defines the dataset that contains the Terms table. Second, the TableAdapter object provides commands that can be used to work with the Terms table in the database. Third, the TableAdapterManager object provides for writing the data in two or more related tables to the database so that referential integrity is maintained. Fourth, the BindingSource object specifies the data source (the Terms table) that the controls are bound to, and it provides functionality for working with the data source. Finally, the BindingNavigator defines the toolbar that contains the controls for working with the data source.

Before I go on, I want to point out that in addition to commands, the TableAdapter object provides a built-in connection and a data adapter object that manages the flow of data between the database and the dataset. As you'll see in chapter 4, it can also contain more than one command that retrieves data from the database. A TableAdapter object can only be created by using Visual Studio design tools like the Data Source Configuration Wizard.

I also want to mention that, in general, you shouldn't have any trouble figuring out how to use the binding navigator toolbar. However, you may want to know that if you click the Add button to add a new row and then decide you don't want to do that, you can click the Delete button to delete the new row. However, there's no way to cancel out of an edit operation. Because of that, you may want to add a button to the toolbar that provides this function. You'll learn how to do that in the next chapter.

A form after the Terms table has been dragged onto it

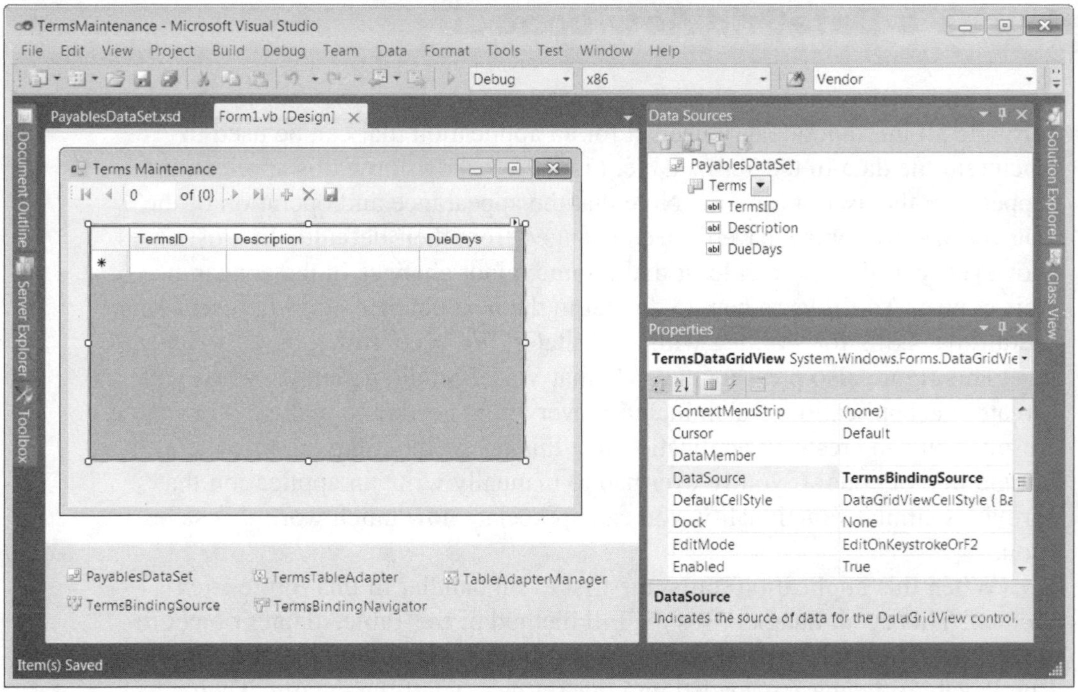

The controls and objects that are created when you drag a data source to a form

Control/object	Description
DataGridView control	Displays the data from the data source in a grid.
BindingNavigator control	Defines the toolbar that can be used to navigate, add, and delete rows in the DataGridView control and save data to the database.
BindingSource object	Identifies the data source that the controls on the form are bound to and provides functionality for working with the data source.
DataSet object	Provides access to all of the tables, views, stored procedures, and functions that are available to the project.
TableAdapter object	Provides a data adapter, a connection, and commands for reading data from and writing data to the specified table in the database.
TableAdapterManager object	Provides for writing data in related tables to the database while maintaining referential integrity.

Description

- To bind a DataGridView control to a table in a dataset, just drag the table from the Data Sources window onto the form. Then, Visual Studio automatically adds a DataGridView control to the form along with the other controls and objects it needs. Because the DataGridView control is bound to the table, it can be referred to as a *bound control.*
- To bind a DataGridView control to a data table, Visual Studio uses a technique called complex data binding. This means that the control is bound to more than one data element, in this case, all the rows and columns in the table.

Figure 3-8 How to generate a DataGridView control from a data source

A Terms Maintenance application that uses a DataGridView control

At this point, the DataGridView control and binding navigator toolbar provide all the functionality needed for an application that can be used to maintain the data in the Terms table. Figure 3-9 shows how this application appears to the user at runtime. Note that the appearance and operation of the DataGridView control haven't been changed from their defaults. In most cases, however, you'll want to at least make some minor changes in the appearance of this control. You'll learn how to do that in the next chapter when I present some additional skills for working with the DataGridView control.

This figure also presents the code that Visual Studio generates when you create this application, which includes everything needed to make it work. As a result, you can create an application like this one without having to write a single line of code. If you've ever had to manually write an application that provides similar functionality, you can appreciate how much work this saves you.

When this application starts, the first event handler in this figure is executed. This event handler uses the Fill method of the TableAdapter object to load data into the DataSet object. In this example, the data in the Terms table of the Payables database is loaded into the Terms table of the dataset. Then, because the DataGridView control is bound to this table, the data is displayed in this control and the user can use it to modify the data in the table by adding, updating, or deleting rows.

When the user changes the data in the DataGridView control, those changes are saved to the dataset. However, the changes aren't saved to the database until the user clicks the Save button in the toolbar. Then, the second event handler in this figure is executed. This event handler starts by calling the Validate method of the form, which causes the Validating and Validated events of the control that's losing focus to be fired. Although you probably won't use the Validated event, you may use the Validating event to validate a row that's being added or modified. However, I've found that this event doesn't work well with the binding navigator toolbar, so you won't see it used in this book.

Next, the EndEdit method of the BindingSource object applies any pending changes to the dataset. That's necessary because when you add or update a row, the new or modified row isn't saved until you move to another row.

Finally, the UpdateAll method of the TableAdapterManager object saves the data in the DataSet object to the Payables database. When this method is called, it checks each row in each table of the dataset to determine if it's a new row, a modified row, or a row that should be deleted. Then, it causes the appropriate SQL Insert, Update, and Delete statements to be executed for these rows. As a result, the Update method works efficiently since it only updates the rows that need to be updated. In addition, the Insert, Update, and Delete statements are executed in a sequence that maintains referential integrity.

Now that you understand this code, you should notice that it doesn't provide for any exceptions that may occur during this processing. Because of that,

The user interface for the Terms Maintenance application

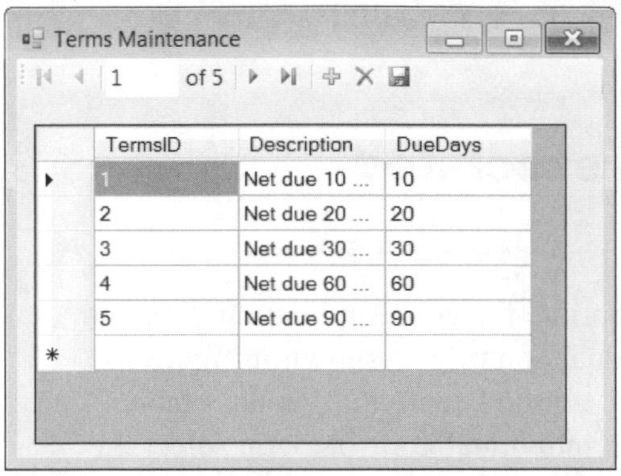

The code that's generated by Visual Studio

```
Private Sub Form1_Load(ByVal sender As System.Object,
        ByVal e As System.EventArgs) Handles MyBase.Load
    'TODO: This line of code loads data into the 'PayablesDataSet.Terms'
    'table. You can move, or remove it, as needed.
    Me.TermsTableAdapter.Fill(Me.PayablesDataSet.Terms)
End Sub

Private Sub TermsBindingNavigatorSaveItem_Click(
        ByVal sender As System.Object, ByVal e As System.EventArgs) _
        Handles TermsBindingNavigatorSaveItem.Click
    Me.Validate()
    Me.TermsBindingSource.EndEdit()
    Me.TableAdapterManager.UpdateAll(Me.PayablesDataSet)
End Sub
```

The syntax of the Fill method

```
TableAdapter.Fill(DataSet.TableName)
```

The syntax of the UpdateAll method

```
TableAdapterManager.UpdateAll(DataSet)
```

Description

- Visual Studio automatically generates the code shown above and places it in the source code file when you drag a data source onto a form. If necessary, you can edit this code.
- The generated code uses the Fill method of the TableAdapter object that's generated for the table to read data from the database, and it uses the UpdateAll method of the TableAdapterManager object that's generated for the dataset to write data to the database. It also uses the EndEdit method of the BindingSource object to save any changes that have been made to the current row to the dataset.
- The Validate method causes the Validating and Validated events of the control that is losing the focus to be fired. You can use the Validating event to perform any required data validation for the form.

Figure 3-9 A Terms Maintenance application that uses a DataGridView control

you need to add the appropriate exception handling code for any production applications that you develop so that they won't crash. You'll learn how to do that later in this chapter.

How to change the controls associated with a data source

If the DataGridView control isn't appropriate for your application, you can bind the columns of a data source to individual controls as shown in figure 3-10. Here, the data source consists of several columns from the Vendors table.

To associate the columns in a table with individual controls, you select the Details option from the drop-down list that's available when you select the table in the Data Sources window. This is illustrated in the first screen in this figure. Then, if you drag that table from the Data Sources window onto a form, Visual Studio generates a label and a bound control for each column in the table.

For most string and numeric columns, Visual Studio generates a TextBox control. That's the case for the Vendors table, as you'll see in the next figure. If you want to change the type of control that's associated with a column, though, you can select the column in the Data Sources window and then use the drop-down list that's displayed to select a different type of control. You can see the list of controls that are available in the second screen in this figure.

If you want to use a control that isn't in this list, you can select the Customize option at the bottom of the list. Then, you can select one or more controls that you want to add to the list from the Options dialog box that's displayed. In most cases, though, you'll use the controls that are included in the list by default.

How to change the default control for a data table

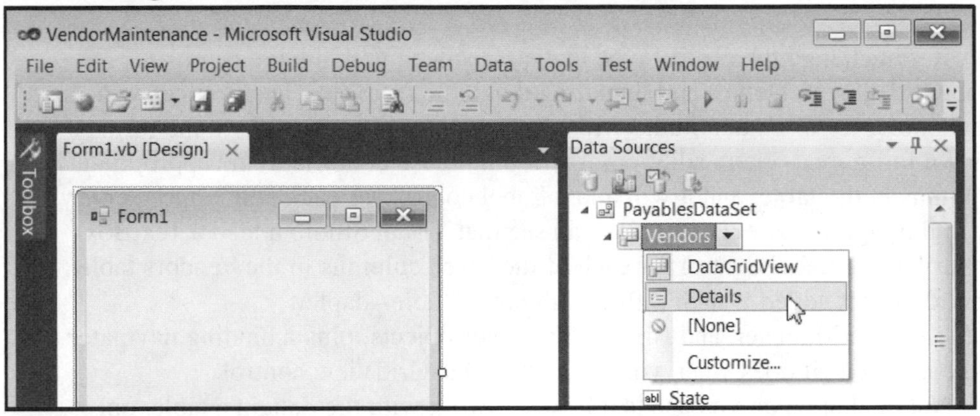

How to change the default control for a column in a data table

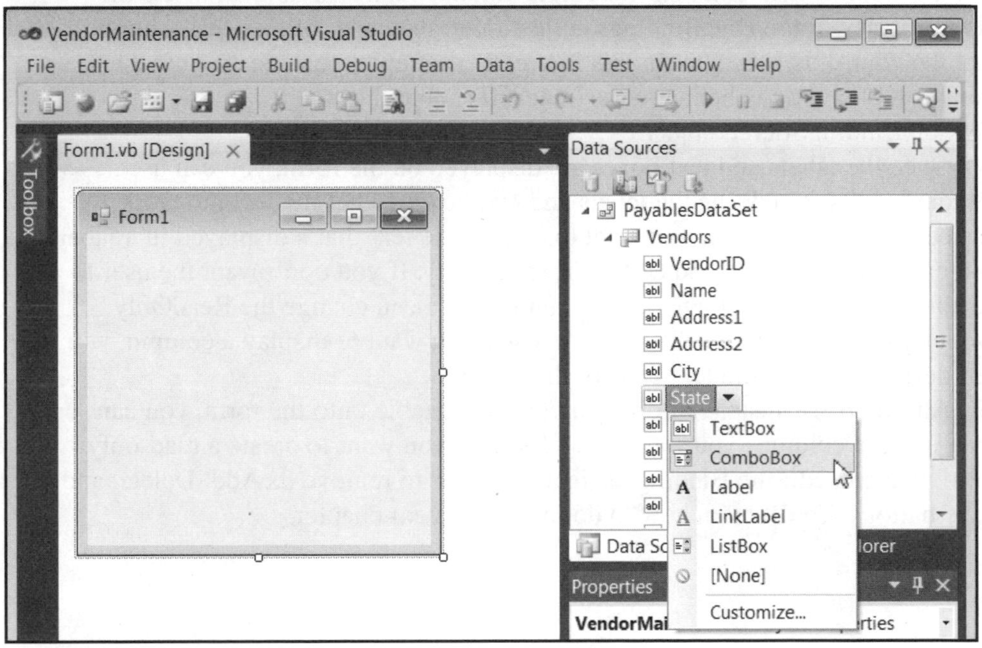

Description

- By default, a data table is associated with a DataGridView control. To change this default so that each column in the table is displayed in a separate control, select the Details option from the drop-down list for the table.
- By default, most string and numeric columns within a data table are associated with the TextBox control. To change this default, select the type of control you want to use from the drop-down list for the column.
- To use a control type that isn't included in the list by default, select the Customize option and then select the type of control you want to use from the Options dialog box that's displayed to add it to the list.

Figure 3-10 How to change the controls associated with a data source

How to generate detail controls from a data source

If you change the control type that's associated with a table from DataGridView to Details and then drag that table from the Data Sources window onto a form, Visual Studio will add the appropriate controls to the form as shown in figure 3-11. In addition, it will bind those controls to the appropriate columns in the table, and it will add a Label control for each column to identify it. In this figure, for example, you can see that Visual Studio added a TextBox control and a Label control for each of the seven columns in the Vendors table. In addition, it added DataSet, BindingSource, TableAdapter, TableAdapterManager, and BindingNavigator objects, plus a binding navigator toolbar, just as it does when you generate a DataGridView control.

Notice that when you use text boxes to work with the data in a table, only one row of the table is displayed at a time. Then, Visual Studio uses *simple data binding* to bind each text box to a single column value. To do that, it sets the Text property in the DataBindings collection to the name of the data column that the control is bound to. In this figure, for example, you can see that the Vendor ID text box is bound to the VendorID column of the VendorsBindingSource object.

Once the labels and text boxes are displayed on the form, you can use standard skills for editing the labels and text boxes to get the form to work correctly. For example, if you want to change the text that's displayed in a label, you can select the label and edit its Text property. If you don't want the user to be able to enter data for a particular column, you can change the ReadOnly property of the text box to True. Or, if you don't want to display a column, you can delete the label and text box for that column.

Alternatively, instead of dragging the entire table onto the form, you can drag just the columns you want. In addition, if you want to create a read-only form, you can edit the BindingNavigator toolbar to remove its Add, Delete, and Save buttons. You'll learn how to do that in the next chapter.

A form after the Vendors table has been dragged onto it

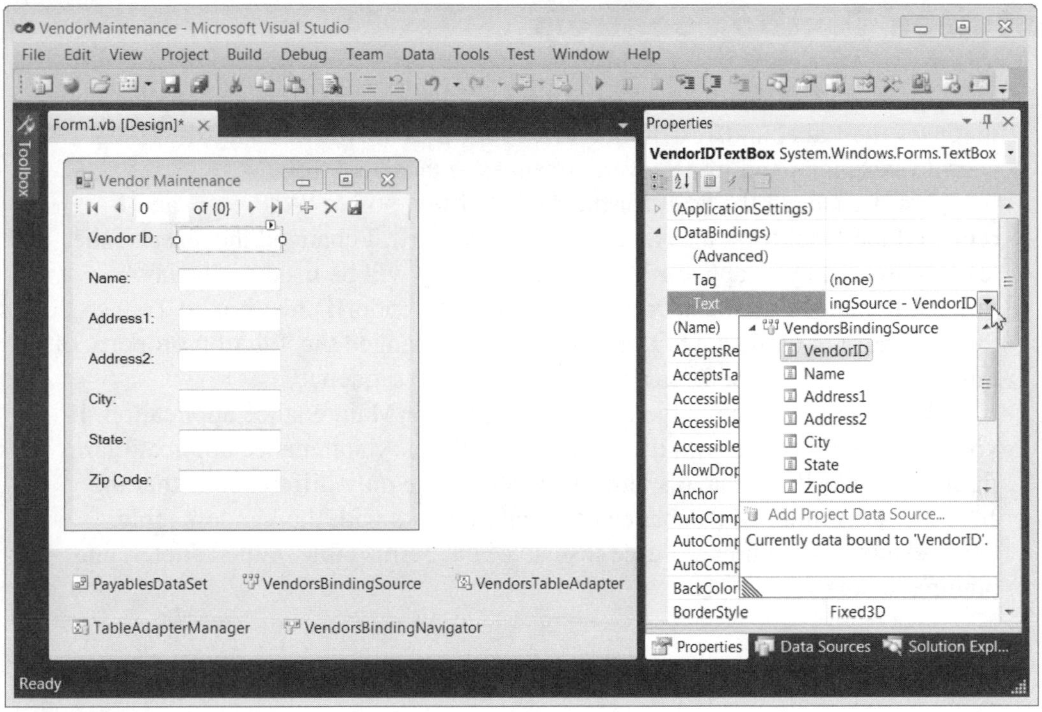

Description

- When you drag a table whose columns are associated with individual controls to a form, Visual Studio automatically adds the controls along with labels that identify the columns. It also adds a binding navigator toolbar and the objects for working with the bound data just as it does for a DataGridView control.
- To display the value of a column in a text box, Visual Studio sets the Text property in the DataBindings collection to the name of the data column. This is known as *simple data binding* because the control is bound to a single column value. To change the binding, you can use the drop-down list for the Text property as shown above.

Note

- When you drag individual controls to a form, don't drop them at the top of the form. If you do, the toolbar will overlay the first label and text box and make them difficult to move.

Figure 3-11 How to generate detail controls from a data source

A Vendor Maintenance application that uses TextBox controls

Figure 3-12 shows the user interface for a Vendor Maintenance application that uses the Label and TextBox controls shown in the previous figure. However, I rearranged and made several changes to those controls.

First, I changed the label for the Address1 text box to "Address:" and I removed the label from the Address2 text box. Next, I changed the sizes of the text boxes so they're appropriate for the data they will be used to display. Finally, I changed the ReadOnly property of the VendorID text box to True so the user can't enter data into this control, and I changed the TabStop property of this text box to False so it isn't included in the tab sequence.

This figure also shows the code for the Vendor Maintenance application. If you compare this code with the code for the Terms Maintenance application in figure 3-9, you'll see that it's almost identical. The only difference is that the code for the Vendor Maintenance application works with the Vendors table, table adapter, and binding source instead of the Terms table, table adapter, and binding source.

The user interface for the Vendor Maintenance application

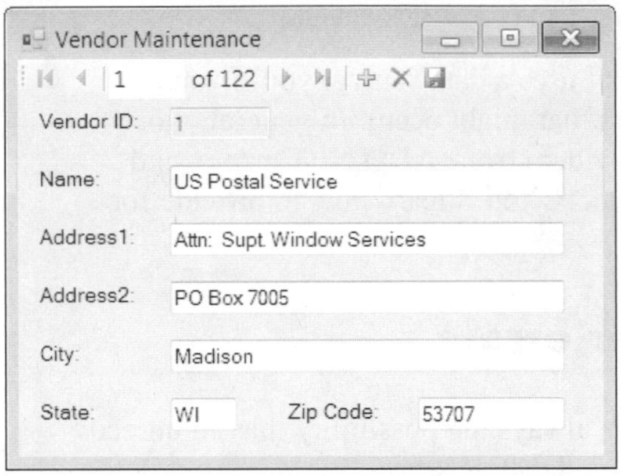

The code for the application

```
Public Class Form1

    Private Sub Form1_Load(ByVal sender As System.Object,
            ByVal e As System.EventArgs) Handles MyBase.Load
        'TODO: This line of code loads data into the
        'PayablesDataSet.Vendors' table.
        'You can move, or remove it, as needed.
        Me.VendorsTableAdapter.Fill(Me.PayablesDataSet.Vendors)
    End Sub

    Private Sub VendorsBindingNavigatorSaveItem_Click(
            ByVal sender As System.Object, ByVal e As System.EventArgs) _
            Handles VendorsBindingNavigatorSaveItem.Click
        Me.Validate()
        Me.VendorsBindingSource.EndEdit()
        Me.TableAdapterManager.UpdateAll(Me.PayablesDataSet)
    End Sub

End Class
```

Figure 3-12 A Vendor Maintenance application that uses TextBox controls

How to handle data errors

When you develop an application that uses a data source, you'll want to provide code that handles any data errors that might occur. In general, those errors fall into three categories: data provider errors, ADO.NET errors, and errors that the DataGridView control detects. You'll learn how to provide for these errors in the topics that follow.

How to handle data provider errors

When you access a database, there is always the possibility that an unrecoverable error might occur. For example, the database server might be shut down when you try to access it, or the network connection to the database server might be broken. Either way, your applications should usually anticipate such problems by catching any database exceptions that might occur.

Figure 3-13 shows the exceptions thrown by the .NET data providers when an unrecoverable error occurs. You can refer to these errors as *data provider errors*. As you can see, each data provider has its own exception class. So, if you're using the SQL Server data provider, you should catch exceptions of the SqlException class.

The code example in this figure shows how you can catch a SqlException that might occur when attempting to fill a dataset using a table adapter. Here, the shaded lines show the code that has been added to the generated code. This code will display an error message when a SqlException occurs, and it uses the Number and Message properties of the SqlException class to display details about the exception. It also uses the GetType method to indicate the type of exception that occurred.

Although it's uncommon, more than one server error can occur as the result of a single database operation. In that case, an error object is created for each error. These objects are stored in a collection that you can access through the Errors property of the exception object. Each error object contains a Number and Message property just like the exception object. However, because the Number and Message properties of the exception object are set to the Number and Message properties of the first error in the Errors collection, you don't usually need to work with the individual error objects.

.NET data provider exception classes

Name	Description
SqlException	Thrown if a server error occurs when accessing a SQL Server database.
OdbcException	Thrown if a server error occurs when accessing an ODBC database.
OleDbException	Thrown if a server error occurs when accessing an OLE DB database.

Common members of the .NET data provider exception classes

Property	Description
`Number`	An error number that identifies the type of error.
`Message`	A message that describes the error.
`Source`	The name of the provider that generated the error.
`Errors`	A collection of error objects that contain information about the errors that occurred during a database operation.
Method	**Description**
`GetType()`	Gets the type of the current exception.

Code that catches a SQL exception

```
Private Sub Form1_Load(ByVal sender As System.Object, _
        ByVal e As System.EventArgs) Handles MyBase.Load
    Try
        Me.VendorsTableAdapter.Fill(Me.PayablesDataSet.Vendors)
    Catch ex As SqlException
        MessageBox.Show("SQL Server error # " & ex.Number & _
            ": " & ex.Message, ex.GetType.ToString)
    End Try
End Sub
```

Description

- Whenever the data provider (SQL Server, ODBC, or OLE DB) encounters a situation it can't handle, a data provider exception is thrown. You can handle these types of exceptions by catching them and displaying appropriate error messages.
- The Number and Message properties pinpoint the specific server error that caused the data provider exception to be thrown.
- The SqlException class is stored in the System.Data.SqlClient namespace.

Figure 3-13 How to handle data provider errors

How to handle ADO.NET errors

When you work with bound controls, *ADO.NET errors* can occur when the data in those controls is saved to the dataset (not the database), or when an Insert, Update, or Delete statement can't be executed against the database. Figure 3-14 presents some of the most common of those errors.

Here, ConstraintException and NoNullAllowedException are subclasses of the DataException class, so you can catch either of these errors by catching DataException errors. In contrast, DBConcurrencyException isn't a subclass of the DataException class, so you must catch DBConcurrencyException errors separately. All of the ADO.NET exception classes are members of the System.Data namespace.

The error-handling code in this figure catches errors caused by the EndEdit method of a binding source and the UpdateAll method of a table adapter manager. The first exception, DBConcurrencyException, occurs if the number of rows that are affected by an insert, update, or delete operation is zero, which typically indicates that concurrency errors have occurred. Then, a message box is used to display an error message, and the Fill method of the table adapter is used to retrieve the current data from the database and load it into the Vendors data table. That will help prevent further concurrency errors from occurring.

Although you might think that a concurrency error would be generated by the database rather than ADO.NET, that's not the case. To understand why, you need to realize that the Update and Delete statements that are generated for a table adapter contain code that checks that a row hasn't changed since it was retrieved. But if the row has changed, the row with the specified criteria won't be found and the SQL statement won't be executed. When the table adapter discovers that the row wasn't updated or deleted, however, it realizes there was a concurrency error and throws an exception.

Like other exception classes provided by the .NET Framework, each ADO.NET exception class has a Message property and a GetType method that you can use to display information about the error. You can see how this property and method are used in the second Catch block in this figure, which catches any other ADO.NET exceptions that may occur. This Catch block displays a dialog box that uses the Message property and the GetType method of the DataException object to describe the error. Then, it uses the CancelEdit method of the binding source to cancel the current edit operation.

Incidentally, to test your handling of concurrency exceptions, you can start two instances of Visual Studio and run the same application from both of them. Then, you can access and update the same row from both instances.

Common ADO.NET exception classes

Class	Description
DBConcurrencyException	The exception that's thrown by the data adapter if the number of rows affected by an insert, update, or delete operation is zero. This exception is typically caused by a concurrency violation.
DataException	The general exception that's thrown when an ADO.NET error occurs.
ConstraintException	The exception that's thrown if an operation violates a constraint. This is a subclass of the DataException class.
NoNullAllowedException	The exception that's thrown when an add or update operation attempts to save a null value in a column that doesn't allow nulls. This is a subclass of the DataException class.

Common members of the ADO.NET exception classes

Property	Description
`Message`	A message that describes the exception.
Method	**Description**
`GetType()`	Gets the type of the current exception.

Code that handles ADO.NET errors

```
    Try
        Me.VendorsBindingSource.EndEdit()
        Me.TableAdapterManager.UpdateAll(Me.PayablesDataSet)
    Catch ex As DBConcurrencyException
        MessageBox.Show("A concurrency error occurred. " &
            "The row was not updated.", "Concurrency Exception")
        Me.VendorsTableAdapter.Fill(Me.PayablesDataSet.Vendors)
    Catch ex As DataException
        MessageBox.Show(ex.Message, ex.GetType.ToString)
        VendorsBindingSource.CancelEdit()
    Catch ex As SqlException
        MessageBox.Show("SQL Server error # " & ex.Number &
            ": " & ex.Message, ex.GetType.ToString)
End Try
```

Description

- An ADO.NET exception is an exception that occurs on any ADO.NET object. All of these exceptions are members of the System.Data namespace.
- In most cases, you'll catch specific types of exceptions if you want to perform special processing when those exceptions occur. Then, you can use the DataException class to catch other ADO.NET exceptions that are represented by its subclasses.

Figure 3-14 How to handle ADO.NET errors

How to handle data errors for a DataGridView control

Because the DataGridView control was designed to work with data sources, it can detect some types of data entry errors before they're saved to the dataset. If, for example, a user doesn't enter a value for a column that's required by the data source, or if a user tries to add a new row with a primary key that already exists, the DataGridView control will raise the DataError event. Then, you can code an event handler for this event as shown in figure 3-15.

The second parameter that's received by this event handler has properties you can use to display information about the error. The one you'll use most often is the Exception property, which provides access to the exception object that was thrown as a result of the error. Like any other exception object, this object has a Message property that provides a description of the error. You can also use the RowIndex and ColumnIndex properties of the second parameter to identify the row and column that caused the data error.

An event of the DataGridView control

Event	Description
`DataError`	Raised when the DataGridView control detects a data error such as a value that isn't in the correct format or a null value where a null value isn't valid.

Three properties of the DataGridViewDataErrorEventArgs class

Property	Description
`Exception`	The exception that was thrown as a result of the error. You can use the Message property of this object to get additional information about the exception.
`RowIndex`	The index for the row where the error occurred.
`ColumnIndex`	The index for the column where the error occurred.

Code that handles a data error for a DataGridView control

```
Private Sub TermsDataGridView_DataError(ByVal sender As System.Object,
        ByVal e As System.Windows.Forms.DataGridViewDataErrorEventArgs) _
        Handles TermsDataGridView.DataError
    Dim row As Integer = e.RowIndex + 1
    Dim errorMessage As String = "A data error occurred." & vbCrLf &
        "Row: " & row & vbCrLf &
        "Error: " & e.Exception.Message
    MessageBox.Show(errorMessage, "Data Error")
End Sub
```

Description

- You can code an event handler for the DataError event of the DataGridView control to handle any data errors that occur when working with the DataGridView control.
- You can use the Exception, RowIndex, and ColumnIndex properties of the second parameter of the event handler to display a meaningful error message.

Figure 3-15 How to handle data errors for a DataGridView control

How to use the Dataset Designer

The *Dataset Designer* lets you work with a dataset schema using a graphic interface. In the topics that follow, you'll learn three basic skills for working with the Dataset Designer. Then, in chapter 5, you'll learn some additional skills for using this designer.

How to view the schema for a dataset

To learn more about a dataset, you can display its schema in the Dataset Designer. In figure 3-16, for example, you can see the schema for the Payables dataset used by the Vendor Maintenance application. For this simple application, this dataset contains just the Vendors table since this is the only table used by the application. The key icon in this table indicates that the VendorID column is the primary key for the table.

For each table in a dataset, the dataset schema also includes a table adapter that lists the queries that can be used with the table. Each table adapter includes at least a *main query* named Fill that determines the columns that are used when you drag the table from the Data Sources window. This query is also used to generate the Insert, Update, and Delete statements for the table. In addition, the table adapter includes any other queries you've defined for the table. You'll learn more about defining additional queries in the next two chapters.

If you click on a table adapter in the Dataset Designer, you'll see that its properties in the Properties window include the ADO.NET objects that the table adapter defines. That includes a Connection object, as well as SelectCommand, InsertCommand, UpdateCommand, and DeleteCommand objects. If you expand any of these command objects, you can look at the CommandText property that defines the SQL statement it executes. In this figure, for example, you can see the beginning of the Select statement for the SelectCommand object that's used by the Fill query of the table adapter for the Vendors table. If you click on the ellipsis button for this property, you can work with the query using the Query Builder that's described in chapter 5.

Note that the Dataset Designer also makes it easy to set the properties for a column in a table that's in the dataset. To do that, just select a column and use the Properties window. For instance, you can use this technique to set the DefaultValue property for a column in the dataset, which is something that you often have to do.

The schema displayed in the Dataset Designer

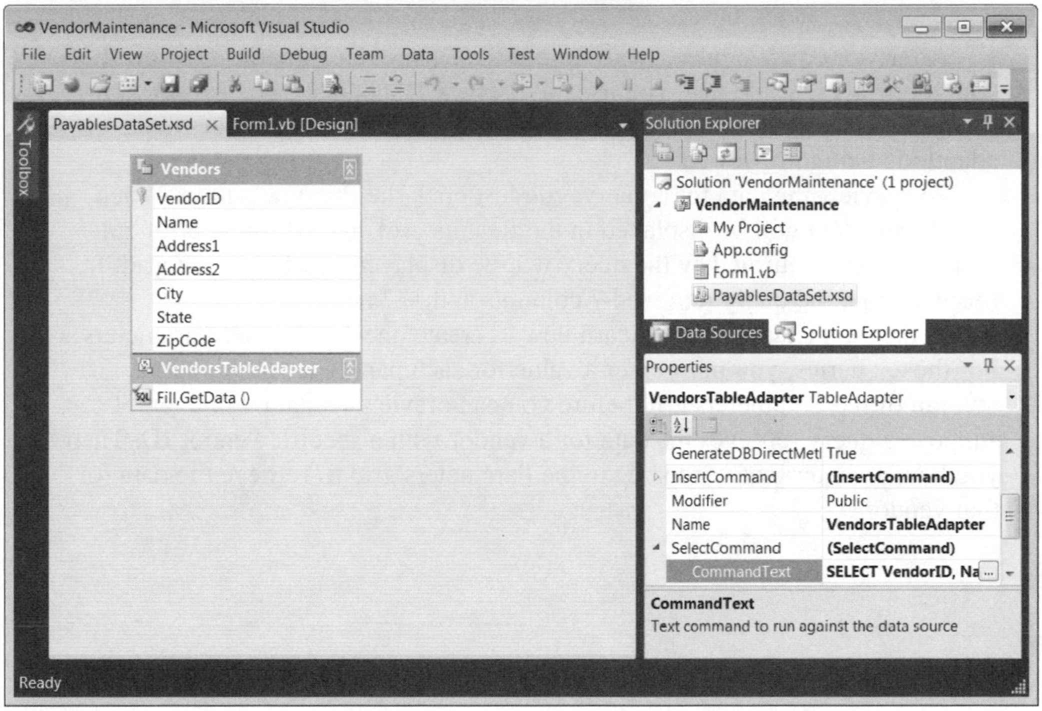

Description

- To view the schema for the dataset of a data source, double-click on the schema file for the dataset (.xsd) in the Solution Explorer, or select the schema file and click the View Designer button at the top of the Solution Explorer. The schema is displayed in the *Dataset Designer*.
- To view the properties for a table adapter in the Properties window, select the table adapter in the Dataset Designer. These properties include the Connection object that's used to connect to the database, and the SelectCommand, InsertCommand, UpdateCommand, and DeleteCommand objects that are used to work with the data in the database.
- For each table adapter, the query named Fill is the *main query*. This query determines the columns that are used when you drag a table from the Data Sources window onto a form. The Insert, Update, and Delete statements for the table are also based on this query.
- To view the properties for a query, select the query in the Dataset Designer.
- To work with the SQL statement in a CommandText property, you can click on the ellipsis button that appears when that property is selected. This displays the statement in the Query Builder, which you'll learn about in chapter 5.
- To view and set the properties for a column in a table, select the column. This is an easy way to set the DefaultValue property for a column.

Figure 3-16 How to view the schema for a dataset

How to preview the data for a query

After you create a query, you can use the Dataset Designer to preview the data it retrieves. To do that, you use the Preview Data dialog box as shown in figure 3-17. Here, the data returned by the Fill query for the Vendors table adapter is being previewed.

To preview the data for a query, you just click the Preview button. When you do, the data will be displayed in the Results grid, and the number of columns and rows returned by the query will be displayed just below the grid. In this example, the query retrieved 7 columns and 122 rows.

In the next chapter, you'll learn how to create queries that use parameters. For those queries, you must enter a value for each parameter in the Value column of the Parameters grid before you can preview its data. For example, suppose a query retrieves the data for a vendor with a specific vendor ID. Then, you have to enter that vendor ID in the Parameters grid to retrieve the data for that vendor.

The Preview Data dialog box

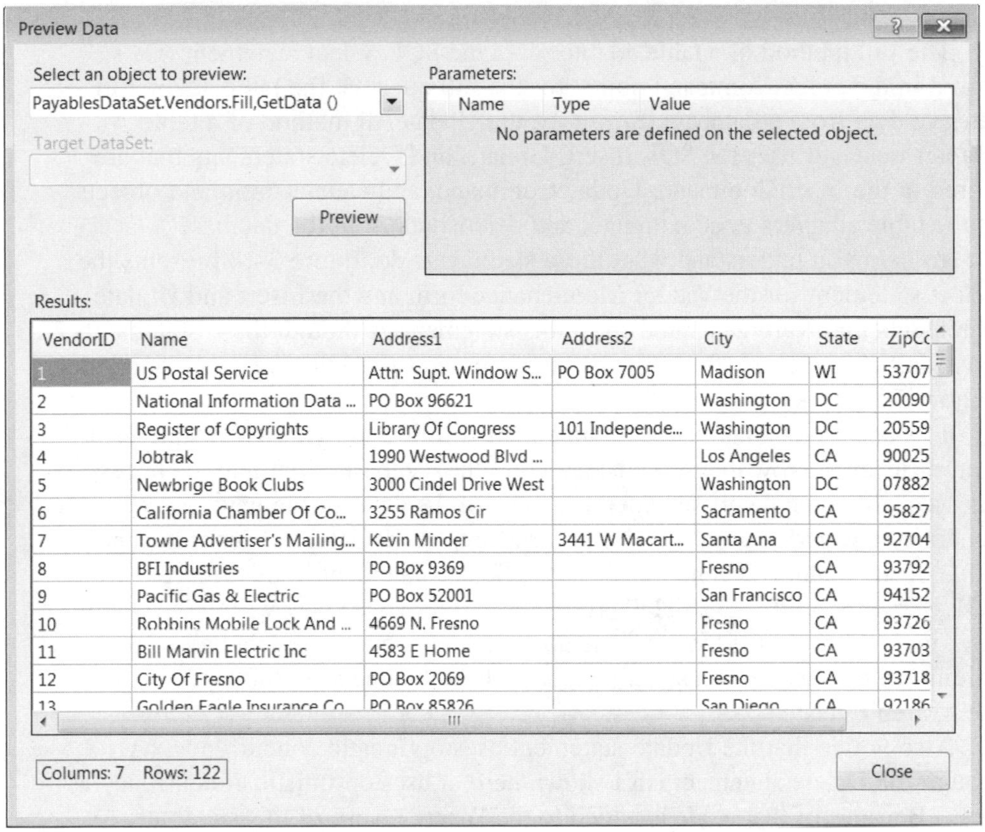

Description

- To display the Preview Data dialog box for a query, right-click on the query in the Dataset Designer and select the Preview Data command, or select the query and then use the Data→Preview Data command.
- To preview the data, click the Preview button. When you do, the data will be displayed in the Results grid, and the number of columns and rows returned by the query will be displayed just below the Results grid.
- If a query requires parameters, you must enter a value for each parameter in the Value column of the Parameters grid. See chapter 4 for more information on query parameters.
- When the data is displayed in the grid as shown in this figure, you can sort the dataset on any field by clicking on the header of a column. This is a standard feature of grid controls, and you can do the same thing to sort data in a DataGridView control.

Figure 3-17 How to preview the data for a query

How to interpret the generated SQL statements

The Fill method of a table adapter uses the SQL Select statement that's stored in the SelectCommand object for the Fill query of the table adapter to retrieve data from a database. Similarly, the UpdateAll method of a table adapter manager uses the SQL Insert, Update, and Delete statements that are stored in the InsertCommand, UpdateCommand, and DeleteCommand objects of the table adapters to add, update, and delete data from the database.

To help you understand what these statements do, figure 3-18 presents the Select statement for the Vendor Maintenance form and the Insert and Update statements that were generated from this statement. Although these statements may look complicated, the information presented here will give you a good idea of how they work.

To start, notice that the Insert statement is followed by a Select statement that retrieves the row that was just added to the database. That may be necessary in cases where the database generates some of the data for the new row. When a vendor row is added to the database, for example, the database generates the value of the VendorID column. Then, the Select statement in this figure uses the SQL Server SCOPE_IDENTITY function to retrieve the row with this ID. For now, just realize that if the database doesn't generate or calculate any of the column values, this Select statement, as well as the one after the Update statement, aren't needed.

Also notice that the Update statement uses optimistic concurrency. (Although the Delete statement isn't shown here, it uses optimistic concurrency as well.) Because of that, code is added to the Where clause of this statement to check whether any of the column values have changed since they were retrieved from the database. This code compares the current value of each column in the database against the original value of the column, which is stored in the dataset. If one or more columns can contain a null value, it also checks if both the original value and the current value of those columns are null. That's the case for the Address2 column in the Vendors table. This is necessary because one null value isn't considered equal to another null value. Then, if none of the values have changed, the operation is performed. Otherwise, it's not.

Finally, notice that most of the statements in this figure use one or more parameters. For example, parameters are used in the Values clause of the Insert statement and the Set clause of the Update statement to refer to the current values of the columns in the dataset. Parameters are also used in the Where clause of the Update statement to refer to the original values of the columns in the dataset. The wizard inserts these parameters when it creates the command objects for a table adapter. Then, before each statement is executed, Visual Studio substitutes the appropriate value for each variable.

This should give you more perspective on how the dataset is refreshed and how optimistic concurrency is provided when you use ADO.NET. Because of the disconnected data architecture, these features can't be provided by the database management system or by ADO.NET. Instead, they are provided by the SQL statements that are generated by the Data Source Configuration Wizard.

SQL that retrieves vendor rows

```
SELECT     VendorID, Name, Address1, Address2, City, State, ZipCode
FROM       Vendors
```

SQL that inserts a vendor row and refreshes the dataset

```
INSERT INTO Vendors
             (Name, Address1, Address2, City, State, ZipCode)
VALUES       (@Name,@Address1,@Address2,@City,@State,@ZipCode);

SELECT     VendorID, Name, Address1, Address2, City, State, ZipCode
FROM       Vendors
WHERE      (VendorID = SCOPE_IDENTITY())
```

SQL that updates a vendor row and refreshes the dataset

```
UPDATE    Vendors
SET       Name = @Name, Address1 = @Address1, Address2 = @Address2,
          City = @City, State = @State, ZipCode = @ZipCode
WHERE     ((VendorID = @Original_VendorID) AND
          (Name = @Original_Name) AND (Address1 = @Original_Address1) AND
          (@IsNull_Address2 = 1) AND (Address2 IS NULL) AND
          (City = @Original_City) AND (State = @Original_State) AND
          (ZipCode = @Original_ZipCode)
          OR
          (VendorID = @Original_VendorID) AND
          (Name = @Original_Name) AND (Address1 = @Original_Address1) AND
          (Address2 = @Original_Address2) AND (City = @Original_City) AND
          (State = @Original_State) AND (ZipCode = @Original_ZipCode));

SELECT     VendorID, Name, Address1, Address2, City, State, ZipCode
FROM       Vendors
WHERE      (VendorID = @VendorID)
```

Description

- By default, the Data Source Configuration Wizard adds code to the Where clause of the Update and Delete statements that checks that the data hasn't changed since it was retrieved. (Although the Delete statement isn't shown here, its Where clause is identical to the Where clause of the Update statement.)
- By default, the Data Source Configuration Wizard adds a Select statement after the Insert and Update statements to refresh the new or modified row in the dataset.
- If a column can contain a null value, code is added to the Where clause of the Update and Delete statements that checks if both the original column value and the current value of the column in the database are null. That's necessary because two null values aren't considered equal.
- The SQL statements use parameters to identify the new values for an insert or update operation. Parameters are also used for the original column values, which are used to check that a row hasn't changed for an update or delete operation. And one is used in the Where clause of the Select statement after the Update statement to refer to the current row. The values for these parameters are stored in and retrieved from the dataset.

Figure 3-18 How to interpret the generated SQL statements

Perspective

Now that you've completed this chapter, you should be able to use a data source to create simple applications that let you view and maintain the data in one table of a database. That should give you some idea of how quickly and easily you can create applications when you use the data source feature. And in the next two chapters, you'll learn how you can use data sources and datasets to build more complex applications.

Terms

data source
schema
typed dataset
binding a control
bound control
complex data binding
simple data binding
data provider error
ADO.NET error
Dataset Designer
main query

Before you do any of the exercises...

Before you do any of the exercises in this book, you need to download the directories and files for this book from our web site and install them on your PC. When you do, a directory named ADO.NET 4 VB will be created on your C drive. This directory will contain the subdirectories and files you need to do the exercises. For example, you can build the applications for this chapter in the C:\ADO.NET 4 VB\Chapter 03 directory. You also need to install SQL Server Express and create the Payables database that you've downloaded as explained in appendix A.

Exercise 3-1 Build a DataGridView application

In this exercise, you'll build the application shown in figure 3-9. That will show you how to build a simple application with data sources, a dataset, and a DataGridView control.

Build the form and test it with valid data

1. Start a new application named TermsMaintenance in your chapter 3 directory, and use the techniques in figures 3-1 through 3-8 to create the data source and drag it onto the form. Then, adjust the size of the form and the DataGridView control as needed, but don't change anything else.

2. Test the application with valid data in three phases. First, sort the rows by clicking on a column header, and size one of the columns by dragging its column separator. Second, change the data in one column of a row, and move to another row to see that the data is changed in the dataset. Third, add a new row with valid data in all columns, and move to another row to see that the row has been added. At this point, the changes have been made to the dataset only, not the database. Now, click the Save button in the toolbar to save the changes to the database.

Test the form with invalid data and provide exception handling

3. Test the application with invalid data by deleting the data in the Description column of a row and moving to another row. This should cause a NoNullAllowedException that's automatically handled by the DataGridView control so the application doesn't crash.
4. Add an event handler for the DataError event of the DataGridView control as shown in figure 3-15. To start the code for that handler, click on the control, click on the Events button in the Properties window, and double-click on the DataError event. Then, write the code for the event, and redo the testing of step 3 to see how your code works.
5. When you're through experimenting, end the application and close the project.

Exercise 3-2 Build an application with text boxes

In this exercise, you'll build the application shown in figure 3-12. That will show you how to use data sources with controls like text boxes.

Build the form and test it with valid data

1. Start a new application named VendorMaintenance in your chapter 3 directory, and create a data source for the fields in the Vendor table that are used by the form in figure 3-12. Then, use the techniques in figures 3-10 and 3-11 to drag the data source fields onto the form as text boxes. At this point, the form should look like the one in figure 3-11.
2. Test the application with valid data in three phases. First, use the toolbar to navigate through the rows. Second, change the data in one column of a row, move to another row, and return to the first row to see that the data has been changed in the dataset. Third, add a new row with valid data in all columns, move to another row, and return to the added row to see that the row has been added to the dataset. Now, click the Save button to save the dataset to the database.

Test the form with invalid data and provide exception handling

3. Add a new row to the dataset, but don't enter anything into the City field. Then, click on the Save button. This should cause a NoNullAllowedException, since City is a required field.
4. Add exception handling code for an ADO.NET DataException as shown in figure 3-14 to catch this type of error. This code replaces the default code in the VendorsBindingNavigatorSaveItem_Click event handler. But note that you also need to add an Imports statement for System.Data.SqlClient to the form. Then, run the application and redo the testing of step 3 to see how this error is handled now.
5. Delete the data in the Name column of a row, which means that the column contains an empty string. Next, move to another row, and return to the first row to see that the row has been accepted into the dataset. Then, click on the Save button and discover that this doesn't throw an exception because an empty string isn't the same as a null value. This indicates that data validation is required because an empty string isn't an acceptable value in the database. In the next chapter, you'll learn one way to provide data validation.
6. Adjust the controls on the form and any related properties so the form looks like the one in figure 3-12. This should take just a minute or two.

Use the Dataset Designer

7. Use one of the techniques in figure 3-16 to view the schema for the dataset in the Dataset Designer.
8. Click on the table adapter in the Dataset Designer and review its properties in the Properties window. Then, look at the Select statement that's used for getting the data into the dataset. To do that, click on the arrow in front of SelectCommand, and click on the ellipsis button for CommandText. This opens up the Query Builder, which you'll learn about in chapter 5, and there you can see the Select statement that's used for getting the data into the dataset. Then, close the Query Builder.
9. Right-click on the query in the Dataset Designer, and preview the data that will be retrieved by that query as shown in figure 3-17.
10. When you're through experimenting, close the project.

4

How to work with bound controls and parameterized queries

In the last chapter, you learned the basic skills for developing applications by using data sources and datasets. Now, you'll learn some additional skills for building database applications that way. Specifically, you'll learn how to work with bound controls, how to use parameterized queries, how to customize the generated toolbars, and how to work with a DataGridView control.

How to work with bound text boxes and combo boxes

The topics that follow show you how to work with bound text boxes and combo boxes. First, you'll learn how to format the data that's displayed in text boxes. Second, you'll learn how to bind data to a combo box. And third, you'll learn how to work with the BindingSource object to make sure that the data and controls are synchronized.

How to format the data displayed in a text box

In the last chapter, you learned how to use bound text boxes to work with the data in a Vendors table. However, because the columns of that table contain string data, it wasn't necessary to format the data when it was displayed. In many cases, though, you'll want to format the data so it's displayed properly.

Figure 4-1 shows how you can apply standard formatting to the data that's displayed in a bound text box. To do that, you use the Formatting and Advanced Binding dialog box. From this dialog box, you can select the format you want to apply from the Format Type list. Then, you can enter appropriate values for the options that are displayed to the right of this list. In this figure, for example, a Date Time format is being applied to the text box that's bound to the InvoiceDate column of the Invoices table.

The dialog box that you can use to apply formatting to a column

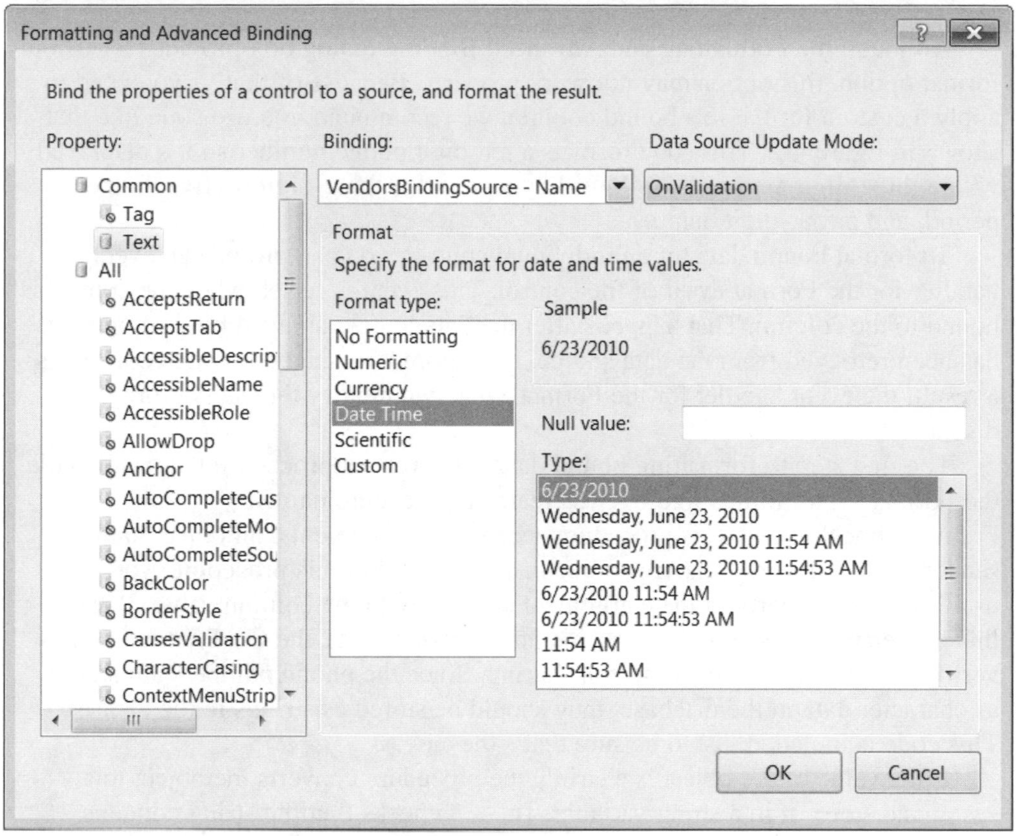

Description

- To display the Formatting and Advanced Binding dialog box, select the text box whose data you want to format, expand the DataBindings group in the Properties window, and then click the ellipsis button that appears when you select the Advanced option.
- To apply a format, select the format you want to use from the Format Type list and enter any additional options that appear to the right of the list. Numeric, Currency, and Scientific let you enter the number of decimal places to be displayed. Date Time lets you select from a number of date and time formats. And Custom lets you enter a custom format.
- Each format also lets you enter the value you want to display in place of a null value. The default is an empty string.
- If you select the Custom format, a note is displayed indicating that the format may not be applied and that you should use the Format or Parse event of the Binding object to apply it instead. See figure 4-2 for more information.

Figure 4-1 How to format the data displayed in a text box

How to use custom formatting

Although the Formatting and Advanced Binding dialog box provides a Custom format option, this option may not work properly. Because of that, if you need to apply a custom format to a bound column, we recommend you use code like that shown in figure 4-2. This code formats a ten-digit phone number so it's displayed with a three-digit area code, followed by a period, a three-digit prefix, another period, and a four-digit number.

To format bound data for an individual control, you can provide an event handler for the Format event of the control. This event is raised when the control is bound to the column. That happens after the data to be displayed by the control has been retrieved from the data source, but before it's assigned to the control. As a result, the event handler for the Format event can modify the data before it's displayed.

The first step to formatting bound data is to create a procedure that can handle the Format event. In this figure, I've created a procedure named FormatPhoneNumber. This procedure accepts two arguments: an object named sender and a ConvertEventArgs object named e. Within this procedure, you can use the Value property of the e argument to work with the column value. Because this property returns an object, the method starts by using the GetType method to verify that the value of the object is a string. Since the phone numbers are stored as character data in the database, they should be stored as strings in the dataset. This code is included just to be sure that's the case.

If the value of the object is a string, the procedure converts the object to a string and stores it in a string variable. Then, it checks that the string contains numeric data and that it has ten digits. In other words, it checks that it contains a standard 10-digit phone number. If so, it formats the variable and assigns the result to the Value property.

Once you've created a procedure to serve as the event handler, the next step is to wire the procedure to the Format event. To understand how this wiring works, you need to realize that the Format event is not raised directly by a control. Instead, this event is raised by the Binding object that's created for each bound property of the control. To wire an event handler to the Format event, then, you must first retrieve the Binding object for the bound property of the control. Then, you can add your event handler to the binding object's Format event.

The second code example in this figure shows the two lines of code needed to do that. The first line declares a Binding variable and assigns the binding object for the Text property of the PhoneTextBox to it. This code accesses the Binding object through the control's DataBindings property. This property returns a collection of all the data bindings for the control, indexed by the name of the property each binding refers to.

The second line in this example associates the Format event of the Binding object with the event handler. To do that, it uses an AddHandler statement. Note in this statement that the AddressOf operator is used to implicitly create an instance of the FormatPhoneNumber event handler at runtime.

If you format data in this way, you need to consider the possible implications of saving the formatted data back to the database. For instance, the phone number

A procedure that formats a phone number that's stored as a string

```
Private Sub FormatPhoneNumber(ByVal sender As Object,
        ByVal e As ConvertEventArgs)
    If e.Value.GetType.ToString = "System.String" Then
        Dim s As String = e.Value.ToString
        If IsNumeric(s) Then
            If s.Length = 10 Then
                e.Value = s.Substring(0, 3) & "." &
                          s.Substring(3, 3) & "." &
                          s.Substring(6, 4)
            End If
        End If
    End If
End Sub
```

Code that wires the procedure to the Format event of a Binding object

```
Dim b As Binding = PhoneTextBox.DataBindings("Text")
AddHandler b.Format, AddressOf FormatPhoneNumber
```

A procedure that removes phone number formatting

```
Private Sub UnformatPhoneNumber(ByVal sender As Object,
    ByVal e As ConvertEventArgs)
    If e.Value.GetType.ToString = "System.String" Then
        Dim s As String = e.Value.ToString
        e.Value = s.Replace(".", "")
    End If
End Sub
```

Code that wires the procedure to the Parse event of a Binding object

```
AddHandler b.Parse, AddressOf UnformatPhoneNumber
```

Description

- To apply formatting to a column using code, you can wire an event handler to the Format event of the Binding object for the control. The Format event is raised when the control is bound to the column.
- In the Format event handler, you can use the Value property of the ConvertEventArgs argument to retrieve and format the value of the data to be bound to the control. Because the Value property returns an object, you'll want to check the type of this property to be sure it's what you expect. Then, you can convert the value to the appropriate type.
- To wire the Format event handler, you start by getting the Binding object for the control. To do that, you use the control's DataBindings property with the name of the bound property as an index. Then, you use the AddHandler statement to associate the Format event of the Binding object with the event handler.
- To remove the formatting, you can create a procedure for the task and then call that procedure when the Parse event of the binding object fires. This Parse event occurs when the value of bound data has changed and the application is attempting to save data back to the database.

Figure 4-2 How to use custom formatting

column in the database for this example provides for only 10 characters. So, if you try to save the 13 characters of the formatted phone number in this column, you'll get an error.

To prevent this, you can use a procedure that undoes the formatting before the data is saved. You can see such a procedure in the third code example in this figure. Here, the three occurrences of the period character are removed by the use of the Replace function.

This procedure can be called by the Parse event of the Binding object. This event fires when the user tries to save changed data back to the database. You can see the code that adds this event handler in the fourth code example in this figure.

How to bind a combo box to a data source

Figure 4-3 shows how to bind a combo box so it displays all of the rows in one table and updates a column in another table. In the Vendor Maintenance form shown in this figure, for example, the combo box is bound to the States table and is used to update the State column in the Vendors table. The easiest way to create a combo box like this is to use the Data Sources window to change the control that's associated with the column in the main table to a combo box before you drag the table to the form. Then, you can use the combo box's smart tag menu to set the binding properties.

To start, you'll need to select the Use Data Bound Items check box to display the binding properties as shown here. Then, you can set these properties.

In this figure, the DataSource property of the State combo box is set to StatesBindingSource (which points to the States table), the DisplayMember property is set to the StateName column (which provides the full name of the state), and the ValueMember property is set to the StateCode column (which provides the two-letter code for the state). That way, this combo box will list the full name of each state in the visible portion of the combo box.

Finally, the SelectedValue property is used to bind the ValueMember property to a column in another data source. In this case, the SelectedValue property is set to the State column of the VendorsBindingSource. That way, the StateCode column of the States table is bound to the State column of the Vendors table. Then, when the data for a vendor is displayed, the state that's selected in the combo box is determined by the State column of the Vendors table. Also, if the user selects a different item from the combo box list, the States column in the Vendors table is changed to the value selected by the user.

In addition to the four properties in the smart tag menu, you may also need to set a couple of other properties when you bind a combo box. In particular, you can set the DropDownStyle property to DropDownList to prevent the user from entering text into the text portion of the combo box. Then, you can set the Text property in the DataBindings group to None so the application doesn't bind the value stored in this property to the data source. *If this property isn't set correctly, the combo box won't work properly.*

A combo box that's bound to a data source

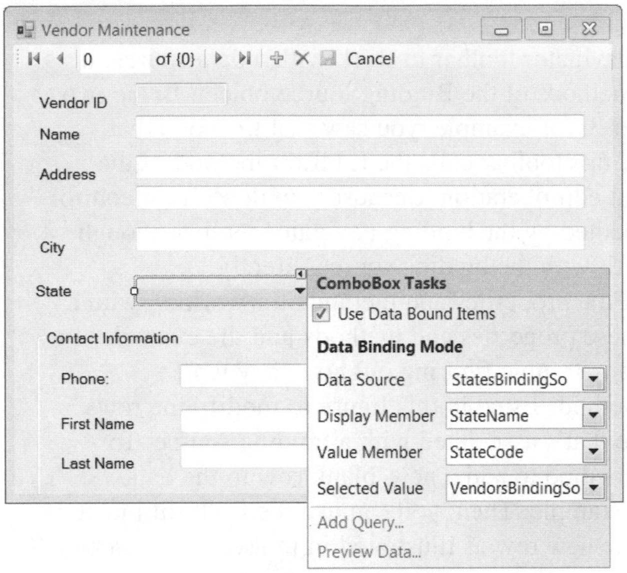

Combo box properties for binding

Property	Description
DataSource	The name of the data table that contains the data displayed in the list.
DisplayMember	The name of the data column whose data is displayed in the list.
ValueMember	The name of the data column whose value is stored in the list. This value is returned by the SelectedValue property of the control.
SelectedValue	Gets the value of the currently selected item. You can use this property to bind the ValueMember property to a column in another data source.

Description

- To access the most common properties for binding a combo box, you can display the smart tag menu for the combo box and select the Use Data Bound Items check box. This will display the properties shown above.
- To set the DataSource property, display the drop-down list; expand the Other Data Sources node, the Project Data Sources node, and the node for the dataset; and select the table you want to use as the data source. This adds BindingSource and TableAdapter objects for the table to the form. Then, you can set the DisplayMember and ValueMember properties to columns in this table.
- The SelectedValue property is typically bound to a column in the main table. That way, if you select a different item from the combo box, the value of the bound column is set to the value of the ValueMember property for the selected item.
- When you bind a combo box to a data source, you'll typically set the DropDownStyle property of the combo box to DropDownList so the user can only select a value from the list. You'll also want to change the (DataBindings) - Text property to (none) to remove the binding from the text box portion of the combo box.

Figure 4-3 How to bind a combo box to a data source

How to use code to work with a binding source

When you use the binding navigator toolbar to work with a data source, it works by using properties and methods of the BindingSource object. In the two applications presented in chapter 3, for example, you saw that the code that's generated for the Save button of this toolbar calls the EndEdit method of the binding source to end the current edit operation. Because you don't have control over most of the code that's executed by the binding navigator toolbar, though, you may sometimes want to work with the binding source directly.

Figure 4-4 presents some of the properties and methods for working with a binding source. If you review these properties and methods and the examples in this figure, you shouldn't have any trouble figuring out how they work.

You can use the first four methods listed in this figure to modify the rows that are stored in the data source that's associated with a binding source. To start, you can use the AddNew method to add a new, blank row to the data source as illustrated in the first example. Then, you can use the EndEdit method to save the data you enter into the new row as illustrated in the second example. You can also use this method to save changes you make to an existing row.

If an error occurs when you try to save changes to a row, or if the user decides to cancel an edit operation, you can use the CancelEdit method to cancel the changes as illustrated in the third example. Note, however, that you don't have to explicitly start an edit operation. The binding source takes care of that automatically when you make changes to a row. Finally, you can use the RemoveCurrent method to remove the current row from the data source as illustrated in the fourth example.

You can use the last four methods in this figure to move to the first, previous, next, or last row in a data source. You can also use the Position property to get or set the index of the current row. And you can use the Count property to get the number of rows in the data source.

To illustrate how you might use these properties and methods, the last example in this figure presents an event handler that responds to the Click event of a button. This event handler uses the MoveNext method to move to the next row in the data source. Then, it uses the Position property to get the index of the current row, and it adds one to the result since the index is zero-based. Finally, it uses the Count property to get the total number of rows in the data source, and it displays the position and count in a text box. This is similar to the display that's included in the binding navigator toolbar.

Common properties and methods of the BindingSource class

Property	Description
`Position`	The index of the current row in the data source.
`Count`	The number of rows in the data source.
Method	**Description**
`AddNew()`	Adds a new, blank row to the data source.
`EndEdit()`	Saves changes to the current row.
`CancelEdit()`	Cancels changes to the current row.
`RemoveCurrent()`	Removes the current row from the data source.
`MoveFirst()`	Moves to the first row in the data source.
`MovePrevious()`	Moves to the previous row in the data source, if there is one.
`MoveNext()`	Moves to the next row in the data source, if there is one.
`MoveLast()`	Moves to the last row in the data source.

A statement that adds a new row to a data source

```
Me.VendorsBindingSource.AddNew()
```

A statement that saves the changes to the current row and ends the edit

```
Me.VendorsBindingSource.EndEdit()
```

A statement that cancels the changes to the current row

```
Me.VendorsBindingSource.CancelEdit()
```

A statement that removes the current row from a data source

```
Me.VendorsBindingSource.RemoveCurrent()
```

Code that moves to the next row and displays the position and count

```
Private Sub btnNext_Click(ByVal sender As System.Object,
        ByVal e As System.EventArgs) Handles btnNext.Click
    Me.VendorsBindingSource.MoveNext()
    Dim position As Integer = VendorsBindingSource.Position + 1
    txtPosition.Text = position & " of " & VendorsBindingSource.Count
End Sub
```

Description

- The binding source ensures that all controls that are bound to the same data table are synchronized. That way, when you move to another row, the data-bound controls will display the values in that row.
- If a form provides for updating the rows in a data table, moving from one row to another causes any changes made to the current row to be saved to the data table.
- When you add a new row using the AddNew method, the Position property of the binding source is set to one more than the position of the last row in the data table.
- You can use the EndEdit and CancelEdit methods to save or cancel the changes to an existing row or a new row that was added using the AddNew method.

Figure 4-4 How to use code to work with a binding source

How to work with parameterized queries

In the last chapter, you learned how the Data Source Configuration Wizard uses parameters in the SQL statements it generates. A query like this that contains parameters is called a *parameterized query*. In the topics that follow, you'll learn one way to create parameterized queries for your forms.

How to create a parameterized query

For some applications, such as the Terms Maintenance application presented in the previous chapter, it's acceptable (or even preferable) to fill the table in the dataset with every row in the database table. However, if a database table contains many columns and rows, this can have a negative impact on the performance of your application. In addition, for some types of applications, you will only want to allow the user to retrieve certain rows from a table. In either case, the solution is to use a parameterized query.

Fortunately, Visual Studio provides an easy way to create a parameterized query, as shown in figure 4-5. When you use this technique, Visual Studio generates a toolbar that lets the user enter the parameters for the query. It also generates the code that fills the table in the dataset with the results of the query.

To create a parameterized query, you can begin by displaying the smart tag menu for any control that's bound to the data source. Then, you can select the Add Query command from this menu. When you do, Visual Studio will display a Search Criteria Builder dialog box like the one shown here. This dialog box lets you enter the name and parameters for the query.

By default, a query is named FillBy, but you can change it to anything you want. I recommend that you name a query based on the function it performs. In this figure, for example, the query has been named FillByVendorID because it will be used to retrieve a vendor row based on the vendor ID.

After you enter the query name, you can modify the Where clause of the query so it includes one or more parameters. In SQL Server, you specify a parameter by coding an @ sign in front of the parameter name. In this figure, for example, the query will return all rows where the value in the VendorID column equals the value of the @VendorID parameter that's entered by the user.

When you finish specifying the query in the Search Criteria Builder dialog box, Visual Studio automatically adds a toolbar to your form. This toolbar contains one or more text boxes that let the user enter the parameters that are needed by the query and a button that lets the user execute the query. You can see this toolbar in the Vendor Maintenance form shown in this figure.

Using this toolbar, the user can retrieve a single row that contains the vendor's data by entering the ID for the vendor and then clicking the FillByVendorID button. In this figure, for example, the user has displayed the row for the vendor with an ID of 34. That's why the binding navigator toolbar shows that only one row exists in the Vendors data table.

The dialog box for creating a parameterized query

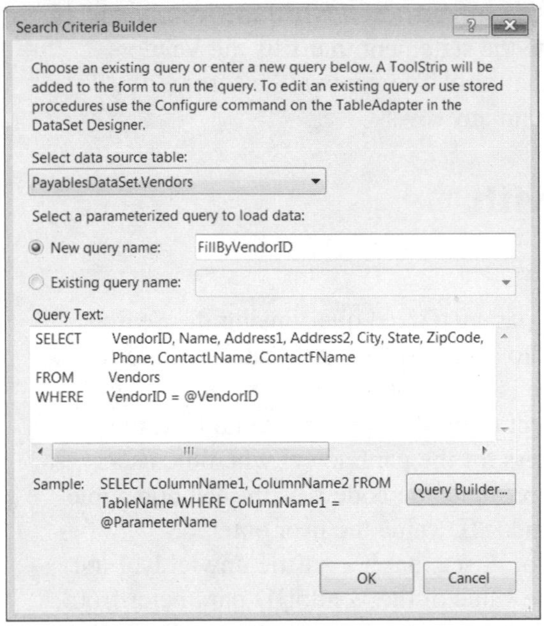

The Vendor Maintenance form with a toolbar for the query

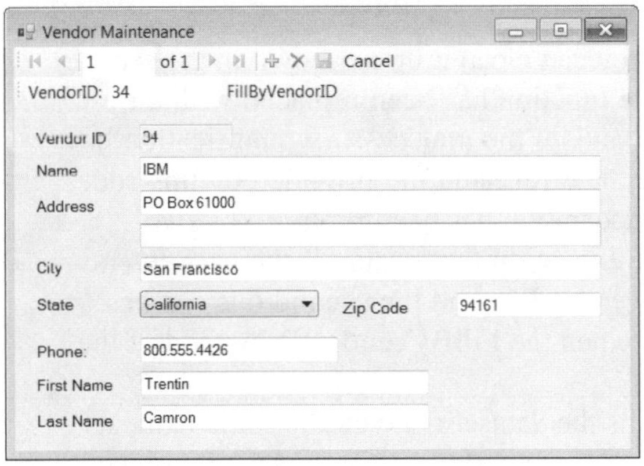

Description

- You can add a *parameterized query* to a data table using the Search Criteria Builder dialog box. To display this dialog box, display the smart tag menu for a control that's bound to the data table and then select the Add Query command.
- When you finish specifying the query in the Search Criteria Builder dialog box, Visual Studio automatically adds a toolbar to your form. This toolbar contains the text boxes that let the user enter the parameters that are needed by the query, and it contains a button that lets the user execute the query.
- You can add more than one parameterized query to a data table using the Search Criteria Builder. Each query you add is displayed in its own toolbar. Because of that, you may want to modify one of the toolbars so that it provides for all the queries.

Figure 4-5 How to create a parameterized query

Although the parameterized query in this example retrieves a single row from the Vendors table, all of the rows are still retrieved when the form loads. If that's not what you want, you can delete the statement that fills the Vendors table from the Load event handler for the form. Then, when the form is first displayed, the Vendors table won't contain any rows.

How to use code to work with a parameterized query

As I mentioned, when you create a parameterized query using the Search Criteria Builder dialog box, Visual Studio automatically generates code to fill the data table using the query. This code is shown at the top of figure 4-6. It calls a method of the TableAdapter object to fill the appropriate table in the dataset based on the values the user enters for the parameters when the user clicks the button in the toolbar. In this example, the code fills the Vendors table with the row for the vendor with the vendor ID value the user entered.

If you review the generated code, you'll see that it's a little unwieldy. First, it uses the CType function to convert the value of the VendorID parameter from a String type to an Integer type. Second, it qualifies references to the Exception class and the MessageBox class even though that isn't necessary within the context of this form.

To make this code easier to read, you can clean it up as shown in the second example in this figure. Here, the CType function has been replaced with the more concise Convert.ToInt32 method and all the unnecessary qualification has been removed. In addition, to enhance the error handling provided by this code, the Catch block that catches a generic exception has been replaced by two Catch blocks. The first one catches the exception that occurs if the user enters anything other than an integer for the vendor ID. And the second one catches any SQL Server exception that occurs when the FillByVendorID method of the table adapter is executed.

As you can see, the method that fills the dataset is given the same name as the query, and it works similarly to the Fill method of the TableAdapter object that you learned about in the previous chapter. The difference is that the method for a parameterized query lets you specify the parameter or parameters that are required by the query. In this figure, for example, the FillByVendorID method of the VendorsTableAdapter object requires a single parameter of the Integer type. To get this parameter, the code gets the string that's entered by the user into the text box on the toolbar, and it converts this string to an Integer type.

Note that the FillByVendorID method of the table adapter fills the Vendors table of the dataset with only one row. Then, if the user makes any changes to that row, he or she must click the Save button to save those changes to the database. If the user retrieves another row instead, that row fills the dataset and the changes are lost. Similarly, the user must click the Save button to save a deletion before moving to another row. Although this user interface works, it isn't very intuitive. As a result, you'll typically want to modify interfaces like this one.

The generated code for a parameterized query

```
Private Sub FillByVendorIDToolStripButton_Click(
    ByVal sender As System.Object, ByVal e As System.EventArgs) _
    Handles FillByVendorIDToolStripButton.Click

    Try
        Me.VendorsTableAdapter.FillByVendorID(
            Me.PayablesDataSet.Vendors, CType(
               VendorIDToolStripTextBox.Text, Integer))
    Catch ex As System.Exception
        System.Windows.Forms.MessageBox.Show(ex.Message)
    End Try

End Sub
```

The same code after it has been cleaned up and enhanced

```
Private Sub FillByVendorIDToolStripButton_Click(
    ByVal sender As System.Object, ByVal e As System.EventArgs) _
    Handles FillByVendorIDToolStripButton.Click

    Try
        Dim vendorID As Integer =
            Convert.ToInt32(VendorIDToolStripTextBox.Text)
        Me.VendorsTableAdapter.FillByVendorID(
            Me.PayablesDataSet.Vendors, vendorID)
    Catch ex As FormatException
        MessageBox.Show("Vendor ID must be an integer.", "Entry Error")
    Catch ex As SqlException
        MessageBox.Show("SQL Server error # " & ex.Number &
            ": " & ex.Message, ex.GetType.ToString)
    End Try

End Sub
```

The syntax of the method for filling a table using a parameterized query

```
TableAdapter.QueryName(DataSet.TableName, param1 [,param2]...)
```

Description

- When you finish specifying a query in the Search Criteria Builder dialog box, Visual Studio automatically generates the code that uses the appropriate method to fill the table in the dataset when the user clicks the button in the toolbar.
- If necessary, you can modify the generated code to make it easier to read or to change the way it works.

Figure 4-6 How to use code to work with a parameterized query

How to work with a ToolStrip control

When you create a parameterized query, Visual Studio automatically generates a ToolStrip control that lets the user enter the parameter for the query. Although this ToolStrip control works well for simple applications, you may want to modify it as your applications become more complex. For example, you may want to change the text on the button that executes the query. Or, you may want to add additional text boxes and buttons that work with other queries. Fortunately, the ToolStrip control is easy to customize.

Before I go on, you should know that the binding navigator toolbar that gets generated when you drag a data source onto a form is a customized ToolStrip control. As a result, you can work with this toolbar just as you would any other ToolStrip control. If, for example, a form won't provide for inserts, updates, and deletes, you can remove the Add, Delete, and Save buttons from this toolbar. You can also add controls that perform customized functions.

How to use the Items Collection Editor

To work with the items on a ToolStrip control, you use the Items Collection Editor shown in figure 4-7. To start, you can add an item by selecting the type of control you want to add from the combo box in the upper left corner and clicking the Add button. This adds the item to the bottom of the Members list. Then, if necessary, you can move the item using the up and down arrow buttons to the right of the Members list.

You can also use the Items Collection Editor to set the properties for a new or existing item. To do that, just select the item in the Members list and use the Properties list at the right side of the dialog box to set the properties. The table in this figure lists the four properties you're most likely to change. Note that when you add a new Button control, the DisplayStyle property is set to Image by default. If you want to display the text that you specify for the Text property instead of an image, then, you need to change the DisplayStyle property to Text.

Finally, you can use the Items Collection Editor to delete an existing item. To do that, just select the item and click the Delete button to the right of the Members list.

The Items Collection Editor for an enhanced ToolStrip control

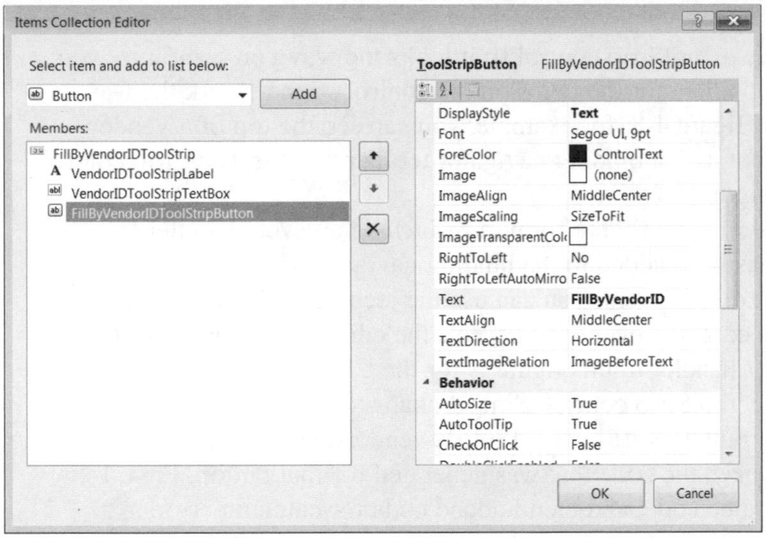

Common properties of ToolStrip items

Property	Description
DisplayStyle	Indicates whether a button displays an image, text, or both an image and text.
Image	The image that's displayed on a button if you select Image or ImageAndText for the DisplayStyle property.
Text	The text that's displayed on a button if you select Text or ImageAndText for the DisplayStyle property.
Width	The width of the item.

Description

- To display the Items Collection Editor dialog box, display the smart tag menu for the ToolStrip and select the Edit Items command.
- To add an item, select the type of control you want to add from the combo box and click the Add button. To add a separator bar, choose Separator. You can also add an item by using the drop-down list that's displayed when the ToolStrip is selected in the Form Designer.
- To move an item, select the item in the Members list and click the up and down arrows to the right of the list.
- To delete an item, select it in the Members list and click the Delete button to the right of the list.
- To set the properties for an item, select the item in the Members list and use the Properties list on the right side of the dialog box to set the properties. You can also set the properties of an item by selecting it in the Form Designer and then using the Properties window.

Note

- Because the BindingNavigator control is a ToolStrip control, you can also use the Items Collection Editor to work with the BindingNavigator control.

Figure 4-7 How to use the Items Collection Editor for a ToolStrip control

How to code an event handler for a ToolStrip item

After you modify a ToolStrip control so it looks the way you want it to, you need to code event handlers for the items on the control so they work the way you want them to. In figure 4-8, for example, you can see the top of a Vendor Maintenance form that uses a binding navigator toolbar and the ToolStrip control that was defined in figure 4-7.

For this application to work, the form must include an event handler for the Cancel button that has been added to the binding navigator toolbar. To generate the code for the start of that event, you can use the technique that's summarized in this figure. In this case, the event just cancels the editing that has been started.

The second event handler in this figure is for the Click event of the Get Vendor button on the ToolStrip control. Since I changed the text for the button but not its name, the button is still named FillByVendorIDToolStripButton. In this case, I just enhanced the code that was generated for that button. First, I cleaned up the generated code, and then I added code for catching errors.

How to code a custom event handler for a control on a binding navigator toolbar

In the last chapter, you learned that when a binding navigator toolbar is added to a form, an event handler is added for the Click event of the toolbar's Save button. That way, you can modify this event handler if you need to. In some cases, you'll want to modify the code that's executed for one of the other controls on the toolbar. For example, you may want to display a confirmation dialog box before a row is deleted. Since the event handler for the Click event of the Delete button isn't exposed by the toolbar, however, you can't modify it directly. Fortunately, there is a way to use a custom event handler with an item on a binding navigator toolbar.

To start, you need to keep the code that's built into the toolbar for an item from being executed. To do that, you can use the properties that are listed in the Items group of the Properties window for the toolbar. These properties associate an action with the toolbar item that initiates the action. For example, the DeleteItem property identifies the toolbar item that initiates the delete action, and the AddItem property identifies the toolbar item that initiates the add action.

To remove the association between an action and a toolbar item so that the default code isn't executed for that item, you change the appropriate Item property to "(none)". For example, to stop the RemoveCurrent method of the binding source from being executed when the Delete button is clicked, you change the DeleteItem property to "(none)". Then, you can code your own custom event handler for the Click event of this button. Note that this code must execute the RemoveCurrent method since it's no longer executed by default. You can use a similar technique to use custom event handlers for the other controls on a binding navigator toolbar. In most cases, though, the built-in code is sufficient.

Customized toolbars for a Vendor Maintenance application

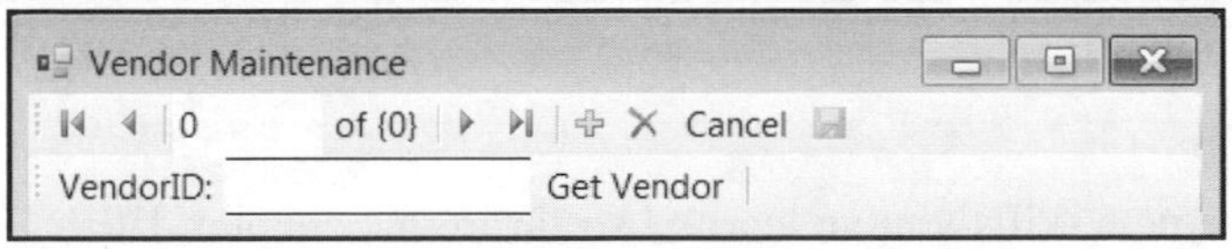

The event handler for the Cancel button on the BindingNavigator Toolstrip control

```
Private Sub BindingNavigatorCancelItem_Click(
        ByVal sender As System.Object, ByVal e As System.EventArgs) _
        Handles BindingNavigatorCancelItem.Click

    VendorsBindingSource.CancelEdit()

End Sub
```

The event handler for the Get Vendor button on the FillByVendorID ToolStrip control

```
Private Sub FillByVendorIDToolStripButton_Click(
        ByVal sender As System.Object, ByVal e As System.EventArgs) _
        Handles FillByVendorIDToolStripButton.Click

    Try
        Dim vendorID As Integer =
            Convert.ToInt32(VendorIDToolStripTextBox.Text)
        Me.VendorsTableAdapter.FillByVendorID(
            Me.PayablesDataSet.Vendors, vendorID)
    Catch ex As FormatException
        MessageBox.Show("Vendor ID must be an integer.", "Entry Error")
    Catch ex As SqlException
        MessageBox.Show("SQL Server error # " & ex.Number &
            ": " & ex.Message, ex.GetType.ToString)
    End Try

End Sub
```

Description

- To code an event handler for a ToolStrip item, display the form in the Form Designer, click on the item to select it, and click on the Events button of the Properties window to display the list of events for the item. Then, you can use standard techniques to generate or select an event handler for a specified event.
- The BindingNavigator ToolStrip control includes properties that identify the ToolStrip items that are associated with specific actions. For example, The DeleteItem property identifies the item that causes a row to be deleted, and the AddItem property identifies the item that causes a row to be added.
- You can code a custom event handler for any of the items on a BindingNavigator ToolStrip control. To do that, change the appropriate Item property to "(none)" so that no action is associated with that item. Then, add your own custom event handler for the item.

Figure 4-8 How to code an event handler for a ToolStrip item

An enhanced Vendor Maintenance application

To illustrate some of the new skills you've learned so far in this chapter, I'll now present an enhanced version of the Vendor Maintenance application that you saw in the last chapter.

The user interface

Figure 4-9 presents the user interface for the Vendor Maintenance application. Figure 4-9 presents the user interface for the Vendor Maintenance application. This time, the application uses a parameterized query to retrieve a row from the Vendors table based on its vendor ID; the form uses a combo box that lets the user select a state; and the generated toolbars have been modified.

The code

Figure 4-9 also presents the code for the Vendor Maintenance application. Since you've already seen most of this code, you shouldn't have any trouble understanding how it works. So I'll just point out a few highlights.

First, the FormatPhoneNumber procedure is the event handler for the Format event of the phone number text box. It puts periods into the phone number before it is displayed. Then, to remove the formatting of the phone number before it's saved to the database, the UnformatPhoneNumber procedure handles the Parse event of that text box. This procedure just removes the periods from the number.

Second, the procedure for the Click event of the Cancel button contains a single statement that cancels the current edit operation. Since this operation can't cause any exceptions, you don't have to use a Try...Catch statement with it.

Third, the event handler for the Click event of the Save button calls a function named IsValidData. This procedure checks that the user has entered a value into each control on the form that requires a value. To do that, the IsValidData function calls the IsPresent function for each control. Then, if a control doesn't contain a value, this function displays an error message, moves the focus to the appropriate control, and returns a value of False, which means that the IsValidData function also returns a value of False.

Finally, before the IsValidData function checks the controls, it checks whether the Count property of the Vendors binding source is greater than zero. If it isn't, it means that the only vendor in the Vendors data table was deleted. In that case, the controls on the form will be empty and the validation shouldn't be performed.

Incidentally, if you have any problems understanding the data validation code or any of the other code that isn't related to ADO.NET, we recommend that you get a copy of *Murach's Visual Basic 2010*. It will answer all your questions.

The user interface for the Vendor Maintenance application

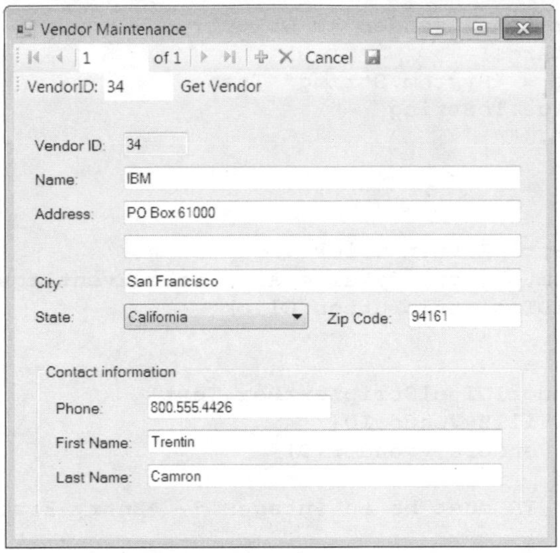

The code for the application **Page 1**

```
Imports System.Data.SqlClient

Public Class Form1

    Private Sub Form1_Load(ByVal sender As System.Object,
            ByVal e As System.EventArgs) Handles MyBase.Load

        Dim b As Binding = PhoneTextBox.DataBindings("Text")
        AddHandler b.Format, AddressOf FormatPhoneNumber
        AddHandler b.Parse, AddressOf UnformatPhoneNumber

        Try
            Me.StatesTableAdapter.Fill(Me.PayablesDataSet.States)
            Me.VendorsTableAdapter.Fill(Me.PayablesDataSet.Vendors)
        Catch ex As SqlException
            MessageBox.Show("SQL Server error # " & ex.Number &
                ": " & ex.Message, ex.GetType.ToString)
        End Try
    End Sub

    Private Sub FormatPhoneNumber(ByVal sender As Object,
            ByVal e As ConvertEventArgs)
        If e.Value.GetType.ToString = "System.String" Then
            Dim s As String = e.Value.ToString
            If IsNumeric(s) Then
                If s.Length = 10 Then
                    e.Value = s.Substring(0, 3) & "." &
                              s.Substring(3, 3) & "." &
                              s.Substring(6, 4)
                End If
            End If
        End If
    End Sub
```

Figure 4-9 An enhanced Vendor Maintenance application (part 1 of 3)

The code for the application **Page 2**

```
Private Sub UnformatPhoneNumber(ByVal sender As Object,
        ByVal e As ConvertEventArgs)
    If e.Value.GetType.ToString = "System.String" Then
        Dim s As String = e.Value.ToString
        e.Value = s.Replace(".", "")
    End If
End Sub

Private Sub FillByVendorIDToolStripButton_Click(
          ByVal sender As System.Object, ByVal e As System.EventArgs) _
          Handles FillByVendorIDToolStripButton.Click
    Try
        Dim vendorID As Integer =
            Convert.ToInt32(VendorIDToolStripTextBox.Text)
        Me.VendorsTableAdapter.FillByVendorID(
            Me.PayablesDataSet.Vendors, vendorID)
    Catch ex As FormatException
        MessageBox.Show("Vendor ID must be an integer.", "Entry Error")
    Catch ex As SqlException
        MessageBox.Show("SQL Server error # " & ex.Number &
            ": " & ex.Message, ex.GetType.ToString)
    End Try
End Sub

Private Sub BindingNavigatorCancelItem_Click(
        ByVal sender As System.Object, ByVal e As System.EventArgs) _
        Handles BindingNavigatorCancelItem.Click
    VendorsBindingSource.CancelEdit()
End Sub

Private Sub VendorsBindingNavigatorSaveItem_Click(
        ByVal sender As System.Object, ByVal e As System.EventArgs) _
        Handles VendorsBindingNavigatorSaveItem.Click
    If IsValidData() Then
        Try
            Me.VendorsBindingSource.EndEdit()
            Me.TableAdapterManager.UpdateAll(Me.PayablesDataSet)
        Catch ex As ArgumentException
            ' This block catches exceptions such as a value that's beyond
            ' the maximum length for a column in a dataset.
            MessageBox.Show(ex.Message, "Argument Exception")
            VendorsBindingSource.CancelEdit()
        Catch ex As DBConcurrencyException
            MessageBox.Show("A concurrency error occurred. " &
                "The row was not updated.", "Concurrency Exception")
            Me.VendorsTableAdapter.Fill(Me.PayablesDataSet.Vendors)
        Catch ex As DataException
            MessageBox.Show(ex.Message, ex.GetType.ToString)
            VendorsBindingSource.CancelEdit()
        Catch ex As SqlException
            MessageBox.Show("SQL Server error # " & ex.Number &
                ": " & ex.Message, ex.GetType.ToString)
        End Try
    End If
End Sub
```

Figure 4-9 An enhanced Vendor Maintenance application (part 2 of 3)

The code for the application **Page 3**

```
    Private Function IsValidData() As Boolean
        If VendorsBindingSource.Count > 0 Then
            Return IsPresent(NameTextBox, "Name") AndAlso
                IsPresent(Address1TextBox, "Address1") AndAlso
                IsPresent(CityTextBox, "City") AndAlso
                IsPresent(StateComboBox, "State") AndAlso
                IsPresent(ZipCodeTextBox, "Zip code")
        Else
            Return True
        End If
    End Function

    Private Function IsPresent(ByVal control As Control,
            ByVal name As String) As Boolean
        If control.GetType.ToString = "System.Windows.Forms.TextBox" Then
            Dim textBox As TextBox = CType(control, TextBox)
            If textBox.Text = "" Then
                MessageBox.Show(name & " is a required field.", "Entry Error")
                textBox.Select()
                Return False
            Else
                Return True
            End If
        ElseIf control.GetType.ToString = "System.Windows.Forms.ComboBox" Then
            Dim comboBox As ComboBox = CType(control, ComboBox)
            If comboBox.SelectedIndex = -1 Then
                MessageBox.Show(name & " is a required field.", "Entry Error")
                comboBox.Select()
                Return False
            Else
                Return True
            End If
        End If
    End Function

End Class
```

Figure 4-9 An enhanced Vendor Maintenance application (part 3 of 3)

How to work with a DataGridView control

In chapter 3, you saw how easy it is to use a DataGridView control to work with the data in a table of a dataset. Now, you'll learn how to modify a DataGridView control so it looks and functions the way you want. In addition, you'll learn how to work with a DataGridView control in code.

How to modify the properties of a DataGridView control

When you generate a DataGridView control from a data source, Visual Studio sets many of the properties of this control and the other objects it creates the way you want them. However, if you want to modify any of these properties, you can do that just as you would for any other type of object. In particular, you'll probably want to edit the properties of the DataGridView control to change its appearance and function.

For the examples in the next five topics, I'll use a DataGridView control that displays data from the Invoices table. This control will let the user modify selected columns of the invoices. It won't let the user add or delete invoices. As you'll see in the next figure, the data source that's used to generate the DataGridView control includes all the columns from the Invoices table except for the TermsID column.

To change the most common properties of a DataGridView control, you can use its smart tag menu as shown in figure 4-10. From this menu, you can create a read-only data grid by removing the check marks from the Enable Adding, Enable Editing, and Enable Deleting check boxes. Or, you can let a user reorder the columns in the grid by checking the Enable Column Reordering check box. In this example, you can see that I removed the check marks from the Enable Adding and Enable Deleting check boxes so the grid won't provide for these functions.

In addition to editing the properties for the grid, you may want to edit the properties for the columns of the grid. For example, you may want to apply currency formatting to a column, or you may want to change the column headings or widths. To do that, you can select the Edit Columns command to display the Edit Columns dialog box shown in the next figure.

By default, when you run an application that uses a DataGridView control, you can sort the rows in a column by clicking in the header at the top of the column. The first time you do this, the rows are sorted in ascending sequence by the values in the column; the next time, in descending sequence. Similarly, you can drag the column separators to change the widths of the columns. Last, if the Enable Column Reordering option is checked, the user can reorder the columns by dragging them. These features let the user customize the presentation of the data.

The smart tag menu for a DataGridView control

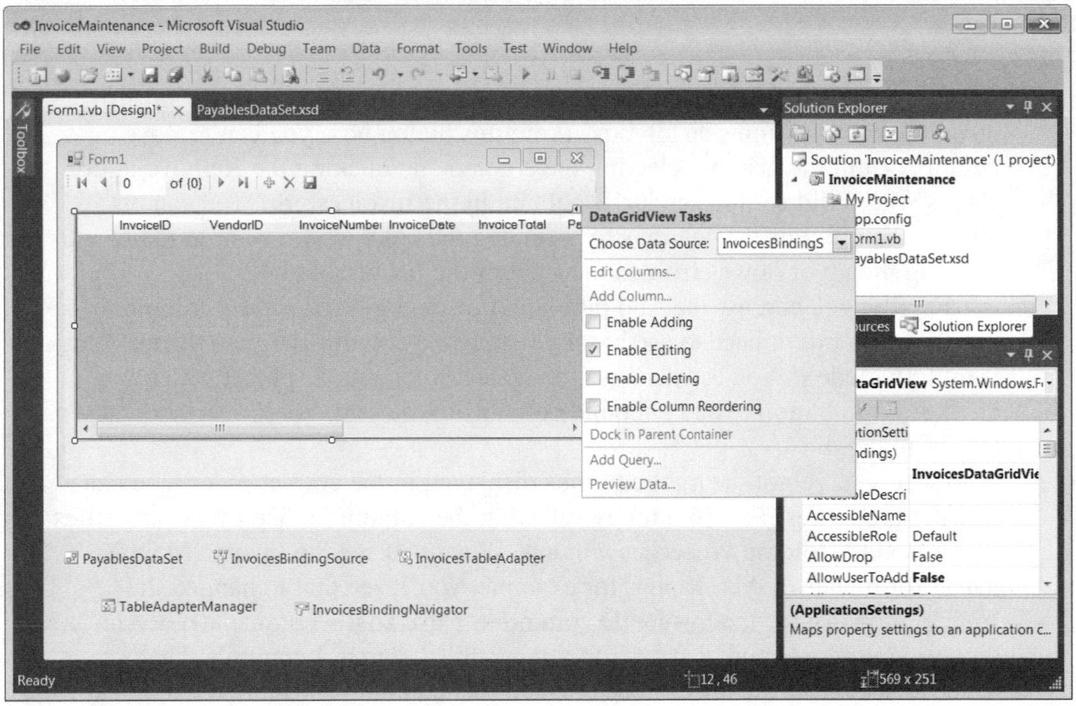

Description

- You can use the smart tag menu of a DataGridView control to edit its most commonly used properties.
- To edit the columns, select the Edit Columns command to display the Edit Columns dialog box. Then, you can edit the columns as described in the next figure.
- To prevent a user from adding, updating, or deleting data that's displayed in the DataGridView control, uncheck the Enable Adding, Enable Editing, or Enable Deleting check boxes.
- To allow a user to reorder the columns in a DataGridView control by dragging them, check the Enable Column Reordering check box.
- You can edit other properties of a DataGridView control by using the Properties window for the control.

Figure 4-10 How to modify the properties of a DataGridView control

How to edit the columns of a DataGridView control

Figure 4-11 shows how to edit the columns of a DataGridView control using the Edit Columns dialog box. From this dialog box, you can remove columns from the grid by selecting the column and clicking the Remove button. That's what I did for the VendorID column in the Invoices grid. You can also change the order of the columns by selecting the column you want to move and clicking the up or down arrow to the right of the list of columns.

Finally, you can use the Add button in this dialog box to add a column to the grid. You might need to do that if you delete a column and then decide you want to include it. You can also use the dialog box that's displayed when you click the Add button to add unbound columns to the grid. You'll learn how to do that in figure 4-13.

Once you've got the right columns displayed in the correct order, you can edit the properties for a column by selecting the column to display its properties in the Bound Column Properties window. When you see the Invoice Maintenance form later in this chapter, for example, you'll see that I changed the Visible property for the InvoiceID column to False so it's not displayed. Although you might think that I could remove this column, I couldn't. That's because, as you'll see later in this chapter, this column is used by the application even though it isn't displayed.

I also changed the HeaderText property for each of the visible columns by adding a space between the two words in each column name, and I changed the Width property of each column as appropriate. I also changed the ReadOnly property of the InvoiceNumber, InvoiceDate, and InvoiceTotal columns to True so that these columns can't be modified. Finally, I used the DefaultCellStyle property to apply a date format to the InvoiceDate, DueDate, and PaymentDate columns and numeric formatting and right alignment to the InvoiceTotal, PaymentTotal, and CreditTotal columns. You'll see the dialog boxes for doing that in the next figure.

The dialog box for editing the columns of a DataGridView control

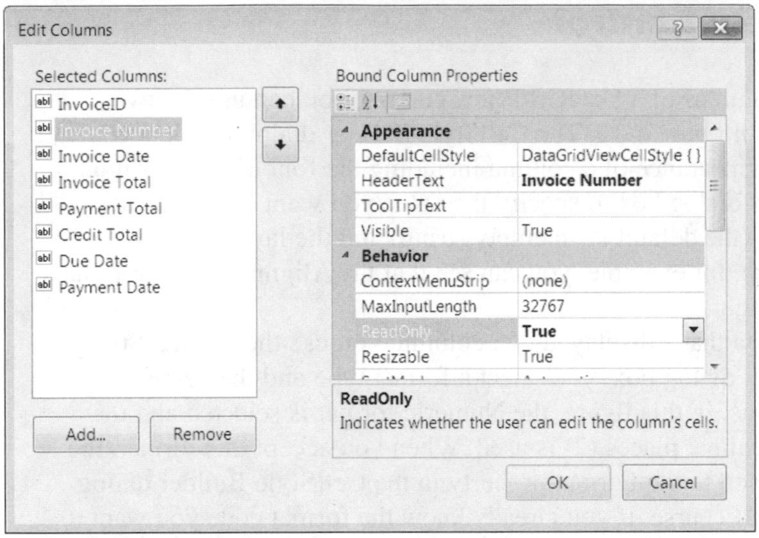

Common properties of a column

Property	Description
HeaderText	The text that's displayed in the column header.
Width	The number of pixels that are used for the width of the column.
DefaultCellStyle	The style that's applied to the cell. You can use the dialog boxes shown in figure 4-12 to set style elements such as color, format, and alignment.
Visible	Determines if the column is visible in the control.
ReadOnly	Determines if the data in the column can be modified.
SortMode	Determines if the data in the grid can be sorted by the values in the column and how the sorting is performed. The default option is Automatic, which uses the built-in sorting mechanism. To provide for custom sorting, select the Programmatic option. To turn off sorting, select the NotSortable option.

Description

- You can use the Edit Columns dialog box to control which columns are displayed in the grid and to edit the properties of those columns. To display this dialog box, choose the Edit Columns command from the smart tag menu for the control.
- To remove columns from the grid, select the column and click the Remove button.
- To add a column to the grid, click the Add button and then complete the dialog box that's displayed. This dialog box lets you add both bound and unbound columns. See figure 4-13 for more information on adding unbound columns.
- To change the order of the columns, select the column you want to move and click the up or down arrow to the right of the list of columns.
- To edit the properties for a column, select the column and use the Bound Column Properties window to edit the properties.

Figure 4-11 How to edit the columns of a DataGridView control

How to format the data in the columns of a DataGridView control

To format the columns of a DataGridView control, you can use the two dialog boxes shown in figure 4-12. The CellStyle Builder dialog box lets you specify the general appearance of a column including the font and colors it uses. You can also use this dialog box to specify the value you want displayed in place of a null value (the default is an empty string) and the layout of the column. In this figure, for example, you can see that the Alignment property has been set to MiddleRight.

To format the data that's displayed in a column, you use the Format String dialog box. From this dialog box, you select a format type and then enter any other available options. In this figure, the Numeric format is selected and the default number of decimal places (2) is used. When you accept this format, the format code is assigned to the Format property in the CellStyle Builder dialog box as shown here. Of course, if you already know the format code you want to use, you can enter it directly into the CellStyle Builder dialog box.

The dialog boxes for formatting the columns of a DataGridView control

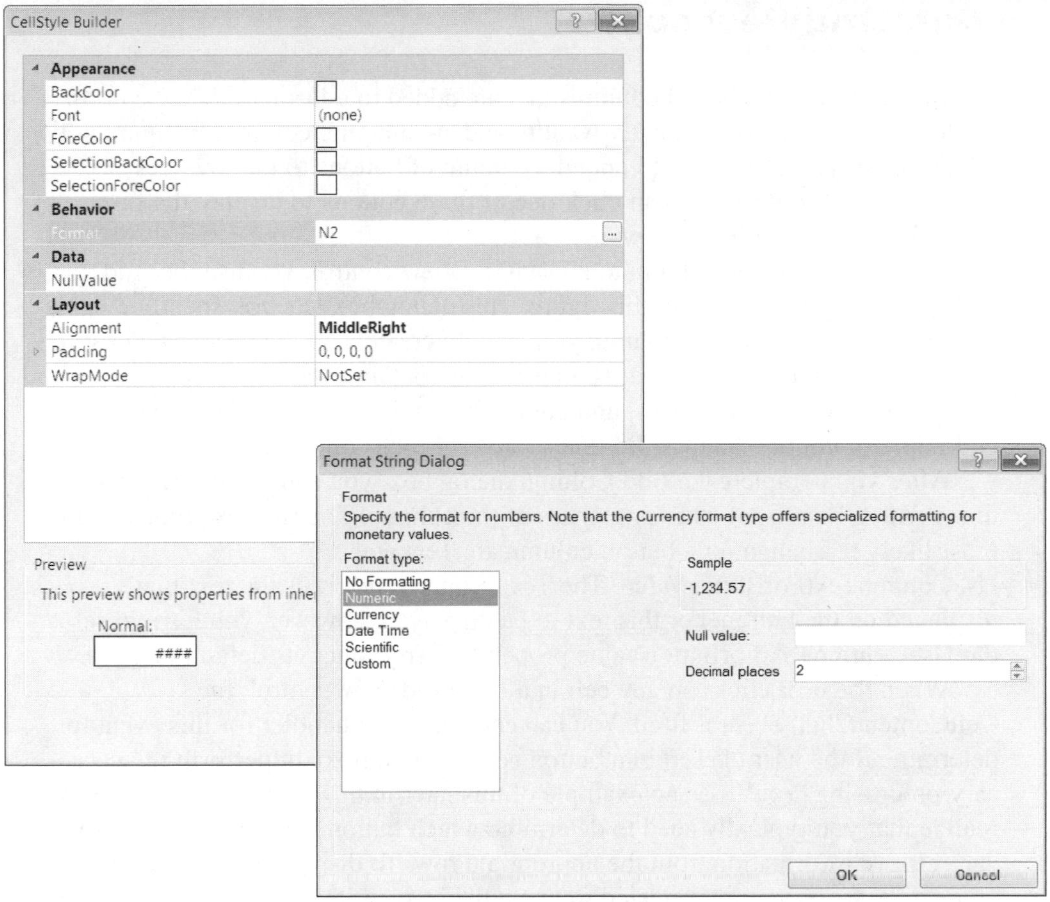

Description

- To display the CellStyle Builder dialog box, click the ellipsis button that appears when you select the DefaultCellStyle property in the Edit Columns dialog box.
- To apply a format to a column, select the Format property and then click the ellipsis button to display the Format String dialog box. Select the format you want to use from the Format Type list and enter any options that appear to the right of the list.

Figure 4-12 How to format the data in the columns of a DataGridView control

How to add an unbound column to a DataGridView control

In addition to the bound columns that are added to a DataGridView control by default, you may occasionally want to add an unbound column. In figure 4-13, for example, you can see that I added a column of buttons to the Invoices DataGridView control. You can click one of these buttons to display the line items for the invoice in that row.

To add an unbound column to a DataGridView control, you use the Add Column dialog box shown in this figure. This dialog box lets you specify a name for the column, the type of column you want to create, and the header text for the column. Although you can create columns that contain a variety of controls, including buttons, check boxes, and combo boxes, you're most likely to create columns that contain buttons. So that's what I'll focus on in this topic.

After you complete the Add Column dialog box, you can use the Edit Columns dialog box to set other properties of the column. The two properties you're most likely to change for a button column are Text and UseColumnTextForButtonValue. The Text property specifies the text that's displayed on the button. For this text to be displayed, however, you have to set the UseColumnTextForButtonValue property to True since its default is False.

When the user clicks on any cell in a DataGridView control, the CellContentClick event is fired. You can code an event handler for this event to determine if the user clicked in a button column and, if so, to perform the necessary processing. You'll see an example of this later in this chapter. For now, just realize that you typically need to determine which button was clicked so that you can retrieve information from the appropriate row. To display the line items for an invoice, for example, you need to know the invoice ID. That's why I included the InvoiceID column in the DataGridView control even though it's not visible.

The Add Column dialog box

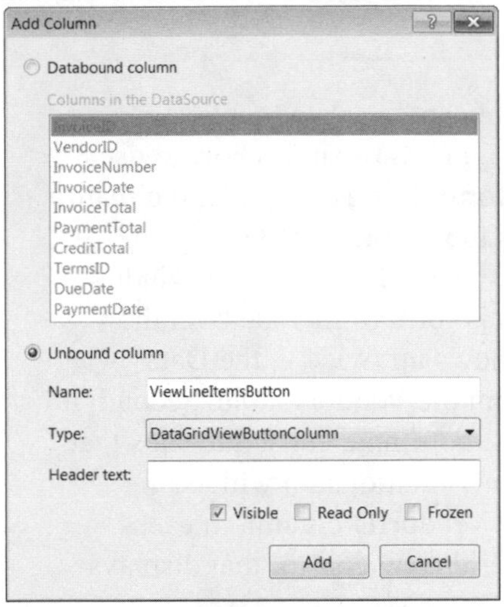

Common properties for button columns

Property	Description
`Text`	The text that's displayed on a button cell if the UseColumnTextForButtonValue property is set to True.
`UseColumnTextForButtonValue`	Determines whether the value of the Text property is displayed on button cells. The default is False.

A DataGridView control with an unbound button column

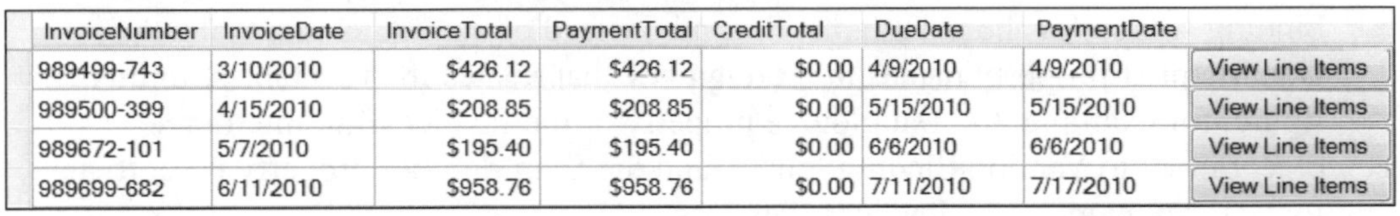

InvoiceNumber	InvoiceDate	InvoiceTotal	PaymentTotal	CreditTotal	DueDate	PaymentDate	
989499-743	3/10/2010	$426.12	$426.12	$0.00	4/9/2010	4/9/2010	View Line Items
989500-399	4/15/2010	$208.85	$208.85	$0.00	5/15/2010	5/15/2010	View Line Items
989672-101	5/7/2010	$195.40	$195.40	$0.00	6/6/2010	6/6/2010	View Line Items
989699-682	6/11/2010	$958.76	$958.76	$0.00	7/11/2010	7/17/2010	View Line Items

Description

- To add an unbound column to a DataGridView control, display the Edit Columns dialog box and click the Add button to display the Add Column dialog box. Then, select the Unbound Column option, enter a name for the column, select a column type, and enter the optional header text.
- You can create unbound columns that contain a variety of controls. However, you're most likely to use columns that contain buttons.
- When you create an unbound button column, you usually leave the header text blank. Then, you can use the Text and UseColumnTextForButtonValue properties to display text on the buttons in the column.
- To respond to the user clicking on a button column, you use the CellContentClick event. Within that event handler, you can use the second argument that's passed to it to get the index of the row and column that was clicked.

Figure 4-13 How to add an unbound column to a DataGridView control

How to use a DataGridView control to create a Master/Detail form

A form that displays the data from a main table and a related table is commonly referred to as a *Master/Detail form*. Figure 4-14 shows how to use a DataGridView control to create a Master/Detail form. In this example, the main table is the Vendors table, and the related table is the Invoices table.

The first thing you should notice in this figure is the Data Sources window. Although you would expect the data source for this form to include both the Vendors and Invoices tables, the Invoices table shows up twice in the Data Sources window. First, it shows up separately from the Vendors table. Second, it shows up subordinate to the Vendors table. This subordinate entry indicates that the Vendors and Invoices tables have a one-to-many relationship with each other. It's this relationship, which is based on the VendorID column in each table, that Visual Studio uses to generate a DataGridView control that displays the appropriate data.

To create a DataGridView control that displays data from a table that's related to the main table for a form, you simply drag the subordinate table to the form. When you do, Visual Studio generates the DataGridView control along with the appropriate BindingSource and TableAdapter objects. In addition, it sets the properties of the BindingSource object so the data from the related table will be displayed.

To understand how this works, this figure also presents the properties of the BindingSource object that accomplish the binding for the DataGridView control. First, instead of naming a dataset, the DataSource property names the binding source for the main table. Second, instead of naming a data table, the DataMember property names the foreign key that relates the two tables. In this figure, for example, the DataSource property of the InvoicesBindingSource object is set to VendorsBindingSource, and the DataMember property is set to a foreign key named FK_Invoices_Vendors.

Of course, you can also set the DataSource and DataMember properties of a binding source manually to create a Master/Detail form. That's what I did for the Invoice Maintenance form shown here because I added the DataGridView control before I added the controls that display the Vendor data.

When you create a Master/Detail form, you should realize that you must retrieve all of the rows you want to be able to display from the detail table. For example, because the Invoice Maintenance form shown here lets the user display all the invoices for any vendor, the invoices for all vendors must be retrieved when the form is loaded. If the Invoices table contains a large number of rows, that may not be what you want. In that case, you can create a parameterized query to retrieve the invoices just for the vendor the user selects. You'll see an example of that when I present a complete Invoice Maintenance application later in this chapter.

A form that uses a DataGridView control to display data from a related table

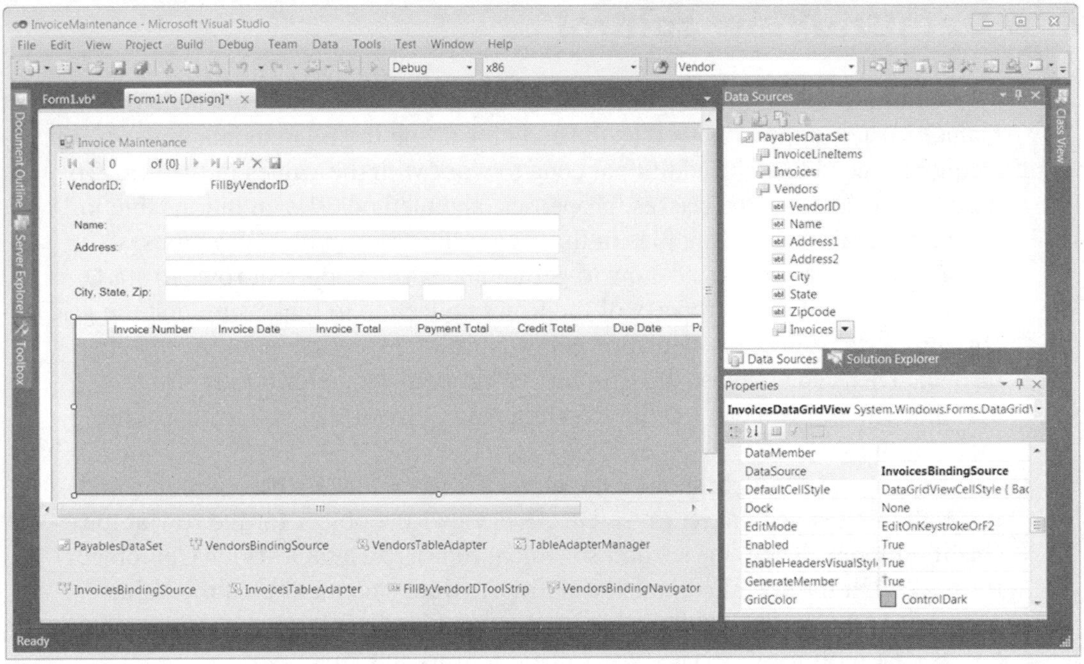

Two BindingSource properties for displaying data from a related table

Property	Description
`DataSource`	The source of the data for the BindingSource object. To display data from a table that's related to the main table for the form, this property should be set to the BindingSource object for the main table.
`DataMember`	A sub-list of the data source for the BindingSource object. To display data from a table that's related to the main table for the form, this property should be set to the foreign key that relates the two tables.

The property settings for the InvoicesBindingSource object

Property	Setting
DataSource	VendorsBindingSource
DataMember	FK_Invoices_Vendors

Description

- If a table has a one-to-many relationship with another table, the many table will appear subordinate to the main table in the Data Sources window. Then, you can drag the subordinate table to a form to create a DataGridView control that displays the rows in the subordinate table that are related to the current row in the main table.

Figure 4-14 How to use a DataGridView control to create a Master/Detail form

How to work with the values in a DataGridView control

Although Visual Studio generates the objects you need to work with a DataGridView control as well as the code for filling the related data table, you'll frequently need to write additional code to work with the values in the grid. To do that, you can use the classes, properties, and methods shown in the table in figure 4-15. The code examples in this figure illustrate some common uses.

The first example shows how to get the index of the current row. To start, you can use the Count property of the Rows collection to make sure that the grid contains at least one row. This prevents a NullReferenceException from being thrown. Then, you can use the CurrentCell property of the grid to return the current cell, and you can use the RowIndex property of that cell to return the index of the row.

The second example shows how to get the value that's stored within a cell. Here, the first statement returns a DataGridViewRow object for the row at the specified index. Then, the second statement returns a DataGridViewCell object for the cell at the specified index. Finally, the third statement uses the Value property of the cell to get the value that's stored in the cell. Note that this property is cast to the appropriate type since it returns an Object type.

The third example shows how to set the value of a cell in a row. This works like the second example, but in reverse.

The fourth example shows how to use a For Each...Next statement to loop through all of the rows in a grid. Within the loop, the first two statements get the value that's stored in the fourth cell (in this case, the invoice total), and the third statement adds that value to a grand total.

The fifth example shows how to refresh the grid so it reflects any changes that have been made to it. Most of the time, the DataGridView control refreshes itself automatically. But if it doesn't, you can use the Refresh method as shown in this example.

The sixth example shows an event handler for the CellDoubleClick event of a DataGridView control. You'll code an event handler like this if you want to allow the user to select a row in the grid by double-clicking on it. Then, you can use the RowIndex property of the second argument that's passed to this event handler to determine which row the user clicked.

How to delete a row from a DataGridView control

The last example in figure 4-15 shows how to delete a row from a DataGridView control. To do that, you use the Rows property to get the collection of rows and then use the RemoveAt method of that collection to remove the row at the specified index. Note that if the DataGridView control is bound to a data table, this also marks the row as deleted in that table. Then, if the table adapter manager is later used to update the database, the row is deleted from the database.

Important properties and methods for working with a DataGridView control

Class	Property/Method	Description
DataGridView	Rows	Gets a collection of DataGridViewRow objects.
DataGridView	CurrentCell	Gets a DataGridViewCell object for the current cell.
DataGridView	Refresh	Refreshes the grid so it shows any changes that have been made to the underlying data source.
DataGridViewRow	Cells	Gets a collection of DataGridViewCell objects.
DataGridViewCell	Value	Gets or sets the value that's stored in the cell.
DataGridViewCell	RowIndex	Gets the index for the row that contains the cell.

How to get the index of the currently selected row

```
If InvoicesDataGridView.Rows.Count > 0 Then
    Dim rowIndex As Integer = InvoicesDataGridView.CurrentCell.RowIndex
End If
```

How to get the value of the first cell in the selected row

```
Dim row As DataGridViewRow = InvoicesDataGridView.Rows(rowIndex)
Dim cell As DataGridViewCell = row.Cells(0)
Dim invoiceID As Integer = CInt(cell.Value)
```

How to set the value of the first cell in the selected row

```
Dim invoiceID As Integer = 10
Dim row As DataGridViewRow = InvoicesDataGridView.Rows(rowIndex)
row.Cells(0).Value = invoiceID
```

How to loop through all rows in the grid

```
Dim grandTotal As Decimal = 0
For Each row As DataGridViewRow In InvoicesDataGridView.Rows
    Dim cell As DataGridViewCell = row.Cells(3)
    Dim invoiceTotal As Decimal = CDec(cell.Value)
    grandTotal += invoiceTotal
Next
```

How to refresh the grid

```
InvoicesDataGridView.Refresh()
```

A method that handles the CellDoubleClick event

```
Private Sub InvoicesDataGridView_CellDoubleClick(
        ByVal sender As System.Object,
        ByVal e As System.Windows.Forms.DataGridViewCellEventArgs) _
        Handles InvoicesDataGridView.CellDoubleClick
    Dim rowIndex As Integer = e.RowIndex
    Me.DisplayLineItems(rowIndex)
End Sub
```

How to delete a row

```
InvoicesDataGridView.Rows.RemoveAt(rowIndex)
```

Figure 4-15 How to work with the values and delete a row in a DataGridView control

An Invoice Maintenance application

Now that you've learned some additional skills for working with a DataGridView control, you're ready to see an Invoice Maintenance application that uses some of those skills.

The user interface

Figure 4-16 presents the user interface for the Invoice Maintenance application. As you can see, this application consists of two forms. The Invoice Maintenance form lets the user retrieve the data for a vendor by entering a vendor ID into the toolbar and then clicking the Get Vendor button. The data for the vendor is then displayed in the text boxes on the form, and the invoices for the vendor are displayed in the DataGridView control. At that point, the user can modify the data in the Payment Total, Credit Total, Due Date, and Payment Date columns of any invoice.

To save any changes made to the invoices to the database, the user must click the Update Database button. Although I could have used the Save button in the binding navigator toolbar for the DataGridView control for this purpose, none of the other controls in the toolbar were needed for this application. So I chose to delete the toolbar and use a standard button instead.

In addition to modifying the data in the DataGridView control, the user can click the View Line Items button for any invoice to display the Line Items form. This form retrieves the line items for the selected invoice and displays them in a DataGridView control.

Before I go on, you should realize that this isn't a realistic application for a couple of reasons. First, you probably wouldn't use a DataGridView control to let the user modify invoice data. Instead, you would let the user modify the data for one invoice at a time. Second, if the user forgets to click the Update Database button after entering some invoice changes, the changes won't be saved when the user selects the next vendor. For the purposes of illustrating the skills presented in this chapter, though, the Invoice Maintenance application is sufficient.

The Invoice Maintenance form

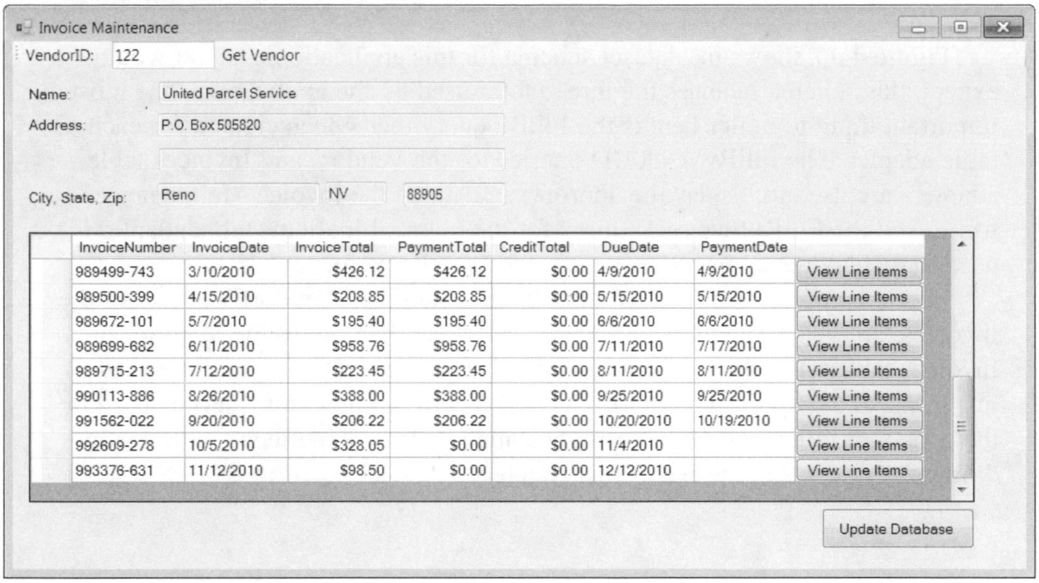

The Line Items form

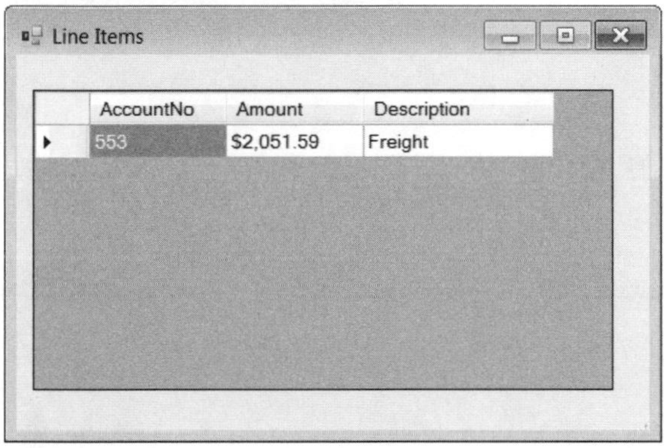

Description

- The Invoice Maintenance form displays the Invoices for a selected vendor and lets the user modify the data in the Payment Total, Credit Total, Due Date, and Payment Date columns.
- The user can also display the line items for an invoice by clicking the View Line Items button for that invoice.
- Because this application doesn't let the user add or delete invoices, the binding navigator toolbar has been omitted from the Invoice Maintenance form and an Update Database button has been added to the form. This button performs the same function as the Save button in the binding navigator toolbar.

Figure 4-16 The user interface for the Invoice Maintenance application

The dataset schema

Figure 4-17 shows the dataset schema for this application. As you would expect, this schema includes the three tables used by the application. The most important thing to notice here is the FillBy query that's been created for each table adapter. The FillByVendorID queries for the Vendors and Invoices table adapters are used to display the appropriate data on the Invoice Maintenance form. And the FillByInvoiceID query for the InvoiceLineItems table adapter is used to display the appropriate data on the Line Items form.

Please note, however, that you don't need the FillByVendorID query for the Invoices table when you use a Master/Detail form that relates the Vendors and Invoices tables. For this application, this FillByVendorID query will be used just to make the application more efficient. You'll see how this query is used in the code that follows. And you can get some hands-on experience with this by doing exercise 4-2 at the end of this chapter.

The dataset schema

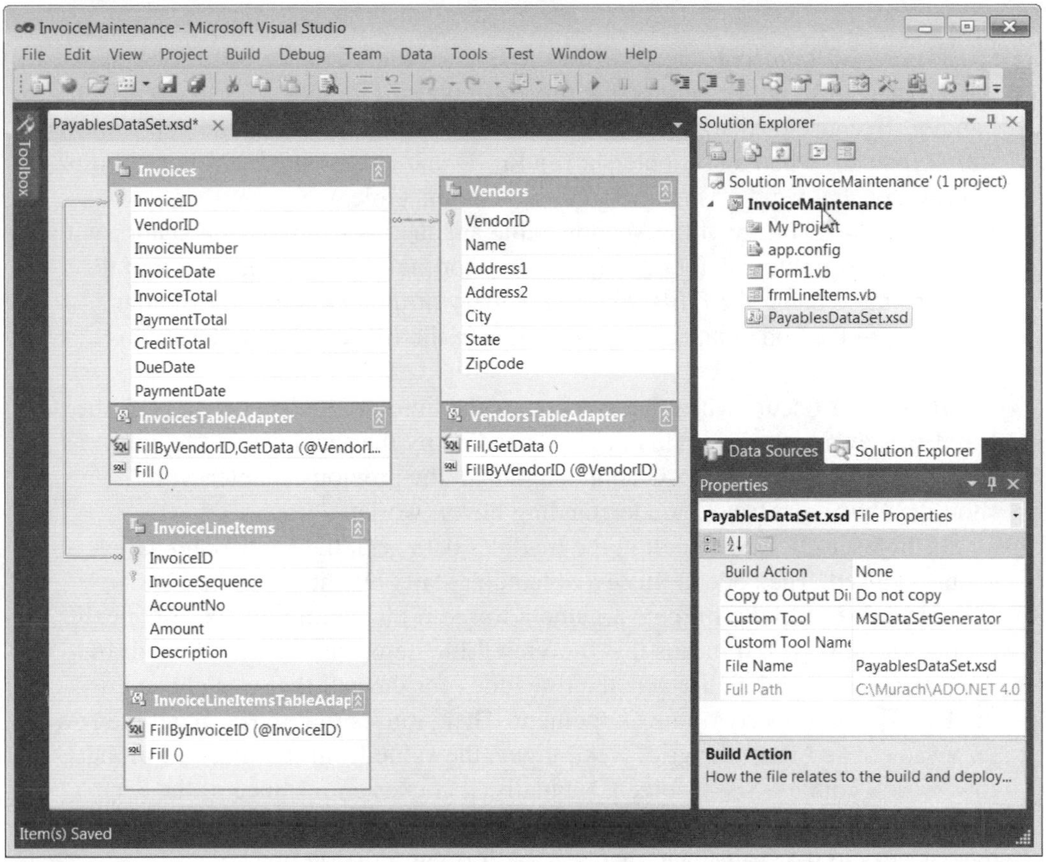

Description

- The Payables dataset defines the three tables used by this application: Vendors, Invoices, and InvoiceLineItems.
- The FillByVendorID query for the Vendors table adapter is used to retrieve the vendor data that's displayed on the Invoice Maintenance form. This query is based on the vendor ID the user enters into the toolbar on the form.
- The FillByVendorID query for the Invoices table adapter is used to retrieve the invoice data that's displayed by the DataGridView control on the Invoice Maintenance form. This query is also based on the vendor ID the user enters into the toolbar on the form.
- The FillByInvoiceID query for the InvoiceLineItems table adapter is used to retrieve the line item data that's displayed on the Line Items form. This query is based on the InvoiceID of the invoice whose View Line Items button is clicked on the Invoice Maintenance form.

Figure 4-17 The dataset schema for the Invoice Maintenance application

The code for the Invoice Maintenance form

Figure 4-18 presents the code for the Invoice Maintenance form. The first thing you should notice here is that this form doesn't include a Load event handler. Because of that, no data is loaded into the dataset when the application starts. Instead, when a user enters a vendor ID and clicks the Get Vendor button, the row for that vendor is loaded into the Vendors table using the FillByVendorID query of the Vendors table adapter. In addition, if a vendor with the ID the user enters is found, any invoices for the vendor are loaded into the Invoices table using the FillByVendorID query of the Invoices table adapter. You can see the code that accomplishes this in the first event handler in this figure.

If an error occurs when the user enters data into the Invoices data grid, the DataError event is raised. This event is handled by the second event handler shown here. Because you saw code like this in the previous chapter, you shouldn't have any trouble understanding how it works.

If the user clicks on a cell in the Invoices data grid, the CellContentClick event is raised. The code in this event handler starts by checking the ColumnIndex property of the e argument to see if the column index of the cell is equal to 8. If it is, it means that the View Line Items button was clicked. In that case, the event handler gets the row index for the cell that was clicked using the RowIndex property of the e argument. Then, it uses that index to get the row that was clicked from the grid. Next, it gets the value from the first cell in that row, which contains the invoice ID. Finally, it creates an instance of the Line Items form, assigns the invoice ID to the form's Tag property so the form will have access to that value, and displays the form as a dialog box.

The code for the Invoice Maintenance form **Page 1**

```
Imports System.Data.SqlClient

Public Class frmInvoiceMaintenance

    Private Sub FillByVendorIDToolStripButton_Click(
            ByVal sender As System.Object, ByVal e As System.EventArgs) _
            Handles FillByVendorIDToolStripButton.Click
        Try
            Dim vendorID As Integer =
                Convert.ToInt32(VendorIDToolStripTextBox.Text)
            Me.VendorsTableAdapter.FillByVendorID(
                Me.PayablesDataSet.Vendors, vendorID)
            Me.InvoicesTableAdapter.FillByVendorID(
                Me.PayablesDataSet.Invoices, vendorID)
        Catch ex As FormatException
            MessageBox.Show("Vendor ID must be an integer.", "Entry Error")
        Catch ex As SqlException
            MessageBox.Show("SQL Server error # " & ex.Number &
                ": " & ex.Message, ex.GetType.ToString)
        End Try
    End Sub

    Private Sub InvoicesDataGridView_DataError(
            ByVal sender As System.Object,
            ByVal e As System.Windows.Forms.DataGridViewDataErrorEventArgs) _
            Handles InvoicesDataGridView.DataError
        Dim row As Integer = e.RowIndex + 1
        Dim errorMessage As String = "A data error occurred." & vbCrLf &
            "Row: " & row & vbCrLf &
            "Error: " & e.Exception.Message
        MessageBox.Show(errorMessage, "Data Error")
    End Sub

    Private Sub InvoicesDataGridView_CellContentClick(
        ByVal sender As System.Object,
        ByVal e As System.Windows.Forms.DataGridViewCellEventArgs) _
        Handles InvoicesDataGridView.CellContentClick
        If e.ColumnIndex = 8 Then ' View Line Items button clicked
            ' Get the ID of the selected invoice
            Dim i As Integer = e.RowIndex
            Dim row As DataGridViewRow = InvoicesDataGridView.Rows(i)
            Dim cell As DataGridViewCell = row.Cells(0)
            Dim invoiceID As Integer = CInt(cell.Value)

            ' Display the Line Items form
            Dim lineItemsForm As New frmLineItems
            lineItemsForm.Tag = invoiceID
            lineItemsForm.ShowDialog()
        End If
    End Sub
```

Figure 4-18 The code for the Invoice Maintenance application (part 1 of 2)

The last event handler for the Invoice Maintenance form is the one that handles the Click event of the Update Database button. It works much like the code you saw earlier in this chapter for the Click event of the Save button in the Vendor Maintenance application. The main difference is that this event handler doesn't start by validating the data. That's not necessary because the only four columns the user can modify contain either decimal or date time data. And if the user enters data that can't be converted to these data types, the error will be handled by the event handler for the DataError event of the data grid.

The code for the Line Items form

Figure 4-18 also presents the code for the Line Items form. This form consists of a single event handler for the Load event of the form. To start, this event handler retrieves the invoice ID that was stored in the Tag property of the form. Then, it uses this value in the FillByInvoiceID query of the Invoice Line Items table adapter to retrieve the line items for the invoice.

The code for the Invoice Maintenance form — Page 2

```
    Private Sub btnUpdate_Click(ByVal sender As System.Object,
            ByVal e As System.EventArgs) Handles btnUpdate.Click
        Try
            Me.InvoicesBindingSource.EndEdit()
            Me.TableAdapterManager.UpdateAll(Me.PayablesDataSet)
        Catch ex As DBConcurrencyException
            MessageBox.Show("A concurrency error occurred.",
                "Concurrency Error")
            Me.InvoicesTableAdapter.Fill(Me.PayablesDataSet.Invoices)
        Catch ex As DataException
            MessageBox.Show(ex.Message, ex.GetType.ToString)
            Me.InvoicesBindingSource.CancelEdit()
        Catch ex As SqlException
            MessageBox.Show("Database error # " & ex.Number &
                ": " & ex.Message, ex.GetType.ToString)
        End Try
    End Sub

End Class
```

The code for the Line Items form

```
Imports System.Data.SqlClient

Public Class frmLineItems

    Private Sub frmLineItems_Load(ByVal sender As System.Object,
            ByVal e As System.EventArgs) Handles MyBase.Load

        Try
            ' Get the invoice ID
            Dim invoiceID As Integer = CInt(Me.Tag)
            ' Fill the InvoiceLineItems table
            Me.InvoiceLineItemsTableAdapter.FillByInvoiceID(
                Me.PayablesDataSet.InvoiceLineItems, invoiceID)
        Catch ex As InvalidCastException
            MessageBox.Show("Invoice ID not an integer.", "Property Error")
        Catch ex As SqlException
            MessageBox.Show("SQL Server error # " & ex.Number &
                ": " & ex.Message, ex.GetType.ToString)
        End Try

    End Sub

End Class
```

Perspective

Now that you've completed this chapter, you should be able to use data sources and datasets to develop substantial database applications. You should also realize how quickly you can prototype these applications. But if you do the exercises that follow, which guide you through the development of the chapter applications from scratch, you should start to see that using data sources isn't quite as easy as it may at first appear.

As I said earlier, if you have any trouble following some of the non-ADO.NET code in this book, we recommend that you get a copy of *Murach's Visual Basic 2010*. It is a terrific reference that will help you quickly learn or refresh your memory about how some aspect of Visual Basic works.

Terms

parameterized query
Master/Detail form

Exercise 4-1 Build the Vendor Maintenance application

This exercise will guide you through the development of the application in figure 4-9. You'll learn a lot by doing that.

Build the user interface

1. Start a new project named VendorMaintenance in your chapter 4 directory. Then, create a data source for the columns in the Vendors table that are used by the form in figure 4-9, plus the StateCode and StateName columns in the States table.
2. Drag the first five data source columns in the Vendors table onto the form as text boxes, but leave enough room at the top for two toolbars. Next, drag the State column onto the form as a combo box, and the ZipCode column as a text box. Then, rearrange the controls and change any required properties so those controls look like the ones in figure 4-9.
3. Drag a GroupBox control onto the form, adjust its size, and drag the last three Vendor columns from the Data Source window into the group box as text boxes. Then, rearrange them and change any required properties as shown in figure 4-9.
4. Use the procedure in figure 4-3 to bind the State combo box on the form to the States table in the data source. Then, set the DropDownStyle property for the combo box to DropDownList, and set its (DataBindings) – Text property to (none).

5. Test the application to see how this user interface works. Use the combo box to change one of the State entries. End the application, and review the code that has been generated for the form.

Add a parameterized query

6. Use the procedure in figure 4-5 to add a parameterized query named FillByVendorID that finds the Vendor row for a specific vendor ID. Then, note the toolbar that has been added to the form. Now, review the code that has been added to the application, and review the schema for the application.
7. Test the application to see how it works. First, use the binding navigator toolbar to move through the rows. Then, enter a vendor ID of 8 in the second toolbar and click the FillByVendorID button. Now, go back to the binding navigator toolbar, and you'll discover that you can't use it to go through the rows any more because the dataset contains only one row.
8. With the application still running, use the second toolbar to select the vendor with VendorID 10. Choose a new state from the combo box, but don't click the Save button. Then, go to VendorID 20, select a new state, and click the Save button. Now, go back to VendorID 10 to see that the state has reverted to what it was originally. Finally, go to VendorID 20 to see that the state has been changed. This shows that you must click the Save button after each change if you want the changes to be made to the database. That's because the dataset consists of only one row at a time.
9. Add a valid row to the dataset and click the Save button. Then, note that the binding navigator toolbar lets you navigate between the previous row and the one you just added because two rows are now in the dataset. As soon as you use the second toolbar to go to a different row, though, the first toolbar shows only one row in the dataset.
10. Delete the row that you added in step 9 by going to that row and clicking the Delete button, which makes the row disappear. Then, click the Save button to apply the deletion to the database. If you don't do that, the row won't be deleted. When you're done, end the application.

Modify the toolbars

11. Use the procedure in figure 4-7 to add a Cancel button to the binding navigator toolbar and to change the text on the FillByVendorID button in the second toolbar to Get Vendor. Then, use the procedure in figure 4-8 to start the event handler for the Cancel button, and add the one line of code that it requires.
12. Test these changes to see how they work. At this point, the application should work like the one in figure 4-9. You just need to enhance the code so it provides for formatting and data validation.

Enhance the code

13. Add the FormatPhoneNumber procedure in figure 4-9 to the form. Then, in the Load event handler for the form, add the code for wiring the Format event of the Phone text box to the FormatPhoneNumber procedure. Now, test this enhancement to make sure the phone number is formatted correctly.

14. Add the UnformatPhoneNumber procedure in figure 4-9 to the form. Then, wire it to the Parse event of the of the PhoneTextBox Binding object.
15. Comment out the code for filling the Vendors table in the Load event handler, and run the application. As you'll see, only the State combo box has a value when the application starts because no vendor has been selected. However, this value is simply the first state in the list, not necessarily the correct state for the first vendor. To remove this from the display, use this statement in the Form Load event to set the index for the State combo box to -1:

    ```
    StateComboBox.SelectedIndex = -1
    ```

    Then, test this change.
16. At this point, you have a prototype of the application. Although you could add the data validation and error handling code that's shown in figure 4-9, that isn't always necessary for a prototype. Just experiment more if you want to, and then end the application.

Add another parameterized query to the form

17. Add a parameterized query named FillByState that gets all the vendor rows for a specific state based on the state code. Next, run the application and use the third toolbar to get all of the rows for a specific state code like CA. Note that the binding navigator toolbar lets you navigate through these rows.
18. Add a separator at the right of the controls on the FillByVendorID ToolStrip, followed by a label, text box, and button that look like the three controls on the FillByState ToolStrip. Then, delete the FillByState ToolStrip.
19. Modify the code for the form so the FillByState button in the FillByVendorID ToolStrip gets the vendor rows by state. Then, test this enhancement. When you've got it working right, close the project.

Exercise 4-2 Build the Invoice Maintenance application

This exercise will guide you through the development of the application in figure 4-16. Here again, you'll learn a lot by doing that. But you may find that this takes a lot longer than you thought.

Build the user interface for the Invoice Maintenance form

1. Start a new project named InvoiceMaintenance in your chapter 4 directory. Then, create a data source for the tables and columns shown in the schema in figure 4-17.
2. Drag the columns in the Vendors table onto the form as text boxes, and adjust them as shown in figure 4-16. Then, drag the Invoices table that's subordinate to the Vendors table onto the form as a DataGridView control.
3. Run the application and use the binding navigator toolbar to scroll through the vendor rows. When a row that has related Invoice rows is selected, you'll see

that the invoice rows are displayed. Now, close the application, and review the code that has been generated for it.

4. Delete the binding navigator toolbar, then comment out the code in the Load event handler for the form that fills the Vendors table (but not the Invoices table). Next, use the procedure in figure 4-5 to create a parameterized query named FillByVendorID that gets the Vendor data for a specific VendorID. Then, run the form, enter VendorIDs, and see how the Vendor and Invoice data is displayed.
5. Use the procedures in figures 4-10 and 4-11 to disable adding and deleting rows in the DataGridView control, to turn off the Visible property of the InvoiceID column, to remove the VendorID column, to set the header text widths of the visible columns as appropriate, to format the date columns, and to set the ReadOnly property for the InvoiceNumber, InvoiceDate, and InvoiceTotal columns to True. Then, set the formatting for the three total columns to Numeric with 2 decimal places, and set their Alignment properties to MiddleRight. Now, run the form to make sure that you've got everything right.
6. Use the procedure in figure 4-13 to add an unbound DataGridViewButtonColumn named ViewLineItemsButton to the DataGridView control. Then, set the Text property for this column to "View Line Items", set the UseColumnTextForButtonValue property to True, and adjust the column width. Now, run the form to make sure this is working right.

Build the user interface for the Line Items form

7. Add a new form to the project and name it frmLineItems. Next, drag the InvoiceLineItems table onto this form. Then, create a parameterized query named FillByInvoiceID that gets the InvoiceLineItems rows for a specific InvoiceID.
8. Delete the toolbars that were generated by the queries, and set the properties of the DataGridView control so the form looks like the one in figure 4-16.
9. Add the code for the CellContentClick event of the DataGridView control on the Invoice Maintenance form, as shown in figure 4-18. This code starts by checking whether column 8 (counting from 0) was clicked, which should be the column that the View Line Items buttons are in. If so, it gets the invoice ID from the row that was clicked, saves it as the Tag property of a new Line Items form, and displays a new Line Items form.
10. Modify the code for the Load event of the Line Items form, as shown in figure 4-18. This code starts by getting the invoice ID from the Tag property of the new form. Then, it fills the InvoiceLineItems table in the dataset. For this statement, you can just copy and modify the statement that was generated for the event handler for the Click event of the FillByInvoiceID ToolStrip button. Now, delete the code for the other event handlers for this form.
11. Test the application to make sure that the Line Items form is displayed when you click on a View Line Items button for an invoice.

Change the way the application gets the invoice data

12. Review the code for the Load event handler for the Invoice Maintenance form. There, you can see that all the rows in the Invoices table are loaded into the dataset when the form is loaded. Then, the dataset rows for a specific VendorID are displayed in the DataGridView control each time the VendorID changes. For some applications, that may be okay, but if there are thousands of invoice rows in the dataset that may be inefficient.
13. To change the way that works, create a parameterized query named FillByVendorID for the DataGridView control that gets the Invoice rows for a specific VendorID. Delete the ToolStrip that gets generated and delete the code for the Click event of its ToolStripButton. Then, modify the code in the event handler for the Click event of the FillByVendorIDToolStripButton so it looks like the code in figure 4-18.
14. Delete the Load event handler for this form. Then, test the application again. It should work the same as it did before, but now only the invoice rows for the selected vendor are in the Invoices table in the dataset.

Complete the application

15. At this point, you have a prototype of the application, and you should have learned a lot about how building applications with data sources and datasets works. Now, if you want to finish this application, you just need to: (1) add an Update Database button to the bottom of the Invoice Maintenance form as shown in figure 4-16; (2) code the event handler for this button's Click event; (3) add the error handling code for both forms; and (4) make sure all of the properties for both forms and all of the controls on both forms are set right.

5

How to use the Dataset Designer

In chapter 3, you learned how to use the Dataset Designer to view the schema of a dataset and to preview the data in a query. Now, in this chapter, you'll learn how to use the Dataset Designer to work with queries and schema. You'll also learn the basic skills for using code to work with a dataset.

Then, you'll see how these techniques can be applied to another application. This application will give you a good idea of how powerful these techniques are. But it will also show you some of the limitations of working with data sources and datasets.

How to work with an existing dataset schema

When you use the Data Source Configuration Wizard to create one or more data sources as described in chapter 3, a dataset schema is created for you. Then, you can use the skills in the topics that follow to work with that schema.

Basic skills for using the Dataset Designer

Figure 5-1 presents some basic skills for using the Dataset Designer. To start, you can display the properties for an object in the Properties window by clicking on the object in the Designer window. To display the properties for a column, for example, just click on the column. Then, you can change the properties for the column.

In particular, if you'll be adding rows to a table that contain columns that are defined with default values in the database (which aren't automatically set by the dataset), you can change the DefaultValue properties of those columns so you don't have to specify values for them in the rows that you add.

You can also display the properties for the dataset by clicking on any empty area in the designer window. Then, you can change the properties as necessary. For example, you may want to set the Hierarchical Update property to False so that a table adapter manager isn't generated for the dataset. That makes sense if an application doesn't provide for updates or it only provides for updating a single table. It also makes sense if an application inserts rows into two or more tables that are related by identity columns. You'll see an example of this in the Invoice Entry application that's presented later in this chapter. If a table adapter manager isn't generated for the dataset, you can use the table adapters to perform update operations instead as you'll see in figure 5-13.

When you want to delete a column, I recommend that you first select the column by left-clicking in the colored border which is located to the left of the column name. If you do this, you will see that the action selects and highlights the whole of the column entry, including its background. Now, when you right-click on the column, you can select Delete from the context menu, and the column will be deleted correctly. If you don't do this, then your right-click may simply delete the text that represents the column name, and you will receive a Failed to Rename Object error message. Another good reason for using this approach is that it's quite easy to delete the whole table by mistake if you haven't selected and highlighted a column.

The Dataset Designer is most useful for working with queries. To start, you can use it to preview the data in a query as you saw in chapter 3. You can also use it to add new queries and edit existing queries. For example, suppose you want to add a query to the Invoice Maintenance application of the last chapter that lets you select vendors based on the Name column. If you use the technique presented in the last chapter to do that, a separate toolbar would be created for

The Dataset Designer

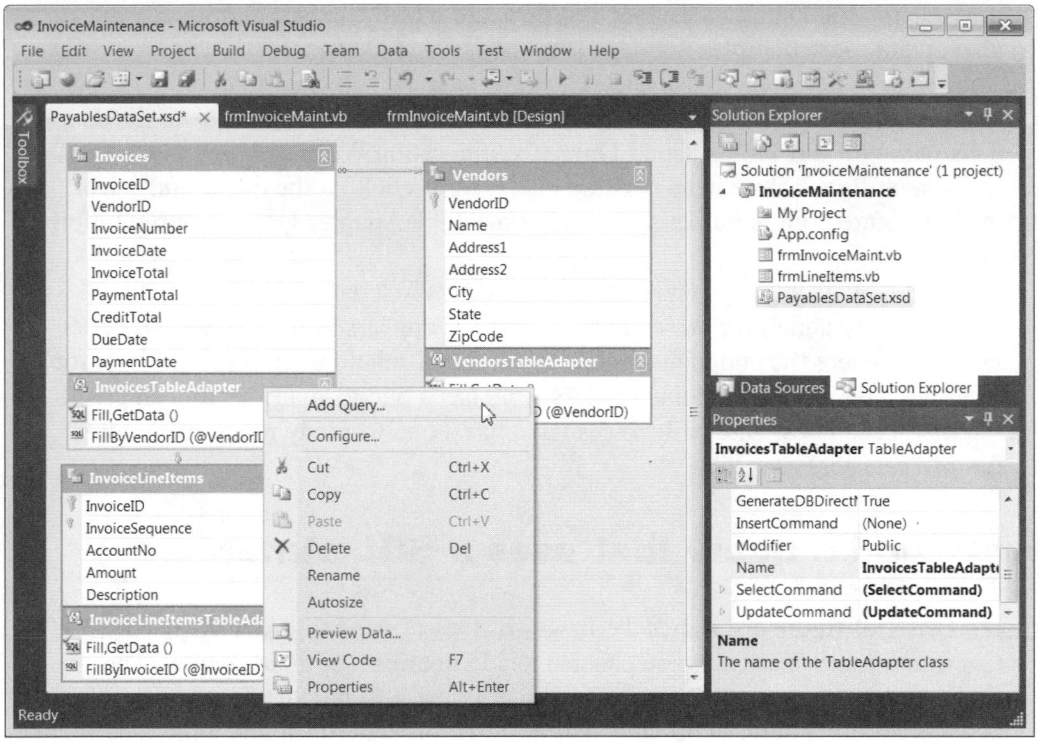

Description

- To display the Dataset Designer for a dataset, double-click the dataset class in the Solution Explorer. Or, select the dataset class and then click the View Designer button at the top of the Solution Explorer.
- To view the properties for a table, column, table adapter, or query, click the object in the Dataset Designer. To view the properties for the dataset, click in an empty area of the designer.
- To delete a column from a table, right-click the column in the Dataset Designer and select the Delete command. This will update the Select, Insert, Update, and Delete statements that are used by the table adapter for the table. It will also delete the column from the data source.
- To add a query, select the table adapter you want to add the query to, and then right-click on the table adapter and select the Add Query command. Then, use the wizard shown in figure 5-2 to define the query.
- To edit a query, right-click on the query and select the Configure command. Then, use the wizard steps shown in part 2 of figure 5-2 to edit the query.
- To preview the data that's returned by a query, right-click on the query and select the Preview Data command. Then, use the Preview Data dialog box that you saw in figure 3-17 of chapter 3 to preview the data.

Figure 5-1 Basic skills for using the Dataset Designer

the query, which probably isn't what you want. Instead, you can create the query using the Dataset Designer and then add it to the existing toolbar. You can also create more complex queries using the Dataset Designer.

To add a new query, just select the table adapter you want to add the query to. Then, right-click on the table adapter and select the Add Query command. This will start the TableAdapter Query Configuration Wizard, which you'll see in the next figure. To edit an existing query, right-click on the query and select the Configure command. This, too, starts the TableAdapter Query Configuration Wizard.

By the way, when you add two related tables to a dataset, a data relation is automatically added for those tables. A relation appears in the Dataset Designer as a link, where the endpoints indicate the type of relationship. In figure 5-1, for example, you can see that the Vendors table has a one-to-many relationship with the Invoices tables, and the Invoices table has a one-to-many relationship with the InvoiceLineItems table.

How to add a query that uses a SQL statement

Part 1 of figure 5-2 shows the first two steps of the TableAdapter Query Configuration Wizard that you can use to add queries to a table adapter. The first step lets you specify whether you want to use a SQL statement, create a new stored procedure, or use an existing stored procedure. In this topic, you'll learn how to add a query that uses a SQL statement. You'll learn how to use stored procedures later in this chapter.

The second step of the wizard lets you specify the type of SQL statement you want to generate. Although most queries return rows, it's also common to create queries that return a single value. You'll see an example of this type of query in just a minute. You can also use this step to create a custom query that inserts, updates, or deletes a row. However, the standard Insert, Update, and Delete statements that are generated by default for a table adapter are adequate for most applications.

The wizard step for choosing a command type

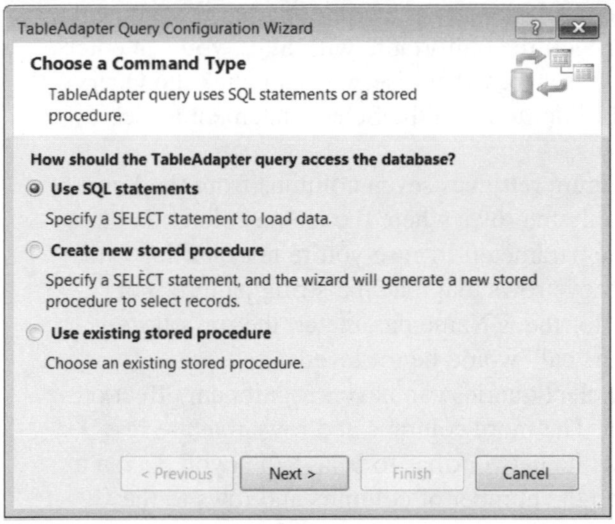

The wizard step for choosing a query type

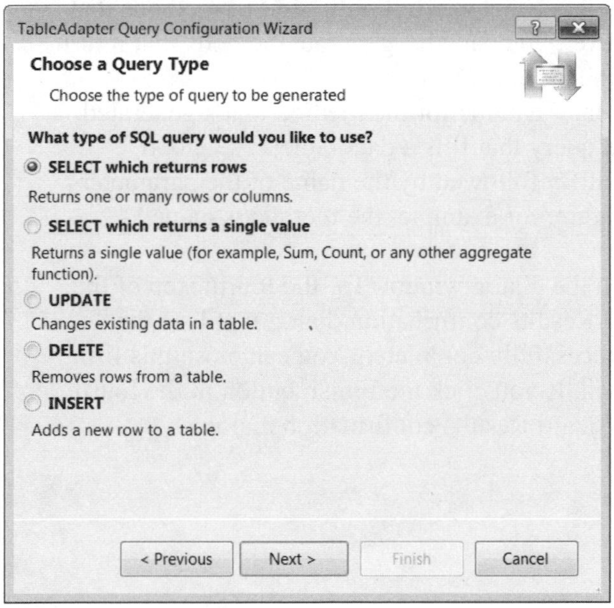

Description

- To add a query, you use the TableAdapter Query Configuration Wizard. The first step of this wizard lets you specify whether you want to use a SQL statement or a new or existing stored procedure for the query.
- If you choose to use an SQL statement, the second step of the wizard lets you choose what type of query you want to create. In most cases, you'll create a Select statement that retrieves one or more rows and columns from the database.

Figure 5-2 How to add a query that uses a SQL statement (part 1 of 2)

Part 2 of figure 5-2 shows the third and fourth steps of the TableAdapter Query Configuration Wizard. The third step lets you enter the Select statement you want to use to retrieve data. If you're comfortable with SQL, you can enter the Select statement directly into this step. Otherwise, you can click the Query Builder button to use the Query Builder to build the Select statement as described later in this chapter.

The Select statement in this figure retrieves seven columns from the Vendors table. However, it retrieves only the rows where the Name column is like the value specified by the @Name parameter. In case you're not familiar with the LIKE keyword, it lets you retrieve rows that match a string pattern. For example, if you specified "cal%" for the @Name parameter, the rows for all vendors with names that start with "cal" would be retrieved.

It's important to realize that Select queries can have a significant effect on the performance of an application. The more columns and rows that are returned by a query, the more traffic the network has to bear. When you design a query, then, you should try to keep the number of columns and rows to the minimum required by the application.

The fourth step of the wizard lets you select the types of methods that are generated for the table adapter. In this chapter, we'll only use Fill methods that fill a data table in a dataset. However, you can also generate methods that return DataTable objects that are independent of a dataset.

The fourth step also lets you enter a name for the method that's generated. When generating a parameterized query that fills a data table, it's a good practice to begin the name with FillBy followed by the name of the parameter that's used by the query. In this figure, for example, the method is named FillByName.

If you click the Next button in the dialog window for the fourth step of the wizard, you'll be shown a Wizard Results confirmation dialog that lists the details of the actions that were successfully completed. You can close this fifth dialog by clicking the Finish button. If you click the Finish button in the fourth dialog, you won't be shown the Wizard Results confirmation dialog.

The wizard step for specifying a Select statement

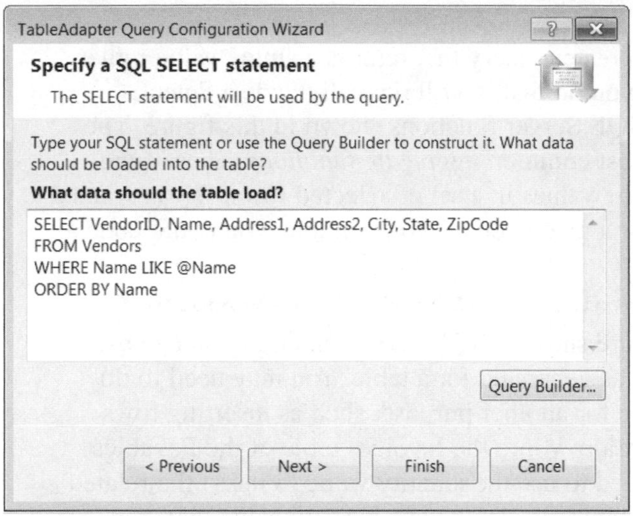

The wizard step for choosing and naming the methods

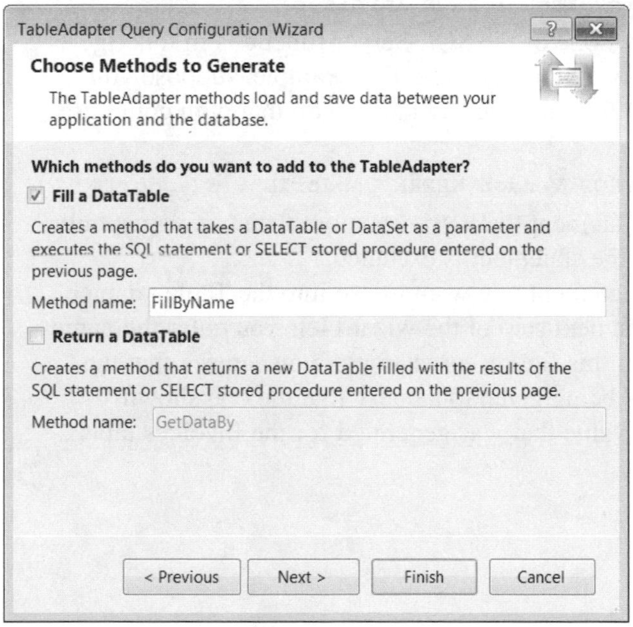

Description

- If you choose to create a Select statement that retrieves one or more rows, the third step of the wizard lets you specify the Select statement. You can either type the Select statement into the area provided, or you can click the Query Builder button to use the Query Builder as shown later in this chapter.
- The fourth step of the wizard lets you select and name the methods that will be added to the table adapter. In most cases, you can include just the method that fills the data table.

Figure 5-2 How to add a query that uses a SQL statement (part 2 of 2)

How to add a query that returns a single value

Figure 5-3 shows how you create a query that returns a single value rather than an entire result set. When you do that, you'll typically code a Select statement that uses one of the SQL Server functions shown in this figure. The first table shows some of the most common *aggregate functions*. These functions perform a calculation on the values in a set of selected rows. If you wanted to get a count of the invoices for a given vendor, for example, you could code a Select statement like this:

```
SELECT COUNT(*) FROM Invoices WHERE VendorID = @VendorID
```

The second table in this figure shows a SQL Server function you can use to get the last identity value that was generated for a table. You may need to do that if you need to use this value for another purpose, such as inserting rows into a related table. If you insert a row into the Invoices table of the Payables database, for example, you'll need to use the identity value to insert the related rows into the InvoiceLineItems table. To get the last identity value that was generated for the Invoices table, you would code a Select statement like this:

```
SELECT IDENT_CURRENT('Invoices') FROM Invoices
```

Although you'll typically use one of the SQL Server functions in this figure to return a single value, that's not always the case. For example, suppose you want to get the default terms ID for a selected vendor. To do that, you could use a Select statement like this:

```
SELECT DefaultTermsID FROM Vendor WHERE VendorID = @VendorID
```

Note that if you code a Select statement that retrieves more than one value, only the first value is returned when the statement is executed.

After you enter the Select statement you want to use into the TableAdapter Query Configuration Wizard, the next step of the wizard lets you enter the name you want to use for the query. In this figure, for example, you can see that the name "GetLastIdentityValue" is being given to a query like the one shown above that gets the last identity value that was generated for the Invoices table.

The wizard step for entering the name of the function

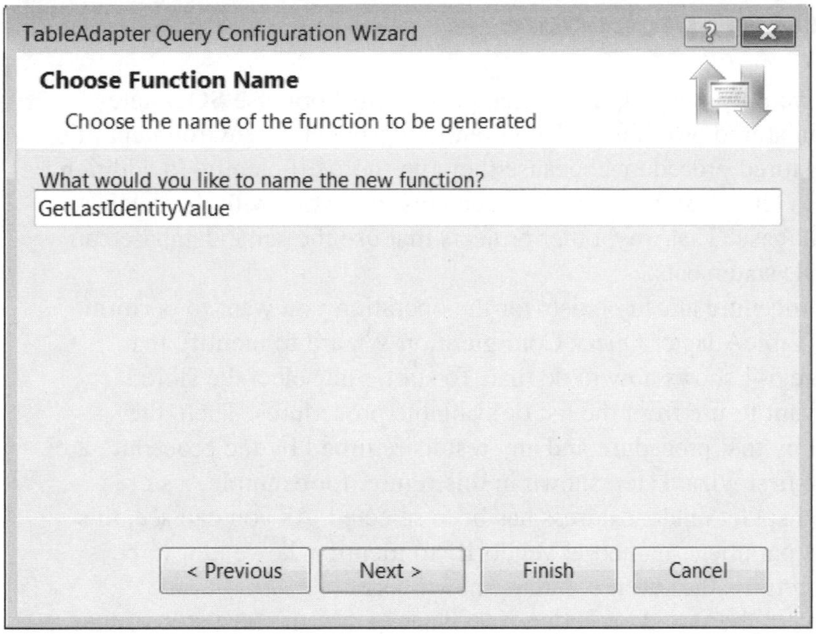

The SQL Server aggregate functions

Function syntax	Description
`AVG([ALL|DISTINCT] expression)`	The average of the non-null values in the expression.
`SUM([ALL|DISTINCT] expression)`	The total of the non-null values in the expression.
`MIN([ALL|DISTINCT] expression)`	The lowest non-null value in the expression.
`MAX([ALL|DISTINCT] expression)`	The highest non-null value in the expression.
`COUNT([ALL|DISTINCT] expression)`	The number of non-null values in the expression.
`COUNT(*)`	The number of rows selected by the query.

A SQL Server function that you can use to get an identity value

Function syntax	Description
`IDENT_CURRENT('TableName')`	Returns the last value generated for the identity column of the specified table.

Description

- If you choose to create a query that returns a single value from the second step of the wizard, the third step lets you enter the Select statement as shown in part 2 of figure 5-2. This Select statement can return the value of an *aggregate function*, any other SQL Server function that returns a single value, or any other single value.
- The fourth step lets you enter the name of the query, also called a *function* since it returns a single value.

Figure 5-3 How to add a query that returns a single value

How to add a query that uses an existing stored procedure

For illustrative purposes, all of the examples in this book use SQL statements rather than stored procedures. However, in a production environment, it's common to use stored procedures because they run more efficiently. In addition, stored procedures let you store the SQL statements that work with the database as part of the database. That way, other projects that use the same database can use the same SQL statements.

If a stored procedure already exists for the operation you want to perform, you can use the TableAdapter Query Configuration Wizard to identify that procedure. Figure 5-4 shows how to do that. To start, you select the stored procedure you want to use from the list of available procedures. Then, the parameters used by that procedure and any results returned by the procedure are displayed. In the first wizard step shown in this figure, for example, a stored procedure named spGetVendorAddress has been selected. As you can see, this procedure uses a parameter named @VendorID to identify the vendor to be retrieved, and it returns the seven columns shown here.

After you select the stored procedure you want to use, the next step of the wizard lets you choose the type of data that's returned by the procedure. For the procedure in this figure, the Tabular Data option is selected since the procedure returns one or more rows and columns. Then, when you click the Next button, the next step lets you select and name the methods you want to add to the TableAdapter just as it does if you had entered a Select statement that returns rows and columns.

If the stored procedure you select returns a single value, you can select the A Single Value option. Then, the wizard will display the step you saw in the last figure that lets you enter a name for the query.

Finally, if the query doesn't return any data, you can select the No Value option. This is the option you'll select if the stored procedure executes an Insert, Update, or Delete statement. Then, the next step lets you enter a name for the query just as it does for a stored procedure that returns a single value.

The wizard step for choosing an existing stored procedure

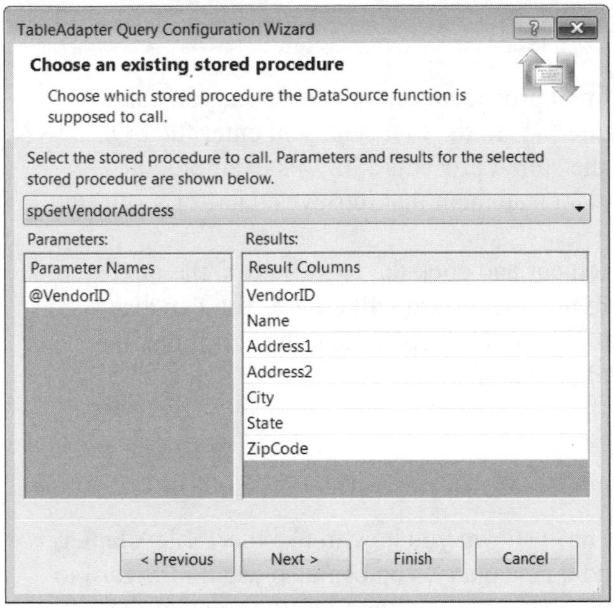

The wizard step for choosing the type of data that's returned

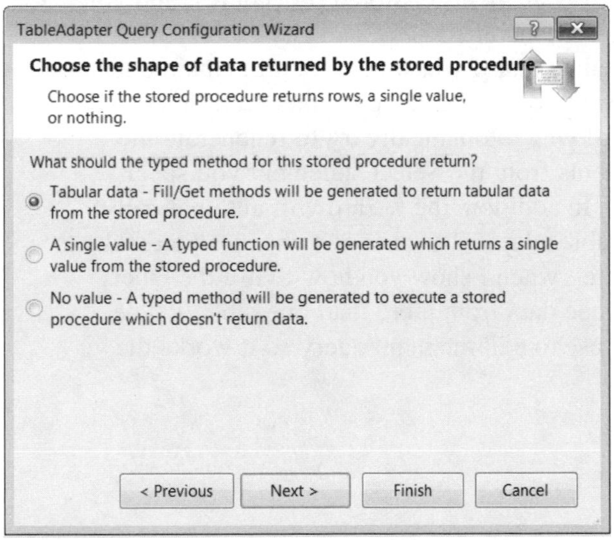

Description

- If you choose to use an existing stored procedure from the first step of the wizard, the second step lets you choose the stored procedure you want to use, and it displays the parameters and results for the selected procedure.
- The third step of the wizard lets you choose whether the stored procedure returns rows and columns, a single value, or no value. The step that's displayed next depends on the option you choose.

Figure 5-4 How to add a query that uses an existing stored procedure

How to add a query that creates a new stored procedure

If you want to create a new stored procedure for an operation, you can use the two wizard steps shown in figure 5-5. In the first step, you enter the SQL statement you want to include in the stored procedure. In this example, the stored procedure will contain a Select statement that retrieves data for a selected vendor.

After you enter the Select statement and click the Next button, the next step lets you name the stored procedure that the wizard will create. You can also click the Preview SQL Script button from this step to view the script that the wizard will use to create the stored procedure.

How to edit a query

Although the last four figures have shown you how to use the TableAdapter Query Configuration Wizard to add a new query, you can also use this wizard to edit an existing query. When you do that, however, the first two steps of the wizard shown in part 1 of figure 5-2 aren't displayed. That means that you can't change whether the query uses SQL statements or stored procedures, and you can't change the type of query that's generated.

Before I go on, you should realize that if you want to edit the main query for a table adapter, you may not want to use the TableAdapter Configuration Wizard. That's because this wizard will automatically try to regenerate the Insert, Update, and Delete statements from the Select statement you specify, which may not be what you want. In addition, the wizard will automatically update any other queries for the table adapter based on the changes you make to the main query. Later in this chapter, when I show you how to use the Query Builder to create queries that include data from more than one table, I'll describe another technique you can use to edit the main query so it works the way you want it to.

The wizard step for entering the Select statement

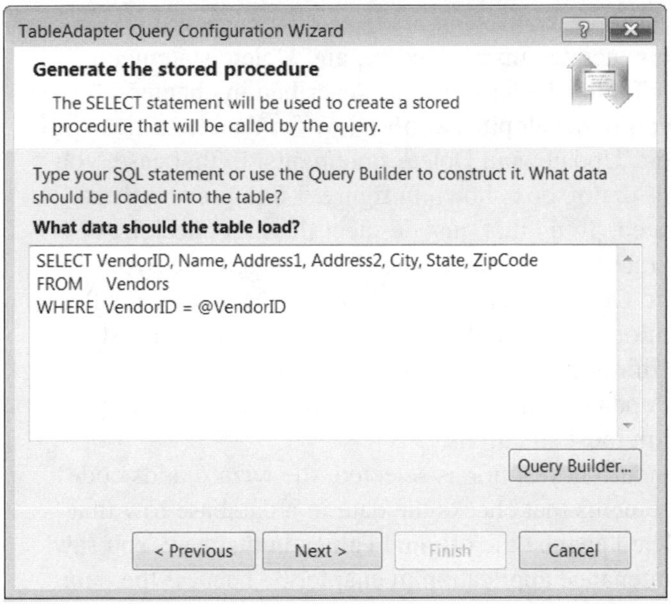

The wizard step for naming the stored procedure

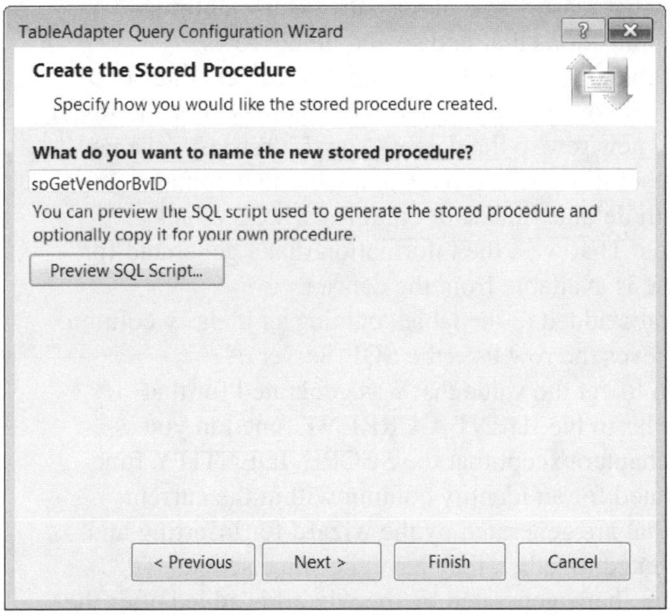

Description

- If you choose to create a stored procedure from the first step of the wizard, the second step lets you enter the Select statement that will be used to create the stored procedure.
- The third step of the wizard lets you enter the name for the stored procedure. You can also preview the SQL script that will be generated from this step.

Figure 5-5 How to add a query that creates a new stored procedure

How to set the advanced SQL generation options

By default, Visual Studio generates Insert, Update, and Delete statements from the main query for each TableAdapter object as described in chapter 3. However, if the application you're developing won't allow for data modification, you won't need the Insert, Update, and Delete statements. In that case, you can use the Advanced Options dialog box shown in figure 5-6 to prevent these statements from being generated. To do that, just deselect the first check box.

Even if you want to generate Insert, Update, and Delete statements, you may want to use the Advanced Options dialog box to control the statements that are generated. The second option, for example, determines whether optimistic concurrency is used, and the third option determines if the dataset will be refreshed after each insert or update operation. These options are selected by default, which is appropriate in most situations.

If the Use Optimistic Concurrency option is selected, the wizard adds code to the Update and Delete statements that checks the data in a database row that is going to be updated or deleted against the original values in that row. You saw this code for the Vendor Maintenance application in chapter 3. Then, if the data has changed, the update or delete is refused and a concurrency exception is thrown. That prevents one user from making changes to rows that have been changed by another user. For that reason, you almost always use optimistic concurrency for multi-user applications that update and delete rows.

If the Refresh the Data Table option is selected, the wizard generates two additional Select statements. As you saw in chapter 3, one comes after the Insert statement that's used to add a new row to the database, and it retrieves the new row into the dataset. This is useful if you add rows to a table that contains an identity column, columns with default values, or columns whose values are calculated from other columns. That way, the information that's generated for these columns by the database is available from the dataset.

By the way, if the row that's added to the table contains an identity column, the Select statement that retrieves the row uses the SQL Server SCOPE_IDENTITY function to get the value that was generated for that column. This function is similar to the IDENT_CURRENT function you learned about earlier in this chapter except that the SCOPE_IDENTITY function gets the last value generated for an identity column within the current scope. Since the statements that are generated by the wizard for inserting and retrieving a new row are executed together, they have the same scope.

The other Select statement that's generated by the wizard is added after the Update statement that's used to modify a row. This ensures that the dataset has current information following an update. Of course, if the values that are generated by the database aren't used by your application, it isn't necessary to refresh the dataset with this information, and it would be inefficient to do that. In many cases, though, you need to refresh the dataset for your application if you want it to work properly.

The dialog boxes for setting advanced SQL generation options

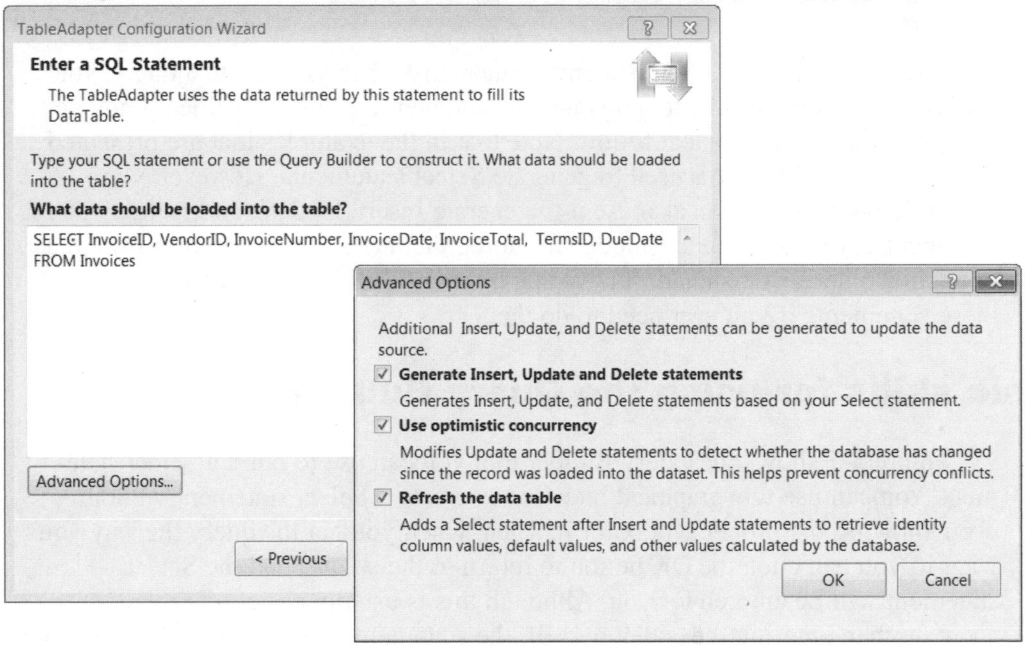

Description

- To display the Advanced Options dialog box, right-click on the main query for a table adapter in the Dataset Designer and select the Configure command to display the TableAdapter Configuration Wizard. Then, click the Advanced Options button.
- The Advanced Options dialog box lets you set the options related to the generation of the Insert, Update, and Delete statements that will be used to update the database.
- If your application doesn't need to add, change, or delete rows in the database table, you should remove the check mark from the Generate option. Then, the other options become unavailable.
- The Use Optimistic Concurrency option determines whether or not the application checks that the rows that are updated or deleted haven't been changed by another user since they were retrieved. If this option is selected, the wizard adds code to the Update and Delete statements to provide for this checking.
- If you remove the check mark from the Use Optimistic Concurrency option, rows are updated and deleted whether or not they've been changed by another user since they were retrieved.
- The Refresh the Data Table option determines whether or not the table in the dataset is refreshed after an insert or update operation. If this option is selected, a Select statement that retrieves the affected row is executed after each Insert and Update statement.

Figure 5-6 How to set the advanced SQL generation options

How to use the Query Builder

Instead of entering a SQL statement manually when you create a query, you can use the Query Builder to generate the statement for you. You'll learn how to do that in the two topics that follow. Note that in the examples that are presented here, the Query Builder is used to generate Select statements. However, you should know that you can also use it to generate Insert, Update, and Delete statements. Although the techniques for doing that are slightly different from the ones shown here, you shouldn't have any trouble figuring out how to generate these statements if you ever need to do that.

Basic skills for using the Query Builder

Figure 5-7 shows the Query Builder tool you can use to build a Select statement. You can use this graphical interface to create a Select statement without even knowing the proper syntax for it. Then, when you get the query the way you want it, you can click the OK button to return to the wizard and the Select statement will be entered for you. Although this is usually easier and more accurate than entering the code yourself, the statement that's generated often contains unnecessary parentheses and qualifiers that can make it more difficult to read. However, you can modify the statement after it's entered into the wizard.

When the Query Builder first opens, the current table is displayed in the *diagram pane*. In this figure, for example, the Vendors table is displayed in the diagram pane. If you need to add other tables to this pane, you can right-click on the pane and select the Add Table command. You'll learn more about creating queries with multiple tables in the next topic.

In the *grid pane*, you can see the columns that are going to be included in the query. To add columns to this pane, you just check the boxes before the column names listed in the diagram pane. Once the columns have been added to the grid pane, you can use the Sort Type column to identify any columns that should be used to sort the returned rows and the Sort Order column to give the order of precedence for the sort if more than one column is identified. Here, for example, the rows will be sorted in ascending sequence by the Name column.

Similarly, you can use the Filter column to establish the criteria to be used to select the rows that will be retrieved by the query. For example, to retrieve only the rows where the Name column matches a specified pattern, you can specify "LIKE @Name" in the Filter column for the Name column as shown here.

As you create the query, the *SQL pane* shows the resulting Select statement. You can also run this query at any time to display the selected rows in the *results pane*. That way, you can be sure that the query works the way you want it to. To run the query, click the Execute Query button. Then, you will be prompted to enter any parameters that are required by the query. If you experience any difficulty with getting the query to work properly, you can use the initial letter or letters, followed by the percentage symbol, as you enter the parameter. The percentage symbol acts as a wild card that represents all the remaining letters.

The Query Builder

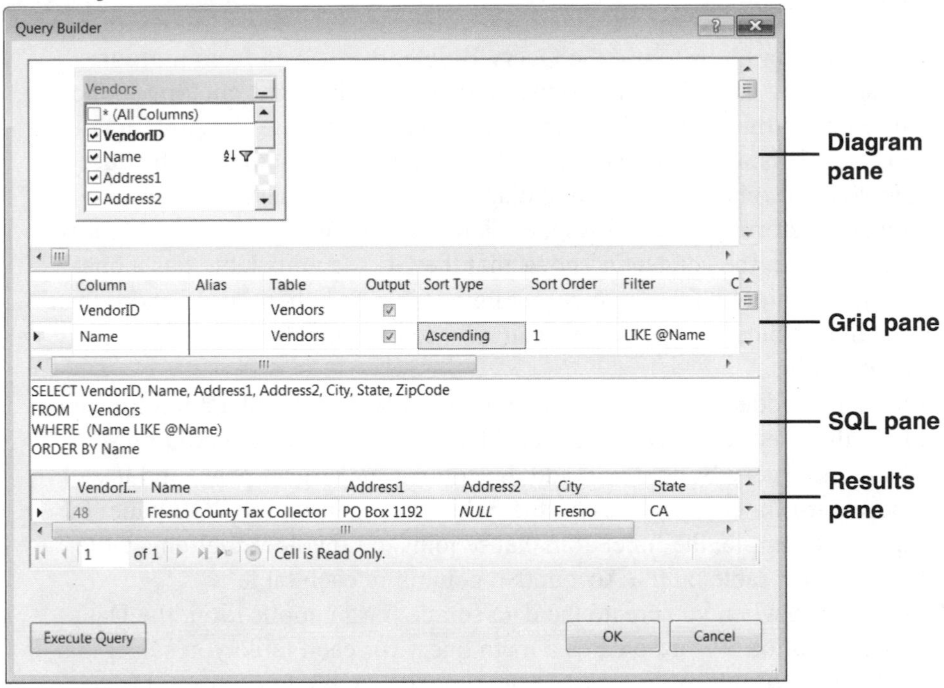

Description

- To display the Query Builder, click the Query Builder button from the wizard step that lets you enter a SQL statement. Or, in the Properties window, click on the ellipsis to the right of the CommandText property of a query.
- By default, the current table is displayed in the *diagram pane*.
- To include a column in a query, click on the box to its left. Then, that column is added to the *grid pane*. Or, select all the columns by checking the * (All Columns) item.
- To create a calculated column, enter an expression in the Column column and then enter the name you want to use for the column in the Alias column.
- To sort the returned rows by one or more columns, select the Ascending or Descending option from the Sort Type column for those columns in the sequence you want them sorted. You can also use the Sort Order column to set the sort sequence.
- To specify selection criteria (like a specific value that the column must contain to be selected), enter the criteria in the Filter column.
- To use a column for sorting or for specifying criteria without including it in the query results, remove the check mark from the Output column.
- As you select columns and specify sort and selection criteria, the Query Builder builds the SQL statement and displays it in the *SQL pane*.
- To display the results of a query, click the Execute Query button. Then, if necessary, enter any parameters required by the query. When you're done, the results are displayed in the *results pane*.

Figure 5-7 Basic skills for using the Query Builder

How to get data from multiple tables

Figure 5-8 shows how to use the Query Builder to get data from multiple tables. To start, you can add tables to the diagram pane by right-clicking in the pane and selecting the Add Table command. Then, you can use the Add Table dialog box that's displayed to select the tables you want to include in the query.

When you add related tables to the diagram pane, the Query Builder includes a connector icon that shows the relationship between the tables. In this figure, for example, the connector shows that the GLAccounts table has a one-to-many relationship with the InvoiceLineItems table. In other words, more than one row in the InvoiceLineItems table can refer to the same row in the GLAccounts table.

Once you've added a table to the diagram pane, you can add a column from that table to the query by selecting the check box to the left of the column's name. Then, the Query Builder will add the column to the grid pane, and it will add the necessary Inner Join clause to the Select statement in the SQL pane. In this figure, for example, the Inner Join clause joins the InvoiceLineItems table to the GLAccounts table on the AccountNo column in each table.

As you know, when you create the data source for an application, the Data Source Configuration Wizard creates a main query for each table you select that retrieves the data for that table. Most of the time, that's what you want. Occasionally, though, you'll want to include one or more columns from another table in the main query for a table. Later in this chapter, for example, you'll see a main query that uses the Select statement shown in this figure. Although you might think that you could create this query by modifying the main query using the TableAdapter Configuration Wizard, you don't usually want to do that because this wizard automatically attempts to generate Insert, Update, and Delete statements from the Select statement you specify. If the Select statement contains data from more than one table, however, it won't be able to do that. As a result, you won't be able to insert, update, or delete rows in the table.

To get around this problem, you can display the Query Builder for the main query from the Properties window. To do that, just select the query in the Dataset Designer and click on the ellipsis to the right of the CommandText property. When you finish editing the query and click the OK button, one or two dialog boxes will be displayed. The first dialog box will ask if you want to regenerate the updating commands based on the new command text. In other words, do you want to modify the Insert, Update, and Delete statements so that they match the Select statement. Since Visual Studio can't generate these statements from a Select statement that contains data from more than one table, you won't want to do that. Instead, you'll want the Insert, Update, and Delete statements to remain unchanged so they include only the columns from the main table. If additional queries are defined for the table adapter, the second dialog box will ask if you want to update the other queries based on the changes you made to the main query. In most cases, you won't want to do that.

A query that gets data from two tables

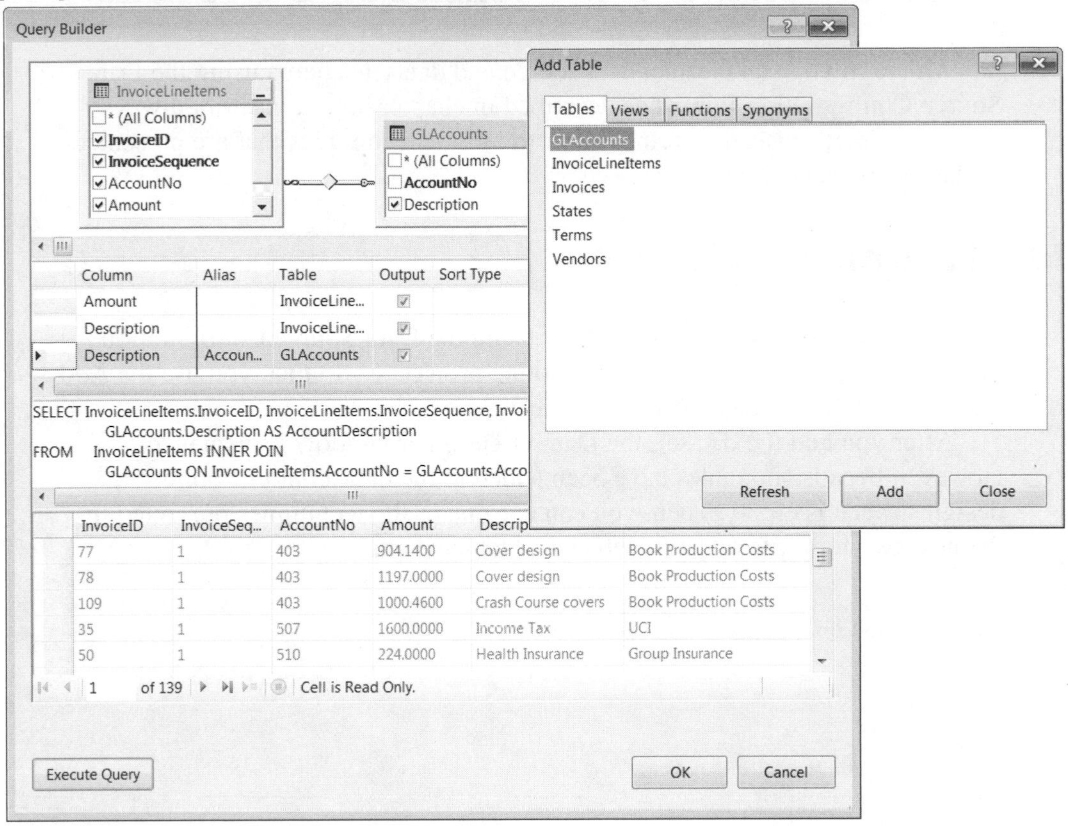

Description

- To add tables to the diagram pane, right-click in the diagram pane and select the Add Table command. Then, you can use the dialog box that's displayed to select the tables you want to include in the query.
- If the tables you add to a query are related, the Query Builder adds connector icons that show the relationships between the tables.
- To add a column from a table to the query, select the check box to the left of the column's name in the diagram pane. When you do, the Query Builder will add the column to the grid pane, and it will add the necessary Inner Join clause to the Select statement in the SQL pane.
- To edit the Select statement that's used by a main query so it includes data from more than one table, select the appropriate query in the Dataset Designer. Then, in the Properties window, click on the ellipsis to the right of the CommandText property, and use the Query Builder to edit the query. Finally, respond to the resulting dialog box to control whether the Insert, Update, and Delete statements for the query are updated.
- If you modify the main query for a table adapter that contains other queries, another dialog box will be displayed that asks if you want to update the other queries based on the changes made to the main query. In most cases, you'll respond No to this dialog box.

Figure 5-8 How to get data from multiple tables

How to create a new dataset schema

Although you can create a data source and dataset schema using the Data Source Configuration Wizard as described in chapter 3, you may not always want to do that. Instead, you may want to use the techniques that are presented in the topics that follow.

How to create a dataset

To create a dataset schema without using the Data Source Configuration Wizard, you start by adding a dataset to the project. To do that, you use the Add New Item dialog box as shown in figure 5-9.

After you add the dataset, the Dataset Designer window is displayed. However, because no tables have been added to the dataset at this point, the design surface is empty. Then, you can use one of the techniques presented in the next two topics to add data tables and table adapters.

The Dataset Designer window for a new dataset class

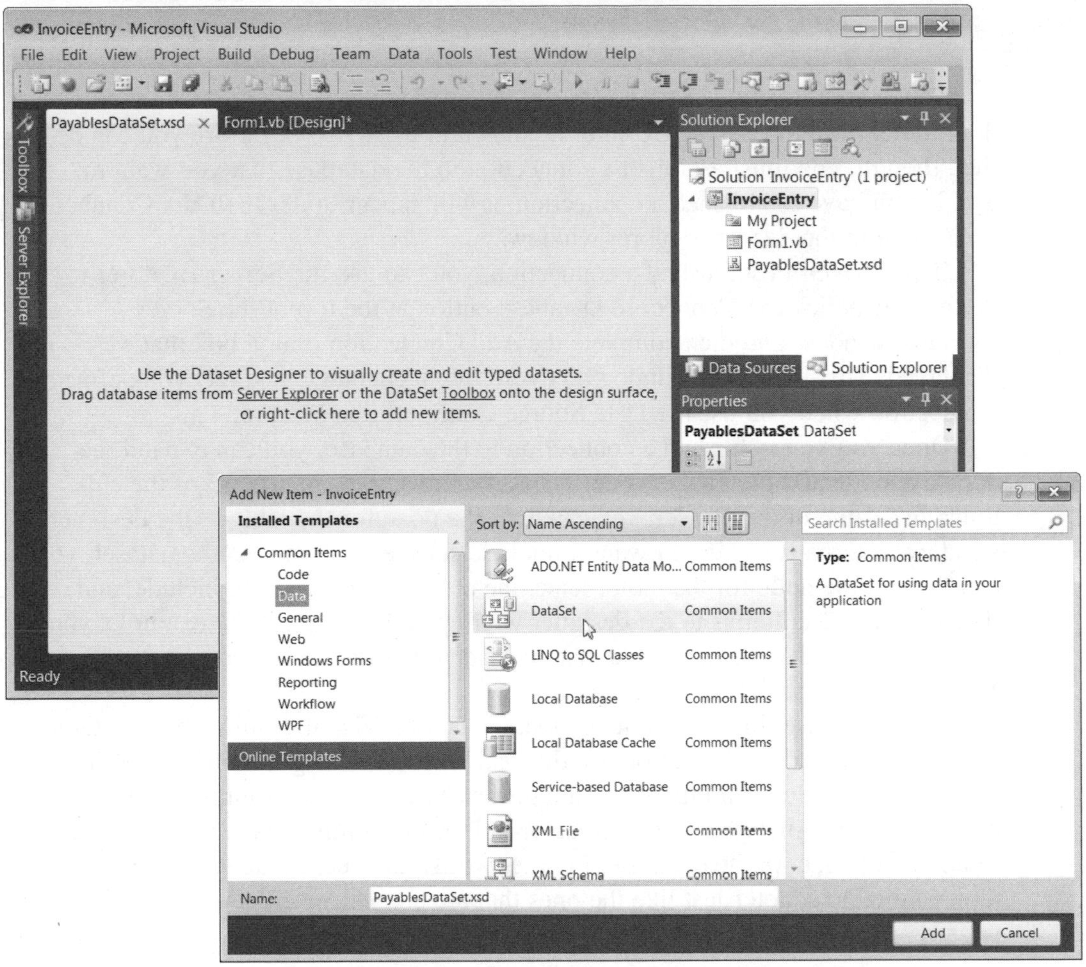

Description

- To display the Add New Item dialog box, right-click on the project in the Solution Explorer and select Add→New Item or select the Add New Item command from the Project menu.
- To create a dataset class, select Data from the Categories list, then select the DataSet template, enter a name for the dataset, and click the Add button.
- To add items to the dataset, you can drag them from the Server Explorer as shown in figure 5-10. You can also drag components from the Toolbox or right-click on the design surface and use the shortcut menu that's displayed to add components as shown in figure 5-11.

Figure 5-9 How to use the Dataset Designer to create a dataset class

How to create a data table and table adapter using the Server Explorer

The easiest way to add a new data table and table adapter to a dataset is to drag items from the Server Explorer as shown in figure 5-10. Before you can do that, though, you must establish a connection to the database that you want to use. If you have established a connection, it will appear under the Data Connections node in the Server Explorer window.

If you haven't established a connection, you can use the Server Explorer to do that. Just click the Connect to Database button at the top of the Server Explorer window and then complete the Add Connection dialog box that's displayed. This is the same dialog box you saw in chapter 3 that lets you define a connection when you use the Data Source Configuration Wizard.

Once you've established a connection to the database, you can expand the database node and the Tables node. Then, if you want to include all of the columns in a table in the dataset, you can drag the node for the table to the designer window. Alternatively, if you want to include selected columns in the dataset, you can expand the node for the table, select the columns you want to include, and then drag those columns to the designer window. In this figure, for example, you can see that I created a data table that consists of the first seven columns in the Vendors table.

When you use this technique to create a dataset, Visual Studio creates a table adapter just as it does when you use the Data Source Configuration Wizard. This table adapter includes a Fill query that retrieves the selected columns from the database. It also includes Insert, Update, and Delete commands that can be used to update the data in the database. In other words, this technique creates a data table and table adapter just like the ones that are created when you use the wizard.

The Dataset Designer after columns are dragged from the Server Explorer

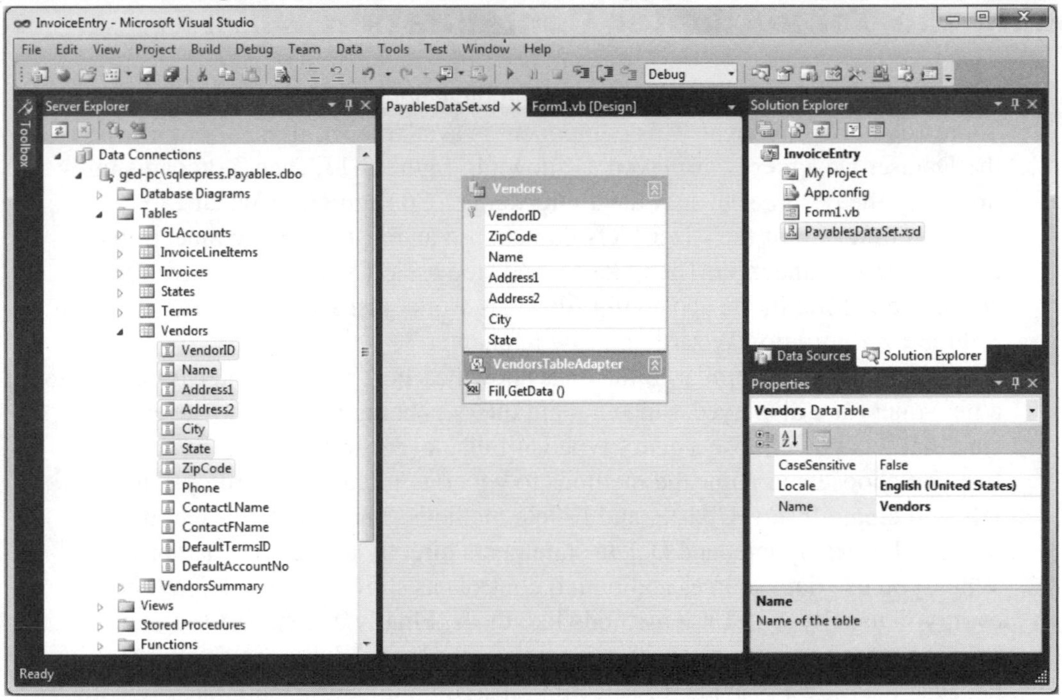

Description

- To display the Server Explorer, use the View→Server Explorer command.
- To use the Server Explorer to add a data table to a dataset, select the columns you want to include in the table and then drag them to the design surface. If you want to include all of the columns, you can drag the table rather than its columns.
- In addition to the data table, a table adapter is created with a Fill query that defines the Select statement that's used to retrieve data from the table. This query is also used to generate Insert, Update, and Delete statements for the table adapter.

Express Edition difference

- The Server Explorer is called the Database Explorer.

Figure 5-10 How to create a data table and table adapter using the Server Explorer

How to create a data table and table adapter using the TableAdapter Configuration Wizard

Another way to create a data table and table adapter is to use the TableAdapter component. This component is available from the Toolbox when the Dataset Designer is displayed as shown in figure 5-11.Then, you can simply drag it to the designer to start the TableAdapter Configuration Wizard.

The first step of the wizard lets you choose an existing data connection or create a new connection. Then, the second step asks if you want to save the connection string in the app.config file. This works just like it does for the Data Source Configuration Wizard you saw in chapter 3.

After that, steps similar to the ones shown earlier in this chapter for creating a new query are displayed. Since a main query is being created, however, the step that lets you choose a query type isn't displayed. In addition, the step that lets you choose and name the methods to generate includes a third option that lets you create Insert, Update, and Delete methods. These methods can be used to issue Insert, Update, and Delete statements directly against the database. When you use data sources and bound controls as shown in this chapter, however, you usually won't use methods like these. Finally, the steps for using existing stored procedures or creating new stored procedures are different because they must provide for selecting, inserting, updating, and deleting data.

You may have noticed that in addition to the TableAdapter component, the Toolbox provides Query, DataTable, and Relation components. You can use the Query component to add a query to a table adapter by dragging it from the Toolbox to the appropriate table. This works the same as using the Add Query command in the shortcut menu for a table adapter.

You can use the DataTable and Relation components to create a custom dataset schema. But if you use this technique to create a dataset, a table adapter isn't created. Because of that, you have to work with the dataset using a data adapter. Since you'll rarely need to create a custom dataset schema, I won't show you how to do that in this book.

At this point, you may be wondering when you would use the Data Source Configuration Wizard or the Server Explorer to create data tables and table adapters and when you would use the TableAdapter Configuration Wizard. In general, I think you should use the TableAdapter Configuration Wizard any time you want to generate Select, Insert, Update, and Delete statements other than the defaults. That's because when you use this wizard, you can make the necessary changes as you create the table adapter. If you don't want to refresh the data table after an insert or update operation, for example, you can set the appropriate option when you specify the Select statement. In contrast, if you use the Data Source Configuration Wizard or the Server Explorer to create the table adapter, you have to modify the main query as shown in figure 5-6 to change this option.

The Dataset Designer after a TableAdapter is dragged from the Toolbox

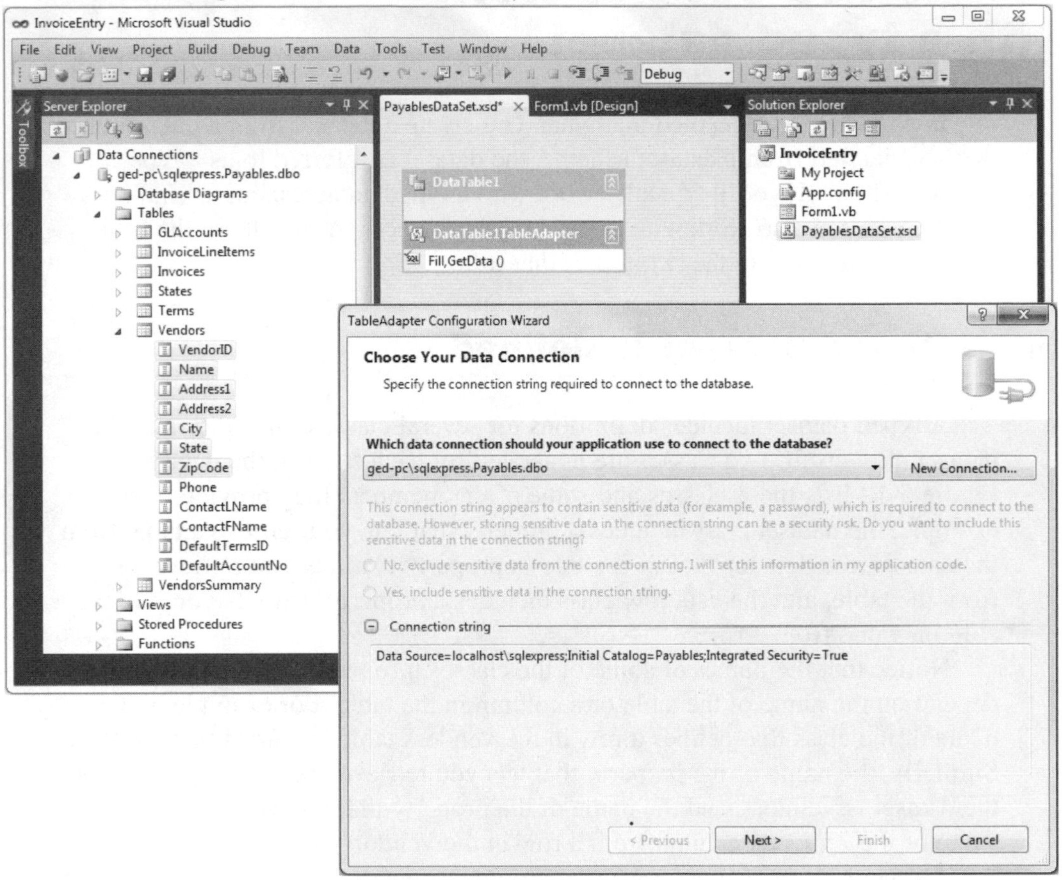

Description

- To start the TableAdapter Configuration Wizard, drag the TableAdapter component from the Toolbox or right-click in the Dataset Designer and select the Add→TableAdapter command.
- The first step of the TableAdapter Configuration Wizard lets you choose an existing data connection or create a new connection. Then, the second step asks you if you want to save the connection string in the application configuration file. The remaining steps are similar to the ones shown earlier in this chapter for adding and editing a query.
- The TableAdapter Configuration Wizard lets you specify the exact query you want to use to retrieve data, it lets you use an existing stored procedure for the main query, it lets you create and use a new stored procedure for the main query, and it lets you set the SQL generation options the way you want them. Because of that, you may want to use this wizard to create your data tables and table adapters instead of using the Data Source Configuration Wizard or the Server Explorer.

Figure 5-11 How to create a data table and table adapter using the TableAdapter Configuration Wizard

How to use code to work with a typed dataset

In chapter 3, you learned that when you create a dataset from a dataset class that's generated from a dataset schema, the dataset is referred to as a typed dataset. Although you'll typically work with a typed dataset using a binding source, you can also work with a typed dataset directly. You'll learn the basic skills for doing that in the two topics that follow.

How a typed dataset is defined

A typed dataset includes definitions for several classes. In addition to the dataset class itself, two classes are generated for each table in the dataset. Figure 5-12 lists these classes and some of the members they provide. For example, the dataset class includes a property that lets you retrieve a table from the dataset, the data table class includes a property that lets you retrieve a row from the table, and the data row class includes a property that lets you retrieve a column value from a row.

Notice that the names of some of the classes, properties, and methods depend on the name of the table or a column in the table. For example, the name of the class that defines a row in the Vendors table is named VendorsRow. Similarly, the name of the property that lets you retrieve the Vendors table from the dataset is Vendors, and the name of the property that lets you retrieve the value of the ZipCode column from a row in the Vendors table is ZipCode.

Although it isn't necessary for you to understand the details of how a typed dataset is implemented, you do need to be aware of the properties and methods that are provided by a typed dataset so you can use them when necessary. In the next figure, for example, you'll see some typical code for working with typed datasets. This code should help you understand how to use these properties and methods.

Classes defined by a typed dataset

Class	Description	Example
Dataset	The dataset itself.	PayablesDataSet
Data table	A table in the dataset.	VendorsDataTable
Data row	A row in the data table.	VendorsRow

Property defined by a dataset class

Property	Description	Example
tablename	Gets a table.	Vendors

Members defined by a data table class

Property	Description	
Count	Gets the number of rows in the table.	
Item	Gets the row with the specified index.	
Method	**Description**	**Example**
New*tablename*Row	Creates a new row based on the table definition.	NewVendorsRow
Add*tablename*Row	Adds the specified data row to the table, or adds a row with the specified values to the table.	AddVendorsRow

Members defined by a data row class

Property	Description	Example
columnname	Gets or sets the value of a column.	ZipCode
Method	**Description**	**Example**
BeginEdit	Places the row in edit mode.	
EndEdit	Saves changes to the current row to the data table.	
CancelEdit	Cancels changes to the current row.	
Delete	Marks the row as deleted.	
Is*columnname*Null	Returns a Boolean value that indicates if the column contains a null value.	IsAddress2Null
Set*columnname*Null	Assigns a null value to the column.	SetAddress2Null

Description

- When you create a dataset schema, Visual Studio generates a typed dataset that includes definitions for the dataset class, the data table classes, and the data row classes.
- The Is…Null and Set…Null methods are generated only for data columns that allow null values. Then, if necessary, you can use these methods to determine what value is assigned to a control that displays the value of the column and what value is assigned to the column based on the value of the control.

Figure 5-12 How a typed dataset is defined

How to work with a typed dataset

Figure 5-13 shows how to work with the data in a typed dataset. To start, you declare a variable that will hold the row as illustrated by the first example in this figure. Here, a variable named vendorRow is declared with a type of PayablesDataSet.VendorsRow. That way, you can use the properties defined by the VendorsRow class to get and set the value of each column in a row as you'll see in a moment.

After you declare a variable to hold a row, you can retrieve a row and assign it to that variable. To retrieve a row, you can use the Item property of the table to refer to the row by its index as illustrated in the first example. Here, the row at index 0 is retrieved and assigned to the vendorRow variable. Notice that because Item is the default property of a table, it can be omitted as shown.

The rest of the code in this example retrieves values from individual columns of the row and assigns them to the appropriate properties of controls on a form. Here, you can see that the value of each column is retrieved using a property of the row. To retrieve the value of the Name column, for example, the Name property is used.

The second example illustrates how you modify the data in an existing row. This code starts by executing a BeginEdit method, which places the row in *edit mode*. Then, the statements that follow assign new values to the columns in the row. To do that, these statements use properties of the data row to refer to the columns just as in the first example. Once the new values have been assigned, the EndEdit method is executed to commit the changes.

The third example in this figure shows how you add new rows to a data table. To do that, you use the New*tablename*Row method of the table, and you assign the result to a data row variable. Then, you assign values to the columns in the row just as you do for an existing row. When you're done, you use the Add*tablename*Row method of the table to add the new row to the table.

The statement in the fourth example in this figure uses the Delete method to mark a row as deleted. However, this row isn't permanently deleted until you update the database. That makes sense because if the Delete method actually deleted the row, there would be no way of knowing it had been deleted and it wouldn't be deleted from the database.

The fifth example in this figure shows an UpdateAll method for the table adapter manager. As you've already learned, this method saves changes made to the dataset to the database.

If a table adapter manager isn't generated for a dataset, you can use the Update method of a table adapter to save the changes made to a single table to the database as shown in the sixth example. You'll see one situation where you'll want to use this method in the Invoice Entry application that's presented next.

By default, when you create a dataset object by dragging a data source to a form, the dataset object is given the same name as the dataset class it's created from. Because of that, it can be difficult to distinguish between the two when you refer to them in code. To make your code clear, then, you should always use the keyword Me to refer to a dataset object as shown in this figure.

Code that retrieves a row and assigns column values to form controls

```
Dim vendorRow As PayablesDataSet.VendorsRow
vendorRow = Me.PayablesDataSet.Vendors(0)
VendorIDTextBox.Text = vendorRow.VendorID.ToString
NameTextBox.Text = vendorRow.Name
...
ZipCodeTextBox.Text = vendorRow.ZipCode
```

Code that modifies the values in the data row

```
vendorRow.BeginEdit()
vendorRow.Name = NameTextBox.Text
...
vendorRow.ZipCode = ZipCodeTextBox.Text
vendorRow.EndEdit()
```

Code that adds a new row to a dataset

```
vendorRow = Me.PayablesDataSet.Vendors.NewVendorsRow
vendorRow.Name = NameTextBox.Text
...
vendorRow.ZipCode = ZipCodeTextBox.Text
Me.PayablesDataSet.Vendors.AddVendorsRow(vendorRow)
```

A statement that marks the row as deleted

```
vendorRow.Delete()
```

A statement that updates the database with the changes

```
TableAdapterManager.UpdateAll(Me.PayablesDataSet)
```

Another way to update the database

```
VendorsTableAdapter.Update(Me.PayablesDataSet.Vendors)
```

Description

- To declare a variable for a row in a data table, you use the class for the data row that's defined by the dataset.
- To retrieve a row from a data table, you can use the Item property of the table and the index of the row. Since Item is the default property, you can omit it as shown above.
- To get or set the values of the columns in a row, use the properties of the row that have the same names as the columns in the data table.
- After you assign new values to the columns in a row, you can use the EndEdit method to commit the changes. To cancel the changes, you can use the CancelEdit method.
- To create a new row based on the schema of a table, you use the New*tablename*Row method of the table and assign the result to a data row variable.
- After you assign values to the columns in the row, you use the Add*tablename*Row method of the table to add the row to the table.
- The Delete method of a row marks the row for deletion. The row isn't actually deleted until the UpdateAll method of the table adapter manager or the Update method of the table adapter is executed.

Figure 5-13 How to work with a typed dataset

The Invoice Entry application

Now that you've seen how to use the Dataset Designer to work with data tables and table adapters, you're ready to see an Invoice Entry application that uses a variety of custom queries. As you review this application, keep in mind that it isn't necessarily implemented using the most professional techniques. In fact, one of the main purposes for presenting this application is to illustrate how difficult it can be to implement an application using data sources and bound controls. That will help you better appreciate the skills you'll learn in the next section of this book.

The user interface

Figure 5-14 presents the two forms of the Invoice Entry application. When this application starts, it displays a blank Add Invoice form. Then, the user can use the toolbar to select a vendor by vendor ID or by name.

If the user enters all or part of a name and clicks the Find button next to the Name text box, the Select Vendor form is displayed. This form displays all the vendors with names that match the name pattern in a DataGridView control. The user can also click this Find button without entering a value in the Name text box, in which case all the vendors are listed in the DataGridView control. Then, the user can double-click on a row to select a vendor or click on the row and then click the OK button. In either case, control returns to the Add Invoice form and the information for the vendor is displayed.

Once a vendor is selected, the user can enter the data for an invoice into the remaining controls on the form. Specifically, the user must enter an invoice number and invoice date along with the line item information. In addition, the user can change the terms or leave them at the vendor's default. In either case, the due date for the invoice is calculated automatically based on the invoice date and the terms.

To enter a line item, the user selects an account from the Account combo box, enters a description and amount in the appropriate text boxes, and clicks the Add button. Then, a line item is added to the DataGridView control, and the invoice total is calculated and displayed. The user can also delete a line item from the grid by clicking the Delete button to the right of the line item. However, the user can't make any changes directly to the data in the grid.

When all the line items for the invoice have been added, the user can click the Accept Invoice button. Then, the new invoice and its line items are saved to the database and a blank Add Invoice form is displayed. The user can also click the Cancel Invoice button to clear the Add Invoice form without saving the invoice.

The Add Invoice form

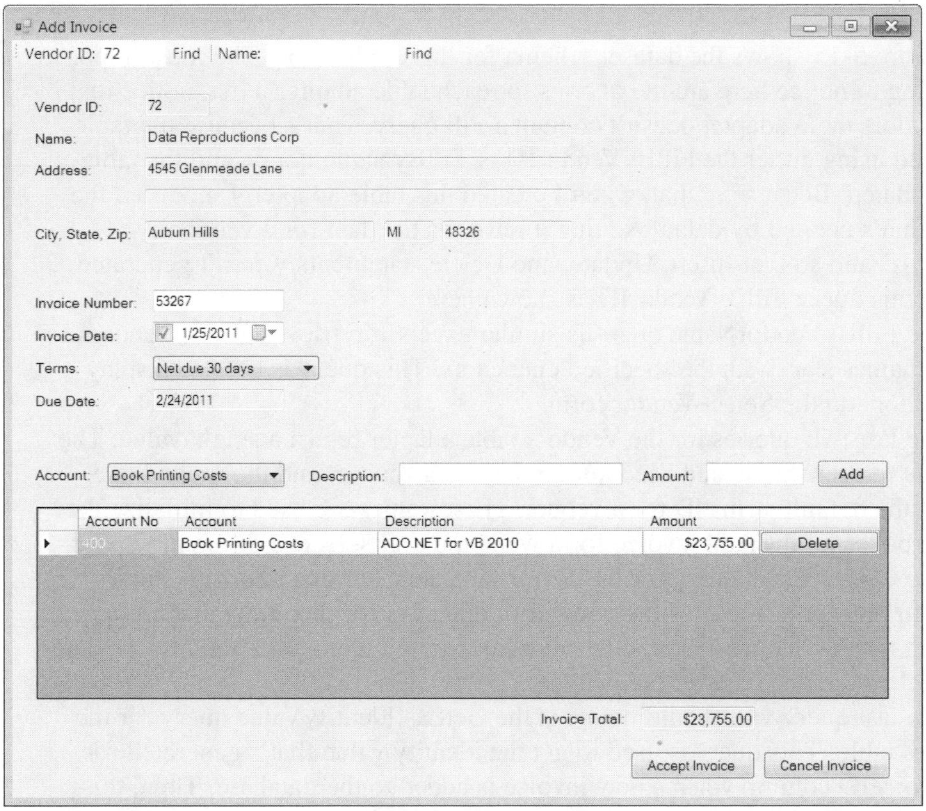

The Select Vendor form

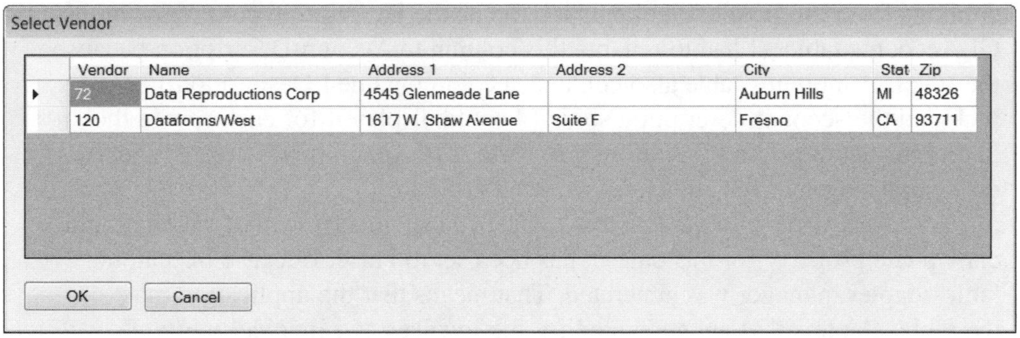

Description

- To add an invoice, the user must select a vendor, enter the invoice information, and enter one or more line items.
- To select a vendor, the user can enter a vendor ID in the toolbar and click the first Find button or enter all or part of the vendor name, click the second Find button, and then select the vendor from the Select Vendor form that's displayed.
- To enter a line item, the user selects an account, enters a description and amount, and clicks the Add button. The user can also delete a line item by clicking its Delete button.

Figure 5-14 The user interface for the Invoice Entry application

The dataset schema

Figure 5-15 shows the dataset schema for this application. The most important thing to notice here are the queries for each table adapter. First, notice that the Vendors table adapter doesn't contain a Fill query. That's because the table is loaded using either the FillByVendorID or FillByName query, and the table isn't updated. Because of that, when I created this table adapter, I modified the query that's created by default so that it retrieves the data for a vendor by vendor ID and so that Insert, Update, and Delete statements weren't generated. I named this query FillByVendorID as shown here.

The FillByVendorName query is similar except it retrieves all the vendors whose names start with the specified characters. This query is used to display the vendors on the Select Vendor form.

The last two queries for the Vendors table adapter return a single value. The first one returns the default account number for a vendor, and the second one returns the default terms ID for a vendor. These values are used to initialize the combo boxes on the Add Invoice form when the user selects a different vendor.

The GetDueDays query for the Terms table adapter also returns a single value. In this case, it returns the number of due days for the terms that are selected for the invoice. Then, this value can be used along with the invoice date to calculate the due date for the invoice.

The last query you should notice is the GetLastIdentityValue query for the Invoices table. This query is used to get the identity value that's generated for the InvoiceID column when a new invoice is added to the database. Then, this value can be used for the InvoiceID column of each line item for the invoice.

You should also notice that the InvoiceLineItems data table includes all the columns from the InvoiceLineItems table plus the Description column from the GLAccounts table. (I had to rename this column to AccountDescription because the InvoiceLineItems table also contains a column named Description.) I included the account description so that I could display it for each row in the line items data grid on the Add Invoice form. I'll explain how I created the query that's used to load this table in the next figure.

Although you can't see it in this figure, you should know that the Hierarchical Update property for this dataset has been set to False. Because of that, no table adapter manager was generated. That means that the application must use the table adapters that are generated for the Invoices and InvoiceLineItems tables to update the database.

The dataset schema

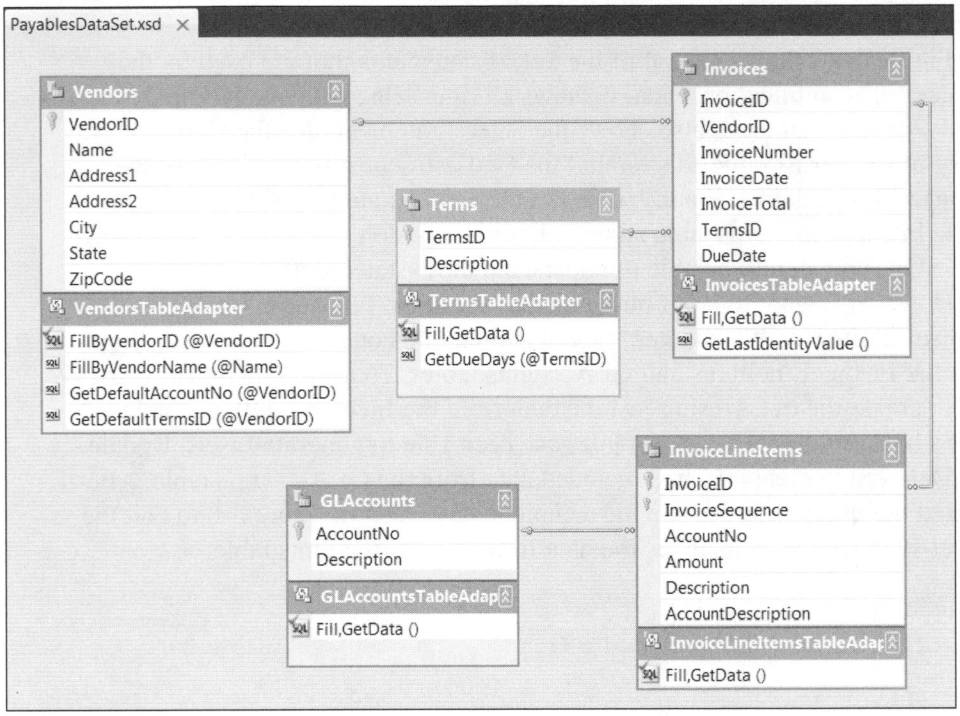

Description

- The FillByVendorID query for the Vendors table adapter is used to retrieve the vendor data that's displayed on the Add Invoice form. This query is based on the vendor ID entered by the user into the toolbar on the form.
- The FillByVendorName query for the Vendors table adapter is used to retrieve the vendors that are displayed in the Select Vendor form. This query is based on a name pattern entered by the user into the toolbar on the Add Invoice form.
- The GetDefaultAccountNo and GetDefaultTermsID queries for the Vendors table adapter are used to retrieve the default account number and terms ID for the selected vendor. These values are used to initialize the Account and Terms combo boxes. These queries are based on the vendor ID for the selected vendor.
- The GetDueDays query for the Terms table adapter is used to retrieve the due days for the selected terms. This value is used to calculate the due date for the invoice.
- The Fill queries for the Terms and GLAccounts table adapters are used to display the lists in the Terms and Account combo boxes on the Add Invoice form.
- The GetLastIdentityValue query for the Invoices table adapter is used to get the ID of the last invoice that was added to the database.
- The Fill query for the InvoiceLineItems table adapter has been modified so it includes the account description from the GLAccounts table. This description is included in the data grid on the Add Invoice form.

Figure 5-15 The dataset schema for the Invoice Entry application

Some of the Select statements

Figure 5-16 shows several of the Select statements that are used by the Invoice Entry application. First, it shows all four Select statements for the Vendors table adapter. It also shows the Select statements for the GetDueDays query of the Terms table adapter and the GetLastIdentityValue query of the Invoices Table adapter. Finally, it shows the Select statement for the Fill query of the InvoiceLineItems table adapter. Even if you don't have much experience with SQL, you should be able to understand these statements.

However, I want to point out one thing about the Fill query for the InvoiceLineItems table adapter. As you can see, this query includes data from both the InvoiceLineItems and GLAccounts tables. To accomplish that, I first had to create the query using just the data from the InvoiceLineItems table. That's because the wizard wouldn't have been able to generate Insert, Update, and Delete statements if I had included data from the GLAccounts table. After I created the query, I had to use the technique described in figure 5-8 to edit the Select statement so it includes the data from the GLAccounts table.

The custom Select statements for the Vendors table adapter

FillByVendorID(@VendorID)

```
SELECT    VendorID, Name, Address1, Address2, City, State, ZipCode
FROM      Vendors
WHERE     VendorID = @VendorID
```

FillByVendorName(@Name)

```
SELECT    VendorID, Name, Address1, Address2, City, State, ZipCode
FROM      Vendors
WHERE     Name LIKE @Name
ORDER BY  Name
```

GetDefaultAccountNo(@VendorID)

```
SELECT    DefaultAccountNo
FROM      Vendors
WHERE     VendorID = @VendorID
```

GetDefaultTermsID(@VendorID)

```
SELECT    DefaultTermsID
FROM      Vendors
WHERE     VendorID = @VendorID
```

The custom Select statement for the Terms table adapter

GetDueDays(@TermsID)

```
SELECT    DueDays
FROM      Terms
WHERE     TermsID = @TermsID
```

The custom Select statement for the Invoices table adapter

GetLastIdentityValue()

```
SELECT   IDENT_CURRENT('Invoices')
FROM     Invoices
```

The Select statement for the InvoiceLineItems table adapter

Fill()

```
SELECT    InvoiceLineItems.InvoiceID, InvoiceLineItems.InvoiceSequence,
          InvoiceLineItems.AccountNo, InvoiceLineItems.Amount,
          InvoiceLineItems.Description,
          GLAccounts.Description AS AccountDescription
FROM      InvoiceLineItems INNER JOIN GLAccounts
          ON InvoiceLineItems.AccountNo = GLAccounts.AccountNo
```

Notes

- The Fill queries for the Terms and GLAccounts table adapters have been configured so no Insert, Update, and Delete statements are generated.
- The Fill queries for the Invoices and InvoiceLineItems table adapters have been configured so the dataset isn't updated after an insert operation.

Figure 5-16 Some of the Select statements for the Invoice Entry application

The code for the Add Invoice form

Figure 5-17 shows the code for the Add Invoice form. To start, this class declares an Integer variable named invoiceSequence. This variable is used to keep track of the InvoiceSequence column that's added to the InvoiceLineItems table, with a value of 1 for the first line item for each invoice, 2 for the second line item, and so on. As a result, this variable is 0 when the application starts, increased by 1 as each line item is added, and reset to zero when an invoice is accepted or canceled.

At the start of the Load event handler for the form, you should notice that the wiring for the SelectedIndexChanged event of the Terms combo box is removed so the event handler for this event isn't executed when the combo box is loaded. Then, this wiring is added back at the end of the Load event handler. In practice, you often need to add this type of code to Load event handlers to prevent the unwanted execution of other event handlers.

The rest of the code in the Load event handler starts by loading the Terms and GLAccounts tables and then initializing the combo boxes that are bound to these tables so that no item is selected. In addition, the date that's displayed in the Invoice Date date time picker is set to the current date, and the checked property of this control is set to False. As you'll see, this property is tested later to determine if the user has selected an invoice date. This is necessary because the date that's initially displayed in this control isn't saved to the data table.

Finally, the Load event handler calls the DisableControls procedure. This procedure disables all of the controls on the form except for the toolbar. That way, the user must select a vendor before entering the data for an invoice.

To select a vendor, the user must enter a vendor ID or name pattern into the toolbar and then click the appropriate Find button. If the user enters a vendor ID and clicks the associated Find button, the Click event handler for this button uses the FillByVendorID method of the Vendors table adapter to fill this table with the appropriate row. Then, the Count property of the Vendors table is used to determine if a vendor with the ID the user entered was found. If not, an error message is displayed and the Vendor ID text box in the toolbar is cleared.

The code for the Add Invoice form **Page 1**

```
Imports System.Data.SqlClient
Public Class frmAddInvoice

    Dim invoiceSequence As Integer

    Private Sub frmAddInvoice_Load(ByVal sender As Object,
            ByVal e As System.EventArgs) Handles Me.Load

        RemoveHandler TermsIDComboBox.SelectedIndexChanged,
            AddressOf TermsIDComboBox_SelectedIndexChanged

        ' Initialize the combo boxes and date time picker
        Me.TermsTableAdapter.Fill(Me.PayablesDataSet.Terms)
        TermsIDComboBox.SelectedIndex = -1

        Me.GLAccountsTableAdapter.Fill(Me.PayablesDataSet.GLAccounts)
        AccountNoComboBox.SelectedIndex = -1

        InvoiceDateDateTimePicker.Value = DateTime.Today
        InvoiceDateDateTimePicker.Checked = False

        ' Disable the controls on the form so the user can't enter
        ' any data until a vendor is selected
        Me.DisableControls()

        AddHandler TermsIDComboBox.SelectedIndexChanged,
            AddressOf TermsIDComboBox_SelectedIndexChanged
    End Sub

    Private Sub DisableControls()
        InvoiceNumberTextBox.Enabled = False
        InvoiceDateDateTimePicker.Enabled = False
        TermsIDComboBox.Enabled = False
        AccountNoComboBox.Enabled = False
        DescriptionTextBox.Enabled = False
        AmountTextBox.Enabled = False
        btnAdd.Enabled = False
        btnAccept.Enabled = False
        btnCancel.Enabled = False
    End Sub

    Private Sub FillByVendorIDToolStripButton_Click(
            ByVal sender As System.Object, ByVal e As System.EventArgs) _
            Handles FillByVendorIDToolStripButton.Click

        Try
            ' Load the Vendors table with the selected vendor
            Dim vendorID As Integer =
                Convert.ToInt32(VendorIDToolStripTextBox.Text)
            Me.VendorsTableAdapter.FillByVendorID(
                Me.PayablesDataSet.Vendors, vendorID)

            If Me.PayablesDataSet.Vendors.Count = 0 Then
                MessageBox.Show("No vendor found with ID " & vendorID & ".",
                                "Vendor Not Found")
                VendorIDToolStripTextBox.Text = ""
```

Figure 5-17 The code for the Add Invoice form (part 1 of 7)

If the vendor is found, the event handler calls the EnableControls procedure to enable the form controls so the user can enter the invoice data. Then, it executes the CancelEdit method of the Invoices binding source to cancel any edit operation. This is necessary because a new invoice row is added later in this event handler. Then, if the user selects a different vendor without adding or canceling the invoice, this code must cancel the current edit before it adds another new row.

Similarly, the next statement removes any rows that may have been added to the line items data grid. To do that, it uses a For statement that loops through the rows in the grid. Notice that to get the number of rows in the grid, this statement uses the Count property of the Rows collection of the grid. Also notice that the loop moves from the last row in the data grid to the first. That's because if you removed the rows from first to last, the second row would become the first row when the first row was deleted and this loop wouldn't work correctly.

After the invoice is cancelled and the data grid is cleared, the Click event handler executes the AddNew method of the Invoices binding source to add a new invoice row. Then, it sets the value of the Vendor ID text box. This is necessary because this text box isn't bound to the VendorID column of the Vendors table. Instead, it's bound to the VendorID column of the Invoices table. That way, when an invoice is accepted, the value of the VendorID column can be taken from this control.

Next, this event handler sets the value of the Invoice Date date time picker to the current date and sets the Checked property to False. This is necessary because if the user has changed the date, the date won't be reset if a new vendor is selected.

The last group of statements in this event handler initializes the two combo boxes on the form. To do that, the GetDefaultTermsID and GetDefaultAccountNo queries are used to get the default terms ID and account number for the selected vendor. Then, these values are used to select the appropriate items in the combo boxes.

The code for the Add Invoice form **Page 2**

```
        Else
            ' Enable the form controls so the user can enter the invoice
            Me.EnableControls()

            ' Remove the new invoice row that was added if a vendor
            ' was previously selected
            Me.InvoicesBindingSource.CancelEdit()

            ' Remove any line items that have been added
            For i As Integer = InvoiceLineItemsDataGridView.Rows.Count - 1 _
                    To 0 Step -1
                InvoiceLineItemsDataGridView.Rows.RemoveAt(i)
            Next

            ' Add a new row to the Invoices table
            Me.InvoicesBindingSource.AddNew()

            VendorIDTextBox.Text = vendorID.ToString

            ' Initialize the invoice date to the current date
            InvoiceDateDateTimePicker.Value = DateTime.Today
            InvoiceDateDateTimePicker.Checked = False

            ' Get the vendor defaults and initialize the combo boxes
            Dim defaultTermsID As Integer =
                CInt(Me.VendorsTableAdapter.GetDefaultTermsID(vendorID))
            TermsIDComboBox.SelectedValue = defaultTermsID

            Dim defaultAccountNo As Integer =
                CInt(Me.VendorsTableAdapter.GetDefaultAccountNo(vendorID))
            AccountNoComboBox.SelectedValue = defaultAccountNo

            InvoiceNumberTextBox.Select()
        End If

    Catch ex As FormatException
        MessageBox.Show("Vendor ID must be an integer.", "Entry Error")
        VendorIDToolStripTextBox.Select()
    Catch ex As SqlException
        MessageBox.Show("Database error # " & ex.Number &
            ": " & ex.Message, ex.GetType.ToString)
    End Try
End Sub

Private Sub EnableControls()
    InvoiceNumberTextBox.Enabled = True
    InvoiceDateDateTimePicker.Enabled = True
    TermsIDComboBox.Enabled = True
    AccountNoComboBox.Enabled = True
    DescriptionTextBox.Enabled = True
    AmountTextBox.Enabled = True
    btnAdd.Enabled = True
    btnAccept.Enabled = True
    btnCancel.Enabled = True
End Sub
```

Figure 5-17 The code for the Add Invoice form (part 2 of 7)

The event handler for the SelectedIndexChanged event of the TermsID combo box is executed when the item that's selected in the box changes. This event handler calls the CalculateDueDate procedure, which uses the GetDueDays query of the Terms table adapter to get the due days for the selected terms. Then, it calculates the due date by adding the due days to the invoice date, and it displays the due date on the form.

If the user enters a name pattern in the toolbar and clicks the associated Find button, the Click event handler for this button displays the Select Vendor form as a dialog box so the user can select the vendor from those that match the pattern. This name pattern is passed to the Select Vendor form using its Tag property. Then, if the user selects a vendor, the vendor ID is retrieved from the Tag property. Finally, the Click event handler for the Find button associated with the Vendor ID text box is executed to get the selected vendor. Note that for this to work, the ID of the selected vendor must first be assigned to the Vendor ID text box. That's because the Click event handler uses the value in this text box in the methods it executes.

The next event handler is executed if the user changes the value of the invoice date. This event handler calls the CalculateDueDate procedure to recalculate the due date based on the new invoice date. Before it does that, though, it checks the Vendor ID text box to see if it contains a value. That's because the value of a date time picker control is set to the current date by default. And when that happens, the ValueChanged event is fired. But you don't want the code in the event handler for this event to be executed until after the user has selected a vendor.

The code for the Add Invoice form

Page 3

```
Private Sub TermsIDComboBox_SelectedIndexChanged(
        ByVal sender As System.Object, ByVal e As System.EventArgs) _
        Handles TermsIDComboBox.SelectedIndexChanged
    Me.CalculateDueDate()
End Sub

Private Sub CalculateDueDate()
    Dim termsID As Integer = CInt(TermsIDComboBox.SelectedValue)
    Dim dueDays As Integer = CInt(Me.TermsTableAdapter.GetDueDays(termsID))
    Dim invoiceDate As Date = InvoiceDateDateTimePicker.Value
    Dim dueDate As Date = invoiceDate.AddDays(dueDays)
    DueDateTextBox.Text = dueDate.ToShortDateString
End Sub

Private Sub FillByNameToolStripButton_Click(
        ByVal sender As System.Object, ByVal e As System.EventArgs) _
        Handles FillByNameToolStripButton.Click

    Try
        ' Create a search string for the name
        Dim name As String = NameToolStripTextBox.Text & "%"

        ' Display the Select Vendor form
        Dim selectVendorForm As New frmSelectVendor
        selectVendorForm.Tag = name
        Dim result As DialogResult = selectVendorForm.ShowDialog

        If result = Windows.Forms.DialogResult.OK Then
            ' Get the ID of the selected vendor
            Dim vendorID As Integer = CInt(selectVendorForm.Tag)

            If vendorID = -1 Then ' No rows matched the search string
                MessageBox.Show("No vendors were found with that name. " &
                    "Please try again.", "No Vendors Found")
                NameToolStripTextBox.Select()
            Else
                ' Fill the dataset with the vendor row
                VendorIDToolStripTextBox.Text = vendorID.ToString
                FillByVendorIDToolStripButton.PerformClick()
                NameToolStripTextBox.Text = ""
            End If
        End If

    Catch ex As Exception
        MessageBox.Show(ex.Message, ex.GetType.ToString)
    End Try
End Sub

Private Sub InvoiceDateDateTimePicker_ValueChanged(
        ByVal sender As System.Object, ByVal e As System.EventArgs) _
        Handles InvoiceDateDateTimePicker.ValueChanged
    If VendorIDTextBox.Text <> "" Then
        Me.CalculateDueDate()
    End If
End Sub
```

Figure 5-17 The code for the Add Invoice form (part 3 of 7)

When the user enters the data for a line item and clicks the Add button, the Click event handler for this button starts by calling the IsValidLineItem procedure. This procedure checks that the user has entered a description and an amount and that the amount is a decimal value. To do that, it uses the IsPresent and IsDecimal procedures on the next page.

If the data is valid, this event handler continues by executing the AddNew method of the InvoiceLineItems binding source to add a new row to the InvoiceLineItems table, which also adds a row to the data grid. Then, it gets the new row from the grid and sets the values of its cells. Notice that the value of the cell that contains the InvoiceID (cell 0, which isn't visible) is set to 1. That's because a value must be assigned to this cell before the row can be added to the table, but the actual value will be taken from the value that's generated by the database when the invoice is inserted. For this reason, a temporary value of 1 is assigned to this cell.

After the values of all the cells in the row are set, the EndEdit method of the binding source is executed to save the row to the dataset. Then, the GetInvoiceTotal procedure is called. This procedure loops through the rows in the data grid to accumulate the invoice total and then displays the total on the form. Finally, the Description and Amount text boxes are cleared and the focus is moved to the Description text box to prepare for the next entry.

The code for the Add Invoice form

Page 4

```
Private Sub btnAdd_Click(ByVal sender As System.Object,
        ByVal e As System.EventArgs) Handles btnAdd.Click

    ' Check that the line item data is valid
    If IsValidLineItem() Then

        ' Add a new row to the InvoiceLineItems table
        InvoiceLineItemsBindingSource.AddNew()

        ' Set the values of the row in the data grid
        Dim rowIndex As Integer =
            InvoiceLineItemsDataGridView.Rows.Count - 1
        Dim row As DataGridViewRow =
            InvoiceLineItemsDataGridView.Rows(rowIndex)
        Dim cell As DataGridViewCell
        cell = row.Cells(0)
        cell.Value = 1
        invoiceSequence += 1
        cell = row.Cells(1)
        cell.Value = invoiceSequence
        cell = row.Cells(2)
        cell.Value = AccountNoComboBox.SelectedValue
        cell = row.Cells(3)
        cell.Value = AccountNoComboBox.Text
        cell = row.Cells(4)
        cell.Value = DescriptionTextBox.Text
        cell = row.Cells(5)
        cell.Value = AmountTextBox.Text

        ' Save the line item to the table
        InvoiceLineItemsBindingSource.EndEdit()

        ' Calculate the invoice total
        Me.GetInvoiceTotal()

        ' Prepare for the next entry
        DescriptionTextBox.Text = ""
        AmountTextBox.Text = ""
        DescriptionTextBox.Select()
    End If
End Sub

Private Function IsValidLineItem() As Boolean
    If IsPresent(DescriptionTextBox, "Description") AndAlso
       IsPresent(AmountTextBox, "Amount") AndAlso
       IsDecimal(AmountTextBox, "Amount") Then
        Return True
    Else
        Return False
    End If
End Function
```

Figure 5-17 The code for the Add Invoice form (part 4 of 7)

If the user clicks a cell in the data grid, the event handler for the CellContentClick event is executed. This event handler starts by checking if the column index of the column that was clicked is equal to 6, which means that the user clicked the Delete button. In that case, the event handler removes the row from the grid. In addition, it resets the sequence number for each line item so that the numbers are in sequence. For example, if the grid has two line items and the first line item is deleted, this code changes the sequence number for the second line item, which is now the first line item, to 1. Last, this event handler recalculates the invoice total and moves the focus to the Description text box.

If the user clicks the Accept Invoice button, the Click event handler for this button starts by calling the IsValidInvoice procedure to be sure that the user has entered an invoice number, selected an invoice date, and added at least one line item. If so, the event handler continues by executing the EndEdit method of the Invoices binding source to save the invoice to the dataset. Then, it adds the invoice to the database using the Update method of the Invoices table adapter.

Note that I couldn't use a table adapter manager to add both the invoice and line item rows at the same time. That's because before the line items can be added, the value of the InvoiceID column must be set. But this value isn't generated until the invoice is added to the database. So I had to add the invoice first and then get the generated invoice ID.

To get the value that was generated for the InvoiceID column, this event handler uses the GetLastIdentityValue query. Then, it assigns this value to the InvoiceID column of each line item, and it updates the InvoiceLineItems table using the Update method of the InvoiceLineItems table adapter.

The next three statements clear the Vendors, Invoices, and InvoiceLineItems tables. These tables must be cleared so that no data is displayed in the bound controls. Note that these operations are performed directly on the dataset. That's because, if you remove them using the binding source, they'll be marked as deleted in the dataset and not actually removed. Then, when the Update method is executed for the Invoices and InvoiceLineItems tables, it will try to delete the existing rows from the database and an error will occur.

The last three statements in this event handler prepare the form for the next entry. The first statement resets the value of the variable that holds the invoice sequence to zero. The second statement calls a procedure named ClearControls, which initializes some of the controls on the form. And the third statement calls the DisableControls procedure so the user must select another vendor before entering the next invoice.

The next event handler for this form is executed when the user clicks the Cancel Invoice button. This event handler starts by cancelling the edit operation on the Invoices table. Then, it clears the Vendors and InvoiceLineItems rows from the dataset. Finally, it prepares the form for another entry.

The final event handler is executed when the user closes the form. This event handler calls the PerformClick method of the Cancel Invoice button, so this has the same effect as if the user had physically clicked the button. Without this line of code, an error will occur if the user closes the form while a vendor's details are displayed, but a new invoice hasn't been added.

The code for the Add Invoice form Page 5

```
Private Function IsPresent(ByVal textBox As TextBox,
        ByVal name As String) As Boolean
    If textBox.Text = "" Then
        MessageBox.Show(name & " is a required field.", "Entry Error")
        textBox.Select()
        Return False
    Else
        Return True
    End If
End Function

Private Function IsDecimal(ByVal textbox As TextBox,
        ByVal name As String) As Boolean
    Try
        Convert.ToDecimal(textbox.Text)
        Return True
    Catch ex As FormatException
        MessageBox.Show(name & " must be a decimal value.", "Entry Error")
        textbox.Select()
        textbox.SelectAll()
        Return False
    End Try
End Function

Private Sub GetInvoiceTotal()
    Dim cell As DataGridViewCell
    Dim amount As Decimal
    Dim invoiceTotal As Decimal
    For Each row As DataGridViewRow In InvoiceLineItemsDataGridView.Rows
        cell = row.Cells(5)
        amount = CDec(cell.Value)
        invoiceTotal += amount
    Next
    InvoiceTotalTextBox.Text = FormatCurrency(invoiceTotal)
End Sub

Private Sub InvoiceLineItemsDataGridView_CellContentClick(
        ByVal sender As System.Object,
        ByVal e As System.Windows.Forms.DataGridViewCellEventArgs) _
        Handles InvoiceLineItemsDataGridView.CellContentClick

    If e.ColumnIndex = 6 Then

        ' Remove the line item when the user clicks the Delete button
        InvoiceLineItemsDataGridView.Rows.RemoveAt(e.RowIndex)

        ' Reset the invoice sequence for all line items
        Dim cell As DataGridViewCell
        Dim row As DataGridViewRow
        For i As Integer = 1 To InvoiceLineItemsDataGridView.Rows.Count
            row = InvoiceLineItemsDataGridView.Rows(i - 1)
            cell = row.Cells(1)
            invoiceSequence = i
            cell.Value = invoiceSequence
        Next
```

Figure 5-17 The code for the Add Invoice form (part 5 of 7)

The code for the Add Invoice form **Page 6**

```
            Me.GetInvoiceTotal()
            DescriptionTextBox.Select()
        End If
    End Sub

    Private Sub btnAccept_Click(ByVal sender As System.Object,
            ByVal e As System.EventArgs) Handles btnAccept.Click

        If IsValidInvoice() Then
            Try
                ' Save the invoice to the Invoices data table
                InvoicesBindingSource.EndEdit()

                ' Update the Invoices table
                InvoicesTableAdapter.Update(Me.PayablesDataSet.Invoices)

                ' Get the generated invoice ID
                Dim invoiceID As Integer =
                    CInt(InvoicesTableAdapter.GetLastIdentityValue)

                ' Set the final invoice ID for all line items
                Dim cell As DataGridViewCell
                For Each row As DataGridViewRow
                        In InvoiceLineItemsDataGridView.Rows
                    cell = row.Cells(0)
                    cell.Value = invoiceID
                Next

                ' Update the InvoiceLineItems table
                InvoiceLineItemsTableAdapter.Update(
                    Me.PayablesDataSet.InvoiceLineItems)

                ' Clear the data tables
                Me.PayablesDataSet.Vendors.Rows.Clear()
                Me.PayablesDataSet.Invoices.Rows.Clear()
                Me.PayablesDataSet.InvoiceLineItems.Rows.Clear()

                ' Prepare the form for another entry
                invoiceSequence = 0
                Me.ClearControls()
                Me.DisableControls()

            Catch ex As ConstraintException
                MessageBox.Show("A constraint violation has occurred. " &
                    "The row was not added.", "Constraint Error")
            Catch ex As DataException
                MessageBox.Show(ex.Message, ex.GetType.ToString)
            Catch ex As SqlException
                MessageBox.Show("Database error # " & ex.Number &
                    ": " & ex.Message, ex.GetType.ToString)
            End Try
        End If
    End Sub
```

Figure 5-17 The code for the Add Invoice form (part 6 of 7)

The code for the Add Invoice form — Page 7

```
    Private Function IsValidInvoice() As Boolean
        If IsPresent(InvoiceNumberTextBox, "Invoice Number") Then
            If InvoiceDateDateTimePicker.Checked = True Then
                If InvoiceLineItemsDataGridView.Rows.Count > 0 Then
                    Return True
                Else
                    MessageBox.Show("You must enter at least one line item.",
                        "Entry Error")
                    DescriptionTextBox.Select()
                    Return False
                End If
            Else
                MessageBox.Show("You must select an invoice date.",
                    "Entry Error")
                InvoiceDateDateTimePicker.Select()
                Return False
            End If
        Else
            Return False
        End If
    End Function

    Private Sub ClearControls()
        VendorIDToolStripTextBox.Text = ""
        VendorIDTextBox.Text = ""
        InvoiceDateDateTimePicker.Value = DateTime.Today
        InvoiceDateDateTimePicker.Checked = False
        TermsIDComboBox.SelectedIndex = -1
        DueDateTextBox.Text = ""
        AccountNoComboBox.SelectedIndex = -1
    End Sub

    Private Sub btnCancel_Click(ByVal sender As System.Object,
            ByVal e As System.EventArgs) Handles btnCancel.Click

        ' Cancel the current edit operation
        InvoicesBindingSource.CancelEdit()

        ' Clear the data tables
        Me.PayablesDataSet.Vendors.Rows.Clear()
        Me.PayablesDataSet.InvoiceLineItems.Rows.Clear()

        ' Prepare the form for another entry
        invoiceSequence = 0
        Me.ClearControls()
        Me.DisableControls()
    End Sub

    Private Sub frmAddInvoice_FormClosing(ByVal sender As Object,
        ByVal e As System.Windows.Forms.FormClosingEventArgs) _
            Handles Me.FormClosing
        btnCancel.PerformClick()
    End Sub
End Class
```

Figure 5-17 The code for the Add Invoice form (part 7 of 7)

The code for the Select Vendor form

Figure 5-18 presents the code for the Select Vendor form. The Load event handler for this form starts by getting the name pattern that was assigned to the Tag property of the form. Then, it uses the FillByVendorName query of the Vendors table adapter to retrieve all the vendors whose names match that pattern. If no names match the pattern, a value of -1 is assigned to the Tag property of the form and the DialogResult property of the form is set to DialogResult.OK, which closes the form.

If one or more vendor names match the pattern, the user can double-click in the DataGridView control to select a vendor. Then, the CellDoubleClick event handler gets the index of the selected row, and that index is passed to the GetVendorID function. This function gets the vendor ID from that row, which is then assigned to the Tag property of the form. Finally, the DialogResult property of the form is set to DialogResult.OK.

The GetVendorID function starts by using the index of the selected row to retrieve the row from the DataGridView control. Next, it gets the cell at index zero, which is the cell that contains the vendor ID. Then, it gets the value of this cell and returns this value.

If the user selects a row in the DataGridView control and clicks the OK button, the Click event handler uses the CurrentCell property of the grid and the RowIndex property of the cell to get the index of the selected row. Then, it calls the GetVendorID function to get the vendor ID from the row, it assigns that value to the Tag property of the form, and it sets the DialogResult property of the form to DialogResult.OK.

The code for the Select Vendor form

```
Public Class frmSelectVendor

    Private Sub frmSelectVendor_Load(ByVal sender As System.Object,
            ByVal e As System.EventArgs) Handles MyBase.Load

        ' Get the vendor rows that match the search string
        Dim name As String = Me.Tag.ToString
        Me.VendorsTableAdapter.FillByVendorName(
            Me.PayablesDataSet.Vendors, name)

        If VendorsDataGridView.Rows.Count = 0 Then
            ' No rows matched the search string
            Me.Tag = -1
            Me.DialogResult = Windows.Forms.DialogResult.OK
            Me.Close()
        End If
    End Sub

    Private Sub VendorsDataGridView_CellDoubleClick(
            ByVal sender As System.Object,
            ByVal e As System.Windows.Forms.DataGridViewCellEventArgs) _
            Handles VendorsDataGridView.CellDoubleClick
        Dim rowIndex As Integer = e.RowIndex
        Me.Tag = Me.GetVendorID(rowIndex)
        Me.DialogResult = Windows.Forms.DialogResult.OK
        Me.Close()
    End Sub

    Private Function GetVendorID(ByVal rowIndex As Integer) As Integer
        Dim row As DataGridViewRow = VendorsDataGridView.Rows(rowIndex)
        Dim cell As DataGridViewCell = row.Cells(0)
        Dim vendorID As Integer = CInt(cell.Value)
        Return vendorID
    End Function

    Private Sub btnOK_Click(ByVal sender As System.Object,
            ByVal e As System.EventArgs) Handles btnOK.Click
        Dim rowIndex As Integer = VendorsDataGridView.CurrentCell.RowIndex
        Me.Tag = Me.GetVendorID(rowIndex)
        Me.DialogResult = Windows.Forms.DialogResult.OK
        Me.Close()
    End Sub

    Private Sub btnCancel_Click(ByVal sender As System.Object,
            ByVal e As System.EventArgs) Handles btnCancel.Click
        Me.Close()
    End Sub

End Class
```

Figure 5-18 The code for the Select Vendor form

Perspective

Now that you've completed this chapter, you should be able to use data sources, datasets, and bound controls to develop serious applications. And yet, you should also have a good feel for why you may not want to use this development technique as your applications get more complicated. In particular, you should realize that using bound controls limits the control you have over the operations that an application performs.

One alternative is to develop three-layer applications, and you'll learn how to do that in the five chapters of the next section. When you use that development technique, you have complete control over how your applications work. You can use the code in the database and business classes in more than one application. And your applications are often easier to debug and maintain.

In most companies, of course, there's a place for both development techniques. When you need to develop a "quick-and-dirty" application or prototype the user interface for a larger application, using data sources and datasets is often the best approach. But when you need to develop a sophisticated production application, using a three-layer approach usually makes sense. As a result, most developers need to learn both approaches to application development.

Beyond that, you have other alternatives for working with datasets and bound controls. First, you can use LINQ as described in chapter 17. Second, you can use the Entity Framework as described in chapter 18. As you'll see in those chapters, each of these techniques has advantages and disadvantages.

Terms

aggregate function
diagram pane
grid pane
SQL pane
results pane
edit mode

Exercise 5-1 Build the Invoice Entry application

For this exercise, you'll build the application that's presented in figure 5-14 from scratch. That will give you a good feel for the strengths and limitations of using data sources and datasets. As you develop this application, you can of course refer to the documentation that's presented in figures 5-15 through 5-17. But even with that, it could take you two hours or more to build this application.

Before you start this application, you may want to run the book application that you've downloaded from our web site, which should be in your Book applications\Chapter 05 directory. That way, you'll have a better understanding of how this application works.

Development guidelines

- Use the Dataset Designer to create the dataset class for this application as shown in figure 5-9, and use the Server Explorer to add tables to the dataset as shown in figure 5-10.
- Like any form, you should build the Add Invoice form from the top down with the data for one table at a time: (1) the controls that present the vendor data; (2) the controls that get the data for a new invoice; (3) the controls that get the data for a line item; and (4) the DataGridView control that presents the line items that have been entered for the current invoice.
- For each portion of the form, you can: (1) use the Server Explorer to add the required data table to the dataset; (2) drag the table or columns from the Data Sources window onto the form; (3) use the Dataset Designer to add the required queries; (4) use the Form Designer to set the required properties and make the required adjustments to the form; and (5) add the event handlers and modify the generated code as needed.
- Since the Select Vendor form just provides another way to get the data for a specific vendor, you can build this form and write the related code any time after you get the FillByVendorID portion of the Add Invoice form working right.
- As you build the application, you don't need to set all the properties right or add all the code for error handling. You just need to set the properties and add the code that affects the way the application works. Once you get the application working right, you can add those finishing touches.

Development notes

- If you have any trouble figuring out how to do something, you can open the book application and see how it does it. In fact, you may want to open this application in a separate instance of Visual Studio. Then, you can switch back and forth between your application and the book application whenever you want to.
- If you make a mistake as you're building the application, you can often undo it by clicking the Undo button or pressing Ctrl+Z. That's often better than trying to fix your mistake.
- To display the check box in a DateTimePicker control like the Invoice Date control, set the ShowCheckBox property to True. This box is automatically checked when a user selects a date, so you can use the Checked property of the control to determine whether the user has selected a date.
- When you create the InvoiceLineItems data table, be sure to configure it so the table isn't refreshed after an insert operation. Then, you can use the technique described in figure 5-8 to edit the Select statement for the main query so it includes the Description column from the GLAccounts table. When you accept this query, be sure to click the No button in the dialog box that's displayed so that the Insert, Update, and Delete statements that are generated from the main query aren't modified based on the change you made.

Section 3

Three-layer Windows Forms applications

In section 2, you learned how to use data sources, datasets, and the Dataset Designer to build Windows Forms applications. Now, you'll learn a completely different way to develop Windows Forms applications.

In this section, you'll learn how to develop three-layer applications that consist of presentation, business, and database classes. When you use this approach to application development, you write Visual Basic code to do everything. As a result, you have complete control over the way your applications work, but you write a lot more code.

One of the benefits of this approach is that you are often able to use the code in your business and database classes for more than one application. Another benefit is that your applications are usually easier to test, debug, and maintain. For these reasons, this development approach is commonly used for serious production applications.

6

How to work with connections, commands, and data readers

In this chapter, you'll learn how to use connections, commands, and data readers for building three-layer applications. Then, you'll see these techniques used in a simple application. When you're done with this chapter, you'll be able to develop simple three-layer applications of your own.

How to create and work with connections and commands

Before you can execute a SQL statement, you must create the command object that will contain it. In addition, you must create the connection object that the command will use to connect to the database.

How to create and work with connections

Figure 6-1 shows how you create and work with a connection for a SQL Server database. As you can see from the syntax at the top of this figure, you can specify a connection string when you create the connection. If you do, this string is assigned to the ConnectionString property. Otherwise, you have to assign a value to this property after you create the connection object. This is illustrated by the first two examples in this figure.

The first example also shows how you can use the Open and Close methods to open and close a connection. Note, though, that instead of using the Close method to close a connection, you can use the Dispose method. This method closes the connection and releases all of the resources used by the connection, which means that you can no longer use the connection. Because of that, you'll want to use Dispose only when you no longer need to use a connection.

This figure also shows some of the common values that you specify in a connection string. For a SQL Server database, you typically specify the name of the server where the database resides, the name of the database, and the type of security to be used. You can also specify the additional values shown in this figure, as well as others. For more information on these values, see the Visual Studio documentation.

To create a connection for an OLE DB provider, you use code similar to that shown in this figure. The main difference is the information that you provide for the connection string. The connection string for a Jet (Access) OLE DB provider, for example, is shown in the last example in this figure. Because the requirements for each provider differ, you may need to consult the documentation for that provider to determine what values to specify.

Before I go on, you should realize that the connection strings for production applications are frequently stored in configuration files outside the application. That way, they can be accessed by any application that needs them, and they can be modified without having to modify each application that uses them. For example, you'll see an application that uses a connection string that's stored in an XML file in chapter 10.

Two constructors for the SqlConnection class

```
New SqlConnection()
New SqlConnection(connectionString)
```

Common properties and methods of the SqlConnection class

Property	Description
`ConnectionString`	Provides information for accessing a SQL Server database.
Method	**Description**
`Open()`	Opens the connection using the specified connection string.
`Close()`	Closes the connection.
`Dispose()`	Releases all resources used by the connection.

Common values used in the ConnectionString property

Name	Description
Data Source/Server	The name of the instance of SQL Server you want to connect to.
Initial Catalog/Database	The name of the database you want to access.
Integrated Security	Determines whether the connection is secure. Valid values are True, False, and SSPI. SSPI uses Windows integrated security and is equivalent to True.
User ID	The user ID that's used to log in to SQL Server.
Password/Pwd	The password that's used to log in to SQL Server.
Persist Security Info	A Boolean value that determines whether sensitive information, such as the password, is returned as part of the connection. The default is False.
Workstation ID	The name of the workstation that's connecting to SQL Server.

Code that creates, opens, and closes a SQL connection

```
Dim connectionString As String =
    "Data Source=localhost\sqlexpress;Initial Catalog=Payables;" &
    "Integrated Security=True"
Dim connection As New SqlConnection()
connection.ConnectionString = connectionString
connection.Open()
...
connection.Close()
```

Another way to create a SqlConnection object

```
Dim connection As New SqlConnection(connectionString)
```

A connection string for the Jet OLE DB provider

```
Provider=Microsoft.Jet.OLEDB.4.0;Data Source=C:\Databases\Payables.mdb
```

Description

- You can set the ConnectionString property after you create a connection or as you create it by passing the string to the constructor of the connection class.
- The values you specify for the ConnectionString property depend on the type of database you're connecting to.

Figure 6-1 How to create and work with connections

How to create a connection string using the SqlConnectionStringBuilder class

Figure 6-2 presents another technique you can use to create a connection string. This technique uses the SqlConnectionStringBuilder class. If you review the properties of this class in this figure, you'll see that, except for the ConnectionString property, they correspond with the values that you can include in a connection string.

The first example in this figure illustrates how you can use the SqlConnectionStringBuilder class to build the same connection string you saw in the last figure. The first statement in this example creates the connection string builder. Then, the next three statements set properties that identify the server, the database, and the security to be used to connect to the server.

The second example shows how you use a connection string builder with a connection. To do that, you use the ConnectionString property of the connection string builder to get the connection string it contains. Then, you use that value to assign a connection string to the connection.

Although this may seem like a roundabout way to create a connection string, it has some distinct advantages. First, you don't have to remember all the different values that you can code for a connection string. Instead, you can use IntelliSense to locate the properties you need. In addition, this technique makes it easy to construct connection strings at runtime. If you need to include a user ID and password that the user enters into a form, for example, you can do that easily by assigning the appropriate control properties to the UserID and Password properties of the connection string builder.

How to create a connection in a Using block

Figure 6-2 also shows how to use a Using block to create and dispose of a connection. As you can see, you create the connection as part of the Using statement, and you open the connection within the Using block. Then, when the Using block ends, the Dispose method of the connection is called automatically. This ensures that the resources for the connection are released as soon as it's no longer needed. This is particularly useful for connections that are only needed for a short period of time.

A constructor for the SqlConnectionStringBuilder class

```
New SqlConnectionStringBuilder()
```

Common properties for working with a SqlConnectionStringBuilder

Property	Description
ConnectionString	The connection string associated with the connection string builder.
DataSource	The name of the instance of SQL Server you want to connect to.
InitialCatalog	The name of the database you want to access.
IntegratedSecurity	A Boolean value that indicates if the connection is secure. False indicates that a user ID and password are included in the connection string, and True indicates that Windows integrated security is used.
UserID	The user ID that's used to log in to SQL Server.
Password	The password that's used to log in to SQL Server.
PersistSecurityInfo	A Boolean value that determines whether sensitive information, such as the password, is returned as part of the connection. The default is False.
WorkstationID	The name of the workstation that's connecting to SQL Server.

Code that creates a connection string using a connection string builder

```
Dim builder As New SqlConnectionStringBuilder
builder.DataSource = "localhost\sqlexpress"
builder.InitialCatalog = "Payables"
builder.IntegratedSecurity = True
```

Code that uses the connection string to create a connection

```
Dim connection As New SqlConnection(builder.ConnectionString)
```

Code that creates a connection in a Using block

```
Using connection As New SqlConnection(connectionString)
    connection.Open()
    ...
End Using
```

Description

- The SqlConnectionStringBuilder class provides an easy way to manage the information that's contained in a connection string. This class defines a collection of key/value pairs that correspond with the information that you can include in a connection string.
- You can access the connection values stored in a connection string builder by using its properties as shown above or by specifying the name of a key like this:

  ```
  builder("Data Source") = "localhost\sqlexpress"
  ```
- After you define a connection string builder, you can use its ConnectionString property to access the connection string it defines.
- To be sure that the resources used by a connection are released when you're done using the connection, you can create the connection within a Using block. Then, the resources are released automatically when the Using block ends.

Figure 6-2 Two more techniques for working with connections

How to create and work with commands

After you define the connection to the database, you create the command objects that contain the SQL statements you want to execute against the database. Figure 6-3 shows three constructors for the SqlCommand class. The first one doesn't require arguments. When you use this constructor, you must set the Connection property to the connection to be used by the command, and you must set the CommandText property to the text of the SQL statement before you execute the command. This is illustrated by the first example in this figure.

The second constructor accepts the SQL command text as an argument. Then, you just have to set the Connection property before you execute the command. The third constructor accepts both the connection and the command text as arguments. The second code example in this figure uses this constructor.

Another property you may need to set is the CommandType property. This property determines how the value of the CommandText property is interpreted. The values you can specify for this property are members of the CommandType enumeration that's shown in this figure. The default value is Text, which causes the value of the CommandText property to be interpreted as a SQL statement. If the CommandText property contains the name of a stored procedure, however, you'll need to set this property to StoredProcedure. Finally, if the CommandText property contains the name of a table, you'll need to set this property to TableDirect. Then, all the rows and columns will be retrieved from the table. Note that this setting is available only for the OLE DB data provider.

The last property that's shown in this figure, Parameters, lets you work with the collection of parameters for a command. You'll see how to use this property in the next chapter.

To execute a query that a command contains, you use the Execute methods of the command shown in this figure. To execute a command that returns a result set, you use the ExecuteReader method of the command. In contrast, you use the ExecuteScalar method to execute a query that returns a single value, and you use the ExecuteNonQuery method to execute an action query. You'll learn how to use all three of these methods in the remaining topics of this chapter.

Three constructors for the SqlCommand class

```
New SqlCommand()
New SqlCommand(commandText)
New SqlCommand(commandText, connection)
```

Common properties and methods of the SqlCommand class

Property	Description
`Connection`	The connection used to connect to the database.
`CommandText`	A SQL statement or the name of a stored procedure.
`CommandType`	A member of the CommandType enumeration that determines how the value in the CommandText property is interpreted.
`Parameters`	The collection of parameters for the command (see chapter 7 for details).
Method	**Description**
`ExecuteReader()`	Executes the query identified by the CommandText property and returns the result as a SqlDataReader object.
`ExecuteScalar()`	Executes the query identified by the CommandText property and returns the first column of the first row of the result set.
`ExecuteNonQuery()`	Executes the query identified by the CommandText property and returns an integer that indicates the number of rows that were affected.

CommandType enumeration members

Member	Description
`Text`	The CommandText property contains a SQL statement. This is the default.
`StoredProcedure`	The CommandText property contains the name of a stored procedure.
`TableDirect`	The CommandText property contains the name of a table (OLE DB only).

Code that creates a SqlCommand object that executes a Select statement

```
Dim selectCommand As New SqlCommand()
selectCommand.Connection = connection
Dim selectStatement As String =
    "SELECT VendorID, Name, Address1, Address2, City, State, ZipCode " &
    "FROM Vendors ORDER BY Name"
selectCommand.CommandText = selectStatement
```

Another way to create a SqlCommand object

```
Dim selectCommand As New SqlCommand(selectStatement, connection)
```

Description

- The CommandText and Connection properties are set to the values you pass to the constructor of the command class. If you don't pass these values to the constructor, you must set the CommandText and Connection properties after you create the command object.
- If you set the CommandText property to the name of a stored procedure, you must set the CommandType property to StoredProcedure.

Figure 6-3 How to create and work with commands

How to work with queries that return a result set

When you execute a command object that contains a Select statement, the command object returns the result set in a data reader object. Then, to work with that result set, you use properties and methods of the data reader object. You'll learn how to do that in the topics that follow.

How to create and work with a data reader

Figure 6-4 presents the basic skills for creating and working with a data reader. To create a data reader, you use the ExecuteReader method of a command object that contains a Select statement. Notice that when you execute this method, you can specify a behavior. The behavior you specify must be a member of the CommandBehavior enumeration. Some of the most common members of this enumeration are listed in this figure. You can use these members to simplify your code or to improve the efficiency of your application.

After you create a data reader, you can use the properties and methods shown in this figure to work with it. To retrieve the next row of data in the result set, for example, you use the Read method. Note that you must execute the Read method to retrieve the first row of data. It's not retrieved automatically when the data reader is created.

To access a column in the most recently retrieved row, you use the Item property. Like many of the other objects you've seen previously, the Item property is the default property of a data reader. Because of that, you can omit it.

The code example in this figure illustrates how you use a data reader. First, the connection that's used by the SqlCommand object is opened. Although it's not shown here, this command contains a Select statement that retrieves columns from the States table. Then, the ExecuteReader method of the command is used to retrieve the data and create a data reader that can process the state rows. Because the CloseConnection behavior is included on this method, the connection will be closed automatically when the data reader is closed. The ExecuteReader method also opens the data reader and positions it before the first row in the result set.

Next, a List() object that can hold State objects is created and a Do While statement is used to loop through the rows in the result set. The condition on this statement executes the Read method of the data reader. This works because the Read method returns a Boolean value that indicates whether the result set contains additional rows. As long as this condition is true, the application processes the row that was retrieved. In this case, the application creates a State object for each row and adds it to the List() object. After all of the rows have been processed, the data reader is closed.

Two ways to create a SqlDataReader object

```
sqlCommand.ExecuteReader()
sqlCommand.ExecuteReader(behavior)
```

Common CommandBehavior enumeration members

Member	Description
`CloseConnection`	Closes the connection when the data reader is closed.
`Default`	Equivalent to specifying no command behavior.
`SingleResult`	Only a single result set is returned.
`SingleRow`	Only a single row is returned.

Common properties and methods of the SqlDataReader class

Property	Description
`IsClosed`	Gets a value that indicates if the data reader is closed.
`Item(index)`	Gets the value of the column with the specified name or position in the row.
Method	**Description**
`Close()`	Closes the data reader. If the command executes a stored procedure that includes output parameters or a return value, this method also sets these values.
`NextResult()`	Advances the data reader to the next result set and returns a Boolean value that indicates whether there are additional result sets.
`Read()`	Retrieves the next row and returns a Boolean value that indicates whether there are additional rows.

Code that uses a data reader to populate a list with State objects

```
connection.Open()
Dim reader As SqlDataReader =
    selectCommand.ExecuteReader(CommandBehavior.CloseConnection)
Dim stateList As New List(Of State)
Do While reader.Read()
    Dim state As New State
    state.StateCode = reader("StateCode").ToString
    state.StateName = reader("StateName").ToString
    stateList.Add(state)
Loop
reader.Close()
```

Description

- You must open the connection that's used by the data reader before you execute the ExecuteReader method of the command object.
- The data reader is opened automatically when it's created. While it's open, no other data readers can be opened on the same connection. The exception is if you're using an Oracle data reader, in which case other Oracle data readers can be open at the same time.
- When you first create a data reader, it's positioned before the first row in the result set. To retrieve the first row, you have to execute the Read method.
- You can combine two or more command behavior members using the & operator.

Figure 6-4 How to create and work with a data reader

Although most commands execute a single Select statement and return a single result set, a command can also execute two or more Select statements and return two or more result sets. That way, only one trip is made to the server for all the statements. To combine two or more Select statements, you code a semicolon between them. For example, suppose you want to retrieve vendor, terms, and account information. To do that, you could code three Select statements in a single command like this:

```
SELECT * From Vendors;
SELECT TermsID, Description FROM Terms;
SELECT AccountNo, Description FROM GLAccounts
```

To process the three result sets returned by these statements, you would read the vendor rows in the first result set. Then, you would use the NextResult method to move to the result set that contains the terms, and you would read the rows in that result set. Finally, you would repeat this process for the rows in the third result set.

How to improve the efficiency of column lookups

When you retrieve a column from a data reader using the column name as shown in the previous figure, the data reader has to search for the appropriate column. To make the retrieval operation more efficient, you can specify the position of the column instead of its name. One way to do that is to use a literal value. For example, you can use a statement like this to retrieve the value of the first column in the States data reader:

```
state.StateCode = reader(0).ToString
```

This technique is error prone, though, because you can easily specify the wrong position for a column. In addition, if the columns that are retrieved change, you may have to modify your code to accommodate the new column positions.

An alternative is to use the GetOrdinal method of the data reader to get the position, or *ordinal*, of a column with the specified name. Then, you can assign the result of that method to a variable and use the variable to refer to the column. To understand how this works, take a look at the code example in figure 6-5. Here, the command contains a Select statement that will return a result set with three columns.

After the connection is opened and the ExecuteReader method is executed, the GetOrdinal method is used to get the position of each of the columns. Notice that this method must locate the column using its name just as the code in the previous figure did. In this case, though, the column is looked up by name only once. Then, within the loop that processes the rows in the result set, the columns are accessed by their ordinals.

When you refer to a column using its ordinal, you can also use the other methods listed in this figure. These methods let you specify the type of data that's retrieved. The three columns in the code in this figure, for example, are retrieved using the GetString, GetDateTime, and GetDecimal methods. This can improve the efficiency of the operation by eliminating unnecessary data conversion.

Common methods for improving the efficiency of column lookups

Method	Description
`GetOrdinal(name)`	Gets the position of the column with the specified name. The position is zero-based.
`GetBoolean(position)`	Gets the value of the column at the specified position as a Boolean.
`GetDateTime(position)`	Gets the value of the column at the specified position as a date and time.
`GetDecimal(position)`	Gets the value of the column at the specified position as a decimal.
`GetInt16(position)`	Gets the value of the column at the specified position as a 16-bit signed integer.
`GetInt32(position)`	Gets the value of the column at the specified position as a 32-bit signed integer.
`GetInt64(position)`	Gets the value of the column at the specified position as a 64-bit signed integer.
`GetString(position)`	Gets the value of the column at the specified position as a string.

Code that uses type-specific Get methods and ordinals

```
Dim selectStatement As String =
    "SELECT InvoiceNumber, InvoiceDate, InvoiceTotal " &
    "FROM Invoices " &
    "WHERE InvoiceTotal - PaymentTotal - CreditTotal > 0"
Dim selectCommand As New SqlCommand(selectStatement, connection)
connection.Open()
Dim reader As SqlDataReader = selectCommand.ExecuteReader()
Dim invNoOrd As Integer = reader.GetOrdinal("InvoiceNumber")
Dim invDateOrd As Integer = reader.GetOrdinal("InvoiceDate")
Dim invTotalOrd As Integer = reader.GetOrdinal("InvoiceTotal")
Dim invoiceList As New List(Of Invoice)
Do While reader.Read
    Dim invoice As New Invoice
    invoice.InvoiceNumber = reader.GetString(invNoOrd)
    invoice.InvoiceDate = reader.GetDateTime(invDateOrd)
    invoice.InvoiceTotal = reader.GetDecimal(invTotalOrd)
    invoiceList.Add(invoice)
Loop
reader.Close()
connection.Close()
```

Description

- Instead of retrieving a column by name, you can retrieve it by its position, or *ordinal*, in the row. That improves the efficiency of the retrieval operation because the data reader can retrieve the column directly rather than looking for it by name.
- If you know that the position of a column won't change, you can specify the position as a literal value. Otherwise, you can use the GetOrdinal method to get its position.
- When you use the Item property to get the value of a column, the value is returned with the Object data type. To improve efficiency, you can use one of the type-specific Get methods to retrieve a column value with the appropriate type.

Figure 6-5 How to improve the efficiency of column lookups

An Invoices by Due Date application that uses a data reader

To illustrate how you can use a data reader to work with the data returned by a Select statement, I'll present an application that lists invoices by due date. Although this is a simple application, you'll see that it consists of three classes in addition to the form class. That will help you understand how you can separate the business and database processing from the processing for the user interface.

The user interface

Figure 6-6 presents the design of the Invoices by Due Date form. As you can see, this form includes information for each invoice with a balance due. This information is displayed in a ListView control, which can be used to display a collection of items in one of five different views. This control is a common control that's available from the Toolbox, not a data control.

To display the invoices, I set the View property of the ListView control to Details, which displays the data in a row and column format. In addition, I used the ColumnHeader Collection Editor for the control to specify the column headings and widths shown here. If you aren't familiar with the ListView control, you may want to consult the Visual Studio documentation on this control to learn more about how it works.

The class design

Figure 6-6 also summarizes the classes used by this application. Like all of the applications in this section of the book, this one has a three-layer architecture that consists of presentation, business, and database classes. To refresh your memory about how this works, please refer back to figure 2-11 in chapter 2.

For this application, the business and database classes are stored in a class library named PayablesData. That way, they can be used by other applications that require the data or operations they provide.

The Invoice class is a business class that represents a single invoice. It has six public properties that represent the data from the Invoices table that's used by this application and a method that calculates and returns the unpaid balance of an invoice.

The InvoiceDB and PayablesDB classes are database classes that contain one method each that works directly with the database. The GetInvoicesDue method in the InvoiceDB class returns a List() object that holds one Invoice object for each invoice in the Invoices table with a balance due. The GetConnection method in the PayablesDB class returns a connection to the Payables database.

The Invoices by Due Date form

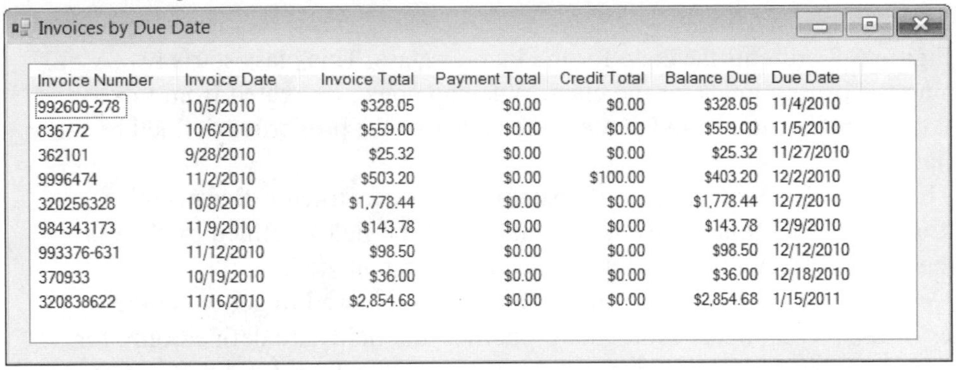

Invoice Number	Invoice Date	Invoice Total	Payment Total	Credit Total	Balance Due	Due Date
992609-278	10/5/2010	$328.05	$0.00	$0.00	$328.05	11/4/2010
836772	10/6/2010	$559.00	$0.00	$0.00	$559.00	11/5/2010
362101	9/28/2010	$25.32	$0.00	$0.00	$25.32	11/27/2010
9996474	11/2/2010	$503.20	$0.00	$100.00	$403.20	12/2/2010
320256328	10/8/2010	$1,778.44	$0.00	$0.00	$1,778.44	12/7/2010
984343173	11/9/2010	$143.78	$0.00	$0.00	$143.78	12/9/2010
993376-631	11/12/2010	$98.50	$0.00	$0.00	$98.50	12/12/2010
370933	10/19/2010	$36.00	$0.00	$0.00	$36.00	12/18/2010
320838622	11/16/2010	$2,854.68	$0.00	$0.00	$2,854.68	1/15/2011

Properties and methods of the Invoice class

Property	Description
`InvoiceNumber`	The invoice number assigned by the vendor.
`InvoiceDate`	The date the invoice was issued.
`InvoiceTotal`	The total amount of the invoice.
`PaymentTotal`	The total payments that have been applied to the invoice.
`CreditTotal`	The total credits that have been applied to the invoice.
`DueDate`	The date the invoice is due.
Method	**Description**
`BalanceDue()`	The unpaid balance of the invoice.

Method of the InvoiceDB class

Method	Description
`GetInvoicesDue()`	Returns a List() object that contains all of the invoices in the Invoices table with unpaid balances.

Method of the PayablesDB class

Method	Description
`GetConnection()`	Returns a SqlConnection object for the Payables database.

Description

- The Invoices by Due Date form uses a ListView control to display a list of all the invoices with a balance due. A data reader is used to retrieve the rows that are displayed.
- To make this work, the View property of the ListView control is set to Details, which causes the data items to be displayed in columns. In addition, the column headers shown above were added using the ColumnHeader Collection Editor.
- The Invoice, InvoiceDB, and PayablesDB classes that are used by this application are stored in a class library named PayablesData.

Figure 6-6 An Invoices by Due Date application that uses a data reader

The code for the Invoice class

Figure 6-7 presents the code for the Invoice class. This class starts by defining the private fields for the class. When an object is created from this class, these fields can be used to store the values of the properties defined by the class.

This class also contains a single parameterless constructor. Because this constructor doesn't contain any statements, all of the fields defined by the class will be assigned default values when the class is instantiated.

Next, this class contains six properties that can be used to get or set the values of the private fields. Note that properties and fields are defined only for the data that's used by the Invoices by Due Date application. I did that just to keep this code as simple as possible. In a production application, however, this class would define properties for all of the columns in the Invoices table. That way, any application that accessed this table could use this class.

The Invoice class also contains one method. This method calculates the balance due for an invoice using the invoice total, payment total, and credit total fields and then returns the value to the calling procedure. If you look back at figure 6-6, you'll see that this is the value that's displayed in the next to last column of the ListView control.

The code for the Invoice class

```
Public Class Invoice
    Private m_InvoiceNumber As String
    Private m_InvoiceDate As Date
    Private m_InvoiceTotal As Decimal
    Private m_PaymentTotal As Decimal
    Private m_CreditTotal As Decimal
    Private m_DueDate As Date

    Public Sub New()

    End Sub

    Public Property InvoiceNumber() As String
        Get
            Return m_InvoiceNumber
        End Get
        Set(ByVal value As String)
            m_InvoiceNumber = value
        End Set
    End Property

    Public Property InvoiceDate() As Date
        Get
            Return m_InvoiceDate
        End Get
        Set(ByVal value As Date)
            m_InvoiceDate = value
        End Set
    End Property

    Public Property InvoiceTotal() As Decimal
        Get
            Return m_InvoiceTotal
        End Get
        Set(ByVal value As Decimal)
            m_InvoiceTotal = value
        End Set
    End Property
    .
    .
    Public Property DueDate() As Date
        Get
            Return m_DueDate
        End Get
        Set(ByVal value As Date)
            m_DueDate = value
        End Set
    End Property

    Public Function BalanceDue() As Decimal
        Return m_InvoiceTotal - m_PaymentTotal - m_CreditTotal
    End Function

End Class
```

Figure 6-7 The code for the Invoice class

The code for the InvoiceDB class

Figure 6-8 presents the code for the InvoiceDB class. This class consists of a single method named GetInvoicesDue that returns a list of Invoice objects. This method starts by creating a new List() object that can hold Invoice objects. Then, it creates a connection by calling the GetConnection method of the PayablesDB class. I'll describe the code for this class in just a minute.

Next, this method defines the Select statement that will be used to retrieve invoices from the Invoices table. Notice that this statement only retrieves invoices with a balance due (InvoiceTotal – PaymentTotal – CreditTotal > 0). In addition, it sorts the invoices by due date.

After it creates the connection and defines the Select statement, this method creates a command object that uses that Select statement and connection. Then, it opens the connection and uses the ExecuteReader method to execute the command. Next, it uses the data reader that's created by the ExecuteReader method to get each invoice that's returned by the Select statement. For each invoice, it creates a new Invoice object and adds it to the invoice list. Then, after all the invoices have been processed, it closes the data reader and the connection and then returns the list of Invoice objects to the calling procedure.

Notice that the statements that open the connection and data reader and process the rows in the data reader are coded within the Try block of a Try…Catch…Finally statement. Then, if a SqlException occurs, the Catch block throws the exception to the calling procedure. Because of that, the procedure that calls this method should catch this exception. Whether or not an exception occurs, the statement that closes the connection is coded within the Finally block. That way, if the statement that opens the connection is successful but the statement that executes the command isn't, the connection is still closed.

The code for the PayablesDB class

Figure 6-8 also presents the code for the PayablesDB class. This class contains a single method named GetConnection that returns a connection to the Payables database. As you've already seen, the InvoiceDB class calls this method to get the connection that's used by the command it executes. Note that the connection string is hard coded into this method. As I explained earlier, however, the connection string for a production application is typically stored in an external configuration file. Then, the GetConnection method would read the connection string from this file. That way, you could change the location of the database without recompiling the application.

At this point, you may be wondering why I coded the GetConnection method in a separate class rather than in the InvoiceDB class. The reason is that this method isn't specific to the Invoices table. Because of that, it can be used to get a connection for any method in any database class in the class library. Although this class library only contains one other database class, a complete class library would probably contain a database class for each table in the database.

The code for the InvoiceDB class

```
Imports System.Data.SqlClient

Public Class InvoiceDB

    Public Shared Function GetInvoicesDue() As List(Of Invoice)
        Dim invoiceList As New List(Of Invoice)
        Dim connection As SqlConnection = PayablesDB.GetConnection
        Dim selectStatement As String =
            "SELECT InvoiceNumber, InvoiceDate, InvoiceTotal, " &
                "PaymentTotal, CreditTotal, DueDate " &
            "FROM Invoices " &
            "WHERE InvoiceTotal - PaymentTotal - CreditTotal > 0 " &
            "ORDER BY DueDate"
        Dim selectCommand As New SqlCommand(selectStatement, connection)
        Try
            connection.Open()
            Dim reader As SqlDataReader = selectCommand.ExecuteReader()
            Dim invoice As Invoice
            Do While reader.Read
                invoice = New Invoice
                invoice.InvoiceNumber = reader("InvoiceNumber").ToString
                invoice.InvoiceDate = CDate(reader("InvoiceDate"))
                invoice.InvoiceTotal = CDec(reader("InvoiceTotal"))
                invoice.PaymentTotal = CDec(reader("PaymentTotal"))
                invoice.CreditTotal = CDec(reader("CreditTotal"))
                invoice.DueDate = CDate(reader("DueDate"))
                invoiceList.Add(invoice)
            Loop
            reader.Close()
        Catch ex As SqlException
            Throw ex
        Finally
            connection.Close()
        End Try
        Return invoiceList
    End Function

End Class
```

The code for the PayablesDB class

```
Imports System.Data.SqlClient

Public Class PayablesDB

    Public Shared Function GetConnection() As SqlConnection
        Dim connectionString As String =
            "Data Source=localhost\sqlexpress;Initial Catalog=Payables;" &
            "Integrated Security=True"
        Return New SqlConnection(connectionString)
    End Function

End Class
```

Figure 6-8 The code for the InvoiceDB and PayablesDB classes

The code for the Invoices by Due Date form

Figure 6-9 presents the code for the Invoices by Due Date form. It is stored in a class named frmInvoicesDue, and this is the presentation class for this application.

To start, this form imports the PayablesData namespace, which is the namespace for the class library that contains the Invoice, InvoiceDB, and PayablesDB classes. For this to work, a reference to the class library must be added to the project that contains the Invoices by Due Date form. To do that, you can use the Project→Add Reference command, and then select the PayablesData project from the Projects tab of the Add Reference dialog box.

The code within the form class provides for populating the ListView control when the form is loaded. To start, it declares a variable that will contain a list of Invoice objects and then assigns the list that's returned by the GetInvoicesDue method of the InvoiceDB class to that list. Because the GetInvoicesDue method can throw a SqlException, this method is coded within the Try block of a Try...Catch statement. Then, if an exception occurs, the Catch block displays an error message and closes the form.

After the invoices are loaded into the invoice list, this code checks to see if the list contains at least one item. If so, it loads the items into the ListView control. Otherwise, it displays a message indicating that all the invoices are paid in full and it closes the form.

To load the invoices into the ListView control, this code uses a For...Next statement that loops through the invoices in the invoice list. For each invoice, it adds the InvoiceNumber property to the list of items in the control. That causes the invoice number to be displayed in the first column of the control. Then, the other properties of each invoice are added as subitems. That causes these values to be displayed in columns following the invoice number.

If you aren't familiar with the ListView control, you may want to consult the Visual Studio documentation on this control to learn more about how it works. In general, though, when its View property is set to Details, it works like any collection of rows that contain columns.

The code for the Invoices by Due Date form

```
Imports PayablesData

Public Class frmInvoicesDue

    Private Sub frmInvoicesDue_Load(ByVal sender As System.Object,
            ByVal e As System.EventArgs) Handles MyBase.Load
        Dim invoiceList As List(Of Invoice)
        Try
            invoiceList = InvoiceDB.GetInvoicesDue
            If invoiceList.Count > 0 Then
                Dim invoice As Invoice
                For i As Integer = 0 To invoiceList.Count - 1
                    invoice = invoiceList(i)
                    lvInvoices.Items.Add(invoice.InvoiceNumber)
                    lvInvoices.Items(i).SubItems.Add(
                        CDate(invoice.InvoiceDate).ToShortDateString)
                    lvInvoices.Items(i).SubItems.Add(
                        FormatCurrency(invoice.InvoiceTotal))
                    lvInvoices.Items(i).SubItems.Add(
                        FormatCurrency(invoice.PaymentTotal))
                    lvInvoices.Items(i).SubItems.Add(
                        FormatCurrency(invoice.CreditTotal))
                    lvInvoices.Items(i).SubItems.Add(
                        FormatCurrency(invoice.BalanceDue))
                    lvInvoices.Items(i).SubItems.Add(
                        CDate(invoice.DueDate).ToShortDateString)
                Next
            Else
                MessageBox.Show("All invoices are paid in full.",
                    "No Balance Due")
                Me.Close()
            End If
        Catch ex As Exception
            MessageBox.Show(ex.Message, ex.GetType.ToString)
            Me.Close()
        End Try
    End Sub

End Class
```

Figure 6-9 The code for the Invoices by Due Date form

How to work with queries that don't return a result set

In addition to executing queries that return result sets, you can use a command to execute queries that return a single value or that perform an action against the database. You'll learn how to work with commands that execute these two types of queries in the last two topics of this chapter. And you'll get a chance to use queries that return scalar values if you do exercise 6-2.

How to execute a query that returns a scalar value

The first code example in figure 6-10 shows you how to execute a command that returns a single value, called a *scalar value*. To do that, you execute the ExecuteScalar method of the command. In this case, the command contains a Select statement that retrieves the total balance due for all the invoices in the Invoices table. This type of summary value is often called an *aggregate value*.

A scalar value can also be the value of a single column, a calculated value, or any other value that can be retrieved from the database. In the Vendor Maintenance application that's presented in the next chapter, for example, you'll see how the ExecuteScalar method is used to retrieve the value of an identity column that's generated for a row that's added to a database.

Since the ExecuteScalar method returns an Object type, you must cast that object to an appropriate data type to get its value. In this example, the object is cast to a Decimal value.

To avoid any confusion, I should make it clear that it is possible to use the ExecuteScalar method with a Select statement that retrieves more than one value. In that case, though, the ExecuteScalar method returns only the first value and the others are discarded.

How to execute an action query

As you know, you can use an Insert, Update, or Delete statement to perform actions against a database. For that reason, these statements are often referred to as *action queries*. To execute an action query, you use the ExecuteNonQuery method of a command as shown in the second code example in figure 6-10.

This example executes a command that contains a Delete statement that will delete all of the invoices in the Invoices table that have a balance due of zero. Notice that the ExecuteNonQuery method returns an integer that indicates the number of rows in the database that were affected by the operation. In this case, the value is used to display a message to the user. In other cases, you can use it to check if the operation was successful.

Code that creates and runs a command that returns an aggregate value

```
Dim selectCommand As New SqlCommand()
selectCommand.Connection = connection
selectCommand.CommandText =
    "SELECT SUM(InvoiceTotal - PaymentTotal - CreditTotal) " &
    "AS BalanceDue FROM Invoices"
connection.Open()
Dim balanceDue As Decimal = CDec(selectCommand.ExecuteScalar)
connection.Close()
```

Code that creates and executes a command that deletes rows

```
Dim deleteCommand As New SqlCommand()
deleteCommand.Connection = connection
deleteCommand.CommandText =
    "DELETE FROM Invoices " &
    "WHERE InvoiceTotal - PaymentTotal - CreditTotal = 0"
Try
    connection.Open()
    Dim rowCount As Integer = deleteCommand.ExecuteNonQuery()
    MessageBox.Show(rowCount & " rows deleted")
Catch ex As SqlException
    MessageBox.Show("SQL Server error # " & ex.Number &
        ": " & ex.Message, ex.GetType.ToString)
Finally
    connection.Close()
End Try
```

How to execute queries that return a single value

- You use the ExecuteScalar method of a command object to retrieve a single value, called a *scalar value*.
- The value that's returned can be the value of a single column and row in the database, a calculated value, an *aggregate value* that summarizes data in the database, or any other value that can be retrieved from the database.
- If the Select statement returns more than one column or row, only the value in the first column and row is retrieved by the ExecuteScalar method.

How to execute action queries

- You use the ExecuteNonQuery method of a command object to execute an Insert, Update, or Delete statement, called an *action query*. This method returns an integer that indicates the number of rows that were affected by the query.
- You can also use the ExecuteNonQuery method to execute statements that affect the structure of a database object. For more information, see the documentation for your database management system.

Figure 6-10 How to execute queries that don't return a result set

Perspective

In this chapter, you learned the essential skills for working with commands and data readers in a three-layer application. When you work this way, your code has to handle all of the functions that are dealt with automatically by the table adapter and table adapter manager when you use data sources and datasets. This means that you have to write more code, but it also means that you have complete control over how the data is processed.

Terms

ordinal
scalar value
aggregate value
action query

Exercise 6-1 Review the Invoices by Due Date application

In this exercise, you'll review the Invoices by Due Date application that's presented in this chapter. That will give you a better idea of how it works.

1. Open the DisplayInvoicesDue application that's in your Chapter 6 directory.
2. In the Solution Explorer, notice that this solution includes two projects: DisplayInvoicesDue and PayablesData. Then, expand the PayablesData project to see that it contains the business and database classes that are used by this application: Invoice, InvoiceDB, and PayablesDB.
3. Double-click on any one of the classes in the PayablesData project to review its code.
4. Display the code for the Invoices by Due Date form (frmInvoicesDue) and note the Imports statement at the top of the file. For this to work, the application must include a reference to the PayablesData project.
5. To see the required reference, expand the References folder for the project in the Solution Explorer. If you don't see this folder, select the project and then click the Show All Files button at the top of the Solution Explorer window.
6. Run the application to see how it works. Then, when you're done experimenting, close the application.

Exercise 6-2 Enhance the Invoices by Due Date application

In this exercise, you'll enhance the Invoices by Due Date application. This will give you a chance to work with commands that return scalar values. When you're done, the form for the application should look like this:

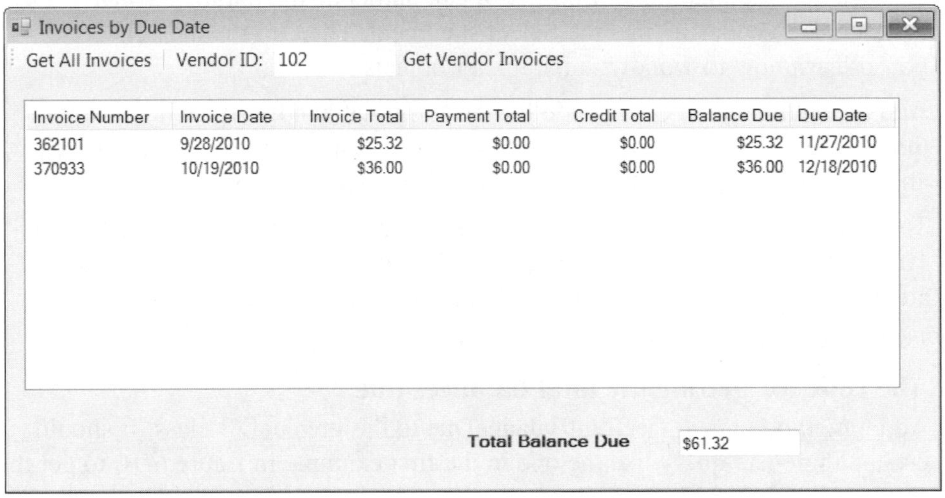

Enhance the interface

1. Open the DisplayInvoicesDue application in your Chapter 6 directory.
2. Add a ToolStrip control to the top of the Invoices by Date Due form and add the buttons, separators, label, and text box shown above to it. Then, set the properties for these controls.
3. Add a label and text box below the ListView control as shown above. Then, set the properties for these controls.
4. Modify the code for the form so it displays the unpaid invoices for all vendors when the user clicks on the Get All Invoices button in the toolbar instead of when the form is loaded. To do that, you just need to move the code from the Load event handler to the Click event handler for the Get All Invoices button. Or, if you prefer, you can copy the code from the Load event handler to the Click event handler and then comment out the code for the Load event handler.
5. Test this modification to see how it works.

Add the code for getting the invoices for a single vendor

6. Add a method named GetVendorInvoicesDue to the InvoiceDB class that gets the unpaid invoices for a single vendor. This method should have one parameter that accepts a vendor ID as an Integer, and it should return a list of Invoice objects that represent the unpaid invoices for that vendor ID. The easiest way to code this method is to copy and modify the code for the GetInvoicesDue method. For now, you can hardcode the parameter that contains the vender ID into the Select statement. Then, in the next chapter, you'll learn how to work with parameter objects.
7. Add an event handler to the code for the form that handles the Click event of the Get Vendor Invoices toolbar button. The easiest way to do that is to copy and modify the code for the Click event of the Get All Invoices button.
8. Test and debug this enhancement until it works right. Try vendor IDs 99 and 102, and make sure the ListView control is cleared before any invoices are added to it. To do that, you can use this command:

   ```
   lvInvoices.Items.Clear()
   ```

Add the code for getting the total balances due

9. Add a method named GetTotalBalanceDue to the InvoiceDB class. It should use an aggregate query like the one in the first example in figure 6-10 to get the sum of all the unpaid invoices.
10. Add a method named GetVendorBalanceDue to the InvoiceDB class. It should have one parameter that receives a vendor ID, and it should get the sum of all of the unpaid invoices for that vendor. Again, you can hardcode the vendor ID parameter into the Select statement.
11. Add the code to the form class that uses the methods that you created in steps 9 and 10 to display the total balance due for all unpaid invoices or just one vendor's unpaid invoices when the buttons in the toolbars are clicked.
12. Test and debug this enhancement until it works right.

7

How to work with parameters and stored procedures

This chapter builds on the skills you learned in the last chapter by presenting some additional techniques for working with commands. Specifically, you'll learn how to work with commands that use parameters to retrieve, insert, update, and delete data. And you'll learn how to execute a stored procedure from a command. When you complete this chapter, you'll have all the skills you need for working with commands in the three-layer applications that you develop.

How to create and work with parameters

In chapter 4, you learned how to generate a parameterized query from a bound control that was created using a data source. In that case, the parameters were generated for you based on the Select statement you defined. When you work with commands directly, however, you have to create the parameters yourself. You'll learn how to do that in just a minute. But first, you need to know how to use parameters in the SQL statements you code.

How to use parameters in SQL statements

A *parameter* is a variable that's used in a SQL statement. Parameters let you create statements that retrieve or update database data based on variable information. For example, an application that maintains the Vendors table can use a parameter in the Where clause of a Select statement to retrieve a specific row from the Vendors table based on the value of the VendorID column. A Select statement that uses parameters in the Where clause is called a *parameterized query*. You can also use parameters in other types of SQL statements, including Insert, Update, and Delete statements.

To use parameters in a SQL statement, you use placeholders as shown in figure 7-1. These placeholders indicate where the parameters should be inserted when the statement is executed. Unfortunately, database management systems don't use a standard syntax for coding placeholders.

For example, the first Select statement in this figure is for SQL Server. As you can see, you use a *named variable* to identify a parameter. Note that the name of the variable must begin with an at sign (@) and is usually given the same name as the column it's associated with. Oracle also uses named variables, but the names must begin with a colon (:) as illustrated in the second Select statement. In contrast, the placeholder for an OLE DB or ODBC parameter is a question mark, as shown in the third Select statement.

The fourth example in this figure shows how you can use parameters in an Insert statement. Here, a row is being inserted into the Vendors table. To do that, a variable is included in the Values clause for each required column in the table.

All of the parameters in the first four examples are *input parameters* because they provide input to the database. In contrast, the last example uses *output parameters*, which receive values from the database. Here, the Select statement retrieves six columns from a single row of the Vendors table just as the Select statement in the first example does, but in this case the column values are stored in output parameters.

When you use output parameters, you don't have to use a data reader to get the values, which can improve the efficiency of an application. However, you'll probably want to use this technique only when you're retrieving a small number of values. Otherwise, the parameters can get unwieldy.

A SQL Server Select statement that uses a parameter

```
SELECT Name, Address1, Address2, City, State, ZipCode
FROM Vendors
WHERE VendorID = @VendorID
```

An Oracle Select statement that uses a parameter

```
SELECT Name, Address1, Address2, City, State, ZipCode
FROM Vendors
WHERE VendorID = :VendorID
```

An OLE DB or ODBC Select statement that uses a parameter

```
SELECT Name, Address1, Address2, City, State, ZipCode
FROM Vendors
WHERE VendorID = ?
```

A SQL Server Insert statement that uses parameters

```
INSERT Vendors (Name, Address1, Address2, City, State, ZipCode)
VALUES (@Name, @Address1, @Address2, @City, @State, @ZipCode)
```

A SQL Server Select statement that uses output parameters

```
SELECT @Name = Name, @Address1 = Address1, @Address2 = Address2,
    @City = City, @State = State, @ZipCode = ZipCode
FROM Vendors
WHERE VendorID = @VendorID
```

Description

- A *parameter* lets you place variable information in a SQL statement.
- When you use a parameter in the Where clause of a Select statement, the resulting query is often called a *parameterized query* because the results of the query depend on the value of the parameter.
- Parameters are often used in Insert or Update statements to provide the values for the database row or rows to be inserted or updated. Likewise, you can use parameters in a Delete statement to indicate which row or rows should be deleted.
- In most cases, you'll use *input parameters* to pass values to the database. However, you can also use *output parameters* in the Select clause of a Select statement to retrieve data from the database. This can be more efficient than using a data reader.
- To use parameters, you code a SQL statement with placeholders for the parameters. Then, you create a parameter object that defines each parameter, and you add it to the Parameters collection of the command object that contains the SQL statement.
- The placeholder for a parameter in a SQL Server command is a *named variable* whose name begins with an at sign (@). For Oracle, the variable name begins with a colon (:). In most cases, you'll give the variable the same name as the column it's associated with.
- If you're using the OLE DB or ODBC data provider, you code the placeholder for a parameter as a question mark.

Figure 7-1 How to use parameters in SQL statements

How to create parameters

After you define a SQL statement that contains parameters, you create the parameter objects. Figure 7-2 shows you how to do that. Here, you can see four constructors for the SqlParameter class. Although there are others, these are the ones you're most likely to use. You can create a parameter for an OLE DB, ODBC, or Oracle command using similar techniques.

Before you can use a parameter, you must assign a name to it. In addition, if the parameter will be used for input, you must also assign a value to it. And if the parameter will be used for output and it will hold string data, you must assign a size to it. If you don't pass these values as arguments to the constructor when you create the parameter, you can do that using some of the properties shown in this figure.

Note here that you can specify the data type using either the DbType or SqlDbType property for a SQL Server parameter. Because the data type is inferred from the value of the parameter, you usually won't set the type for an input parameter. However, you may want to specify the type for an output parameter so you can specify the name when you create the parameter.

The first example in this figure shows how to create a parameter object using the first constructor for the SqlParameter class. This parameter is assigned to a variable named vendorIDParm. Then, this variable is used to set the parameter's properties.

The second example shows how to create a parameter using a single statement. This statement uses the second constructor for the SqlParameter class to create a parameter named @VendorID with the value specified by the vendorID variable.

In contrast to the first two examples, the third example creates an output parameter. To do that, it uses the fourth constructor to specify the name, type, and size for the parameter. Then, it sets the Direction property of the parameter to ParameterDirection.Output.

When you assign a name to a SQL Server or Oracle parameter, that name must be the same as the name that's specified in the SQL statement. That's because ADO.NET associates the parameters with the placeholders by name. As a result, if a statement uses two or more parameters, you can add them to the Parameters collection in any sequence. In contrast, OLE DB and ODBC parameters must be added to the collection in the same order that they appear in the SQL statement. In that case, ADO.NET associates the parameters with the placeholders by sequence since the placeholders aren't named.

Four constructors for the SqlParameter class

```
New SqlParameter()
New SqlParameter(name, value)
New SqlParameter(name, type)
New SqlParameter(name, type, size)
```

Common properties of the SqlParameter class

Property	Description
DbType	A member of the DbType enumeration that determines the type of data that the parameter can hold.
Direction	A member of the ParameterDirection enumeration that determines if the parameter will be used for input, output, both input and output, or to hold the return value from a stored procedure or function. The default is Input.
IsNullable	A Boolean value that indicates if the parameter accepts nulls. The default is False.
ParameterName	The name of the parameter.
Size	The maximum size of the value that the parameter can hold.
SqlDbType	A member of the SqlDbType enumeration that determines the type of data that the parameter can hold. This property is synchronized with the DbType property.
Value	The value of the parameter stored as an Object type.

Code that creates an input parameter

```
Dim vendorIDParm As New SqlParameter()
vendorIDParm.ParameterName = "@VendorID"
vendorIDParm.Value = vendorID
```

Another way to create an input parameter

```
Dim vendorIDParm As New SqlParameter("@VendorID", vendorID)
```

Code that creates an output parameter

```
Dim nameParm As New SqlParameter("@Name", SqlDbType.VarChar, 50)
nameParm.Direction = ParameterDirection.Output
```

Description

- When you create a parameter, you can specify the parameter name along with a value, a data type, or a data type and size. If you don't specify the appropriate values, you can set the values of the associated properties after you create the parameter.
- In addition to a name, you must set the value for an input parameter and a direction for an output parameter. You must also set the size for an output parameter if it will contain string data.
- When you create parameters for a SQL Server or Oracle command, you must give them the same names you used in the SQL statement. Then, you can add the parameters to the Parameters collection in any order you want since ADO.NET refers to them by name.
- Because the parameters for an OLE DB or ODBC command aren't named in the SQL statement, the parameters can be given any name you want. However, they must be added to the Parameters collection in the same order that they appear in the statement.

Figure 7-2 How to create parameters

How to work with parameters

After you create a parameter, you must add it to the Parameters collection of the command that will use the parameter. This is illustrated in the first example in figure 7-3. Here, the Parameters property of the command is used to refer to the Parameters collection. Then, the Add method of that collection is used to add the vendorIDParm parameter that was created in the previous figure.

You can also use one of the overloaded Add methods to create a parameter and add it to the Parameters collection in a single statement. These methods let you specify a name and type or a name, type, and size, and they return the parameter that's created. That way, you can store the parameter in a variable so you can refer to it later if you need to.

Another way to create a parameter and add it to the Parameters collection is to use the AddWithValue method. This is illustrated in the second example in this figure, and this is the easiest way to create an input parameter. Like the Add methods, the AddWithValue method returns the parameter that's created in case you want to refer to it later.

If you don't create a variable to hold a parameter, you can refer to it through the Parameters collection as illustrated in the third example. Here, the value of the @VendorID parameter is set to the value of a variable named vendorID.

The last example in this figure shows how to work with a command that uses output parameters. Although it's not shown here, this command contains the last Select statement shown in figure 7-1. The first thing you should notice is that the ExecuteNonQuery method is used to execute this command, even though it contains a Select statement. That's because you don't need a data reader to get the results of the query. Instead, the results will be stored in the output parameters.

After you execute a command that contains output parameters, you can refer to the parameters using the same techniques you use to refer to input parameters. In this example, parameter variables are used to display the parameter values in text boxes. Notice that the values of the parameters are converted to strings. That's necessary because the Value property is an Object type.

Common properties and methods of the Parameters collection

Property	Description
`Item(index)`	Gets the parameter with the specified name or position from the collection.
Method	**Description**
`Add(parameter)`	Adds the specified parameter to the collection.
`Add(name, type)`	Adds a parameter with the specified name and type to the collection.
`Add(name, type, size)`	Adds a parameter with the specified name, type, and size to the collection.
`AddWithValue(name, value)`	Adds a parameter with the specified name and value to the collection.

A statement that adds a parameter to the Parameters collection

```
selectCommand.Parameters.Add(vendorIDParm)
```

A statement that creates an input parameter and adds it to the Parameters collection

```
selectCommand.Parameters.AddWithValue("@VendorID", vendorID)
```

A statement that changes the value of an existing parameter

```
selectCommand.Parameters("@VendorID").Value = vendorID
```

Code that executes a command with a Select statement that uses output parameters

```
selectCommand.ExecuteNonQuery()
txtName.Text = nameParm.Value.ToString
txtAddress1.Text = address1Parm.Value.ToString
txtAddress2.Text = address2Parm.Value.ToString
txtCity.Text = cityParm.Value.ToString
txtState.Text = stateParm.Value.ToString
txtZipCode.Text = zipCodeParm.Value.ToString
```

Description

- To work with the parameters for a command, you use the Parameters property of the command. This property returns a SqlParameterCollection object that contains all the parameters for the command.
- To add an existing parameter to the Parameters collection, you use the Add method. You can also use the Add method to create a parameter with the specified name and type or name, type, and size, and add that parameter to the Parameters collection.
- You can use the AddWithValue method of the Parameters collection to create a parameter with the specified name and value and add that parameter to the collection.
- All the Add methods return the parameter that's created so you can assign it to a variable.
- To execute a command that contains a Select statement that uses output parameters, you use the ExecuteNonQuery method of the command. Then, when the method is executed, the returned values are stored in the output parameters.

Figure 7-3 How to work with parameters

A Vendor Maintenance application that uses parameters

To illustrate the use of parameters, the following topics present a Vendor Maintenance application. As you'll see, this application uses a parameter in the Select statement that retrieves a single vendor from the Vendors table. It uses parameters in the Insert statement to specify the column values for the new vendor. And it uses parameters in the Update statement to specify the new column values as well as parameters that provide the old column values that are used for concurrency checking. Although this presentation is lengthy, it's worth taking the time to go through it because it will give you a thorough understanding of how you build three-layer applications with commands.

The user interface

Figure 7-4 presents the user interface for the Vendor Maintenance application. As you can see, this application consists of two forms. The Vendor Maintenance form lets the user select an existing vendor and then displays the basic information for that vendor on the form. Then, the user can click the Modify button to modify the information for the vendor or the Add button to add a new vendor.

If the user clicks the Add or Modify button, the Add/Modify Vendor form is displayed. Note that the title of this form changes depending on whether a vendor is being added or modified. In this case, the user that was selected in the Vendor Maintenance form is being modified.

In addition to the name and address information that's displayed in the Vendor Maintenance form, the Add/Modify Vendor form lets the user enter contact information and select default terms and a default account. After entering the appropriate values, the user can click the Accept button or press the Enter key to accept the new or modified vendor. Alternatively, the user can click the Cancel button or press the Esc key to cancel the operation.

At this point, you may be wondering why I used two forms to implement the Vendor Maintenance application. The answer is that, in the real world, most maintenance applications aren't this simple. In many cases, in fact, the maintenance of a table will be combined with other functions. In chapter 10, for example, you'll see a Payable Entry application that lets you add and modify vendors at the same time that you enter new invoices. Even if the table maintenance is provided by a separate application, however, it can be easier to implement the application using two forms because it simplifies the program logic.

The Vendor Maintenance form

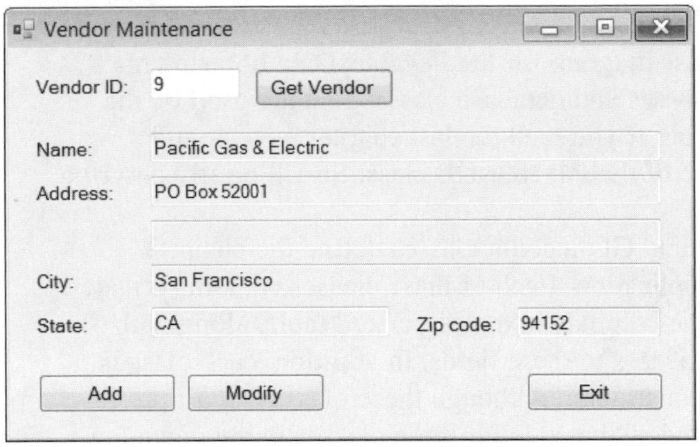

The Add/Modify Vendor form

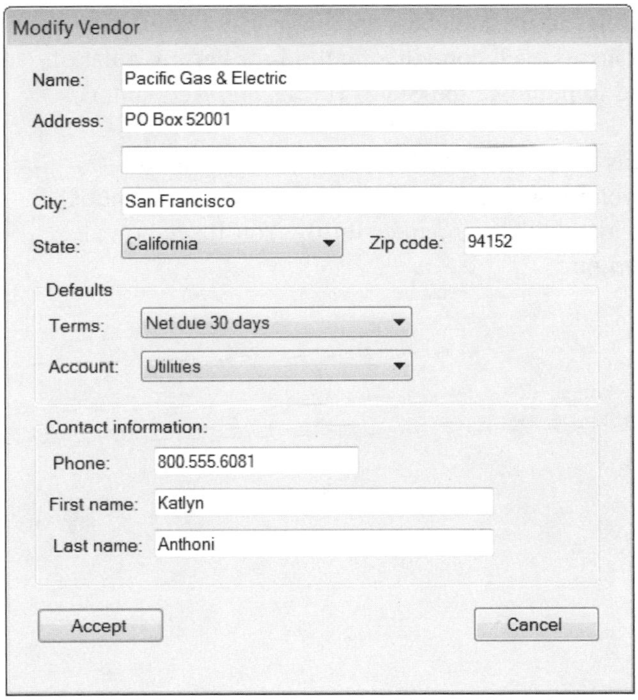

Description

- To add a new vendor, the user clicks the Add button on the Vendor Maintenance form to display a blank Add Vendor form. Then, the user enters the data for the new vendor and clicks the Accept button to return to the Vendor Maintenance form.
- To modify the data for an existing vendor, the user enters the vendor ID and clicks the Get Vendor button to display the basic information for that vendor. Then, the user clicks the Modify button to display the Modify Vendor form, makes the appropriate modifications, and clicks the Accept button to return to the Vendor Maintenance form.

Figure 7-4 The user interface for the Vendor Maintenance application

The class diagram for the PayablesData library

Figure 7-5 presents the class diagram for the PayablesData library. This diagram shows the business classes and database classes that are used by the Vendor Maintenance application. If you read the last chapter, you should already understand the purpose of the PayablesDB class. So I'll briefly describe the other classes here.

The Vendor, State, Terms, and GLAccount classes define the business objects that are used by this application. Each of these classes contains private fields that hold the values of the columns in the associated table, along with public properties that provide access to these fields. In addition, each class is defined with a parameterless constructor. Although these classes aren't presented in this chapter, you can view the code for these classes in the downloaded VendorMaintenance application that's in the Chapter 7 folder.

The VendorDB, StateDB, TermsDB, and GLAccountDB classes provide methods for working with the tables in the Payables database. The StateDB, TermsDB, and GLAccountDB classes each contain a method for getting a list of objects. These lists are then used to populate the State, Terms, and Account combo boxes.

The VendorDB class contains three methods. The GetVendor method returns a Vendor object for the vendor with a specified ID. And the AddVendor and UpdateVendor methods do just what their names imply. You'll see how these methods work in the next figure.

The class diagram for the PayablesData library

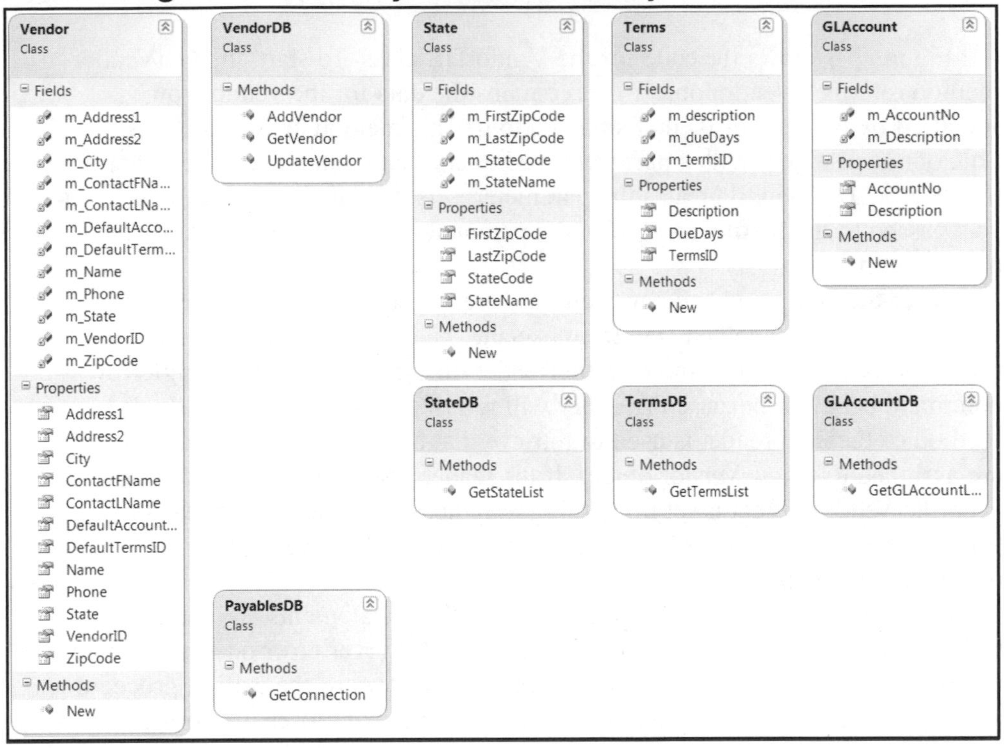

Description

- The PayablesData library contains the classes that define the business objects used by the Vendor Maintenance application and the database classes that are used to work with the Payables database.
- The business objects are defined by the Vendor, State, Terms, and GLAccount classes. These objects will hold data from the associated tables in the Payables database.
- The classes that end with DB, including VendorDB, StateDB, TermsDB, GLAccountDB, and PayablesDB, are the database classes. These classes provide shared members for working with the Payables database.
- The StateDB, TermsDB, and GLAccountDB classes provide public methods for getting lists of data from the States, Terms, and GLAccounts tables. The VendorDB class provides public methods for getting the data for a vendor, adding a vendor, and updating a vendor. And the PayablesDB class provides a public method for getting a connection to the Payables database.

Notes

- To create a class diagram like this, right-click on a project or class in the Solution Explorer and select the View Class Diagram command.
- The Class Diagram feature isn't available in the Express edition of Visual Basic.

Figure 7-5 The class diagram for the PayablesData library

The code for the VendorDB class

Figure 7-6 shows the code for the VendorDB class. To start, the GetVendor method returns a Vendor object that contains the data for the vendor row specified by the vendor ID that's passed to it. This method creates a SqlCommand object with a parameterized query that contains a placeholder for the vendor ID. Then, it creates the parameter, sets its value to the vendorID that was passed to the method, and adds the parameter to the Parameters collection of the command.

After the command and parameter are created, the connection is opened and the ExecuteReader method is used to execute the command and create a data reader object. Notice that the ExecuteReader method specifies the SingleRow command behavior because the query will return just one row. Then, the Read method of the data reader is used to retrieve that row, and the values of that row are assigned to a new Vendor object. If the reader doesn't contain a row, however, the Vendor object is set to Nothing to indicate that the vendor wasn't found. Then, the reader and connection are closed and the Vendor object is returned to the calling procedure.

Like the code you saw in the last chapter, these statements are coded within a Try...Catch...Finally statement. Then, if a SQL Server error occurs when any of these statements is executed, the exception is thrown to the calling procedure so it can handle the error. In addition, the statement that closes the connection is coded within the Finally block so the connection is closed whether or not an exception occurs.

The AddVendor method adds a new row to the Vendors table. This method receives a Vendor object that contains the data for the new row. Then, a command object that contains an Insert statement with a parameter for each column in the row is created.

The code for the VendorDB class Page 1

```
Imports System.Data.SqlClient

Public Class VendorDB

    Public Shared Function GetVendor(ByVal vendorID As Integer) As Vendor
        Dim vendor As New Vendor
        Dim connection As SqlConnection = PayablesDB.GetConnection
        Dim selectStatement As String =
            "SELECT VendorID, Name, Address1, Address2, City, State, " &
                "ZipCode, Phone, ContactFName, ContactLName, " &
                "DefaultAccountNo, DefaultTermsID " &
            "FROM Vendors " &
            "WHERE VendorID = @VendorID"
        Dim selectCommand As New SqlCommand(selectStatement, connection)
        selectCommand.Parameters.AddWithValue("@VendorID", vendorID)
        Try
            connection.Open()
            Dim reader As SqlDataReader =
                selectCommand.ExecuteReader(CommandBehavior.SingleRow)
            If reader.Read Then
                vendor.VendorID = CInt(reader("VendorID"))
                vendor.Name = reader("Name").ToString
                vendor.Address1 = reader("Address1").ToString
                vendor.Address2 = reader("Address2").ToString
                vendor.City = reader("City").ToString
                vendor.State = reader("State").ToString
                vendor.ZipCode = reader("ZipCode").ToString
                vendor.Phone = reader("Phone").ToString
                vendor.ContactFName = reader("ContactFName").ToString
                vendor.ContactLName = reader("ContactLName").ToString
                vendor.DefaultAccountNo = CInt(reader("DefaultAccountNo"))
                vendor.DefaultTermsID = CInt(reader("DefaultTermsID"))
            Else
                vendor = Nothing
            End If
            reader.Close()
        Catch ex As SqlException
            Throw ex
        Finally
            connection.Close()
        End Try
        Return vendor
    End Function

    Public Shared Function AddVendor(ByVal vendor As Vendor) As Integer
        Dim connection As SqlConnection = PayablesDB.GetConnection
        Dim insertStatement As String =
            "INSERT Vendors " &
            "(Name, Address1, Address2, City, State, ZipCode, Phone, " &
            "ContactFName, ContactLName, DefaultTermsID, DefaultAccountNo) " &
            "VALUES (@Name, @Address1, @Address2, @City, @State, @ZipCode, " &
            "@Phone, @ContactFName, @ContactLName, @DefaultTermsID, " &
            "@DefaultAccountNo)"
        Dim insertCommand As New SqlCommand(insertStatement, connection)
```

Figure 7-6 The code for the VendorDB class (part 1 of 5)

After the command is created, the parameters for the command are created. If a column doesn't allow nulls, the appropriate property of the Vendor object is assigned to the parameter. But if a column allows nulls, the property is first checked to see if it contains an empty string. If so, the Value field of the DBNull class is used to assign a null value to the parameter. Otherwise, the value of the property is assigned to the parameter.

Next, the connection is opened and the ExecuteNonQuery method of the command object is executed within a Try...Catch...Finally statement that catches SQL Server exceptions. Then, if an exception occurs, this method throws the exception so it can be handled by the calling procedure. Otherwise, another command object that contains a Select statement that retrieves the ID of the vendor that was just added is created. Then, this command is executed using the ExecuteScalar method. Finally, the vendor ID that's returned by this statement is returned to the calling procedure.

The code for the VendorDB class — Page 2

```
        insertCommand.Parameters.AddWithValue("@Name", vendor.Name)
        insertCommand.Parameters.AddWithValue("@Address1", vendor.Address1)
        If vendor.Address2 = "" Then
            insertCommand.Parameters.AddWithValue("@Address2", DBNull.Value)
        Else
            insertCommand.Parameters.AddWithValue("@Address2",
                vendor.Address2)
        End If
        insertCommand.Parameters.AddWithValue("@City", vendor.City)
        insertCommand.Parameters.AddWithValue("@State", vendor.State)
        insertCommand.Parameters.AddWithValue("@ZipCode", vendor.ZipCode)
        If vendor.Phone = "" Then
            insertCommand.Parameters.AddWithValue("@Phone", DBNull.Value)
        Else
            insertCommand.Parameters.AddWithValue("@Phone", vendor.Phone)
        End If
        If vendor.ContactFName = "" Then
            insertCommand.Parameters.AddWithValue("@ContactFName",
                DBNull.Value)
        Else
            insertCommand.Parameters.AddWithValue("@ContactFName",
                vendor.ContactFName)
        End If
        If vendor.ContactLName = "" Then
            insertCommand.Parameters.AddWithValue("@ContactLName",
                DBNull.Value)
        Else
            insertCommand.Parameters.AddWithValue("@ContactLName",
                vendor.ContactLName)
        End If
        insertCommand.Parameters.AddWithValue("@DefaultTermsID",
            vendor.DefaultTermsID)
        insertCommand.Parameters.AddWithValue("@DefaultAccountNo",
            vendor.DefaultAccountNo)
        Try
            connection.Open()
            insertCommand.ExecuteNonQuery()
            Dim selectStatement As String =
                "SELECT IDENT_CURRENT('Vendors') FROM Vendors"
            Dim selectCommand As New SqlCommand(selectStatement, connection)
            Dim vendorID As Integer = CInt(selectCommand.ExecuteScalar)
            Return vendorID
        Catch ex As SqlException
            Throw ex
        Finally
            connection.Close()
        End Try
    End Function
```

Figure 7-6 The code for the VendorDB class (part 2 of 5)

The UpdateVendor method receives two arguments: a Vendor object named oldVendor that contains the original data for the vendor row to be updated, and another Vendor object named newVendor that supplies the updated values for the vendor. The properties of these objects are used to set the values of the parameters defined by the Update statement associated with the command object. Notice that the properties of the oldVendor object are assigned to parameters in the Where clause of the Update statement. That way, the Update statement will update the row only if none of the vendor columns have been changed since the vendor was retrieved.

Also notice how the Update statement handles columns that can contain nulls. First, it checks if the value of the column in the database is equal to the value that was originally retrieved just as it does for the other columns. In addition, it checks if both the database value and the original value are equal to NULL. That's necessary because two nulls aren't considered equal.

After the parameter values are set, this method uses the ExecuteNonQuery method to execute the Update statement. If no error occurs, the value that's returned by the ExecuteNonQuery method is tested to determine whether the update was successful. If it wasn't, it probably means that the vendor has been modified or deleted by another user. In that case, this method returns False to the calling procedure. Otherwise, it returns True.

The code for the VendorDB class

Page 3

```
Public Shared Function UpdateVendor(ByVal oldVendor As Vendor,
    ByVal newVendor As Vendor) As Boolean
    Dim connection As SqlConnection = PayablesDB.GetConnection
    Dim updateStatement As String =
         "UPDATE Vendors SET " &
           "Name = @NewName, " &
           "Address1 = @NewAddress1, " &
           "Address2 = @NewAddress2, " &
           "City = @NewCity, " &
           "State = @NewState, " &
           "ZipCode = @NewZipCode, " &
           "Phone = @NewPhone, " &
           "ContactFName = @NewContactFName, " &
           "ContactLName = @NewContactLName, " &
           "DefaultTermsID = @NewDefaultTermsID, " &
           "DefaultAccountNo = @NewDefaultAccountNo " &
         "WHERE VendorID = @OldVendorID " &
           "AND Name = @OldName " &
           "AND Address1 = @OldAddress1 " &
           "AND (Address2 = @OldAddress2 " &
             " OR Address2 IS NULL AND @OldAddress2 IS NULL) " &
           "AND City = @OldCity " &
           "AND State = @OldState " &
           "AND ZipCode = @OldZipCode " &
           "AND (Phone = @OldPhone " &
             " OR Phone IS NULL AND @OldPhone IS NULL) " &
           "AND (ContactFName = @OldContactFName " &
             " OR ContactFName IS NULL AND @OldContactFName IS NULL) " &
           "AND (ContactLName = @OldContactLName " &
             " OR ContactLName IS NULL AND @OldContactLName IS NULL) " &
           "AND DefaultTermsID = @OldDefaultTermsID " &
           "AND DefaultAccountNo = @OldDefaultAccountNo"
    Dim updateCommand As New SqlCommand(updateStatement, connection)
    updateCommand.Parameters.AddWithValue("@NewName",
        newVendor.Name)
    updateCommand.Parameters.AddWithValue("@NewAddress1",
        newVendor.Address1)
    If newVendor.Address2 = "" Then
        updateCommand.Parameters.AddWithValue("@NewAddress2",
            DBNull.Value)
    Else
        updateCommand.Parameters.AddWithValue("@NewAddress2",
            newVendor.Address2)
    End If
    updateCommand.Parameters.AddWithValue("@NewCity",
        newVendor.City)
    updateCommand.Parameters.AddWithValue("@NewState",
        newVendor.State)
    updateCommand.Parameters.AddWithValue("@NewZipCode",
        newVendor.ZipCode)
```

Figure 7-6 The code for the VendorDB class (part 3 of 5)

The code for the VendorDB class **Page 4**

```
        If newVendor.Phone = "" Then
            updateCommand.Parameters.AddWithValue("@NewPhone",
                DBNull.Value)
        Else
            updateCommand.Parameters.AddWithValue("@NewPhone",
                newVendor.Phone)
        End If
        If newVendor.ContactFName = "" Then
            updateCommand.Parameters.AddWithValue("@NewContactFName",
                DBNull.Value)
        Else
            updateCommand.Parameters.AddWithValue("@NewContactFName",
                newVendor.ContactFName)
        End If
        If newVendor.ContactLName = "" Then
            updateCommand.Parameters.AddWithValue("@NewContactLName",
                DBNull.Value)
        Else
            updateCommand.Parameters.AddWithValue("@NewContactLName",
                newVendor.ContactLName)
        End If
        updateCommand.Parameters.AddWithValue("@NewDefaultTermsID",
            newVendor.DefaultTermsID)
        updateCommand.Parameters.AddWithValue("@NewDefaultAccountNo",
            newVendor.DefaultAccountNo)
        updateCommand.Parameters.AddWithValue("@OldVendorID",
            oldVendor.VendorID)
        updateCommand.Parameters.AddWithValue("@OldName",
            oldVendor.Name)
        updateCommand.Parameters.AddWithValue("@OldAddress1",
            oldVendor.Address1)
        If oldVendor.Address2 = "" Then
            updateCommand.Parameters.AddWithValue("@OldAddress2",
                DBNull.Value)
        Else
            updateCommand.Parameters.AddWithValue("@OldAddress2",
                oldVendor.Address2)
        End If
        updateCommand.Parameters.AddWithValue("@OldCity",
            oldVendor.City)
        updateCommand.Parameters.AddWithValue("@OldState",
            oldVendor.State)
        updateCommand.Parameters.AddWithValue("@OldZipCode",
            oldVendor.ZipCode)
        If oldVendor.Phone = "" Then
            updateCommand.Parameters.AddWithValue("@OldPhone",
                DBNull.Value)
        Else
            updateCommand.Parameters.AddWithValue("@OldPhone",
                oldVendor.Phone)
        End If
```

Figure 7-6 The code for the VendorDB class (part 4 of 5)

The code for the VendorDB class — Page 5

```
        If oldVendor.ContactFName = "" Then
            updateCommand.Parameters.AddWithValue("@OldContactFName",
                DBNull.Value)
        Else
            updateCommand.Parameters.AddWithValue("@OldContactFName",
               oldVendor.ContactFName)
        End If
        If oldVendor.ContactLName = "" Then
            updateCommand.Parameters.AddWithValue("@OldContactLName",
                DBNull.Value)
        Else
            updateCommand.Parameters.AddWithValue("@OldContactLName",
                oldVendor.ContactLName)
        End If
        updateCommand.Parameters.AddWithValue("@OldDefaultTermsID",
            oldVendor.DefaultTermsID)
        updateCommand.Parameters.AddWithValue("@OldDefaultAccountNo",
            oldVendor.DefaultAccountNo)

        Try
            connection.Open()
            Dim count As Integer = updateCommand.ExecuteNonQuery
            If count > 0 Then
                Return True
            Else
                Return False
            End If
        Catch ex As SqlException
            Throw ex
        Finally
            connection.Close()
        End Try
    End Function

End Class
```

Figure 7-6 The code for the VendorDB class (part 5 of 5)

The code for the StateDB class

Figure 7-7 shows the code for the StateDB class. This class contains a single method named GetStateList that returns a generic List() object that contains one State object for each of the rows in the States table, sorted by state name.

To get this list, the GetStateList method creates a SqlCommand object with a Select statement that retrieves the appropriate data. Then, it calls the ExecuteReader method of this command to create a data reader that can be used to read each state. Once the data reader is created, this method uses this reader to read each row in the table, it creates a State object for each row, and it adds each State object to the List() object. Finally, it closes the data reader and returns the list of State objects.

Although they're not shown here, the TermsDB and GLAccountDB classes contain methods similar to the GetStateList method. Instead of creating a list of State objects, however, the GetTermsList method in the TermsDB class returns a list of Terms objects. And the GetGLAccountList method in the GLAccountDB class returns a list of GLAccount objects. If you want to view the code for these classes, it's available in the VendorMaintenance application in the Chapter 7 folder.

The code for the StateDB class

```
Imports System.Data.SqlClient

Public Class StateDB

    Public Shared Function GetStateList() As List(Of State)
        Dim stateList As New List(Of State)
        Dim connection As SqlConnection = PayablesDB.GetConnection
        Dim selectStatement As String =
            "SELECT StateCode, StateName, FirstZipCode, LastZipCode " &
            "FROM States " &
            "ORDER BY StateName"
        Dim selectCommand As New SqlCommand(selectStatement, connection)
        Try
            connection.Open()
            Dim reader As SqlDataReader = selectCommand.ExecuteReader()
            Dim state As State
            Do While reader.Read
                state = New State
                state.StateCode = reader("StateCode").ToString
                state.StateName = reader("StateName").ToString
                state.FirstZipCode = CInt(reader("FirstZipCode"))
                state.LastZipCode = CInt(reader("LastZipCode"))
                stateList.Add(state)
            Loop
            reader.Close()
        Catch ex As SqlException
            Throw ex
        Finally
            connection.Close()
        End Try
        Return stateList
    End Function

End Class
```

Note

- The code for the TermsDB and GLAccountDB classes is similar to the code for the StateDB class. The GetTermsList method in the TermsDB class retrieves data from the Terms table and stores it in a list of Terms objects. The GetGLAccountList method in the GLAccountDB class retrieves data from the GLAccounts table and stores it in a list of GLAccount objects.

Figure 7-7 The code for the StateDB class

The code for the Vendor Maintenance form

Figure 7-8 shows the code for the Vendor Maintenance form. Because this form doesn't contain a Load event handler, no data is displayed when the form is first displayed. Then, the user must enter a vendor ID and click the Get Vendor button to retrieve the data for a vendor or click the Add button to add a new vendor.

The event handler for the Click event of the Get Vendor button starts by calling the IsPresent and IsInt32 methods in a class named Validator to check that the user entered a vendor ID and that the vendor ID is an integer. Although I won't show you the Validator class here, it contains shared methods that check for various data types and formats. These methods are similar to the procedures that were used in the Vendor Maintenance application in chapter 4 to validate the data for a vendor. You can view the code for the Validator class in the VendorMaintenance application in the Chapter 7 folder.

If the vendor ID is an integer, this value is passed to a procedure named GetVendor. This procedure starts by calling the GetVendor method of the VendorDB class to get the vendor with the specified ID, and the Vendor object that's returned by this method is stored in a variable named vendor. If the object contains a value of Nothing, a message is displayed indicating that the vendor wasn't found. Otherwise, a procedure named DisplayVendor is called to display the properties of the Vendor object in the text boxes on the form. This procedure also enables the Modify button so the user can modify the selected vendor. (This button is disabled when the form is first displayed.)

Notice that the statements of the GetVendor procedure are coded within a Try…Catch statement. That's because, if a SQL Server error occurs during the execution of the GetVendor method in the VendorDB class, the exception is thrown to the calling procedure. Because of that, this procedure must catch the exception. You'll see this same technique used for all the methods of the database classes that are called by this application.

If the user clicks the Add button, the Click event handler for this button displays the Add/Modify Vendor form as a dialog box. But first, it sets the public addVendor field of this form to True so the form will know that a new vendor is being added. If the vendor is added successfully, the new vendor is retrieved from the Add/Modify Vendor form. Then, the data for the new vendor is displayed on the form and the Modify button is enabled.

The code for the Vendor Maintenance form — Page 1

```
Imports PayablesData

Public Class frmVendorMaintenance

    Dim vendor As Vendor

    Private Sub btnGetVendor_Click(ByVal sender As System.Object,
        ByVal e As System.EventArgs) Handles btnGetVendor.Click
        If Validator.IsPresent(txtVendorID) AndAlso
           Validator.IsInt32(txtVendorID) Then
            Dim vendorID As Integer = CInt(txtVendorID.Text)
            Me.GetVendor(vendorID)
        End If
    End Sub

    Private Sub GetVendor(ByVal vendorID As Integer)
        Try
            vendor = VendorDB.GetVendor(vendorID)
            If vendor Is Nothing Then
                MessageBox.Show("No vendor found with this ID. " &
                    "Please try again.", "Vendor Not Found")
            Else
                Me.DisplayVendor()
            End If
        Catch ex As Exception
            MessageBox.Show(ex.Message, ex.GetType.ToString)
        End Try
    End Sub

    Private Sub DisplayVendor()
        txtName.Text = vendor.Name
        txtAddress1.Text = vendor.Address1
        txtAddress2.Text = vendor.Address2
        txtCity.Text = vendor.City
        txtState.Text = vendor.State
        txtZipCode.Text = vendor.ZipCode
        btnModify.Enabled = True
    End Sub

    Private Sub btnAdd_Click(ByVal sender As System.Object,
            ByVal e As System.EventArgs) Handles btnAdd.Click
        Dim addModifyVendorForm As New frmAddModifyVendor
        addModifyVendorForm.addVendor = True
        Dim result As DialogResult = addModifyVendorForm.ShowDialog
        If result = DialogResult.OK Then
            vendor = addModifyVendorForm.vendor
            txtVendorID.Text = vendor.VendorID.ToString
            Me.DisplayVendor()
        End If
    End Sub
```

Figure 7-8 The code for the Vendor Maintenance form (part 1 of 2)

The Click event handler for the Modify button is similar. However, it sets the addVendor field of the Add/Modify Vendor form to False to indicate that a vendor is being modified. In addition, it sets the public vendor field to the current Vendor object. That way, the form can display this data without having to retrieve it from the database again.

If the vendor is modified successfully, the updated vendor is retrieved from the Add/Modify Vendor form and the new data for the vendor is displayed on the form. If a concurrency error occurs, however, the result of the Add/Modify Vendor form is set to DialogResult.Retry. Then, a procedure named ClearControls is called. This procedure assigns empty strings to the text boxes on the form and disables the Modify button. Last, the GetVendor procedure is called to retrieve and display the current data for the vendor if that vendor still exists.

The code for the Vendor Maintenance form Page 2

```
    Private Sub btnModify_Click(ByVal sender As System.Object,
            ByVal e As System.EventArgs) Handles btnModify.Click
        Dim addModifyVendorForm As New frmAddModifyVendor
        addModifyVendorForm.addVendor = False
        addModifyVendorForm.vendor = vendor
        Dim result As DialogResult = addModifyVendorForm.ShowDialog
        If result = DialogResult.OK Then
            vendor = addModifyVendorForm.vendor
            Me.DisplayVendor()
        ElseIf result = DialogResult.Retry Then
            Me.ClearControls()
            Me.GetVendor(vendor.VendorID)
        End If
    End Sub

    Private Sub ClearControls()
        txtName.Text = ""
        txtAddress1.Text = ""
        txtAddress2.Text = ""
        txtCity.Text = ""
        txtState.Text = ""
        txtZipCode.Text = ""
        btnModify.Enabled = False
    End Sub

    Private Sub btnExit_Click(ByVal sender As System.Object,
            ByVal e As System.EventArgs) Handles btnExit.Click
        Me.Close()
    End Sub

End Class
```

Figure 7-8 The code for the Vendor Maintenance form (part 2 of 2)

The code for the Add/Modify Vendor form

Figure 7-9 shows the code for the Add/Modify Vendor form. This form starts by declaring the two public fields that are also used by the Vendor Maintenance form.

When the form is first loaded, the Load event handler starts by calling the LoadComboBoxes procedure. This procedure uses the methods of the StateDB, TermsDB, and GLAccountDB classes to get generic lists that contain State, Terms, and GLAccount objects. Then, it binds the three combo boxes on the form to these lists. Note that the list that contains the State objects is declared at the module-level. That's because it's also used by the IsValidData function, which you can see on page 3 of this listing.

If a new vendor is being added, the Load event handler continues by setting the Text property of the form to "Add Vendor" and initializing the combo boxes so that no items are selected. Otherwise, it sets the Text property of the form to "Modify Vendor" and calls the DisplayVendorData procedure. This procedure displays the current data for the vendor on the form. Notice that if the Phone property of the Vendor object contains data, the phone number is formatted by calling the FormattedPhoneNumber function. After that, the user can enter the data for a new vendor or modify the data for an existing vendor.

If the user clicks the Accept button, the Click event handler for this button starts by calling the IsValidData function. This function calls the IsPresent, IsInt32, IsStateZipCode, and IsPhoneNumber methods of the Validator class to determine if the data is valid. Note that because a phone number is optional, the IsPhoneNumber method is called only if a phone number has been entered.

If the data is valid, the event handler continues by checking whether a vendor is being added. If so, the vendor field is set to a new Vendor object and the PutVendorData procedure is called. This procedure sets the properties of the Vendor object to the values that the user entered on the form.

Next, the event handler executes the AddVendor method of the VendorDB class and assigns the new vendor ID that's returned by this method to the VendorID property of the Vendor object. Then, if no SQL Server error occurs, the DialogResult property of the form is set to DialogResult.OK, which causes the form to be closed and control to be returned to the Vendor Maintenance form. Otherwise, the exception is caught and an error message is displayed.

If a vendor is being modified, this procedure starts by creating a new Vendor object and storing it in the newVendor variable. Then, it sets the VendorID property of that object to the VendorID property of the current Vendor object since the vendor ID can't be changed, and it calls the PutVendorData procedure to set the rest of the properties. Next, it calls the UpdateVendor method of the VendorDB class and passes it both the old and new Vendor objects. If a concurrency error occurs, a value of False is returned. In that case, an error message is displayed and the DialogResult property of the form is set to DialogResult.Retry. Otherwise, the new Vendor object is assigned to the original Vendor object and the DialogResult property is set to DialogResult.OK. In either case, the form is closed.

The code for the Add/Modify Vendor form Page 1

```
Imports PayablesData

Public Class frmAddModifyVendor
    Public addVendor As Boolean
    Public vendor As Vendor
    Private stateList As List(Of State)

    Private Sub frmAddModifyVendor_Load(ByVal sender As System.Object,
            ByVal e As System.EventArgs)
        Me.LoadComboBoxes()
        If addVendor Then
            Me.Text = "Add Vendor"
            cboStates.SelectedIndex = -1
            cboTerms.SelectedIndex = -1
            cboAccounts.SelectedIndex = -1
        Else
            Me.Text = "Modify Vendor"
            Me.DisplayVendorData()
        End If
    End Sub

    Private Sub LoadComboBoxes()
        Try
            stateList = StateDB.GetStateList
            cboStates.DataSource = stateList
            cboStates.DisplayMember = "StateName"
            cboStates.ValueMember = "StateCode"

            Dim termsList As List(Of Terms)
            termsList = TermsDB.GetTermsList
            cboTerms.DataSource = termsList
            cboTerms.DisplayMember = "Description"
            cboTerms.ValueMember = "TermsID"

            Dim accountList As List(Of GLAccount)
            accountList = GLAccountDB.GetGLAccountList
            cboAccounts.DataSource = accountList
            cboAccounts.DisplayMember = "Description"
            cboAccounts.ValueMember = "AccountNo"
        Catch ex As Exception
            MessageBox.Show(ex.Message, ex.GetType.ToString)
        End Try
    End Sub

    Private Sub DisplayVendorData()
        txtName.Text = vendor.Name
        txtAddress1.Text = vendor.Address1
        txtAddress2.Text = vendor.Address2
        txtCity.Text = vendor.City
        cboStates.SelectedValue = vendor.State
        txtZipCode.Text = vendor.ZipCode
        cboTerms.SelectedValue = vendor.DefaultTermsID
        cboAccounts.SelectedValue = vendor.DefaultAccountNo
```

Figure 7-9 The code for the Add/Modify Vendor form (part 1 of 3)

The code for the Add/Modify Vendor form — Page 2

```
        If vendor.Phone = "" Then
            txtPhone.Text = ""
        Else
            txtPhone.Text = FormattedPhoneNumber(vendor.Phone)
        End If
        txtFirstName.Text = vendor.ContactFName
        txtLastName.Text = vendor.ContactLName
    End Sub

    Private Function FormattedPhoneNumber(ByVal phone As String) As String
        Return phone.Substring(0, 3) & "." &
            phone.Substring(3, 3) & "." &
            phone.Substring(6, 4)
    End Function

    Private Sub btnAccept_Click(ByVal sender As System.Object,
            ByVal e As System.EventArgs) Handles btnAccept.Click
        If IsValidData() Then
            If addVendor Then
                vendor = New Vendor
                Me.PutVendorData(vendor)
                Try
                    vendor.VendorID = VendorDB.AddVendor(vendor)
                    Me.DialogResult = DialogResult.OK
                Catch ex As Exception
                    MessageBox.Show(ex.Message, ex.GetType.ToString)
                End Try
            Else
                Dim newVendor As New Vendor
                newVendor.VendorID = vendor.VendorID
                Me.PutVendorData(newVendor)
                Try
                    If Not VendorDB.UpdateVendor(vendor, newVendor) Then
                        MessageBox.Show("Another user has updated or " &
                            "deleted that vendor.", "Database Error")
                        Me.DialogResult = DialogResult.Retry
                    Else
                        vendor = newVendor
                        Me.DialogResult = DialogResult.OK
                    End If
                Catch ex As Exception
                    MessageBox.Show(ex.Message, ex.GetType.ToString)
                End Try
            End If
        End If
    End Sub
```

Figure 7-9 The code for the Add/Modify Vendor form (part 2 of 3)

The code for the Add/Modify Vendor form — Page 3

```
Private Function IsValidData() As Boolean
        If Validator.IsPresent(txtName) AndAlso
               Validator.IsPresent(txtAddress1) AndAlso
               Validator.IsPresent(txtCity) AndAlso
               Validator.IsPresent(cboStates) AndAlso
               Validator.IsPresent(txtZipCode) AndAlso
               Validator.IsInt32(txtZipCode) AndAlso
               Validator.IsPresent(cboTerms) AndAlso
               Validator.IsPresent(cboAccounts) Then
            Dim firstZip As Integer
                = stateList(cboStates.SelectedIndex).FirstZipCode
            Dim lastZip As Integer
                = stateList(cboStates.SelectedIndex).LastZipCode
            If Validator.IsStateZipCode(txtZipCode, firstZip, lastZip) Then
                If txtPhone.Text <> "" Then
                    If Validator.IsPhoneNumber(txtPhone) Then
                        Return True
                    Else
                        Return False
                    End If
                Else
                    Return True
                End If
            Else
                Return False
            End If
        Else
            Return False
        End If
    End Function

    Private Sub PutVendorData(ByVal vendor As Vendor)
        vendor.Name = txtName.Text
        vendor.Address1 = txtAddress1.Text
        vendor.Address2 = txtAddress2.Text
        vendor.City = txtCity.Text
        vendor.State = cboStates.SelectedValue.ToString
        vendor.ZipCode = txtZipCode.Text
        vendor.DefaultTermsID = CInt(cboTerms.SelectedValue)
        vendor.DefaultAccountNo = CInt(cboAccounts.SelectedValue)
        vendor.Phone = txtPhone.Text.Replace(".", "")
        vendor.ContactFName = txtFirstName.Text
        vendor.ContactLName = txtLastName.Text
    End Sub

End Class
```

Figure 7-9 The code for the Add/Modify Vendor form (part 3 of 3)

How to work with stored procedures

Instead of using Select, Insert, Update, and Delete statements that are coded in your application, you can use stored procedures that contain the statements you need. A *stored procedure* is a database object that contains one or more SQL statements.

In the topics that follow, you'll learn how to work with stored procedures. But keep in mind as you read these topics that they're not meant to teach you how to code stored procedures. They're just meant to give you an idea of how stored procedures work and how you can use them from Visual Basic applications. When you're ready to learn how to code your own stored procedures, please see our book, *Murach's SQL Server 2008 for Developers*.

An introduction to stored procedures

When you send a SQL statement to a database management system for processing, the DBMS must compile and optimize the query before it executes it. In contrast, because a stored procedure is stored with the database, it only has to be compiled and optimized the first time it's executed. Because of that, stored procedures can improve the efficiency of a database application.

Figure 7-10 illustrates how a stored procedure works. At the top of this figure, you can see a Create Procedure statement that creates a stored procedure named spGetVendorAddress. This stored procedure contains a Select statement that retrieves data for a vendor from the Vendors table based on the Vendor ID. Notice that this stored procedure requires a parameter, which is defined at the beginning of the procedure.

To execute a stored procedure, you use a command object as demonstrated in this figure. Here, the CommandText property is set to the name of the stored procedure, and the CommandType property is set to CommandType.StoredProcedure. In addition, a parameter that will contain the value that's passed to the stored procedure is added to the Parameters collection of the command. Then, the connection is opened and the command is executed. Because the stored procedure in this example contains a Select statement, the ExecuteReader method is used to execute the command and store the result set in a data reader. But you can use the ExecuteNonQuery method to execute a stored procedure that contains an Insert, Update, or Delete statement, and you can use the ExecuteScalar method to execute a stored procedure that returns a single value.

When you use a stored procedure in a three-layer application, you execute it from a database class. In the Vendor Maintenance application, for example, the command in the GetVendor method in the VendorDB class in figure 7-6 (part 1) could be replaced with a command that uses a stored procedure. In other words, when you call a method like this in a database class, it will work equally well whether it uses a query or a stored procedure. And you can change a method in a database class so it uses a stored procedure without changing anything else in the application.

SQL code for creating a stored procedure that retrieves a row

```
CREATE PROCEDURE spGetVendorAddress (@VendorID int)
AS
SELECT VendorID, Name, Address1, Address2, City, State, ZipCode
FROM Vendors
WHERE (VendorID = @VendorID)
```

Visual Basic code that creates and executes a command that uses the stored procedure

```
Dim selectCommand As New SqlCommand()
selectCommand.Connection = connection
selectCommand.CommandText = "spGetVendorAddress"
selectCommand.CommandType = CommandType.StoredProcedure
selectCommand.Parameters.AddWithValue("@VendorID", vendorID)
connection.Open()
Dim reader As SqlDataReader = selectCommand.ExecuteReader()
.
.
```

Concepts

- A *stored procedure* consists of one or more SQL statements that have been compiled and stored with the database.
- Stored procedures can improve database performance because the SQL statements in each procedure are only compiled and optimized the first time they're executed. In contrast, SQL statements that are sent from a Visual Basic application have to be compiled and optimized every time they're executed.
- You can use parameters to pass values from an application to the stored procedure or from the stored procedure to the application. Stored procedures can also pass back a return value, which is typically used to indicate whether or not an error occurred.

How to use stored procedures from Visual Basic

- To use a stored procedure in a Visual Basic application, you set the CommandText property of a command to the name of the stored procedure, and you set the CommandType property to CommandType.StoredProcedure.
- If a stored procedure uses input parameters, you must add parameter objects to the Parameters collection just as you do when you use SQL statements directly. You must also add parameter objects for output parameters or a return value returned by the procedure. See figure 7-11 for details.
- To execute a stored procedure, you use the method of the command object that's appropriate for the processing that's done by the procedure. To execute a stored procedure that returns a result set, for example, you use the ExecuteReader method.

Figure 7-10 An introduction to stored procedures

How to work with output parameters and return values

The stored procedure you saw in the last figure used just an input parameter. But stored procedures can also use output parameters, and they can return a return value. Figure 7-11 illustrates how this works.

At the top of this figure, you can see a stored procedure that inserts a new row into the Vendors table. This procedure uses input parameters for each of the required columns in this table. In addition, it uses an output parameter that will return the identity value that's generated for the Vendor ID column. To assign a value to this parameter, the procedure uses a Set statement. As you can see, this statement assigns the value of the SCOPE_IDENTITY function to this parameter. SCOPE_IDENTITY is a SQL Server system function that returns the last value that was generated for an identity column within the current scope. In this case, the scope is the stored procedure.

This procedure also includes a Return statement that passes a return value back to the program. In this case, the procedure simply returns the value of the @@ERROR system function, which will contain the error number that was generated by the Insert statement. If no error was generated, this function will return a value of zero.

The Visual Basic code shown in this figure illustrates how you can use the output parameter and return value included in this stored procedure. To do that, you add parameter objects to the Parameters collection of the command that will execute the stored procedure. To indicate that a parameter will receive a return value or output from the stored procedure, you set its Direction property as shown here. Then, after the query is executed, you can get the values of the parameters through the Parameters collection. In this example, the @Error parameter is checked to see if it has a value of zero, which indicates that no error occurred. Then, the value of the @VendorID parameter is assigned to the VendorID property of a Vendor object. Otherwise, some other processing is performed.

If you understand how to use commands to execute queries, you shouldn't have any trouble using them with stored procedures. Before you use an existing stored procedure, though, you'll need to find out how it's defined, what parameters it uses, and whether it includes a Return statement. That way, you can define your command objects accordingly.

SQL code for creating a stored procedure that returns output parameters and a return value

```
CREATE PROCEDURE spInsertVendor
    ( @Name varchar(50), @Address1 varchar(50),
      @Address2 varchar(50), @City varchar(50),
      @State char(2), @ZipCode varchar(20),
      @VendorID int OUTPUT )
AS
INSERT INTO Vendors(Name, Address1, Address2, City, State, ZipCode)
VALUES (@Name, @Address1, @Address2, @City, @State, @ZipCode)
SET @VendorID = SCOPE_IDENTITY()
RETURN @@ERROR
```

Visual Basic code that executes the stored procedure

```
Dim insertCommand As New SqlCommand("spInsertVendor", connection)
insertCommand.CommandType = CommandType.StoredProcedure
insertCommand.Parameters.AddWithValue("@Name", vendor.Name)
insertCommand.Parameters.AddWithValue("@Address1", vendor.Address1)
insertCommand.Parameters.AddWithValue("@Address2", vendor.Address2)
insertCommand.Parameters.AddWithValue("@City", vendor.City)
insertCommand.Parameters.AddWithValue("@State", vendor.State)
insertCommand.Parameters.AddWithValue("@ZipCode", vendor.ZipCode)
insertCommand.Parameters.Add("@VendorID", SqlDbType.Int)
insertCommand.Parameters("@VendorID").Direction =
    ParameterDirection.Output
insertCommand.Parameters.Add("@Error", SqlDbType.Int)
insertCommand.Parameters("@Error").Direction =
    ParameterDirection.ReturnValue
.
.
connection.Open()
insertCommand.ExecuteNonQuery()
If CInt(insertCommand.Parameters("@Error").Value) = 0 Then
    vendor.VendorID = CInt(insertCommand.Parameters("@VendorID").Value)
Else
.
.
End If
connection.Close()
```

Description

- If a stored procedure includes output parameters or a Return statement, you must add parameters to the command that executes the stored procedure. These parameters will receive the values returned by the stored procedure.
- The Direction property of an output parameter must be set to ParameterDirection.Output. The Size property must also be set if the parameter is defined with a string data type.
- The Direction property of the parameter that receives the return value must be set to ParameterDirection.ReturnValue.

Figure 7-11 How to work with output parameters and return values

Perspective

In this chapter, you learned the skills for working with parameters and stored procedures. These are essential skills for working with commands as you develop database applications. In the next chapter, you'll learn an essential skill for working with a series of related commands.

Terms

parameter
parameterized query
input parameter
output parameter
stored procedure

Exercise 7-1 Enhance the Vendor Maintenance application

In this exercise, you'll enhance the Vendor Maintenance application that's presented in this chapter. That will give you a chance to work with parameters and stored procedures. It will also demonstrate that it's relatively easy to make changes to a three-layer application.

Review the application

1. Open the Vendor Maintenance application that's in your Chapter 7 directory. Then, use the Solution Explorer to review the files for this application.
2. In the PayablesData project, note that each business class is matched with a DB class. In the VendorMaintenace project, note that the Validator class provides the methods for validating data.
3. Test the application to see how it works. First, modify a row. Then, add a new row.

Add a delete function to the application

4. Add a Delete button to the Vendor Maintenance form to the right of the Modify button.

5. Add a DeleteVendor method to the VendorDB class that deletes the current vendor row. This method should have one parameter that accepts a Vendor object, and it should return a Boolean value of True if the deletion works and False if it doesn't.

   Like the UpdateVendor method in the VendorDB class, the deletion shouldn't be done if the vendor data has changed since it was retrieved from the database. Also, if a SQL exception occurs during the operation, the exception should be thrown to the calling procedure.

   One way to code this method is to copy and modify the code for the UpdateVendor method. Recall from figure 1-11 that the Delete statement doesn't require any values to be Set and note that only one SQL parameter is needed. So your completed DeleteVendor method will be much shorter than the UpdateVendor method.

6. Add a Click event handler for the Delete button. This event handler should start by using a message box to confirm that the user wants to delete the current vendor. If the user confirms, the event handler should execute the DeleteVendor method in the VendorDB class.

   Then, if the method returns True, the controls on the form should be cleared. If the method returns False, an error message should be displayed that indicates that another user updated or deleted the current vendor before the delete operation. And if the method throws a SQL exception, the exception message should be displayed.

7. Test and debug this enhancement until it works right.

Use a stored procedure for the GetVendor method in the VendorDB class

8. Use the View menu to display the Server Explorer (Database Explorer if you are using Visual Basic 2010 Express edition). Then, expand the nodes for the Payables database until you reach Stored Procedures. There, you can see that the database includes a stored procedure named spGetVendor, and if you double-click on it you can see the details of the stored procedure.

9. Modify the GetVendor method in the VendorDB class so it uses the spGetVendor stored procedure instead of the coded Select statement. To do that, comment out the statements that you won't need. Then, use figure 7-10 as a guide for writing the statements that you do need for using the stored procedure.

10. Test and debug this enhancement until it works right. Note that this enhancement doesn't require changes to any of the presentation or business classes.

8

How to work with transactions

In the last two chapters, you learned how to issue one database command at a time. Now, you'll learn how to work with groups of related commands so none of the commands in the group are applied to the database unless all of the commands are. This is an important skill for critical applications. And this is a feature that you can't implement when you use data sources and datasets.

How to use transactions

In chapter 5, you saw an Invoice Entry application that added one invoice row to the Invoices table and one or more line item rows to the InvoiceLineItems table for each invoice that the user entered. In a case like this, you want to be sure that all of the database commands for each invoice are executed successfully. For instance, you don't want the invoice row to get added to the database unless the line item rows are added too. To prevent that from happening, you can use transactions.

A *transaction* is a group of related database commands that you combine into a single logical unit. Then, you can make sure that all of the commands in the transaction can be completed successfully before you *commit* them. And if one or more of the commands aren't done successfully, you can *rollback* all of the commands.

How to start a transaction

Figure 8-1 presents the methods you use to create and work with transactions. To start a transaction, you use the BeginTransaction method of a connection object as shown in the first example in this figure. This creates a transaction object that you can use to work with the transaction.

Note that before you execute the BeginTransaction method, you must open the connection. Also note that the SqlTransaction class doesn't have a public constructor. As a result, the only way to create a SqlTransaction object is to use the BeginTransaction method of the connection object.

How to associate commands with a transaction

To use a transaction, you associate it with one or more commands. To do that, you assign the transaction object to the Transaction property of each command as shown in the second and third examples in figure 8-1. Note that each of the commands must be associated with the same connection object on which the transaction was started.

How to commit or rollback a transaction

After you associate a transaction with a command, any SQL statement you execute using that command becomes part of the transaction. Then, if all of the commands in the transaction execute without error, you can *commit* the transaction. That means that all of the changes that have been made to the database since the beginning of the transaction are made permanent. To commit a transaction, you use the Commit method of the transaction as shown in the fourth example in figure 8-1.

The syntax for creating a transaction object

```
sqlConnection.BeginTransaction()
```

Common methods of the SqlTransaction class

Method	Description
`Commit()`	Commits the changes to the database, making them permanent.
`Rollback()`	Reverses the changes made to the database to the beginning of the transaction.

Code that begins a transaction on a connection

```
Dim payableTransaction As SqlTransaction
connection.Open()
payableTransaction = connection.BeginTransaction
```

Code that associates the transaction with a command

```
Dim insertInvoiceCommand As New SqlCommand
insertInvoiceCommand.Connection = connection
insertInvoiceCommand.Transaction = payableTransaction
```

Code that associates the transaction with another command

```
Dim insertLineItemCommand As New SqlCommand
insertLineItemCommand.Connection = connection
insertLineItemCommand.Transaction = payableTransaction
```

Code that commits the transaction

```
payableTransaction.Commit()
```

Code that rolls back the transaction

```
payableTransaction.Rollback()
```

Description

- A *transaction* is a group of SQL statements that are combined into a logical unit. By default, each SQL statement is treated as a separate transaction.
- When you *commit* a transaction, the changes made to the database become permanent. Until it's committed, you can undo all of the changes since the beginning of the transaction by *rolling back* the transaction.
- The BeginTransaction method of a connection begins a transaction on an open connection and returns a transaction object. To associate a transaction with a command, you set the Transaction property of the command to the transaction object.
- If you close a connection while a transaction is pending, the changes are rolled back.

Figure 8-1 How to create and work with transactions

In contrast, if any of the commands cause an error, you can reverse, or *rollback*, all of the changes made to the database since the beginning of the transaction. To rollback a transaction, you use the Rollback method of the transaction as shown in the last example in figure 8-1.

How to work with save points

In most cases, if you need to rollback a transaction, you'll rollback the entire transaction. Occasionally, though, you may need to rollback just part of a transaction. To do that, you use *save points* as illustrated in figure 8-2.

To set a save point, you use the Save method of the transaction. On this method, you specify the name you want to use for the save point. Then, to roll a transaction back to a save point, you name the save point on the Rollback method. The example in this figure illustrates how this works.

The code in this example starts by creating a command that contains a Delete statement that deletes the vendor with a specified ID. This command is associated with a transaction named vendorTransaction. The next group of statements deletes the vendor with a vendor ID of 124 and then sets a save point named Vendor1. The next group of statements is similar except that it deletes the vendor with a vendor ID of 125 and then sets a save point named Vendor2. The two statements after that delete the vendor with a vendor ID of 126.

After that, the next statement rolls back the transaction to the Vendor2 save point. That means that any processing that was done after the Vendor2 save point is rolled back, which means that the third delete operation is rolled back. Then, the next statement rolls back the transaction to the Vendor1 save point, which rolls back the second delete operation. Finally, the transaction is committed. Since the only delete operation that hasn't already been rolled back is the one that deleted row 124, this row is deleted permanently.

Methods of the SqlTransaction class for working with save points

Method	Description
Save(savePointName)	Creates a save point with the specified name within the transaction.
Rollback(savePointName)	Reverses the changes made to the database to the specified save point.

Code that uses a transaction with two save points

```
Dim vendorTransaction As SqlTransaction
connection.Open()
vendorTransaction = connection.BeginTransaction

Dim deleteStatement As String =
    "DELETE FROM Vendors WHERE VendorID = @VendorID"
Dim deleteCommand As New SqlCommand(deleteStatement, connection)
deleteCommand.Parameters.Add("@VendorID", SqlDbType.Int)
deleteCommand.Connection = connection
deleteCommand.Transaction = vendorTransaction

deleteCommand.Parameters("@VendorID").Value = 124
deleteCommand.ExecuteNonQuery()
vendorTransaction.Save("Vendor1")

deleteCommand.Parameters("@VendorID").Value = 125
deleteCommand.ExecuteNonQuery()
vendorTransaction.Save("Vendor2")

deleteCommand.Parameters("@VendorID").Value = 126
deleteCommand.ExecuteNonQuery()

vendorTransaction.Rollback("Vendor2")
vendorTransaction.Rollback("Vendor1")

vendorTransaction.Commit()
```

Description

- To partially rollback a transaction, you can use *save points*. To set a save point, you use the Save method of the transaction.
- To rollback a transaction to a save point, you code the save point name on the Rollback method. If you don't code a save point name on this method, the entire transaction is rolled back.
- After you rollback to a save point, you must still execute the Commit method if you want to commit the rest of the transaction.

An introduction to concurrency and locking

When two or more users have access to the same database, it's possible for them to be working with the same data at the same time. As you learned in chapter 2, this is called *concurrency*. Concurrency isn't a problem when two users retrieve the same data at the same time. If they then try to update that data, however, that can be a problem. In the topics that follow, you'll learn how SQL Server uses locking to prevent concurrency problems. You'll also learn how you can control the types of problems that are allowed.

The four concurrency problems that locks can prevent

Figure 8-3 describes the four types of concurrency problems that locks can prevent. Depending on the nature of the data you're working with, these problems may not adversely affect a database. In fact, for many systems, these problems happen infrequently. Then, when they do occur, they can be corrected by simply resubmitting the query that caused the problem. On some database systems, however, these problems can affect data integrity in a serious way.

To help prevent concurrency problems, SQL Server uses *locking*. In most cases, the default locking behavior prevents serious data integrity problems from occurring. In some cases, though, you may want to change the default locking behavior. ADO.NET lets you do that by setting the transaction isolation level.

Four types of concurrency problems

Problem	Description
Lost updates	Occur when two transactions select the same row and then update the row based on the values originally selected. Since each transaction is unaware of the other, the later update overwrites the earlier update.
Dirty reads	Occur when a transaction selects data that isn't committed by another transaction. For example, transaction A changes a row. Transaction B then selects the changed row before transaction A commits the change. If transaction A then rolls back the change, transaction B has selected a row that doesn't exist in the database.
Nonrepeatable reads	Occur when two Select statements of the same data result in different values because another transaction has updated the data in the time between the two statements. For example, transaction A selects a row. Transaction B then updates the row. When transaction A selects the same row again, the data is different.
Phantom reads	Occur when you perform an update or delete on a set of rows when another transaction is performing an insert or delete that affects one or more rows in that same set of rows. For example, transaction A updates the payment total for each invoice that has a balance due. Transaction B inserts a new, unpaid, invoice while transaction A is still running. After transaction A finishes, there is still an invoice with a balance due.

Description

- SQL Server uses *locking* to help prevent concurrency problems. *Locks* delay the execution of a transaction if it conflicts with a transaction that's already running.
- In a large system with many users, you should expect these kinds of problems to occur. In general, you don't need to take any action except to anticipate the problem. In many cases, if the query is resubmitted, the problem goes away.
- On some systems, if two transactions overwrite each other, the validity of the database is compromised and resubmitting one of the transactions won't eliminate the problem. If you're working on such a system, you must anticipate these concurrency problems and account for them in your code.
- You should consider concurrency problems as you write your code. If one of these problems would affect data integrity, you can change the default locking behavior by setting the transaction isolation level as shown in the next figure.

Note

- Although you can use locking to prevent lost updates, you can also prevent them by comparing the original values retrieved from the database with the current values in the database in the Where clause of the Update statement as you saw in the last chapter.

Figure 8-3 The four concurrency problems that locks can prevent

How to work with isolation levels

Figure 8-4 shows how you change the *transaction isolation level* for a transaction. To do that, you specify the isolation level on the BeginTransaction method using one of the members of the IsolationLevel enumeration. The table in this figure indicates which of the four concurrency problems an IsolationLevel will prevent or allow. For example, if you set the isolation level to Serializable as shown in the statement in this figure, all four concurrency problems will be prevented.

When you set the isolation level to Serializable, each transaction is completely isolated from every other transaction and concurrency is severely restricted. The server does this by locking each resource, preventing other transactions from accessing it. Since each transaction must wait for the previous transaction to commit, the transactions are executed serially, one after another.

Since the Serializable isolation level eliminates all possible concurrency problems, you may think that this is the best option. However, this option requires more server overhead to manage all of the locks. In addition, access time for each transaction is increased, since only one transaction can work with the data at a time. For most systems, this will actually eliminate few concurrency problems but will cause severe performance problems.

The lowest isolation level is ReadUncommitted, which allows all four of the concurrency problems to occur. It does this by performing Select queries without setting any locks and without honoring any existing locks. Since this means that your Select statements will always execute immediately, this setting provides the best performance. Since other transactions can retrieve and modify the same data, however, this setting can't prevent concurrency problems.

The default isolation level, ReadCommitted, is acceptable for most applications. However, the only concurrency problem it prevents is dirty reads. Although it can prevent some lost updates, it can't prevent them all.

The RepeatableRead level allows more concurrency than the Serializable level but less than the ReadCommitted level. As you might expect, then, it results in faster performance than Serializable and permits fewer concurrency problems than ReadCommitted.

The Snapshot level uses a SQL Server feature called *row versioning*. With row versioning, any data that's retrieved by a transaction that uses Snapshot isolation is consistent with the data that existed at the start of the transaction. To accomplish that, SQL Server maintains a snapshot of the original version of a row each time it's modified.

When you use row versioning, locks aren't required for read operations, which improves concurrency. However, the need to maintain row versions requires additional resources and can degrade performance. In most cases, then, you'll use row versioning only when data consistency is imperative.

The syntax for changing the isolation level for a transaction

```
connection.BeginTransaction(isolationLevel)
```

Common members of the IsolationLevel enumeration

Member	Description
ReadUncommitted	Allows all concurrency problems.
ReadCommitted	Prevents dirty reads, but not lost updates, nonrepeatable reads, or phantom reads. This is the default isolation level for SQL Server.
RepeatableRead	Prevents dirty reads, lost updates, and nonrepeatable reads, but not phantom reads.
Snapshot	Prevents all concurrency problems by using row versioning instead of locking.
Serializable	Prevents all concurrency problems.

Code that sets the isolation level for a transaction so all concurrency problems are prevented

```
connection.BeginTransaction(IsolationLevel.Serializable)
```

Description

- Since SQL Server manages locking automatically, you can't control every aspect of locking for your transactions. However, you can set the isolation level in your code.
- The *transaction isolation level* controls the degree to which transactions are isolated from one another. The server isolates transactions by using more restrictive locking behavior. If you isolate your transactions from other transactions, concurrency problems are reduced or eliminated.
- You specify the transaction isolation level by passing a member of the IsolationLevel enumeration to the BeginTransaction method. The default transaction isolation level is ReadCommitted. At this level, some lost updates, nonrepeatable reads, and phantom reads can occur, but this is acceptable for most transactions.
- The ReadUncommitted isolation level doesn't set any locks and ignores locks that are already held. This level results in the highest possible performance for your query, but at the risk of every kind of concurrency problem. For this reason, you should only use this level for data that is rarely updated.
- The RepeatableRead level places locks on all data that's used in a transaction, preventing other users from updating that data. However, this isolation level still allows inserts, so phantom reads can occur.
- The Snapshot level was introduced with SQL Server 2005. It uses *row versioning* rather than locks to provide read consistency. With row versioning, each time a transaction modifies a row, SQL Server stores an image of the row as it existed before the modification. That way, read operations that use row versioning retrieve the row as it existed at the start of the transaction.
- The Serializable level places a lock on all data that's used in a transaction. Since each transaction must wait for the previous transaction to commit, the transactions are handled in sequence. This is the most restrictive of the five isolation levels shown in this figure.

Figure 8-4 How to work with isolation levels

A Transfer Payment application that uses transactions

To illustrate the use of transactions, the rest of this chapter presents a simple application. It lets the user reverse an incorrect invoice payment and apply the payment to the correct invoice. For each transfer, a transaction is used to make sure that a payment isn't reversed unless it is also applied to the correct invoice.

The user interface

Figure 8-5 presents the user interface for this application. First, the user gets the invoice information for the invoice that the payment amount should be transferred from. Then, the user gets the invoice information for the invoice that the payment should be transferred to. At this point, if everything looks okay, the user can enter the transfer amount and click the Make Transfer button.

Of course, this application is unrealistically simple. For instance, you probably wouldn't get the invoice data without also getting some vendor data to make sure you've got the right invoice, and a real world application would almost certainly include a list of invoice numbers that the user can choose from. So please keep in mind that the purpose of this application is to illustrate the use of transactions, not business practices.

Nevertheless, this application does represent a type of application that is relatively common. That is, an application that lets a user fix a clerical error. For no matter how well designed a user interface is, a careless user can make errors that need to be fixed with applications like this one.

The Transfer Payment form

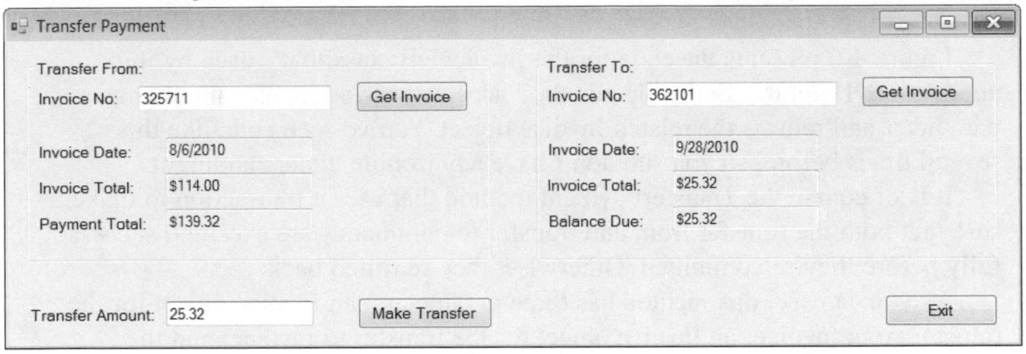

The dialog box that's displayed after the transfer is processed

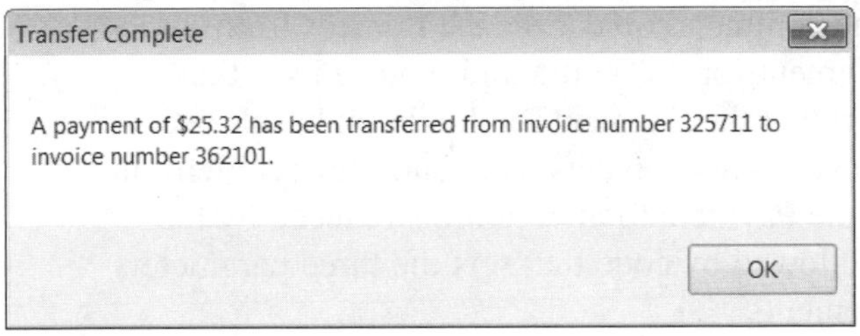

Description

- Due to clerical errors, invoice payments are sometimes applied to the wrong invoices. In those cases, you need to reverse any payments that are applied to the wrong invoices and apply those amounts to the right invoices. That's what this application provides for.
- To transfer a payment from one invoice to another, the user enters the invoice number for the first invoice, clicks the first Get Invoice button, enters the invoice number for the second invoice, and clicks the second Get Invoice button. Then, if the data that's displayed is for the right invoices, the user enters the amount to be transferred and clicks the Make Transfer button.
- If the transfer is successful, the dialog box shown above is displayed. Otherwise, an error message is displayed. In either case, the form is cleared so the user can transfer another payment.
- This application requires the use of transactions because the transfer amount shouldn't be reversed from the first invoice without also applying it to the second invoice. If an error occurs during this process, the database operations should be rolled back.

Figure 8-5 The user interface for the Transfer Payment application

The code for the InvoiceDB class

Figure 8-6 presents the code for the InvoiceDB class that's used by this application. Here, the GetInvoice method accepts a string invoice number as a parameter and returns the related Invoice object. You've seen code like this several times before, so you shouldn't have any trouble understanding it.

It is of course the TransferPayment method that uses a transaction to make sure that both the transfer from and transfer to commands are executed successfully before they're committed. Otherwise, they're rolled back.

As you can see, this method has three parameters: an Invoice object for the transfer from invoice; an Invoice object for the transfer to invoice; and the payment amount as a Decimal type. To start, this method creates a connection object and a transaction object. These will be used later.

Next, this method creates the command object for the transfer from. In the Where clause of the Update statement for this command, you can see that parameters are used to make sure that the PaymentTotal column hasn't been changed since the row was retrieved. This prevents a concurrency problem. In the Set clause, you can see that the PaymentTotal column is reduced by the payment amount. This code is followed by code that sets the three parameters that are used by the Update statement.

The code for the InvoiceDB class

Page 1

```
Imports System.Data.SqlClient

Public Class InvoiceDB

Public Shared Function GetInvoice(ByVal invoiceNo As String) As Invoice
        Dim invoice As New Invoice
        Dim connection As SqlConnection = PayablesDB.GetConnection
        Dim selectStatement As String =
            "SELECT InvoiceNumber, InvoiceDate, " &
            "InvoiceTotal, PaymentTotal " &
            "FROM Invoices " &
            "WHERE InvoiceNumber = @InvoiceNumber"
        Dim selectCommand As New SqlCommand(selectStatement, connection)
        selectCommand.Parameters.AddWithValue("@InvoiceNumber", invoiceNo)
        Try
            connection.Open()
            Dim reader As SqlDataReader =
                selectCommand.ExecuteReader(CommandBehavior.SingleRow)
            If reader.Read Then
                invoice.InvoiceNumber = reader("InvoiceNumber").ToString
                invoice.InvoiceDate = CDate(reader("InvoiceDate"))
                invoice.InvoiceTotal = CDec(reader("InvoiceTotal"))
                invoice.PaymentTotal = CDec(reader("PaymentTotal"))
            Else
                invoice = Nothing
            End If
            reader.Close()
        Catch ex As SqlException
            Throw ex
        Finally
            connection.Close()
        End Try
        Return invoice
    End Function

    Public Shared Function TransferPayment(ByVal fromInvoice As Invoice,
        ByVal toInvoice As Invoice, ByVal payment As Decimal) As Boolean
        Dim connection As SqlConnection = PayablesDB.GetConnection
        Dim paymentTran As SqlTransaction = Nothing

        Dim fromCommand As New SqlCommand
        fromCommand.Connection = connection
        fromCommand.CommandText =
            "UPDATE Invoices " &
            "SET PaymentTotal = PaymentTotal - @Payment " &
            "WHERE InvoiceNumber = @InvoiceNumber " &
            "  AND PaymentTotal = @PaymentTotal"
        fromCommand.Parameters.AddWithValue("@Payment", payment)
        fromCommand.Parameters.AddWithValue("@InvoiceNumber",
                fromInvoice.InvoiceNumber)
        fromCommand.Parameters.AddWithValue("@PaymentTotal",
                fromInvoice.PaymentTotal)
```

Figure 8-6 The code for the InvoiceDB class (part 1 of 2)

The next set of statements creates the command object for the transfer to. This works like the statements for the transfer from command object, but the PaymentTotal column is increased by the payment amount.

The rest of the code in this method starts the transaction, associates the two commands with the transaction, and executes the commands. Then, if one of the commands doesn't return a value that's greater than zero, which indicates a concurrency problem, the transaction is rolled back and the method returns a value of False. Or, if a SQL exception is caught by the Catch block, the transaction is rolled back and the exception is thrown to the calling method. But if both commands are successful, the transaction is committed and the method returns a value of True.

The code for the InvoiceDB class **Page 2**

```
        Dim toCommand As New SqlCommand
        toCommand.Connection = connection
        toCommand.CommandText =
            "UPDATE Invoices " &
            "SET PaymentTotal = PaymentTotal + @Payment " &
            "WHERE InvoiceNumber = @InvoiceNumber " &
            "  AND PaymentTotal = @PaymentTotal"
        toCommand.Parameters.AddWithValue("@Payment", payment)
        toCommand.Parameters.AddWithValue("@InvoiceNumber",
            toInvoice.InvoiceNumber)
        toCommand.Parameters.AddWithValue("@PaymentTotal",
            toInvoice.PaymentTotal)

        Try
            connection.Open()
            paymentTran = connection.BeginTransaction
            fromCommand.Transaction = paymentTran
            toCommand.Transaction = paymentTran

            Dim count As Integer = fromCommand.ExecuteNonQuery
            If count > 0 Then
                count = toCommand.ExecuteNonQuery
                If count > 0 Then
                    paymentTran.Commit()
                    Return True
                Else
                    paymentTran.Rollback()
                    Return False
                End If
            Else
                paymentTran.Rollback()
                Return False
            End If
        Catch ex As SqlException
            If paymentTran IsNot Nothing Then
                paymentTran.Rollback()
            End If
            Throw ex
        Finally
            connection.Close()
        End Try
    End Function

End Class
```

Figure 8-6 The code for the InvoiceDB class (part 2 of 2)

The code for the Transfer Payment form

To show you how the TransferPayment method of the InvoiceDB database class is used by the Transfer Payment form, figure 8-7 presents the code for the Click event of its Make Transfer button. If you want to see the other event handlers for this form, you can of course open the application that you've downloaded from our web site. But you shouldn't have any trouble envisioning what the other event handlers do.

As you can see in this figure, the code for the Click event handler of the Make Transfer button consists of nested If statements that check the validity of all the data before executing the TransferPayment method of the InvoiceDB class. If anything is invalid, the related Else clause displays an appropriate error message. But if everything is valid, the TransferPayment method is executed.

When the TransferPayment method is executed, it returns True, returns False, or throws a SQL exception. As a result, the call for this method is coded as the condition for an If statement within the Try block of a Try...Catch statement. Then, if the method returns True, a message is displayed that documents the payment transfer. If the method returns False, a message is displayed that indicates that a concurrency error probably occurred. And if the method throws a SQL exception, the exception message is displayed.

Note that once the result is returned from the TransferPayment method of the InvoiceDB class, the fromInvoice and toInvoice variables are set to Nothing after the ClearControls procedure is called. This is done whether or not the transfer was successful. If these variables aren't set to Nothing, the user could transfer a payment without retrieving another to or from invoice.

The code for the Click event of the Make Transfer button

```
Private Sub btnTransfer_Click(ByVal sender As System.Object,
        ByVal e As System.EventArgs) Handles btnTransfer.Click
    If Validator.IsPresent(txtTransferAmount) AndAlso
        Validator.IsDecimal(txtTransferAmount) Then
        If fromInvoice IsNot Nothing AndAlso toInvoice IsNot Nothing Then
            Dim transferAmount As Decimal = CDec(txtTransferAmount.Text)
            If transferAmount <= fromInvoice.PaymentTotal Then
                If transferAmount <= toInvoice.BalanceDue Then
                    Try
                        If InvoiceDB.TransferPayment(fromInvoice,
                                toInvoice, transferAmount) Then
                            Dim message As String =
                                "A payment of " &
                                FormatCurrency(transferAmount) &
                                " has been transferred from " &
                                "invoice number " &
                                fromInvoice.InvoiceNumber &
                                " to invoice number " &
                                toInvoice.InvoiceNumber & "."
                            MessageBox.Show(Message, "Transfer Complete")
                        Else
                            MessageBox.Show("The transfer was not " &
                                "processed. Another user may have " &
                                "posted a payment to one of the " &
                                "invoices.", "Transfer Not Processed")
                        End If
                    Catch ex As Exception
                        MessageBox.Show(ex.Message, ex.GetType.ToString)
                    Finally
                        Me.ClearControls()
                        fromInvoice = Nothing
                        toInvoice = Nothing
                    End Try
                Else
                    MessageBox.Show("Transfer amount cannot be more " &
                        "than the balance due.", "Data Entry Error")
                End If
            Else
                MessageBox.Show("Transfer amount cannot be more " &
                    "than the payment total.", "Data Entry Error")
            End If
        Else
            MessageBox.Show("You must select the From and To invoices " &
                "before transferring a payment.", "Data Entry Error")
        End If
    End If
End Sub
```

Figure 8-7 The code for the Transfer Payment form

Perspective

In this chapter, you've learned how to use transactions, which is an important skill for critical database applications. Although the application in this chapter is simplistic, you'll see the use of transactions in a more realistic application in chapter 10. And the exercise for that chapter will give you a chance to work with the code for using transactions.

Now that you know how to use transactions, you have a complete set of skills for building three-layer database applications. When you use these skills, you have complete control over how your applications work. The code in your business and database classes can be used in more than one application. Your applications are relatively easy to test, debug, maintain, and enhance. And you can use transactions to make sure that all of the database commands in a group have been done successfully before you commit them.

In the next chapter, though, you'll learn how to use a feature of Visual Studio that lets you build three-layer applications and still get the benefits of using bound controls. This feature is called object data sources, and every professional should know how to use it.

Terms

transaction
commit
rollback
save point
locking
dirty read
nonrepeatable read
phantom read
transaction isolation level
row versioning
lost update

9

How to work with object data sources

In section 2 of this book, you learned how to use data sources and datasets to work with the data in a database. This lets you quickly create forms that use controls that are bound to the database. However, it doesn't give you as much control over how your applications work as you may need.

In the last three chapters, you learned how to use code to access a database. Although you can't build applications as quickly with this approach and you can't use data binding, you do have complete control over the way the data access code works.

In this chapter, you'll learn how you can get the best of both worlds by using object data sources, which are data sources that get their data from business objects. This lets you get the benefits of data binding and have complete control over how the data access code works.

An introduction to object data sources

The following topics introduce you to object data sources and the three-layer architecture that they let you implement.

How three-layer Windows applications work with object data sources

As you learned in chapter 2, most development experts recommend a *three-layer architecture* that separates the presentation, business, and data access components of the application. The *presentation layer* includes the forms that define the user interface. The *middle layer* includes classes that represent business entities. It may also include classes that implement business rules such as data validation requirements or discount policies. The *database layer* consists of the classes that manage the data access for the business objects and the database itself.

When you use *object data sources*, as figure 9-1 shows, you still use a three-layer architecture that includes business and database classes. Then, the object data source is stored in the presentation layer so it can be used for data binding. In this case, it's used to bind controls on a form to the data in a business object, which is created from a business class in the middle layer. This means that you can use data binding in the presentation layer and still use code to control the data access operations.

When you use an object data source, you create a database class to handle the data access for the business object. This class typically provides at least one method that retrieves data from the database and stores it in the business object. It can also provide methods to insert, update, and delete data.

The three-layer architecture in Visual Studio 2008

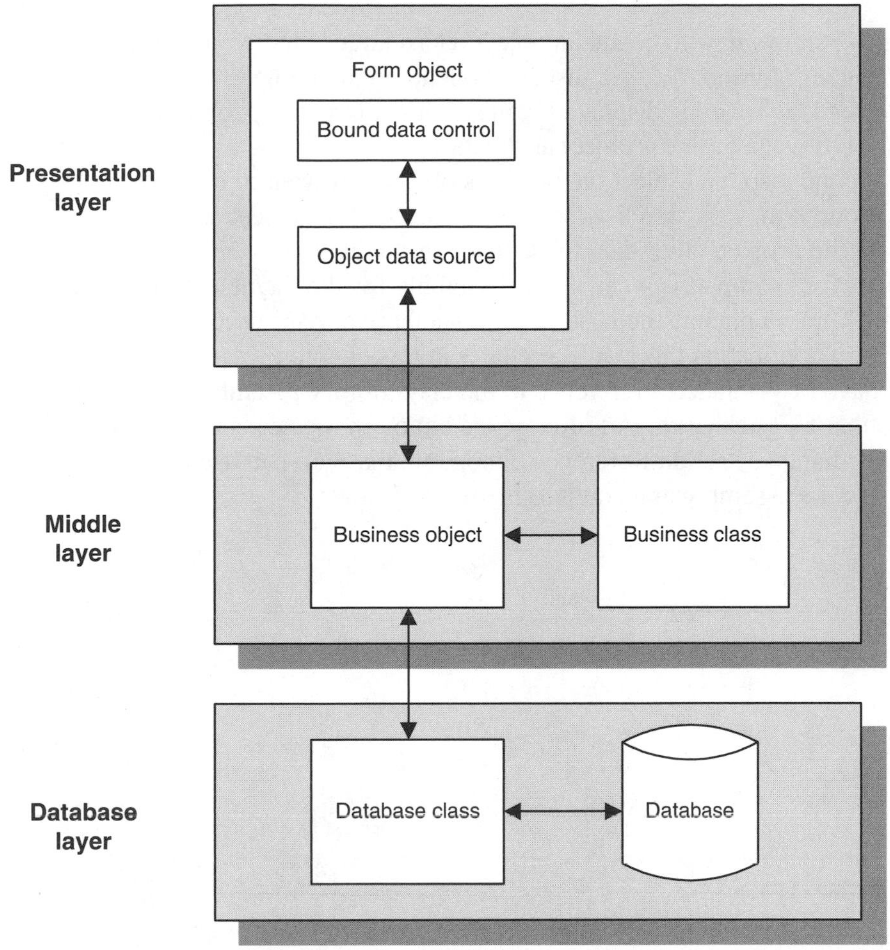

Description

- An *object data source* is a data source that gets its data from a business object rather than directly from a database. To work with the data in a business object, an application uses a database class.
- An application that uses object data sources has a *three-layer architecture* where the object data sources are part of the *presentation layer*, the business classes are part of the *middle layer*, and the database classes are part of the *database layer*.
- The business classes that define the business objects used by an application and the database classes that work with those objects are typically stored in a class library.
- Once you create an object data source, you can drag it to a form to create controls that are bound to the properties of the business object it's based on.

Figure 9-1 How three-layer Windows applications work with object data sources

How to create an object data source

Figure 9-2 shows how to create an object data source. First, you start the Data Source Configuration Wizard just as you learned in chapter 3. Then, when the first step of the wizard is displayed, you select the Object option to indicate that you want to use a business object as the data source.

In the second step, you select the business object you want to bind the object data source to. This step lists any assemblies that have been added as references to the project, other than those that begin with Microsoft or System. In this figure, for example, you can see an assembly for the PayablesData class library. This library contains the business and database classes used by the Payment Entry application that you'll see later in this chapter.

If you haven't yet added a reference to the class library assembly you need, you can do that by clicking the Add Reference button in the second step of the Wizard. This displays an Add Reference dialog box that you can use to locate the dll file for the assembly and add it to the project.

The first dialog box of the Data Source Configuration Wizard

How to select the object for the data source

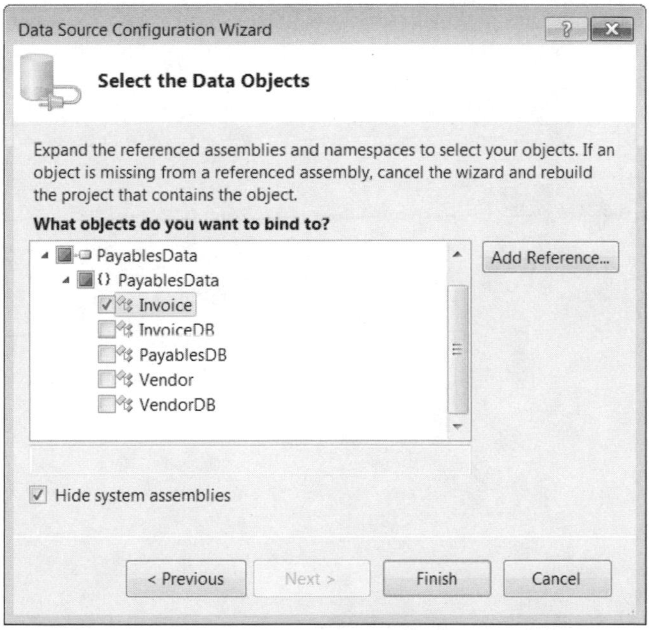

Description

- To create an object data source, select the Object option from the first step of the Data Source Configuration Wizard. Then, select the business object you want to use as the source of data from the list of objects in the second step.

Figure 9-2 How to create an object data source

How to use an object data source

After you create an object data source, it appears in the Data Sources window as shown in figure 9-3. Here, you can see the Invoice business object in the PayablesData class library that was selected in the previous figure. When you expand this object, you can see all of the public properties it defines.

To work with an object data source, you can drag a business object to a form. By default, a DataGridView control, binding source, and binding navigator are generated as shown here. You can also change the default control for a business object by selecting the Details option from the drop-down list for the table. Then, if you drag that business object from the Data Sources window onto a form, Visual Studio generates a label and a bound control for each property of the business object. This works just like it does for a data source that gets its data from a database.

As you might expect, you don't use datasets with object data sources. Because of that, Visual Studio doesn't generate a dataset schema when you create an object data source, and it doesn't create a dataset when you drag an object data source to a form. In addition, it doesn't create a table adapter or table adapter manager since they're used strictly with datasets.

A form after the Invoice data source has been dragged onto it

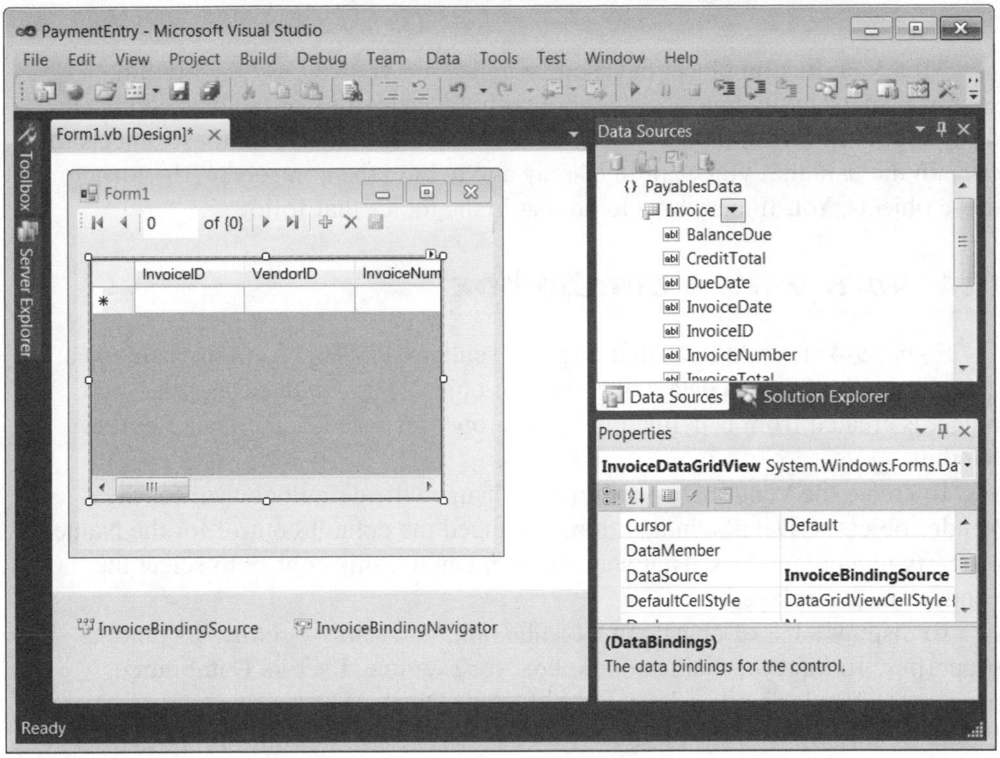

Description

- When you create an object data source, it appears in the Data Sources window. Then, you can drag the entire business object or individual properties of the business object to the form to create bound controls. This is identical to the way that you work with tables and columns in a data source that gets its data from a database.
- Unlike a data source that gets it data from a database, an object data source doesn't store its data in a dataset. Because of that, no dataset schema file is generated when the data source is created, and no dataset, table adapter, or table adapter manager are created when you drag the data source to a form.
- Although a binding navigator is added to the form when you drag an object data source onto it, you won't typically use this control.
- The binding source for an object data source provides for working with the properties of the data source at design time. At runtime, however, the application must create the object that contains the data that will be displayed in the controls and then bind the controls to the object. See figures 9-4 and 9-5 for details.

How to work with bound controls

After you drag an object data source to a form, you can use the binding source Visual Studio generates to work with the properties of the data source at design time. In addition, you'll need to use code to create the business objects that contain the data that you want to display and to bind the controls on the form to those objects. You'll learn how to do that in the topics that follow.

How to work with a combo box

Figure 9-4 shows a form that displays vendor data. This form uses an object data source that gets its data from a Vendor object. The Vendor class that this object is created from is defined with the properties listed in the Data Sources window.

To create the Vendor Display form, I changed the default control for the Vendor object to Details. In addition, I changed the default control for the Name property to a combo box. That way, the user can use this control to select the vendor that's displayed.

To display a list of objects in a combo box, you start by setting its binding properties. To bind the Name combo box, for example, I set its DataSource property to VendorBindingSource, and I set its DisplayMember property to Name. In addition, I removed the binding from the Text property of the control, which is set by default.

Note that I didn't set the ValueMember property of the combo box. That's because, when the user selects a vendor from the combo box, the selected vendor is retrieved from the list of vendors using the SelectedIndex property. Later in this chapter, when I present the Payment Entry application, I'll show you another way to retrieve a vendor by setting the ValueMember property.

Next, you use code like that shown in the first example in this figure to create the list of objects to be displayed and bind it to the combo box. The first statement in this example creates a variable that can store a list of Vendor objects. Then, the second statement uses the GetVendorList method of a class named VendorDB to get all the vendors from the database and store them in this list. Finally, the last statement sets the DataSource property of the combo box to this list.

Note that this last statement overrides the DataSource property that's set at design time. In contrast, you set this property to the binding source at design time so you can set the other binding properties of the control. That's necessary because the object you want to bind to isn't available at design time.

How to work with a text box

When you create a text box from an object data source, its Text property is automatically bound to the appropriate property of the binding source. Then, to display a value in the text box, you use code like that shown in the second example in figure 9-4.

A combo box and text boxes that are bound to an object data source

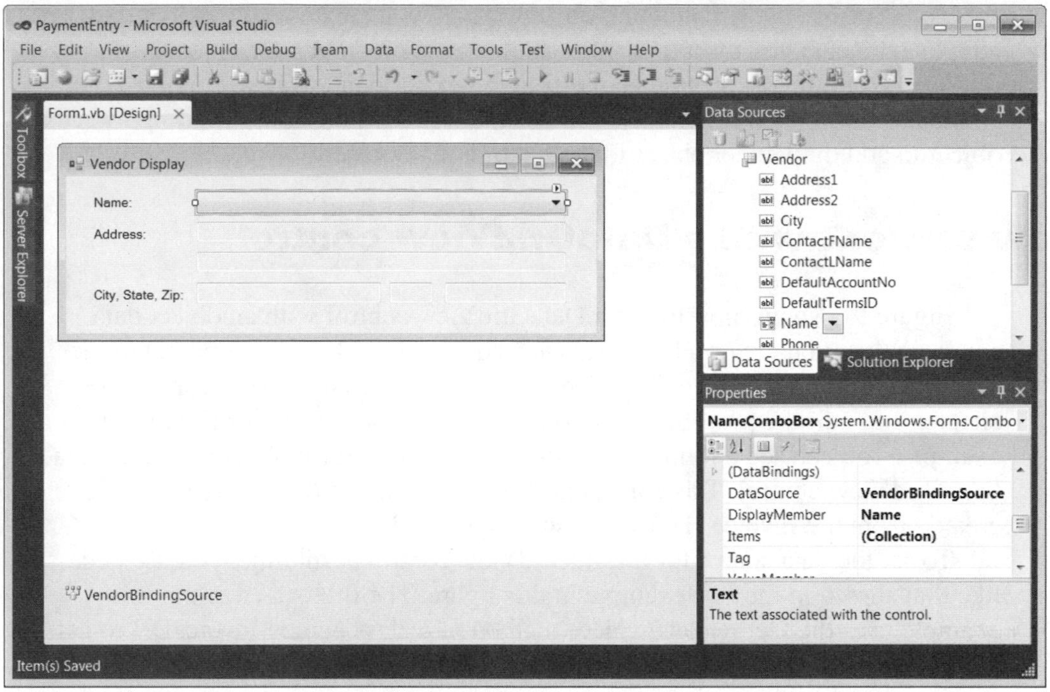

Code that creates a List() object and binds the combo box to it

```
Private vendorList As List(Of Vendor)
vendorList = VendorDB.GetVendorList
NameComboBox.DataSource = vendorList
```

Code that binds the text boxes to a Vendor object

```
VendorBindingSource.Clear()
Dim vendor As Vendor = vendorList(NameComboBox.SelectedIndex)
VendorBindingSource.Add(vendor)
```

Description

- If you generate a combo box from a property of an object data source, you'll need to set its binding properties as described in figure 4-3 of chapter 4.
- To bind a combo box to an object, you create the object from a class that implements the IList interface, such as the List() class. Then, you set the DataSource property of the combo box to that object.
- To bind text boxes to an object, you first clear the binding source to remove any existing object that the controls are bound to. Then, you create the object that contains the data you want to display and add it to the binding source.

Figure 9-4 How to use text boxes and combo boxes with an object data source

To start, you use the Clear method of the BindingSource object to remove any objects from the list of bound objects. Then, you create a new object that contains the data you want to display. In this example, a Vendor object is retrieved from the list that the Name combo box is bound to based on the vendor the user selected. Finally, you use the Add method of the BindingSource object to add the Vendor object to the list of bound objects.

How to work with a DataGridView control

Figure 9-5 shows how to use a DataGridView control with an object data source. When you create a DataGridView control, its columns are bound to the properties of the business object. Then, you can use the skills you learned in chapter 4 to edit the properties and columns of the control. In this figure, for example, you can see a form that displays the invoices for a selected vendor in a DataGridView control. This control is bound to an object data source that was created from the Invoice class you saw in figure 9-3.

To set the data source for a DataGridView control at runtime, you use code like that shown in the first example in this figure. The first statement in this example uses the GetVendorInvoices method of a class named InvoiceDB to get all the invoices for the specified vendor. These invoices are stored in a List(Of Invoice) variable. Then, the second statement sets the DataSource property of the DataGridView control to this list.

To work with the objects in a DataGridView control, you can use code like that shown in the second example. This code uses a For Each…Next loop to iterate through each row in the grid to calculate the total balance due for a vendor. Within this loop, it uses the DataBoundItem property of each row to get the business object that's stored in that row. Then, it casts the Object type that's returned by this property to the Invoice type so it can be stored in an Invoice variable. Finally, the BalanceDue property of the Invoice object is added to the balance due for the vendor.

When a DataGridView control is bound to an object data source, a CurrencyManager object is used to manage the list of business objects that's displayed by the control. If the list of objects changes, you can use the CurrencyManager object to synchronize the grid with the list. To do that, you use code like that shown in the third example in this figure.

The first statement in this example uses the BindingContext property of the DataGridView control to get the CurrencyManager object for this control. Notice that the object that's returned by this property must be cast to the CurrencyManager type. That's because the object type depends on the data source that's passed to the BindingContext property. Then, the second statement uses the Refresh method of the CurrencyManager object to display the current list of objects in the DataGridView control.

A form with a DataGridView control that's bound to an object data source

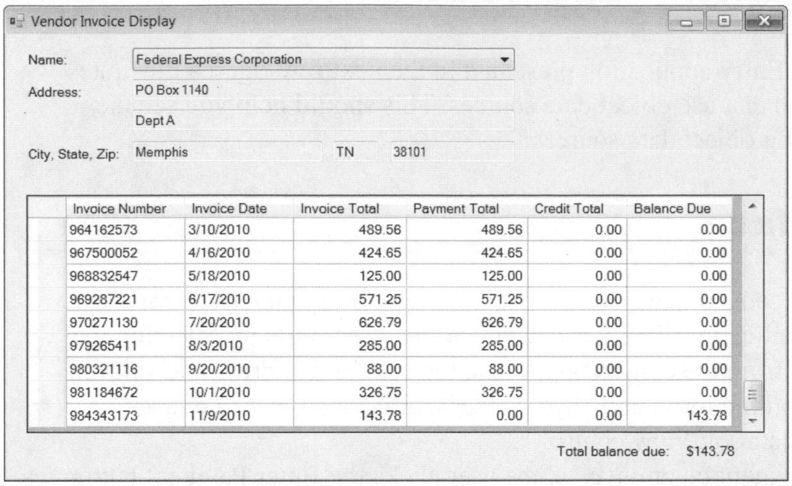

Code that creates a List() object and binds a DataGridView control to it

```
Dim invoiceList As List(Of Invoice) = InvoiceDB.GetVendorInvoices(vendorID)
InvoiceDataGridView.DataSource = invoiceList
```

Code that retrieves business objects from the DataGridView control

```
Dim balanceDue As Decimal = 0
For Each row As DataGridViewRow In InvoiceDataGridView.Rows
    Dim invoice As Invoice = CType(row.DataBoundItem, Invoice)
    balanceDue += invoice.BalanceDue
Next
```

Code that refreshes the data displayed in the DataGridView control

```
Dim cm As CurrencyManager = CType( _
    InvoiceDataGridView.BindingContext(invoiceList), CurrencyManager)
cm.Refresh()
```

Description

- When you generate a DataGridView control from an object data source, the columns in the control are bound to the properties of the business object. You can edit these columns as described in chapter 4.
- You can set the DataSource property of a DataGridView control to an object created from any class that implements a list. This includes the generic List() class and its subclasses as well as the older ArrayList class and the DataSet and DataTable classes.
- You can use the DataBoundItem property of a DataGridViewRow object to get the business object that's stored in that row.
- If an application lets you add, modify, or delete items in a DataGridView control, you can use the BindingContext property of the control to get the CurrencyManager object that manages the list of bound objects. Then, you can use the Refresh method of the CurrencyManager object to refresh the list so the current list is displayed.

Figure 9-5 How to use a DataGridView control with an object data source

A Payment Entry application

The Payment Entry application presented in the next few figures illustrates how an application can use object data sources. This should help you see the advantages of using object data sources.

The user interface

Figure 9-6 presents the two forms that make up the user interface for the Payment Entry application. To enter a payment, the user starts by selecting the vendor to be paid from the combo box. Then, the vendor's address is displayed in the text boxes on the form, and any invoices that have a balance due are displayed in the DataGridView control.

To make a payment on an invoice, the user clicks the Enter Payment button for that invoice. Then, the Payment Entry form is displayed. From this form, the user can enter the payment amount and then click the Accept button to post the payment and return to the Vendor Invoices form. Alternatively, the user can click the Cancel button to return to the Vendor Invoices form without posting a payment.

The Vendor Invoices form

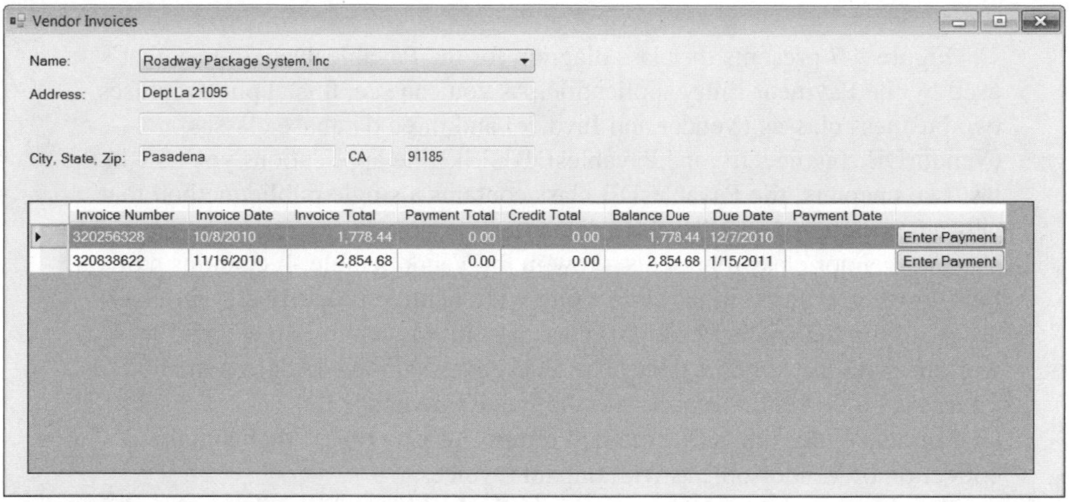

The Payment Entry form

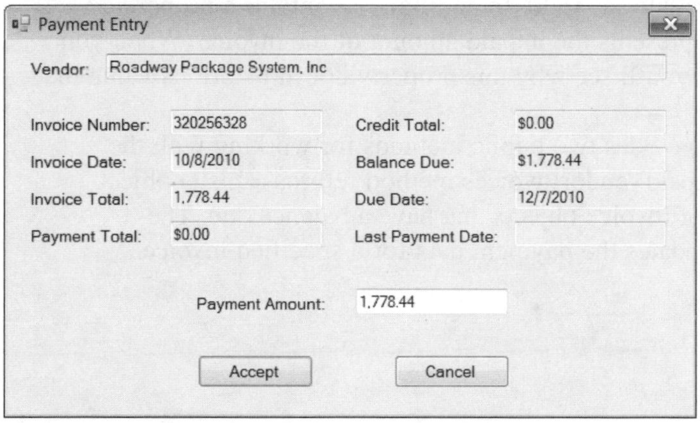

Description

- The Vendor Invoices form lets the user select a vendor from a combo box that lists all the vendors with unpaid invoices. Then, all the unpaid invoices are displayed in a DataGridView control.
- To enter a payment for an invoice, the user clicks the Enter Payment button for that invoice in the DataGridView control to display the Payment Entry form. Then, the user enters the payment amount and clicks the Accept button.
- The Name combo box is bound to a list of Vendor objects created from the Vendor class, the text boxes that display the vendor data are bound to a Vendor object that's created from the Vendor class, the DataGridView control is bound to a list of Invoice objects created from the Invoice class, and the text boxes that display the invoice data are bound to an Invoice object that's created from the Invoice class.

Figure 9-6 The user interface for the Payment Entry application

The class diagram for the PayablesData library

Figure 9-7 presents the class diagram for the PayablesData library that's used by the Payment Entry application. As you can see, this application uses two business classes (Vendor and Invoice) and three database classes (VendorDB, InvoiceDB, and PayablesDB). Like the applications you saw in the last two chapters, the PayablesDB class contains a single public method that gets a connection to the Payables database.

The Vendor class represents a row in the Vendors table. It contains a private field for each column in the table along with a public property that provides access to the field. The VendorDB class provides two public methods for working with the Vendors table. The GetVendorNameAndAddress method returns a single Vendor object with the specified Vendor ID. The GetVendorsWithBalanceDue method returns a List() object that contains a collection of Vendor objects with unpaid invoices.

The Invoice class represents a row in the Invoices table. Like the Vendor class, it contains a private field for each column in the table along with a public property that provides access to the field. In addition, it contains a property named BalanceDue that represents the unpaid amount of the invoice. When you see the code for this class, you'll see why this property doesn't store its value in a private field.

The InvoiceDB class provides two public methods for working with the Invoices table. The GetUnpaidVendorInvoices method returns a List() object that contains a collection of Invoice objects that have a balance due. The UpdatePayment method updates the payment data for a specified invoice.

The class diagram for the PayablesData library

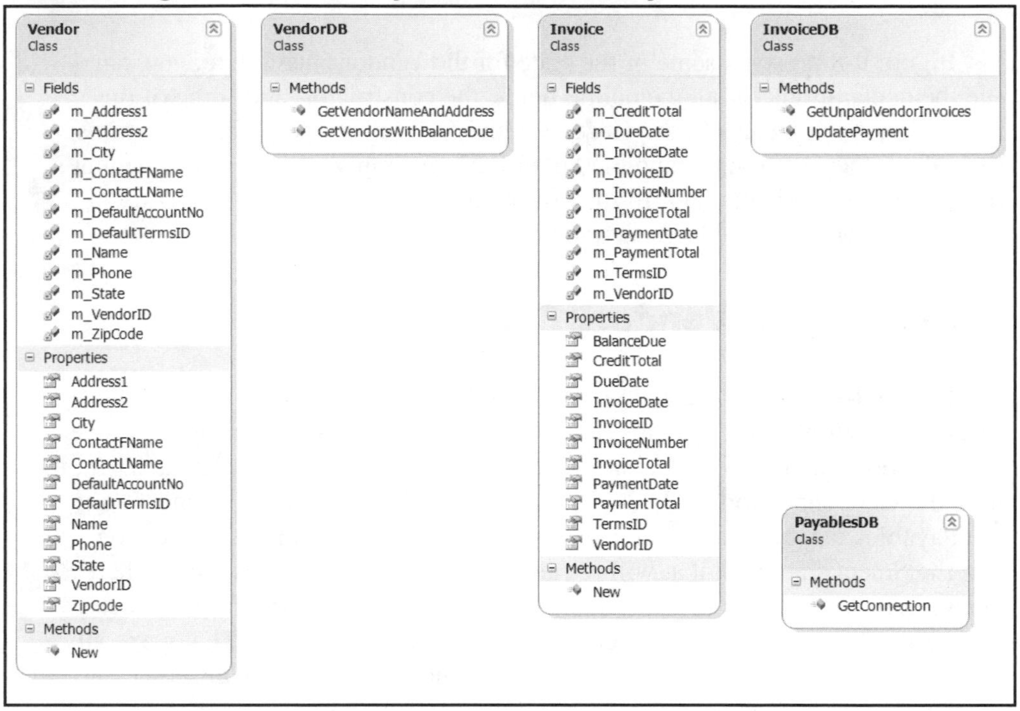

Description

- The PayablesData library contains the classes that define the business objects used by the Payment Entry application and the database classes that are used to work with the Payables database.
- The business objects are defined by the Vendor and Invoice classes. These objects will hold data from the Vendors and Invoices tables in the Payables database.
- The VendorDB, InvoiceDB, and PayablesDB classes are the database classes. These classes provide shared members for working with the Payables database.
- The VendorDB class provides public methods for getting a single vendor and a list of vendors that have unpaid invoices from the Vendors table. The InvoiceDB class provides public methods for getting the unpaid invoices for a vendor and for updating the payment data for an invoice. And the PayablesDB class provides a public method for getting a connection to the Payables database.

Figure 9-7 The class diagram for the PayablesData library

The code for the Vendor class

Figure 9-8 presents some of the code for the Vendor class. Here, you can see the declarations for all the public fields, the constructor, and some of the properties. As you can see, the Get procedure for each property simply returns the value of a private field, and the Set procedure simply assigns the value that's passed to it to a private field. If you understand how properties work, you shouldn't have any trouble understanding this code.

The code for the VendorDB class

Figure 9-9 presents the code for the VendorDB class. The GetVendorsWithBalanceDue method of this class starts by declaring a variable that will hold the List() of Vendor objects that's returned by the method. Then, it uses the GetConnection method of the PayablesDB class to get a connection to the Payables database, and it creates a command object using the connection and the Select statement that will retrieve the vendors. In this case, the Where clause contains another Select statement that retrieves the sum of the invoices for the vendor and checks whether that sum is greater than zero. That way, only the vendors who have unpaid invoices will be included in the result set.

Once the command object is created, this method continues by opening the connection and executing the command to create a data reader. Then, for each vendor that's returned, it creates a Vendor object, sets the VendorID and Name properties of the object, and adds the object to the list of Vendor objects. Note that because this list will be used only to load the Name combo box on the Vendor Invoices form, it isn't necessary to set the other properties of the Vendor objects. Instead, the vendor ID of the selected vendor will be used to retrieve the vendor from the Vendors table. That makes the application more efficient because it retrieves only the data it needs. This method ends by closing the data reader and the connection and returning the list of vendors to the calling procedure.

The GetVendorNameAndAddress method is similar to the GetVendor method you saw in the Vendor Maintenance application in chapter 7. The only difference is that the GetVendor method retrieved all the columns from the Vendors table, because all the columns were used by the Vendor Maintenance application. In contrast, the Payment Entry application uses only the vendor ID and name and address columns. So that's all the GetVendorNameAndAddress method retrieves. That reduces network traffic and improves efficiency.

Also notice that if a row isn't returned—in other words, if a row isn't found with the specified vendor ID—the Vendor object is set to Nothing. Although this application doesn't check for this condition because a vendor wouldn't be deleted if it had unpaid invoices, this method could be used by other applications that retrieve a vendor by vendor ID.

The code for the Vendor class

```
Public Class Vendor
    Private m_VendorID As Integer
    Private m_Name As String
    Private m_Address1 As String
    Private m_Address2 As String
    Private m_City As String
    Private m_State As String
    Private m_ZipCode As String
    Private m_Phone As String
    Private m_ContactLName As String
    Private m_ContactFName As String
    Private m_DefaultTermsID As Integer
    Private m_DefaultAccountNo As Integer

    Public Sub New()

    End Sub

    Public Property VendorID() As Integer
        Get
            Return m_VendorID
        End Get
        Set(ByVal value As Integer)
            m_VendorID = value
        End Set
    End Property

    Public Property Name() As String
        Get
            Return m_Name
        End Get
        Set(ByVal value As String)
            m_Name = value
        End Set
    End Property

    Public Property Address1() As String
        Get
            Return m_Address1
        End Get
        Set(ByVal value As String)
            m_Address1 = value
        End Set
    End Property
    .
    .
    Public Property DefaultAccountNo() As Integer
        Get
            Return m_DefaultAccountNo
        End Get
        Set(ByVal value As Integer)
            m_DefaultAccountNo = value
        End Set
    End Property

End Class
```

Figure 9-8 The code for the Vendor class

The code for the VendorDB class

Page 1

```
Imports System.Data.SqlClient

Public Class VendorDB

    Public Shared Function GetVendorsWithBalanceDue() As List(Of Vendor)
        Dim vendorList As New List(Of Vendor)
        Dim connection As SqlConnection = PayablesDB.GetConnection
        Dim selectStatement As String =
            "SELECT VendorID, Name " &
            "FROM Vendors " &
            "WHERE (SELECT SUM(InvoiceTotal - PaymentTotal - CreditTotal) " &
            "       FROM Invoices " &
            "       WHERE Invoices.VendorID = Vendors.VendorID) " &
            "           > 0 " &
            "ORDER BY Name"
        Dim selectCommand As New SqlCommand(selectStatement, connection)
        Try
            connection.Open()
            Dim reader As SqlDataReader = selectCommand.ExecuteReader()
            Dim vendor As Vendor
            Do While reader.Read
                vendor = New Vendor
                vendor.VendorID = CInt(reader("VendorID"))
                vendor.Name = reader("Name").ToString
                vendorList.Add(vendor)
            Loop
            reader.Close()
        Catch ex As SqlException
            Throw ex
        Finally
            connection.Close()
        End Try
        Return vendorList
    End Function
```

Figure 9-9 The code for the VendorDB class (part 1 of 2)

The code for the VendorDB class — Page 2

```
    Public Shared Function GetVendorNameAndAddress(
            ByVal vendorID As Integer) As Vendor
        Dim vendor As New Vendor
        Dim connection As SqlConnection = PayablesDB.GetConnection
        Dim selectStatement As String =
            "SELECT VendorID, Name, Address1, Address2, City, State, ZipCode " &
            "FROM Vendors " &
            "WHERE VendorID = @VendorID"
        Dim selectCommand As New SqlCommand(selectStatement, connection)
        selectCommand.Parameters.AddWithValue("@VendorID", vendorID)

        Try
            connection.Open()
            Dim reader As SqlDataReader =
                selectCommand.ExecuteReader(CommandBehavior.SingleRow)
            If reader.Read Then
                vendor.VendorID = CInt(reader("VendorID"))
                vendor.Name = reader("Name").ToString
                vendor.Address1 = reader("Address1").ToString
                vendor.Address2 = reader("Address2").ToString
                vendor.City = reader("City").ToString
                vendor.State = reader("State").ToString
                vendor.ZipCode = reader("ZipCode").ToString
            Else
                vendor = Nothing
            End If
            reader.Close()
        Catch ex As SqlException
            Throw ex
        Finally
            connection.Close()
        End Try
        Return vendor
    End Function

End Class
```

Figure 9-9 The code for the VendorDB class (part 2 of 2)

The code for the Invoice class

Like the Vendor class, the Invoice class shown in figure 9-10 contains private fields, a constructor, and public properties that provide access to the private fields. I want to point out two things about this class, though. First, in addition to the properties that provide access to the private fields, this class contains a property named BalanceDue that returns the balance due for an invoice. To do that, it returns the result of subtracting the payment total and the credit total from the invoice total. Because the value of this property can't be set directly, it's defined as a read-only property, and it doesn't need to be a private field because there is no Set clause in the property declaration.

Second, the m_PaymentDate field and the PaymentDate property are declared as nullable types. That's necessary because the PaymentDate column in the Invoices table can contain a null. If you didn't define this field and property as nullable and the column contained a null value, the field would be set to the default date of 01/01/01. Then, this value would be returned by the property and displayed in the DataGridView control, which isn't what you want.

For the PaymentDate property to work correctly, the Get procedure uses the HasValue property of the field to determine if it stores a value or contains a null. Then, if it stores a value, the procedure returns the date. Otherwise, it returns Nothing.

The code for the InvoiceDB class

Figure 9-11 presents the code for the InvoiceDB class. The GetUnpaidVendorInvoices method of this class receives a vendor ID and returns a List() that contains a collection of Invoice objects for the vendor that have a balance due. Because you've seen code like this before, you shouldn't have any trouble understanding it. However, I do want to point out that to determine if the payment date is null, this method uses the IsDBNull function. Then, if it is null, the PaymentDate property is set to Nothing. Otherwise, it's set to the payment date.

The UpdatePayment method of this class receives two Invoice objects named oldInvoice and newInvoice. The oldInvoice object contains the original data for the invoice and is used to check that another user hasn't modified or deleted the invoice since it was retrieved. The newInvoice object is used to assign new values to the PaymentTotal and PaymentDate columns.

After the connection and command are created, this method creates the necessary parameters and adds them to the Parameters collection. Then, it opens the connection and executes the command. If the command is successful, True is returned to the calling procedure. If the command in unsuccessful, however, it most likely means that a concurrency error occurred. In that case, False is returned to the calling procedure. In either case, the connection is closed.

The code for the Invoice class

```
Public Class Invoice
    Private m_InvoiceID As Integer
    Private m_VendorID As Integer
    Private m_InvoiceNumber As String
    Private m_InvoiceDate As Date
    Private m_InvoiceTotal As Decimal
    Private m_PaymentTotal As Decimal
    Private m_CreditTotal As Decimal
    Private m_TermsID As Integer
    Private m_DueDate As Date
    Private m_PaymentDate As Nullable(Of Date)

    Public Sub New()

    End Sub

    Public Property InvoiceID() As Integer
        Get
            Return m_InvoiceID
        End Get
        Set(ByVal value As Integer)
            m_InvoiceID = value
        End Set
    End Property

    Public Property VendorID() As Integer
        Get
            Return m_VendorID
        End Get
        Set(ByVal value As Integer)
            m_VendorID = value
        End Set
    End Property
    .
    .
    Public Property PaymentDate() As Nullable(Of Date)
        Get
            If m_PaymentDate.HasValue Then
                Return CDate(m_PaymentDate)
            Else
                Return Nothing
            End If
        End Get
        Set(ByVal value As Nullable(Of Date))
            m_PaymentDate = value
        End Set
    End Property

    Public ReadOnly Property BalanceDue() As Decimal
        Get
            Return m_InvoiceTotal - m_PaymentTotal - m_CreditTotal
        End Get
    End Property

End Class
```

Figure 9-10 The code for the Invoice class

The code for the InvoiceDB class

Page 1

```
Imports System.Data.SqlClient

Public Class InvoiceDB

    Public Shared Function GetUnpaidVendorInvoices(
            ByVal vendorID As Integer) As List(Of Invoice)
        Dim invoiceList As New List(Of Invoice)
        Dim connection As SqlConnection = PayablesDB.GetConnection
        Dim selectStatement As String =
            "SELECT InvoiceID, VendorID, InvoiceNumber, InvoiceDate, " &
                "InvoiceTotal, PaymentTotal, CreditTotal, " &
                "TermsID, DueDate, PaymentDate " &
            "FROM Invoices " &
            "WHERE VendorID = @VendorID " &
            "  AND InvoiceTotal - PaymentTotal - CreditTotal > 0 " &
            "ORDER BY InvoiceDate"
        Dim selectCommand As New SqlCommand(selectStatement, connection)
        selectCommand.Parameters.AddWithValue("@VendorID", vendorID)
        Try
            connection.Open()
            Dim reader As SqlDataReader = selectCommand.ExecuteReader()
            Dim invoice As Invoice
            Do While reader.Read
                invoice = New Invoice
                invoice.InvoiceID = CInt(reader("InvoiceID"))
                invoice.VendorID = CInt(reader("VendorID"))
                invoice.InvoiceNumber = reader("InvoiceNumber").ToString
                invoice.InvoiceDate = CDate(reader("InvoiceDate"))
                invoice.InvoiceTotal = CDec(reader("InvoiceTotal"))
                invoice.PaymentTotal = CDec(reader("PaymentTotal"))
                invoice.CreditTotal = CDec(reader("CreditTotal"))
                invoice.TermsID = CInt(reader("TermsID"))
                invoice.DueDate = CDate(reader("DueDate"))
                If IsDBNull(reader("PaymentDate")) Then
                    invoice.PaymentDate = Nothing
                Else
                    invoice.PaymentDate = CDate(reader("PaymentDate"))
                End If
                invoiceList.Add(invoice)
            Loop
            reader.Close()
        Catch ex As SqlException
            Throw ex
        Finally
            connection.Close()
        End Try
        Return invoiceList
    End Function
```

Figure 9-11 The code for the InvoiceDB class (part 1 of 2)

The code for the InvoiceDB class **Page 2**

```
    Public Shared Function UpdatePayment(ByVal oldInvoice As Invoice,
            ByVal newInvoice As Invoice) As Boolean
        Dim connection As SqlConnection = PayablesDB.GetConnection
        Dim updateStatement As String =
            "UPDATE Invoices " &
            "SET PaymentTotal = @NewPaymentTotal, " &
            "PaymentDate = @NewPaymentDate " &
            "WHERE InvoiceID = @OldInvoiceID " &
            "  AND VendorID = @OldVendorID " &
            "  AND InvoiceNumber = @OldInvoiceNumber " &
            "  AND InvoiceDate = @OldInvoiceDate " &
            "  AND InvoiceTotal = @OldInvoiceTotal " &
            "  AND PaymentTotal = @OldPaymentTotal " &
            "  AND CreditTotal = @OldCreditTotal " &
            "  AND TermsID = @OldTermsID " &
            "  AND DueDate = @OldDueDate " &
            "  AND (PaymentDate = @OldPaymentDate " &
            "   OR PaymentDate IS NULL AND @OldPaymentDate IS NULL)"
        Dim updateCommand As New SqlCommand(updateStatement, connection)
        updateCommand.Parameters.AddWithValue("@NewPaymentTotal",
            newInvoice.PaymentTotal)
        updateCommand.Parameters.AddWithValue("@NewPaymentDate",
            newInvoice.PaymentDate)
        updateCommand.Parameters.AddWithValue("@OldInvoiceID",
            oldInvoice.InvoiceID)
        updateCommand.Parameters.AddWithValue("@OldVendorID",
            oldInvoice.VendorID)
        .
        .
        updateCommand.Parameters.AddWithValue("@OldDueDate", oldInvoice.DueDate)
        If Not oldInvoice.PaymentDate.HasValue Then
            updateCommand.Parameters.AddWithValue("@OldPaymentDate",
                DBNull.Value)
        Else
            updateCommand.Parameters.AddWithValue("@OldPaymentDate",
                oldInvoice.PaymentDate)
        End If

        Try
            connection.Open()
            Dim count As Integer = updateCommand.ExecuteNonQuery
            If count > 0 Then
                Return True
            Else
                Return False
            End If
        Catch ex As SqlException
            Throw ex
        Finally
            connection.Close()
        End Try
    End Function

End Class
```

Figure 9-11 The code for the InvoiceDB class (part 2 of 2)

The code for the Vendor Invoices form

Figure 9-12 presents the code for the Vendor Invoices form. This form starts by declaring three variables. The first variable, named vendor, will store a Vendor object that the text boxes on the form are bound to. The second variable, named vendorList, will store the list of Vendor objects that the Name combo box will be bound to. The third variable, named invoiceList, will store the list of Invoice objects that the DataGridView control will be bound to.

The event handler for the Load event of the form populates these three variables. To do that, it calls two procedures named GetVendorList and GetVendorData. The GetVendorList procedure uses the GetVendorsWithBalanceDue method of the VendorDB class to populate the vendorList variable with all the vendors that have unpaid invoices. Then, it sets the DataSource property of the Name combo box to this list so that the combo box displays a list of vendor names. This works because the DisplayMember property of the combo box was set to the Name property of the Vendor object at design time using the BindingSource object.

The GetVendorData procedure displays the data for the currently selected vendor. When the application starts, this vendor will be the first one in the list that was returned by the GetVendorList procedure. The GetVendorData procedure starts by getting the vendor ID from the Name combo box. This works because the ValueMember property of the combo box was set to the VendorID property of the Vendor object at design time. Then, it calls the GetVendorNameAndAddress method of the VendorDB class to get the data for the selected vendor, and it stores the Vendor object that's returned in the vendor variable. Next, it clears the Vendor binding source and adds the Vendor object to that binding source. This binds the text boxes on the form to the Vendor object so they display the vendor data.

The next statement in the GetVendorData procedure calls the GetUnpaidVendorInvoices method of the InvoiceDB class to populate the invoiceList variable with all the unpaid invoices for the vendor. Then, it sets the DataSource property of the DataGridView control to this list, which causes the invoices to be displayed in this control.

If the user selects a different vendor from the combo box, the event handler for the SelectedIndexChanged event is executed. This event handler calls the GetVendorData procedure to retrieve the data for the selected vendor along with a list of the vendor's unpaid invoices.

The code for the Vendor Invoices form — Page 1

```
Imports PayablesData

Public Class frmVendorInvoices

    Private vendor As Vendor
    Private vendorList As List(Of Vendor)
    Private invoiceList As List(Of Invoice)

    Private Sub frmVendorInvoices_Load(ByVal sender As System.Object,
            ByVal e As System.EventArgs) Handles MyBase.Load
        Me.GetVendorList()
        Me.GetVendorData()
    End Sub

    Private Sub GetVendorList()
        Try
            ' Get the list of Vendor objects
            ' and bind the combo box to the list
            vendorList = VendorDB.GetVendorsWithBalanceDue
            NameComboBox.DataSource = vendorList
        Catch ex As Exception
            MessageBox.Show(ex.Message, ex.GetType.ToString)
        End Try
    End Sub

    Private Sub GetVendorData()
        Dim vendorID As Integer = CInt(NameComboBox.SelectedValue)
        Try
            ' Get a Vendor object for the selected vendor
            ' and bind the text boxes to the object
            vendor = VendorDB.GetVendorNameAndAddress(vendorID)
            VendorBindingSource.Clear()
            VendorBindingSource.Add(vendor)
            ' Get the list of Invoice objects
            ' and bind the DataGridView control to the list
            invoiceList = InvoiceDB.GetUnpaidVendorInvoices(vendorID)
            InvoiceDataGridView.DataSource = invoiceList
        Catch ex As Exception
            MessageBox.Show(ex.Message, ex.GetType.ToString)
        End Try
    End Sub

    Private Sub NameComboBox_SelectedIndexChanged(ByVal sender As System.Object,
        ByVal e As System.EventArgs) Handles NameComboBox.SelectedIndexChanged
        Me.GetVendorData()
    End Sub
```

Figure 9-12 The code for the Vendor Invoices form (part 1 of 2)

If the user clicks an Enter Payment button in the DataGridView control, the event handler for the CellContentClick event is executed. This event handler starts by checking that the user clicked in the column with this button and not another column in the grid. If the button column was clicked, it gets the index for the row that was clicked and retrieves the row. Then, it uses the DataBoundItem property of the row to get the Invoice object that's stored in the row.

After that, this event handler creates a new instance of the Payment Entry form. Then, it sets the public vendorName field of this form to the name of the selected vendor, it sets the public invoice field to the selected invoice, and it displays the form as a dialog box.

If the payment is posted successfully, the BindingContext property of the DataGridView control is used to get the CurrencyManager object for this control. Then, if the invoice was paid in full, the invoice is removed from the list of invoices. If additional invoices remain in the list, the currency manager is then refreshed so the invoice that was removed is no longer displayed in the data grid. If no more invoices remain in the list, however, the GetVendorList and GetVendorData procedures are called to refresh the list of names in the combo box and display the data for the first vendor. If the invoice is not paid in full, the invoice in the invoice list is replaced with the new invoice, and the currency manager is refreshed so it displays the updated data for the invoice.

If a concurrency error occurs during the update of the invoice, the DialogResult property of the Payment Entry form is set to DialogResult.Retry. Then, the GetUnpaidVendorInvoices method is called to get an updated list of invoices. If there is still at least one unpaid invoice, the DataSource property of the DataGridView control is set to this list. Otherwise, the GetVendorList and GetVendorData procedures are called to refresh the vendor list and display the data for the first vendor.

The code for the Vendor Invoices form **Page 2**

```
    Private Sub InvoiceDataGridView_CellContentClick(
            ByVal sender As System.Object,
            ByVal e As System.Windows.Forms.DataGridViewCellEventArgs) _
            Handles InvoiceDataGridView.CellContentClick
        If e.ColumnIndex = 11 Then ' The Enter Payment button was clicked
            ' Get the invoice from the row
            Dim i As Integer = e.RowIndex
            Dim row As DataGridViewRow = InvoiceDataGridView.Rows(i)
            Dim invoice As Invoice = CType(row.DataBoundItem, Invoice)

            ' Display the Payment Entry form to accept the payment
            Dim acceptPaymentForm As New frmPaymentEntry
            acceptPaymentForm.vendorName = NameComboBox.Text
            acceptPaymentForm.invoice = invoice
            Dim result As DialogResult = acceptPaymentForm.ShowDialog

            If result = DialogResult.OK Then
                Dim cm As CurrencyManager = CType(
                    InvoiceDataGridView.BindingContext(invoiceList),
                      CurrencyManager)
                If acceptPaymentForm.invoice.BalanceDue = 0 Then
                    ' Remove the invoice from the list
                    invoiceList.RemoveAt(i)
                    If invoiceList.Count > 0 Then
                        ' Refresh the data grid
                        cm.Refresh()
                    Else
                        ' Get a current vendor list and refresh the display
                        Me.GetVendorList()
                        Me.GetVendorData()
                    End If
                Else
                    ' Replace the invoice and refresh the data grid
                    invoiceList(i) = acceptPaymentForm.invoice
                    cm.Refresh()
                End If
            ElseIf result = DialogResult.Retry Then
                ' A concurrency exception occurred
                invoiceList = InvoiceDB.GetUnpaidVendorInvoices(vendor.VendorID)
                If invoiceList.Count > 0 Then
                    InvoiceDataGridView.DataSource = invoiceList
                Else
                    Me.GetVendorList()
                    Me.GetVendorData()
                End If
            End If
        End If
    End Sub

End Class
```

Figure 9-12 The code for the Vendor Invoices form (part 2 of 2)

The code for the Payment Entry form

Figure 9-13 presents the code for the Payment Entry form. This form starts by declaring the two public fields whose values are set by the Vendor Invoices form: vendorName and invoice. Then, the event handler for the Load event of the form assigns the vendor name to the appropriate text box on the form, and it adds the Invoice object in the invoice variable to the Invoice binding source so that the invoice data is displayed on the form. Finally, it displays the balance due for the invoice in the Payment text box. That way, the user can just press the Enter key to pay the invoice in full.

When the user presses the Enter key or clicks the Accept button, the event handler for the Click event of this button starts by checking that the payment amount the user entered is valid. To do that, it uses three methods of the Validator class. First, it calls the IsPresent method to check that the user entered a value. Second, it calls the IsDecimal method to check that the user entered a decimal value. Third, it calls the IsWithinRange method to check that the user entered a value between 1 and the balance due.

If the payment amount is valid, this event handler continues by creating a new Invoice object. Then, it calls the PutNewInvoice procedure to assign values to the properties of that object. Notice that because only the payment total and payment date values will be updated, most of the values for the new invoice are taken from the original invoice. Also notice that the payment date is set to the current date.

After the appropriate values are assigned to the new invoice, the UpdatePayment method of the InvoiceDB class is called to update the payment information for the invoice. If the update is unsuccessful, a message is displayed indicating that another user updated or deleted the invoice, and the DialogResult property of the form is set to DialogResult.Retry. If the update is successful, however, the new Invoice object is assigned to the original Invoice object and the DialogResult property of the form is set to DialogResult.OK.

The code for the Payment Entry form

```
Imports PayablesData

Public Class frmPaymentEntry

    Public vendorName As String
    Public invoice As Invoice

    Private Sub frmPaymentEntry_Load(ByVal sender As System.Object,
            ByVal e As System.EventArgs) Handles MyBase.Load
        txtVendor.Text = vendorName
        InvoiceBindingSource.Add(invoice)
        txtPayment.Text = FormatNumber(invoice.BalanceDue)
    End Sub

    Private Sub btnAccept_Click(ByVal sender As System.Object,
            ByVal e As System.EventArgs) Handles btnAccept.Click
        If Validator.IsPresent(txtPayment) AndAlso
           Validator.IsDecimal(txtPayment) AndAlso
           Validator.IsWithinRange(txtPayment, 1,
               CDec(FormatNumber(invoice.BalanceDue))) Then
            Dim newInvoice As New Invoice
            Me.PutNewInvoice(newInvoice)
            Try
                If Not InvoiceDB.UpdatePayment(invoice, newInvoice) Then
                    MessageBox.Show("Another user has updated or deleted " &
                        "that invoice.",
                        "Database Error")
                    Me.DialogResult = DialogResult.Retry
                Else
                    invoice = newInvoice
                    Me.DialogResult = DialogResult.OK
                End If
            Catch ex As Exception
                MessageBox.Show(ex.Message, ex.GetType.ToString)
            End Try
        End If
    End Sub

    Private Sub PutNewInvoice(ByVal newInvoice As Invoice)
        newInvoice.InvoiceID = invoice.InvoiceID
        newInvoice.VendorID = invoice.VendorID
        newInvoice.InvoiceNumber = invoice.InvoiceNumber
        newInvoice.InvoiceDate = invoice.InvoiceDate
        newInvoice.InvoiceTotal = invoice.InvoiceTotal
        Dim payment As Decimal = CDec(txtPayment.Text)
        newInvoice.PaymentTotal = invoice.PaymentTotal + payment
        newInvoice.CreditTotal = invoice.CreditTotal
        newInvoice.TermsID = invoice.TermsID
        newInvoice.DueDate = invoice.DueDate
        newInvoice.PaymentDate = DateTime.Today
    End Sub

End Class
```

Figure 9-13 The code for the Payment Entry form

Perspective

As you've seen in this chapter, object data sources provide a powerful way to develop database applications. Like standard data sources, they let you develop forms that use bound controls. Unlike standard data sources, however, they let you write your own data access code, which gives you complete control over how the data is processed.

Terms

three-layer architecture
presentation layer
middle layer
database layer
object data source

Exercise 9-1 Build the Payment Entry application

In this exercise, you'll start to build the application that's presented in this chapter, but you'll use the existing PayablesData library. As a result, you won't have to code the business or database classes. This exercise will demonstrate how the use of object data sources can make it easier for you to build three-layer applications.

Start the application and set up the PayablesData library

1. Start a new project named PaymentEntry in your chapter 9 directory.
2. Add a new class library project to the solution named PayablesData. To do that, you can right-click on the solution in the Solution Explorer, select Add→New Project, click on the Class Library template, and proceed from there.
3. Add the five classes in the PayablesData library that's in the PaymentEntry application in the Book applications\Chapter 09 directory to the new PayablesData project. To do that, you can right-click on the PayablesData project in the Solution Explorer, select Add→Existing Item, and proceed from there.
4. Use the Build→Build PayablesData command to build the PayablesData project and create the DLL file for the class library. (If you are using Visual Basic 2010 Express Edition, right-click on the name of the PayablesData project in the Solution Explorer, then select Build from the shortcut menu).

Build the Vendor Invoices form

5. Use the procedure in figure 9-2 to create an object data source for the Vendor class in the PayablesData library. In the step for selecting the object, click on the Add Reference button and add a reference to the PayablesData library. Then, create a second object data source, this time for the Invoice class.
6. Use the procedure in figure 9-3 to drag the properties for the Vendor class onto the form so they look like the ones in figure 9-6. Then, drag the Invoice class onto the form so it creates a DataGridView control like the one that's also shown in figure 9-6.
7. Set the properties for the Name combo box using the procedure shown in figure 4-3 of chapter 4. In this case, you set DataSource to VendorBindingSource, DisplayMember to Name, and ValueMember to VendorID. Also, set the DropDownStyle property to DropDownList, and *be sure to change the (DataBindings) – Text property to none to remove the binding from the text box portion of the combo box.*
8. Test the application to see how it works. At this time, no data is displayed because the business objects that are bound to the controls haven't been populated with data.
9. Add the code for the Load event handler that's shown in figure 9-12 (part 1), and add the code for the two procedures that it calls. That will populate the business objects. Then, add the event handler for the SelectedIndexChanged event for the Name combo box.
10. Test the application to see that the form shows the data for any vendor that you select from the combo box. This should give you some idea of how the use of object data sources can help you build three-layer applications more quickly.

Build the Payment Entry form and complete the application

11. If you think you can learn more by building the rest of this application, you should be able to do so without much trouble. And if you have problems, you can refer to the complete application in the Book applications\Chapter 09 directory.

10

A complete Payable Entry application

In the last four chapters, you've seen examples of applications that use business and database classes. However, the examples in those chapters have been relatively simple so you could focus on the database programming skills that they require.

Now that you've learned those skills, you're ready to see how they all fit together in a comprehensive, real-world application. To help you do that, this chapter presents a Payable Entry application that's significantly more complicated than any of the examples you've seen so far. This application uses object data sources and transactions, and it should give you many programming ideas that you can apply to your own applications.

The user interface and class diagram

The Payable Entry application lets the user enter a new invoice (or payable) for a selected vendor, and each invoice consists of invoice data and line item data. This application lets the user add or modify vendors. And it lets the user display the line items for an existing invoice.

For each new invoice, one row is added to the Invoices table in the database, and for each line item for that invoice, one row is added to the InvoiceLineItems table. To make sure that all of the rows for a related invoice are added successfully, this application uses transactions.

This is a three-layer application that uses object data sources, because I think that's the best way to develop applications like this. As you will see, using object data sources reduces the amount of code that you have to write, but still retains the benefits that you get from developing three-layer applications.

The user interface

Figure 10-1 presents four of the forms that make up the user interface for the Payable Entry application. When this application starts, the Vendor Invoices form is displayed. From this form, the user can enter a vendor ID and click the Get Vendor button to retrieve the vendor and invoice information for that vendor and display it on the form.

The user can also search for a vendor by clicking the Find Vendor button. This displays the Find Vendor form, which lets the user enter a name and state for the search criteria. In this figure, for example, all of the vendors whose names start with the letters "co" are displayed. Then, the user can select a vendor from this list.

The user can also add or modify a vendor by clicking the Add Vendor or Modify Vendor button on the Vendor Invoices form. This displays the Add/Modify Vendor form you saw in chapter 7. Because this form works just like the form presented in that chapter, it's not repeated here.

If the selected vendor has any existing invoices, the user can click the View Line Items button for that invoice on the Vendor Invoices form. Then, a Line Items form like the one shown in the second part of this figure is displayed.

The Vendor Invoices form

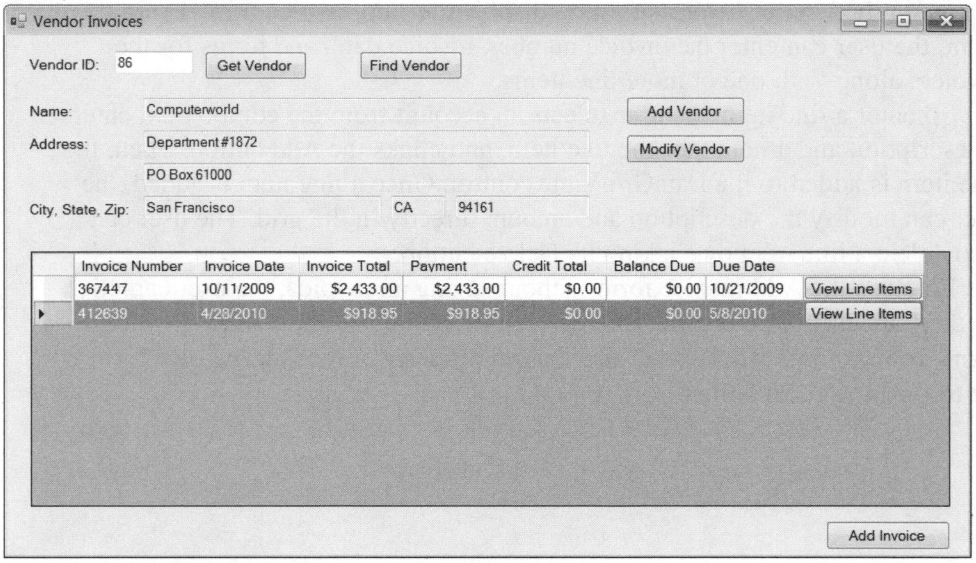

The Find Vendor form

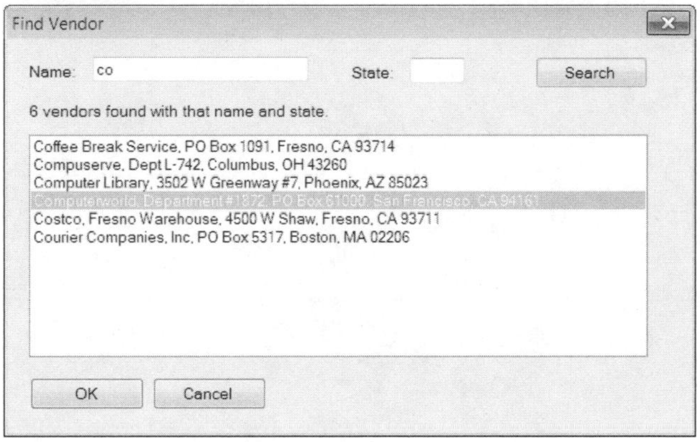

Description

- To select a vendor, the user can enter the vendor ID and click the Get Vendor button or click the Find Vendor button to display the Find Vendor form.
- From the Find Vendor form, the user can enter all or part of a name and a state code and then click the Search button to list all the vendors that match the criteria. Then, the user can highlight a vendor and click the OK button or double-click a vendor to select that vendor.
- After a vendor is selected, the name and address information for that vendor is displayed on the Vendor Invoices form, along with any existing invoices for that vendor.
- The user can also add or modify a vendor by clicking the Add Vendor or Modify Vendor button on the Vendor Invoices form. This displays a form like the one used by the Vendor Maintenance application in chapter 7.

Figure 10-1 The user interface for the Payable Entry application (part 1 of 2)

To add an invoice for a selected vendor, the user clicks the Add Invoice button on the Vendor Invoices form to display the Add Invoice form. From this form, the user can enter the invoice number, invoice date, and terms for the invoice, along with one or more line items.

To enter a line item, the user selects an account from the combo box, enters a description and amount for the line item, and clicks the Add button. Then, the line item is added to the DataGridView control. Once a line item is added, the user can modify the description and amount directly in the grid. The user can also delete a line item by clicking its Delete button.

To close the Add Invoice form without saving an invoice, the user can click on the Cancel Invoice button. This will return the user to the Vendor Invoices form. To make this work, the CancelButton property of the Add Invoice form is set to the btnCancel button.

The Line Items form

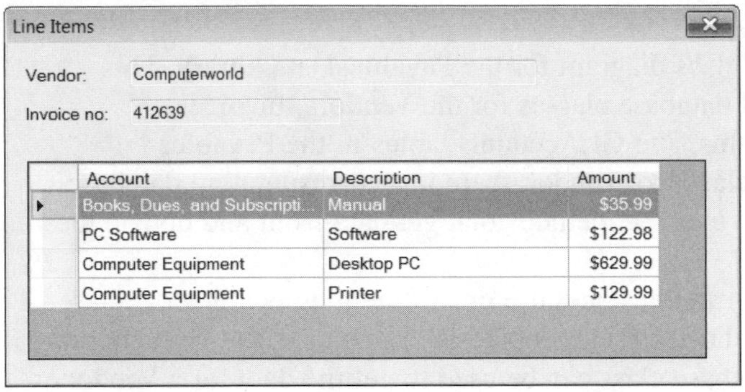

The Add Invoice form

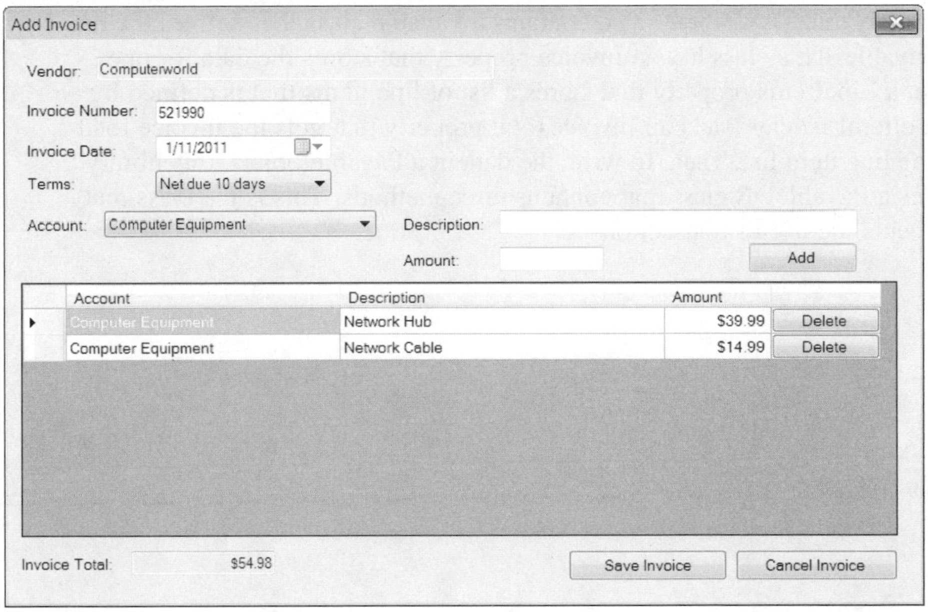

Description

- To display the line items for an invoice, the user clicks the View Line Items button for the invoice on the Vendor Invoices form.
- To enter a new invoice for a vendor, the user clicks the Add Invoice button on the Vendor Invoices form to display the Add Invoice form. Then, the user enters the invoice information and clicks the Save Invoice button.
- To enter a line item, the user selects an account, enters a description and amount, and clicks the Add button. The user can also modify the description and amount for a line item directly in the DataGridView control or delete a line item by clicking its Delete button.
- After an invoice is processed, the Add Invoice form is closed and the Vendor Invoices form is redisplayed with the new invoice. To return to the Vendor Invoices form without processing the invoice, the user can click the Cancel Invoice button.

Figure 10-1 The user interface for the Payable Entry application (part 2 of 2)

The class diagram for the PayablesData library

Figure 10-2 presents the class diagram for the PayablesData library. This library includes business and database classes for the Vendors, Invoices, InvoiceLineItems, States, Terms, and GLAccounts tables in the Payables database. For each business class like Vendor, there is a corresponding database class like VendorDB that provides the methods that get data from and update the data in the related table.

When you use object data sources, you use one of the methods in a database class to get the data for the related business object. For instance, the GetVendor method in the VendorDB database class can be used to get the data for a Vendor business object. Then, the business object is the data source for the controls that are bound to it.

The PayablesData library also contains a Payable class that defines the data for a payable. This class has an Invoice property that stores the data for one invoice, a LineItems property that stores a list of line items that is defined by the LineItemList class, and an InvoiceTotal property that gets the invoice total from the line item list. Then, to write the data in a Payable object, this library provides a PayableDB class that contains three methods. This is the class that implements the use of transactions.

The class diagram for the PayablesData library

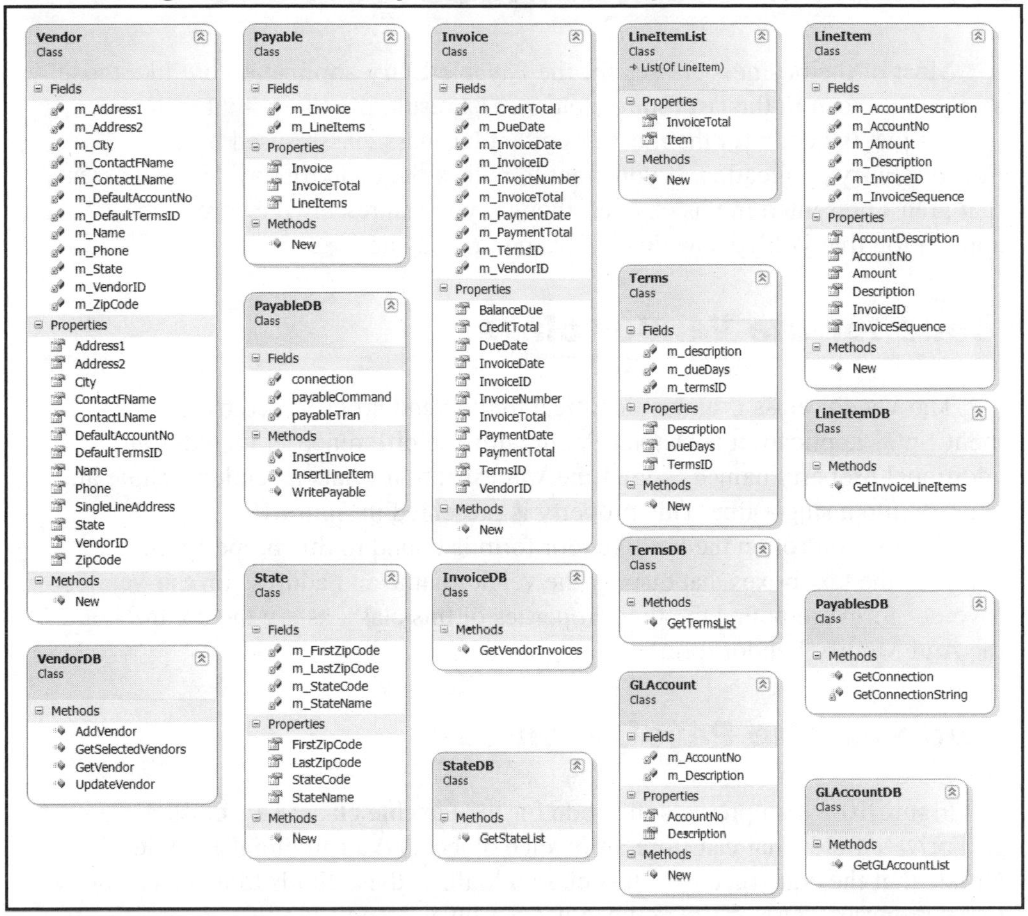

Description

- The Payable Entry application uses a business class named Payable to create a business object that holds the invoice and line item data for a payable. Then, it uses the public, shared WritePayable method of the PayableDB class to add the payable to the Invoice and InvoiceLineItems tables of the Payables database.
- The line items that are stored in a Payable object are defined by the LineItemList class. This class inherits the List() class, overloads the Item property of that class, and adds a custom InvoiceTotal property.
- Each line item is defined by the LineItem class. This class contains a property for each column in the InvoiceLineItems table, plus a property for the Description column of the GLAccounts table.

Figure 10-2 The class diagram for the PayablesData library

The code for the business classes

Most of the business classes for the Payable Entry application are like those that you've seen in the last four chapters. As a result, the topics that follow present just the code for the most important business classes used by the Payable Entry application. If you want to review the code for any of the classes that aren't presented in this chapter, though, you can review the complete application that you've downloaded from our web site.

The code for the Vendor class

The Vendor class is almost identical to the Vendor class used by the Payment Entry application in chapter 9, but with one difference. It includes an additional property named SingleLineAddress that formats a vendor's name and address into a single line. This property is presented in figure 10-3.

The list control on the Find Vendor form is bound to this property. In contrast, the text boxes that display the vendor name and address on the Vendor Invoices form are bound to other properties of this class, as are the controls on the Add/Modify Vendor form.

The code for the Payable class

Figure 10-3 also presents the code for the Payable class. This class declares two private fields that can store an Invoice object and a LineItemList object. Notice that the constructor for this class initializes these fields to instances of the appropriate class. Then, you can use the Invoice and LineItems properties to retrieve these objects, and you can use the properties of these objects to work with the values they contain.

The last property of the Payable class, InvoiceTotal, gets the total of the line items. To do that, it uses the InvoiceTotal property of the LineItemList object. You'll see the code for this property in the next figure.

The code for the SingleLineAddress property in the Vendor class

```
Public Class Vendor
    .
    .
    .
    Public ReadOnly Property SingleLineAddress() As String
        Get
            Dim s As String
            s = Name & ", " & Address1 & ", "
            If Address2 <> "" Then
                s &= Address2 & ", "
            End If
            s &= City & ", " & State & " " & ZipCode
            Return s
        End Get
    End Property
End Class
```

The code for the Payable class

```
Public Class Payable
    Private m_Invoice As Invoice
    Private m_LineItems As LineItemList

    Public Sub New()
        m_Invoice = New Invoice
        m_LineItems = New LineItemList
    End Sub

    Public ReadOnly Property Invoice() As Invoice
        Get
            Return m_Invoice
        End Get
    End Property

    Public ReadOnly Property LineItems() As LineItemList
        Get
            Return m_LineItems
        End Get
    End Property

    Public ReadOnly Property InvoiceTotal() As Decimal
        Get
            Return m_LineItems.InvoiceTotal
        End Get
    End Property
End Class
```

Figure 10-3 The code for the Vendor and Payable classes

The code for the LineItem class

Figure 10-4 presents the code for the LineItem class. This class declares one private field and one public property for each column in the InvoiceLineItems table. In addition, it declares a private field and a public property for the Description column in the GLAccounts table. That way, this column can be displayed in the DataGridView control on the Add Invoice form, which is bound to the LineItem class.

The code for the LineItemList class

Figure 10-4 also presents the code for the LineItemList class. This class inherits the List() class and defines a list of LineItem objects. It consists of a constructor that calls the default constructor of the base class and two properties.

The Item property overloads the Item property defined by the List() class. It returns a line item from the list based on the index that's passed to it. Notice that if the index value doesn't fall within the range of indexes for the list, a value of Nothing is returned.

The InvoiceTotal property returns the total of all the line items in the list. To do that, it uses a For...Next statement to loop through the line items and accumulate a total of the Amount property.

The code for the State class

Figure 10-5 presents the code for the State class. It declares a private field and a public property for each column in the States table. The State combo box on the Add/Modify Vendor form displays the values of the StateName property and stores the values of the StateCode property of this class. Similar code is used for the Terms and GLAccount classes, which aren't presented here.

The code for the LineItem class

Page 1

```
Public Class LineItem

    Private m_InvoiceID As Integer
    Private m_InvoiceSequence As Integer
    Private m_AccountNo As Integer
    Private m_AccountDescription As String
    Private m_Amount As Decimal
    Private m_Description As String

    Public Sub New()

    End Sub

    Public Property InvoiceID() As Integer
        Get
            Return m_InvoiceID
        End Get
        Set(ByVal value As Integer)
            m_InvoiceID = value
        End Set
    End Property

    Public Property InvoiceSequence() As Integer
        Get
            Return m_InvoiceSequence
        End Get
        Set(ByVal value As Integer)
            m_InvoiceSequence = value
        End Set
    End Property

    Public Property AccountNo() As Integer
        Get
            Return m_AccountNo
        End Get
        Set(ByVal value As Integer)
            m_AccountNo = value
        End Set
    End Property

    Public Property AccountDescription() As String
        Get
            Return m_AccountDescription
        End Get
        Set(ByVal value As String)
            m_AccountDescription = value
        End Set
    End Property
```

Figure 10-4 The code for the LineItem and LineItemList classes (part 1 of 2)

The code for the LineItem class **Page 2**

```
    Public Property Amount() As Decimal
        Get
            Return m_Amount
        End Get
        Set(ByVal value As Decimal)
            m_Amount = value
        End Set
    End Property

    Public Property Description() As String
        Get
            Return m_Description
        End Get
        Set(ByVal value As String)
            m_Description = value
        End Set
    End Property

End Class
```

The code for the LineItemList class

```
Public Class LineItemList
    Inherits List(Of LineItem)

    Public Sub New()
        MyBase.New()
    End Sub

    Default Public Overloads ReadOnly Property Item(ByVal i As Integer) _
            As LineItem
        Get
            If i < 0 OrElse i > MyBase.Count - 1 Then
                Return Nothing
            Else
                Return MyBase.Item(i)
            End If
        End Get
    End Property

    Public ReadOnly Property InvoiceTotal() As Decimal
        Get
            Dim total As Decimal
            Dim lineItem As LineItem
            For i As Integer = 0 To MyBase.Count - 1
                lineItem = MyBase.Item(i)
                total += lineItem.Amount
            Next
            Return total
        End Get
    End Property

End Class
```

Figure 10-4 The code for the LineItem and LineItemList classes (part 2 of 2)

The code for the State class

```
Public Class State
    Private m_StateCode As String
    Private m_StateName As String
    Private m_FirstZipCode As Integer
    Private m_LastZipCode As Integer

    Public Sub New()

    End Sub

    Public Property StateCode() As String
        Get
            Return m_StateCode
        End Get
        Set(ByVal value As String)
            m_StateCode = value
        End Set
    End Property

    Public Property StateName() As String
        Get
            Return m_StateName
        End Get
        Set(ByVal value As String)
            m_StateName = value
        End Set
    End Property

    Public Property FirstZipCode() As Integer
        Get
            Return m_FirstZipCode
        End Get
        Set(ByVal value As Integer)
            m_FirstZipCode = value
        End Set
    End Property

    Public Property LastZipCode() As Integer
        Get
            Return m_LastZipCode
        End Get
        Set(ByVal value As Integer)
            m_LastZipCode = value
        End Set
    End Property

End Class
```

Figure 10-5 The code for the State class

The code for the database classes

Most of the database classes for the Payable Entry application use methods like the ones that you've been studying in the last four chapters. As a result, the topics that follow present just the code for the most important database classes and methods. If you want to review the code for any of the classes that aren't presented in this chapter, though, you can review the complete application that you've downloaded from our web site.

The code for the VendorDB class

Figure 10-6 presents the code for just the GetSelectedVendors method in the VendorDB class. The other methods in this class are like the ones that you've seen in the last four chapters.

The GetSelectedVendors method is used by the Find Vendor form to retrieve the vendors that meet the name and state criteria the user enters. Notice how the Where clause of the Select statement for this method is coded. It uses the Like operator to retrieve vendors with a name and state *like* the name and state the user enters. Then, a percent sign (%) is added at the end of the values for the @Name and @State parameters. This indicates that any characters can follow the characters the user enters.

If, for example, the user enters "comp" for the name and doesn't enter anything for the state, this statement retrieves all the vendors that have a name that begins with "comp", such as Compuserve and Computerworld. However, if the user also enters "ca" for the state, the search will be further refined so it only retrieves vendors that have a name that begins with "comp" in a state that begins with "ca".

For each vendor that's retrieved, a Vendor object is created and added to a list of Vendor objects. Then, when all the vendors have been retrieved, the vendor list is returned to the calling procedure.

The code for the GetSelectedVendors method

```
Imports System.Data.SqlClient

Public Class VendorDB

    Public Shared Function GetSelectedVendors(ByVal name As String,
            ByVal state As String) As List(Of Vendor)
        Dim vendorList As List(Of Vendor) = New List(Of Vendor)
        Dim connection As SqlConnection = PayablesDB.GetConnection
        Dim selectStatement As String =
            "SELECT VendorID, Name, Address1, Address2, City, State, " &
                "ZipCode, Phone, ContactFName, ContactLName, " &
                "DefaultAccountNo, DefaultTermsID " &
            "FROM Vendors " &
            "WHERE (Name LIKE @Name) AND (State LIKE @State) " &
            "ORDER BY Name"
        Dim selectCommand As SqlCommand =
            New SqlCommand(selectStatement, connection)
        selectCommand.Parameters.AddWithValue("@Name", name & "%")
        selectCommand.Parameters.AddWithValue("@State", state & "%")
        Try
            connection.Open()
            Dim reader As SqlDataReader = selectCommand.ExecuteReader()
            Dim vendor As Vendor
            Do While reader.Read
                vendor = New Vendor
                vendor.VendorID = CInt(reader("VendorID"))
                vendor.Name = reader("Name").ToString.Trim
                vendor.Address1 = reader("Address1").ToString
                vendor.Address2 = reader("Address2").ToString
                vendor.City = reader("City").ToString.Trim
                vendor.State = reader("State").ToString.Trim
                vendor.ZipCode = reader("ZipCode").ToString.Trim
                vendor.Phone = reader("Phone").ToString
                vendor.ContactFName = reader("ContactFName").ToString
                vendor.ContactLName = reader("ContactLName").ToString
                vendor.DefaultAccountNo = CInt(reader("DefaultAccountNo"))
                vendor.DefaultTermsID = CInt(reader("DefaultTermsID"))
                vendorList.Add(vendor)
            Loop
            reader.Close()
        Catch ex As SqlException
            Throw ex
        Finally
            connection.Close()
        End Try
        Return vendorList
    End Function
    .
    .
    .
End Class
```

Figure 10-6 The code for the VendorDB class

The code for the PayableDB class

Figure 10-7 presents the code for the PayableDB class. Since this class uses transactions and performs the main function of the Payable Entry application, I'll describe it in detail. To start, this class declares three private fields that will hold the connection, command, and transaction objects.

The WritePayable method gets a Payable object as a parameter and returns an integer value that represents an invoice ID. It starts by calling the GetConnection method of the PayablesDB class to get a connection to the Payables database. Next, it opens the connection, starts a transaction on the connection, creates a command object, and sets its Connection and Transaction properties.

At this point, a SQL statement has not been assigned to the command object. That's because the same command object will be used to insert rows into the Invoices and InvoiceLineItems tables. That way, you only have to associate the transaction with a single command object. Another way to do this, however, would be to use two command objects: one for inserting a row into the Invoices table and one for inserting a row into the InvoiceLineItems table. Then, you would have to associate the transaction with both command objects if you wanted them to be executed as part of the same transaction.

After the connection and command objects are established, the WritePayable method writes the payable data to the database. To do that, it starts by calling the InsertInvoice procedure to insert the invoice into the Invoices table. Because this procedure uses properties of the Payable object, that object is passed to it. Then, the invoice ID for the new invoice that's returned by this procedure is saved in a local variable named invoiceID.

If the InsertInvoice procedure is successful, the WritePayable method continues by calling the InsertLineItem procedure for each line item in the Payable object's LineItems collection. Before it does that, though, it sets the Invoice ID property of each line item to the value that was returned by the InsertInvoice procedure, and it sets the InvoiceSequence property to the appropriate value.

If the invoice and all of the line items are written successfully, the WritePayable method commits the transaction and returns the generated invoice ID to the calling procedure. However, if an error occurs while inserting a row into the Invoices or InvoiceLineItems table, the code in the Catch block rolls back the transaction and throws the exception to the calling procedure.

The InsertInvoice procedure starts by setting the CommandText property of the command object to the Insert statement that will be used to insert the invoice. As you can see, this statement will use parameters to specify the values that are assigned to the columns in the invoice row. Then, the next statement clears the Parameters collection of the command object. That's necessary because this command is used to insert rows into both the Invoices and InvoiceLineItems tables. So different parameters will need to be created for each Insert statement. The next group of statements creates the parameters used by the statement that inserts an invoice.

The code for the PayableDB class

Page 1

```
Imports System.Data.SqlClient

Public Class PayableDB
    Private Shared connection As SqlConnection
    Private Shared payableCommand As SqlCommand
    Private Shared payableTran As SqlTransaction

    Public Shared Function WritePayable(ByVal payable As Payable) As Integer

        Try
            connection = PayablesDB.GetConnection
            connection.Open()
            payableTran = connection.BeginTransaction

            payableCommand = New SqlCommand
            payableCommand.Connection = connection
            payableCommand.Transaction = payableTran

            Dim invoiceID As Integer = InsertInvoice(payable)
            Dim invoiceSequence As Integer = 0
            For Each li As LineItem In payable.LineItems
                li.InvoiceID = invoiceID
                invoiceSequence += 1
                li.InvoiceSequence = invoiceSequence
                InsertLineItem(li)
            Next
            payableTran.Commit()
            Return invoiceID
        Catch ex As SqlException
            payableTran.Rollback()
            Throw ex
        Finally
            connection.Close()
        End Try

    End Function

Private Shared Function InsertInvoice(ByVal payable As Payable) As Integer
     payableCommand.CommandText =
         "INSERT INTO Invoices " &
         "(VendorID, InvoiceNumber, InvoiceDate, InvoiceTotal, " &
         "TermsID, DueDate) " &
         "VALUES (@VendorID, @InvoiceNumber, @InvoiceDate, @InvoiceTotal, " &
         "@TermsID, @DueDate)"
     payableCommand.Parameters.Clear()

     payableCommand.Parameters.AddWithValue("@VendorID",
         payable.Invoice.VendorID)
     payableCommand.Parameters.AddWithValue("@InvoiceNumber",
         payable.Invoice.InvoiceNumber)
     payableCommand.Parameters.AddWithValue("@InvoiceDate",
         payable.Invoice.InvoiceDate)
     payableCommand.Parameters.AddWithValue("@InvoiceTotal",
         payable.Invoice.InvoiceTotal)
```

Figure 10-7 The code for the PayableDB class (part 1 of 2)

After the parameters have been created, the InsertInvoice procedure calls the command's ExecuteNonQuery method to execute the Insert statement. Then, it changes the command's CommandText property to "SELECT IDENT_CURRENT('Invoices') FROM Invoices" and executes this statement using the ExecuteScalar method. This SQL statement returns the identity value that was generated for the invoice. This value is then returned to the WritePayable method.

The InsertLineItem procedure works similarly. It sets the CommandText property of the command object to an Insert statement that can be used to insert a line item. Then, it clears the Parameters collection of the command and creates the required parameters. Finally, it calls the ExecuteNonQuery method to insert the row.

Notice that neither the InsertInvoice nor the InsertLineItem procedure uses a Try…Catch statement to catch SQL Server exceptions. That's because each of these procedures is called within the scope of the Try…Catch statement in the WritePayable method. As a result, if a SQL Server exception occurs within either of these procedures, the Catch block in the WritePayable method will be executed.

The code for the PayableDB class **Page 2**

```
        payableCommand.Parameters.AddWithValue("@TermsID",
            payable.Invoice.TermsID)
        payableCommand.Parameters.AddWithValue("@DueDate",
            payable.Invoice.DueDate)

        payableCommand.ExecuteNonQuery()

        payableCommand.CommandText _
            = "SELECT IDENT_CURRENT('Invoices') FROM Invoices"
        Dim invoiceID As Integer = CInt(payableCommand.ExecuteScalar)
        Return invoiceID

    End Function

    Private Shared Sub InsertLineItem(ByVal li As LineItem)
        payableCommand.CommandText =
            "INSERT INTO InvoiceLineItems " &
            "(InvoiceID, InvoiceSequence, AccountNo, Description, Amount) " &
            "VALUES (@InvoiceID, @InvoiceSequence, @AccountNo, " &
            "@Description, @Amount)"
        payableCommand.Parameters.Clear()

        payableCommand.Parameters.AddWithValue("@InvoiceID", li.InvoiceID)
        payableCommand.Parameters.AddWithValue("@InvoiceSequence",
            li.InvoiceSequence)
        payableCommand.Parameters.AddWithValue("@AccountNo", li.AccountNo)
        payableCommand.Parameters.AddWithValue("@Description", li.Description)
        payableCommand.Parameters.AddWithValue("@Amount", li.Amount)

        payableCommand.ExecuteNonQuery()

    End Sub

End Class
```

Figure 10-7 The code for the PayableDB class (part 2 of 2)

The code for the PayablesDB class

Figure 10-8 presents the code for the PayablesDB class. Unlike the PayablesDB class used by the applications in the last four chapters, the GetConnection method in this class gets the connection string from an XML file. This file is stored in the bin\Debug directory for the application, but it would normally be stored in a central location. That way, the connection string could be used by other applications.

The code for the StateDB class

Figure 10-8 also presents the code for the StateDB class. This class contains a method named GetStateList that returns a list of all the states in the States table. This method is used to get the list of states that's displayed in the State combo box on the Add/Modify Vendor form. This code is typical of the code in the TermsDB and GLAccountDB classes.

The code for the PayablesDB class

```
Imports System.Data.SqlClient
Imports System.Xml

Public Class PayablesDB

    Public Shared Function GetConnection() As SqlConnection
        Return New SqlConnection(GetConnectionString)
    End Function

    Private Shared Function GetConnectionString() As String
        Dim xmlReader As New XmlTextReader("csPayables.xml")
        Return xmlReader.ReadElementString("Connection")
    End Function

End Class
```

The code for the StateDB class

```
Imports System.Data.SqlClient

Public Class StateDB

    Public Shared Function GetStateList() As List(Of State)
        Dim stateList As New List(Of State)
        Dim connection As SqlConnection = PayablesDB.GetConnection
        Dim selectStatement As String =
            "SELECT StateCode, StateName, FirstZipCode, LastZipCode " &
            "FROM States " &
            "ORDER BY StateName"
        Dim selectCommand As New SqlCommand(selectStatement, connection)
        Try
            connection.Open()
            Dim reader As SqlDataReader = selectCommand.ExecuteReader()
            Dim state As State
            Do While reader.Read
                state = New State
                state.StateCode = reader("StateCode").ToString
                state.StateName = reader("StateName").ToString
                state.FirstZipCode = CInt(reader("FirstZipCode"))
                state.LastZipCode = CInt(reader("LastZipCode"))
                stateList.Add(state)
            Loop
            reader.Close()
        Catch ex As SqlException
            Throw ex
        Finally
            connection.Close()
        End Try
        Return stateList
    End Function

End Class
```

Figure 10-8 The code for the PayablesDB and StateDB classes

The code for the forms

The code for the forms used by the Payable Entry application follows.

The code for the Vendor Invoices form

Figure 10-9 presents the code for the Vendor Invoices form. This form starts by declaring a public variable named vendor that will store the Vendor object for the currently selected vendor. This variable is declared as public so it can be used by other forms of this application.

If the user enters a vendor ID and clicks the Get Vendor button, the Click event handler for that button calls the GetVendor procedure. This procedure calls the GetVendor method of the VendorDB class. If the vendor is found, the Vendor binding source is cleared, the new vendor is added to the binding source so its data is displayed on the form, and the Modify Vendor button is enabled. (This button is disabled when the form is first displayed.) If the vendor isn't found, an error message is displayed, the Vendor binding source is cleared so no data is displayed on the form, and the Modify Vendor button is disabled.

If the vendor is found, the Click event handler for the Get Vendor button continues by calling the GetVendorInvoices procedure. This procedure calls the GetVendorInvoices method of the InvoiceDB class to get a list of the invoices for the selected vendor. Then, the DataSource property of the DataGridView control is set to this list, the CurrencyManager object for this control is retrieved, and the currency manager is refreshed so the invoices are displayed.

If the vendor isn't found, the event handler checks if the invoice list is not equal to Nothing. In other words, it checks if the GetVendorInvoices method has been called previously so the invoice list has been initialized. If it has, the invoice list is cleared and the currency manager for the DataGridView control is refreshed so no invoices are displayed.

If the user clicks the Find Vendor button, the Click event handler for that button creates an instance of the Find Vendor form and displays it as a dialog box. Then, if the user selects a vendor, that vendor is added to the Vendor binding source and the vendor's invoices are retrieved.

The event handlers for the Add Vendor and Modify Vendor buttons are similar to those event handlers in the Vendor Maintenance application you saw in chapter 7. The main difference is that, in this application, the data for a vendor is displayed by adding the Vendor object to the Vendor binding source. In addition, a new List (Of Invoice) is created to hold the invoices for the new vendor, and the DataGridView control is bound to this list.

If the user clicks the View Line Items button for an invoice, the CellContentClick event handler for the data grid starts by retrieving the invoice from the selected row. Then, it creates an instance of the Line Items form, sets the public invoiceID and invoiceNumber variables of that form, and displays the form.

Finally, the Click event handler for the Add Invoice button first checks that a vendor has been selected. If not, an error message is displayed. Otherwise, an instance of the Add Invoice form is created and displayed as a dialog box. Then,

The code for the Vendor Invoices form **Page 1**

```
Imports PayablesData

Public Class frmVendorInvoices
    Public vendor As Vendor
    Private invoiceList As List(Of Invoice)
    Private cm As CurrencyManager

    Private Sub btnGetVendor_Click(ByVal sender As System.Object,
            ByVal e As System.EventArgs) Handles btnGetVendor.Click
        If Validator.IsPresent(txtVendorID) AndAlso
           Validator.IsInt32(txtVendorID) Then
            Dim vendorID As Integer = CInt(txtVendorID.Text)
            Me.GetVendor(vendorID)
            If vendor IsNot Nothing Then
                Me.GetVendorInvoices(vendorID)
            Else
                If invoiceList IsNot Nothing Then
                    invoiceList.Clear()
                    cm.Refresh()
                End If
            End If
        End If
    End Sub

    Private Sub GetVendor(ByVal vendorID As Integer)
        Try
            vendor = VendorDB.GetVendor(vendorID)
            If vendor IsNot Nothing Then
                VendorBindingSource.Clear()
                VendorBindingSource.Add(vendor)
                btnModifyVendor.Enabled = True
            Else
                MessageBox.Show("No vendor found with this ID. " &
                    "Please try again.", "Vendor Not Found")
                VendorBindingSource.Clear()
                btnModifyVendor.Enabled = False
            End If
        Catch ex As Exception
            MessageBox.Show(ex.Message, ex.GetType.ToString)
        End Try
    End Sub

    Private Sub GetVendorInvoices(ByVal vendorID As Integer)
        Try
            invoiceList = InvoiceDB.GetVendorInvoices(vendorID)
            InvoiceDataGridView.DataSource = invoiceList
            cm = CType(InvoiceDataGridView.BindingContext(invoiceList),
                CurrencyManager)
            cm.Refresh()
        Catch ex As Exception
            MessageBox.Show(ex.Message, ex.GetType.ToString)
        End Try
    End Sub
```

Figure 10-9 The code for the Vendor Invoices form (part 1 of 3)

The code for the Vendor Invoices form **Page 2**

```
Private Sub btnFindVendor_Click(ByVal sender As System.Object,
        ByVal e As System.EventArgs) Handles btnFindVendor.Click
    Dim findVendorForm As New frmFindVendor
    Dim result As DialogResult = findVendorForm.ShowDialog()
    If result = DialogResult.OK Then
        txtVendorID.Text = vendor.VendorID.ToString
        VendorBindingSource.Clear()
        VendorBindingSource.Add(vendor)
        Me.GetVendorInvoices(vendor.VendorID)
        btnModifyVendor.Enabled = True
    End If
End Sub

Private Sub btnAddVendor_Click(ByVal sender As System.Object,
        ByVal e As System.EventArgs) Handles btnAddVendor.Click
    Dim addModifyVendorForm As New frmAddModifyVendor
    addModifyVendorForm.addVendor = True
    Dim result As DialogResult = addModifyVendorForm.ShowDialog
    If result = DialogResult.OK Then
        txtVendorID.Text = vendor.VendorID.ToString
        VendorBindingSource.Clear()
        VendorBindingSource.Add(vendor)
        invoiceList = New List(Of Invoice)
        InvoiceDataGridView.DataSource = invoiceList
        cm = CType(InvoiceDataGridView.BindingContext(invoiceList),
            CurrencyManager)
        btnModifyVendor.Enabled = True
    End If
End Sub

Private Sub btnModifyVendor_Click(ByVal sender As System.Object,
        ByVal e As System.EventArgs) Handles btnModifyVendor.Click
    Dim addModifyVendorForm As New frmAddModifyVendor
    addModifyVendorForm.addVendor = False
    Dim result As DialogResult = addModifyVendorForm.ShowDialog
    If result = DialogResult.OK Then
        VendorBindingSource.Clear()
        VendorBindingSource.Add(vendor)
    ElseIf result = DialogResult.Retry Then
        Me.GetVendor(vendor.VendorID)
        Me.GetVendorInvoices(vendor.VendorID)
    End If
End Sub
```

Figure 10-9 The code for the Vendor Invoices form (part 2 of 3)

The code for the Vendor Invoices form **Page 3**

```
    Private Sub InvoiceDataGridView_CellContentClick(
            ByVal sender As System.Object,
            ByVal e As System.Windows.Forms.DataGridViewCellEventArgs) _
            Handles InvoiceDataGridView.CellContentClick
        If e.ColumnIndex = 9 Then
            Dim i As Integer = e.RowIndex
            Dim row As DataGridViewRow = InvoiceDataGridView.Rows(i)
            Dim invoice As Invoice = CType(row.DataBoundItem, Invoice)

            Dim lineItemsForm As New frmLineItems
            lineItemsForm.invoiceID = invoice.InvoiceID
            lineItemsForm.invoiceNumber = invoice.InvoiceNumber
            lineItemsForm.ShowDialog()
        End If
    End Sub

    Private Sub btnAddInvoice_Click(ByVal sender As System.Object,
            ByVal e As System.EventArgs) Handles btnAddInvoice.Click
        If txtVendorID.Text = "" Then
            MessageBox.Show("You must select a vendor.", "Entry Error")
        Else
            Dim addInvoiceForm As New frmAddInvoice
            Dim result As DialogResult = addInvoiceForm.ShowDialog
            If result = DialogResult.OK Then
                invoiceList.Add(addInvoiceForm.payable.Invoice)
                cm.Refresh()
            End If
        End If
    End Sub

End Class
```

Figure 10-9 The code for the Vendor Invoices form (part 3 of 3)

if an invoice is added successfully, it's added to the invoice list and the currency manager for the DataGridView control is refreshed so the invoice is displayed.

The code for the Find Vendor form

Figure 10-10 presents the code for the Find Vendor form. The first event handler for this form is executed when the user enters the name and state criteria for the vendors to be displayed and clicks the Search button. This event handler starts by calling the GetSelectedVendors method of the VendorDB class to get a list of Vendor objects.

As you saw earlier in this chapter, the GetSelectedVendors method uses the values the user entered into the Name and State text boxes to determine which Vendor objects to return. Then, this list of Vendor objects is stored in the vendorList variable that's declared at the module level, and the DataSource property of the list box is set to this list. Because the DisplayMember property of the list box was set to the SingleLineAddress property of the Vendor class at design time, the information for each vendor will be displayed in a single line as shown in figure 10-1.

After it sets the DataSource property of the list box, this event handler uses a Select Case statement to display a message in the label above the list box. This message indicates whether any vendors were found with the specified name and state and, if so, how many were found.

Once a list of vendors is displayed, the user can highlight a vendor and click the OK button. Then, the event handler for the Click event of this button sets the vendor variable that's declared in the Vendor Invoices form to the selected Vendor object and sets the DialogResult property of the form to DialogResult.OK. The same processing is performed if the user double-clicks on a vendor. If the user clicks the Cancel button, however, the DialogResult property of the form is automatically set to DialogResult.Cancel since the CancelButton property of the form is set to this button.

The code for the Find Vendor form

```
Imports PayablesData

Public Class frmFindVendor

    Private vendorList As List(Of Vendor)

    Private Sub btnSearch_Click(ByVal sender As System.Object,
            ByVal e As System.EventArgs) Handles btnSearch.Click

        vendorList = VendorDB.GetSelectedVendors(txtLastName.Text,
            txtState.Text)
        SingleLineAddressListBox.DataSource = vendorList

        Select Case vendorList.Count
            Case 0
                lblMessage.Text = "No vendors found with that name and state."
            Case 1
                lblMessage.Text = "One vendor found with that name and state."
            Case Else
                lblMessage.Text = SingleLineAddressListBox.Items.Count &
                    " vendors found with that name and state."
        End Select

        SingleLineAddressListBox.SelectedIndex = -1
        btnOK.Enabled = False

    End Sub

    Private Sub SingleLineAddressListBox_SelectedIndexChanged(
            ByVal sender As System.Object, ByVal e As System.EventArgs) _
            Handles SingleLineAddressListBox.SelectedIndexChanged
        btnOK.Enabled = True
    End Sub

    Private Sub btnOK_Click(ByVal sender As System.Object,
            ByVal e As System.EventArgs) Handles btnOK.Click
        frmVendorInvoices.vendor =
            vendorList(SingleLineAddressListBox.SelectedIndex)
        Me.DialogResult = DialogResult.OK
    End Sub

    Private Sub SingleLineAddressListBox_DoubleClick(
            ByVal sender As System.Object, ByVal e As System.EventArgs) _
            Handles SingleLineAddressListBox.DoubleClick
        frmVendorInvoices.vendor =
           vendorList(SingleLineAddressListBox.SelectedIndex)
        Me.DialogResult = DialogResult.OK
    End Sub

End Class
```

Figure 10-10 The code for the Find Vendor form

The code for the Add Invoice form

Figure 10-11 presents the code for the Add Invoice form. This form starts by declaring a public variable named payable that will hold a Payable object. It's declared as public so that after a payable is added, the Vendor Invoices form can retrieve the Invoice object from the Payable object and add it to the list of invoices that are displayed on the form.

When this form is displayed, the Load event handler starts by displaying the vendor name in the Vendor text box, initializing the Text property of the Invoice Number text box to an empty string, and initializing the Value property of the Invoice Date date time picker to the current date. This is necessary because these controls are unbound. Then, it calls the GetTermsList method of the TermsDB class to get a list of terms, and it assigns this list to the DataSource property of the Terms combo box. It also sets the SelectedValue property of the combo box to the DefaultTermsID property of the Vendor object so the default terms are selected by default. Similar processing is performed for the Account combo box. Finally, a new Payable object is created and assigned to the payable variable; the LineItems property of this object, which contains a collection of LineItem objects, is assigned to the DataSource property of the DataGridView control; and the CurrencyManager object is retrieved from this control.

If the user clicks the Add button to add a line item, the Click event handler for that button starts by checking that the description and amount are valid. If so, a new LineItem object is created, its properties are set, and it's added to the LineItems collection of the Payable object. Then, the CurrencyManager object for the DataGridView control is refreshed so the new line item is displayed. Finally, the invoice total is retrieved from the Payable object and displayed on the form, the Description and Amount text boxes are cleared, and the focus is moved to the Account combo box so another line item can be entered.

If the user clicks the Delete button for a line item, the event handler for the CellContentClick event of the DataGridView control removes the line item from the LineItems collection of the Payable object. Then, it refreshes the CurrencyManager object so the line item is no longer displayed, it displays the new invoice total, and it moves the focus to the Account combo box.

The code for the Add Invoice form **Page 1**

```
Imports PayablesData
Public Class frmAddInvoice
    Public payable As Payable
    Private cm As CurrencyManager
    Private termsList As List(Of Terms)

    Private Sub frmAddInvoice_Load(ByVal sender As System.Object,
            ByVal e As System.EventArgs) Handles MyBase.Load
        txtVendor.Text = frmVendorInvoices.vendor.Name
        InvoiceNoTextBox.Text = ""
        InvoiceDateDateTimePicker.Value = DateTime.Today
        termsList = TermsDB.GetTermsList
        TermsIDComboBox.DataSource = termsList
        TermsIDComboBox.SelectedValue =
            frmVendorInvoices.vendor.DefaultTermsID

        Dim accountList As List(Of GLAccount) = GLAccountDB.GetGLAccountList
        AccountNoComboBox.DataSource = accountList
        AccountNoComboBox.SelectedValue =
            frmVendorInvoices.vendor.DefaultAccountNo
        payable = New Payable
        LineItemDataGridView.DataSource = payable.LineItems
        cm = CType(LineItemDataGridView.BindingContext(payable.LineItems),
            CurrencyManager)
        InvoiceNoTextBox.Select()
    End Sub

    Private Sub btnAdd_Click(ByVal sender As System.Object,
            ByVal e As System.EventArgs) Handles btnAdd.Click
        If IsValidData() Then
            Dim lineItem As New LineItem
            lineItem.AccountNo = CInt(AccountNoComboBox.SelectedValue)
            lineItem.AccountDescription = AccountNoComboBox.Text
            lineItem.Description = txtDescription.Text
            lineItem.Amount = CDec(txtAmount.Text)
            payable.LineItems.Add(lineItem)
            cm.Refresh()
            txtInvoiceTotal.Text = FormatCurrency(payable.InvoiceTotal)
            txtDescription.Text = ""
            txtAmount.Text = ""
            AccountNoComboBox.Select()
        End If
    End Sub

    Private Sub LineItemDataGridView_CellContentClick(
            ByVal sender As System.Object,
            ByVal e As System.Windows.Forms.DataGridViewCellEventArgs) _
            Handles LineItemDataGridView.CellContentClick
        If e.ColumnIndex = 6 Then
            payable.LineItems.RemoveAt(e.RowIndex)
            cm.Refresh()
            txtInvoiceTotal.Text = FormatCurrency(payable.InvoiceTotal)
            AccountNoComboBox.Select()
        End If
    End Sub
```

Figure 10-11 The code for the Add Invoice and Line Items forms (part 1 of 2)

The last event handler is executed when the user clicks the Save Invoice button. This event handler starts by making sure that at least one line item has been entered. If so, it sets the properties of the Invoice object that's stored in the Payable object. Then, it calls the WritePayable method of the PayableDB class to add the invoice and line items to the Payables database. If the invoice ID that's returned by this method is equal to zero, it indicates that the invoice wasn't added. In that case, an error message is displayed and the DialogResult property of the form is set to DialogResult.Cancel. Otherwise, the invoiceID property of the Invoice object is set to the new invoice ID and the DialogResult property of the form is set to DialogResult.OK.

The code for the Line Items form

Figure 10-11 also presents the code for the Line Items form. This form declares two public variables: invoiceID and invoiceNumber. The values of these variables are set by the Vendor Invoices form before this form is displayed.

The Load event for this form starts by calling the GetInvoiceLineItems method of the LineItemDB class to get the line items for the selected invoice and store them in a list. Then, the DataSource property of the DataGridView control is set to this list so it displays the line items. Finally, the vendor name and invoice number are displayed in the text boxes on the form.

The code for the Add Invoice form **Page 2**

```
    Private Sub btnSave_Click(ByVal sender As System.Object,
            ByVal e As System.EventArgs) Handles btnSave.Click
        If payable.LineItems.Count = 0 Then
            MessageBox.Show("You must add at least one line item.", "Error")
            AccountNoComboBox.Select()
        Else
            payable.Invoice.VendorID = frmVendorInvoices.vendor.VendorID
            payable.Invoice.InvoiceNumber = InvoiceNoTextBox.Text
            payable.Invoice.InvoiceDate = InvoiceDateDateTimePicker.Value
            payable.Invoice.InvoiceTotal = payable.LineItems.InvoiceTotal
            payable.Invoice.TermsID = CInt(TermsIDComboBox.SelectedValue)
            Dim dueDays As Integer =
                termsList(TermsIDComboBox.SelectedIndex).DueDays
            payable.Invoice.DueDate =
                payable.Invoice.InvoiceDate.AddDays(dueDays)
            Try
                Dim invoiceID As Integer = PayableDB.WritePayable(payable)
                If invoiceID = 0 Then
                    MessageBox.Show("A database error occurred. " &
                        "The invoice was not posted.", "Database Error")
                    Me.DialogResult = DialogResult.Cancel
                Else
                    payable.Invoice.InvoiceID = invoiceID
                    Me.DialogResult = DialogResult.OK
                End If
            Catch ex As Exception
                MessageBox.Show(ex.Message, ex.GetType.ToString)
            End Try
        End If
    End Sub

    Private Function IsValidData() As Boolean
        Return Validator.IsPresent(txtDescription) AndAlso
               Validator.IsPresent(txtAmount) AndAlso
               Validator.IsDecimal(txtAmount)
    End Function

End Class
```

The code for the Line Items form

```
Imports PayablesData
Public Class frmLineItems
    Public invoiceID As Integer
    Public invoiceNumber As String

    Private Sub frmLineItems_Load(ByVal sender As System.Object,
            ByVal e As System.EventArgs) Handles MyBase.Load
        Dim lineItemList As List(Of LineItem) =
            LineItemDB.GetInvoiceLineItems(invoiceID)
        LineItemDataGridView.DataSource = lineItemList
        txtVendor.Text = frmVendorInvoices.vendor.Name
        txtInvoiceNo.Text = invoiceNumber
    End Sub
End Class
```

Figure 10-11 The code for the Add Invoice and Line Items forms (part 2 of 2)

The code for the Add/Modify Vendor form

Figure 10-12 presents the code for the Add/Modify Vendor form. Although this form works like the Add/Modify Vendor form in chapter 7, its code is somewhat different since it uses object data sources. As a result, you may want to compare the code in this chapter to the code in figure 7-9 in chapter 7.

This form starts by declaring a public variable named addVendor that indicates whether a vendor is being added or modified. This variable is set by the Vendor Invoices form before the form is displayed. In addition, three private variables are declared: newVendor will store a Vendor object that contains any changes the user makes; oldVendor will store a Vendor object that contains the original data for the vendor, and phoneBinding will store the Binding object for the Phone text box.

The Load event handler for the form starts by calling the LoadComboBoxes procedure, which gets the list of objects to be displayed in each box and sets its DataSource property to the list. Here, the DisplayMember and ValueMember properties of the boxes don't have to be set because they're set at design time.

Next, if a vendor is being added, an instance of the Vendor object is created and stored in the newVendor variable. But if a vendor is being modified, the Vendor object for the current vendor is stored in the oldVendor variable. In addition, a new Vendor object is created and stored in the newVendor variable, and the PutNewVendor procedure is called to assign the properties of the oldVendor object to the newVendor object. At this point, the oldVendor and newVendor objects have identical data.

The next set of statements retrieve the Binding object for the Phone text box and wire its Format and Parse events to event handlers. The Format event handler formats the phone number when it's displayed in the text box. In contrast, the Parse event handler removes the formatting when the value in the control changes so the formatting characters won't be stored in the database. Last, the Load event handler adds the newVendor object to the Vendor binding source. This causes the current data for the vendor to be displayed on the form.

If the user clicks the Accept button, the Click event handler for this button starts by checking if the data is valid. If it is and a vendor is being added, the AddVendor method of the VendorDB class is called to add the vendor to the database, and the vendorID that's returned by this method is stored in the VendorID property of the newVendor object. Then, this object is assigned to the Vendor object declared by the Vendor Invoices form, and the DialogResult property of the form is set to DialogResult.OK.

If a vendor is being modified, this event handler calls the UpdateVendor method of the VendorDB class, and both the oldVendor and newVendor objects are passed to this method. That way, the oldVendor object can be used to perform concurrency checking. If the update is successful, the Vendor object declared by the Vendor Invoices form is set to the newVendor object, and the DialogResult property of the form is set to DialogResult.OK. Otherwise, an error message is displayed indicating that the vendor row has been updated or deleted, and the DialogResult property is set to DialogResult.Retry.

The code for the Add/Modify Vendor form — Page 1

```
Imports PayablesData

Public Class frmAddModifyVendor

    Public addVendor As Boolean
    Private oldVendor As Vendor
    Private newVendor As Vendor
    Private phoneBinding As Binding

    Private Sub frmAddModifyVendor_Load(ByVal sender As System.Object,
            ByVal e As System.EventArgs) Handles MyBase.Load

        Me.LoadComboBoxes()

        If addVendor Then
            Me.Text = "Add Vendor"
            newVendor = New Vendor
        Else
            Me.Text = "Modify Vendor"
            oldVendor = frmVendorInvoices.vendor
            newVendor = New Vendor
            Me.PutNewVendor()
        End If

        phoneBinding = PhoneTextBox.DataBindings("Text")
        AddHandler phoneBinding.Format, AddressOf FormatPhoneNumber
        AddHandler phoneBinding.Parse, AddressOf UnformatPhoneNumber

        VendorBindingSource.Add(newVendor)

    End Sub

    Private Sub LoadComboBoxes()
        Try
            stateList = StateDB.GetStateList
            StateComboBox.DataSource = stateList

            Dim termsList As List(Of Terms)
            termsList = TermsDB.GetTermsList
            cboTerms.DataSource = termsList

            Dim accountList As List(Of GLAccount)
            accountList = GLAccountDB.GetGLAccountList
            cboAccounts.DataSource = accountList
        Catch ex As Exception
            MessageBox.Show(ex.Message, ex.GetType.ToString)
        End Try
    End Sub
```

Figure 10-12 The code for the Add/Modify Vendor form (part 1 of 3)

The code for the Add/Modify Vendor form **Page 2**

```
Private Sub FormatPhoneNumber(ByVal sender As Object,
        ByVal e As ConvertEventArgs)
    If e.Value IsNot Nothing Then
        If e.Value.GetType.ToString = "System.String" Then
            Dim s As String = e.Value.ToString
            If IsNumeric(s) Then
                If s.Length = 10 Then
                    e.Value = s.Substring(0, 3) & "." &
                              s.Substring(3, 3) & "." &
                              s.Substring(6, 4)
                End If
            End If
        End If
    End If
End Sub

Private Sub UnformatPhoneNumber(ByVal sender As Object,
        ByVal e As ConvertEventArgs)
    Dim s As String = e.Value.ToString
    s = s.Replace(".", "")
    If IsNumeric(s) Then
        If s.Length = 10 Then
            e.Value = s
        End If
    End If
End Sub

Private Sub PutNewVendor()
    newVendor.VendorID = oldVendor.VendorID
    newVendor.Name = oldVendor.Name
    newVendor.Address1 = oldVendor.Address1
    newVendor.Address2 = oldVendor.Address2
    newVendor.City = oldVendor.City
    newVendor.State = oldVendor.State
    newVendor.ZipCode = oldVendor.ZipCode
    newVendor.DefaultTermsID = oldVendor.DefaultTermsID
    newVendor.DefaultAccountNo = oldVendor.DefaultAccountNo
    newVendor.Phone = oldVendor.Phone
    newVendor.ContactFName = oldVendor.ContactFName
    newVendor.ContactLName = oldVendor.ContactLName
End Sub
```

Figure 10-12 The code for the Add/Modify Vendor form (part 2 of 3)

The code for the Add/Modify Vendor form **Page 3**

```
Private Sub btnAccept_Click(ByVal sender As System.Object,
        ByVal e As System.EventArgs) Handles btnAccept.Click
    If IsValidData() Then
        If addVendor Then
            Try
                newVendor.VendorID = VendorDB.AddVendor(newVendor)
                frmVendorInvoices.vendor = newVendor
                Me.DialogResult = DialogResult.OK
            Catch ex As Exception
                MessageBox.Show(ex.Message, ex.GetType.ToString)
            End Try
        Else
            Try
                If VendorDB.UpdateVendor(oldVendor, newVendor) Then
                    frmVendorInvoices.vendor = newVendor
                    Me.DialogResult = DialogResult.OK
                Else
                    MessageBox.Show("Another user has updated or deleted " &
                       "that vendor.", "Database Error")
                    Me.DialogResult = DialogResult.Retry
                End If
            Catch ex As Exception
            MessageBox.Show(ex.Message, ex.GetType.ToString)
                End Try
        End If
    End If
End Sub

Private Function IsValidData() As Boolean
  If Validator.IsPresent(NameTextBox) AndAlso
         Validator.IsPresent(Address1TextBox) AndAlso
         Validator.IsPresent(CityTextBox) AndAlso
         Validator.IsPresent(StateComboBox) AndAlso
         Validator.IsPresent(ZipCodeTextBox) AndAlso
         Validator.IsPresent(cboTerms) AndAlso
         Validator.IsPresent(cboAccounts) AndAlso
         Validator.IsInt32(ZipCodeTextBox) Then
   Dim firstZip As Integer =
      stateList(StateComboBox.SelectedIndex).FirstZipCode
   Dim lastZip As Integer = stateList(StateComboBox.SelectedIndex).LastZipCode
   If Validator.IsStateZipCode(ZipCodeTextBox, firstZip, lastZip) Then
      If PhoneTextBox.Text <> "" Then
         If Validator.IsPhoneNumber(PhoneTextBox) Then
            Return True
         Else
            Return False
         End If
      Else
         Return True
      End If
   End If
  Else
     Return False
  End If
End Function
```

Figure 10-12 The code for the Add/Modify Vendor form (part 3 of 3)

Perspective

Now that you've seen the code for the Payable Entry application, you should have a better feel for how you can use object data sources. As you've seen, they're particularly useful for working with controls like the DataGridView control that's designed for working with bound data. But they also make it easier to work with the data in standard controls like text boxes and combo boxes.

You should also have a better idea of when and how transactions should be used. In particular, you've seen how you can use special database classes to implement the use of transactions.

At this point, you may also be thinking that developing all of the code that's required for a three-layer application is a lot of hard work. Although that's true, you should keep in mind that all of the code for the business and database classes can be reused by other applications. So you only have to write this code once.

In fact, if you work in a shop with other programmers, some of this code may already be written for you. In that case, you may need to add new properties and methods to these classes to provide additional functionality, but that should be easy to do once you develop some basic properties and methods like the ones shown in this chapter.

Exercise 10-1 Revise the code for using transactions in the Payable Entry application

In this exercise, you'll modify the way transactions are used by the Payable Entry application that has been presented in this chapter. That will give you some practice working with transactions.

1. Open the Payable Entry application in your chapter 10 directory.
2. Review the code in the PayableDB class that implements the use of transactions. Note that it uses just one command object for three different types of SQL statements, so the properties of the command have to be changed each time a new type of SQL statement is executed.
3. Modify the code in the PayableDB class so it uses a separate command object for each type of SQL statement that is executed, but still implements the use of transactions. (You may need to refer back to chapter 8 to refresh your memory on how to associate a transaction between commands.)
4. Test your modifications.

Section 4

How to use ADO.NET with web applications

In the first three sections of this book, you've learned how to use ADO.NET to work with a database from Windows Forms applications. Now, the four chapters in this section show you how to access and update a database from an ASP.NET web application.

In chapter 11, you'll learn how to use the SQL data source control and the GridView control for quickly building web applications. In chapter 12, you'll learn more about using the GridView control. In chapter 13, you'll learn how to use the DetailsView control. And in chapter 14, you'll learn how to use object data source controls, which let you build three-layer web applications using some of the skills that you learned in section 3.

Please keep in mind that the focus of these chapters is on database programming, not all aspects of web development. If you're already familiar with ASP.NET, these chapters should be easy for you to follow. If you aren't familiar with ASP.NET, these chapters will show that database programming for web applications uses the same basic skills as database programming for Windows applications. For a book that presents all of the skills that you need for building professional web applications, we recommend *Murach's ASP.NET 4 Web Programming with VB 2010.*

11

How to use SQL data sources

To make it easy to connect to a SQL Server database and work with its data, ASP.NET 4 offers a SQL data source control. In this chapter, you'll learn how to use this control, which lets you access data with little or no programming. Along the way, you'll learn the basic skills for using the GridView control.

How to create a SQL data source control

To access the data in a SQL Server database from an ASP.NET web application, you can use a SQL data source control. Then, you can bind the ASP.NET data controls like the GridView control to the data source. As you will see, this is similar to using a data source in a Windows application.

How to add a SQL data source control to a form

Figure 11-1 shows how to add a *SQL data source control* to a form. To do that, you open the Data group of the Toolbox, drag the SqlDataSource control onto the form, and drop it. Since a data source control isn't displayed on the page when the application is run, it doesn't matter where you drop this control. But it does make sense to place it near the control that it will be bound to.

When you drop the SQL data source control on a page, its smart tag menu will appear. Then, you can choose the Configure Data Source command to configure the data source using the Data Source Configuration Wizard as shown in the topics that follow. Once you've configured the data source control, you can bind controls to it so they can work with the data source defined by the control.

This figure also shows the aspx code for a simple SQL data source control, along with the basic attributes of this control. In an ASP.NET web application, aspx code is generated for the controls that you place on a form. As this chapter progresses, you'll see many examples of aspx code.

In addition to the ID and Runat attributes, a SQL data source control has a ConnectionString attribute that specifies the connection to the database. In most cases, you'll store the connection string in the web.config file as shown later in this chapter. The ProviderName attribute specifies the data provider that will be used to access the database. For a SQL data source control, the default is System.Data.SqlClient. Finally, the SelectCommand attribute specifies the Select statement or stored procedure that will be used to retrieve data from the database.

A SQL data source control in the Web Forms Designer

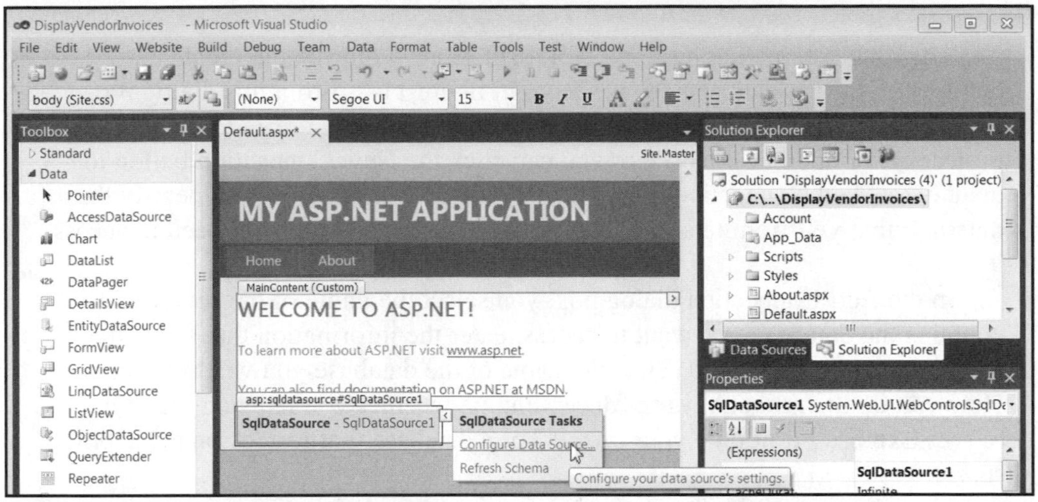

Aspx code generated for a basic SQL data source control

```
<asp:SqlDataSource ID="SqlDataSource1" runat="server"
    ConnectionString="<%$ ConnectionStrings:PayablesConnectionString %>"
    SelectCommand="SELECT [VendorID], [Name] FROM [Vendors]
                   ORDER BY [Name]">
</asp:SqlDataSource>
```

Basic SQL data source control attributes

Attribute	Description
ID	The ID for the SQL data source control.
Runat	Must specify "server".
ConnectionString	The connection string. In most cases, you should use a <%$ expression to specify the name of a connection string saved in the web.config file (see figure 11-3).
ProviderName	The name of the provider used to access the database. The default is System.Data.SqlClient.
SelectCommand	The SQL Select statement or stored procedure executed by the data source to retrieve data.

Description

- To create a *SQL data source control*, drag the control from the Data group of the Toolbox onto the form. Then, choose Configure Data Source from the control's smart tag menu and proceed from there.
- Once the SQL data source control has been configured, you can bind controls to it so they get their data from the SQL data source.
- You can also create a SQL data source control using the Choose Data Source command in the smart tag menu of a bindable control. See figures 11-13 and 11-14 for details.

Figure 11-1 How to add a SQL data source control to a form

How to define the connection

The first step in configuring a SQL data source control is to create the connection for the data source, as shown in figure 11-2. From this dialog box, you can select an existing connection (one you've already created for this project or for another project), or you can click the New Connection button to display the Add Connection dialog box. This dialog box helps you identify the database that you want to access and provide the information you need to access it.

In the Add Connection dialog box, you select the name of the server that contains the database you want to access, enter the information that's required to log on to the server, and select the name of the database you want to access. How you do that, though, varies depending on whether you're using the SQL Server Express Edition on your own PC or a database that resides on a database server.

If you're using SQL Server Express on your own PC, you can type localhost\sqlexpress for the server name. Alternatively, you can select the server name from the drop-down list, which will include your computer name like this: ANNEPC\SQLEXPRESS. If you will be porting your applications from one computer to another, though, it's best to use localhost. That way, you won't have to change the server name to refer to the correct computer.

For the logon information, you can click on the Use Windows Authentication option. Then, SQL Server Express will use the login name and password that you use for your computer as the name and password for the database too. As a result, you won't need to provide a separate user name and password in this dialog box. Last, you select the name of the database that you want to connect to. When you're done, you can click on the Test Connection button to be sure that the connection works.

In contrast, if you're using a database on a server computer, you need to get the connection information from the network or database administrator. That will include the server name, logon information, and database name. Once you establish a connection to a database, you can use that connection for all of the other applications that use that database.

The dialog boxes for defining a connection

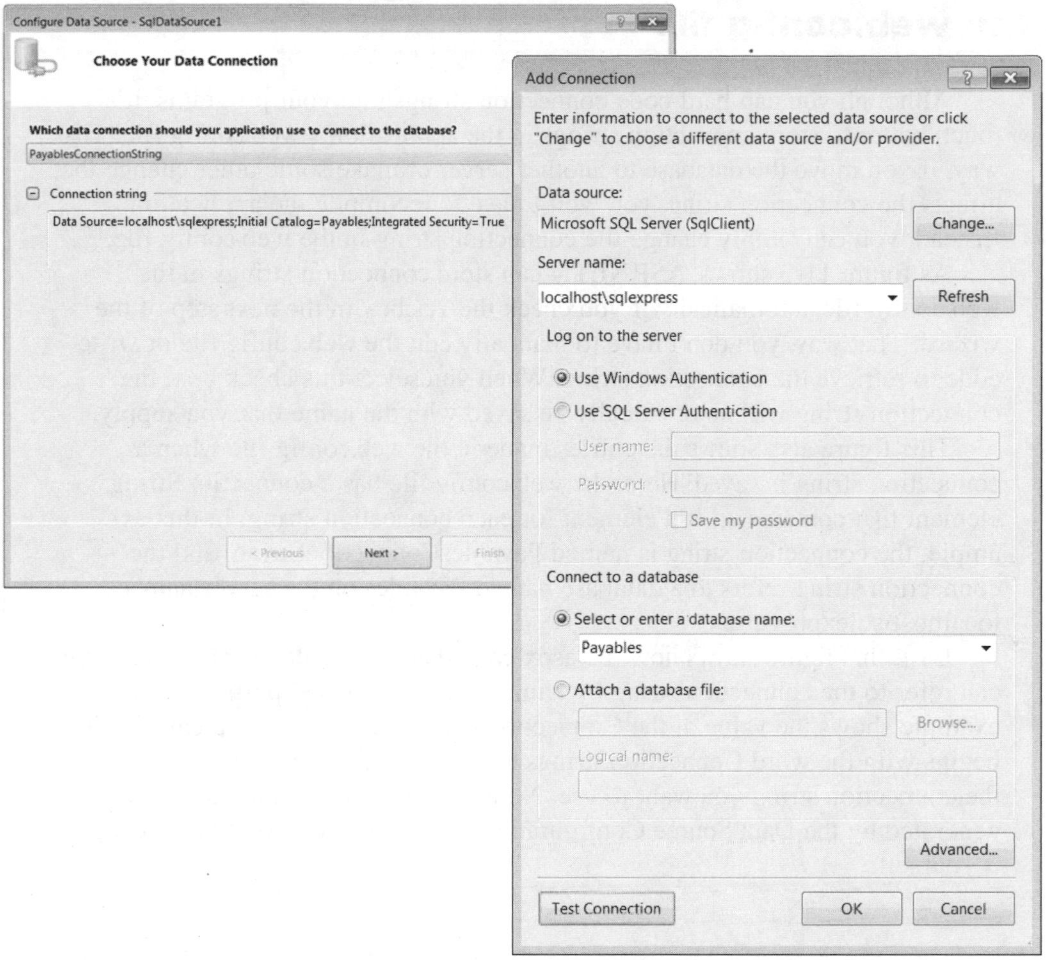

Description

- The first Configure Data Source dialog box asks you to identify the data connection for the database you want to use. If you've previously created a connection for that database, you can select it from the drop-down list. To see the connection string for that connection, click the + button below the drop-down list.
- To create a new connection, click the New Connection button to display the Add Connection dialog box. Then, enter the name of the database server in the Server Name text box or select it from the drop-down list. For SQL Server Express, you can use localhost\sqlexpress as the server name.
- After you enter the server name, select the authentication mode you want to use (we recommend Windows Authentication). Then, select the database you want to connect to from the Select or Enter a Database Name drop-down list.
- To be sure that the connection is configured properly, you can click the Test Connection button.

Figure 11-2 How to define the connection

How to save the connection string in the web.config file

Although you can hard-code connection strings into your programs, it's much better to store connection strings in the application's web.config file. That way, if you move the database to another server or make some other change that affects the connection string, you won't have to recompile the application. Instead, you can simply change the connection string in the web.config file.

As figure 11-3 shows, ASP.NET 4 can store connection strings in the web.config file automatically if you check the Yes box in the next step of the wizard. That way, you don't have to manually edit the web.config file or write code to retrieve the connection string. When you select this check box, the connection string will automatically be saved with the name that you supply.

This figure also shows the entries made in the web.config file when a connection string is saved. Here, the web.config file has a connectionString element that contains an add element for each connection string. In this example, the connection string is named PayablesConnectionString, and the connection string refers to a database named Payables on the server named localhost\sqlexpress.

Last, this figure shows how the aspx code that's generated for a data source can refer to the connection string by name. Here, the shaded portion of the example shows the value of the ConnectionString attribute. As you can see, it begins with the word ConnectionStrings followed by a colon and the name of the connection string you want to use. Note that this code is automatically generated by the Data Source Configuration Wizard, so you don't have to write it yourself.

The dialog box for saving the connection string in the web.config file

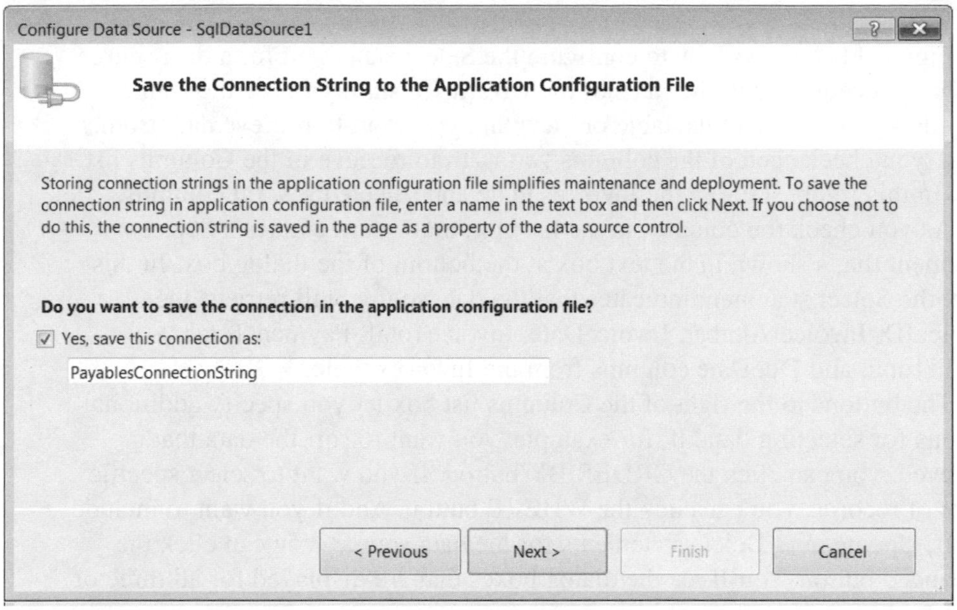

The ConnectionStrings section of the web.config file

```
<connectionStrings>
    <add name="PayablesConnectionString"
      connectionString="Data Source=localhost\sqlexpress;
      Initial Catalog=Payables;Integrated Security=True"
      providerName="System.Data.SqlClient" />
</connectionStrings>
```

Aspx code that refers to a connection string in the web.config file

```
<asp:SqlDataSource ID="SqlDataSource1" runat="server"
    ConnectionString="<%$ ConnectionStrings:PayablesConnectionString %>"
    SelectCommand="SELECT [VendorID], [Name] FROM [Vendors]
                   ORDER BY [Name]">
</asp:SqlDataSource>
```

Description

- ASP.NET 4 applications can store connection strings in the web.config file.
- If you choose to save the connection string in the web.config file, the ConnectionString attribute of the data source control will include a special code that retrieves the connection string from that file.
- If you choose not to save the connection string in the web.config file, the ConnectionString attribute of the data source control will specify the actual connection string.
- We recommend that you always save the connection string in the web.config file. Then, if the location of the database changes, you can change the connection string in the web.config file rather than in each page that uses the connection.

Figure 11-3 How to save the connection string in the web.config file

How to configure the Select statement

Figure 11-4 shows how to configure the Select statement for a data source as you proceed through the steps of the wizard. To start, you use the Name drop-down list to select the table or view that you want to retrieve data from. Then, you check each of the columns you want to retrieve in the Columns list box. In this figure, I chose the Invoices table and selected several columns.

As you check the columns in the list box, the wizard creates a Select statement that's shown in the text box at the bottom of the dialog box. In this case, the Select statement indicates that the data source will retrieve the InvoiceID, InvoiceNumber, InvoiceDate, InvoiceTotal, PaymentTotal, CreditTotal, and DueDate columns from the Invoices table.

The buttons to the right of the Columns list box let you specify additional options for selecting data. If, for example, you want to sort the data that's retrieved, you can click the ORDER BY button. If you want to select specific types of records, you can click the WHERE button. And if you want to include Insert, Update, and Delete statements for the data source, you can click the Advanced button. You'll see the dialog boxes that are displayed for all three of these buttons in this chapter.

When you finish specifying the data you want the data source to retrieve, you click the Next button. This takes you to a page that includes a Test Query button. If you click this button, the wizard immediately retrieves the data that you specified. You can then look over this data to make sure the query retrieves the data you expected. If it doesn't, you can click the Back button and adjust the query.

How to create an Order By clause

Figure 11-4 also shows the dialog box that's displayed when you click the ORDER BY button in the first dialog box. This dialog box lets you select up to three sort columns. In the example in this figure, the data that's retrieved from the Invoices table is sorted by Invoice Date in ascending sequence.

The dialog boxes for defining the Select statement and sorting the results

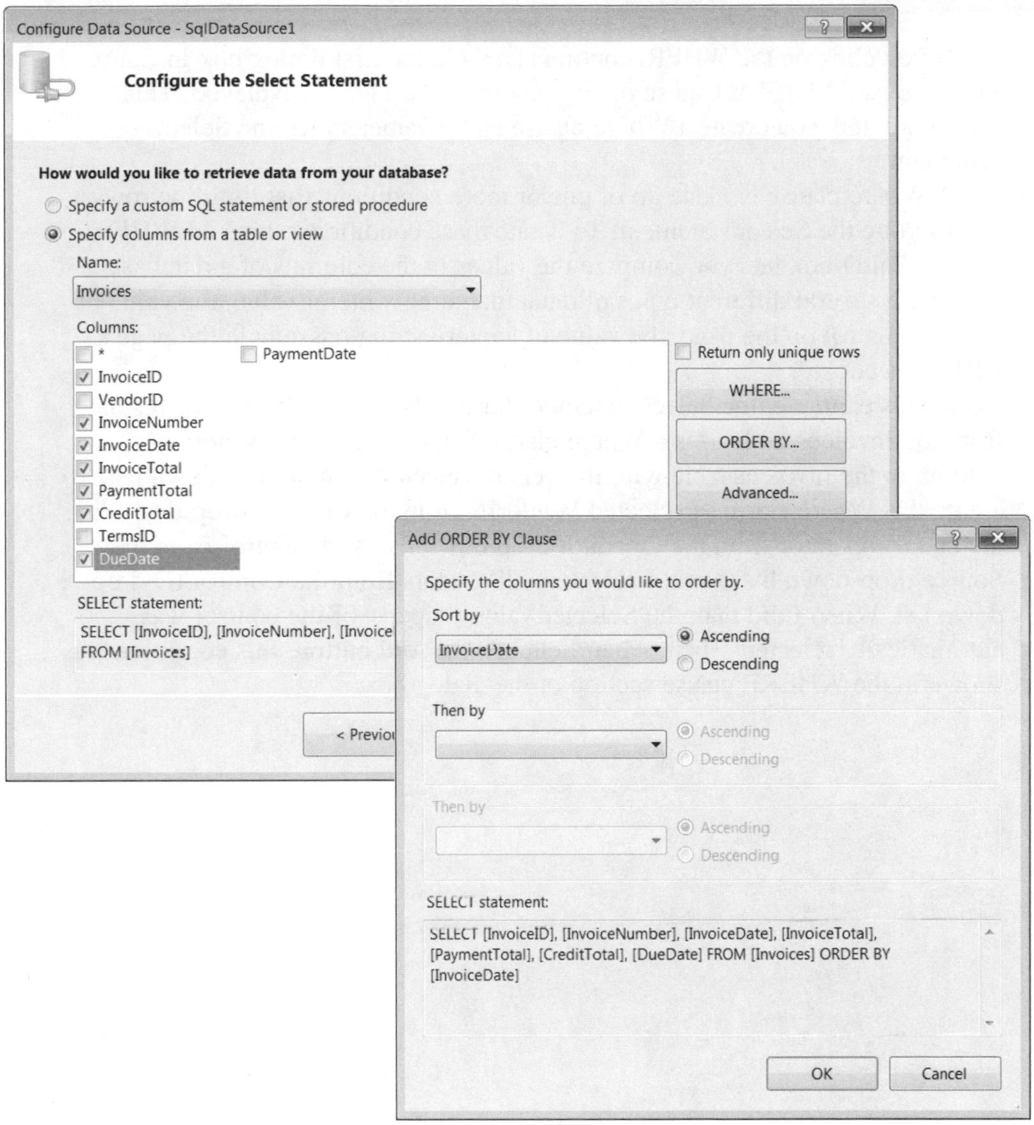

Description

- If you want Visual Studio to configure the Select statement for you, select the second option from the dialog box that's displayed (this is the default), select the table or view, and then select the columns you want retrieved.
- If you want to sort the resulting rows, you can click the ORDER BY button to display the Add ORDER BY Clause dialog box. This dialog box lets you sort by up to three columns in either ascending or descending sequence.
- If you want to specify selection criteria, you can click the WHERE button. See figure 11-5 for details.

Figure 11-4 How to configure the Select statement and create an Order By clause

How to create a Where clause

If you click on the WHERE button shown in the first dialog box in figure 11-4, the Add WHERE Clause dialog box in figure 11-5 is displayed. This dialog box lets you create a Where clause and parameters for the Select statement.

A Where clause is made up of one or more conditions that limit the rows retrieved by the Select statement. To create these conditions, the Add WHERE Clause dialog box lets you compare the values in the columns of a database table with several different types of data, including a literal value, the value of another control on the page, the value of a query string passed via the page's URL, or a cookie.

In this example, the Select statement for the data source that retrieves data from the Invoices table uses a Where clause that compares the VendorID column in the Invoices table with the vendor selected from a drop-down list. To create this Where clause, I selected VendorID from the Column drop-down list, the equals operator from the Operator drop-down list, and Control from the Source drop-down list. Next, I selected ddlVendors from the Control ID drop-down list. When I did that, the SelectedValue property of the control was automatically selected. Then, when I clicked the Add button, this condition was shown in the WHERE clause section of the dialog box.

The Add WHERE Clause dialog box

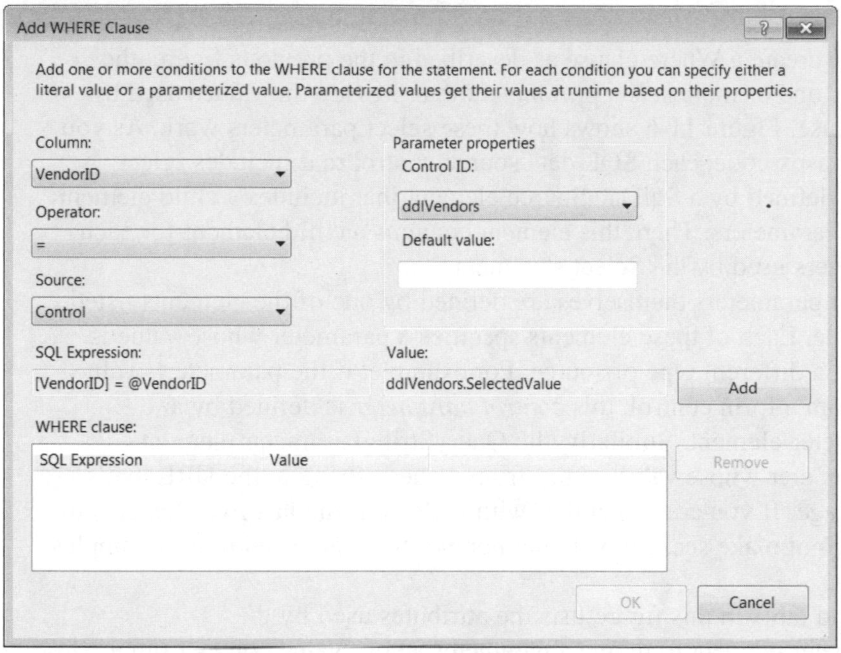

The WHERE clause section after a condition has been added

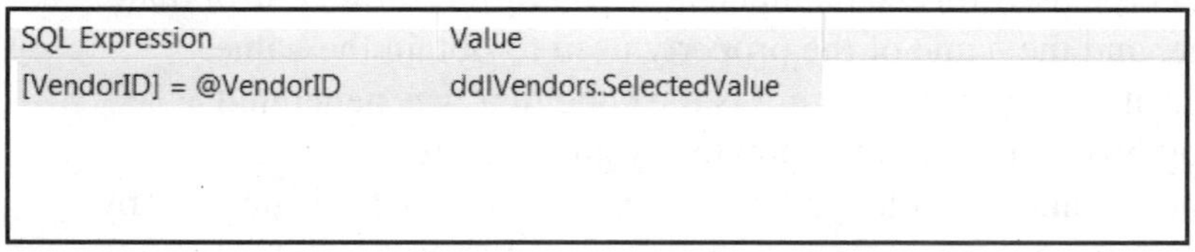

Description

- The Add WHERE Clause dialog box lets you specify a Where clause for the Select statement.
- The Where clause consists of one or more conditions that you construct by using the controls in this dialog box. To create a condition, you select the column you want to compare, the operator you want to use for the comparison, and the source of the data to use for the comparison. Then, you must click Add to add the condition to the list of Where clause conditions.
- The source of the data for the comparison can be a literal value, the value of another control on the form, a cookie, an HTML form field, a profile property, a query string in the URL for the page, or a value stored in session state.

Remember

- After you select the column, operator, and source for the comparison, be sure to click the Add button to add the condition to the generated Where clause. Otherwise, the condition won't be added to the Where clause.

Figure 11-5 How to create a Where clause

How select parameters work

When you create a Where clause as described in the previous figure, the wizard creates one or more *select parameters* that provide the values used by the Where clause. Figure 11-6 shows how these select parameters work. As you can see in the aspx code, each SQL data source control that includes select parameters is defined by a SqlDataSource element that includes a child element named SelectParameters. Then, this element contains a child element for each of the parameters used by the Select statement.

The select parameters themselves are defined by one of the elements listed in the first table. Each of these elements specifies a parameter whose value is obtained from a different type of source. For example, if the parameter's value is obtained from a form control, this *control parameter* is defined by a ControlParameter element. Similarly, the QueryStringParameter element defines a parameter whose value comes from a query string in the URL that's used for the page. If you aren't familiar with ASP.NET, the last five elements in this table may not make sense to you, but none of them are used in the examples in this section.

The second table in this figure lists the attributes used by the ControlParameter element to define a parameter whose value comes from a form control. As you can see, these attributes provide the name of the parameter, the SQL data type used for the parameter, the ID of the form control that provides the value, and the name of the property used to obtain the value.

The aspx code at the top of this figure is the code that was generated as a result of the dialog boxes shown in the previous figures. Here, the Select statement uses one parameter named @VendorID. This parameter is defined by a ControlParameter element whose Name attribute is set to VendorID. The SQL data type for this parameter is Int32, and the parameter's value is obtained from the SelectedValue property of the form control whose ID is ddlVendors.

The aspx code for a data source control that includes a select parameter

```
<asp:SqlDataSource ID="SqlDataSource1" runat="server"
    ConnectionString="<%$ ConnectionStrings:PayablesConnectionString %>"
    SelectCommand="SELECT InvoiceID, InvoiceNumber, InvoiceDate,
    InvoiceTotal, PaymentTotal, CreditTotal, DueDate FROM Invoices
        WHERE (VendorID = @VendorID)
        ORDER BY InvoiceDate">
    <SelectParameters>
        <asp:ControlParameter ControlID="ddlVendors" Name="VendorID"
            PropertyName="SelectedValue" Type="Int32" />
    </SelectParameters>
</asp:SqlDataSource>
```

Elements used to define select parameters

Element	Description
SelectParameters	Contains a child element for each parameter used by the data source's Select statement.
Parameter	Defines a parameter with a constant value.
ControlParameter	Defines a parameter that gets its value from a control on the page.
QueryStringParameter	Defines a parameter that gets its value from a query string in the URL used to request the page.
FormParameter	Defines a parameter that gets its value from an HTML form field.
SessionParameter	Defines a parameter that gets its value from an item in session state.
ProfileParameter	Defines a parameter that gets its value from a profile property.
CookieParameter	Defines a parameter that gets its value from a cookie.

The ControlParameter element

Attribute	Description
Name	The parameter name.
Type	The SQL data type of the parameter.
ControlID	The ID of the web form control that supplies the value for the parameter.
PropertyName	The name of the property from the web form control that supplies the value for the parameter.

Description

- The SelectParameters element defines the *select parameters* that are used by the Select statement of a data source. The aspx code that defines these parameters is generated automatically when you use the Add WHERE Clause dialog box to create parameters.
- A *control parameter* is a parameter whose value is obtained from another control on a web form, such as the value selected from a drop-down list. Control parameters are defined by the ControlParameter element.
- Once you understand how to use control parameters, you shouldn't have any trouble learning how to use the other types of parameters on your own.

Figure 11-6 How select parameters work

How to use custom SQL statements or stored procedures

Although you can use the technique shown in figures 11-4 and 11-5 to configure a Select statement, you will frequently need to create Select statements that are more complicated than this technique provides for. In that case, you can write your own custom SQL statements. Alternatively, you can use existing stored procedures with an SQL data source control.

How to use custom SQL statements

If you want to provide your own custom SQL statements for a data source control, you can select the first option from the first dialog box you saw back in figure 11-4. Then, when you click the Next button, the dialog box shown in figure 11-7 is displayed. As you can see, this dialog box includes tabs that let you enter Select, Update, Insert, and Delete statements for the data source. You can also click on the Query Builder button to open the Query Builder, which lets you visually create SQL statements. For more information on how to use the Query Builder, see chapter 5.

How to use stored procedures

The dialog box shown in figure 11-7 also lets you use stored procedures with a data source. To do that, just select the Stored Procedure option to display a list of the stored procedures that have been defined for the database. Then, select the stored procedure you want to use. If you want to use stored procedures to perform update, insert, and delete operations as well, select the appropriate stored procedures from the UPDATE, INSERT, and DELETE tabs.

The dialog box for entering a custom Select statement or stored procedure

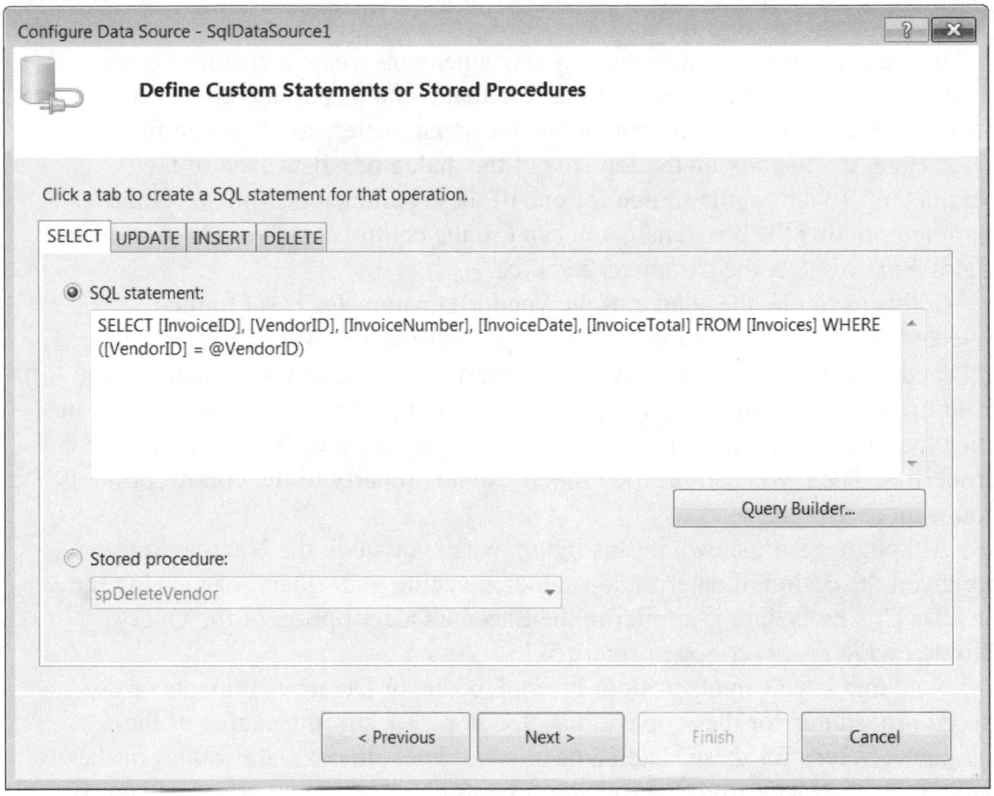

Description

- To use custom SQL statements or stored procedures, select the first option from the first dialog box shown in figure 11-4. Then, the dialog box shown above is displayed.
- To use a custom Select statement to retrieve data, enter the statement on the SELECT tab or click the Query Builder button to use the Query Builder to build the statement. For information on using the Query Builder, see chapter 5.
- To use a stored procedure to retrieve data, select the Stored Procedure option and then select the stored procedure you want to use from the list of available stored procedures.
- If you want to use the data source to update, insert, or delete data in the database, you must also enter custom statements on or select stored procedures from the UPDATE, INSERT, and DELETE tabs.

Figure 11-7 How to use custom SQL statements or stored procedures

How to define the parameters for a custom SQL statement or stored procedure

If you specify one or more parameters when you create a custom Select statement, or if you use a stored procedure that contains parameters to retrieve data, the next dialog box lets you define those parameters as shown in figure 11-8. Here, the list box on the left side of the dialog box lists each of the parameters. To define the source for one of these parameters, you select the parameter in this list box. Then, you can use the controls on the right side of the dialog box to select the parameter's source.

In this example, the source of the VendorID parameter is set to the SelectedValue property of the control named ddlVendors. When I selected the ddlVendors control, the SelectedValue property was selected by default. If you want to use a different property as the source for a parameter, however, you can click the Show Advanced Properties link to display a list of the parameter properties. Then, you can set the PropertyName property to the control property you want to use.

Although it isn't shown in this figure, when you click the Next button you are given the option of entering a parameter, testing your query, or viewing the results. This procedure is similar to the Execute Query option of the Query Builder, which is described in figure 5-7.

Note that if you create custom Insert, Update, or Delete statements or use stored procedures for these operations, you don't specify the source of the parameter values for these statements or procedures. Instead, the values of these parameters are taken from the row that's being inserted, updated, or deleted. If you want to include parameters that provide for optimistic concurrency, you can do that too. In that case, though, you have to set two additional properties of the data source control as described in this figure. This will make more sense when you see how to update data in the next two chapters.

The dialog box for defining parameters

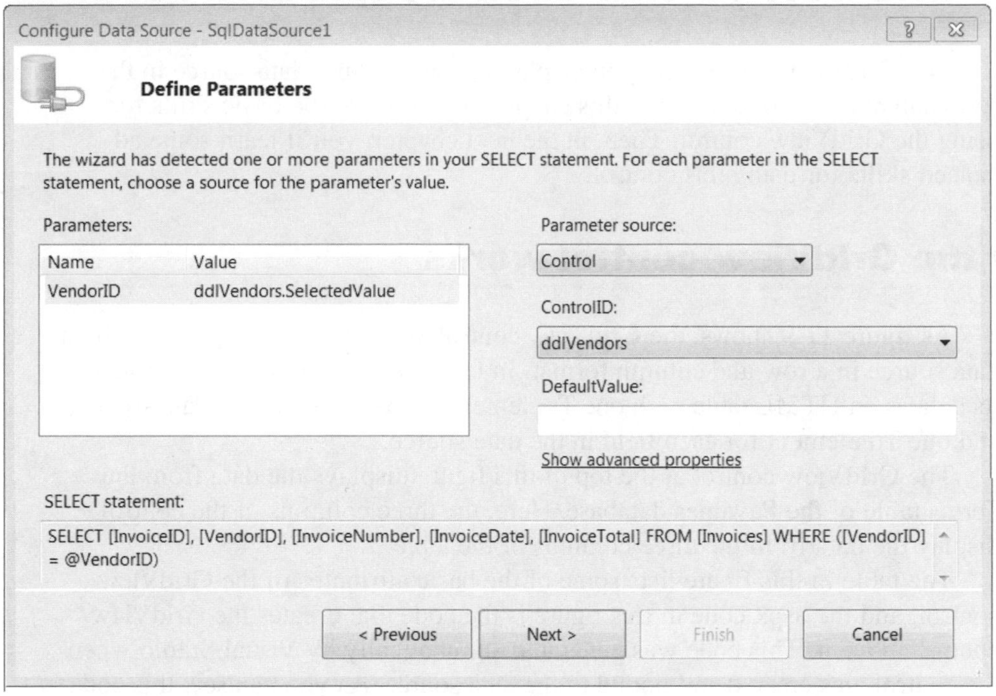

Parameter sources

Source	Description
Control	The parameter's value comes from a control on the page.
QueryString	The parameter's value comes from a query string in the URL used to request the page.
Form	The parameter's value comes from an HTML form field.
Session	The parameter's value comes from an item in session state.
Profile	The parameter's value comes from a profile property.
Cookie	The parameter's value comes from a cookie.

Description

- If a custom Select statement or the stored procedure for a retrieval operation uses parameters, the next dialog box lets you define those parameters. To define a parameter, you specify the source of its value.
- If you specify a custom Insert, Update, or Delete statement or select stored procedures for these operations, the values in the current row are automatically assigned to the parameters in the SQL statements or stored procedures.
- If you use optimistic concurrency in an Update or Delete statement, you need to set the ConflictDetection attribute of the data source control to CompareAllValues, and you need to set the OldValuesParameterFormatString attribute to indicate the format used for the names of the parameters for the old values.

Figure 11-8 How to define the parameters for a custom SQL statement or stored procedure

Introduction to the GridView control

The GridView control lets you display the data from a data source in the rows and columns of a table. In this chapter, you'll learn the basic skills for using the GridView control. Then, in the next chapter, you'll learn some advanced skills for using this control.

How the GridView control works

As figure 11-9 shows, the GridView control displays the data provided by a data source in a row and column format. In fact, the GridView control renders its data as an HTML table with one Tr element for each row in the data source, and one Td element for each field in the data source.

The GridView control at the top of this figure displays the data from the Terms table of the Payables database. Here, the three columns of the control display the data from the three columns of the table.

The table in this figure lists some of the basic attributes of the GridView control, and the aspx code in this figure is the code that creates the GridView control above it. This code was generated automatically by Visual Studio when the control was created and bound to the data source. As you can see, this code contains a Columns element that contains the child elements that define the fields to be displayed. In this code example, the Columns element includes three BoundField elements: one for each of the columns in the data source.

An automatically generated GridView control

TermsID	Description	DueDays
1	Net due 10 days	10
2	Net due 20 days	20
3	Net due 30 days	30
4	Net due 60 days	60
5	Net due 90 days	90

The aspx code for the GridView control

```
<asp:GridView ID="GridView1" runat="server" DataSourceID="SqlDataSource1"
    AutoGenerateColumns="False" DataKeyNames="TermsID">
    <Columns>
        <asp:BoundField DataField="TermsID" HeaderText="TermsID"
            InsertVisible="False" ReadOnly="True"
            SortExpression="TermsID" />
        <asp:BoundField DataField="Description" HeaderText="Description"
            SortExpression="Description" />
        <asp:BoundField DataField="DueDays" HeaderText="DueDays"
            SortExpression="DueDays" />
    </Columns>
</asp:GridView>
```

Basic attributes of the GridView control

Attribute	Description
ID	The ID of the control.
Runat	Must specify "server".
DataSourceID	The ID of the data source to bind to.
DataKeyNames	The names of the primary key fields separated by commas.
AutoGenerateColumns	Specifies whether the control's columns should be automatically generated.
SelectedIndex	Specifies the row to be initially selected.

Description

- The GridView control displays data from a data source in a row and column format. The data is rendered as an HTML table.
- To create a GridView control, drag the control from the Data group of the Toolbox.
- To bind a GridView control to a data source, use the smart tag menu's Choose Data Source command. See figure 11-13 for more information.
- Each column of the data source is defined by a BoundField element. See figures 11-10 and 11-11 for information on how to define and format these and other fields.

Figure 11-9 How the GridView control works

How to define the fields in a GridView control

By default, a GridView control displays one column for each column in the data source. If that's not what you want, you can choose Edit Columns from the control's smart tag menu to display the Fields dialog box shown in figure 11-10. Then, you can use this dialog box to delete or hide the fields that you don't want to display, change the order of the fields, add additional fields, and adjust the properties of the fields.

The Available Fields list box lists all of the available sources for GridView fields, while the Selected Fields list box shows the fields that are already included in the GridView control. To add an additional field to the GridView control, select the field you want to add in the Available Fields list box and click Add. To change the properties for a field, select the field in the Selected Fields list and use the Properties list.

The table in this figure lists some of the properties you're most likely to want to change. For example, the HeaderText property determines the text that's displayed for the field's header row, and the ReadOnly property determines if the field can be modified. You'll learn about modifying the data in a GridView control in the next chapter.

If you want to format fields that contain numbers or dates, you can use the DataFormatString property to specify the type of formatting. For example, for a field that contains a decimal value, you can specify a string of {0:c} to apply standard currency formatting to the value. And for a field that contains a date, you can use the {0:d} formatting to display the short date form. The full list of formatting codes is available on Microsoft's MSDN site.

The Fields dialog box

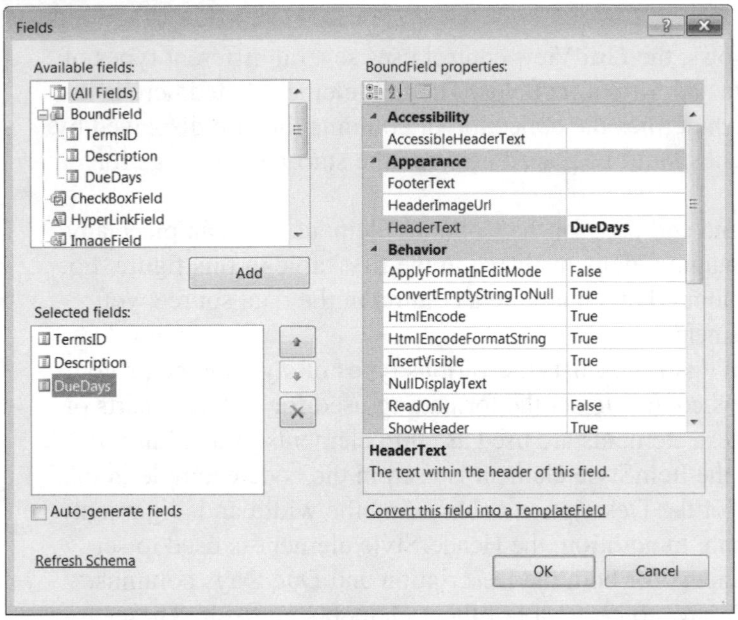

Commonly used field properties

Property	Description
DataField	For a bound field, the name of the column in the underlying data source that the field should be bound to.
DataFormatString	A format string used to format the data. For example, use {0:c} to format a decimal value as currency.
ItemStyle.width	The width of the field.
ReadOnly	True if the field is used for display only.
Visible	False if the field is not displayed. Typically used for identity columns.
NullDisplayText	The text that's displayed if the data field is null.
ConvertEmptyStringToNull	If True (the default), empty strings are treated as nulls when data is updated in the database. Set this property to False if the underlying database field doesn't allow nulls.
HeaderText	The text that's displayed in the header row for the field.
ShowHeader	True if the header should be displayed for this field.

Description

- By default, the GridView control displays one column for each column in the data source.
- To define the fields you want to display in a GridView control, display the Fields dialog box by selecting the Edit Columns command in the control's smart tag menu.
- You can also add a column by choosing the Add New Column command from the smart tag menu. See chapter 12 for details.

Figure 11-10 How to define the fields in a GridView control

Elements used to create and format fields

As figure 11-11 shows, the GridView control uses several different types of child elements to create and format its fields. The first element listed here is the Columns element, which defines the collection of columns that are displayed by the control. This element should be placed between the start and end tags for the GridView control.

Between the start and end tags for the Columns element, you can place any combination of the remaining elements listed in the first table in this figure. For example, to create a column that's bound to a column in the data source, you use the BoundField element.

The second table in this figure lists the various types of style elements you can use with a GridView control to set the formatting used for different parts of the control. Some of these elements are used as child elements of a column element. For example, the ItemStyle element is used in the code example in this figure to set the width for the Description column and the width and alignment for the Due Days column. In addition, the HeaderStyle element is used to set the alignment of the headers for both the Description and Due Days columns.

Note that you don't have to create all of these elements yourself. These elements are created automatically when you use the Fields dialog box as described in the previous figure, when you use the Properties window to specify the styles for an element, or when you apply a scheme to the GridView control using the Auto Format command in the control's smart tag menu.

Column field elements

Element	Description
Columns	The columns that are displayed by a GridView control.
asp:BoundField	A field bound to a data source column.
asp:ButtonField	A field that displays a button.
asp:CheckBoxField	A field that displays a check box.
asp:CommandField	A field that contains Select, Edit, Delete, Update, or Cancel buttons.
asp:HyperlinkField	A field that displays a hyperlink.
asp:ImageField	A field that displays an image.
asp:TemplateField	Lets you create a column with custom content.

Style elements

Element	Description
RowStyle	The style used for data rows.
AlternatingRowStyle	The style used for alternating data rows.
SelectedRowStyle	The style used when the row is selected.
EditRowStyle	The style used when the row is being edited.
EmptyDataRowStyle	The style used when the data source is empty.
ItemStyle	The style used for an individual field.
HeaderStyle	The style used to format the header row.
FooterStyle	The style used to format the footer row.
PagerStyle	The style used to format the GridView's pager row.

The aspx code for a control that uses field and style elements

```
<asp:GridView ID="GridView1" runat="server" AutoGenerateColumns="False"
    DataKeyNames="TermsID" DataSourceID="SqlDataSource1">
    <Columns>
        <asp:BoundField DataField="TermsID" HeaderText="TermsID"
            InsertVisible="False" ReadOnly="True"
            SortExpression="TermsID" Visible="False" />
        <asp:BoundField DataField="Description" HeaderText="Description" >
            <ItemStyle Width="125px" />
            <HeaderStyle HorizontalAlign="Left" />
        </asp:BoundField>
        <asp:BoundField DataField="DueDays" HeaderText="Due Days" >
            <ItemStyle HorizontalAlign="Right" Width="80px" />
            <HeaderStyle HorizontalAlign="Right" />
        </asp:BoundField>
    </Columns>
</asp:GridView>
```

Description

- The GridView control uses several child elements to define the column fields in a row and the styles used to format the data.
- You can set some of the style elements from the Fields dialog box shown in figure 11-10, from the Properties window, or by using the Auto Format command in the smart tag menu.

Figure 11-11 Elements used to create and format fields

How to use a SQL data source

Now that you know how to create a SQL data source control and you know the basic skills for using a GridView control, you're ready to learn how to use a SQL data source. To illustrate these skills, I'll use an application that uses two SQL data sources.

A Vendor Invoices application that uses two data sources

Figure 11-12 shows a simple one-page application that demonstrates the use of two SQL data sources. The drop-down list at the top of the page is bound to a SQL data source that gets the vendors from which the company makes purchases. Then, when the user selects a vendor from this list, the invoices for the selected vendor are retrieved from a second SQL data source, which is bound to a GridView control that's below the drop-down list. As a result, the invoices are displayed in the GridView control.

Since this application relies entirely on the data binding that's established in the Web Forms Designer, the only Visual Basic that's required is for handling any errors that occur as the page is processed. But, as you will see in the code in figure 11-16, that code can be minimal. In fact, even complicated applications that insert, update, and delete database data can often be written with little or no database code.

That's not to say that most ASP.NET database applications are code-free. In chapters 12 and 13, for example, you'll see applications that require database handling code. In particular, these applications require code to detect database errors and concurrency violations and display appropriate error messages. Also, as you'll learn in chapter 14, you can use object data sources to build three-layer applications that require extensive amounts of database handling code.

The Vendor Invoices application displayed in a web browser

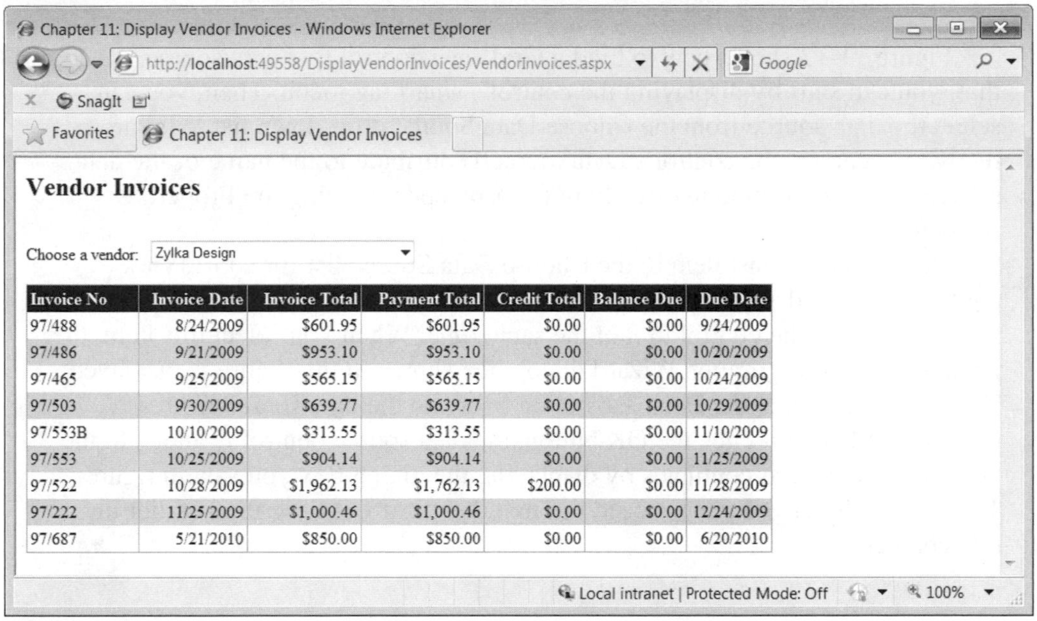

Description

- The Vendor Invoices application uses two SQL data source controls to get vendor and invoice data from a SQL Server database and display it in two bound controls.
- The drop-down list near the top of the form displays the vendors. This control is bound to the first data source control.
- The GridView control, which is bound to the second data source control, displays the invoices for the vendor that's selected in the drop-down list.
- This application requires no Visual Basic code to handle the retrieval or display of data.

Figure 11-12 A Vendor Invoices application that uses two data sources

How to bind a GridView control to a data source

Figure 11-13 shows how to bind a GridView control to a data source. To do that, you can start by displaying the control's smart tag menu. Then, you can select the data source from the Choose Data Source drop-down list. Alternatively, you can set the control's DataSourceID attribute to the name of the data source you want to bind to directly in the aspx code or using the Properties window.

Notice that the last item in the Choose Data Source list for a GridView control is <New data source…>. You can use this item to create a new data source and bind the control to it at the same time. When you select this item, the Data Source Configuration Wizard dialog box shown in this figure is displayed. Then, you can select the Database option to create the data source from a database. When you click the OK button, the data source control is added to the form and the wizard continues by displaying the dialog box you saw in figure 11-2. From there, you can proceed through the wizard as described earlier in this chapter.

The smart tag menu for binding a GridView control to a data source

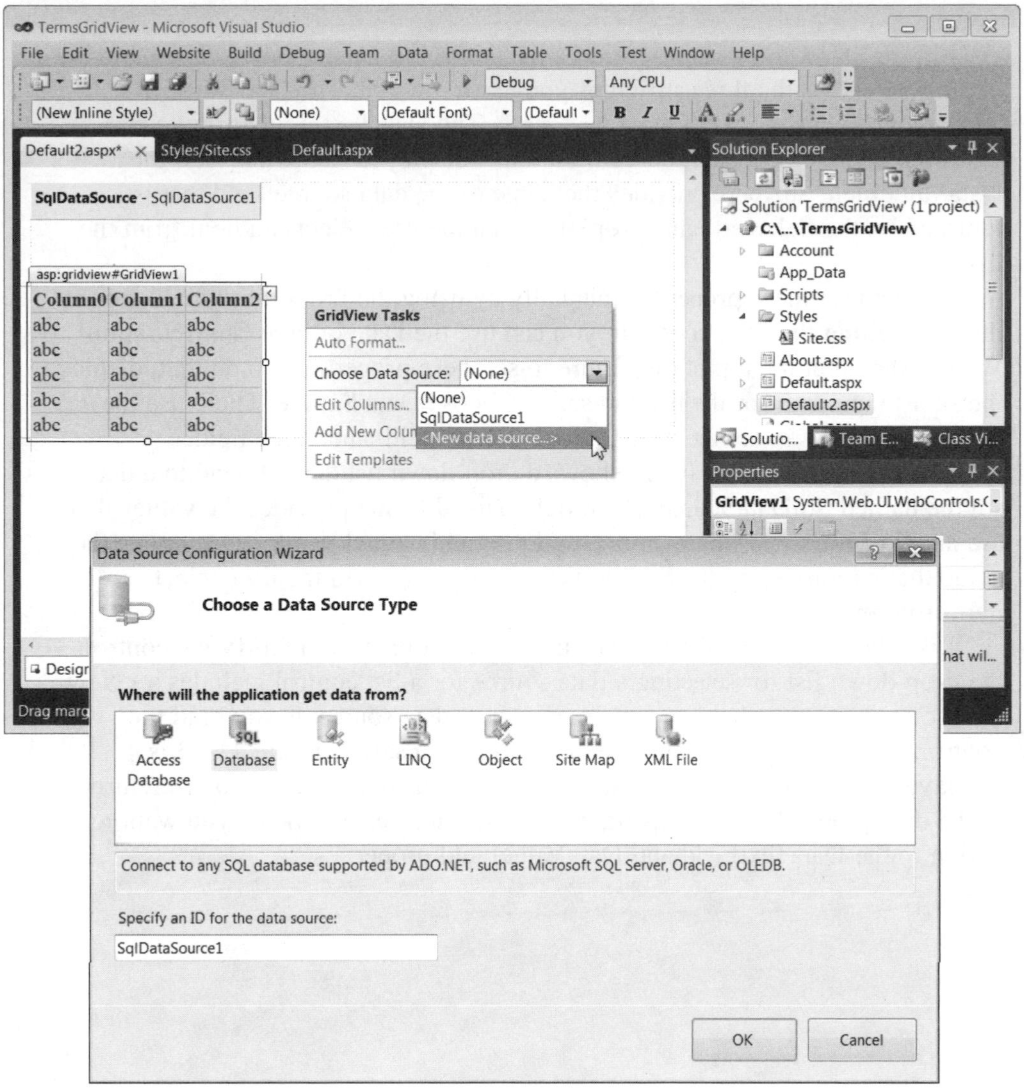

Description

- To bind a GridView control to a data source, display the control's smart tag menu and select the data source from the Choose Data Source drop-down list.
- If you haven't created the data source, you can create it by selecting the <New data source…> item from the Choose Data Source list. Then, the Data Source Configuration Wizard dialog box shown above is displayed.
- To create a data source from a database, select the Database option and, optionally, enter an ID for the data source. Then, configure the data source as shown earlier in this chapter.

Figure 11-13 How to bind a GridView control to a data source

How to bind a list control to a data source

Figure 11-14 shows how to bind a list control to a data source. The table in this figure shows the three attributes you use to do that. The DataSourceID attribute provides the ID of the data source. The DataTextField attribute provides the name of the data source field that's displayed in the list. And the DataValueField attribute provides the name of the data source field that is returned by the SelectedValue property when the user selects an item from the list.

You can set these properties manually by using the Properties window or by directly editing the aspx code. Or, you can use the Data Source Configuration Wizard shown at the top of this figure to set these properties. To do that, display the smart tag menu for the list and select Choose Data Source. Then, use the wizard's controls to set the data source, display field, and value field.

The aspx code in this figure shows a drop-down list that's bound to a data source named SqlDataSource1. The field named Name provides the values that are displayed in the drop-down list, and the field named VendorID supplies the value that's returned by the SelectedValue property when the user selects an item from the list.

Like the drop-down list for selecting a data source for a GridView control, the drop-down list for selecting a data source for a list control includes a <New data source...> item that lets you create a new data source as you bind the control. If you select this item, the dialog box you saw in figure 11-13 is displayed. Then, when you're done configuring the data source, you're returned to the dialog box shown in this figure so you can select the fields you want to assign to the DataTextField and DataValueField properties.

The Data Source Configuration Wizard for binding a drop-down list

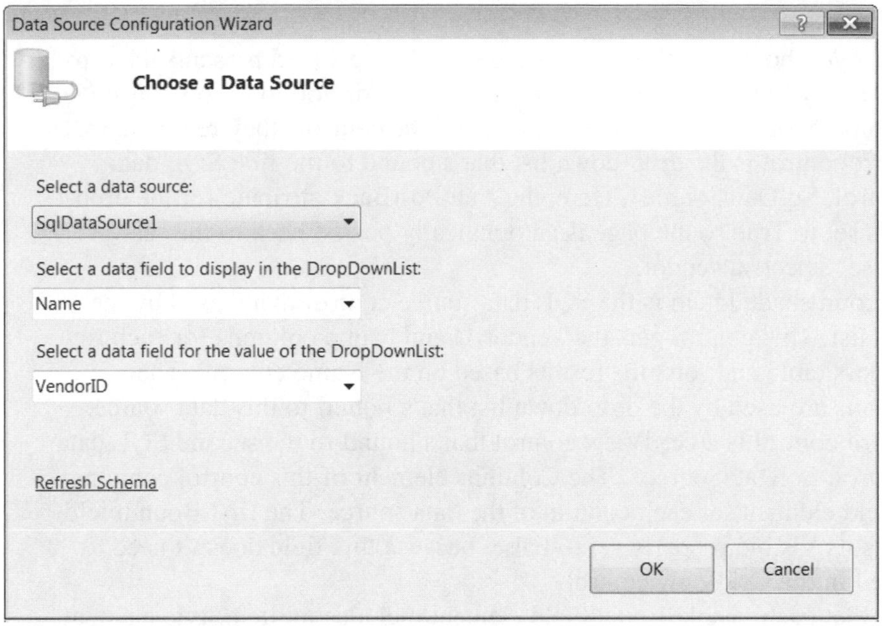

List control attributes for data binding

Attribute	Description
DataSourceID	The ID of the data source to bind the list to.
DataTextField	The name of the data source field that should be displayed in the list.
DataValueField	The name of the data source field whose value should be returned by the SelectedValue property of the list.

The aspx code for a drop-down list that's bound to a SQL data source

```
<asp:DropDownList ID="ddlVendors" runat="server"  Width="248px"
    AutoPostBack="True" DataSourceID="SqlDataSource1"
    DataTextField="Name" DataValueField="VendorID">
</asp:DropDownList>
```

Description

- You can bind any of the controls that inherit the ListControl class to a data source. That includes the list box control, the drop-down list control, the check box list control, the radio button list control, and the bulleted list control.
- You can use the Data Source Configuration Wizard to select the data source for a list control, the data field to display in the list, and the data value to return for the selected item. If the data source doesn't already exist, you can select the <New data source...> item from the drop-down list to display the dialog box shown in figure 11-13.
- You can also use the DataTextFormatString attribute of a list control to specify a format string you want to apply to the text that's displayed in the control.

Figure 11-14 How to bind a list control to a data source

The aspx file for the Vendor Invoices page

To show you how everything works together, figure 11-15 presents the aspx code for the Vendor Invoices page. To make it easier for you to follow this code, I've shaded parts of the data source controls and the controls they're bound to.

The first control is the drop-down list that's bound to the first SQL data source control, SqlDataSource1. Here, the AutoPostBack attribute for the drop-down list is set to True so the page is automatically posted back to the server when the user selects a vendor.

The second shaded item is the SQL data source control that's used by the drop-down list. This control gets the VendorID and Name columns for each row in the Vendors table and sorts the results based on the Name column. Then, these columns are used by the drop-down list that's bound to this data source.

The third control is a GridView control that's bound to the second SQL data source control, SqlDataSource2. The Columns element of this control contains a BoundField element for each column of the data source. The first BoundField element has its Visible property set to False, because this field doesn't need to be displayed in the GridView control.

Notice that each visible BoundField element includes an ItemStyle element that specifies the width of the field and a HeaderStyle element that specifies the alignment of the header text. In most cases, the ItemStyle of the visible BoundField elements specifies the alignment of the data within the field.

Incidentally, if you have experience with previous versions of ASP.NET and Visual Studio, you'll find that the Default.aspx web form that's automatically created by Visual 2010 has additional content. To avoid confusion, that extra content is omitted from the aspx pages that are presented in this book. To create web pages with the same content as the pages in this book, you can use the Website→Add New Item→Web Form command.

The VendorInvoices.aspx file Page 1

```
<%@ Page Language="VB" AutoEventWireup="false"
    CodeFile="VendorInvoices.aspx.vb" Inherits="VendorInvoices" %>

<!DOCTYPE html PUBLIC "-//W3C//DTD XHTML 1.0 Transitional//EN"
"http://www.w3.org/TR/xhtml1/DTD/xhtml1-transitional.dtd">

<html xmlns="http://www.w3.org/1999/xhtml" >
<head runat="server">
    <title>Chapter 11: Display Vendor Invoices</title>
</head>
<body>
  <form id="form1" runat="server">
    <div>
        <h2>Vendor Invoices</h2><br />
        Choose a vendor:  
        <asp:DropDownList ID="ddlVendors" runat="server"  Width="248px"
            AutoPostBack="True" DataSourceID="SqlDataSource1"
            DataTextField="Name" DataValueField="VendorID">
        </asp:DropDownList>
        <asp:SqlDataSource ID="SqlDataSource1" runat="server"
            ConnectionString="<%$ ConnectionStrings:PayablesConnectionString %>"
            SelectCommand="SELECT [VendorID], [Name] FROM [Vendors]
                           ORDER BY [Name]">
        </asp:SqlDataSource><br /><br />
        <asp:GridView ID="grdInvoices" runat="server"
            AutoGenerateColumns="False"
            DataSourceID="SqlDataSource2" BackColor="White"
            BorderColor="#999999" BorderStyle="Solid"
            BorderWidth="1px" CellPadding="3" ForeColor="Black"
            GridLines="Vertical">
           <Columns>
             <asp:BoundField DataField="InvoiceID" HeaderText="InvoiceID"
                 SortExpression="InvoiceID" Visible="False" >
             </asp:BoundField>
             <asp:BoundField DataField="InvoiceNumber"
                 HeaderText="Invoice No" SortExpression="InvoiceNumber" >
                 <ItemStyle Width="100px" />
                 <HeaderStyle HorizontalAlign="Left" />
             </asp:BoundField>
             <asp:BoundField DataField="InvoiceDate"
                 DataFormatString="{0:d}"
                 HeaderText="Invoice Date" SortExpression="InvoiceDate" >
                 <ItemStyle Width="95px" HorizontalAlign="Right" />
                 <HeaderStyle HorizontalAlign="Right" />
             </asp:BoundField>
             <asp:BoundField DataField="InvoiceTotal"
                 DataFormatString="{0:c}"
                 HeaderText="Invoice Total" SortExpression="InvoiceTotal" >
                 <ItemStyle Width="100px" HorizontalAlign="Right" />
                 <HeaderStyle HorizontalAlign="Right" />
             </asp:BoundField>
```

Figure 11-15 The aspx file for the Vendor Invoices page (part 1 of 2)

To format the GridView control as shown in figure 11-12, I applied the Black & Blue 1 scheme to the control. That caused several attributes to be added to this control. In addition, it caused the style elements to be added at the end of the aspx code for this control. Note that since a footer isn't displayed and row selection and paging aren't enabled, the only two elements that affect this control are the HeaderStyle and AlternatingRowStyle elements.

The fourth control, SqlDataSource2, uses a Select statement that retrieves data from the Invoices table. Here, the Where clause specifies that only those rows whose VendorID column equals the value of the VendorID parameter should be retrieved. To make this work, the ControlParameter element specifies that the value of the VendorID parameter is obtained from the SelectedValue property of the ddlVendors control.

The VendorInvoices.aspx file **Page 2**

```
            <asp:BoundField DataField="PaymentTotal"
                DataFormatString="{0:c}" HeaderText="Payment Total" >
                <ItemStyle Width="110px" HorizontalAlign="Right" />
                <HeaderStyle HorizontalAlign="Right" />
            </asp:BoundField>
            <asp:BoundField DataField="CreditTotal"
                DataFormatString="{0:c}"
                HeaderText="Credit Total" >
                <ItemStyle HorizontalAlign="Right" Width="90px" />
                <HeaderStyle HorizontalAlign="Right" />
            </asp:BoundField>
            <asp:BoundField DataField="BalanceDue"
                DataFormatString="{0:c}"
                HeaderText="Balance Due" SortExpression="BalanceDue">
                <ItemStyle Width="90px" HorizontalAlign="Right" />
                <HeaderStyle HorizontalAlign="Right" />
            </asp:BoundField>
            <asp:BoundField DataField="DueDate"
                DataFormatString="{0:d}" HeaderText="Due Date"
                SortExpression="DueDate">
                <ItemStyle Width="75px" HorizontalAlign="Right" />
                <HeaderStyle HorizontalAlign="Right" />
            </asp:BoundField>
          </Columns>
          <FooterStyle BackColor="#CCCCCC" />
          <SelectedRowStyle BackColor="#000099" Font-Bold="True"
              ForeColor="White" />
          <PagerStyle BackColor="#999999" ForeColor="Black"
              HorizontalAlign="Center" />
          <HeaderStyle BackColor="Black" Font-Bold="True"
              ForeColor="White" />
          <AlternatingRowStyle BackColor="#CCCCCC" />
      </asp:GridView>
      <asp:SqlDataSource ID="SqlDataSource2" runat="server"
        ConnectionString="<%$ ConnectionStrings:PayablesConnectionString %>"
        SelectCommand="SELECT InvoiceID, InvoiceNumber, InvoiceDate,
            InvoiceTotal, PaymentTotal, CreditTotal,
            InvoiceTotal - PaymentTotal - CreditTotal AS BalanceDue,
            DueDate
            FROM Invoices
            WHERE (VendorID = @VendorID)
            ORDER BY InvoiceDate">
        <SelectParameters>
           <asp:ControlParameter ControlID="ddlVendors" Name="VendorID"
               PropertyName="SelectedValue" Type="Int32" />
        </SelectParameters>
      </asp:SqlDataSource>
    </div>
  </form>
</body>
</html>
```

Figure 11-15 The aspx file for the Vendor Invoices page (part 2 of 2)

The code-behind file for the Vendor Invoices page

Figure 11-16 shows the *code-behind file* for the Vendor Invoices page. This is the file that contains the Visual Basic code for the web page. However, because the SQL data source control handles all the data processing for this page, the only event handler that's needed is one that handles any errors that occur during this processing.

The code in this event handler gets the Exception object, stores it in session state, and then uses the Response.Redirect method to display an error page. Because control is passed to another page, the Exception object has to be stored in session state in order for it to be used by the code for the error page. In an ASP.NET application, the data that's stored in session state is retained as the user moves from one page to another, but all other data is lost.

The aspx code for the Error page

In the aspx code for the Error page that control is redirected to, you can see a heading, some text, and a label that will be used to display the message of the Exception object.

The code-behind file for the Error page

In the code-behind file for the Error page, you can see that the Exception object is moved from session state into a variable named ex. Then, the Message property of the Exception object in that variable is stored in the label control on the Error page.

The VendorInvoices.aspx.vb file

```
Partial Class VendorInvoices
    Inherits System.Web.UI.Page

    Protected Sub Page_Error(ByVal sender As Object,
            ByVal e As System.EventArgs) Handles Me.Error
        Dim ex As Exception
        ex = Server.GetLastError
        Session("Exception") = ex
        Response.Redirect("ErrorPage.aspx")
    End Sub

End Class
```

The ErrorPage.aspx file

```
<%@ Page Language="VB" AutoEventWireup="false"
    CodeFile="ErrorPage.aspx.vb" Inherits="ErrorPage" %>

<!DOCTYPE html PUBLIC "-//W3C//DTD XHTML 1.0 Transitional//EN"
    "http://www.w3.org/TR/xhtml1/DTD/xhtml1-transitional.dtd">

<html xmlns="http://www.w3.org/1999/xhtml" >
<head runat="server">
    <title>Chapter 11: Display Vendor Invoices</title>
</head>
<body>
    <form id="form1" runat="server">
    <div>
        <h2>Unexpected error</h2><br />
        The following error has occurred:
        <asp:Label ID="lblError" runat="server"
            ForeColor="Red"></asp:Label></div>
    </form>
</body>
</html>
```

The ErrorPage.aspx.vb file

```
Partial Class ErrorPage
    Inherits System.Web.UI.Page

    Protected Sub Page_Load(ByVal sender As Object,
            ByVal e As System.EventArgs) Handles Me.Load
        If Not IsPostBack Then
            Dim ex As Exception = Session("Exception")
            lblError.Text = ex.Message
        End If
    End Sub

End Class
```

Figure 11-16 The VendorInvoices code-behind file and the code for the Error page

How to use the advanced features of a data source control

The SQL data source control provides several advanced features that you may want to use in your applications. These features are explained in the topics that follow.

How to create a data source control that can update the database

Like the table adapters you use with data in a Windows application, a SQL data source can include Insert, Update, and Delete statements that let you automatically update the underlying database based on changes made by the user to bound data controls. If you configure the Select statement from a table or view, Visual Studio can automatically generate the Insert, Update, and Delete statements from the Select statement. But if you use a custom Select statement to retrieve the data from the database, you have to use custom Insert, Update, and Delete statements as described earlier in this chapter. And if you retrieve data using a stored procedure, you have to use stored procedures to insert, update, and delete data.

To automatically generate these statements, you can check the first box in the dialog box shown in figure 11-17. This dialog box is displayed when you click the Advanced button in the first dialog box shown in figure 11-4. You can also check the box for optimistic concurrency, which enhances the generated statements so they check whether updated or deleted rows have changed since the data source retrieved the original data.

The code in this figure shows the aspx elements that are generated when you request Insert, Update, and Delete statements without using optimistic concurrency. Here, the InsertCommand, UpdateCommand, and DeleteCommand attributes provide the statements, and the InsertParameters, UpdateParameters, and DeleteParameters child elements define the parameters used by these statements. Because optimistic concurrency isn't used, these statements will update the database whether or not the data has changed since it was originally retrieved, which could lead to corrupt data.

If you check the Use Optimistic Concurrency check box, though, the update and delete commands will include Where clauses that compare the value of each column with the value originally retrieved. Because these values are passed as parameters, the generated aspx code will also include additional elements that define these parameters. The SqlDataSource element will also include two additional attributes to indicate that optimistic concurrency should be used and to indicate the format that should be used for the names of the parameters that will hold the original column values. Then, if the value of any column has changed since it was originally retrieved, the update or delete operation will be refused, and your application needs to provide code that handles that situation. You'll see how that works in chapter 12.

The Advanced SQL Generation Options dialog box

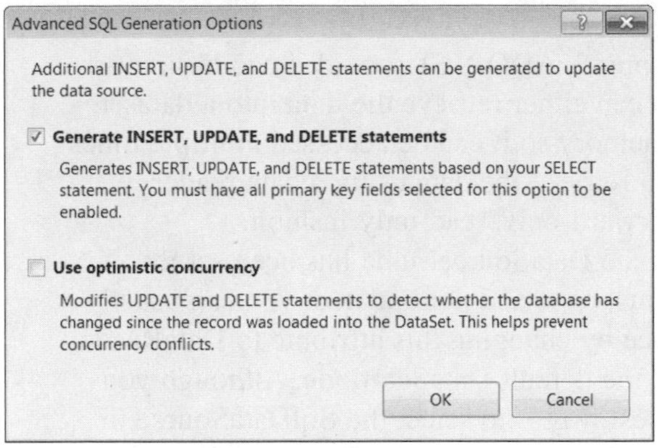

The aspx code for a SQL data source control that uses action queries

```
<asp:SqlDataSource ID="SqlDataSource1" runat="server"
    ConnectionString="<%$ ConnectionStrings:PayablesConnectionString %>"
    DeleteCommand="DELETE FROM [Terms] WHERE [TermsID] = @TermsID"
    InsertCommand="INSERT INTO [Terms] ([Description], [DueDays])
        VALUES (@Description, @DueDays)"
    SelectCommand="SELECT [TermsID], [Description], [DueDays]
        FROM [Terms] ORDER BY [DueDays]"
    UpdateCommand="UPDATE [Terms] SET [Description] = @Description,
        [DueDays] = @DueDays WHERE [TermsID] = @TermsID">
    <DeleteParameters>
        <asp:Parameter Name="TermsID" Type="Int32" />
    </DeleteParameters>
    <InsertParameters>
        <asp:Parameter Name="Description" Type="String" />
        <asp:Parameter Name="DueDays" Type="Int16" />
    </InsertParameters>
    <UpdateParameters>
        <asp:Parameter Name="Description" Type="String" />
        <asp:Parameter Name="DueDays" Type="Int16" />
        <asp:Parameter Name="TermsID" Type="Int32" />
    </UpdateParameters>
</asp:SqlDataSource>
```

Description

- If you configure the Select statement for a data source by selecting columns from a table or view, you can automatically generate Insert, Update, and Delete statements from the Select statement by using the Advanced SQL Generation Options dialog box.
- To display the Advanced SQL Generation Options dialog box, click the Advanced button in the dialog box in figure 11-4. Then, check the appropriate boxes to generate Insert, Update, and Delete statements, or to generate versions that use optimistic concurrency
- The InsertCommand, UpdateCommand, and DeleteCommand attributes in the aspx code define the Insert, Update, and Delete statements used by a data source. If these statements require parameters, the InsertParameters, UpdateParameters, and DeleteParameters elements specify those parameters.

Figure 11-17 How to create a data source control that can update the database

How to change the data source mode

As you may remember from chapter 2, ADO.NET provides two basic ways to retrieve data from a database. You can either retrieve the data into a dataset, which retains a copy of the data in memory so it can be accessed multiple times and updated if necessary. Or, you can retrieve the data using a data reader, which lets you retrieve the data in forward-only, read-only fashion.

In figure 11-18, you can see that the DataSourceMode has been set to DataReader. If the data will be read just once and not updated, you can usually improve the application's performance by changing this attribute to DataReader mode. Otherwise, you can leave it at the default DataSet mode. Although you can change this code manually, the best way is to select the SqlDataSource in the Design pane, then change the DataSourceMode in the Properties Window of Visual Studio.

How to use caching

ASP.NET's caching feature lets you save the data retrieved by a data source in cache memory on the server. That way, the next time the data needs to be retrieved, the cached data is used instead of getting it from the database again. Since this reduces database access, it often improves an application's overall performance.

To enable caching, you simply set the EnableCaching attribute for a SQL data source to True, as shown in figure 11-18. Then, you can use the CacheDuration attribute to specify how long in seconds data should be kept in the cache. If, for example, the cached data rarely changes, you can set a long cache duration value such as 30 minutes or more. If the data changes frequently, you can set a shorter cache duration value.

But what if the data in the database changes before the duration expires? In that case, the user will view data that is out of date. Sometimes, that's okay so you don't have to worry about it. Otherwise, you can minimize the chance of this happening by setting a shorter duration time.

The DataSourceMode attribute

Attribute	Description
DataSourceMode	DataSet or DataReader. The default is DataSet, but you can specify DataReader if the data source is read-only.

A SQL data source control that uses a data reader

```
<asp:SqlDataSource ID="SqlDataSource1" runat="server"
    ConnectionString="<%$ ConnectionStrings:PayablesConnectionString %>"
    DataSourceMode="DataReader"
    SelectCommand="SELECT [VendorID], [Name]
        FROM [Vendors]
        ORDER BY [Name]">
</asp:SqlDataSource>
```

SqlDataSource attributes for caching

Attribute	Description
EnableCaching	A Boolean value that indicates whether caching is enabled for the data source. The default is False.
CacheDuration	The length of time in seconds that the cached data should be saved in cache storage.
CacheExpirationPolicy	If this attribute is set to Absolute, the cache duration timer is started the first time the data is retrieved and is not reset to zero until after the time has expired. If this attribute is set to Sliding, the cache duration timer is reset to zero each time the data is retrieved. The default is Absolute.

A SQL data source control that uses caching

```
<asp:SqlDataSource ID="SqlDataSource1" runat="server"
    ConnectionString="<%$ ConnectionStrings:PayablesConnectionString %>"
    EnableCaching="True" CacheDuration="60"
    SelectCommand="SELECT [VendorID], [Name]
        FROM [Vendors]
        ORDER BY [Name]">
</asp:SqlDataSource>
```

Description

- The DataSourceMode attribute lets you specify that data should be retrieved using a data reader rather than a dataset. For read-only data, a data reader is usually more efficient.
- The data source caching attributes let you specify that data should be stored in cache storage for a specified period of time. For data that changes infrequently, caching can improve performance.

Figure 11-18 How to change the data source mode and use caching

Perspective

In this chapter, you've learned how to use ASP.NET 4's SQL data source control. However, we've only scratched the surface of what this data source can do. As you will see, the real power of a SQL data source lies in what it can do in combination with data controls like the GridView control that you'll learn more about in the next chapter and the DetailsView control that you'll learn about in chapter 13.

I also want to point out what many developers feel is a weakness of the SQL data source control. Because this control can directly specify the SQL statements used to access and update a database, it violates one of the basic principles of good application design. That is, the code that's used to manage the application's user interface should be separated from the code that's used to access the application's database and perform its business logic. Clearly, when you use the SQL data source control, the database code is mixed with the presentation code.

Fortunately, ASP.NET 4 provides two ways to minimize or eliminate this problem. First, the SQL data source control can use stored procedures rather than SQL statements. That way, the SQL statements that access and update the database are placed in the database itself, separate from the presentation code. Second, you can use object data source controls rather than SQL data source controls. When you use object data source controls, you can create and use separate data access classes, so the data access code isn't in the aspx file at all. You'll learn how that works in chapter 14.

Terms

SQL data source control
select parameter
control parameter
code-behind file

How to open and run web applications from VS

If you don't already know how to use ASP.NET but would like to open and run the book applications for this section, here's a brief guide to doing that:

- To open a web application from Visual Studio, use the File→Open Web Site command. Then, navigate to the directory for the application, click on the directory for the application, and click the Open button.
- To set the starting page for the application, find the aspx file for the page in the Solution Explorer, right-click on it, and select Set as Start Page.
- To run the application, click on the Start Debugging button in the toolbar just as you would for a Windows Form project. This will display the starting page in your default web browser.

Exercise 11-1 Create a databound web application

In this exercise, you'll complete a web application that's similar to the Vendor Invoices application shown in figure 11-12. Because this exercise carefully guides you through the development process, you should be able to do this whether or not you have ASP.NET experience. When you're done, the web form should look like this:

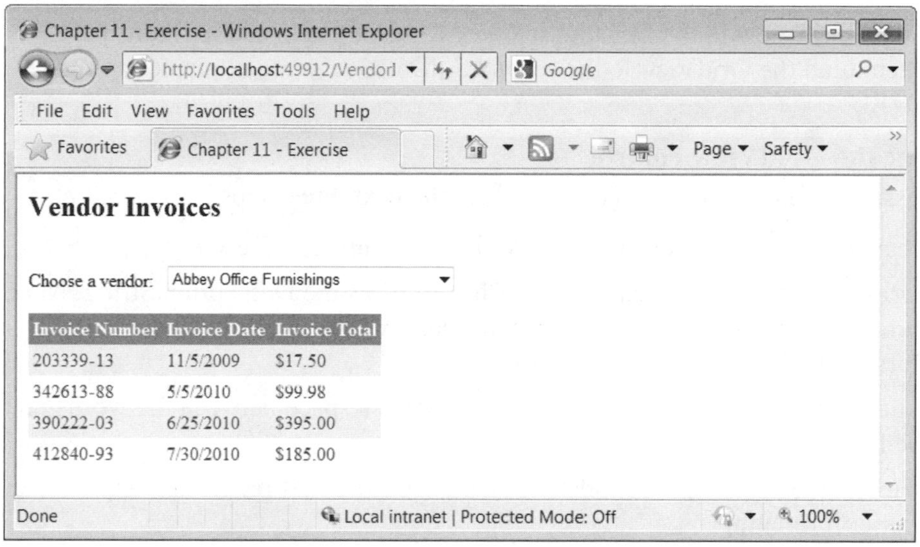

Create a data source and bind it to the DropDownList control

1. Use the File→Open Web Site command to open the VendorInvoices web site in your Chapter 11 directory. Then, look at the Default.aspx file in Design View, and note that a DropDownList control has already been created.
2. Create a SqlDataSource as shown in the first three figures of this chapter. Use the Vendors table of the Payables database and save the connection string as PayablesConnectionString. Then, configure the Select statement by including the VendorID and VendorName fields from the Vendors table, and ordering the data by the VendorName field, as shown in figure 11-4.
3. Bind the DropDownList to this SqlDataSource. As part of this process, set the data field that will be displayed to the VendorName field, and the data field for the value to the VendorID field. Refer to figures 11-13 and 11-14 if you need to refresh your memory.

Create another data source and bind it to a GridView control

4. Create a second SqlDataSource. Use the PayablesConnectionString you created in step 2 above and select the Invoices table. Select the InvoiceID, InvoiceNumber, InvoiceDate, and InvoiceTotal fields from the Invoices table, and order the data by invoice date.

   Then, create a Where clause that limits the data to the invoices for the vendor currently selected in the ddlVendors DropDownList. You can use the explanations in figure 11-5 to guide you.

5. Add a GridView to the Default.aspx web form, as explained in figure 11-9. Then, bind the GridView to the second SqlDataSource, as explained in figure 11-13.

Format the GridView control

If necessary, you can refer to figure 11-10 for the next three steps.

6. Change the Visible property of the VendorID column to False.
7. Format the InvoiceDate column by using {0:d} as the DataFormatString. Next, format the InvoiceTotal column to show currency by using {0:c} as the DataFormatString.
8. Edit the header text for each column so there is a space between the words in the headers.
9. Select the Auto Format command in the control's smart menu, and apply classic formatting.
10. Run the project, select different vendors from the DropDownList control, and confirm that their invoices are displayed in the GridView control as the choice of vendor changes.

12

How to use the GridView control

In the last chapter, you learned some basic skills for using the GridView control. Now, this chapter presents some additional skills for using this control that will show you how much this ASP.NET control can do for you. As you will see, the GridView control provides automatic paging and sorting. It lets you update and delete data with minimal Visual Basic code. And its appearance is fully customizable.

How to customize the GridView control

The GridView control is one of the most powerful user interface controls available in ASP.NET 4. It provides many options that let you customize its appearance and behavior. In the following topics, you'll learn how to enable sorting, provide for custom paging, add button fields, and use code to work with the data in the control.

How to enable sorting

The GridView control has a built-in ability to let the user sort the rows based on any or all of the columns displayed by the control. As figure 12-1 shows, all you have to do to enable sorting is set the AllowSorting attribute to True. The easiest way to do that is to check the Enable Sorting option in the control's smart tag menu.

To allow sorting for a specific column, you provide a SortExpression attribute for that column. Then, the user can sort the rows in ascending sequence based on the data in that column by clicking the column header. If the user clicks the column header again, the data is sorted in descending sequence.

When the AllowSorting attribute of the GridView is set to true, a SortExpression attribute is automatically generated for each bound field. As a result, if you don't want to allow sorting for one or more columns, you must remove the SortExpression attributes for those columns. To do that, you can use the Fields dialog box to clear the SortExpression properties. Or, you can use the HTML Editor to delete the SortExpression attributes.

The GridView control in this figure allows sorting for four of the five fields displayed by the GridView control. As you can see, the column headers for these fields are underlined to indicate that the fields can be sorted. The two SortExpression attributes shown in the code in this figure simply duplicate the name of the data source column the field is bound to. If, for example, the user clicks the header of the InvoiceDate column, the data is sorted on the InvoiceDate field.

In some cases, you may want the sort expression to be based on two or more columns. To do that, you just use commas to separate the sort field names. For example, if you want all the invoices with the same date to be sorted by invoice total when the user clicks the header for the invoice date column, you can code the SortExpression attribute for the date column like this:

```
SortExpression="InvoiceDate, InvoiceTotal"
```

It's important to note that the GridView control doesn't actually do the sorting. Instead, it relies on the underlying data source to sort the data. As a result, sorting will only work if the data source provides for sorting. For a SQL data source, this means that you need to use the default DataSet mode.

A GridView control with sorting enabled

Invoice No	Invoice Date	Invoice Total	Balance Due	Due Date
992609-278	10/5/2010	$328.05	$328.05	11/4/2010
836772	10/6/2010	$559.00	$559.00	11/5/2010
320256328	10/8/2010	$1,778.44	$1,778.44	12/7/2010
370933	10/19/2010	$36.00	$36.00	12/18/2010
9996474	11/2/2010	$503.20	$403.20	12/2/2010
984343173	11/9/2010	$143.78	$143.78	12/9/2010
993376-631	11/12/2010	$98.50	$98.50	12/12/2010
320838622	11/16/2010	$2,854.68	$2,854.68	1/15/2011

The aspx code for the control shown above

```
<asp:GridView ID="grdInvoices" runat="server" AllowSorting="True"
    DataSourceID="SqlDataSource1" AutoGenerateColumns="False"
    DataKeyNames="InvoiceID" CellPadding="4" ForeColor="#333333"
    GridLines="None">
    <AlternatingRowStyle BackColor="White" />
    <Columns>
      <asp:BoundField DataField="InvoiceID" HeaderText="InvoiceID"
          Visible="False" ReadOnly="True" />
      <asp:BoundField DataField="InvoiceNumber" HeaderText="Invoice No" />
      <asp:BoundField DataField="InvoiceDate" DataFormatString="{0:d}"
          HeaderText="Invoice Date" SortExpression="InvoiceDate" >
          <ItemStyle  HorizontalAlign="Right" />
      </asp:BoundField>
      .
      .
      <asp:BoundField DataField="DueDate" HeaderText="Due Date"
          DataFormatString="{0:d}" SortExpression="DueDate" >
          <ItemStyle HorizontalAlign="Right" />
      </asp:BoundField>
    </Columns>
    <HeaderStyle BackColor="#507CD1" Font-Bold="True" ForeColor="White" />
    <RowStyle BackColor="#EFF3FB" />
</asp:GridView>
```

Description

- To enable sorting, set the AllowSorting attribute of the GridView control to True. Then, a SortExpression attribute will be added automatically to all columns.
- To remove the SortExpression attribute from a column where you don't want to allow sorting, delete the SortExpression in the Fields dialog box or in the HTML editor.
- For sorting to work, the DataSourceMode attribute of the data source must be set to DataSet mode.

Figure 12-1 How to enable sorting

How to enable paging

Paging refers to the ability of the GridView control to display bound data one page at a time, along with paging controls that let the user select which page of data to display next. To enable paging, you simply set the AllowPaging attribute of the control to True as shown in figure 12-2. The easiest way to set this attribute is to check the Enable Paging option in the control's smart tag menu.

When you enable paging, an additional row is displayed at the bottom of the GridView control to display the pager controls. Then, if you want to control how this row is formatted, you can add a PagerStyle element. The simplest way to do that is to select the GridView control in the Design pane, select PagerStyle in the Properties pane, expand the list of settings in the Properties pane, and apply the values you want. Alternatively, you can manually insert the code in the HTML editor pane. In the example in this figure, the PagerStyle element specifies that the background color for the pager row should be light gray and the pager controls should be horizontally centered.

Unlike sorting, the GridView control doesn't delegate the paging function to the underlying data source. Like sorting, however, paging works only for data sources that are in DataSet mode.

A GridView with paging enabled

Invoice No	Invoice Date	Invoice Total	Balance Due	Due Date
320838622	11/16/2010	$2,854.68	$2,854.68	1/15/2011
993376-631	11/12/2010	$98.50	$98.50	12/12/2010
984343173	11/9/2010	$143.78	$143.78	12/9/2010
9996474	11/2/2010	$503.20	$403.20	12/2/2010
370933	10/19/2010	$36.00	$36.00	12/18/2010
320256328	10/8/2010	$1,778.44	$1,778.44	12/7/2010
836772	10/6/2010	$559.00	$559.00	11/5/2010
992609-278	10/5/2010	$328.05	$328.05	11/4/2010
PO2-88D77S8	10/5/2010	$943.35	$0.00	11/4/2010
981184672	10/1/2010	$326.75	$0.00	10/31/2010
1 2 3 4				

The code for the GridView control shown above

```
<asp:GridView ID="grdInvoices" runat="server" AutoGenerateColumns="False"
    DataKeyNames="InvoiceID" DataSourceID="SqlDataSource1"
    AllowPaging="True" CellPadding="4" ForeColor="#333333"
GridLines="None">
    <AlternatingRowStyle BackColor="White" />
    <Columns>
      <asp:BoundField DataField="InvoiceID" Visible="False"
          ReadOnly="True" />
      <asp:BoundField DataField="InvoiceNumber" HeaderText="Invoice No" />
      <asp:BoundField DataField="InvoiceDate" DataFormatString="{0:d}"
          HeaderText="Invoice Date" >
          <ItemStyle Width="95px" HorizontalAlign="Right" />
      </asp:BoundField>
      .
      .
      <asp:BoundField DataField="DueDate" DataFormatString="{0:d}"
          HeaderText="Due Date" >
          <ItemStyle HorizontalAlign="Right" />
      </asp:BoundField>
    </Columns>
    <HeaderStyle BackColor="#507CD1" Font-Bold="True" ForeColor="White" />
    <PagerStyle BackColor="#2461BF" ForeColor="White"
        HorizontalAlign="Center" />
    <RowStyle BackColor="#EFF3FB" />
/asp:GridView>
```

Description

- To enable *paging*, set the AllowPaging attribute to True. Then, add a PagerStyle element to define the appearance of the pager controls. You can also add a PagerSettings element as described in the next figure to customize the way paging works.
- For paging to work, the DataSourceMode attribute of the data source must be set to DataSet mode.

Figure 12-2 How to enable paging

How to customize paging

Figure 12-3 shows how you can customize the way paging works with a GridView control. To start, the two attributes in the first table let you enable paging and specify the number of data rows that will be displayed on each page. The default setting for the second attribute is 10, which is an appropriate value for most GridView controls.

You can also customize the appearance of the pager area by including a PagerSettings element between the start and end tags of a GridView control. Then, you can use the attributes in the second table for the customization. The most important of these attributes is Mode, which determines what buttons are displayed in the pager area. If, for example, you set the mode to NextPrevious, only Next and Previous buttons will be displayed.

If you specify Numeric or NumericFirstLast for the Mode attribute, individual page numbers are displayed in the pager area so the user can go directly to any of the listed pages. You can then use the PageButtonCount attribute to specify how many of these page numbers should be displayed in the pager area. Note that if you specify NumericFirstLast, the first and last buttons are displayed only if the total number of pages exceeds the value you specify for the PageButtonCount attribute and the first or last page number isn't displayed.

The remaining attributes in this table let you control the text or image that's displayed for the various buttons. By default, the values for the First, Previous, Next, and Last buttons use less-than and greater-than signs, but the example shows how you can change the text for these buttons.

The PagerSettings display is context-sensitive and will change if the page currently on view is the first or last page. For example, if the first page is being displayed, only Next and Last will be shown as PagerSettings choices. This makes sense, because there can't be a previous page if you are already on the first page. In the same way, if the last page is being displayed, only First and Prev will be shown as choices.

Attributes of the GridView control that affect paging

Attribute	Description
AllowPaging	Set to True to enable paging.
PageSize	Specifies the number of rows to display on each page. The default is 10.

Attributes of the PagerSettings element

Attribute	Description
Mode	Controls what buttons are displayed in the pager area. You can specify NextPrevious, NextPreviousFirstLast, Numeric, or NumericFirstLast. The default is Numeric.
FirstPageText	The text to display for the first page button. The default is <<, which displays as <<.
FirstPageImageUrl	The URL of an image file used to display the first page button.
PreviousPageText	The text to display for the previous page button. The default is <, which displays as <.
PreviousPageImageUrl	The URL of an image file used to display the previous page button.
NextPageText	The text to display for the next page button. The default is >, which displays as >.
NextPageImageUrl	The URL of an image file used to display the next page button.
LastPageText	The text to display for the last page button. The default is >>, which displays as >>.
LastPageImageUrl	The URL of an image file used to display the last page button.
PageButtonCount	The number of page buttons to display if the Mode is set to Numeric or NumericFirstLast. The default is 10.
Position	The location of the pager area. You can specify Top, Bottom, or TopAndBottom.
Visible	Set to False to hide the pager controls.

Example

A PagerSettings element

```
<PagerSettings Mode="NextPreviousFirstLast"
               NextPageText="Next" PreviousPageText="Prev"
               FirstPageText="First" LastPageText="Last" />
```

The resulting pager area

Description

- You can use the PageSize attribute of the GridView element to specify the number of rows to display on each page.
- You can also add a PagerSettings element to control the appearance of the pager area.

Figure 12-3 How to customize paging

How to use a button field

In addition to the bound fields that you use to display the data in a data source, you can add a variety of other fields to a GridView control. Later in this chapter, for example, you'll learn how to add command fields, which provide specialized buttons for editing and deleting rows. You can also add fields that contain check boxes, hyperlinks, images, and buttons.

In this topic, I'll show you how to use a button field that the user can click to perform a specific function. This is illustrated in figure 12-4. Here, the GridView control contains a button field that lets the user display the line items for an invoice. To do that, the user simply clicks the button that's displayed in the button field.

To define a button field, click on the smart tag of the GridView control, then select Edit Columns. This will open the Fields dialog box. Next, you typically use the three attributes shown in the table in this figure. The aspx code that follows this table shows how these attributes are set for the button field that's displayed in the GridView control at the top of the figure.

To respond when the user clicks a button field, you code an event handler for the RowCommand event of the GridView control as shown in the second code example. This event handler starts by checking the CommandName property of the e argument to determine which button field was clicked. Note that because the GridView control in this example contains a single button field, this code isn't really necessary. I included it only to illustrate how to use the CommandName property.

The next statement in this event handler gets the index of the row whose button was clicked. To do that, it uses the CommandArgument property of the e argument. Unlike a standard button control, you don't set the value of this property when you define a button field. Instead, it's automatically set to the index of a row when the button in that row is clicked. Once you have the index of the row, you can extract information from that row as you'll see in the next figure.

Before I go on, I should point out that you can also use the RowCommand event with the command fields you'll learn about in figure 12-11. However, you're more likely to use them with button fields that perform custom functions as shown here.

A GridView control with a button field

Invoice No	Invoice Date	Invoice Total	Balance Due	Due Date	
320838622	11/16/2010	$2,854.68	$2,854.68	1/15/2011	View Line Items
993376-631	11/12/2010	$98.50	$98.50	12/12/2010	View Line Items
984343173	11/9/2010	$143.78	$143.78	12/9/2010	View Line Items
9996474	11/2/2010	$503.20	$403.20	12/2/2010	View Line Items
370933	10/19/2010	$36.00	$36.00	12/18/2010	View Line Items
320256328	10/8/2010	$1,778.44	$1,778.44	12/7/2010	View Line Items
836772	10/6/2010	$559.00	$559.00	11/5/2010	View Line Items
992609-278	10/5/2010	$328.05	$328.05	11/4/2010	View Line Items
Next Last					

Commonly used button field attributes

Property	Description
ButtonType	The type of button to be displayed. Possible values are Button, Image, and Link. Link is the default.
Text	The text that's displayed on the button.
CommandName	The name of the command that's associated with the button.

The aspx code for the button field shown above

```
<asp:ButtonField ButtonType="Button" CommandName="ViewLineItems"
    Text="View Line Items" />
```

Code that responds to a button being clicked

```
Protected Sub grdInvoices_RowCommand(ByVal sender As Object,
        ByVal e As System.Web.UI.WebControls.GridViewCommandEventArgs) _
        Handles grdInvoices.RowCommand
    If e.CommandName = "ViewLineItems" Then
        Dim rowIndex As Integer = e.CommandArgument
        Me.DisplayLineItems(rowIndex)
    End If
End Sub
```

Description

- To add a button field to a GridView control, display the Fields dialog box, select ButtonField from the Available Fields list, and click the Add button. Then, you can select the button field in the Selected Fields list and set its properties.
- To respond to the user clicking a button field, code an event handler for the RowCommand event of the GridView control. Within this event handler, you can use the CommandName property of the e argument to get the value that was assigned to the CommandName property of the button field, and you can use the CommandArgument property to get the index of the row that contains the button that was clicked.

Figure 12-4 How to use a button field

How to use code to work with the data in a GridView control

In chapter 4, you learned how to use code to work with the data in a DataGridView control. Similarly, when you develop web applications, you can use code to work with the data in a GridView control. To do that, you can use the classes and properties shown in the table in figure 12-5. The code examples in this figure illustrate some of the common uses of these classes and properties.

To start, you can use one of the techniques in the first two examples to get a row from a GridView control. If you've provided a way for the user to select a row in the control, you can use the SelectedRow property of the control to get the selected row. You'll learn how to provide for selecting rows later in this chapter. If you haven't provided a way to select a row, you can retrieve a row by its index as shown in the second example. Notice in both examples that the row variable is declared as a GridViewRow object.

Once you retrieve a row, you can use code like that in the third example to get the contents of a cell in the row. To do that, you use the Cells property of the row to get the collection of TableCell objects in the row, and you use an index to refer to the cell whose contents you want to retrieve. In this example, the second cell in the row is retrieved. Then, the Text property of that cell is used to get the contents of the cell.

You can use different techniques to get the value of the data key that's specified by the DataKeyNames attribute of a GridView control. These techniques are particularly useful if the key column is included in the data source but is not displayed in the control. In that case, the key values aren't stored in the field because they don't need to be displayed. However, the values are stored in DataKey objects that are created automatically when the DataKeyNames attribute of the GridView control is set.

If the GridView control provides for selecting rows, you can use one of the techniques in the next two examples to get the key values. If the data key contains a single field, you can use the SelectedValue property as shown in the first example. If the data key contains two or more fields, you can also use this property to get the value of the first field. Alternatively, you can use code like that in the second example to get the value of each field. Here, the first statement uses the SelectedDataKey property to get the DataKey object for the selected row. Then, the next two statements use index values to retrieve the values of the two key fields.

If the GridView control doesn't provide for selecting rows, you can use one of the techniques in the last two examples to get the key values. To get the value of a data key that contains a single field, or to get the value of the first field in a data key, you can use the DataKeys property to refer to the collection of DataKey objects. Then, you can use a row index to refer to the DataKey object for a specific row, and you can use the Value property to get the value of that DataKey object. To get the values of the fields in a key that has two or more fields, you can use the DataKeys property and a row index to get the DataKey object for a specific row. Then, you can use index values to get the values of the key fields.

Important properties for working with a GridView control

Class	Property	Description
GridView	Rows	Gets a collection of GridViewRow objects.
GridView	SelectedRow	Gets a GridViewRow object for the currently selected row.
GridView	DataKeys	Gets a collection of DataKey objects.
GridView	SelectedDataKey	Gets the DataKey object for the currently selected row.
GridView	SelectedValue	Gets the value of the first field in the data key for the currently selected row.
GridView	SelectedIndex	Gets or sets the index of the currently selected row.
GridViewRow	Cells	Gets a collection of TableCell objects.
TableCell	Text	Gets or sets the contents of the cell.

How to get the currently selected row

```
Dim row As GridViewRow = grdInvoices.SelectedRow
```

How to get a row by its index

```
Dim row As GridViewRow = grdInvoices.Rows(rowIndex)
```

How to get the value of the second cell in a row

```
Dim cell As TableCell = row.Cells(1)
Dim invoiceNo As String = cell.Text
```

How to get the value of the data key for the currently selected row

For a data key that has a single field

```
Dim invoiceID As Integer = grdInvoices.SelectedValue
```

For a data key that has two fields

```
Dim key As DataKey = grdLineItems.SelectedDataKey
Dim invoiceID As Integer = key(0)
Dim invoiceSeq As Integer = key(1)
```

How to get the value of a data key by row index

For a data key that has a single field

```
Dim invoiceID As Integer = grdInvoices.DataKeys(rowIndex).Value
```

For a data key that has two fields

```
Dim key As DataKey = grdLineItems.DataKeys(rowIndex)
Dim invoiceID As Integer = key(0)
Dim invoiceSeq As Integer = key(1)
```

Description

- To use the properties that work with the currently selected row, you must provide a way to select a row. To do that, you can check the Enable Selection option in the control's smart tag menu, or you can add a command field as shown in figure 12-11.
- If the DataKeyNames attribute of a GridView control is set, a DataKey object is automatically created for each row in a GridView control.

Figure 12-5 How to use code to work with the data in a GridView control

A display application that uses two GridView controls

In the following topics, you'll see an enhanced version of the Vendor Invoices application that was presented in the last chapter. As you'll see, this application uses many of the skills you've learned so far in this chapter.

The enhanced Vendor Invoices application

Figure 12-6 presents the enhanced Vendor Invoices application. The Vendor Invoices page of this application displays all the invoices for the vendor that's selected from the drop-down list in a GridView control just as it did in the last chapter. However, the invoices in this version of the application are displayed 10 rows at a time, and numeric page buttons are displayed at the bottom of the GridView control so the user can navigate from page to page. In addition, the user can sort the data by clicking the column headings for the Invoice No, Invoice Date, Invoice Total, Balance Due, and Due Date columns.

The GridView control on the Vendor Invoices page also includes a button field that displays buttons with the text "View Line Items" on them. If the user clicks one of these buttons, the Line Items page is displayed. This page displays the line items for the invoice in a GridView control, and it displays the vendor name and invoice number in text boxes. When this page is displayed, the user can click the Return to Invoices button to return to the Vendor Invoices page.

The Vendor Invoices page

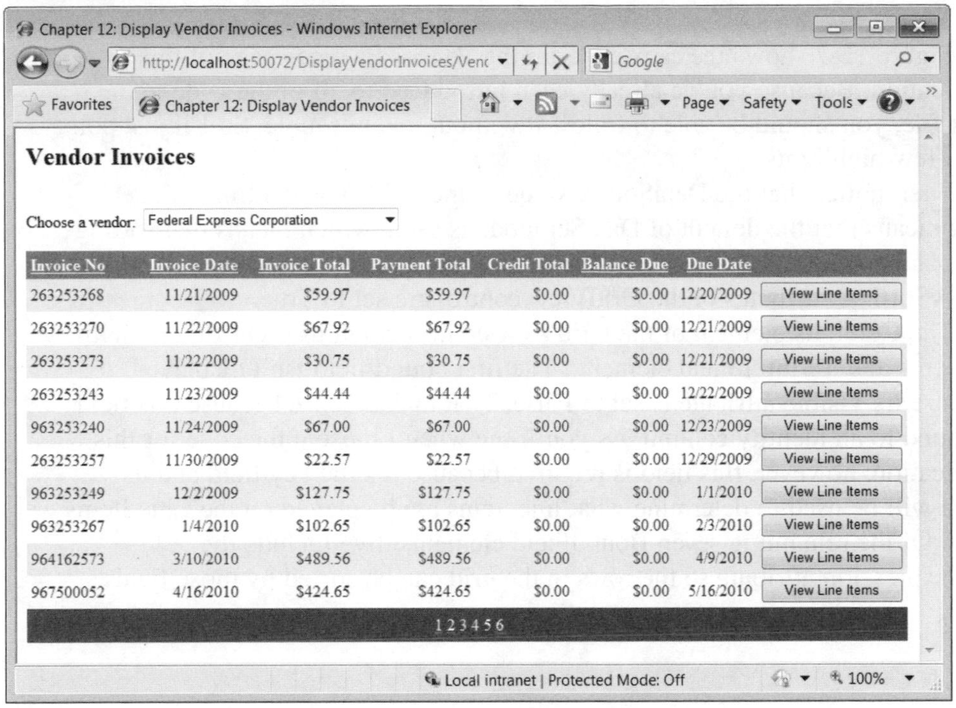

The Line Items page

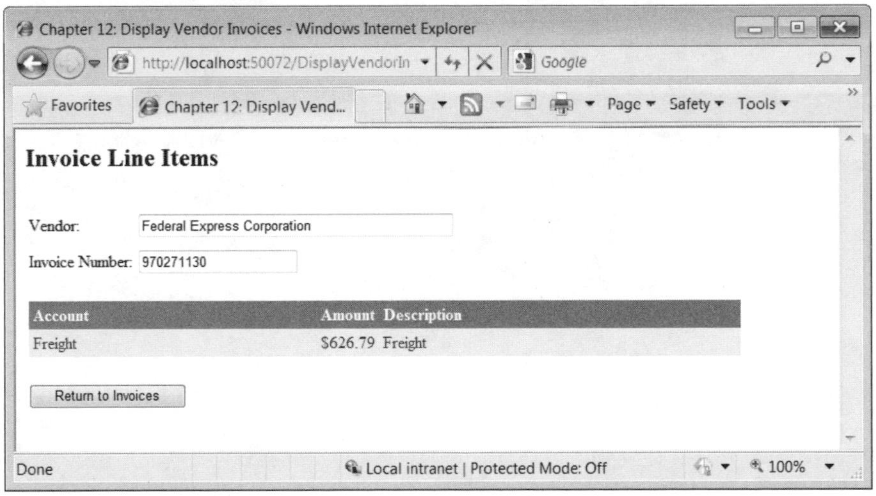

Description

- The Vendor Invoices application lets the user display the Invoices for a vendor in a GridView control that's bound to a SQL data source control. The user can also display the line items for an invoice in another GridView control by clicking the View Line Items button for that invoice.

Figure 12-6 The enhanced Vendor Invoices application

The aspx file for the Vendor Invoices page

Figure 12-7 shows the aspx code for the Vendor Invoices page of this application. Because you've already been introduced to all of the code in the aspx file, you should be able to follow it without much trouble. So I'll just point out a few highlights.

First, notice that the DataSourceMode of the GridView control isn't set. That means that the default of DataSet mode is used, which means that sorting and paging can be enabled. To enable sorting and paging, the AllowPaging and AllowSorting attributes of the GridView control are set to True.

The Columns element of the GridView control contains eight BoundField elements and a ButtonField element. The first bound field isn't displayed because its Visible attribute is set to False. That makes sense because this field is bound to an identity column. As you'll see when I present the code for this application, however, this field is required because it's the key field and its value will be used to determine what line items are displayed on the Line Items page. Of the remaining seven BoundField elements, five include the SortExpression attribute so the rows in the grid can be sorted by those fields.

The VendorInvoices.aspx file **Page 1**

```
<head runat="server">
    <title>Chapter 12: Display Vendor Invoices</title>
</head>
<body>
  <form id="form1" runat="server">
    <div>
        <h2>Vendor Invoices</h2><br />
        Choose a vendor:  
        <asp:DropDownList ID="ddlVendors"
            runat="server" DataSourceID="SqlDataSource1" DataTextField="Name"
            DataValueField="VendorID" Width="248px" AutoPostBack="True">
        </asp:DropDownList>
        <asp:SqlDataSource ID="SqlDataSource1" runat="server"
            ConnectionString=
                "<%$ ConnectionStrings:PayablesConnectionString %>"
            SelectCommand="SELECT [VendorID], [Name] FROM [Vendors]
                ORDER BY [Name]">
        </asp:SqlDataSource> <br /> <br />
        <asp:GridView ID="grdInvoices" runat="server"
            AutoGenerateColumns="False"
            DataKeyNames="InvoiceID" DataSourceID="SqlDataSource2"
            CellPadding="4"
            ForeColor="#333333" GridLines="None"
            AllowPaging="True" AllowSorting="True">
            <Columns>
                <asp:BoundField DataField="InvoiceID" HeaderText="InvoiceID"
                    Visible="False" >
                </asp:BoundField>
                <asp:BoundField DataField="InvoiceNumber"
                    HeaderText="Invoice No"
                    SortExpression="InvoiceNumber" >
                    <ItemStyle Width="100px" />
                    <HeaderStyle HorizontalAlign="Left" />
                </asp:BoundField>
                <asp:BoundField DataField="InvoiceDate"
                    DataFormatString="{0:d}"
                    HeaderText="Invoice Date" SortExpression="InvoiceDate" >
                    <ItemStyle Width="95px" HorizontalAlign="Right" />
                    <HeaderStyle HorizontalAlign="Right" />
                </asp:BoundField>
                <asp:BoundField DataField="InvoiceTotal"
                    DataFormatString="{0:c}"
                    HeaderText="Invoice Total" SortExpression="InvoiceTotal"
                    <ItemStyle HorizontalAlign="Right" Width="100px" />
                    <HeaderStyle HorizontalAlign="Right" />
                </asp:BoundField>
                <asp:BoundField DataField="PaymentTotal"
                    DataFormatString="{0:c}"
                    HeaderText="Payment Total" >
                    <ItemStyle HorizontalAlign="Right" Width="110px" />
                    <HeaderStyle HorizontalAlign="Right" />
                </asp:BoundField>
```

Figure 12-7 The aspx file for the Vendor Invoices page (part 1 of 2)

The style elements that follow the Columns element specify a number of style attributes that were automatically added because I selected Auto Format from the smart tag menu of the GridView control, and then picked the Classic style option. The PagerStyle BackColor, ForeColor and HorizontalAlign attributes are set to the appropriate values for that style. Because no PagerSettings element is included, the pager controls will be displayed as page numbers at the bottom of the grid.

The VendorInvoices.aspx file Page 2

```
            <asp:BoundField DataField="CreditTotal"
                DataFormatString="{0:c}"
                HeaderText="Credit Total" >
                <ItemStyle HorizontalAlign="Right" Width="90px" />
                <HeaderStyle HorizontalAlign="Right" />
            </asp:BoundField>
            <asp:BoundField DataField="BalanceDue"
                DataFormatString="{0:c}"
                HeaderText="Balance Due"
                SortExpression="BalanceDue">
                <ItemStyle HorizontalAlign="Right" Width="90px" />
                <HeaderStyle HorizontalAlign="Right" />
            </asp:BoundField>
            <asp:BoundField DataField="DueDate" DataFormatString="{0:d}"
                HeaderText="Due Date" SortExpression="DueDate">
                <ItemStyle Width="75px" HorizontalAlign="Right" />
                <HeaderStyle HorizontalAlign="Right" />
            </asp:BoundField>
            <asp:ButtonField ButtonType="Button"
                CommandName="ViewLineItems"
                Text="View Line Items" />
        </Columns>
        <EditRowStyle BackColor="#2461BF" />
        <FooterStyle BackColor="#507CD1" Font-Bold="True"
            ForeColor="White" />
        <RowStyle BackColor="#EFF3FB" />
        <SelectedRowStyle BackColor="#D1DDF1" Font-Bold="True"
            ForeColor="#333333" />
        <PagerStyle BackColor="#2461BF" ForeColor="White"
            HorizontalAlign="Center" />
        <HeaderStyle BackColor="#507CD1" Font-Bold="True"
            ForeColor="White" />
        <AlternatingRowStyle BackColor="White" />
        <SortedAscendingCellStyle BackColor="#F5F7FB" />
        <SortedAscendingHeaderStyle BackColor="#6D95E1" />
        <SortedDescendingCellStyle BackColor="#E9EBEF" />
        <SortedDescendingHeaderStyle BackColor="#4870BE" />
    </asp:GridView>
    <asp:SqlDataSource ID="SqlDataSource2" runat="server"
        ConnectionString=
            "<%$ ConnectionStrings:PayablesConnectionString %>"
        SelectCommand="SELECT InvoiceID, InvoiceNumber, InvoiceDate,
            InvoiceTotal, PaymentTotal, CreditTotal,
            InvoiceTotal - PaymentTotal - CreditTotal AS BalanceDue,
            DueDate
        FROM Invoices
        WHERE (VendorID = @VendorID) ORDER BY InvoiceDate">
       <SelectParameters>
           <asp:ControlParameter ControlID="ddlVendors" Name="VendorID"
               PropertyName="SelectedValue" Type="Int32" />
       </SelectParameters>
    </asp:SqlDataSource>
  </div>
 </form>
</body>
```

Figure 12-7 The aspx file for the Vendor Invoices page (part 2 of 2)

The code-behind file for the Vendor Invoices page

Figure 12-8 presents the Visual Basic code for the Vendor Invoices page. It starts with the Page_Load event handler, which is executed each time the page is loaded. This event handler starts by checking if the page is being posted back from itself or control is being passed to it from another page (in this case, the Line Items page). If it isn't being posted back, the code checks if an item named VendorID exists in session state. If it does, this value is stored in the SelectedValue property of the drop-down vendors list.

As you'll see in a minute, this session state item is created the first time the user clicks the View Line Items button for an invoice, which causes the Line Items page to be displayed. Then, if the user clicks the Return to Invoices button on that page, the Page_Load event handler for the Vendor Invoices page correctly sets the SelectedValue property of the drop-down list

If the user clicks one of the View Line Items buttons in the GridView control, the event handler for the RowCommand event is executed. This event handler starts by checking the CommandName property of the e argument to determine if one of the View Line Items buttons was clicked. This is necessary because the column headers that provide for sorting are also implemented as button fields, and you don't want the code in this event handler to be executed if one of these fields is clicked.

Next, the RowCommand event handler uses the CommandArgument property of the e argument to get the index of the row that contains the button that was clicked. Then, it uses the DataKeys property of the grid to get the invoice ID for the invoice in that row, and it uses the Rows property to get the row. Next, it uses the Cells property of the row to get the contents of the second cell, which contains the invoice number. After that, it stores the invoice ID, invoice number, vendor ID, and vendor name in session state. Notice that the vendor ID and vendor name are retrieved from the drop-down list. You've already seen how the vendor ID is used when the Vendor Invoices form is redisplayed. The other session state items are used by the Line Items form, as you'll see in a minute. Finally, the Line Items form is displayed.

The last event handler for this page handles any unexpected exceptions. Like the Vendor Invoices application in the previous chapter, it gets the exception, stores it in session state, and then displays it on an error page.

The code-behind file for the Vendor Invoices page

```
Partial Class VendorInvoices
    Inherits System.Web.UI.Page

    Protected Sub Page_Load(ByVal sender As Object,
            ByVal e As System.EventArgs) Handles Me.Load
        If Not IsPostBack Then
            If Session("VendorID") IsNot Nothing Then
                ' Redisplay the invoices for the previously selected vendor
                ddlVendors.SelectedValue = CInt(Session("VendorID"))
            End If
        End If
    End Sub

    Protected Sub grdInvoices_RowCommand(ByVal sender As Object,
            ByVal e As System.Web.UI.WebControls.GridViewCommandEventArgs) _
            Handles grdInvoices.RowCommand

        If e.CommandName = "ViewLineItems" Then

            ' Get the index of the row with the button that was clicked
            Dim rowIndex As Integer = e.CommandArgument

            ' Get the key value for the row
            Dim invoiceID As Integer = grdInvoices.DataKeys(rowIndex).Value

            ' Get the value in the second cell of the row
            Dim row As GridViewRow = grdInvoices.Rows(rowIndex)
            Dim cell As TableCell = row.Cells(1)
            Dim invoiceNo As String = cell.Text

            Session("InvoiceID") = invoiceID
            Session("InvoiceNo") = invoiceNo
            Session("VendorID") = ddlVendors.SelectedValue
            Session("VendorName") = ddlVendors.SelectedItem.Text
            Response.Redirect("LineItems.aspx")
        End If

    End Sub

    Protected Sub Page_Error(ByVal sender As Object,
            ByVal e As System.EventArgs) Handles Me.Error
        Dim ex As Exception
        ex = Server.GetLastError
        Session("Exception") = ex
        Response.Redirect("ErrorPage.aspx")
    End Sub

End Class
```

Figure 12-8 The code-behind file for the Vendor Invoices page

The aspx file for the Line Items page

Figure 12-9 shows the aspx code for the Line Items page. The only thing I want to point out here is the select parameter for the SQL data source shown on page 2. This parameter is a session parameter that gets its value from an item in session state. In this case, the parameter uses the session state item that contains the invoice ID. That way, only the line items for the invoice the user selected on the Vendor Invoices page are displayed.

You should also notice that an HTML table is used to align the labels and text boxes for this data. In this section, we've used tables to do this type of alignment because we thought most readers would be familiar with HTML tables. Be aware, though, that the modern way to do this is to use CSS instead of tables, which is explained in detail in *Murach's ASP.NET Web Programming with VB 2010.*

The code-behind file for the Line Items page

When the Line Items page is loaded, the Load event handler in figure 12-10 starts by getting the values of the InvoiceNo and VendorName items in session state. Then, it displays these values in the two text boxes on the form. Note that it isn't necessary to explicitly retrieve the value of the InvoiceID item that's used by the SQL data source. That's done automatically by the aspx code.

The next event handler for this page is executed when the user clicks the Return to Invoices button. This event handler simply redirects the browser to the Vendor Invoices page. Finally, the last event handler handles any unexpected exceptions and redirects to the Error page.

The LineItems.aspx file **Page 1**

```
<head runat="server">
    <title>Chapter 12: Display Vendor Invoices</title>
</head>
<body>
  <form id="form1" runat="server">
    <div>
      <h2>Invoice Line Items</h2><br />
      <table>
        <tr>
          <td style="width: 103px">
              <asp:Label ID="Label1" runat="server" Text="Vendor:">
              </asp:Label></td>
          <td style="width: 585px">
              <asp:TextBox ID="txtVendor" runat="server" ReadOnly="True"
                  Width="300px">
              </asp:TextBox></td>
        </tr>
        <tr>
          <td style="width: 103px; height: 5px" />
          <td style="width: 585px; height: 5px" />
        </tr>
        <tr>
          <td style="width: 103px">
              <asp:Label ID="Label2" runat="server" Text="Invoice Number:">
              </asp:Label></td>
          <td style="width: 585px">
              <asp:TextBox ID="txtInvoiceNo" runat="server" ReadOnly="True">
              </asp:TextBox></td>
          </tr>
        <tr>
          <td style="width: 103px; height: 20px"></td>
          <td style="width: 585px; height: 20px"></td>
        </tr>
        <tr>
          <td colspan="2">
              <asp:GridView ID="grdLineItems" runat="server"
                  AutoGenerateColumns="False"
                  DataSourceID="SqlDataSource1" CellPadding="4"
                  ForeColor="#333333" GridLines="None">
                  <Columns>
                    <asp:BoundField DataField="Account" HeaderText="Account">
                      <ItemStyle Width="250px" />
                      <HeaderStyle HorizontalAlign="Left" />
                    </asp:BoundField>
                    <asp:BoundField DataField="Amount"
                      DataFormatString="{0:c}"
                      HeaderText="Amount" >
                      <ItemStyle HorizontalAlign="Right" Width="75px" />
                      <HeaderStyle HorizontalAlign="Right" />
                    </asp:BoundField>
```

Figure 12-9 The aspx file for the Line Items page (part 1 of 2)

The LineItems.aspx file **Page 2**

```
                    <asp:BoundField DataField="Description"
                      HeaderText="Description">
                      <ItemStyle Width="350px" />
                      <HeaderStyle HorizontalAlign="Left" />
                    </asp:BoundField>
                  </Columns>
                  <EditRowStyle BackColor="#2461BF" />
                  <FooterStyle BackColor="#507CD1" Font-Bold="True"
                      ForeColor="White" />
                  <HeaderStyle BackColor="#507CD1" Font-Bold="True"
                      ForeColor="White" />
                  <AlternatingRowStyle BackColor="White" />
                  <PagerStyle BackColor="#2461BF" ForeColor="White"
                      HorizontalAlign="Center" />
                  <RowStyle BackColor="#EFF3FB" />
                  <SelectedRowStyle BackColor="#D1DDF1" Font-Bold="True"
                      ForeColor="#333333" />
                  <SortedAscendingCellStyle BackColor="#F5F7FB" />
                  <SortedAscendingHeaderStyle BackColor="#6D95E1" />
                  <SortedDescendingCellStyle BackColor="#E9EBEF" />
                  <SortedDescendingHeaderStyle BackColor="#4870BE" />
              </asp:GridView>
              <asp:SqlDataSource ID="SqlDataSource1" runat="server"
                  ConnectionString=
                  "<%$ ConnectionStrings:PayablesConnectionString %>"
                  SelectCommand="SELECT GLAccounts.Description AS Account,
                      InvoiceLineItems.Amount, InvoiceLineItems.Description
                  FROM InvoiceLineItems INNER JOIN GLAccounts
                  ON InvoiceLineItems.AccountNo = GLAccounts.AccountNo
                  WHERE (InvoiceLineItems.InvoiceID = @InvoiceID)">
                  <SelectParameters>
                      <asp:SessionParameter Name="InvoiceID"
                          SessionField="InvoiceID" />
                  </SelectParameters>
              </asp:SqlDataSource>
          </td>
        </tr>
        <tr>
          <td style="width: 103px; height: 20px"></td>
          <td style="width: 585px; height: 20px"></td>
        </tr>
        <tr>
          <td colspan="2">
              <asp:Button ID="btnReturn" runat="server"
                  Text="Return to Invoices" />
          </td>
        </tr>
      </table>
    </div>
  </form>
</body>
```

Figure 12-9 The aspx file for the Line Items page (part 2 of 2)

The code-behind file for the Line Items page

```
Partial Class LineItems
    Inherits System.Web.UI.Page

    Protected Sub Page_Load(ByVal sender As Object,
            ByVal e As System.EventArgs) Handles Me.Load
        Dim name As String = Session("VendorName").ToString
        txtVendor.Text = name
        Dim invoiceNo As String = Session("InvoiceNo").ToString
        txtInvoiceNo.Text = invoiceNo
    End Sub

    Protected Sub btnReturn_Click(ByVal sender As Object,
            ByVal e As System.EventArgs) Handles btnReturn.Click
        Response.Redirect("VendorInvoices.aspx")
    End Sub

    Protected Sub Page_Error(ByVal sender As Object,
            ByVal e As System.EventArgs) Handles Me.Error
        Dim ex As Exception
        ex = Server.GetLastError
        Session("Exception") = ex
        Response.Redirect("ErrorPage.aspx")
    End Sub

End Class
```

Figure 12-10 The code-behind file for the Line Items page

How to update GridView data

Another impressive feature of the GridView control is its ability to update data in the underlying data source with little additional code. Before you can set that up, though, you must configure the data source with Update, Delete, and Insert statements, as described in the last chapter. Once you've done that, you can set up a GridView control so it calls the Update and Delete statements, which you'll learn how to do next.

How to work with command fields

A *command field* is a GridView column that contains one or more command buttons. Figure 12-11 shows five of the command buttons that you can include in each row of a GridView control. Please note, however, that the Update and Cancel buttons are displayed only when a user clicks the Edit button to edit a row. You can't display these buttons in separate command fields.

When the user clicks a Delete button, the GridView control calls the data source control's Delete method, which deletes the selected row from the underlying database. Then, the GridView control redisplays the data without the deleted row.

When the user clicks the Edit button, the GridView control places the selected row in *edit mode*. In this mode, the labels used to display the editable bound fields are replaced by text boxes so the user can enter changes. Also, the row is formatted using the style attributes provided by the EditRowStyle element. Finally, the Edit button itself is replaced by Update and Cancel buttons. Then, if the user clicks the Update button, the GridView control calls the data source control's Update method, which updates the underlying database. But if the user clicks the Cancel button, any changes made by the user are discarded and the original values are redisplayed.

The Select button lets the user select a row. Then, the selected row is displayed with the settings in the SelectedRowStyle element. Also, the SelectedIndex and SelectedRow properties are updated to reflect the selected row. The Select button is most often used in combination with a FormView or DetailsView control to create pages that show the details for an item selected from the GridView control. You'll learn how this works in chapter 13.

The two tables in this figure show the attributes of a CommandField element. For instance, you can set the ShowEditButton attribute to True to display an Edit button in a command field. And you can use the EditText attribute to set the text that's displayed on that button.

Although a single command field can display more than one button, it's common to create separate command fields for Select, Edit, and Delete buttons. If you want to include more than one button in a single command field, however, you can do that by selecting the CommandField item in the Available Fields list rather than a specific command field. Then, you can set the Show properties of that command field so it displays the buttons you want.

The Fields dialog box for working with a command field

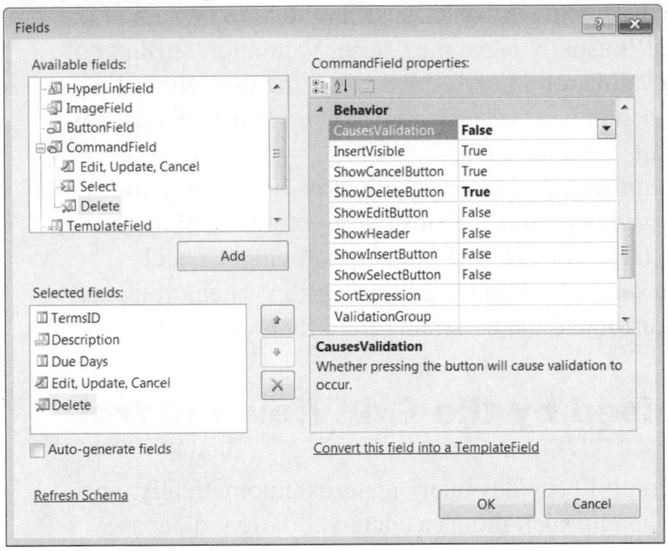

Typical code for defining command fields

```
<asp:CommandField ButtonType="Button" ShowEditButton="True"
     CausesValidation="True" />
<asp:CommandField ButtonType="Button" ShowDeleteButton="True"
     CausesValidation="False" />
```

Attributes of the CommandField element

Attribute	Description
ButtonType	Specifies the type of button displayed in the command field. Valid options are Button, Link, or Image.
CausesValidation	Specifies whether validation should be performed if the user clicks the button.
ValidationGroup	Specifies the name of the group to be validated if CausesValidation is True.

Attributes that show buttons and set the text or images they display

Button	Show	Text	Image
Cancel	ShowCancelButton	CancelText	CancelImage
Delete	ShowDeleteButton	DeleteText	DeleteImage
Edit	ShowEditButton	EditText	EditImage
Select	ShowSelectButton	SelectText	SelectImage
Update	n/a	UpdateText	UpdateImage

Description

- A *command field* adds buttons that let the user edit, delete, or select data in a GridView control.
- The CommandField element also provides for an Insert button, but the GridView control doesn't directly support insert operations.

Figure 12-11 How to work with command fields

It's also common to set the CausesValidation attribute of the Select and Delete buttons to False since these buttons don't cause any data to be sent to the server. On the other hand, you'll usually leave the CausesValidation attribute of the Edit button set to True so validation is performed when the user clicks the Update button. Later in this chapter, you'll learn how to use validation controls with the Edit button by creating template fields.

Although you can add command fields using the Fields dialog box, you should know that you can also add command fields by selecting the appropriate options in the control's smart tag menu. To add Edit, Update, and Cancel buttons, for example, you can select the Enable Editing option. Then, you can use the Fields dialog box to customize the command field that's created.

How to use events raised by the GridView control

Although the GridView control provides many features automatically, you still must write some code to handle such things as data validation, database exceptions, and concurrency errors. As figure 12-12 shows, most of this code will be in the form of event handlers that respond to one or more of the events raised by the GridView control.

If you look at the list of events in the table in this figure, you'll see that several of them come in pairs, with one event raised before an action is taken and the other after the action completes. For example, when the user clicks the Delete button in a GridView row, two events are raised. The RowDeleting event is raised before the row is deleted, and the RowDeleted event is raised after the row has been deleted.

The most common reason to handle the before-action events is to provide data validation. For example, when the user clicks the Update button, you can handle the RowUpdating event to make sure the user has entered valid data. If not, you can set the e argument's Cancel property to True to cancel the update.

In contrast, the after-action events give you an opportunity to make sure the database operation completed successfully. In most applications, you should test for two conditions. First, you should check for any database exceptions by checking the Exception property of the e argument. If this property refers to a valid object, an exception has occurred and you can notify the user with an appropriate error message.

Second, if optimistic concurrency is used, you should check to see if a concurrency violation has occurred. To do that, you can check the AffectedRows property of the e argument. If this property is zero, it means that no rows were affected by the operation. That typically indicates that a concurrency error has occurred, and you can notify the user with an appropriate error message.

When you use optimistic concurrency, remember that the Where clause in an Update or Delete statement tries to find a row that has the same values as when the row was originally retrieved. If that row can't be found, it means that another user has updated one of the columns or deleted the row. Then, the

Events raised by the GridView control

Event	Raised when ...
RowCommand	A button is clicked.
RowCancelingEdit	The Cancel button of a row in edit mode is clicked.
RowDataBound	Data binding completes for a row.
RowDeleted	A row has been deleted.
RowDeleting	A row is about to be deleted.
RowEditing	A row is about to be edited.
RowUpdated	A row has been updated.
RowUpdating	A row is about to be updated.
SelectedIndexChanged	A row has been selected.
SelectedIndexChanging	A row is about to be selected.

An event handler for the RowUpdated event

```
Protected Sub grdTerms_RowUpdated(ByVal sender As Object,
        ByVal e As System.Web.UI.WebControls.GridViewUpdatedEventArgs) _
        Handles grdTerms.RowUpdated
    If e.Exception IsNot Nothing Then
        lblError.Text = "An exception occurred. " &
            e.Exception.Message
        e.ExceptionHandled = True
        e.KeepInEditMode = True
    ElseIf e.AffectedRows = 0 Then
        lblError.Text = "The row was not updated. " &
             "Another user may have updated or deleted those terms. " &
             "Please try again."
    End If
End Sub
```

Description

- The GridView control raises various events that can be handled when data is updated.
- The RowUpdating event is often used for data validation. You can cancel the update or delete operation by setting the e argument's Cancel property to True.
- You can handle the RowUpdated and RowDeleted events to ensure that the row was successfully updated or deleted.
- To determine if a SQL exception has occurred, check the Exception property of the e argument. If an exception has occurred, the most likely cause is a null value for a column that doesn't accept nulls. To suppress the exception, you can set the ExceptionHandled property to True. And to keep the control in edit mode, you can set the KeepInEditMode property to True.
- To determine how many rows were updated or deleted, check the AffectedRows property of the e argument. If this property is zero and an exception has *not* been thrown, the most likely cause is a concurrency error.

Figure 12-12 How to use events raised by the GridView control

update or delete operation never takes place so no rows are affected.

When you try to update a record, one of the most common exceptions is caused by an attempt to store a null value in a database column that doesn't allow null values. This occurs when the user doesn't enter a value in one of the columns that's being updated. In this case, you can display an appropriate error message and set the e argument's ExceptionHandled property to True to suppress further processing of the exception. You can also set the KeepInEditMode property to True to leave the GridView control in edit mode.

How to insert a row in a GridView control

You may have noticed that although the GridView control lets you update and delete rows, it has no provision for inserting new rows. When you use the GridView control in concert with a FormView or DetailsView control, though, you can provide for insert operations with a minimum of code. You'll learn how to do that in chapter 13. Another alternative is to create a page that lets you insert data into a GridView control by using the technique described in figure 12-13.

To provide for insertions, you must first create a set of input controls such as text boxes in which the user can enter data for the row to be inserted. Next, you must provide a button that the user can click to start the insertion. Then, in the event handler for this button, you can set the insert parameter values to the values entered by the user and execute the data source's Insert method to add the new row.

This is illustrated by the code in this figure. Here, if the insertion is successful, the contents of the text boxes are cleared so the user can insert another row. But if an exception is thrown, an error message is displayed. This message indicates that an exception has occurred and uses the Message property of the Exception object to display the message that's stored in that object.

By the way, you should know that the SqlDataSource class also provides properties and methods for updating and deleting rows. Since you can perform these operations using a control like a GridView control that's bound to the data source, however, you're not likely to use these properties and methods. If you ever need to perform an update or delete operation that can't be done using a bound control, however, you can perform the operation directly using the data source. Keep in mind that if you do that, you won't be able to use command fields to initiate the operations. Instead, you can use button fields that you respond to using code similar to the code shown in this figure.

Members of the SqlDataSource class for inserting rows

Method	Description
`Insert`	Executes the Insert command defined for the data source.

Property	Description
`InsertCommand`	The Insert command to be executed.
`InsertParameters(NameString)`	The parameter with the specified name.

Property of the Parameter class for inserting rows

Property	Description
`DefaultValue`	The default value of a parameter. This value is used if no other value is assigned to the parameter.

Code that uses a SQL data source control to insert a row

```
Protected Sub btnAdd_Click(ByVal sender As Object,
        ByVal e As System.EventArgs) Handles btnAdd.Click
    SqlDataSource1.InsertParameters("Description").DefaultValue =
        txtDescription.Text
    SqlDataSource1.InsertParameters("DueDays").DefaultValue =
        txtDueDays.Text
    Try
        SqlDataSource1.Insert()
        txtDescription.Text = ""
        txtDueDays.Text = ""
    Catch ex As Exception
        lblError.Text = "An exception occurred. " &
            ex.Message
    End Try
End Sub
```

Description

- The GridView control doesn't support insert operations, but you can use the GridView's data source to insert rows into the database. When you do, the new row will automatically be shown in the GridView control.
- To provide for inserts, the page should include controls such as text boxes for the user to enter data and a button that the user can click to insert the data.
- To use a SqlDataSource control to insert a database row, first set the DefaultValue property of each insert parameter to the value you want to insert. Then, execute the Insert method.
- The Insert method may throw a SqlException if a SQL Server error occurs. The most likely cause of the exception is a primary key constraint violation.

Figure 12-13 How to insert a row in a GridView control

A maintenance application that uses a GridView control

To give you a better idea of how you can use a GridView control to update, delete, and insert data, the following topics present an application that maintains the Terms table in the Payables database.

The Terms Maintenance application

Figure 12-14 introduces you to the Terms Maintenance application. It lets the user update, delete, and insert rows in the Terms table of the Payables database. Here, a GridView control is used to display the rows in the Terms table along with Edit and Delete buttons. In this figure, the user has clicked the Edit button for the second data row, placing that row in edit mode.

Beneath the GridView control, two text boxes let the user enter data for a new terms row. Then, if the user clicks the Add Terms button, the data entered in these text boxes is used to add a terms row to the database. Although it isn't apparent from this figure, required field validators are used for both text boxes, and a compare validator is used for the Due Days text box to check that the value the user enters is an integer. Also, there's a label control beneath the GridView control that's used to display error messages when an update, delete, or insert operation fails.

The Terms Maintenance application

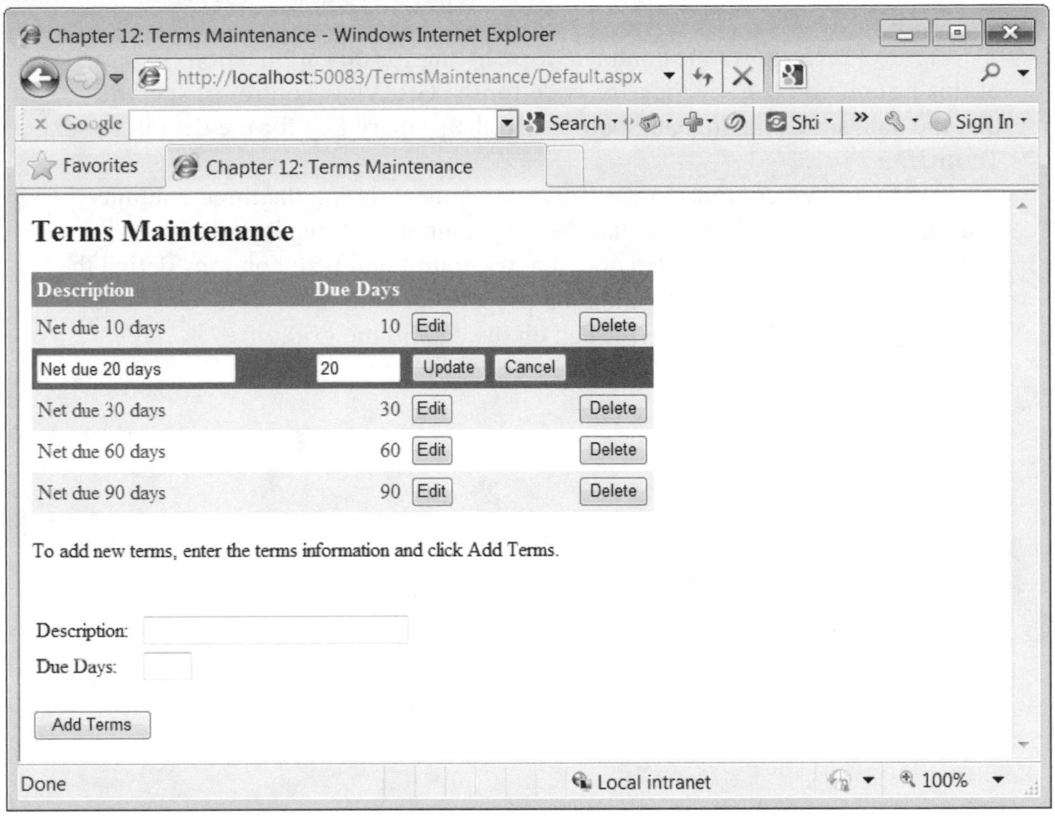

Description

- The Terms Maintenance application uses a GridView control to let the user update or delete rows in the Terms table.
- To edit a terms row, the user clicks the Edit button. This places the GridView control into *edit mode*. The user can then change the Description and Due Days and click the Update button. Or, the user can click the Cancel button to leave edit mode.
- To delete a terms row, the user clicks the Delete button.
- The user can add a terms row to the table by entering data into the text boxes beneath the GridView control and clicking the Add Terms button.
- A required field validator is included for the Description text box, and a required field validator and a compare validator are included for the Due Days text box.
- If an insert, update, or delete operation fails, an error message in displayed in a label above the text boxes for adding a new row.

Figure 12-14 The Terms Maintenance application

The aspx file

Figure 12-15 shows the complete aspx listing for this application. In part 1 of this figure, you can see the aspx code for the GridView control. It specifies that the data source is SqlDataSource1 and the primary key for the data is TermsID.

The first three columns in the Columns element define the three columns from the data source. But note that the first column isn't displayed because it contains an identity value. Also note that the fourth and fifth columns define the command fields. The CausesValidation property of both these fields is left at False since no validation is performed on the data in the grid.

The Default.aspx file Page 1

```
<body>
  <form id="form1" runat="server">
    <div>
        <h2>Terms Maintenance</h2>
        <asp:GridView ID="grdTerms" runat="server" AutoGenerateColumns="False"
            DataKeyNames="TermsID" DataSourceID="SqlDataSource1"
            CellPadding="4" ForeColor="#333333" GridLines="None">
            <EditRowStyle BackColor="#2461BF" />
            <FooterStyle BackColor="#507CD1" Font-Bold="True"
                ForeColor="White" />
            <Columns>
                <asp:BoundField DataField="TermsID" Visible="False" />
                <asp:TemplateField HeaderText="Description">
                    <EditItemTemplate>
                        <asp:TextBox ID="txtGridDescription" runat="server"
                            Text='<%# Bind("Description") %>'></asp:TextBox>
                    </EditItemTemplate>
                    <ItemTemplate>
                        <asp:Label ID="lblGridDescription" runat="server"
                            Text='<%# Bind("Description") %>'></asp:Label>
                    </ItemTemplate>
                    <HeaderStyle HorizontalAlign="Left" />
                    <ItemStyle Width="200px" />
                </asp:TemplateField>
                <asp:BoundField DataField="DueDays" HeaderText="Due Days">
                    <ItemStyle HorizontalAlign="Right" Width="75px" />
                    <HeaderStyle HorizontalAlign="Right" />
                </asp:BoundField>
                <asp:CommandField ButtonType="Button" ShowEditButton="True"
                    CausesValidation="False" />
                <asp:CommandField ButtonType="Button" ShowDeleteButton="True"
                    CausesValidation="False" />
            </Columns>
            <HeaderStyle BackColor="#507CD1" Font-Bold="True"
                ForeColor="White" />
            <AlternatingRowStyle BackColor="White" />
            <PagerStyle BackColor="#2461BF" ForeColor="White"
                HorizontalAlign="Center" />
            <RowStyle BackColor="#EFF3FB" />
            <SelectedRowStyle BackColor="#D1DDF1" Font-Bold="True"
                ForeColor="#333333" />
            <SortedAscendingCellStyle BackColor="#F5F7FB" />
            <SortedAscendingHeaderStyle BackColor="#6D95E1" />
            <SortedDescendingCellStyle BackColor="#E9EBEF" />
            <SortedDescendingHeaderStyle BackColor="#4870BE" />
        </asp:GridView>
```

Notes

- The GridView control is bound to the data source named SqlDataSource1.
- The Columns element includes child elements that define five columns. Three are for the bound fields, the other two are for the command buttons.
- The Visible attribute of the first field, which is bound to the TermsID column, is set to False because this column is an identity column.

Figure 12-15 The aspx file for the Terms Maintenance application (part 1 of 3)

Part 2 of this figure shows the SQL data source control. This data source includes two attributes that you haven't seen before. The ConflictDetection attribute indicates how update and delete operations are handled. By default, this attribute is set to CompareAllValues, which means that optimistic concurrency checking will be done. The OldValuesParameterFormatString attribute indicates the format of the parameter names that are used to hold the original column values. By default, this attribute is set to original_{0}, which means that the name of each original parameter will include the name of the column prefixed with "original_".

As a result of these two attribute values, these statements are used to retrieve, delete, update, and insert category rows:

```
SELECT [TermsID], [Description], [DueDays]
    FROM [Terms]

DELETE FROM [Terms]
    WHERE [TermsID] = @original_TermsID
      AND [Description] = @original_Description
      AND [DueDays] = @original_DueDays

UPDATE [Terms]
    SET [Description] = @Description, [DueDays] = @DueDays
    WHERE [TermsID] = @original_TermsID
      AND [Description] = @original_Description
      AND [DueDays] = @original_DueDays

INSERT INTO [Terms]
    ([Description], [DueDays])
    VALUES (@Description, @DueDays)
```

Here, the Where clauses of the Update and Delete statements implement optimistic concurrency by looking for rows that have the values originally retrieved. Then, the DeleteParameters, UpdateParameters, and InsertParameters elements in the aspx code define the parameters used by all four of these statements.

The Default.aspx file Page 2

```
<asp:SqlDataSource ID="SqlDataSource1" runat="server"
    ConflictDetection="CompareAllValues"
    ConnectionString=
        "<%$ ConnectionStrings:PayablesConnectionString %>"
    OldValuesParameterFormatString="original_{0}"
    SelectCommand="SELECT [TermsID], [Description], [DueDays]
        FROM [Terms]"
    DeleteCommand="DELETE FROM [Terms]
        WHERE [TermsID] = @original_TermsID
          AND [Description] = @original_Description
          AND [DueDays] = @original_DueDays"
    InsertCommand="INSERT INTO [Terms]
        ([Description], [DueDays])
        VALUES (@Description, @DueDays)"
    UpdateCommand="UPDATE [Terms]
        SET [Description] = @Description,
            [DueDays] = @DueDays
        WHERE [TermsID] = @original_TermsID
          AND [Description] = @original_Description
          AND [DueDays] = @original_DueDays">
    <DeleteParameters>
        <asp:Parameter Name="original_TermsID" Type="Int32" />
        <asp:Parameter Name="original_Description" Type="String" />
        <asp:Parameter Name="original_DueDays" Type="Int16" />
    </DeleteParameters>
    <UpdateParameters>
        <asp:Parameter Name="Description" Type="String" />
        <asp:Parameter Name="DueDays" Type="Int16" />
        <asp:Parameter Name="original_TermsID" Type="Int32" />
        <asp:Parameter Name="original_Description" Type="String" />
        <asp:Parameter Name="original_DueDays" Type="Int16" />
    </UpdateParameters>
    <InsertParameters>
        <asp:Parameter Name="Description" Type="String" />
        <asp:Parameter Name="DueDays" Type="Int16" />
    </InsertParameters>
</asp:SqlDataSource><br />
```

Notes

- The Select statement retrieves all rows in the Terms table.
- The Where clauses in the Delete and Update statements provide for optimistic concurrency.

Figure 12-15 The aspx file for the Terms Maintenance application (part 2 of 3)

Finally, part 3 of this figure shows the input controls used to enter the data for a new term. As you can see, the values in both text boxes are validated by ASP.NET validator controls. Both the description and due days values are validated by required field validators that test whether the user has entered data in the text boxes. In addition, the Due Days text box is validated by a compare validator that tests whether the user enters an integer in this text box. All of this validation is done when the user clicks the Add Terms button.

The Default.aspx file Page 3

```
        To add new terms, enter the terms information and click Add Terms.
        <br />
        <asp:Label ID="lblError" runat="server" ForeColor="Red"
            EnableViewState="False"></asp:Label><br /><br />
        <table>
          <tr>
            <td style="width: 80px">Description:</td>
            <td style="width: 124px">
                <asp:TextBox ID="txtDescription" runat="server" Width="200px">
                </asp:TextBox></td>
            <td style="width: 184px">
                <asp:RequiredFieldValidator ID="RequiredFieldValidator1"
                    runat="server" ControlToValidate="txtDescription"
                    ErrorMessage="Description is a required field."
                    Width="184px"></asp:RequiredFieldValidator></td>
          </tr>
          <tr>
            <td style="width: 80px">Due Days:</td>
            <td style="width: 124px">
                <asp:TextBox ID="txtDueDays" runat="server" Width="32px">
                </asp:TextBox></td>
            <td style="width: 184px">
                <asp:RequiredFieldValidator ID="RequiredFieldValidator2"
                    runat="server" ControlToValidate="txtDueDays"
                    ErrorMessage="Due Days is a required field."
                    Display="Dynamic" Width="176px">
                </asp:RequiredFieldValidator>
                <asp:CompareValidator ID="CompareValidator1" runat="server"
                    ErrorMessage="Due Days must be an integer."
                    Operator="DataTypeCheck" ControlToValidate="txtDueDays"
                    Type="Integer" Display="Dynamic" Width="184px">
                </asp:CompareValidator>
            </td>
          </tr>
      </table>
      <br />
      <asp:Button ID="btnAdd" runat="server" Text="Add Terms" />
    </div>
  </form>
</body>
```

Notes

- The text boxes are used to enter data for a new row.
- The required field validators ensure that the user enters data for both the Description and DueDays columns of a new row, and the compare validator ensures that the user enters an integer for the DueDays column.

Figure 12-15 The aspx file for the Terms Maintenance application (part 3 of 3)

The code-behind file

Although it would be nice if you could create a robust database application without writing any Visual Basic code, you must still write code to insert data into a GridView control and to catch and handle any database or concurrency errors that might occur. Figure 12-16 shows this code for the Terms Maintenance application.

As you can see, this code-behind file consists of just four event handlers. The first one, btnAdd_Click, sets the values of the two insert parameters to the values entered by the user when the user clicks the Add Terms button. Then, it calls the Insert method of the data source control. If an exception is thrown, an appropriate error message is displayed. If an exception isn't thrown, the values in the description and due days text boxes are reset to empty strings.

The second event handler, grdTerms_RowUpdated, is executed after a row has been updated. This event handler checks the Exception property of the e argument to determine if an exception has been thrown. If so, an error message is displayed, the ExceptionHandled property is set to True to suppress the exception, and the KeepInEditMode property is set to True to leave the GridView control in edit mode. If an exception hasn't occurred, the e argument's AffectedRows property is checked. If it's zero, it means that a concurrency error has occurred and an appropriate message is displayed.

The third event handler, grdTerms_RowDeleted, is executed after a row has been deleted. This event handler is almost identical to the event handler for the RowUpdated event of the grid. The only difference is that if an exception occurs, the row isn't kept in edit mode since it wasn't in edit mode to begin with. In fact, the KeepInEditMode property isn't available for a delete operation.

Although the first three event handlers handle any exceptions that might occur when a row is inserted, updated, or deleted, they don't handle exceptions that might occur when the data is retrieved. Because of that, a fourth event handler is required to catch these exceptions. You've seen this code in previous applications.

The Default.aspx.vb file

```
Partial Class _Default
    Inherits System.Web.UI.Page

    Protected Sub btnAdd_Click(ByVal sender As Object,
            ByVal e As System.EventArgs) Handles btnAdd.Click
        SqlDataSource1.InsertParameters("Description").DefaultValue =
            txtDescription.Text
        SqlDataSource1.InsertParameters("DueDays").DefaultValue =
            txtDueDays.Text
        Try
            SqlDataSource1.Insert()
            txtDescription.Text = ""
            txtDueDays.Text = ""
        Catch ex As Exception
            lblError.Text = "An exception occurred. " &
                ex.Message
        End Try
    End Sub

    Protected Sub grdTerms_RowUpdated(ByVal sender As Object,
            ByVal e As System.Web.UI.WebControls.GridViewUpdatedEventArgs) _
            Handles grdTerms.RowUpdated
        If e.Exception IsNot Nothing Then
            lblError.Text = "An exception occurred. " &
                e.Exception.Message
            e.ExceptionHandled = True
            e.KeepInEditMode = True
        ElseIf e.AffectedRows = 0 Then
            lblError.Text = "The row was not updated. " &
                "Another user may have updated or deleted those terms. " &
                "Please try again."
        End If
    End Sub

    Protected Sub grdTerms_RowDeleted(ByVal sender As Object,
            ByVal e As System.Web.UI.WebControls.GridViewDeletedEventArgs) _
            Handles grdTerms.RowDeleted
        If e.Exception IsNot Nothing Then
            lblError.Text = "An exception occurred. " &
                e.Exception.Message
            e.ExceptionHandled = True
        ElseIf e.AffectedRows = 0 Then
            lblError.Text = "The row was not deleted. " &
                "Another user may have updated or deleted those terms. " &
                "Please try again."
        End If
    End Sub

    Protected Sub Page_Error(ByVal sender As Object,
            ByVal e As System.EventArgs) Handles Me.Error
        Dim ex As Exception
        ex = Server.GetLastError
        Session("Exception") = ex
        Response.Redirect("ErrorPage.aspx")
    End Sub
End Class
```

Figure 12-16 The code-behind file for the Terms Maintenance application

How to work with template fields

Although using bound fields is a convenient way to include bound data in a GridView control, the most flexible way is to use template fields. A *template field* is simply a field that provides one or more templates that are used to render the column. You can include anything you want in these templates, including labels or text boxes, data binding expressions, and validation controls. In fact, including validation controls for editable GridView columns is one of the main reasons for using template fields.

How to create template fields

Figure 12-17 shows how to create template fields. The easiest way to do that is to first create a regular bound field and then convert it to a template field. This changes the BoundField element to a TemplateField element and, more importantly, generates ItemTemplate and EditItemTemplate elements that include labels and text boxes with appropriate binding expressions. You'll learn more about binding expressions in the next figure.

Once you've converted a bound field to a template, you can edit the template to add any additional elements you want to include, such as validation controls. In the code example in this figure, you can see that I added a RequiredFieldValidator control to the EditItem template for the Description column. That way, the user must enter data into the txtGridDescription text box. I also changed the names of the label and the text box generated for the Item and EditItem templates from their defaults (Label1 and TextBox1) to lblGridDescription and txtGridDescription.

You can also edit the templates from Design view. To do that, you select Edit Templates from the GridView control's smart tag menu to place the control in *template-editing mode*. Then, display the smart tag menu again and select the template you want to edit from the Display drop-down list. In this figure, for example, you can see the EditItem template for the Description column.

Although a text box is included in the EditItem template for a column by default, you should know that you can use other types of controls too. For example, you can use a check box to work with a Boolean column, and you can use a Calendar control to work with a date column. You can also use a drop-down list that lets the user select a value from the list. To do that, you must create a separate data source that retrieves the data for the list. Then, you can bind the drop-down list to this data source by setting the DataTextField and DataValueField attributes as shown in the last chapter, and you can bind the drop-down list to a column in the GridView's data source by setting its SelectedValue attribute using the DataBindings dialog box you'll see in the next figure.

How to edit templates

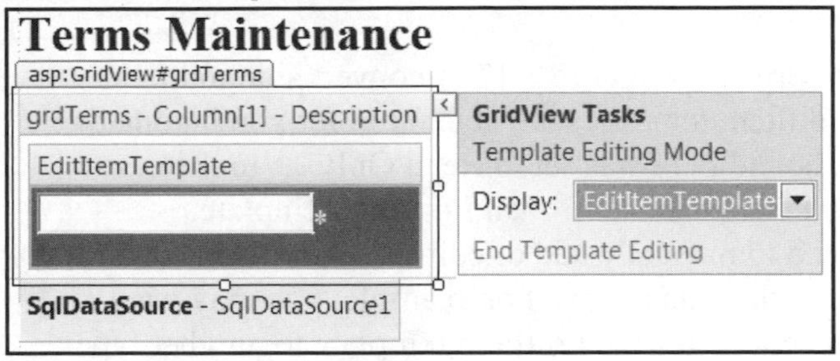

GridView template elements

Element	Description
ItemTemplate	The template used for an individual column.
AlternatingItemTemplate	The template used for alternate rows of a column.
EditItemTemplate	The template used for a column when the row is being edited.
HeaderTemplate	The template used for the column header.
FooterTemplate	The template used for the column footer.

A template field that includes a validation control

```
<asp:TemplateField HeaderText="Description">
    <ItemTemplate>
        <asp:Label ID="lblGridDescription" runat="server"
            Text='<%# Bind("Description") %>'></asp:Label>
    </ItemTemplate>
    <EditItemTemplate>
        <asp:TextBox ID="txtGridDescription" runat="server"
            Text='<%# Bind("Description") %>'></asp:TextBox>
        <asp:RequiredFieldValidator ID="RequiredFieldValidator3"
            runat="server" ControlToValidate="txtGridDescription"
            ErrorMessage="Description is a required field."
            ValidationGroup="Edit">*</asp:RequiredFieldValidator>
    </EditItemTemplate>
    <HeaderStyle HorizontalAlign="Left" />
    <ItemStyle Width="200px" />
</asp:TemplateField>
```

Description

- *Template fields* provide more control over the appearance of the columns in a GridView control. A common reason for using template fields is to add validation controls.
- To create a template field, first use the Fields dialog box to create a bound field. Then, click the Convert This Field into a TemplateField link.
- To edit a template, choose Edit Templates from the smart tag menu for the GridView control. Then, select the template you want to edit in the smart tag menu and edit the template by adding text or other controls. You may also want to change the names of the labels and text boxes that were generated when you converted to a template field. When you're finished, choose End Template Editing in the smart tag menu.

Figure 12-17 How to create template fields

How to bind the controls in a template

If you use the technique described in figure 12-17 to convert a bound field to a template field, Item and EditItem templates are generated for you automatically. Also, unless the original bound field was set to Read Only, as in the case of an identity field, a bound text box is added to each EditItem template.

In some cases, you may need to manually add or edit the controls in a template that you want to bind to the data source. For example, you may want to change the text box that's generated for the EditItem template to another type of control or add a control to the template. In either case, you can bind that control to the data source using the DataBindings dialog box shown in figure 12-18.

From the DataBindings dialog box, you can select the Field Binding option and then select the field you want to bind to from the first drop-down list. If you want to format the bound data, you can also select a format from the second drop-down list. And you can select which property of the control is bound to the data source by selecting that property from the Bindable Properties list. In most cases, however, the property you want is selected by default. In this figure, for example, the Text property of a text box is being bound, which is usually what you want.

As you make selections in the DataBindings dialog box, Visual Studio generates either an Eval or a Bind method that contains the data binding expression that's used to bind the control. These methods provide for displaying data in a control. If the field is Read Only, an Eval method is generated. If the field isn't Read Only, and therefore is editable, a Bind method is generated. You can see the syntax of the Eval and Bind methods in this figure along with three examples.

By default, the Two-way binding checkbox will be checked, unless the original bound field was Read Only. To generate a Bind method, this box should be checked.

Although the drop-down lists in the DataBindings dialog box make it easy to create a data binding expression, you can also create your own custom binding expressions. To do that, you just select the Custom Binding option and then enter the binding expression in the Code Expression text box. You might want to do that, for example, if you need to apply a custom format to the data.

The DataBindings dialog box for binding a text box

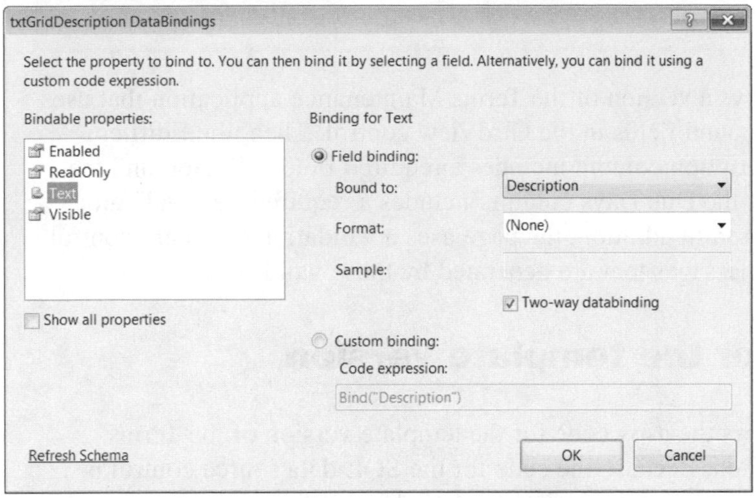

The syntax of the Eval and Bind methods

```
<%# {Eval|Bind}(NameString [,FormatString]) %>
```

Code examples

```
<%# Eval("Description") %>
<%# Eval("InvoiceTotal", "{0:c}") %>
<%# Bind("InvoiceTotal", "{0:c}") %>
```

Description

- To bind a control in a template, select the Edit DataBindings command from the smart tag menu for the control to display the DataBindings dialog box. Then, select the property you want to bind to, select the Field Binding option, and select the field you want to bind to from the Bound To drop-down list.
- If you want to apply a format to the bound data, select a format from the Format drop-down list.
- As you specify the binding for a control, Visual Studio generates a data binding expression that uses the Bind method. You can see this method in the Code Expression box at the bottom of the DataBindings dialog box. To generate an Eval method instead, uncheck the Two-way Databinding option.
- You can also create a custom binding expression by selecting the Custom Binding option and then entering the expression in the Code Expression text box.
- The Eval method provides a read-only display of data from a data source in a control. In contrast, the Bind method provides for *two-way binding*, which means that it can be used to display as well as update data from a data source.

Note

- If the Field Binding option isn't enabled, you can click the Refresh Schema link to enable it.

Figure 12-18 How to bind the controls in a template

The template version of the Terms Maintenance application

Figure 12-19 shows a version of the Terms Maintenance application that uses templates instead of bound fields in the GridView control. Then, the EditItem template for the Description column includes a required field validator, and the EditItem template for the Due Days column includes a required field validator and a compare validator. In addition, the page uses a validation summary control to display any error messages that are generated by these validators.

The aspx code for the template version

Figure 12-20 shows the aspx code for the template version of the Terms Maintenance application. Because the code for the SQL data source control is identical to the code in the file shown in figure 12-15, this figure doesn't show that code. Because you've already been introduced to most of the remaining code, I'll just point out a few highlights.

First, the GridView control uses template fields for the two columns that can be modified. The EditItem templates for these columns include validators that validate the data the user enters into the text boxes in the templates. Here, each validator is assigned to a validation group named Edit. Then, in the CommandField element for the Edit button, the CausesValidation attribute is set to True and the ValidationGroup attribute is set to Edit. As a result, just the validators that belong to the Edit group will be invoked when this button is clicked.

Note that I changed the Bind methods that were generated for the labels in the two Item templates for these columns to Eval methods. Although that wasn't necessary, it illustrates that two-way binding isn't needed in these templates because they don't provide for modifying the data.

Second, the ErrorMessage attribute of each of the Edit validators provides the error message that's displayed in the ValidationSummary control. For this control, you can see that the ValidationGroup is set to Edit so the right messages will be displayed. In addition, the content of each validator specifies that an asterisk will appear to the right of each field in the GridView control when the validator detects an error. If you look closely at the screen in the last figure, you can see that these asterisks are displayed in white on the dark column dividers.

Third, because this version uses a validation group for the validators in the GridView control, it must also use a validation group for the validators that are outside of the GridView control. As a result, the three validators for the text boxes as well as the Add Terms button all have a ValidationGroup attribute that assigns them to the Add group.

Last, page 2 of this code shows the asp controls and the table that is used to display the data below the GridView control. This starts with an ASP.NET ValidationSummary control that displays the error messages that are in the Edit group.

The Terms Maintenance application with template fields

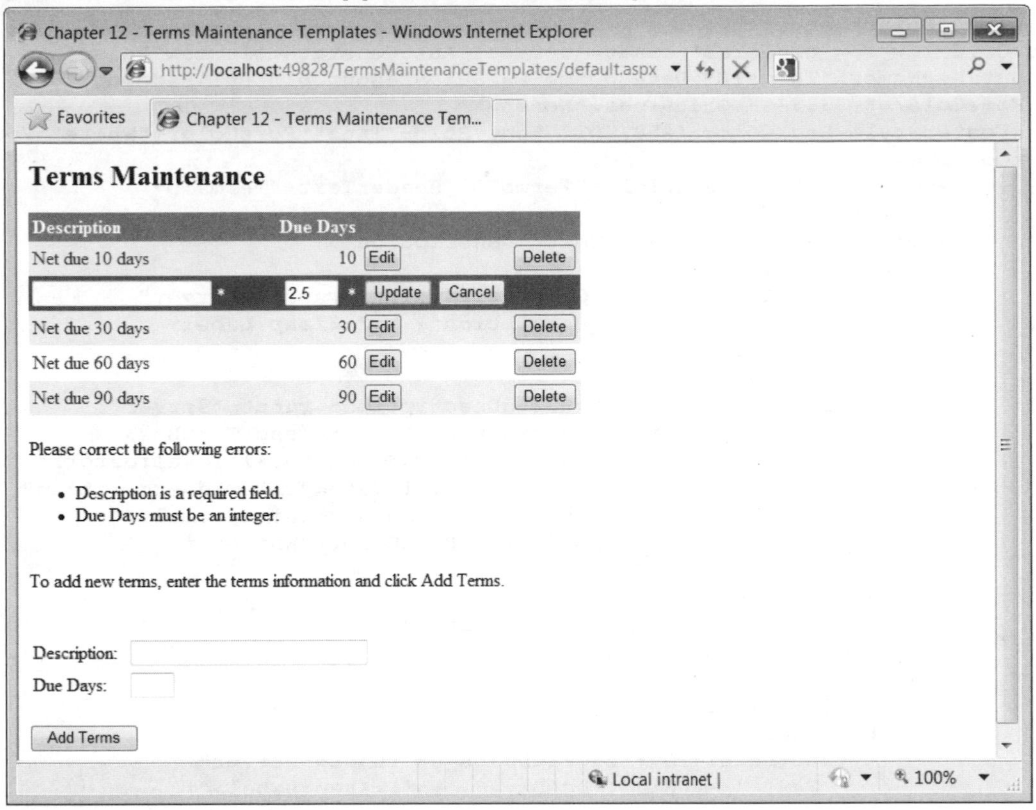

Description

- This version of the Terms Maintenance application uses template fields in the GridView control.
- The EditItem template for the Description field includes a required field validator, and the EditItem template for the Due Days field includes a required field validator and a compare validator.
- A ValidationSummary control is used to display the error messages generated by the validators.

Figure 12-19 The template version of the Terms Maintenance application

The Default.aspx file **Page 1**

```
<h2>Terms Maintenance</h2>
<asp:GridView ID="grdTerms" runat="server" AutoGenerateColumns="False"
    DataKeyNames="TermsID" DataSourceID="SqlDataSource1" CellPadding="3"
    ForeColor="#333333" GridLines="None">
    <FooterStyle BackColor="#507CD1" Font-Bold="True" ForeColor="White" />
    <Columns>
        <asp:BoundField DataField="TermsID" HeaderText="TermsID"
            Visible="False" />
        <asp:TemplateField HeaderText="Description">
            <ItemTemplate>
                <asp:Label ID="lblGridDescription" runat="server"
                 Text='<%# Bind("Description") %>'></asp:Label>
            </ItemTemplate>
            <EditItemTemplate>
                <asp:TextBox ID="txtGridDescription" runat="server"
                  Text='<%# Bind("Description") %>'></asp:TextBox>
                <asp:RequiredFieldValidator ID="RequiredFieldValidator3"
                    runat="server" ControlToValidate="txtGridDescription"
                    ErrorMessage="Description is a required field."
                    ValidationGroup="Edit" ForeColor="White">*
                </asp:RequiredFieldValidator>
            </EditItemTemplate>
            <HeaderStyle HorizontalAlign="Left" />
            <ItemStyle Width="200px" />
        </asp:TemplateField>
        <asp:TemplateField HeaderText="Due Days">
            <ItemTemplate>
                <asp:Label ID="lblGridDueDays" runat="server"
                  Text='<%# Bind("DueDays") %>'></asp:Label>
            </ItemTemplate>
            <EditItemTemplate>
                <asp:TextBox ID="txtGridDueDays" runat="server"
                    Text='<%# Bind("DueDays") %>' Width="40px"></asp:TextBox>
                <asp:RequiredFieldValidator ID="RequiredFieldValidator4"
                    runat="server" ControlToValidate="txtGridDueDays"
                    ErrorMessage="Due Days is a required field."
                    Display="Dynamic" ValidationGroup="Edit"
                    ForeColor="White">*</asp:RequiredFieldValidator>
                <asp:CompareValidator ID="CompareValidator2" runat="server"
                    ControlToValidate="txtGridDueDays" Display="Dynamic"
                    ErrorMessage="Due Days must be an integer."
                    Operator="DataTypeCheck" Type="Integer"
                    ValidationGroup="Edit" ForeColor="White">*
                </asp:CompareValidator>
            </EditItemTemplate>
            <HeaderStyle HorizontalAlign="Right" />
            <ItemStyle HorizontalAlign="Right" Width="75px" />
        </asp:TemplateField>
        <asp:CommandField ButtonType="Button" ShowEditButton="True"
            CausesValidation="True" ValidationGroup="Edit" />
        <asp:CommandField ButtonType="Button" ShowDeleteButton="True"
            CausesValidation="False" />
    </Columns>
</asp:GridView>
```

Figure 12-20 The aspx code for the template version of the Terms Maintenance application (part 1 of 2)

The Default.aspx file **Page 2**

```
<asp:ValidationSummary ID="ValidationSummary1" runat="server"
    HeaderText="Please correct the following errors:"
    ValidationGroup="Edit" /><br />
To add new terms, enter the terms information and click Add Terms.<br />
<asp:Label ID="lblError" runat="server" ForeColor="Red"
    EnableViewState="False"></asp:Label><br /><br />
<table>
  <tr>
    <td style="width: 80px">Description:</td>
    <td style="width: 124px">
        <asp:TextBox ID="txtDescription" runat="server" Width="200px">
        </asp:TextBox></td>
    <td style="width: 184px">
        <asp:RequiredFieldValidator ID="RequiredFieldValidator1"
            runat="server" ControlToValidate="txtDescription"
            ErrorMessage="Description is a required field."
            Display="Dynamic" Width="184px" ValidationGroup="Add">
        </asp:RequiredFieldValidator></td>
  </tr>
  <tr>
    <td style="width: 80px">Due Days:</td>
    <td style="width: 124px">
        <asp:TextBox ID="txtDueDays" runat="server" Width="32px">
        </asp:TextBox></td>
    <td style="width: 184px">
        <asp:RequiredFieldValidator ID="RequiredFieldValidator2"
            runat="server" ControlToValidate="txtDueDays"
            Display="Dynamic" ErrorMessage="Due Days is a required field."
            Width="176px" ValidationGroup="Add">
        </asp:RequiredFieldValidator>
        <asp:CompareValidator ID="CompareValidator1" runat="server"
            Display="Dynamic" ErrorMessage="Due Days must be an integer."
            Operator="DataTypeCheck" ControlToValidate="txtDueDays"
            Type="Integer" Width="184px" ValidationGroup="Add">
        </asp:CompareValidator></td>
  </tr>
</table>
<br />
<asp:Button ID="btnAdd" runat="server" Text="Add Terms"
    ValidationGroup="Add" />
```

Description

- The code for the SQL data source control and the GridView styles has been omitted since it's identical to the code in figure 12-15.
- Two validation groups are used by this form: one for the controls that validate a row that's being edited and one for the controls that validate a row that's being added.

Figure 12-20 The aspx code for the template version of the Terms Maintenance application (part 2 of 2)

Perspective

The GridView control works well for any application that displays a list of items retrieved from a database, and many applications have that need. It's also good for displaying search results, such as product searches for an online catalog or document searches in an online customer support site. And it's good for maintaining tables that have a small amount of data, such as the Terms table shown in this chapter.

In the next chapter, you'll build on your knowledge of the GridView control by learning how to use it in combination with the DetailsView control. This control is designed to display the details for an item that's selected from a GridView control or a list control. And the combination of a GridView control and a DetailsView control can be powerful.

Keep in mind that the goal of this chapter and the next one is to show you how ASP.NET data controls can be used with SQL data sources to display and update the data in a database. Then, chapter 14 will show you how these data controls can be used with object data sources. For a thorough treatment of the ASP.NET data controls, we recommend *Murach's ASP.NET 4 Web Programming with VB 2010.*

Terms

paging
data key
command field
edit mode
template field
template-editing mode
two-way binding

Exercise 12-1 Build the Terms Maintenance application

In this exercise, you start with a partial Terms Maintenance application like the one in figure 12-14. This starting application includes all of the controls except the GridView control as well as some of the Visual Basic code that the application requires. Then, you'll add the GridView control and complete the application.

Create and bind the GridView control

1. Use the File→Open Web Site command to open the TermsMaintenance project in the Chapter 12 directory.
2. Double-click on the Default.aspx file in the Solution Explorer to display the starting page in the Designer. Then, drag a GridView control from the Toolbox and drop it right below the SqlDataSource control.
3. Click on the Source button at the bottom of the Designer to display the aspx code for the page, and make sure that you've dropped the GridView control in the right place. If you haven't, you can move the source code to the right place.
4. In the aspx code, note the table after the GridView control. This table includes the labels and text boxes for getting the data for adding a new row. Note too that this code includes three ASP.NET validators that will check to make sure that the user has entered values for the description and due days and that the due days entry is an integer.
5. Use the GridView control's smart tag menu to assign SqlDataSource1 as its data source, and use the Properties pane to change the ID of the control to grdTerms.
6. Select Refresh Schema from the smart tag menu of the GridView control to create the three bound fields.
7. Select Auto Format from the smart tag menu of the GridView control, and then select Classic to create the look that's shown in figure 12-14.

Add command fields to the GridView control

8. Add a column that contains an Edit, Update, and Cancel command field. Then, change the button type from the default of Link to Button. If necessary, refer to figure 12-11 and recall that you can access the Fields dialog box by selecting Edit Columns from the GridView control's smart tag menu.
9. In the command field properties pane in the Fields dialog box, set the CausesValidation property of the command button to False.
10. Use the same techniques to add a column that contains a Delete command field and set its properties as in steps 6 and 7.

Add and test the code for the edit function

11. Double-click on the Default.aspx.vb file in the Solution Explorer to display the code for the web page. Then, enter the code needed to handle the RowUpdated event of the GridView control. You can see this code in figure 12-12.

12. Run the application. Then, click the Edit button for one of the rows, enter a non-numeric value into the Due Days text box, and click the Update button. This should display an exception message because the database doesn't accept non-numeric values in that column.
13. Delete the non-numeric value and leave the Due Days text box empty. Then, click the Update button again and confirm that an exception message is displayed. This time the exception message should explain that a null value isn't acceptable for this column.
14. Enter an integer value in the Due Days text box and click the Update button. This time, the update should be accepted.

Test the Add Terms function

15. In the Default.aspx.vb file, review the code for the btnAdd_Click function. This is the code that is executed when you click on the Add Terms button.
16. Test this function by clicking the Add Terms button without entering any data in the two text boxes above it. Then, note the messages to the right of the text boxes. These messages are displayed by the ASP.NET validators that you saw in the aspx code back in step 4.
17. Enter a description in the Description text box and a non-numeric value in the Due Days text box, and click on the Add Terms button. This time, the message to the right of the second text box is displayed by the third aspx validator.
18. Enter valid data for both text boxes, and click the Add Terms button. This adds the row to the database and displays the row in the GridView control.

Add and test the code for the delete function

19. In the Default.aspx.vb file, enter the code needed to handle the RowDeleted event of the GridView control. You can see this code in the listing in figure 12-16.
20. Test the delete function by clicking the Delete button for the row you added in step 18. This should work.
21. Test the delete function by clicking the Delete button for one of the old rows. This should display an exception message because a foreign key constraint in the Payables database won't allow the deletion. In other words, the row you're trying to delete is referred to by a foreign key in a row in another table. (Refer back to figure 1-6 if you need to refresh your memory on how this works.)

13

How to use the DetailsView control

In this chapter, you'll learn how to use the DetailsView control. This is another example of how the ASP.NET data controls can help you build web applications. Although this control is designed to work with the GridView control to display the details of the item selected in that control, it can also be used on its own or in combination with other types of list controls such as drop-down lists or list boxes.

How to use the DetailsView control

The following topics present the basics of working with the DetailsView control.

An introduction to the DetailsView control

As figure 13-1 shows, the DetailsView control is designed to display the data for a single row of a data source. To use this control effectively, you must provide some way for the user to select which data row to display. The most common way to do that is to use the DetailsView control in combination with another control such as a GridView control or a drop-down list. At the top of this figure, you can see how the DetailsView control works with a drop-down list, and you'll see how it works with a GridView control later in this chapter.

Alternatively, you can enable paging for the DetailsView control. Then, pager controls appear at the bottom of the DetailsView control that let the user select the row to be displayed. You'll learn how this works in figure 13-4.

As the code example in this figure shows, you use the DataSourceID attribute to specify the data source that a DetailsView control should be bound to. Then, the Fields element contains a set of child elements that define the individual fields to be displayed by the DetailsView control. This is similar to the way the Columns element for a GridView control works.

In figure 13-5, you will see the code for the SQL data source that this DetailsView control is bound to. This data source has a ControlParameter that gets the user's selection from the drop-down list and uses it to get the detailed data that will be displayed in the DetailsView control.

A DetailsView control can be displayed in one of three modes. In ReadOnly mode, the data for the current row in the data source is displayed but can't be modified. In Edit mode, the user can modify the data for the current row. And in Insert mode, the user can enter data that will be inserted into the data source as a new row.

A DetailsView control that displays data for a selected vendor

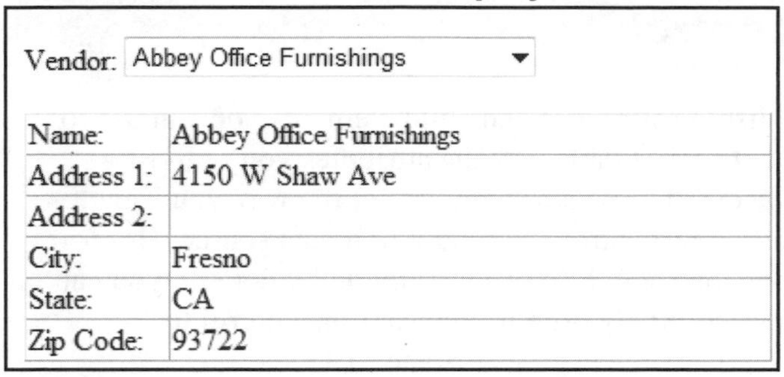

The aspx code for the DetailsView control shown above

```
<asp:DetailsView ID="DetailsView1" runat="server" AutoGenerateRows="False"
    DataSourceID="SqlDataSource2" Height="50px" Width="400px">
    <Fields>
        <asp:BoundField DataField="Name" HeaderText="Name:">
            <ItemStyle Width="325px" />
            <HeaderStyle Width="75px" />
        </asp:BoundField>
        <asp:BoundField DataField="Address1" HeaderText="Address 1:" />
        <asp:BoundField DataField="Address2" HeaderText="Address 2:" />
        <asp:BoundField DataField="City" HeaderText="City:" />
        <asp:BoundField DataField="State" HeaderText="State:" />
        <asp:BoundField DataField="ZipCode" HeaderText="Zip Code:" />
     </Fields>
</asp:DetailsView>
```

Three modes of the DetailsView control

Mode	Description
ReadOnly	Used to display an item from the data source.
Edit	Used to edit an item in the data source.
Insert	Used to insert a new item into the data source.

Description

- The DetailsView control displays data for a single row of a data source. It is usually used in combination with a drop-down list or GridView control that is used to select the row to be displayed.
- By default, the DetailsView element includes a Fields element that contains a BoundField element for each field retrieved from the data source.
- You can edit the fields collection by choosing Edit Fields from the smart tag menu of a DetailsView control.

Figure 13-1 An introduction to the DetailsView control

Attributes and child elements for the DetailsView control

The tables in figure 13-2 list the attributes and child elements you can use to declare a DetailsView control. The first table lists the attributes you're most likely to use for this control. Most of these attributes are set the way you want them when you create a DetailsView control and bind it to a data source. However, if you want to display the control in Edit or Insert mode by default, you can set the DefaultMode attribute accordingly. And if you want the control to provide for paging, you can set the AllowPaging attribute to True.

By the way, the DetailsView control has many other attributes you can use to specify the control's layout and formatting. For example, you can include attributes like Height, Width, BackColor, and ForeColor. To see all of the attributes that are available, you can use the HTML Editor's IntelliSense feature.

The second table in this figure lists the child elements that you can use between the start and end tags of the DetailsView element. Most of these elements provide styles and templates that control the formatting for the different parts of the DetailsView control. You saw the same approach used to apply styles to the GridView in some of the examples in the previous chapter.

The Fields element can contain any of the child elements listed in the third table of this figure. These elements describe the individual data fields that are displayed by the DetailsView control. You can use the HTML Editor to create these elements manually. You can use the Fields dialog box as described in chapter 11 by choosing Edit Fields from the smart tag menu. Or, you can use the Add Field dialog box as described in the next figure.

Although this figure doesn't show it, the child elements in the third table can themselves include child elements to specify formatting information. For example, you can include HeaderStyle and ItemStyle as child elements of a BoundField element to control the formatting for the header and item sections of a bound field. Here again, you can use the HTML Editor's IntelliSense feature to see what child elements are available and what attributes they support.

DetailsView control attributes

Attribute	Description
ID	The ID of this control.
Runat	Must specify "server".
DataSourceID	The ID of the data source to bind the DetailsView control to.
DataKeyNames	A list of field names that form the primary key for the data source.
AutoGenerateRows	If True, a row is automatically generated for each field in the data source. If False, you must define the rows in the Fields element.
DefaultMode	Sets the initial mode of the DetailsView control. Valid options are Edit, Insert, and ReadOnly. The default is ReadOnly.
AllowPaging	Set to True to allow paging.

DetailsView child elements

Element	Description
Fields	The fields that are displayed by a DetailsView control.
RowStyle	The style used for data rows in ReadOnly mode.
AlternatingRowStyle	The style used for alternate rows.
EditRowStyle	The style used for data rows in Edit mode.
InsertRowStyle	The style used for data rows in Insert mode.
CommandRowStyle	The style used for command rows.
EmptyDataRowStyle	The style used for data rows when the data source is empty.
EmptyDataTemplate	The template used when the data source is empty.
HeaderStyle	The style used for the header row.
HeaderTemplate	The template used for the header row.
FooterStyle	The style used for the footer row.
FooterTemplate	The template used for the footer row.
PagerSettings	The settings used to control the pager row.
PagerStyle	The style used for the pager row.
PagerTemplate	The template used for the pager row.

Fields child elements

Element	Description
asp:BoundField	A field bound to a data source column.
asp:ButtonField	A field that displays a button.
asp:CheckBoxField	A field that displays a check box.
asp:CommandField	A field that contains command buttons.
asp:HyperlinkField	A field that displays a hyperlink.
asp:ImageField	A field that displays an image.
asp:TemplateField	A column with custom content.

Figure 13-2 Attributes and child elements for the DetailsView control

How to add fields to a DetailsView control

By default, the Web Forms Designer generates a BoundField element for each column in the data source. Because of that, you usually won't need to add BoundField elements. Instead, you can modify the fields that are generated so they look and work the way you want them to.

However, if you delete a field from a DetailsView control and then decide to add it back, or if you modify the data source to include additional fields and don't refresh the DetailsView control, you can use the Add Field dialog box in figure 13-3 to add the fields. You can also use this dialog box to add other types of fields. Later in this chapter, for example, you'll see how to use this dialog box to add command fields.

To display the Add Field dialog box, you choose Add New Field from the DetailsView control's smart tag menu. Next, you select the type of field you want to add. Then, you set any other settings required by the field. If, for example, you select BoundField as the field type, you'll need to enter the text to display as a heading and identify the data source column you want to bind to.

Each time you use the Add Field dialog box, a child element is added to the Fields element of the DetailsView control. As you can see in the code example in this figure, each BoundField element includes a ReadOnly attribute that's set to True by default as well as a SortExpression attribute. If you don't want the ReadOnly attribute set to True, you can remove the check mark from the Read Only option in the Add Field dialog box. In addition, you can omit the SortExpression attribute since it has no effect on a BoundField element in a DetailsView control.

The Add Field dialog box

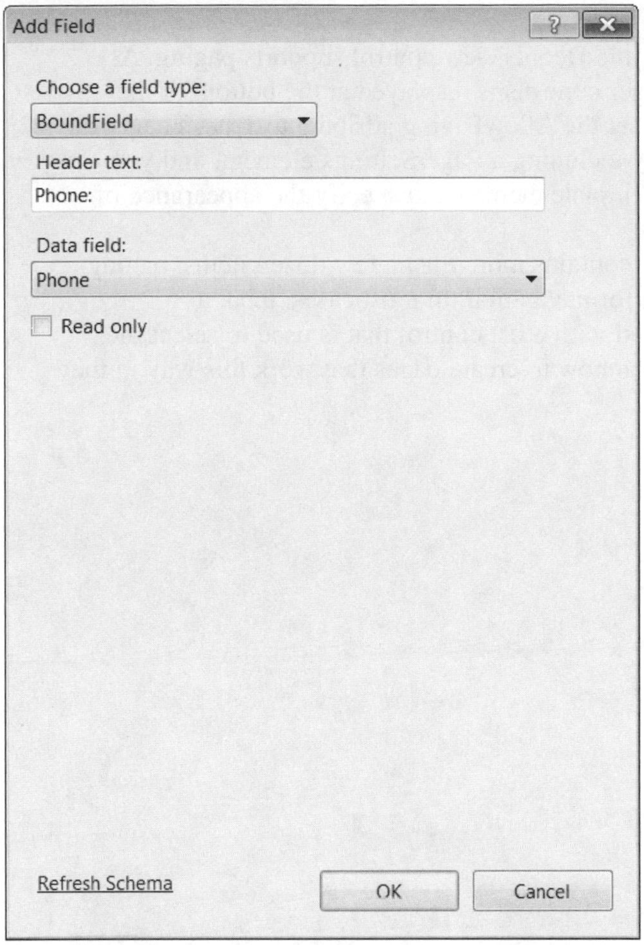

Aspx code generated by the Add Field dialog box

```
<asp:BoundField DataField="Phone" HeaderText="Phone:"
    ReadOnly="True" SortExpression="Phone" />
```

Description

- The DetailsView control supports the same field types as the GridView control.
- You can add a field to a DetailsView control by choosing Add New Field from the smart tag menu. Then, you can use the Add Field dialog box to add the field.
- You can also choose Edit Fields from the smart tag menu to bring up the Fields dialog box that's shown in figure 11-10 of chapter 11.
- By default, the DetailsView control includes one row for each column in the data source.

Figure 13-3 How to add fields to a DetailsView control

How to enable paging

Like the GridView control, the DetailsView control supports paging. As figure 13-4 shows, a row of pager controls is displayed at the bottom of the DetailsView control when you set the AllowPaging attribute to True. Then, you can specify the paging mode by including a PagerSettings element, and you can include PagerStyle and PagerTemplate elements to specify the appearance of the pager controls.

Note that if the data source contains more than a few dozen items, paging isn't a practical way to provide for navigation. In most cases, then, a DetailsView control is associated with a list control that is used to select the item to be displayed. You'll learn how to create pages that work this way in the next figure.

A DetailsView control that allows paging

Name:	American Booksellers Assoc
Address 1:	828 S Broadway
Address 2:	
City:	Tarrytown
State:	NY
Zip Code:	10591
<< < > >>	

The aspx code for the DetailsView control shown above

```
<asp:DetailsView ID="DetailsView1" runat="server" AllowPaging="True"
    AutoGenerateRows="False" DataSourceID="SqlDataSource1"
    Height="50px" Width="400px">
    <PagerSettings Mode="NextPreviousFirstLast" />
    <Fields>
        <asp:BoundField DataField="Name" HeaderText="Name:">
            <ItemStyle Width="325px" />
            <HeaderStyle Width="75px" />
        </asp:BoundField>
        <asp:BoundField DataField="Address1" HeaderText="Address 1:" />
        <asp:BoundField DataField="Address2" HeaderText="Address 2:" />
        <asp:BoundField DataField="City" HeaderText="City:" />
        <asp:BoundField DataField="State" HeaderText="State:" />
        <asp:BoundField DataField="ZipCode" HeaderText="Zip Code:" />
    </Fields>
</asp:DetailsView>
```

Description

- The DetailsView control supports paging, so you can move from one item to the next by using the pager controls. This works much the same as it does for a GridView control, except that data from only one row at a time is displayed.
- For more information about paging, please refer to figure 12-2 in chapter 12.

How to create a Master/Detail page

As figure 13-5 shows, a *Master/Detail page* is a page that displays a list of data items from a data source along with the details for one of the items selected from the list. The list of items can be displayed by any control that allows the user to select an item, including a drop-down list or a GridView control. Then, you can use a DetailsView control to display the details for the selected item. The page shown in figure 13-1 is an example of a Master/Detail page in which the master list is displayed as a drop-down list and a DetailsView control is used to display the details for the selected item.

A Master/Detail page typically uses two data sources. The first retrieves the items to be displayed by the control that contains the list of data items. For efficiency's sake, this data source should retrieve only the data columns necessary to display the list. For example, the data source for the drop-down list in figure 13-1 only needs to retrieve the VendorID and Name columns from the Vendors table in the Payables database.

The second data source provides the data for the selected item. It usually uses a parameter to specify which row should be retrieved from the database. In the example in this figure, the data source uses a parameter that's bound to the drop-down list. That way, this data source automatically retrieves the data for the vendor that's selected by the drop-down list.

A Master/Detail page typically contains:

- A control, such as a drop-down list or a GridView control, that lets the user choose an item to display.
- A data source that retrieves all of the items that are going to be displayed in the list control. Then, the list control should be bound to this data source.
- A DetailsView control that displays the data for the item selected by the user.
- A data source that retrieves the data that's displayed in the DetailsView control. Then, the DetailsView control should be bound to this data source.
- To retrieve the selected item, this second data source can use a parameter that's bound to the SelectedValue property of the control that contains the list of items.

A SQL data source control with a parameter that's bound to a list

```
<asp:SqlDataSource ID="SqlDataSource2" runat="server"
    ConnectionString="<%$ ConnectionStrings:PayablesConnectionString %>"
    SelectCommand="SELECT [Name], [Address1], [Address2], [City], [State],
            [ZipCode], [Phone]
        FROM [Vendors]
        WHERE ([VendorID] = @VendorID)">
    <SelectParameters>
        <asp:ControlParameter ControlID="ddlVendors" Name="VendorID"
            PropertyName="SelectedValue" Type="Int32" />
    </SelectParameters>
</asp:SqlDataSource>
```

Description

- A *Master/Detail page* is a page that displays a list of items from a database along with the details of one item from the list. The DetailsView control is often used to display the details portion of a Master/Detail page.
- The list portion of a Master/Detail page can be displayed by any control that contains a list of data items, including a drop-down list or a GridView control.
- A Master/Detail page usually includes two data sources: one for the master list and the other for the DetailsView control.

Figure 13-5 How to create a Master/Detail page

How to update DetailsView data

Besides displaying data for a specific item from a data source, you can use a DetailsView control to edit, insert, and delete items. You'll learn how to do that in the following topics.

An introduction to command buttons

Much like the GridView control, the DetailsView control uses command buttons to let the user edit and delete data. Thus, the DetailsView control provides Edit, Delete, Update, and Cancel buttons. In addition, the DetailsView control lets the user insert data, so it provides for two more buttons. The New button places the DetailsView control in Insert mode, and the Insert button accepts the data entered by the user and writes it to the data source. These command buttons are summarized in figure 13-6.

There are two ways to provide the command buttons for a DetailsView control. The easiest way is to use the AutoGenerate*xxx*Button attributes, which are listed in the second table and illustrated in the code example. However, when you use these attributes, you have no control over the appearance of the buttons. For that, you must use command fields as described in the next figure.

A DetailsView control with automatically generated command buttons

Name:	City Of Fresno
Address 1:	PO Box 2069
Address 2:	
City:	Fresno
State:	CA
Zip Code:	93718
Edit Delete New	

Command buttons

Button	Description
Edit	Places the DetailsView control in Edit mode.
Delete	Deletes the current item and leaves the DetailsView control in ReadOnly mode.
New	Places the DetailsView control in Insert mode.
Update	Displayed only in Edit mode. Updates the data source, then returns to ReadOnly mode.
Insert	Displayed only in Insert mode. Inserts the data, then returns to ReadOnly mode.
Cancel	Displayed in Edit and Insert mode. Cancels the operation and returns to ReadOnly mode.

Attributes that generate command buttons

Attribute	Description
AutoGenerateDeleteButton	Generates a Delete button.
AutoGenerateEditButton	Generates an Edit button.
AutoGenerateInsertButton	Generates a New button.

A DetailsView element that automatically generates command buttons

```
<asp:DetailsView ID="DetailsView1" runat="server" AutoGenerateRows="False"
    DataKeyNames="VendorID" DataSourceID="SqlDataSource2" Width="400px"
    BackColor="White" GridLines="None" Height="50px" BorderColor="White"
    BorderStyle="Ridge" BorderWidth="2px" CellPadding="3" CellSpacing="1"
    AutoGenerateDeleteButton="True"
    AutoGenerateEditButton="True"
    AutoGenerateInsertButton="True">
```

Description

- The DetailsView control supports six different command buttons.
- You can use the AutoGenerateDeleteButton, AutoGenerateEditButton, and AutoGenerateInsertButton attributes to automatically generate those command buttons.
- To customize command button appearance, use command fields instead of automatically generated buttons, as described in the next figure.

Figure 13-6 An introduction to command buttons

How to add command buttons

Like the GridView control, the DetailsView control lets you use command field elements to specify the command buttons that should be displayed by the control. One way to add command fields to a DetailsView control is to use the Add Field dialog box shown in figure 13-7. Of course, you can also use the Edit Fields dialog box to add command fields, or you can use the HTML Editor to code the CommandField elements manually.

When you select CommandField as the field type, a drop-down list lets you choose whether the command buttons should be displayed as buttons or hyperlinks. In addition, four check boxes appear that let you select which command buttons you want to show in the command field. For a DetailsView control, you typically include all of the command buttons you need in a single command field. That way, all of the buttons will be displayed in a single row of the control. In contrast, if you create a separate command field for each button, the buttons are displayed in separate rows of the control.

Note that the CommandField element includes attributes that let you specify the text or image to be displayed and whether the buttons cause validation. For more information about using these attributes, please refer back to chapter 12.

In the example in this figure, multiple CommandFields have been selected. As a result, the Delete, Edit and New buttons will be displayed side by side in the same row. Alternatively, you can create a separate CommandField for each button by selecting just one of the first three Command Button types. Each button will then be displayed in a separate row of the Details View control.

The Add Field dialog box also lets you add any of the types of child elements that are described in the third table of figure 13-2. To do that, you just select the type of field you want to create from the drop-down list at the top of the dialog box. Then, the appropriate options for that field type are displayed so you can fill in the required details.

The Add Field dialog box for adding a command field

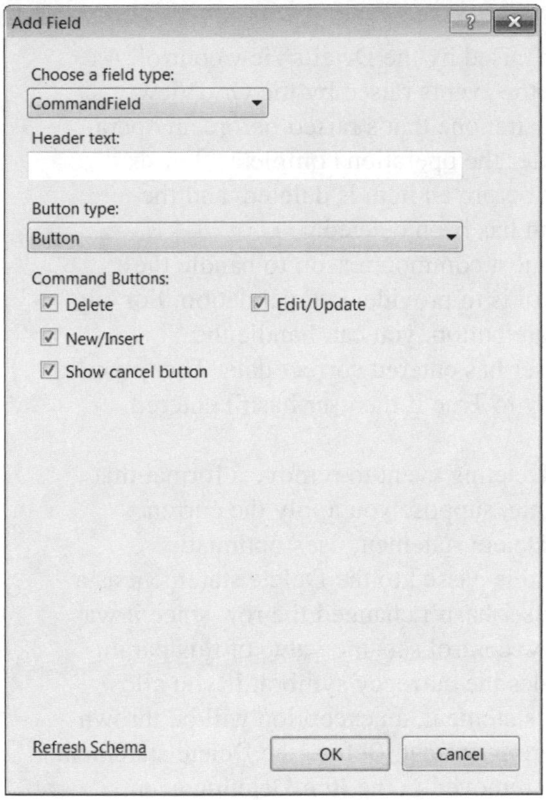

Code generated by the above dialog box

```
<asp:CommandField ButtonType="Button"
    ShowDeleteButton="True"
    ShowEditButton="True"
    ShowInsertButton="True" />
```

Description

- You can add command fields to a DetailsView control to let the user update, insert, and delete data.
- The command fields for a DetailsView control are similar to the command fields for a GridView control. However, the DetailsView control doesn't provide a Select command field, and it does provide New and Insert command fields. For more information about command fields, please refer to figure 12-11 in chapter 12.
- To display the Add Field dialog box, choose Add New Field from the smart tag menu of the DetailsView control.
- When you use the Add Field dialog box to add a command field, a single command field is created for all the buttons you select. That way, all the buttons are displayed in a single row of the DetailsView control. If you create an individual command field for each button, each button is displayed in a separate row of the DetailsView control.

Figure 13-7 How to add command fields

How to handle DetailsView events

Figure 13-8 lists the events that are raised by the DetailsView control. As you can see, these events are similar to the events raised by the GridView control. Most of these events come in pairs: one that's raised before an operation occurs, and another that's raised after the operation completes. For example, the ItemDeleting event is raised before an item is deleted, and the ItemDeleted event is raised after an item has been deleted.

As with the GridView control, the most common reason to handle the before events for the DetailsView control is to provide data validation. For example, when the user clicks the Update button, you can handle the ItemUpdating event to make sure the user has entered correct data. Then, you can set the e argument's Cancel property to True if the user hasn't entered correct data. This cancels the update.

You may also need to use the ItemDeleting event to remove a format that was applied to a bound field. For example, suppose you apply the currency format to a numeric field. Then, if the Delete statement uses optimistic concurrency, the value of the bound field is passed to the Delete statement as a parameter so it can check that another user hasn't changed the row since it was retrieved. Unfortunately, the DetailsView control sets the value of this parameter to its formatted value, which includes the currency symbol. If you allow this value to be passed on to the Delete statement, an exception will be thrown because the parameter value is in the wrong format. Before the Delete statement is executed, then, the formatting can be removed in the ItemDeleting event handler. Note that a similar event handler isn't required when you update a row because the DetailsView control doesn't use the format string in Edit mode by default.

The after-action events let you check that database operations have completed successfully. To do that, you need to check for two types of errors. First, you should check for database exceptions by testing the Exception property of the e argument. If it isn't Nothing, a database exception has occurred. Then, you should display an appropriate error message to let the user know about the problem.

If the data source uses optimistic concurrency, you should also check that there hasn't been a concurrency error. You can do that by testing the AffectedRows property of the e argument. If a concurrency error has occurred, this property will be set to zero meaning that no rows have been changed. Then, you can display an appropriate error message.

If no errors occurred during the update operation, the ItemUpdated event shown in this figure ends by calling the DataBind method for the drop-down list control. This is necessary because view state is enabled for this control. As a result, this control will continue to display the old data unless you call its DataBind method to refresh its data. If view state were disabled for this control, the DataBind call wouldn't be necessary.

Events raised by the DetailsView control

Event	Description
ItemCommand	Raised when a button is clicked.
ItemCreated	Raised when an item is created.
DataBound	Raised when data binding completes for an item.
ItemDeleted	Raised when an item has been deleted.
ItemDeleting	Raised when an item is about to be deleted.
ItemInserted	Raised when an item has been inserted.
ItemInserting	Raised when an item is about to be inserted.
ItemUpdated	Raised when an item has been updated.
ItemUpdating	Raised when an item is about to be updated.
PageIndexChanged	Raised when the index of the displayed item has changed.
PageIndexChanging	Raised when the index of the displayed item is about to change.

An event handler for the ItemUpdated event

```
Protected Sub dvVendor_ItemUpdated(ByVal sender As Object,
        ByVal e As System.Web.UI.WebControls.DetailsViewUpdatedEventArgs) _
        Handles dvVendor.ItemUpdated
    If e.Exception IsNot Nothing Then
        lblError.Text = "An exception occurred. " &
            e.Exception.Message
        e.ExceptionHandled = True
        e.KeepInEditMode = True
    ElseIf e.AffectedRows = 0 Then
        lblError.Text = "Another user has updated or deleted " &
            "that vendor. Please try again."
    Else
        ddlVendors.DataBind()
    End If
End Sub
```

Description

- Like the GridView control, the DetailsView control raises events that can be handled when data is updated. At the minimum, you should use these events to test for database exceptions and concurrency errors.
- To determine if a SQL exception has occurred, test the Exception property of the e argument. If an exception has occurred, you can set the ExceptionHandled property to True to suppress the exception. You can also set the KeepInEditMode property to True to keep the DetailsView control in Edit mode.
- If the AffectedRows property of the e argument is zero and an exception has not been thrown, a concurrency error has probably occurred.
- If the DetailsView control is used on a Master/Detail page, you should call the DataBind method of the master list control after a successful insert, update, or delete operation.

Figure 13-8 How to handle DetailsView events

How to create template fields

Like the GridView control, you can use template fields to control the appearance of the fields in a DetailsView control. You can do that to add validation controls or to use controls other than text boxes as described in the last chapter or to modify the text boxes that are displayed by default. Figure 13-9 illustrates how this works.

At the top of this figure, you can see a DetailsView control that doesn't use templates displayed in Edit mode. Here, the text boxes that are generated by default aren't big enough to display all of the data in the first two fields for the selected vendor. In addition, only the state code is displayed, not the state name, which makes it more difficult for the user to change the state.

The second DetailsView control illustrates how you can use templates to make it easier for the user to work with the data. Here, the text boxes for the first four fields have been enlarged so all the data in these fields can be displayed at once. In addition, the text box for the state code has been replaced by a drop-down list that displays the state name. This control is bound to a separate data source that retrieves the state codes and state names from the States table.

To create template fields for a DetailsView control, you use the same techniques you use to create templates for a GridView control. That is, you convert bound fields to template fields, you switch to template-editing mode, and you select the template you want to edit. The table in this figure lists the five templates that are available for the template fields in a DetailsView control. In most cases, you'll define just the Item, EditItem, and InsertItem templates as shown in the code example in this figure.

A DetailsView control without templates displayed in Edit mode

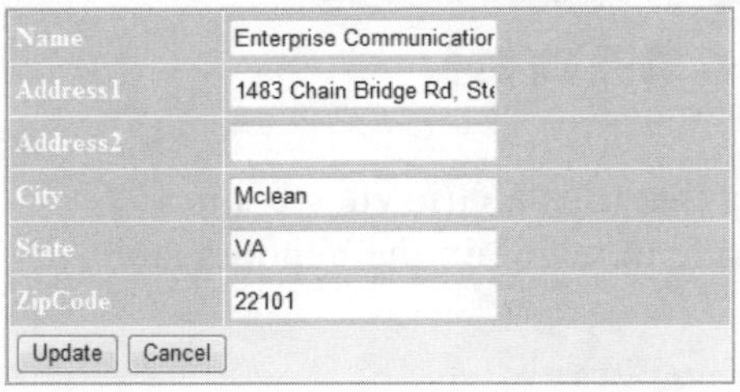

A DetailsView control with custom templates displayed in Edit mode

DetailsView template elements

Element	Description
ItemTemplate	The template used for an individual field.
AlternatingItemTemplate	The template used for alternating fields.
EditItemTemplate	The template used for a field in Edit mode.
InsertItemTemplate	The template used for a field in Insert mode.
HeaderTemplate	The template used for the header text for a field.

The aspx code for a custom template field

```
<asp:TemplateField HeaderText="Name:">
    <ItemTemplate>
        <asp:Label ID="Label4" runat="server"
            Text='<%# Bind("Name") %>'></asp:Label>
    </ItemTemplate>
    <EditItemTemplate>
        <asp:TextBox ID="txtEditName" runat="server"
            Text='<%# Bind("Name") %>' Width="300px"></asp:TextBox>
    </EditItemTemplate>
    <InsertItemTemplate>
        <asp:TextBox ID="txtInsertName" runat="server"
            Text='<%# Bind("Name") %>' Width="300px"></asp:TextBox>
    </InsertItemTemplate>
</asp:TemplateField>
```

Description

- You can use template fields to control the appearance of the fields in a DetailsView control using the same techniques you use to work with template fields in a GridView control. See figure 12-17 in chapter 12 for more information.

Figure 13-9 How to create template fields

A Vendor Maintenance application that uses a DetailsView control

The following topics present an application that uses a GridView control and a DetailsView control in a Master/Detail page to maintain the Vendors table in the Payables database.

The operation of the application

Figure 13-10 shows the operation of the Vendor Maintenance application. This application uses a GridView control to list the vendors on the left side of the page. This control uses paging so the user can scroll through the entire Vendors table.

When the user clicks the Select button for a vendor, the details for that vendor are displayed in the DetailsView control on the right side of the page. Then, the user can use the Edit or Delete buttons to edit or delete the selected vendor. The user can also click the New button to insert a new vendor.

The aspx file

Figure 13-11 shows the Default.aspx file for the Vendor Maintenance application. This file uses a table to control the overall layout of the page. On page 1 of this listing, you can see the GridView control that displays the vendors, as well as the data source for this control. Notice that the SelectedIndex attribute of the GridView control is set to 0. That way, the information for the first vendor will be displayed in the DetailsView control when the page is first displayed.

The DetailsView control is shown on pages 2 and 3 of the listing. Here, the DetailsView element includes the attributes that control the overall appearance of the control. I generated most of these attributes by applying a scheme to the DetailsView control. Then, I edited the attributes to change the colors. You can also see that the scheme added RowStyle, EditRowStyle, and HeaderStyle elements. Since an InsertRowStyle element isn't included, this style will default to the EditRowStyle.

Except for the field for the VendorID column, all of the bound fields have been converted to template fields. Then, the EditItem and InsertItem templates for these fields were modified so the fields are displayed as shown in the second DetailsView control you saw in figure 13-9. In addition, required field validators were added for the Name, Address1, City, and ZipCode fields. Finally, a command field that provides for Edit, Delete, and New buttons was added.

The Vendor Maintenance page

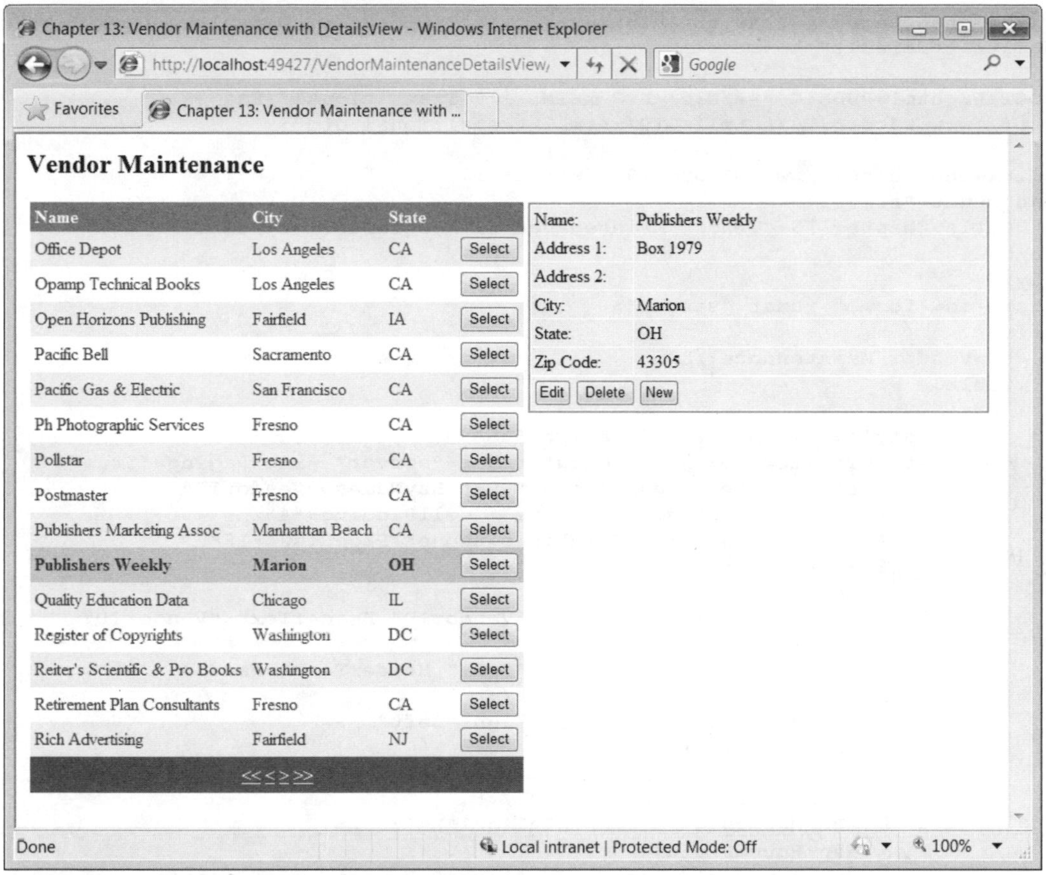

Description

- The Vendor Maintenance application uses GridView and DetailsView controls to let the user update the data in the Vendors table.
- To select a vendor, the user locates the vendor in the GridView control and clicks the Select button. This displays the details for the vendor in the DetailsView control. Then, the user can click the Edit button to change the vendor data or the Delete button to delete the vendor.
- To add a new vendor to the database, the user clicks the New button in the DetailsView control. Then, the user can enter the data for the new vendor and click the Insert button.

Figure 13-10 The operation of the Vendor Maintenance application

The Default.aspx file

Page 1

```
<%@ Page Language="VB" AutoEventWireup="false" CodeFile="Default.aspx.vb"
Inherits="_Default" %>

<!DOCTYPE html PUBLIC "-//W3C//DTD XHTML 1.0 Transitional//EN"
"http://www.w3.org/TR/xhtml1/DTD/xhtml1-transitional.dtd">

<html xmlns="http://www.w3.org/1999/xhtml" >
<head runat="server">
    <title>Chapter 13: Vendor Maintenance with DetailsView</title>
</head>
<body>
  <form id="form1" runat="server">
  <div>
    <h2>Vendor Maintenance</h2>
    <table>
      <tr>
        <td style="width: 520px" valign="top">
          <asp:GridView ID="grdVendors" runat="server" AllowPaging="True"
              AutoGenerateColumns="False" DataKeyNames="VendorID"
              DataSourceID="SqlDataSource1" CellPadding="4"
              ForeColor="#333333"GridLines="None" PageSize="15"
              SelectedIndex="0">
            <Columns>
              <asp:BoundField DataField="VendorID" HeaderText="VendorID"
                  Visible="False" />
              <asp:BoundField DataField="Name" HeaderText="Name">
                <ItemStyle Width="225px" />
                <HeaderStyle HorizontalAlign="Left" />
              </asp:BoundField>
              <asp:BoundField DataField="City" HeaderText="City">
                <ItemStyle Width="130px" />
                <HeaderStyle HorizontalAlign="Left" />
              </asp:BoundField>
              <asp:BoundField DataField="State" HeaderText="State">
                <ItemStyle Width="65px" />
                <HeaderStyle HorizontalAlign="Left" />
              </asp:BoundField>
              <asp:CommandField ButtonType="Button" ShowSelectButton="True" />
            </Columns>
            <SelectedRowStyle BackColor="LightSteelBlue" Font-Bold="True"
                ForeColor="#333333" />
            <PagerStyle BackColor="#2461BF" ForeColor="White"
                HorizontalAlign="Center" />
            <HeaderStyle BackColor="#507CD1" Font-Bold="True"
               ForeColor="White" />
            <AlternatingRowStyle BackColor="White" />
            <RowStyle BackColor="#EFF3FB" />
            <PagerSettings Mode="NextPreviousFirstLast" />
          </asp:GridView>
          <asp:SqlDataSource ID="SqlDataSource1" runat="server"
              ConnectionString=
                  "<%$ ConnectionStrings:PayablesConnectionString %>"
              SelectCommand="SELECT [VendorID], [Name], [City], [State]
                  FROM [Vendors] ORDER BY [Name]">
          </asp:SqlDataSource>
        </td>
```

Figure 13-11 The aspx file for the Vendor Maintenance application (part 1 of 4)

The Default.aspx file **Page 2**

```
<td style="width: 430px" valign="top">
  <asp:DetailsView ID="dvVendor" runat="server" AutoGenerateRows="False"
      DataKeyNames="VendorID" DataSourceID="SqlDataSource2" Height="50px"
      Width="425" BackColor="White" BorderColor="White" BorderStyle="Ridge"
      BorderWidth="2px" CellPadding="3" CellSpacing="1" GridLines="None">
    <Fields>
      <asp:BoundField DataField="VendorID" HeaderText="VendorID"
          Visible="False" />
      <asp:TemplateField HeaderText="Name:">
        <ItemTemplate>
          <asp:Label ID="Label4" runat="server"
              Text='<%# Bind("Name") %>'></asp:Label>
        </ItemTemplate>
        <EditItemTemplate>
          <asp:TextBox ID="txtName" runat="server"
              Text='<%# Bind("Name") %>' Width="300px"></asp:TextBox>
          <asp:RequiredFieldValidator ID="RequiredFieldValidator1"
              runat="server" ControlToValidate="txtName"
              ErrorMessage="Name is a required field.">*
          </asp:RequiredFieldValidator>
        </EditItemTemplate>
        <InsertItemTemplate>
          <asp:TextBox ID="txtName" runat="server"
              Text='<%# Bind("Name") %>' Width="300px"></asp:TextBox>
          <asp:RequiredFieldValidator ID="RequiredFieldValidator5"
              runat="server" ControlToValidate="txtName"
              ErrorMessage="Name is a required field.">*
          </asp:RequiredFieldValidator>
        </InsertItemTemplate>
        <ItemStyle Width="335px" />
        <HeaderStyle Width="90px" />
      </asp:TemplateField>
      .
      .
      <asp:TemplateField HeaderText="State:">
        <ItemTemplate>
          <asp:Label ID="Label1" runat="server"
              Text='<%# Bind("State") %>'></asp:Label>
        </ItemTemplate>
        <EditItemTemplate>
          <asp:DropDownList ID="ddlState" runat="server"
              DataSourceID="SqlDataSource3" DataTextField="StateName"
              DataValueField="StateCode"
              SelectedValue='<%# Bind("State") %>' Width="160px">
          </asp:DropDownList>
        </EditItemTemplate>
        <InsertItemTemplate>
          <asp:DropDownList ID="ddlState" runat="server"
              DataSourceID="SqlDataSource3" DataTextField="StateName"
              DataValueField="StateCode"
              SelectedValue='<%# Bind("State") %>' Width="160px">
          </asp:DropDownList>
        </InsertItemTemplate>
      </asp:TemplateField>
      .
      .
```

Figure 13-11 The aspx file for the Vendor Maintenance application (part 2 of 4)

In part 3 of this figure, you can see the aspx code for the data source that the DetailsView control is bound to. A data source is also included for the drop-down lists that are used to display the states in the EditItem and InsertItem templates for the State field. If you look back at the definitions of these controls, you'll see how they're bound to this data source.

The code-behind file

Figure 13-12 shows the code-behind file for the Default page of the Vendor Maintenance application. Even though this application provides complete maintenance for the Vendors table, only four event handlers are required. The first three event handlers respond to events raised by the DetailsView control. They handle database exceptions and concurrency errors for updates, deletions, and insertions. The last event handler handles any other exceptions that might occur.

Note that the error-handling code for the insert event handler is simpler than the error-handling code for the update and delete event handlers. That's because optimistic concurrency doesn't apply to insert operations. As a result, there's no need to check the AffectedRows property to see if a concurrency error has occurred.

The Default.aspx file **Page 3**

```
        <asp:CommandField ButtonType="Button"
            ShowDeleteButton="True"
            ShowEditButton="True"
            ShowInsertButton="True" />
    </Fields>
    <RowStyle BackColor="#EFF3FB" ForeColor="Black" />
    <EditRowStyle BackColor="LightSteelBlue" Font-Bold="True"
        ForeColor="White" />
    <HeaderStyle BackColor="#4A3C8C" Font-Bold="True"
        ForeColor="#E7E7FF" />
</asp:DetailsView>
<asp:SqlDataSource ID="SqlDataSource2" runat="server"
    ConflictDetection="CompareAllValues"
    ConnectionString="<%$ ConnectionStrings:PayablesConnectionString %>"
    OldValuesParameterFormatString="original_{0}"
    SelectCommand="SELECT [VendorID], [Name], [Address1], [Address2],
            [City], [State], [ZipCode]
        FROM Vendors
        WHERE VendorID = @VendorID"
    DeleteCommand="DELETE FROM [Vendors]
        WHERE [VendorID] = @original_VendorID
          AND [Name] = @original_Name
          AND [Address1] = @original_Address1
          AND ( [Address2] = @original_Address2
           OR Address2 IS NULL AND @original_Address2 IS NULL )
          AND [City] = @original_City
          AND [State] = @original_State
          AND [ZipCode] = @original_ZipCode"
    InsertCommand="INSERT INTO [Vendors]
            ([Name], [Address1], [Address2], [City], [State], [ZipCode])
        VALUES (@Name, @Address1, @Address2, @City, @State, @ZipCode)"
    UpdateCommand="UPDATE [Vendors]
        SET [Name] = @Name, [Address1] = @Address1,
            [Address2] = @Address2, [City] = @City,
            [State] = @State, [ZipCode] = @ZipCode
        WHERE [VendorID] = @original_VendorID
          AND [Name] = @original_Name
          AND [Address1] = @original_Address1
          AND ( [Address2] = @original_Address2
           OR Address2 IS NULL AND @original_Address2 IS NULL )
          AND [City] = @original_City
          AND [State] = @original_State
          AND [ZipCode] = @original_ZipCode">
```

Figure 13-11 The aspx file for the Vendor Maintenance application (part 3 of 4)

The Default.aspx file **Page 4**

```
<SelectParameters>
  <asp:ControlParameter ControlID="grdVendors" Name="VendorID"
      PropertyName="SelectedValue" Type="Int32" />
</SelectParameters>
<DeleteParameters>
  <asp:Parameter Name="original_VendorID" Type="Int32" />
  <asp:Parameter Name="original_Name" Type="String" />
  <asp:Parameter Name="original_Address1" Type="String" />
  <asp:Parameter Name="original_Address2" Type="String" />
  <asp:Parameter Name="original_City" Type="String" />
  <asp:Parameter Name="original_State" Type="String" />
  <asp:Parameter Name="original_ZipCode" Type="String" />
</DeleteParameters>
<UpdateParameters>
  <asp:Parameter Name="Name" Type="String" />
  <asp:Parameter Name="Address1" Type="String" />
  <asp:Parameter Name="Address2" Type="String" />
  <asp:Parameter Name="City" Type="String" />
  <asp:Parameter Name="State" Type="String" />
  <asp:Parameter Name="ZipCode" Type="String" />
  <asp:Parameter Name="original_VendorID" Type="Int32" />
  <asp:Parameter Name="original_Name" Type="String" />
  <asp:Parameter Name="original_Address1" Type="String" />
  <asp:Parameter Name="original_Address2" Type="String" />
  <asp:Parameter Name="original_City" Type="String" />
  <asp:Parameter Name="original_State" Type="String" />
  <asp:Parameter Name="original_ZipCode" Type="String" />
</UpdateParameters>
<InsertParameters>
  <asp:Parameter Name="Name" Type="String" />
  <asp:Parameter Name="Address1" Type="String" />
  <asp:Parameter Name="Address2" Type="String" />
  <asp:Parameter Name="City" Type="String" />
  <asp:Parameter Name="State" Type="String" />
  <asp:Parameter Name="ZipCode" Type="String" />
</InsertParameters>
</asp:SqlDataSource>
<asp:SqlDataSource ID="SqlDataSource3" runat="server"
    ConnectionString="<%$ ConnectionStrings:PayablesConnectionString %>"
    SelectCommand="SELECT [StateCode], [StateName] FROM [States]
        ORDER BY [StateName]">
</asp:SqlDataSource>
<br />
<asp:ValidationSummary ID="ValidationSummary1" runat="server"
    HeaderText="Please correct the following errors:" />
<br />
<asp:Label ID="lblError" runat="server" EnableViewState="False"
    ForeColor="Red"></asp:Label>
        </td>
      </tr>
    </table>
  </div>
  </form>
</body>
</html>
```

Figure 13-11 The aspx file for the Vendor Maintenance application (part 4 of 4)

The Default.aspx.vb file

```
Partial Class _Default
    Inherits System.Web.UI.Page

    Protected Sub dvVendor_ItemDeleted(ByVal sender As Object,
            ByVal e As System.Web.UI.WebControls.DetailsViewDeletedEventArgs) _
            Handles dvVendor.ItemDeleted
        If e.Exception IsNot Nothing Then
            lblError.Text = "An exception occurred. " &
                e.Exception.Message
        ElseIf e.AffectedRows = 0 Then
            lblError.Text = "Another user has updated or deleted " &
              "that vendor. Please try again."
    Else
        grdVendors.DataBind()
    End If
    End Sub

    Protected Sub dvVendor_ItemInserted(ByVal sender As Object,
            ByVal e As System.Web.UI.WebControls.DetailsViewInsertedEventArgs) _
            Handles dvVendor.ItemInserted
        If e.Exception IsNot Nothing Then
            lblError.Text = "An exception occurred. " &
                e.Exception.Message
            e.ExceptionHandled = True
        Else
            grdVendors.DataBind()
        End If
    End Sub

    Protected Sub dvVendor_ItemUpdated(ByVal sender As Object,
            ByVal e As System.Web.UI.WebControls.DetailsViewUpdatedEventArgs) _
            Handles dvVendor.ItemUpdated
        If e.Exception IsNot Nothing Then
            lblError.Text = "An exception occurred. " &
                e.Exception.Message
            e.ExceptionHandled = True
            e.KeepInEditMode = True
        ElseIf e.AffectedRows = 0 Then
            lblError.Text = "Another user has updated or deleted " &
                "that vendor. Please try again."
        Else
            grdVendors.DataBind()
        End If
    End Sub

    Protected Sub Page_Error(ByVal sender As Object,
            ByVal e As System.EventArgs) Handles Me.Error
        Dim ex As Exception
        ex = Server.GetLastError
        Session("Exception") = ex
        Response.Redirect("ErrorPage.aspx")
    End Sub

End Class
```

Figure 13-12 The code-behind file for the Vendor Maintenance application

Perspective

The DetailsView control is a second example of an ASP.NET data control that makes it easier to build web applications. Remember, though, that the emphasis of this book is on the database programming for web applications, not the ASP.NET data controls. That's why this book only presents the GridView and DetailsView controls. To learn how to use the other ASP.NET data controls and for a complete treatment of ASP.NET web programming, we recommend *Murach's ASP.NET 4 Web Programming with VB 2010.*

In the next chapter, you'll learn more about the database programming for web applications. Specifically, you'll learn how to use object data sources to get the data for the data controls. Unlike SQL data sources, object data sources let you separate the data access code from the presentation code and still take advantage of data binding.

Term

Master/Detail page

Exercise 13-1 Create a maintenance application with a DetailsView control

In this exercise, you start with a partial application for the Vendors page that follows. This starting application includes all of the controls except the DetailsView control. Then, you'll add that control and complete the application.

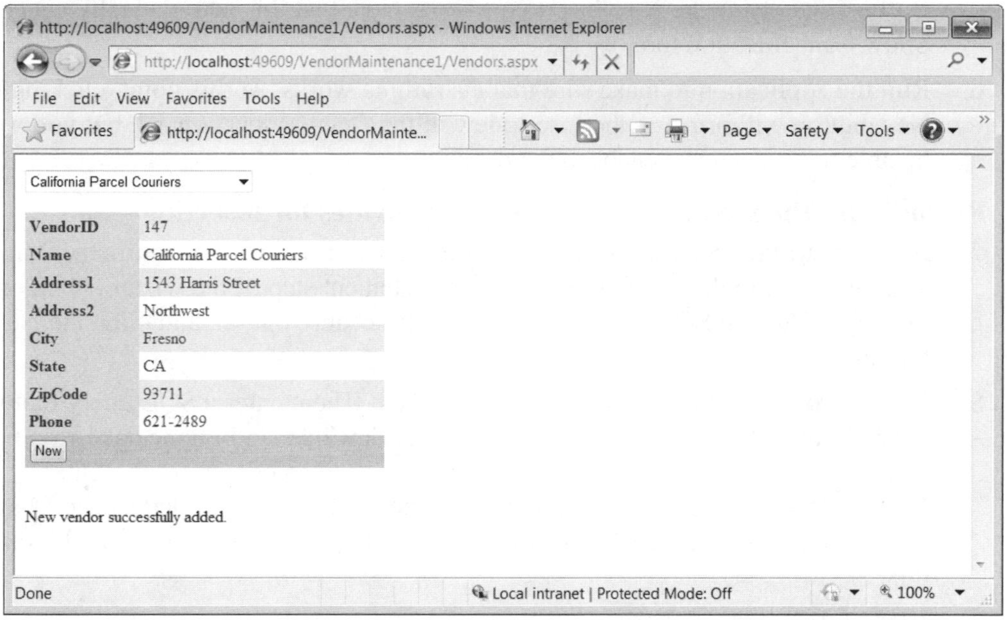

Create and bind the DetailsView control

1. Use the File→Open Web Site command to open the VendorMaintenance web site in the Chapter 13 directory. Then, run this application to see that the drop-down list is populated by the data source that it's bound to.
2. Double-click on the Vendors.aspx file in the Solution Explorer to display the starting page in the Designer. Then, drag a DetailsView control from the Toolbox and drop it right below the SqlDataSource1 control. To put space above and below this control, press the Enter key in the Designer. Then, click the Source button at the bottom of the Designer to see that pressing the Enter key has added <br /> tags to the HTML.
3. In Design view, Drag and drop a second SqlDataSource control right after the DetailsView control. This data source should select the VendorID, Name, Address1, Address2, City, State, ZipCode and Phone fields from the Vendors table in the Payables database. Then, click the WHERE Button, select the VendorID column as the column to compare, and the ddlVendors control for the parameter property. If necessary, look back at figure 11-5 in chapter 11 to see how this works. (Tip: Don't forget to click the Add button before leaving this dialog box).

4. Set the data source of the DetailsView control to SqlDataSource2. Next, click Auto Format and select the Simple style from the list of options. Then, increase the width of this control by clicking on the handle at the right hand edge and dragging outwards until its width is about 350 pixels.
5. Select the Add New Field option from the smart tag menu of the DetailsView control. Then, choose the Field Type of CommandField; change the Button Type to Button; and check the New/Insert checkbox. Note that this automatically checks the Show Cancel Button too.
6. Run the application to make sure that everything works. At this point, clicking the New button will bring up the Insert view of the DetailsView control, but you won't be able to save a new vendor to the database.

Reconfigure the second data source so it provides for inserting

7. In the smart tag menu for the SqlDataSource2 control, click on Configure Data Source. Then, in the Configure the Select Statement step of the wizard, click on the Specify a Custom SQL statement or Stored Procedure option, and click the Next button.
8. In the next dialog box, click on the INSERT tab. Then, enter a SQL query that will insert Name, Address1, Address2, City, State, ZipCode, and Phone data for a new vendor into the Vendors table. You can either enter the code or use the Query Builder. If you use the query builder, enter the field name preceded by the @ symbol (e.g. @Name) in the New Value column. The completed statement should look like this:

```
INSERT INTO [Vendors]
 ([Name], [Address1], [Address2], [City], [State], [ZipCode], [Phone])
VALUES
 (@Name, @Address1, @Address2, @City, @State, @ZipCode, @Phone)
```

   When you're done, go through the rest of the wizard steps without making any changes.

Handle the ItemInserted event

9. To ensure that the DropDownList control is updated to include any vendors that are added, code an ItemInserted event handler for the DetailsView control in the Vendors.aspx.vb file. You can see an example of this in figure 13-12, but you should alter that code so it displays the message "New vendor successfully added." if no exception is raised at run time. Note too that the ID for the label in the form is lblMessage, not lblError, and that you use the DataBind method on the drop-down list, not on grdVendors.
10. Run the project and confirm that you can add new vendors to the database, that the new vendors are added to the drop-down list, and that the success message is displayed after a new vendor has been added.

14

How to use object data sources

This chapter is designed to show you how to use the object data source control as an alternative to the SQL data source control that you've already learned about. The benefit of using an object data source control is that it lets you use a three-layer design in which the code that's used to access the database is kept in data access classes. This lets you separate the presentation code from the data access code, but still lets you use the data binding features of ASP.NET 4.

An introduction to object data sources

The following topics introduce you to object data sources and the three-layer architecture that they let you implement.

How three-layer applications work in ASP.NET 4

As you learned in chapter 2, most development experts recommend a *three-layer architecture* for building applications that separates the presentation, business, and data access components of the application. For a web application, the *presentation layer* includes the web pages that define the user interface. The *middle layer* includes the classes that manage the data access for those pages, and it may also include classes that define business objects such as vendors and invoices or that implement business rules such as data validation requirements or discount policies. The *database layer* consists of the database itself.

To use this architecture and still get the benefit of data binding, ASP.NET 4 provides *object data sources*. Then, an object data source control serves as an interface between the data-bound controls in the presentation layer and the *data access classes* in the middle layer. This means that you can use data binding in the presentation layer without placing the data access code in that layer.

When you use an object data source control, you must create a data access class to handle the data access for the control. This class provides at least one method that retrieves data from the database and returns it in a form that the object data source control can handle. It can also provide methods that insert, update, and delete data. The data access class should be placed in the application's App_Code folder.

When you code a data access class, you can use any techniques you want to access the database. In this chapter, for example, you'll see data access classes that use the ADO.NET classes you've learned about throughout this book. If you have already developed data access classes for the database used by your application, you may be able to use those classes with an object data source. Often, though, it's better to develop the data access classes specifically for the object data source controls that you're going to use. That way, you can design each class so it works as efficiently as possible.

Incidentally, Microsoft uses both the term *business object class* and the term *data object class* to refer to a class that provides data access for an object data source. If you follow the recommendations in this chapter, however, you'll use shared methods to provide the data access functions, so an object will never be instantiated from the class. In addition, we use the term *business object* to refer to an instance of a class that represents a business entity, such as a vendor. To avoid confusion, then, I use the term *data access class* to refer to a class that provides the data access code for an object data source.

The three-layer architecture in ASP.NET 4

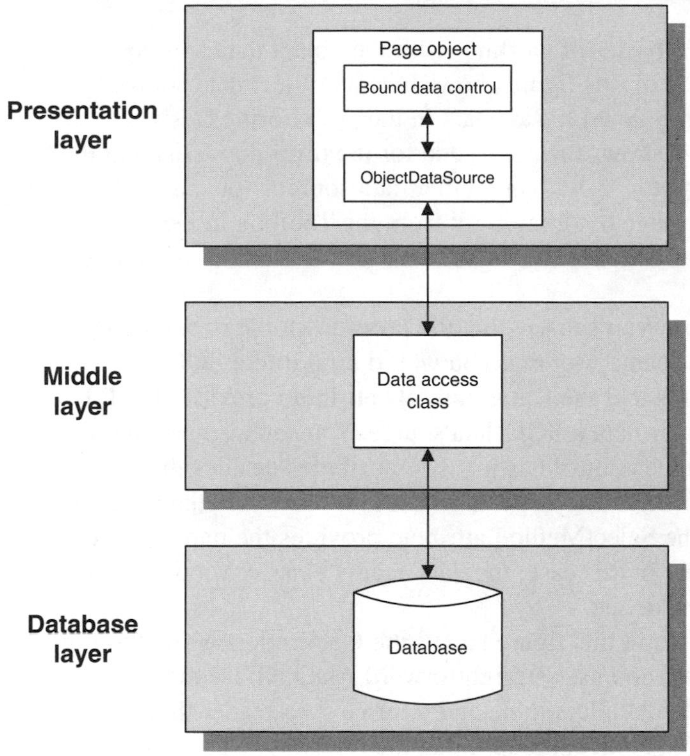

The three layers

- The *presentation layer* consists of the ASP.NET 2.0 pages that manage the appearance of the application. This layer can include bound data controls and object data source controls that bind the data controls to the data.
- The *middle layer* contains the *data access classes* that manage the data access for the application. This layer can also contain business classes that represent business entities such as customers, products, or employees and implement business rules such as credit and discount policies.
- The *database layer* consists of the database that contains the data for the application. Ideally, the SQL statements that provide the database access should be saved in stored procedures within the database, but the SQL statements are often stored in the data access classes.

Description

- An *object data source* is implemented by the object data source control, which lets you use data binding with the *three-layer architecture* for a database application.
- An object data source is similar to a SQL data source. However, instead of directly accessing a database, the object data source gets its data through a data access class that handles the details of database access.

Figure 14-1 How three-layer applications work in ASP.NET 4

How to use the object data source control

Figure 14-2 presents the basics of working with the object data source control. The image at the top of this figure shows how an object data source control that's bound to a drop-down list appears in the Web Forms Designer. Then, the first code example shows the aspx code for the drop-down list and the object data source it's bound to. As with any other data source, you can add an object data source to a web page by dragging it from the Toolbox in Design view or by entering the aspx code for the object data source element in Source view.

In the first code example, you can see that the drop-down list is bound to the object data source in the same way that you would bind it to a SQL data source. The only difference is that the DataSourceID attribute provides the ID of an object data source rather than a SQL data source. You can also see that the code for the object data source control has just two attributes besides the required ID and Runat attributes. The TypeName attribute provides the name of the data access class, and the SelectMethod attribute provides the name of the method used to retrieve data. In this case, the data access class is VendorDB and the select method is GetVendorList.

The second code example in this figure shows the GetVendorList method of the VendorDB class. This method uses straightforward ADO.NET code to retrieve vendor rows from the Vendors table and return a data reader that can be used to read the vendor rows. Notice, though, that the return type for this method is IEnumerable. Because the SqlDataReader class implements the IEnumerable interface, a data reader is a valid return object for this method. (You'll learn more about the return types that are acceptable for a select method in figure 14-9.)

A drop-down list that's bound to an object data source control

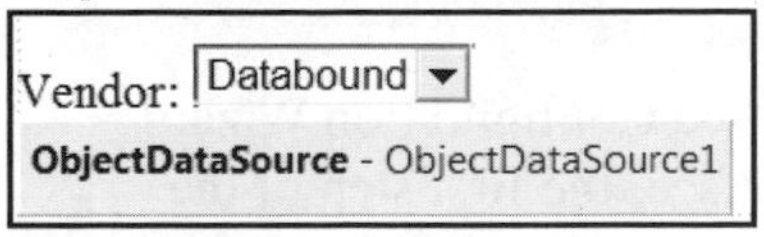

The code for the drop-down list and the object data source control

```
<asp:DropDownList ID="ddlVendors" runat="server"
    DataSourceID="ObjectDataSource1"
    DataTextField="Name" DataValueField="VendorID"
    AutoPostBack="True">
</asp:DropDownList>
<asp:ObjectDataSource ID="ObjectDataSource1" runat="server"
    TypeName="VendorDB"
    SelectMethod="GetVendorList">
</asp:ObjectDataSource>
```

The GetVendorList method of the VendorDB class

```
<DataObjectMethod(DataObjectMethodType.Select)>
Public Shared Function GetVendorList() As IEnumerable
    Dim con As New SqlConnection(PayablesDB.GetConnectionString)
    Dim sel As String = "SELECT VendorID, Name FROM Vendors ORDER BY Name"
    Dim cmd As New SqlCommand(sel, con)
    con.Open()
    Dim rdr As SqlDataReader =
        sel.ExecuteReader(CommandBehavior.CloseConnection)
    Return rdr
End Function
```

Basic attributes of the object data source control

Attribute	Description
ID	The ID of the control.
Runat	Must specify "server".
TypeName	The name of the data access class.
SelectMethod	The name of the method that retrieves the data.
UpdateMethod	The name of the method that updates the data.
DeleteMethod	The name of the method that deletes the data.
InsertMethod	The name of the method that inserts the data.
DataObjectTypeName	The name of a class that provides properties that are used to pass parameter values.
ConflictDetection	Specifies how concurrency conflicts will be detected. CompareAllValues uses optimistic concurrency checking. OverwriteValues, which is the default, does no concurrency checking.

Description

- The object data source control specifies the name of the data access class and the methods used to select, update, delete, and insert data.

Figure 14-2 How to use the object data source control

How to configure an object data source control

Figure 14-3 shows how you can use the Data Source Configuration Wizard to configure an object data source control. As you can see, the first step of the wizard lets you choose the business object that will be associated with this object data source. The selection you make here will be used in the TypeName attribute of the object data source control. (Notice that Microsoft refers to the data access class as a *business object* in this wizard. In other contexts, though, Microsoft refers to the data access class as a *data object* or a *data component*.)

The drop-down list in the first step of the wizard lists all of the classes that are available in the App_Code folder. If you check the "Show Only Data Components" box, only those classes that identify themselves as data components will be listed. In figure 14-11, you'll learn how to mark classes this way.

When you select a data access class and click Next, the Define Data Methods step of the configuration wizard is displayed. Here, you can select the method you want to use to retrieve data for the object data source. The one you select is specified in the SelectMethod attribute of the object data source control. (In this step, the wizard uses a feature called *reflection* to determine all of the available methods, and you'll learn more about reflection in a moment.)

If you choose a select method that requires parameters, the Define Parameters step lets you specify the source for each of the required parameters. Then, the wizard generates the elements that define the parameters required by the object data source. This works the same as it does for a SQL data source.

As you can see in this figure, the Data Source Configuration Wizard also provides tabs that let you specify the methods for update, insert, and delete operations. Later in this chapter, you'll see an application that uses these methods. But for now, I'll just focus on how you can use an object data source to retrieve data.

How to work with bound controls

Although you can bind a control such as a drop-down list or GridView control to an object data source, you can't use the designer to select individual fields like you can when you use a SQL data source. That's because the fields are defined in the data access class and not directly in the data source. When you bind a drop-down list, for example, you have to manually enter the names of the fields you want to display and use for the value of the control. Similarly, when you bind a GridView control, you have to manually enter the name of each field you want to bind and, if the control provides for sorting, you have to enter the name of the field for each sort expression. In addition, you have to enter the appropriate field name or names for the DataKeyNames attribute of the control. Although that makes object data sources more difficult to work with than SQL data sources, the advantages outweigh this added difficulty.

The Data Source Configuration Wizard

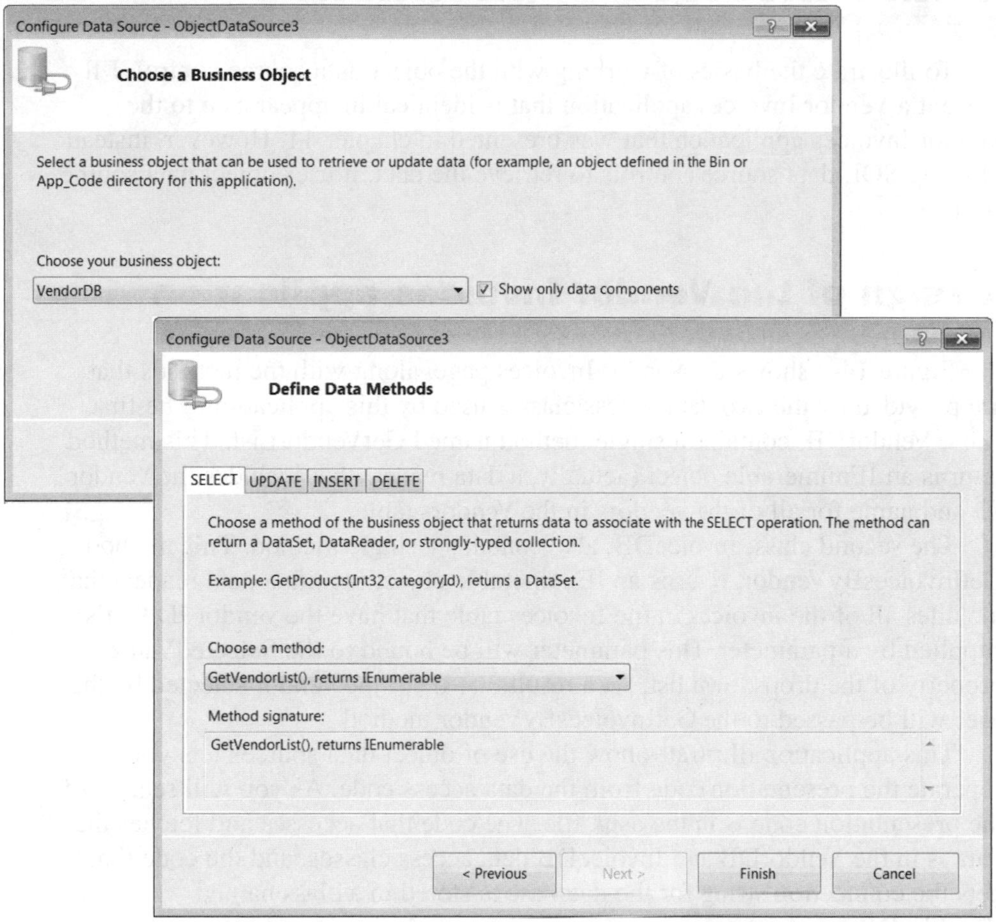

Description

- You can use the Data Source Configuration Wizard to configure an object data source control by choosing Configure Data Source from its smart tag menu.
- The Choose a Business Object step of the wizard lets you select the data access class you want to use.
- The Define Data Methods step of the wizard includes tabs that let you choose the methods you want to use for select, update, insert, and delete operations.
- If you choose a method that requires parameters, a Define Parameters step will appear. This step lets you choose the source of each parameter required by the method. For example, you can specify that a drop-down list should be used as the source for a parameter.
- If you create a new data source from a bound control, the first step of the Data Source Configuration Wizard asks you to choose a data source type. To create an object data source, select the Object option. Then, when you click the Next button, the first dialog box shown above is displayed.

Figure 14-3 How to configure an object data source control

A Vendor Invoices application

To illustrate the basics of working with the object data source control, I'll present a Vendor Invoices application that is identical in appearance to the Vendor Invoices application that was presented in chapter 11. However, instead of using SQL data source controls to retrieve the data, it uses object data source controls.

The design of the Vendor Invoices application

Figure 14-4 shows the Vendor Invoices page, along with the methods that are provided by the two data access classes used by this application. The first class, VendorDB, contains a single method named GetVendorList. This method returns an IEnumerable object (actually, a data reader) that includes the vendor ID and name for all of the vendors in the Vendors table.

The second class, InvoiceDB, also contains a single method. This method, GetInvoicesByVendor, returns an IEnumerable object (again, a data reader) that includes all of the invoices in the Invoices table that have the vendor ID that's supplied by a parameter. This parameter will be bound to the SelectedValue property of the drop-down list. As a result, the ID of the vendor selected by the user will be passed to the GetInvoicesByVendor method.

This application illustrates how the use of object data sources lets you separate the presentation code from the data access code. As you will see, all of the presentation code is in the aspx file. The code that accesses and fetches the data is in the VendorDB and InvoiceDB data access classes, and the code that gets the connection string for the database is stored in a class named PayablesDB.

The aspx file

Figure 14-5 shows the Default.aspx file for the Vendor Invoices application. If you compare this listing with the listing shown in figure 11-15, you'll discover that the only difference is that the SqlDataSource elements have been replaced by object data source elements. In other words, the code for the drop-down list and GridView controls is identical whether the application uses a SQL data source or an object data source.

In the first object data source control, the TypeName attribute specifies VendorDB, and the SelectMethod attribute specifies GetVendorList. As a result, the GetVendorList method in the VendorDB class will be called to retrieve the vendor data when the drop-down list is bound.

For the second object data source control, the TypeName and SelectMethod attributes specify that the GetInvoicesByVendor method of the InvoiceDB class will be used to retrieve the data for the GridView control. In addition, a ControlParameter element within the SelectParameters element is used to declare the VendorID parameter that's required by the GetInvoicesByVendor

The Vendor Invoices application

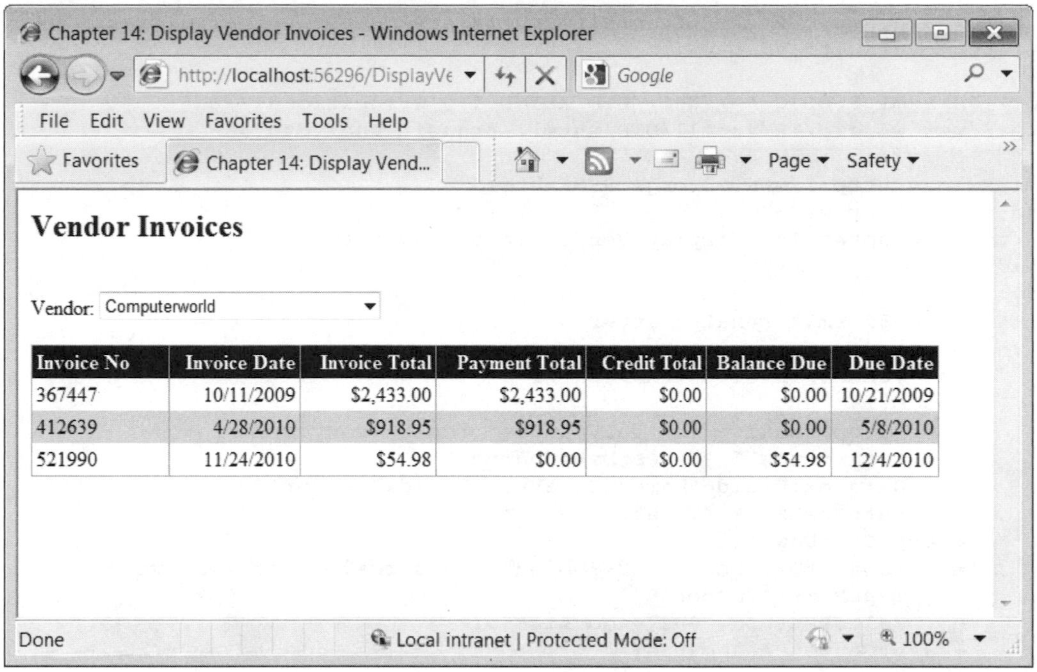

Method of the VendorDB class

Method	Description
GetVendorList() As IEnumerable	Returns an IEnumerable object with the ID and name of all the vendors in the Vendors table.

Method of the InvoiceDB class

Method	Description
GetInvoicesByVendor(VendorID As String) As IEnumerable	Returns an IEnumerable object with the invoice number, invoice date, invoice total, payment total, credit total, balance due, and due date for all invoices in the Invoices table for the specified vendor.

Description

- The Vendor drop-down list is bound to an object data source control that retrieves a list of vendors from the Vendors table. This object data source uses a data access class named VendorDB that contains the shared method that returns the list of vendors.
- The GridView control is bound to a second object data source control that uses a parameterized query to retrieve the invoices for a selected vendor. This object data source uses a data access class named InvoiceDB that contains the shared method that returns the list of invoices. The VendorID for the parameter that's required by this method is taken from the SelectedValue property of the drop-down list.

Figure 14-4 The design of the Vendor Invoices application

The Default.aspx file **Page 1**

```
<%@ Page Language="VB" AutoEventWireup="false" CodeFile="Default.aspx.vb"
Inherits="_Default" %>

<!DOCTYPE html PUBLIC "-//W3C//DTD XHTML 1.0 Transitional//EN"
"http://www.w3.org/TR/xhtml1/DTD/xhtml1-transitional.dtd">

<html xmlns="http://www.w3.org/1999/xhtml" >
<head runat="server">
    <title>Chapter 14: Display Vendor Invoices</title>
</head>
<body>
    <form id="form1" runat="server">
    <div>
        <h2>Vendor Invoices</h2><br />
        Vendor:
        <asp:DropDownList ID="ddlVendors" runat="server"
            DataSourceID="ObjectDataSource1"
            DataTextField="Name" DataValueField="VendorID"
            AutoPostBack="True">
        </asp:DropDownList>
        <asp:ObjectDataSource ID="ObjectDataSource1" runat="server"
            TypeName="VendorDB"
            SelectMethod="GetVendorList">
        </asp:ObjectDataSource>
        <br />
        <br />
        <asp:GridView ID="grdInvoices" runat="server"
            AutoGenerateColumns="False" DataSourceID="ObjectDataSource2"
            BackColor="White" BorderColor="#999999" BorderStyle="Solid"
            BorderWidth="1px" CellPadding="3" ForeColor="Black"
            GridLines="Vertical">
            <Columns>
                <asp:BoundField DataField="InvoiceNumber"
                    HeaderText="Invoice No" SortExpression="InvoiceNumber" >
                    <ItemStyle Width="100px" />
                    <HeaderStyle HorizontalAlign="Left" />
                </asp:BoundField>
                <asp:BoundField DataField="InvoiceDate"
                    DataFormatString="{0:d}" HeaderText="Invoice Date"
                    SortExpression="InvoiceDate" HtmlEncode="False" >
                    <ItemStyle Width="95px" HorizontalAlign="Right" />
                    <HeaderStyle HorizontalAlign="Right" />
                </asp:BoundField>
                <asp:BoundField DataField="InvoiceTotal"
                    DataFormatString="{0:c}" HeaderText="Invoice Total"
                    SortExpression="InvoiceTotal" HtmlEncode="False" >
                    <ItemStyle HorizontalAlign="Right" Width="100px" />
                    <HeaderStyle HorizontalAlign="Right" />
                </asp:BoundField>
                <asp:BoundField DataField="PaymentTotal"
                    DataFormatString="{0:c}" HeaderText="Payment Total"
                    HtmlEncode="False" >
                    <ItemStyle HorizontalAlign="Right" Width="110px" />
                    <HeaderStyle HorizontalAlign="Right" />
                </asp:BoundField>
```

Figure 14-5 The aspx file for the Vendor Invoices application (part 1 of 2)

The Default.aspx file **Page 2**

```
                <asp:BoundField DataField="CreditTotal"
                    DataFormatString="{0:c}" HeaderText="Credit Total"
                    HtmlEncode="False" >
                    <ItemStyle HorizontalAlign="Right" Width="90px" />
                    <HeaderStyle HorizontalAlign="Right" />
                </asp:BoundField>
                <asp:BoundField DataField="BalanceDue"
                    DataFormatString="{0:c}" HeaderText="Balance Due"
                    HtmlEncode="False" SortExpression="BalanceDue">
                    <ItemStyle HorizontalAlign="Right" Width="90px" />
                    <HeaderStyle HorizontalAlign="Right" />
                </asp:BoundField>
                <asp:BoundField DataField="DueDate" DataFormatString="{0:d}"
                    HeaderText="Due Date" HtmlEncode="False"
                    SortExpression="DueDate">
                    <ItemStyle Width="75px" HorizontalAlign="Right" />
                    <HeaderStyle HorizontalAlign="Right" />
                </asp:BoundField>
            </Columns>
            <FooterStyle BackColor="#CCCCCC" />
            <SelectedRowStyle BackColor="#000099" Font-Bold="True"
                ForeColor="White" />
            <PagerStyle BackColor="#999999" ForeColor="Black"
                HorizontalAlign="Center" />
            <HeaderStyle BackColor="Black" Font-Bold="True"
                ForeColor="White" />
            <AlternatingRowStyle BackColor="#CCCCCC" />
        </asp:GridView>
        <asp:ObjectDataSource ID="ObjectDataSource2" runat="server"
            SelectMethod="GetInvoicesByVendor" TypeName="InvoiceDB">
            <SelectParameters>
                <asp:ControlParameter ControlID="ddlVendors" Name="vendorID"
                    PropertyName="SelectedValue" Type="Int32" />
            </SelectParameters>
        </asp:ObjectDataSource>
    </div>
    </form>
</body>
</html>
```

Figure 14-5 The aspx file for the Vendor Invoices application (part 2 of 2)

method. This parameter is bound to the SelectedValue property of the drop-down list.

Because the data binding for this application is defined entirely in the aspx file, the only code in the code-behind file for this page is used to catch any unhandled exceptions that might occur. The only other Visual Basic code for this application is in the data access classes, which are presented next.

The VendorDB class

Figure 14-6 presents the Visual Basic code for the VendorDB class. Although this code should be stored in the project's App_Code folder, this folder isn't added by default to the project. To add it, you right-click on the project name in the Solution Explorer, select Add ASP.NET folder from the context menu, and select App_Code from the list of available folders. After you add this folder, you can use the Website→Add New Item command to add a class file to the App_Code folder.

Before I explain the details of how this method works, I want to point out the DataObject and DataObjectMethod attributes that appear in this class. These attributes are used to identify the class and methods as data objects, and you'll learn how to use them in figure 14-11. For now, just realize that they're used by the Data Source Configuration Wizard to determine which classes and methods to display when you configure an object data source.

The GetVendorList method starts by creating a connection to the Payables database. To get the connection string for this database, it calls the GetConnectionString method of a class named PayablesDB. You'll see the code for this class in the next figure.

Next, this method creates a command object to retrieve data from the Payables database using this Select statement:

```
SELECT VendorID, Name
FROM Vendors
ORDER BY Name
```

This command object is instantiated using this Select statement and the connection object as parameters. Then, the connection is opened, the ExecuteReader method of the command object is called to create a data reader object that contains the requested data, and the data reader is returned to the object data source.

Notice that if an exception occurs when the connection is opened or the data reader is created, the Catch block starts by checking if the data reader was created. If so, the data reader is closed, which also closes the connection since the CommandBehavior.CloseConnection argument was specified on the ExecuteReader method. Otherwise, just the connection is closed.

The VendorDB class

```
Imports Microsoft.VisualBasic
Imports System.ComponentModel
Imports System.Data
Imports System.Data.SqlClient

<DataObject(True)>
Public Class VendorDB

    <DataObjectMethod(DataObjectMethodType.Select)>
    Public Shared Function GetVendorList() As IEnumerable
        Dim con As New SqlConnection(PayablesDB.GetConnectionString)
        Dim sel As String = "SELECT VendorID, Name FROM Vendors ORDER BY Name"
        Dim cmd As New SqlCommand(sel, con)
        Dim rdr As SqlDataReader = Nothing
        Try
            con.Open()
            rdr = cmd.ExecuteReader(CommandBehavior.CloseConnection)
            Return rdr
        Catch ex As Exception
            If rdr IsNot Nothing Then
                rdr.Close()
            Else
                con.Close()
            End If
            Throw ex
        End Try
    End Function

End Class
```

Note

- The DataObject and DataObjectMethod attributes are explained in figure 14-11.

Figure 14-6 The VendorDB class for the Vendor Invoices application

The InvoiceDB class

Figure 14-7 presents the InvoiceDB class. The GetInvoicesByVendor method of this class is slightly more complicated that the GetVendorList method of the VendorDB class because it uses a parameter in its Select statement:

```
SELECT InvoiceNumber, InvoiceDate, InvoiceTotal, PaymentTotal,
    CreditTotal, InvoiceTotal - PaymentTotal - CreditTotal
    AS BalanceDue, DueDate
FROM Invoices
WHERE VendorID = @VendorID
ORDER BY InvoiceDate
```

Here again, a command object is created using the Select statement and a connection object. Then, a parameter named VendorID is added to the command's Parameters collection. Finally, the connection is opened, the command is executed to create a data reader with the requested data, and the data reader is returned to the object data source.

The PayablesDB class

Both the GetVendorList and GetInvoicesByVendor methods call a method named GetConnectionString to retrieve the connection string for the Payables database. You can see this method in the PayablesDB class in figure 14-7. The GetConnectionString method uses the ConfigurationManager class to retrieve the connection string named "PayablesConnectionString" from the web.config file. As a result, the connection string for the Payables database must be stored in this file. Because the Data Source Configuration Wizard can't store the connection string in the web.config file when it creates an object data source, you'll have to store it there yourself. To refresh your memory about how to do that, please refer to figure 11-3 in chapter 11.

The InvoiceDB class

```
Imports Microsoft.VisualBasic
Imports System.ComponentModel
Imports System.Data
Imports System.Data.SqlClient

<DataObject(True)>
Public Class InvoiceDB

    <DataObjectMethod(DataObjectMethodType.Select)>
    Public Shared Function GetInvoicesByVendor(ByVal vendorID As Integer) _
            As IEnumerable
        Dim con As New SqlConnection(PayablesDB.GetConnectionString)
        Dim sel As String =
            "SELECT InvoiceNumber, InvoiceDate, InvoiceTotal, " &
                "PaymentTotal, CreditTotal, " &
                "InvoiceTotal - PaymentTotal - CreditTotal AS BalanceDue," &
                "DueDate " &
            "FROM Invoices " &
            "WHERE VendorID = @VendorID " &
            "ORDER BY InvoiceDate"
        Dim cmd As New SqlCommand(sel, con)
        cmd.Parameters.AddWithValue("@VendorID", vendorID)
        Dim rdr As SqlDataReader = Nothing
        Try
            con.Open()
            rdr = cmd.ExecuteReader(CommandBehavior.CloseConnection)
            Return rdr
        Catch ex As Exception
            If rdr IsNot Nothing Then
                rdr.Close()
            Else
                con.Close()
            End If
            Throw ex
        End Try
    End Function

End Class
```

The PayablesDB class

```
Imports Microsoft.VisualBasic

Public Class PayablesDB

    Public Shared Function GetConnectionString() As String
        Return ConfigurationManager.ConnectionStrings _
            ("PayablesConnectionString").ConnectionString
    End Function

End Class
```

Figure 14-7 The InvoiceDB and PayablesDB classes for the Vendor Invoices application

How to create a data access class

The most challenging aspect of using object data sources is developing the data access classes they require. So the topics that follow explain how to design and implement these classes.

How to design a data access class

As figure 14-8 shows, the data access class used by an object data source can have four different types of methods that are used to select, insert, update, and delete data. You can use any method names that you want for these methods, and you can design the class so it has more than one of each of these types of methods. For example, in addition to the GetVendorList method, the VendorDB class you saw in figure 14-6 might include a select method that retrieves all the vendor columns and rows.

The data access methods can be shared methods or instance methods. If you define them as instance methods, the object data source control will create an instance of the data access class before it calls the method, and then destroy the object after the method has been executed. For this to work, the data access class must provide a parameterless constructor. In Visual Basic, though, a parameterless constructor is provided by default if the class has no constructors.

Because creating and destroying a data access object can be time consuming, I suggest that you use shared methods for the select, insert, update, and delete methods whenever possible. That way, the object data source won't have to create an instance of the data access class when it calls one of the data access methods.

Although you provide the name of the methods called by the object data source control by using the SelectMethod, InsertMethod, UpdateMethod, and DeleteMethod attributes, the object data source control doesn't generate the parameters that will be passed to these methods until runtime. Because of that, the object data source must use a .NET feature called reflection to determine if a method it calls contains the correct parameters. It also uses reflection to determine the return type of a select method. As you'll see in the next figure, this lets you design a select method that can return the selected data in a variety of forms.

In case you haven't encountered reflection before, it's a .NET feature that provides information about compiled classes at runtime. For example, reflection can determine what methods are provided by a particular class. In addition, it can determine what parameters each method requires and the type returned by the method.

By the way, when you create an object data source, you'll notice that Visual Studio generates Parameter elements based on the parameters that are declared by the methods specified by the SelectMethod, InsertMethod, UpdateMethod, and DeleteMethod attributes. As you'll learn in figure 14-10, however, those aren't necessarily the parameters that the object data source will require.

Types of methods in a data access class

Method type	Description
Select	Retrieves data from a database and returns it as an IEnumerable object.
Insert	Inserts data for one row into the underlying database. The values for the new row are passed via parameters.
Update	Updates the data for one row in the underlying database. The values for the new row, along with any values that are used to implement optimistic concurrency, are passed via parameters.
Delete	Deletes a row from the underlying database. The key or keys for the row to be deleted, along with any values that are used to implement optimistic concurrency, are passed via parameters.

How an object data source determines which method to call

- The name of the method used for select, insert, update, and delete operations is specified by the SelectMethod, InsertMethod, UpdateMethod, or DeleteMethod attribute.
- An object data source determines what parameters need to be passed to the data access class methods based on the data fields to be inserted, updated, or deleted and whether or not optimistic concurrency is used.
- An object data source uses reflection to determine the parameter signatures for the insert, update, and delete methods provided by the data access class.
- At runtime, if the class doesn't provide a method with the correct name and parameters, an exception is thrown.

Description

- A data access class can declare public methods that select, insert, update, and delete data. These methods can be instance methods or shared methods.
- You can use any method names you want for the select, insert, update, and delete methods.
- If the select, insert, update, and delete methods are shared methods, the methods are used without creating an instance of the data access class.
- If the select, insert, update, and delete methods are instance methods, an instance of the data access class is created and destroyed for each data access operation. In this case, the data access class must provide a parameterless constructor.
- You can use parameters to pass selection criteria or other data to the select, insert, update, and delete methods. For more information on the parameters used with insert, update, and delete methods, see figure 14-10.
- *Reflection* is a .NET feature that provides information about compiled classes and methods at runtime.

Figure 14-8 How to design a data access class

How to create a select method

Figure 14-9 shows how to design and code a select method that can be used with an object data source. The table at the top of this figure lists the four different types of values that a select method can return. The simplest is the IEnumerable interface, which can return a data reader or a data view since the DataReader and DataView classes implement the IEnumerable interface. Also, the IEnumerable object can be a strongly-typed collection that's created by using the generics feature of Visual Basic.

The select method can also return a DataTable or DataSet object. Because a dataset can contain more than one table, the object data source control simply uses the first table in the dataset. As a result, you must design the select method so the first table in the dataset contains the data you want to access.

The main advantage of returning a dataset rather than a data table or data view is that an object data source can cache a dataset. To enable caching, you can set the EnableCaching attribute to True for the object data source control. In that case, the select method will be called only the first time the data is requested. For more information on caching, which works the same as it does for a SQL data source, please refer back to chapter 11.

You can also pass parameters to the select method. In that case, the object data source control must include a SelectParameters element. This element is added automatically if you use the Data Source Configuration Wizard to create the control. Then, you can create a ControlParameter element that binds a parameter to a control such as a drop-down list. You saw an example of this in figure 14-5.

Allowable return types for a select method

Return type	Description
IEnumerable	A collection such as an ArrayList or HashTable or a strongly-typed collection such as System.Collections.Generic.List. (Because the DataReader and DataView classes implement IEnumerable, the select method can also return a data reader or a data view.)
DataTable	If the select method returns a data table, the object data source control automatically extracts a data view from the table and uses the view for data binding.
DataSet	If the select method returns a dataset, the object data source control extracts a data view from the first data table in the dataset and uses the view for data binding.
Object	If the select method returns an object, the object data source control wraps the object in an IEnumerable collection with just one item, then does the data binding as if the method returned an IEnumerable.

A select method that returns a data reader

```
Public Shared Function GetTerms() As IEnumerable
    Dim con As New SqlConnection(PayablesDB.GetConnectionString)
    Dim sel As String = "SELECT TermsID, Description, DueDays FROM Terms"
    Dim cmd As New SqlCommand(sel, con)
    con.Open()
    Return cmd.ExecuteReader(CommandBehavior.CloseConnection)
End Function
```

A select method that returns a dataset

```
Public Shared Function GetTerms() As DataSet
    Dim con As New SqlConnection(PayablesDB.GetConnectionString)
    Dim sel As String = "SELECT TermsID, Description, DueDays FROM Terms"
    Dim da As New SqlDataAdapter(sel, con)
    Dim ds As New DataSet
    da.Fill(ds, "Terms")
    Return ds
End Function
```

Description

- The select method returns data retrieved from the underlying database. It can return the data in several forms, including a data reader or a dataset.
- If the select method returns a dataset, the object data source can cache the data.
- The select method can also return a strongly-typed generic collection. See figure 14-19 for an example.
- If the select method accepts parameters, the parameters must be declared within the SelectParameters element of the object data source control. Within this element, you can use the ControlParameter element to declare a parameter that's bound to another control on the page.

How to create update, delete, and insert methods

Besides select methods, the data access class used by an object data source can provide methods that update, delete, and insert data in the underlying database. Figure 14-10 presents some guidelines that you should follow when you create these methods.

Undoubtedly the most difficult aspect of working with object data sources is determining how the parameters for update, delete, and insert methods are passed to them from the data source. The reason for this difficulty is that these parameters aren't determined until runtime. Then, the object data source creates a collection of parameters that are passed to the data access class method based on several factors, including (1) the bound fields that are used by the control that is bound to the object data source, (2) the DataKeyNames attribute of the bound control, (3) whether the object data source uses optimistic concurrency checking, and (4) whether the key fields are updatable.

Once the object data source has determined what parameters need to be passed, it uses reflection to determine whether the data access class has a method that accepts the required parameters. If so, the method is called using these parameters. If not, an exception is thrown. This means that you must anticipate the parameters that will be passed to your method so you can code them correctly. Fortunately, though, if you guess wrong, you can use the message displayed by the exception that occurs to determine what parameters were expected and then correct your code.

If the object data source is bound to a GridView or DetailsView control that uses BoundField elements, the parameter names are determined by the DataField attributes of those elements. In contrast, if the object data source is bound to a GridView or DetailsView control that uses TemplateField elements, or if the object data source is bound to a FormView control, the parameter names are determined by the names specified in the Eval and Bind methods of the bound controls. As a result, the parameter names you use in your data access class methods must be the same as the names you use on the DataField attributes or in the Eval and Bind methods.

Note, however, that the order of the parameters doesn't matter. Instead, the object data source uses reflection to determine the names and order of the parameters expected by the data access methods. Then, when it calls those methods, the object data source passes the parameters in the expected order.

The most confusing aspect of how an object data source generates parameters has to do with the cases that require two sets of values to be passed to an update method. That happens if you use optimistic concurrency or if the primary key column is updatable. For optimistic concurrency, both sets of values are needed so the update statement can make sure the data hasn't been changed before it applies the update. And if optimistic concurrency isn't used but the key column is updatable, the update statement needs the original key value so it can properly retrieve the row to be updated.

A typical Update method

```
Public Shared Sub UpdateTerms(ByVal description As String,
        ByVal dueDays As Integer, ByVal original_TermsID As Integer)
    Dim con As New SqlConnection(PayablesDB.GetConnectionString)
    Dim up As String = "UPDATE Terms " &
        "SET Description = @Description, " &
        "    DueDays = @DueDays " &
        "WHERE TermsID = @original_TermsID"
    Dim cmd As New SqlCommand(up, con)
    cmd.Parameters.AddWithValue("Description", description)
    cmd.Parameters.AddWithValue("DueDays", dueDays)
    cmd.Parameters.AddWithValue("original_TermsID", original_TermsID)
    con.Open()
    cmd.ExecuteNonQuery
    con.Close()
End Sub
```

How parameters are generated

- Parameters are automatically generated when an object data source control is bound to a control that lets you update a row in a data source, including the GridView, DetailsView, and FormView controls.
- One parameter is generated for each bound column. If the column is updatable, the parameter is given the same name as the column. Otherwise, the parameter is given the name of the column prefixed with original_.
- If the object data source control uses optimistic concurrency, an additional parameter is generated for each updatable bound column when you call the update method. These parameters hold the original values of the columns.
- If optimistic concurrency isn't used but the key column of the data source is updatable, an additional parameter is generated for the key column when you call the update method. This parameter holds the new value of the key column.
- When you call the delete method, a parameter is always generated to hold the original value of the key column.
- If you create an object data source control that uses optimistic concurrency, Visual Studio automatically adds an OldValuesParameterFormatString attribute with a value of original_{0}. That way, the names of the parameters for the original column values will be different from the names of the parameters for the new column values.
- If you don't use optimistic concurrency but the key column is updatable, you'll need to add the OldValuesParameterFormatString attribute manually.

Description

- To properly design an update, delete, or insert method, you must be aware of how the object data source control generates the parameters that are passed to these methods.
- Although the order in which the parameters appear in your update, delete, and insert methods doesn't matter, your parameter names must match the names generated by the object data source control.
- If your methods don't use the parameter names that the object data source expects, you can use the exceptions that occur at runtime to correct your parameter names.

Figure 14-10 How to create update, delete, and insert methods

If you create an object data source control that uses optimistic concurrency, Visual Studio will automatically add an OldValuesParameterFormatString attribute with a value of original_{0}. That way, the names of the parameters that are generated for an update operation will consist of the column names prefixed with "original_". As a result, if the new value of a field named Description is passed via a parameter named Description, the original value will be passed via a parameter named original_Description. Without the OldValuesParameterFormatString attribute, the names of both parameters would be Description. That's because the default value of the OldValuesParameterFormatString attribute is {0}.

If the key column is updatable and the object data source doesn't use optimistic concurrency, Visual Studio doesn't generate the OldValuesParameterFormatString attribute. Because of this, the name of the parameter that holds the original value of the column will be the same as the name of the parameter that holds the new value of the column. To avoid that, you'll need to set the value of this property yourself.

The names of the parameters that are passed to a delete method also depend on whether the object data source control is created with optimistic concurrency. If optimistic concurrency isn't used, the parameter names are simply the names of the key columns. But if optimistic concurrency is used, the delete parameters will begin with original_.

How to use attributes to mark a data access class

Figure 14-11 shows how you can use *Visual Basic attributes* to identify a data access class and its methods. If you haven't worked with attributes before, they are simply a way of providing declarative information for classes, methods, properties, and so on. Although some of these attributes have meaning at runtime, the attributes in this figure are used at design time. In particular, the Data Source Configuration Wizard uses these attributes to determine which classes in the App_Code folder are data access classes and which methods in the data access class are select, insert, update, and delete methods.

Note, however, that you don't need to use these attributes. The only reason to use them is to help the Data Source Configuration Wizard recognize the data access classes and methods. If you haven't marked your data access classes with these attributes, you can still access them from the wizard by clearing the Show Only Data Components checkbox in the Choose a Business Object step of the wizard (see figure 14-3).

Attributes for marking data access classes

To mark an element as...	Use this attribute...
A data object class	`<DataObject(True)>`
A Select method	`<DataObjectMethod(DataObjectMethodType.Select)>`
An Insert method	`<DataObjectMethod(DataObjectMethodType.Insert)>`
An Update method	`<DataObjectMethod(DataObjectMethodType.Update)>`
A Delete method	`<DataObjectMethod(DataObjectMethodType.Delete)>`

A marked data access class

```
Imports Microsoft.VisualBasic
Imports System.ComponentModel
Imports System.Data
Imports System.Data.SqlClient

<DataObject(True)>
Public Class VendorDB

    <DataObjectMethod(DataObjectMethodType.Select)>
    Public Shared Function GetVendorList() As IEnumerable
        Dim con As New SqlConnection(PayablesDB.GetConnectionString)
        Dim sel As String _
            = "SELECT VendorID, Name FROM Vendors ORDER BY Name"
        Dim cmd As New SqlCommand(sel, con)
        Dim rdr As SqlDataReader = Nothing
        Try
            con.Open()
            rdr = cmd.ExecuteReader(CommandBehavior.CloseConnection)
            Return rdr
        Catch ex As Exception
            If rdr IsNot Nothing Then
                rdr.Close()
            Else
                con.Close()
            End If
            Throw ex
        End Try
    End Function

End Class
```

Description

- You can use DataObject and DataObjectMethod attributes to mark data access classes and methods. Visual Studio uses these attributes to determine which classes and methods to list in the drop-down lists of the Data Source Configuration Wizard.
- The DataObject and DataObjectMethod attributes are stored in the System.ComponentModel namespace.

Figure 14-11 How to use attributes to mark a data access class

A Terms Maintenance application

To give you a better idea of how you can use an object data source to update, delete, and insert data, the following topics present an application that maintains the Terms table in the Payables database. This application is a variation of the Terms Maintenance application that was presented in chapter 12.

The design of the Terms Maintenance application

Figure 14-12 presents the design for this version of the Terms Maintenance application. It uses a GridView control to let the user update and delete terms rows and a DetailsView control to insert new terms rows. Both the GridView and DetailsView controls are bound to a single object data source control. But the DetailsView control is used only in Insert mode so it isn't used to display, update, or delete existing terms rows.

The table in this figure shows the public methods that are provided by the TermsDB class. These four methods provide the select, update, delete, and insert functions. Since all of these methods are defined as shared, an instance of the TermsDB class doesn't have to be created to access the database.

The Terms Maintenance application

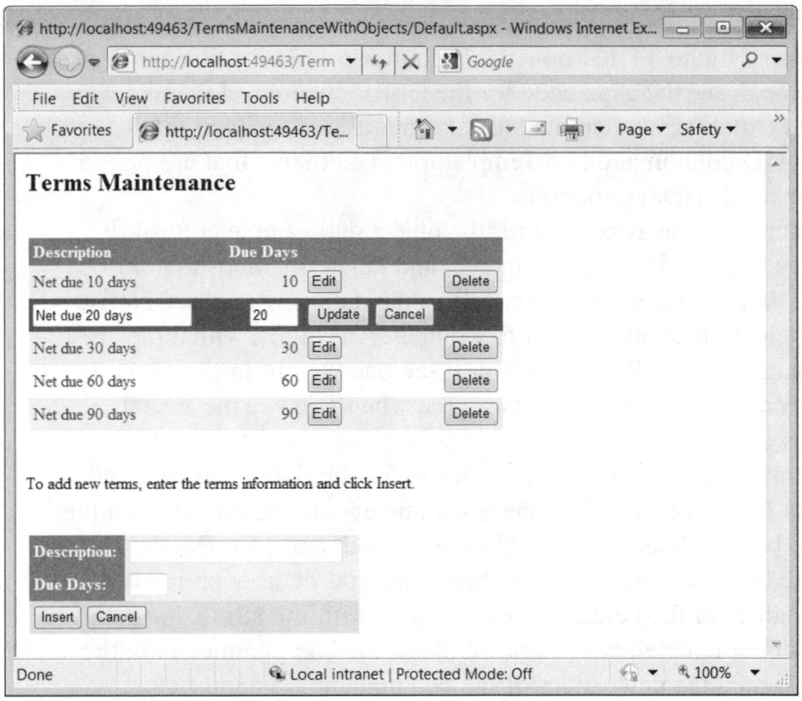

Methods of the TermsDB class

Method type	Signature
Select	`Public Shared Function GetTerms() As IEnumerable`
Update	`Public Shared Function UpdateTerms(ByVal Description As String, ByVal DueDays As Integer, ByVal original_TermsID As Integer, ByVal original_Description As String, ByVal original_DueDays As Integer) As Integer`
Delete	`Public Shared Function DeleteTerms( ByVal original_TermsID As Integer, ByVal original_Description As String, ByVal original_DueDays As Integer) As Integer`
Insert	`Public Shared Sub InsertTerms(ByVal Description As String, ByVal DueDays As Integer)`

Description

- This version of the Terms Maintenance application uses a GridView control to update and delete rows and a DetailsView control to insert rows. These controls are bound to an object data source control that accesses the Terms table of the Payables database.
- The data access class named TermsDB provides the select, insert, update, and delete methods.

The aspx file

The three parts of figure 14-13 show the Default.aspx file for this application. In part 1, you can see the aspx code for the GridView control that displays the terms rows. Its Columns element includes a BoundField element that's bound to the TermsID column and two TemplateField elements that are bound to the Description and DueDays columns.

In part 2, you can see the aspx code for the object data source control. It provides the names of the select, insert, update, and delete methods that will be used to access the data, and it names TermsDB as the data access class. Notice that the ConflictDetection attribute is set to CompareAllValues, which means that optimistic concurrency will be used. You'll see one way to implement optimistic concurrency with an object data source when you see the Visual Basic code for this application.

The object data source also defines parameters for the delete, update, and insert methods. As I mentioned earlier, these parameters are generated from the methods specified by the DeleteMethod, UpdateMethod, and InsertMethod properties of the data source. Because the object data source uses optimistic concurrency, the names of the delete parameters start with the string "original_". In addition, two sets of update parameters are included. The parameters in the first set will be assigned the new values of the two updatable bound fields: Description and DueDays. As you can see, these parameters are given the same names as the bound fields. The parameters in the second set will be assigned the original values of the row that's being updated. These parameters are given the same names as the bound fields, preceded by the string "original_". The first parameter will be used to identify the row to be updated and the second and third parameters will be used to provide for optimistic concurrency.

You can also see the aspx code for the DetailsView control starting at the bottom of part 2 and continuing in part 3. Here, I set the DefaultMode attribute to Insert so this control is always displayed in Insert mode.

The body of the Default.aspx file **Page 1**

```
<body>
  <form id="form1" runat="server">
  <div>
    <h2>Terms Maintenance</h2><br />
    <table>
    <tr>
      <td style="width: 460px" valign="top">
        <asp:GridView ID="grdTerms" runat="server" AutoGenerateColumns="False"
            DataKeyNames="TermsID" DataSourceID="ObjectDataSource1"
            CellPadding="4" ForeColor="#333333" GridLines="None">
            <Columns>
              <asp:BoundField DataField="TermsID" HeaderText="TermsID"
                 Visible="False" />
              <asp:TemplateField HeaderText="Description">
                 <ItemTemplate>
                   <asp:Label ID="lblGridCategory" runat="server"
                       Text='<%# Bind("Description") %>'></asp:Label>
                 </ItemTemplate>
                 <EditItemTemplate>
                   <asp:TextBox ID="txtGridDescription" runat="server"
                       Text='<%# Bind("Description") %>'></asp:TextBox>
                   <asp:RequiredFieldValidator ID="RequiredFieldValidator3"
                       runat="server" ControlToValidate="txtGridDescription"
                       ErrorMessage="Description is a required field."
                       ValidationGroup="Edit" ForeColor="White">*
                   </asp:RequiredFieldValidator>
                 </EditItemTemplate>
                 <HeaderStyle HorizontalAlign="Left" />
                 <ItemStyle Width="225px" />
              </asp:TemplateField>
              <asp:TemplateField HeaderText="Due Days">
                <ItemTemplate>
                  <asp:Label ID="lblGridDueDays" runat="server"
                      Text='<%# Bind("DueDays") %>'></asp:Label>
                </ItemTemplate>
                <EditItemTemplate>
                  <asp:TextBox ID="txtGridDueDays" runat="server"
                     Text='<%# Bind("DueDays") %>' Width="40px"></asp:TextBox>
                  <asp:RequiredFieldValidator ID="RequiredFieldValidator4"
                     runat="server" ControlToValidate="txtGridDueDays"
                     ErrorMessage="Due Days is a required field."
                     Display="Dynamic" ValidationGroup="Edit"
                     ForeColor="White">*
                  </asp:RequiredFieldValidator>
                  <asp:CompareValidator ID="CompareValidator2" runat="server"
                     ControlToValidate="txtGridDueDays" Display="Dynamic"
                     ErrorMessage="Due Days must be an integer."
                     Operator="DataTypeCheck" Type="Integer"
                     ValidationGroup="Edit" ForeColor="White">*
                  </asp:CompareValidator>
                </EditItemTemplate>
                <HeaderStyle HorizontalAlign="Right" />
                <ItemStyle HorizontalAlign="Right" Width="100px" />
              </asp:TemplateField>
```

Figure 14-13 The aspx file for the Terms Maintenance application (part 1 of 3)

The body of the Default.aspx file

Page 2

```
            <asp:CommandField ButtonType="Button" ShowEditButton="True"
                ValidationGroup="Edit" />
            <asp:CommandField ButtonType="Button" ShowDeleteButton="True"
                CausesValidation="False" />
          </Columns>
          <HeaderStyle BackColor="#507CD1" Font-Bold="True"
              ForeColor="White" />
          <AlternatingRowStyle BackColor="White" />
          <EditRowStyle BackColor="#2461BF" />
          <RowStyle BackColor="#EFF3FB" />
      </asp:GridView>
      <asp:ObjectDataSource ID="ObjectDataSource1" runat="server"
          SelectMethod="GetTerms"
          UpdateMethod="UpdateTerms" DeleteMethod="DeleteTerms"
          OldValuesParameterFormatString="original_{0}"
          InsertMethod="InsertTerms" TypeName="TermsDB"
          ConflictDetection="CompareAllValues">
          <DeleteParameters>
              <asp:Parameter Name="original_TermsID" Type="Int32" />
              <asp:Parameter Name="original_Description" Type="String" />
              <asp:Parameter Name="original_DueDays" Type="Int32" />
          </DeleteParameters>
          <UpdateParameters>
              <asp:Parameter Name="description" Type="String" />
              <asp:Parameter Name="dueDays" Type="Int32" />
              <asp:Parameter Name="original_TermsID" Type="Int32" />
              <asp:Parameter Name="original_Description" Type="String" />
              <asp:Parameter Name="original_DueDays" Type="Int32" />
          </UpdateParameters>
          <InsertParameters>
              <asp:Parameter Name="description" Type="String" />
              <asp:Parameter Name="dueDays" Type="Int32" />
          </InsertParameters>
      </asp:ObjectDataSource>
    </td>
    <td style="width: 100px" valign="top">
      <asp:ValidationSummary ID="ValidationSummary1" runat="server"
          HeaderText="Please correct the following errors:"
          ValidationGroup="Edit" Width="240px" />
    </td>
  </tr>
  </table>
  < br /><br />
  To add new terms, enter the terms information and click Insert.<br />
  <asp:Label ID="lblError" runat="server" ForeColor="Red"
      EnableViewState="False"></asp:Label><br />
  <br />
  <table>
  <tr>
    <td style="width: 330px">
      <asp:DetailsView ID="dvTerms" runat="server" AutoGenerateRows="False"
          DataSourceID="ObjectDataSource1" DefaultMode="Insert"
          Height="50px" Width="320px" CellPadding="4" ForeColor="#333333"
          GridLines="None">
```

Figure 14-13 The aspx file for the Terms Maintenance application (part 2 of 3)

The body of the Default.aspx file **Page 3**

```
        <Fields>
          <asp:BoundField DataField="TermsID" HeaderText="TermsID"
              ReadOnly="True" Visible="False" />
          <asp:TemplateField HeaderText="Description:">
              <InsertItemTemplate>
                  <asp:TextBox ID="txtDescription" runat="server"
                      Text='<%# Bind("Description") %>'
                      Width="200px"></asp:TextBox>
                  <asp:RequiredFieldValidator ID="RequiredFieldValidator1"
                      runat="server" ControlToValidate="txtDescription"
                      ErrorMessage="Description is a required field."
                      ValidationGroup="Add" Display="Dynamic">*
                  </asp:RequiredFieldValidator>
              </InsertItemTemplate>
              <ItemStyle Width="230px" />
              <HeaderStyle Width="90px" />
          </asp:TemplateField>
          <asp:TemplateField HeaderText="Due Days:">
              <InsertItemTemplate>
                  <asp:TextBox ID="txtDueDays" runat="server"
                      Text='<%# Bind("DueDays") %>'
                      Width="32px"></asp:TextBox>
                  <asp:RequiredFieldValidator ID="RequiredFieldValidator2"
                      runat="server" ControlToValidate="txtDueDays"
                      Display="Dynamic"
                      ErrorMessage="Due Days is a required field."
                      ValidationGroup="Add">*</asp:RequiredFieldValidator>
                  <asp:CompareValidator ID="CompareValidator1"
                      runat="server" ControlToValidate="txtDueDays"
                          Operator="DataTypeCheck" Type="Integer"
                          ErrorMessage="Due Days must be an integer."
                          Display="Dynamic"
                          ValidationGroup="Add">*</asp:CompareValidator>
              </InsertItemTemplate>
          </asp:TemplateField>
          <asp:CommandField ButtonType="Button" ShowInsertButton="True"
              ValidationGroup="Add" />
        </Fields>
        <CommandRowStyle BackColor="#D1DDF1" Font-Bold="True" />
        <FieldHeaderStyle BackColor="#507CD1" Font-Bold="True"
            ForeColor="White" />
        <InsertRowStyle BackColor="#EFF3FB" ForeColor="White" />
      </asp:DetailsView>
    </td>
    <td style="width: 100px">
      <asp:ValidationSummary ID="ValidationSummary2" runat="server"
          HeaderText="Please correct the following errors:"
          ValidationGroup="Add" Width="248px" />
    </td>
  </tr>
  </table>
</div>
</form>
</body>
```

Figure 14-13 The aspx file for the Terms Maintenance application (part 3 of 3)

The code-behind file

Figure 14-14 shows the code-behind file for the Default.aspx page of the Terms Maintenance application. This file consists of six event handlers that handle the exceptions that might be raised and the concurrency errors that might occur when the object data source's select, update, delete, or insert methods are called.

The first event handler is executed after the data source is updated. This event handler retrieves the return value from the update method using the ReturnValue property of the e argument and assigns it to the AffectedRows property of the e argument. This is necessary because the AffectedRows property isn't set automatically like it is for a SQL data source. For this to work, of course, the update method must return the number of rows that were updated. You'll see the code that accomplishes that in the next figure.

The second event handler is executed after a row in the GridView control is updated, which happens after the data source is updated. This event handler checks the Exception property of the e argument to determine if an exception has been thrown. If so, an error message is displayed, the ExceptionHandled property is set to True to suppress the exception, and the KeepInEditMode property is set to True to leave the GridView control in Edit mode.

If an exception didn't occur, this event handler continues by checking the AffectedRows property of the e argument. The value of this property is passed forward from the AffectedRows property of the object data source's Updated event. If the value of this property is zero, the row was not updated, most likely due to the concurrency checking code that was added to the SQL Update statement. As a result, an appropriate error message is displayed.

The next two event handlers are similar, except they handle the Deleted event of the object data source control and the RowDeleted event of the GridView control. Like the Updated event handler of the object data source control, the Deleted event handler sets the AffectedRows property of the e argument. And, like the RowUpdated event handler of the GridView control, the RowDeleted event handler checks for exceptions and concurrency errors.

The next event handler is executed after a row is inserted using the DetailsView control. It checks whether an exception has occurred and responds accordingly. Note that currency checking isn't necessary here because a concurrency error can't occur for an insert operation.

The last event handler catches any other exceptions that might occur while the page is being processed. Although the code for this event handler isn't shown here, it works just like the Page_Error event handlers you've seen in other applications in this book.

By the way, this code illustrates just one way that you can provide for concurrency errors. Another way is to write the update and delete methods so they throw an exception if a concurrency error occurs. Then, the RowUpdated and RowDeleted event handlers can test the e.Exception property to determine if this exception has been thrown. I prefer the technique illustrated here, though, because the code for the RowUpdated and RowDeleted event handlers is the same as it is when you use a SQL data source.

The Default.aspx.vb file

```
Partial Class _Default
    Inherits System.Web.UI.Page
    Protected Sub ObjectDataSource1_Deleted(ByVal sender As Object,
    ByVal e As System.Web.UI.WebControls.ObjectDataSourceStatusEventArgs) _
    Handles ObjectDataSource1.Deleted
       e.AffectedRows = CInt(e.ReturnValue)
    End Sub

    Protected Sub grdTerms_RowDeleted(ByVal sender As Object,
    ByVal e As System.Web.UI.WebControls.GridViewDeletedEventArgs) _
    Handles grdTerms.RowDeleted
        If e.Exception IsNot Nothing Then
            lblError.Text = "An exception occurred. " & e.Exception.Message
            e.ExceptionHandled = True
        ElseIf e.AffectedRows = 0 Then
            lblError.Text = "The row was not deleted. " &
                "Another user may have updated or deleted those terms. " &
                "Please try again."
        End If
    End Sub

    Protected Sub ObjectDataSource1_Updated(ByVal sender As Object,
    ByVal e As System.Web.UI.WebControls.ObjectDataSourceStatusEventArgs) _
    Handles ObjectDataSource1.Updated
        e.AffectedRows = CInt(e.ReturnValue)
    End Sub

    Protected Sub grdTerms_RowUpdated(ByVal sender As Object,
    ByVal e As System.Web.UI.WebControls.GridViewUpdatedEventArgs) _
    Handles grdTerms.RowUpdated
        If e.Exception IsNot Nothing Then
            lblError.Text = "An exception occurred. " & e.Exception.Message
            e.ExceptionHandled = True
            e.KeepInEditMode = True
        ElseIf e.AffectedRows = 0 Then
            lblError.Text = "The row was not updated. " &
                "Another user may have updated or deleted those terms. " &
                "Please try again."
        End If
    End Sub

    Protected Sub dvTerms_ItemInserted(ByVal sender As Object,
    ByVal e As System.Web.UI.WebControls.DetailsViewInsertedEventArgs) _
    Handles dvTerms.ItemInserted
        If e.Exception IsNot Nothing Then
            lblError.Text = "An exception occurred. " & e.Exception.Message
            e.ExceptionHandled = True
        End If
    End Sub

    Protected Sub Page_Error(ByVal sender As Object,
    ByVal e As System.EventArgs) Handles Me.Error
    ...
    End Sub
End Class
```

Figure 14-14 The code-behind file for the Terms Maintenance application

The TermsDB class

The two parts of figure 14-15 present the TermsDB class that's used as the data access class for this application. This class uses the DataObject attribute to mark the class as a data object class, and it uses the DataObjectMethod attribute to mark the methods as data object methods.

The four public methods in this class provide for the select, insert, delete, and update operations performed by this application. These methods use standard ADO.NET code to access the database. Since this code is straightforward, you shouldn't have any trouble understanding how it works. So I'll just describe it briefly here.

The GetTerms method retrieves all of the rows and columns from the Terms table in the Payables database. This data is then returned as a data reader, and the object data source uses it to populate the GridView control.

To get a connection to the Payables database, the GetTerms method calls the GetConnectionString method of the PayablesDB class. This method is identical to the GetConnectionString method you saw in figure 14-7. It gets the connection string from the web.config file. The GetConnectionString method is also called by the other methods in the TermsDB class.

When the user clicks the Insert button in the DetailsView control, the object data source executes the InsertTerms method. This method is declared with two parameters that correspond to the Description and DueDays columns in the Terms table. A parameter isn't included for the TermsID column because it's an identity column and its value will be generated by the database. When the object data source executes this method, it passes the values that the user entered into the DetailsView control. Then, the method creates and executes a command that uses these parameter values to insert a new row.

The TermsDB.vb file **Page 1**

```
Imports Microsoft.VisualBasic
Imports System.ComponentModel
Imports System.Data
Imports System.Data.SqlClient

<DataObject(True)>
Public Class TermsDB

    <DataObjectMethod(DataObjectMethodType.Select)>
    Public Shared Function GetTerms() As IEnumerable
        Dim con As New SqlConnection(PayablesDB.GetConnectionString)
        Dim sel As String =
            "SELECT TermsID, Description, DueDays FROM Terms"
        Dim cmd As New SqlCommand(sel, con)
        Dim rdr As SqlDataReader = Nothing
        Try
            con.Open()
            rdr = cmd.ExecuteReader(CommandBehavior.CloseConnection)
            Return rdr
        Catch ex As SqlException
            If rdr IsNot Nothing Then
                rdr.Close()
            Else
                con.Close()
            End If
            Throw ex
        End Try
    End Function

    <DataObjectMethod(DataObjectMethodType.Insert)>
    Public Shared Sub InsertTerms(
            ByVal description As String,
            ByVal dueDays As Integer)
        Dim con As New SqlConnection(PayablesDB.GetConnectionString)
        Dim ins As String =
            "INSERT INTO Terms " &
                "(Description, DueDays) " &
            "VALUES(@Description, @DueDays)"
        Dim cmd As New SqlCommand(ins, con)
        cmd.Parameters.AddWithValue("Description", description)
        cmd.Parameters.AddWithValue("DueDays", dueDays)
        Try
            con.Open()
            cmd.ExecuteNonQuery()
        Catch ex As SqlException
            Throw ex
        Finally
            con.Close()
        End Try
    End Sub
```

Figure 14-15 The TermsDB class for the Terms Maintenance application (part 1 of 2)

When the user clicks the Delete button in the GridView control, the object data source executes the DeleteTerms method. This method accepts three parameters: the original terms ID, description, and due days. The values of these parameters are used within the Where clause of the Delete statement that's executed by this method to identify the row to be deleted and to perform concurrency checking.

Notice that this method is written as a function that returns an integer value. Then, when the command that contains the Delete statement is executed, the result is stored in an integer variable, which is returned to the object data source. Because this value indicates the number of rows that were deleted, it can be used as shown in the previous figure to check for a concurrency error.

The last method, UpdateTerms, is executed when the user clicks the Update button in the GridView control. It's declared with five parameters: the current description and due days and the original terms ID, description, and due days. The values of the current description and due days parameters are used to update the terms row, and the values of the original parameters are used to identify the row to be updated and to perform concurrency checking.

Like the DeleteTerms method, the UpdateTerms method returns an integer value that indicates the number of rows that were affected by the update operation. Then, this value can be used to check for a concurrency error.

The TermsDB.vb file **Page 2**

```
    <DataObjectMethod(DataObjectMethodType.Delete)>
    Public Shared Function DeleteTerms(ByVal original_TermsID As Integer,
            ByVal original_Description As String,
            ByVal original_DueDays As Integer) As Integer
        Dim con As New SqlConnection(PayablesDB.GetConnectionString)
        Dim del As String =
            "DELETE FROM Terms " &
            "WHERE TermsID = @original_TermsID " &
            "  AND Description = @original_Description " &
            "  AND DueDays = @original_DueDays"
        Dim cmd As New SqlCommand(del, con)
        cmd.Parameters.AddWithValue("original_TermsID", original_TermsID)
        cmd.Parameters.AddWithValue("original_Description",
            original_Description)
        cmd.Parameters.AddWithValue("original_DueDays", original_DueDays)
        Try
            con.Open()
            Dim i As Integer = cmd.ExecuteNonQuery
            Return i
        Catch ex As SqlException
            Throw ex
        Finally
            con.Close()
        End Try
    End Function

    <DataObjectMethod(DataObjectMethodType.Update)>
    Public Shared Function UpdateTerms(ByVal description As String,
            ByVal dueDays As Integer, ByVal original_TermsID As Integer,
            ByVal original_Description As String,
            ByVal original_DueDays As Integer) As Integer
        Dim con As New SqlConnection(PayablesDB.GetConnectionString)
        Dim up As String = "UPDATE Terms " &
            "SET Description = @Description, DueDays = @DueDays " &
            "WHERE TermsID = @original_TermsID " &
            "  AND Description = @original_Description " &
            "  AND DueDays = @original_DueDays"
        Dim cmd As New SqlCommand(up, con)
        cmd.Parameters.AddWithValue("Description", description)
        cmd.Parameters.AddWithValue("DueDays", dueDays)
        cmd.Parameters.AddWithValue("original_TermsID", original_TermsID)
        cmd.Parameters.AddWithValue("original_Description",
            original_Description)
        cmd.Parameters.AddWithValue("original_DueDays", original_DueDays)
        Try
            con.Open()
            Dim i As Integer = cmd.ExecuteNonQuery
            Return i
        Catch ex As SqlException
            Throw ex
        Finally
            con.Close()
        End Try
    End Function
End Class
```

Figure 14-15 The TermsDB class for the Terms Maintenance application (part 2 of 2)

How to use business objects with object data sources

Although you can use a parameter for each bound field that's required by an insert, update, or delete method in a data access class, that can be cumbersome if more than just a few fields are required. In that case, you may want to use a business object that stores the data for all of the fields. In fact, because it's easier to determine what parameters are required by a method when you use business objects, you might want to use them regardless of the number of fields you're working with.

How to create methods that use business objects

Figure 14-16 shows how to create methods that use business objects. Just as when you create methods that use individual field parameters, you need to determine what parameters are required when you use business objects. This figure summarizes how an object data source generates these parameters.

Any insert or delete method you create requires a single business object as its parameter. This business object must contain all the values required by the method, and you can give it any name you choose. If an update method doesn't provide for optimistic concurrency checking, it too requires a single business object as its parameter.

If an update method provides for optimistic concurrency checking, it requires two parameters as shown in the code at the top of this figure. The first parameter must be a business object that provides the original values for the row to be updated, and the second parameter must be a business object that provides the new values for the row. Then, the method assigns the properties of these objects to the appropriate parameters. Notice that the name of the first parameter is the same as the name of the second parameter, preceded by original_. However, the second parameter can be any name you choose.

Although two parameters are also required if the key column for a table is updatable, you should know that the object data source won't automatically generate two parameters in this case. Because of that, you will need to set the ConflictDetection attribute of the object data source to CompareAllValues even if the update method doesn't provide for optimistic concurrency checking, and you will need to set the OldValuesParameterFormatString attribute accordingly. Then, the first parameter will contain an object with the original values for the row, and you can use the property that contains the value for the key column to identify the row to be updated.

This figure also lists the requirements for a business class that you can use to create the business objects. First, the class must provide a parameterless constructor. Since Visual Basic provides a parameterless constructor by default if a class isn't defined with any constructors, you may be able to omit this constructor. However, I prefer to include it for completeness.

An update method that uses business objects

```
Public Shared Sub UpdateTerms(ByVal original_Terms As Terms,
        ByVal terms As Terms)
    Dim con As New SqlConnection(PayablesDB.GetConnectionString)
    Dim up As String = "UPDATE Terms " &
        "SET Description = @Description, DueDays = @DueDays " &
        "WHERE TermsID = @original_TermsID " &
        "  AND Description = @original_Description " &
        "  AND DueDays = @original_DueDays"
    Dim cmd As New SqlCommand(up, con)
    cmd.Parameters.AddWithValue("Description", terms.Description)
    cmd.Parameters.AddWithValue("DueDays", terms.DueDays)
    cmd.Parameters.AddWithValue("original_TermsID", original_Terms.TermsID)
    cmd.Parameters.AddWithValue("original_Description",
        original_Terms.Description)
    cmd.Parameters.AddWithValue("original_DueDays", original_Terms.DueDays)
    con.Open()
    cmd.ExecuteNonQuery
    con.Close()
End Sub
```

How parameters are generated

- When the insert or delete method is called, one parameter of the business class type is generated and passed to the method. The parameter that's declared in the method can have any name you choose.
- One parameter of the business class type is also generated and passed to the update method when this method is called if optimistic concurrency isn't used. The parameter that's declared in the method can have any name you choose.
- If optimistic concurrency is specified, two parameters are generated and passed to the update method. The first one contains the original values, and the second one contains the new values. The name of the first object must be the name of the second object, preceded by the string that's specified by the OldValuesParameterFormatString attribute.

Requirements for the business class

- The class must provide a parameterless constructor.
- The class must have public properties with names that match the names of the bound fields that are passed to the object data source from the bound control.
- The public properties must have both get and set procedures.

Description

- Instead of using individual parameters for each bound field, you can use an object that's created from a business class that contains a property for each field.
- To use a business class with an object data source control, you set the DataObjectTypeName attribute to the name of the class.

Figure 14-16 How to create methods that use business objects

Second, the class must define a public property for each bound field that's passed from the bound control to the object data source. The names of these properties must be the same as the names specified for the DataField attribute or on the Eval or Bind method. This works just like it does when you use individual parameters for each bound field.

Third, the property for each bound field must include both a get and a set procedure. The object data source uses the set procedures to set the values of the properties based on the values passed to it from the bound control. And the insert, update, and delete methods in the data access class use the get procedures to assign the values of the properties to parameters of command objects.

Once you create the business class, you need to indicate that you want the object data source to use it with the insert, update, and delete methods. To do that, you set the DataObjectTypeName attribute of the control to the name of the class.

The aspx file for a Terms Maintenance application that uses business objects

Figure 14-17 presents part of the aspx file for a version of the Terms Maintenance application that uses business objects. The only difference here is in the definition of the object data source control. As you can see, the DataObjectTypeName attribute of this control is set to a class named Terms. You'll see the definition of this class in the next figure.

In addition to the DataObjectTypeName attribute, you should notice that parameters are included only for the update method. These parameters are included because optimistic concurrency checking is performed by the update method, which means that this method requires two parameters: an object that contains the original values and an object that contains the new values. Because these parameters must be given appropriate names as explained in the last topic, the object data source must include parameters that specify these names. In contrast, the names of the parameters in the insert and delete methods can be anything you like, so they don't have to be defined by the object data source. Similarly, if optimistic concurrency checking isn't performed by an update method, the object data source doesn't need to define any update parameters.

Part of the Default.aspx file that uses business objects

```
...
<asp:GridView ID="grdTerms" runat="server" AutoGenerateColumns="False"
    DataKeyNames="TermsID" DataSourceID="ObjectDataSource1"
    CellPadding="4" ForeColor="#333333" GridLines="None">
    <Columns>
        <asp:BoundField DataField="TermsID" HeaderText="TermsID"
            Visible="False" />
        <asp:TemplateField HeaderText="Description">
            <ItemTemplate>
                <asp:Label ID="lblGridCategory" runat="server"
                    Text='<%# Bind("Description") %>'></asp:Label>
            </ItemTemplate>
            <EditItemTemplate>
                <asp:TextBox ID="txtGridDescription" runat="server"
                    Text='<%# Bind("Description") %>'></asp:TextBox>
                <asp:RequiredFieldValidator ID="RequiredFieldValidator3"
                    runat="server" ControlToValidate="txtGridDescription"
                    ErrorMessage="Description is a required field."
                    ValidationGroup="Edit" ForeColor="White">*
                </asp:RequiredFieldValidator>
            </EditItemTemplate>
            ...
<asp:ObjectDataSource ID="ObjectDataSource1" runat="server"
    DataObjectTypeName="Terms" SelectMethod="GetTerms"
    UpdateMethod="UpdateTerms" DeleteMethod="DeleteTerms"
    InsertMethod="InsertTerms" OldValuesParameterFormatString="original_{0}"
    TypeName="TermsDB" ConflictDetection="CompareAllValues">
    <UpdateParameters>
        <asp:Parameter Name="original_Terms" Type="Object" />
        <asp:Parameter Name="terms" Type="Object" />
    </UpdateParameters>
</asp:ObjectDataSource>
...
<asp:DetailsView ID="dvTerms" runat="server" AutoGenerateRows="False"
    DataSourceID="ObjectDataSource1" DefaultMode="Insert" Height="50px"
    Width="320px" CellPadding="4" ForeColor="#333333" GridLines="None">
    <Fields>
        <asp:BoundField DataField="TermsID" HeaderText="TermsID"
            ReadOnly="True" Visible="False" />
        <asp:TemplateField HeaderText="Description:">
            <InsertItemTemplate>
                <asp:TextBox ID="txtDescription" runat="server"
                    Text='<%# Bind("Description") %>'
                    Width="200px"></asp:TextBox>
                <asp:RequiredFieldValidator ID="RequiredFieldValidator1"
                    runat="server" ControlToValidate="txtDescription"
                    ErrorMessage="Description is a required field."
                    ValidationGroup="Add" Display="Dynamic">*
                </asp:RequiredFieldValidator>
            </InsertItemTemplate>
        ...
```

Figure 14-17 The aspx file for the Terms Maintenance application that uses business objects

The Terms business class

Figure 14-18 presents the Terms business class that's used by the object data source shown in the previous figure. If you've used business classes like this before, you shouldn't have any trouble understanding how it works. In this case, the class includes three public properties that correspond with the three columns of the Terms table. The values of these properties are stored in the three private fields declared by this class. As required for business classes that are used by an object data source, each property is defined with both a get and a set procedure. This class also includes a parameterless constructor that's called when the object data source creates an instance of the class.

A TermsDB class that uses business objects

Figure 14-19 presents a version of the TermsDB class that uses business objects. Notice that although the select method in this class doesn't have to use the business object to store the results of the retrieval operation, it makes sense to do that if the insert, update, and delete methods use business objects. In this case, then, the select method returns a List(Of Terms) object. To do that, it creates an object from the Terms class for each row that's retrieved by the data reader, and it assigns the values in that row to the appropriate properties of the object. Then, it adds that object to the List(Of Terms) object.

The insert method receives a single Terms object. Then, it assigns the Description and DueDays properties of that object to the parameters that are defined in the Values clause of the Insert statement. When the Insert statement is executed, a new row with these values is inserted into the Terms table.

The delete method also receives a single Terms object. This object contains the values that were originally retrieved from the Terms table. The TermsID, Description, and DueDays properties of this object are assigned to the parameters that are defined in the Where clause of the Delete statement. Then, if a row with these values is found, the row is deleted. Otherwise, it indicates that a concurrency error has occurred.

The update method receives two Terms objects. The first one contains the values that were originally retrieved from the Terms table, and the second one contains the new values for the row. The TermsID, Description, and DueDays properties of the first object are assigned to the parameters that are defined in the Where clause of the Update statement, and the Description and DueDays properties of the second object are assigned to the properties that are defined in the Set clause of the Update statement. Then, if a row with the values in the first object is found, the values of the Description and DueDays columns of that row are updated to the values in the second object.

The Terms.vb file

```
Public Class Terms
    Private m_termsID As Integer
    Private m_description As String
    Private m_dueDays As Integer

    Public Sub New()

    End Sub

    Public Property TermsID() As Integer
        Get
            Return m_termsID
        End Get
        Set(ByVal value As Integer)
            m_termsID = value
        End Set
    End Property

    Public Property Description() As String
        Get
            Return m_description
        End Get
        Set(ByVal value As String)
            m_description = value
        End Set
    End Property

    Public Property DueDays() As Integer
        Get
            Return m_dueDays
        End Get
        Set(ByVal value As Integer)
            m_dueDays = value
        End Set
    End Property

End Class
```

Figure 14-18 The Terms business class

A TermsDB.vb file that uses business objects **Page 1**

```
Imports Microsoft.VisualBasic
Imports System.ComponentModel
Imports System.Data
Imports System.Data.SqlClient
Imports System.Collections.Generic

<DataObject(True)>
Public Class TermsDB

    <DataObjectMethod(DataObjectMethodType.Select)>
    Public Shared Function GetTerms() As List(Of Terms)
        Dim termsList As New List(Of Terms)
        Dim con As New SqlConnection(PayablesDB.GetConnectionString)
        Dim sel As String =
            "SELECT TermsID, Description, DueDays FROM Terms"
        Dim cmd As New SqlCommand(sel, con)
        Try
            con.Open()
            Dim rdr As SqlDataReader = cmd.ExecuteReader()
            Dim terms As Terms
            Do While rdr.Read
                terms = New Terms
                terms.TermsID = CInt(rdr("TermsID"))
                terms.Description = rdr("Description").ToString
                terms.DueDays = CInt(rdr("DueDays"))
                termsList.Add(terms)
            Loop
            rdr.Close()
        Catch ex As SqlException
            Throw ex
        Finally
            con.Close()
        End Try
        Return termsList
    End Function

    <DataObjectMethod(DataObjectMethodType.Insert)>
    Public Shared Sub InsertTerms(ByVal terms As Terms)
        Dim con As New SqlConnection(PayablesDB.GetConnectionString)
        Dim ins As String =
            "INSERT INTO Terms " &
                "(Description, DueDays) " &
            "VALUES(@Description, @DueDays)"
        Dim cmd As New SqlCommand(ins, con)
        cmd.Parameters.AddWithValue("Description", terms.Description)
        cmd.Parameters.AddWithValue("DueDays", terms.DueDays)
        Try
            con.Open()
            cmd.ExecuteNonQuery()
        Catch ex As SqlException
            Throw ex
        Finally
            con.Close()
        End Try
    End Sub
```

Figure 14-19 A TermsDB class that uses business objects (part 1 of 2)

A TermsDB.vb file that uses business objects **Page 2**

```
    <DataObjectMethod(DataObjectMethodType.Delete)>
    Public Shared Function DeleteTerms(ByVal terms As Terms) As Integer
        Dim con As New SqlConnection(PayablesDB.GetConnectionString)
        Dim del As String =
            "DELETE FROM Terms " &
            "WHERE TermsID = @TermsID " &
            "  AND Description = @Description " &
            "  AND DueDays = @DueDays"
        Dim cmd As New SqlCommand(del, con)
        cmd.Parameters.AddWithValue("TermsID", terms.TermsID)
        cmd.Parameters.AddWithValue("Description", terms.Description)
        cmd.Parameters.AddWithValue("DueDays", terms.DueDays)
        Try
            con.Open()
            Dim i As Integer = cmd.ExecuteNonQuery
            Return i
        Catch ex As SqlException
            Throw ex
        Finally
            con.Close()
        End Try
    End Function

    <DataObjectMethod(DataObjectMethodType.Update)>
    Public Shared Function UpdateTerms(
            ByVal original_Terms As Terms,
            ByVal terms As Terms) As Integer
        Dim con As New SqlConnection(PayablesDB.GetConnectionString)
        Dim up As String =
            "UPDATE Terms " &
            "SET Description = @Description, " DueDays = @DueDays " &
            "WHERE TermsID = @original_TermsID " &
            "  AND Description = @original_Description " &
            "  AND DueDays = @original_DueDays"
        Dim cmd As New SqlCommand(up, con)
        cmd.Parameters.AddWithValue("Description", terms.Description)
        cmd.Parameters.AddWithValue("DueDays", terms.DueDays)
        cmd.Parameters.AddWithValue("original_TermsID",
            original_Terms.TermsID)
        cmd.Parameters.AddWithValue("original_Description",
            original_Terms.Description)
        cmd.Parameters.AddWithValue("original_DueDays",
            original_Terms.DueDays)
        Try
            con.Open()
            Dim i As Integer = cmd.ExecuteNonQuery
            Return i
        Catch ex As SqlException
            Throw ex
        Finally
            con.Close()
        End Try
    End Function

End Class
```

Figure 14-19 A TermsDB class that uses business objects (part 2 of 2)

How to use paging with object data sources

One complication that arises when you use an object data source is that it doesn't automatically provide for paging with controls like the GridView control. Because of that, you have to set the attributes of the object data source that provide for paging, and you have to provide for paging in the data access class. You'll learn how to do that in the two topics that follow.

How to create an object data source that provides for paging

To create an object data source that provides for paging, you set the four attributes shown in figure 14-20. The EnablePaging attribute simply indicates that the object data source supports paging. The StartRowIndexParameterName and MaximumRowsParameterName attributes specify the names of parameters that will be used by the select method in the data access class to determine which rows are returned by the method. You'll see an example of how that works in the next figure. For now, just realize that when you use a pager control to display another page of data in a bound control, the bound control passes the values that will be assigned to these two parameters to the object data source.

The last attribute, SelectCountMethod, names a method in the data access class that returns a count of the total number of rows that are retrieved by the select method. The control that's bound to the object data source uses this value to determine what pager controls to display. For example, if the bound control uses first, previous, next, and last pager controls, it will be able to determine when the first or last page is displayed so it can omit the first and previous or next and last pager controls. This is illustrated by the GridView control shown at the top of this figure, which is bound to the object data source shown here. In this case, the first page is displayed so the first and previous pager controls aren't included.

A GridView control that provides for paging

Name	City	State	ZipCode
Abbey Office Furnishings	Fresno	CA	93722
American Booksellers Assoc	Tarrytown	NY	10591
American Express	Los Angeles	CA	90096
ASC Signs	Fresno	CA	93703
Ascom Hasler Mailing Systems	Shelton	CT	06484
AT&T	Phoenix	AZ	85062
Aztek Label	Anaheim	CA	92807
Baker & Taylor Books	Charlotte	NC	28217
Bertelsmann Industry Svcs. Inc	Valencia	CA	91355
BFI Industries	Fresno	CA	93792
> >>			

Attributes of the object data source control that are used for paging

Attribute	Description
EnablePaging	True if the object data source control supports paging.
StartRowIndexParameterName	The name of the parameter in the select method of the data access class that receives the index of the first row to be retrieved. The default is startRowIndex.
MaximumRowsParameterName	The name of the parameter in the select method of the data access class that receives the maximum number of rows to be retrieved. The default is maximumRows.
SelectCountMethod	The name of a public method in the data access class that returns the total number of rows that are retrieved by the select method.

The aspx code for an object data source that provides for paging

```
<asp:ObjectDataSource ID="ObjectDataSource1" runat="server"
    SelectMethod="GetVendorsByPage" TypeName="VendorDB"
    EnablePaging="True" StartRowIndexParameterName="startIndex"
    SelectCountMethod="SelectCount" MaximumRowsParameterName="maxRows">
</asp:ObjectDataSource>
```

Description

- To use paging with a control like a GridView control that's bound to an object data source, you must set the four attributes of the object data source control shown above.
- When a pager control on a bound control is clicked, the index of the starting row to be displayed and the maximum number of rows to be displayed are passed to the object data source. The object data source then passes these values to the parameters of the select method specified by the StartRowIndexParameterName and MaximumRowsParameterName attributes of the object data source.
- In addition to the select method that's used to retrieve the rows to be displayed, the data access class must include a method that returns the total number of rows that are retrieved. This method is named on the SelectCountMethod attribute of the object data source, and it's used by the bound control to determine what pager controls to display.

Figure 14-20 How to create an object data source that provides for paging

How to create a data access class that provides for paging

Figure 14-21 shows the code for a data access class that's used by the object data source you saw in the last figure. This class uses a List(Of Vendor) object named vendorList to store the data that's retrieved by the select method. This list is declared at the class level so both the select method and the method that returns the count of rows have access to it. As you can see, the method that returns the count of rows, which is named SelectCount as specified by the SelectCountMethod attribute of the object data source, simply returns the number of items in this list.

The most difficult aspect of creating a data access class that provides for paging is determining what rows the select method should return. To do that, the select method uses the two parameters that are passed to it from the object data source. The names of these parameters are the same as the names specified by the StartRowIndexParameterName and MaximumRowsParameterName attributes of the object data source.

The body of the select method starts by retrieving all the rows specified by the Select statement just as any other select method does. In this case, the select method uses the ExecuteReader method of a command object to create a data reader that contains the requested data from the Vendors table. Then, it retrieves each row of data from the data reader, stores it in a Vendor object, and adds the vendor object to the vendor list.

Next, this method gets a count of the number of rows in the list and stores it in a variable named rowCount. Then, it checks to be sure that the rows specified by the values that were passed to the method aren't beyond the end of the list. That can happen if the total number of rows isn't evenly divisible by the number of rows on a page. For example, the Vendors table contains 122 rows, and 10 rows are displayed on each page (see figure 14-20). That means that the last page will contain only two rows. In that case, the maximum number of rows must be adjusted so only those two rows are returned. If you don't include this code, an error will occur when you try to display the last page indicating that the index is out of range.

The last group of statements in this method retrieves the requested rows from the vendor list and stores them in another List(Of Vendor) object named pageList. To do that, it uses a For...Next loop with a counter variable that varies from a value of 0 to the maximum number of rows minus 1. Then, the first statement within the loop calculates the index of the item to be retrieved from the vendor list by adding the value of the starting index that was passed to the method to the counter variable. Then, the item at that index is added to the page list. Finally, after all the items have been added to the page list, the list is returned to the object data source.

The data access class used by the object data source

```
Imports Microsoft.VisualBasic
Imports System.ComponentModel
Imports System.Data
Imports System.Data.SqlClient
Imports System.Collections.Generic

<DataObject(True)>
Public Class VendorDB

    Private Shared vendorList As List(Of Vendor)

    <DataObjectMethodAttribute(DataObjectMethodType.Select)>
    Public Shared Function GetVendorsByPage(ByVal startIndex As Integer,
            ByVal maxRows As Integer) As List(Of Vendor)
        vendorList = New List(Of Vendor)
        Dim con As New SqlConnection(PayablesDB.GetConnectionString)
        Dim sel As String =
            "SELECT Name, City, State, ZipCode FROM Vendors ORDER BY Name"
        Dim cmd As New SqlCommand(sel, con)
        Try
            con.Open()
            Dim rdr As SqlDataReader = cmd.ExecuteReader
            Dim vendor As Vendor
            Do While rdr.Read
                vendor = New Vendor
                vendor.Name = rdr("Name").ToString
                vendor.City = rdr("City").ToString
                vendor.State = rdr("State").ToString
                vendor.ZipCode = rdr("ZipCode").ToString
                vendorList.Add(vendor)
            Loop
            rdr.Close()
        Catch ex As Exception
            Throw ex
        Finally
            con.Close()
        End Try

        Dim rowCount As Integer = vendorList.Count
        If startIndex + maxRows > rowCount Then
            maxRows = rowCount - startIndex
        End If

        Dim pageList As New List(Of Vendor)
        Dim rowIndex As Integer
        For i As Integer = 0 To maxRows - 1
            rowIndex = i + startIndex
            pageList.Add(vendorList(rowIndex))
        Next
        Return pageList
    End Function

    Public Shared Function SelectCount() As Integer
        Return vendorList.Count
    End Function
End Class
```

Figure 14-21 A data access class that provides for paging

Perspective

In this chapter, you've learned how to work with object data sources. The benefit of this feature is that it lets you save time by using the data binding features of ASP.NET, but still maintains the design principle that says the presentation code should be separate from the data access code. Also, because you write the data access code when you use object data sources, you have complete control over how these methods work.

Unfortunately, this feature has two shortcomings that negate some of the benefits. First, this feature's reliance on reflection means that it must resolve method calls at runtime rather than at compile time, which adds overhead (albeit small) to every data access operation. Second, the way this feature uses parameters often leaves developers guessing at what parameters the object data source control is going to pass to your data access methods, particularly if you use an individual parameter for each column.

As you've seen in this chapter, though, you can simplify this process by using business objects instead of individual parameters. That will help you get the most benefit from this feature.

Terms

three-layer architecture
presentation layer
middle layer
database layer
object data source
data access class
business object class
data object class
reflection
Visual Basic attribute

Exercise 14-1 Create the Display Vendor Invoices application

In this exercise, you'll start from a partial web site, and you'll complete the application that's shown in figure 14-20.

Review the starting application

1. Use the File→Open Web Site command to open the DisplayVendorInvoices web site in your Chapter 14 directory.
2. View the Default.aspx page and note that it already contains a DropDownList control, a GridView control, and one ObjectDataSource control that is assigned to the GridView control. To complete this application, you'll need to create a GetVendorList function in the VendorDB class, you'll need to create an object data source that will use the GetVendorList function as its SelectMethod, and you'll need to bind the drop-down list to this object data source.

Create the GetVendorList function

3. Open the VendorDB file which is located in the App_Code folder. Here, you'll see that the start of a GetVendorList function has been entered.
4. Use the code listing in figure 14-6 as a guide as you enter the code for the GetVendorList function.
5. Use the Build→Rebuild Web Site command to rebuild the web site and thus make the GetVendorList function visible to the rest of the project.

Create an object data source for the drop-down list

6. Add another ObjectDataSource control to the Default.aspx page by dragging it from the Toolbox and dropping it on the Design pane. Then, change the control's ID to ObjectDataSourceVendors.
7. Use the technique in figure 14-3 to configure the new object data source so it will get the data for the drop-down list. VendorDB will be the business object, and GetVendorList will be the required method.

Bind the drop-down list to the object data source

8. Use the smart tag for the DropDownList control to set the data source to ObjectDataSourceVendors.
9. Set Name as the field to display in the drop-down list and VendorID as the value for the drop-down list. Recall from figure 14-3 that you have to enter these values manually because no field names will be displayed for you.
10. Run the application, select a Vendor from the drop-down list, and confirm that the vendor's invoices are displayed correctly.

Exercise 14-2 Create a GridView control that provides paging

In this exercise, you'll create a GridView control like the one in figure 14-12 that provides for paging.

Create an object data source for the GridView control

1. Open the DisplayVendorsWithPaging web site in your Chapter 14 directory. Then, view the Default.aspx page and note that it already contains a GridView control.
2. Create a new object data source by dragging an ObjectDataSource control from the Toolbox and dropping it on the Design pane. Then, change its ID to ObjectDataSourceVendorPaging.
3. In the Properties pane, with the ObjectDataSource still selected, set the TypeName property to VendorDB, so the VendorDB class that's in the App_Code folder can be accessed at run time.
4. Still in the Properties pane, set the SelectMethod property to GetVendorsByPage and the SelectCountMethod property to SelectCount. Those are the names of the methods in the VendorDB class that will be used for this data source, but you will need to enter these names manually.
5. Still in the Properties pane, change the StartRowIndexParameterName property to startIndex and the MaximumRowsParameterName property to maxRows because those are the names used for the parameters of the GetVendorsByPage method in the VendorDB class.
6. Still in the Properties pane, set the EnablePaging property to True.

Edit the GridView and test the application

7. Use the smart tag menu of the GridView control to assign the object data source to the control. When Visual Studio asks if you would like to regenerate the GridView column fields and data keys, choose No.
8. In the smart tag menu, check the EnablePaging item to turn paging on.
9. Run the application and note that paging is enabled, and the default pager setting uses numerals. If you get errors when you run this application, check the properties you set in steps 3 to 6 to ensure that you have entered them all correctly.

Change the pager setting

10. With the GridView control selected, go to the Properties pane and navigate to the PagerSettings property. Expand the PagerSettings properties, select the Mode property, click on the down arrow, and select NextPreviousFirstLast from the list of choices.
11. Run the application again and note that the PagerSettings now use arrows in place of the numerals.

Section 5

Advanced database programming skills

In the first four sections of this book, you learned how to use ADO.NET to build Windows and web applications. Now, you'll learn some advanced database programming skills that can be used for both Windows and web applications.

In chapter 15, you'll learn how to use XML files in your applications. In chapter 16, you'll learn how to use the Report Designer and the ReportViewer controls to generate and display reports.

Then, in chapters 17 and 18, you'll learn how to use two relatively new features of ADO.NET. In chapter 17, you'll learn how to use a query language called LINQ (Language Integrated Query) that lets you query five different types of data sources using Visual Basic instead of SQL. And in chapter 18, you'll learn how to use the Entity Framework, which lets you query the objects of the application, while the framework retrieves and updates the data in the database.

Unlike the chapters in the other sections of this book, the chapters in this section can be read in whatever sequence you prefer. If, for example, you want to know how to add reports to your applications, you can go directly to chapter 16. We do recommend, though, that you read the LINQ chapter before the Entity Framework chapter because it uses LINQ to Entities.

15

How to work with XML data

This chapter shows you how to work with XML data in both Windows and web applications. XML, as you probably know, is commonly used to transfer data from one type of system to another.

An introduction to XML

XML is a text based representation of data that can be read both by humans and machines. A key benefit of using XML is that translating data from other formats into XML makes it possible to exchange data between different types of systems.

What XML is and how it is used

XML (*Extensible Markup Language*) provides a way to store and exchange data by using tags that identify each data element. In some ways, XML is similar to HTML, the markup language that's used to display documents on the web. As a result, if you're familiar with HTML, you'll have no trouble learning how to create *XML documents*.

Figure 15-1 shows a simple XML document that contains information about two vendors. Each vendor has ID, Name, Address1, Address2, City, State, and ZipCode data. In the next two figures, you'll learn how the tags in this XML document work. But even without knowing those details, you can pick out the data for these vendors in the XML document.

This XML document and the documents you'll see in the next two figures are typical of documents that you create from scratch. However, the XML that ADO.NET generates for the data in a dataset is slightly different. You'll see an example of that later in this chapter. You'll also learn how you can control the XML that ADO.NET generates.

XML was designed as a way to represent information so it can be exchanged between dissimilar systems or applications. Initially, its purpose was to overcome some of the shortcomings of HTML as the use of the Internet increased in the late 1990s. XML was also intended to bridge the gap between man and machine by being machine readable and human understandable.

As with many technologies, though, XML expanded as developers found new uses for it. As a result, many supplementary technologies, such as the query languages described in this chapter, have been added to it. In addition, other XML based variations, such as XAML, have been devised.

The .NET Framework uses XML internally for many different purposes. In particular, ADO.NET relies extensively on XML and in fact was created by Microsoft with XML specifically in mind. As a result, if you understand how data and dataset schemas are represented in XML, you'll have a better understanding of how XML is used behind the scenes.

The data for two vendors

Column	First vendor	Second vendor
ID	1	9
Name	U.S. Postal Service	Pacific Gas and Electric
Address1	Attn: Supt. Window Services	Box 52001
Address2	PO Box 7005	
City	Madison	San Francisco
State	WI	CA
ZipCode	53707	94152

The data stored in an XML document

```
<?xml version="1.0" encoding="utf-8" standalone="yes"?>
<!--Vendor information-->
<Vendors>
  <Vendor ID="1">
    <Name>U.S. Postal Service</Name>
    <Address1>Attn: Supt. Window Services</Address1>
    <Address2>PO Box 7005</Address2>
    <City>Madison</City>
    <State>WI</State>
    <ZipCode>53707</ZipCode>
  </Vendor>
  <Vendor ID="9">
    <Name>Pacific Gas and Electric</Name>
    <Address1>Box 52001</Address1>
    <City>San Francisco</City>
    <State>CA</State>
    <ZipCode>94152</ZipCode>
  </Vendor>
</Vendors>
```

Description

- *XML*, the *Extensible Markup Language*, provides a method of structuring information in a text file using special *tags*. A file that contains XML is known as an *XML document.*
- The XML document in this figure contains information for two vendors. Each vendor has an *attribute* called ID and *elements* that provide name and address information. You'll learn more about attributes and elements in the next two figures.
- XML can be used to exchange information between different systems, especially via the Internet.
- Many .NET classes, particularly the ADO.NET and web classes, use XML internally to store or exchange information. In addition, the .NET Framework provides many other classes that are designed for working with XML data.

Figure 15-1 What XML is and how it is used

XML tags, declarations, and comments

Figure 15-2 shows how *tags* are used to structure the data in an XML document. Each XML tag must begin with the < character and must end with the > character , so the first line in the XML document in this figure contains a complete XML tag. Similarly, the next three lines contain complete tags. In contrast, the fifth line contains two tags, <Name> and </Name>, with a text value in between. You'll see how this works in a moment.

The first tag in any XML document is an *XML declaration.* This declaration identifies the document as an XML document and indicates which XML version the document conforms to. In addition, the declaration can identify the character set that's being used for the document (encoding). In this example, the character set is UTF-8, the most common one used for XML documents in English-speaking countries. Note, however, that when you generate XML from Visual Studio, the encoding declaration is omitted by default.

The final item in the declaration (standalone) indicates whether the declarations for all the entities are included within the document, or whether an external DTD, or Document Type Definition, is to be used. As you'll see later in this chapter, a DTD is one way to describe the schema that defines the structure of the XML file.

An XML document can also contain *comments*. These are tags that begin with <!-- and end with -->. Between the tags, you can type anything you want. For instance, the second line in this figure is a comment that indicates what type of information is contained in the XML document. It's often a good idea to include similar comments in your own XML documents.

XML elements

Elements are the building blocks of XML. Each element in an XML document represents a single data item and is identified by two tags: a *start tag* and an *end tag*. The start tag marks the beginning of the element and provides the element's name. The end tag marks the end of the element and repeats the name, prefixed by a slash. For example, <Name> is the start tag for an element named Name, and </Name> is the corresponding end tag.

It's important to realize that XML doesn't provide a predefined set of element names the way HTML does. Instead, the element names are created so they describe the contents of each element. Note that XML names are case-sensitive, and that the name can't begin with the letters xml, a numeral, or an underscore. Also, spaces are not allowed in element names.

A complete element usually consists of the element's start tag, its end tag, and the *content* between the tags. For example, <City>Madison</City> indicates that the content of the City element is *Madison*. And <Address1>Attn: Supt. Window Services</Address1> indicates that the content of the Address1 element is *Attn: Supt. Window Services*. However, tags can also be empty, as you will see in figure 15-8.

A Vendor element and its child elements

```
<?xml version="1.0" encoding="utf-8" standalone="yes"?>
<!--Vendor information-->
<Vendors>
  <Vendor ID="1">
    <Name>U.S. Postal Service</Name>
    <Address1>Attn: Supt. Window Services</Address1>
    <Address2>PO Box 7005</Address2>
    <City>Madison</City>
    <State>WI</State>
    <ZipCode>53707</ZipCode>
  </Vendor>
</Vendors>
```

Vendor element

Name element

City element

A Vendor element with another level of child elements

```
<?xml version="1.0" encoding="utf-8" standalone="yes"?>
<!--Vendor information-->
<Vendors>
  <Vendor ID="1">
    <Name>U.S. Postal Service</Name>
    <StreetAddress>
      <Address1>Attn: Supt. Window Services</Address1>
      <Address2>PO Box 7005</Address2>
      <City>Madison</City>
      <State>WI</State>
      <ZipCode>53707</ZipCode>
    </StreetAddress>
  </Vendor>
</Vendors>
```

XML tags, declarations, and comments

- Each XML tag begins with < and ends with >.
- The first line in an XML document is an *XML declaration* that indicates which version of the XML standard is being used. The declaration can also identify the character set that's being used, and it can indicate whether all entity declarations are included.
- An XML document can include comments that clarify the information it contains. *XML comments* begin with the sequence <!-- and end with -->.

Elements

- An *element* is a unit of XML data that begins with a start tag and ends with an end tag. The start tag provides the name of the element and contains any attributes assigned to the element (see figure 15-3 for the details on attributes). The end tag repeats the name, prefixed with a slash (/).
- The *content* of an element is contained within the element's start and end tags.
- Elements can contain other elements. An element that's contained within another element is a *child element*. An element that contains other child elements is a parent element.
- A child element can itself have child elements, in which case it both a child and a parent.
- The highest-level parent element in an XML document is known as the *root element*. An XML document can have only one root element.

Figure 15-2 XML tags, declarations, comments, and elements

Besides content, elements can contain other elements, known as *child elements*. This lets you add structure to a *parent element*. For example, a parent Vendor element can have child elements that provide details about each vendor, such as the vendor's name and address. In this figure, for example, you can see that the start tags, end tags, and values for the Name, Address1, Address2, City, State, and ZipCode elements are contained between the start and end tags for the Vendor element. As a result, these elements are children of the Vendor element, and the Vendor element is the parent of each of these elements.

The XML in figure 15-2 also shows that a child element can itself be a parent element to additional child elements. For example, the second XML document in this figure shows how an element named StreetAddress can be used to contain the address elements. As a result, the StreetAddress element is a child of the Vendor element and the parent of the Address1, Address2, City, State, and ZipCode elements.

Although figure 15-2 doesn't show it, you should also realize that an element can contain more than one occurrence of a child element. The Vendors element in the XML document you saw in figure 15-1, for example, contained two occurrences of the Vendor element.

The highest-level parent element in an XML document is known as the *root element*, and an XML document can have only one root element. In the examples in figures 15-1 and 15-2, the root element is Vendors. For XML documents that contain repeating information, it's common to use a plural name for the root element to indicate that it contains multiple child elements.

XML attributes

As shown in figure 15-3, *attributes* are a concise way to provide data for XML elements. In the Vendors XML document, for example, each Vendor element has an ID attribute that provides an identifying number for the vendor. Thus, <Vendor ID="1"> contains an attribute named ID whose value is 1.

Here again, XML doesn't provide a set of predefined attributes. Instead, attributes are created as they're needed, using names that describe the content of the attributes. If an element has more than one attribute, the attributes can be listed in any order, but they must be separated from each other by one or more spaces. In addition, each attribute can appear only once within an element.

In many cases, you can choose to use either an element or an attribute to represent a data item. In the Vendors document, for example, I could have used a child element named ID rather than an attribute to represent each vendor's ID. Likewise, I could have used an attribute named Name rather than a child element for the vendor's name.

Because attributes are more concise than child elements, it is tempting to use attributes rather than child elements. However, an element with more than a few attributes soon becomes unwieldy. As a result, most experienced XML developers limit their use of attributes to certain types of information, such as identifiers like vendor ID numbers, product codes, and so on.

An XML document

```
<?xml version="1.0" encoding="utf-8" standalone="yes"?>
<!--Vendor information-->
<Vendors>
  <Vendor ID="1">                                          ID attribute
    <Name>U.S. Postal Service</Name>
    <Address1>Attn: Supt. Window Services</Address1>
    <Address2>PO Box 7005</Address2>
    <City>Madison</City>
    <State>WI</State>
    <ZipCode>53707</ZipCode>
  </Vendor>
</Vendors>
```

Description

- A start tag for an element can include one or more attributes. An attribute consists of an attribute name, an equal sign, and a literal value.
- The value of an attribute must be enclosed in single or double quotes.
- If an element has more than one attribute, the order in which the attributes appear doesn't matter, but the attributes must be separated by one or more spaces.

Differences between attributes and child elements

- The data for an element can be represented using child elements, attributes, or a combination of elements and attributes. The choice of whether to implement a data item as an attribute or as a separate child element is often a matter of preference.
- Two advantages of attributes are that they can appear in any order and they are more concise because they don't require end tags.
- Two advantages of child elements are that they are easier to read and they are more convenient for long string values.

Figure 15-3 XML attributes

An introduction to the XML Schema Definition language

An *XML schema* defines the structure that an XML document must adhere to for the document to be considered *valid*. To achieve this, the schema defines all the detailed requirements for the target XML file. This may include details of the elements and attributes that must exist in the XML file, together with details such as the order and number of child elements and default values. To specify the schema for an XML document, you use a *schema language*.

Two schema languages are supported by the XML standards: *Document Type Definition*, or *DTD*, and *XML Schema Definition*. XML Schema Definition is also known as *XSD*, but it's usually referred to as *XML schema*. XML schemas are generally seen as the long term replacement for DTDs, because they are more flexible and offer support for data types. ADO.NET is designed to work with XML schema.

Figure 15-4 presents a small section of an XML schema that defines a document that contains information about vendors. This schema is for the dataset named PayablesDataSet that contains the Vendors table that you've worked with throughout this book.

In the snippet of the XML schema shown here, you can see that there is a Vendors element that represents the Vendors table of the dataset. There is also one element for each column in the Vendors table, although only the VendorID and Name columns are shown in this snippet. This corresponds to the graphical representation of the dataset that you can see in the Dataset Designer in Visual Studio. For instance, the VendorID element in the schema specifies that the field is read-only, auto-incremented, and has the int data type.

One way to create an XML schema is by typing the correct XSD language elements into an XML document. However, when you want to access the schema for a dataset, it's much easier to let Visual Studio generate this for you. You have already seen two ways to do that in this book. In chapter 3, you learned how to generate the schema from a data source that you created using the Data Source Configuration Wizard. And in chapter 5, you saw how to use the Dataset Designer to generate the schema as you drag elements from the Server Explorer or the Toolbox.

You can view the complete schema by opening the XSD file in the default XML editor provided by Visual Studio. Recall that to do this, you right-click on the XSD file in the Solution Explorer and select Open With→XML (Text) Editor. The resulting file contains more detail than shown in the snippet in this figure, but much of it is similar. If a TableAdapter has been created, details of the connection, commands, and mappings will also be included in the XSD file.

An XML Schema Definition

```
<?xml version="1.0" standalone="yes"?>
<xs:schema id="PayablesDataSet"
targetNamespace="http://tempuri.org/PayablesDataSet.xsd"
xmlns:mstns="http://tempuri.org/PayablesDataSet.xsd"
xmlns="http://tempuri.org/PayablesDataSet.xsd"
xmlns:xs="http://www.w3.org/2001/XMLSchema" xmlns:msdata="urn:schemas-microsoft-
com:xml-msdata" attributeFormDefault="qualified" elementFormDefault="qualified">
  <xs:element name="PayablesDataSet" msdata:IsDataSet="true"
   msdata:UseCurrentLocale="true">
    <xs:complexType>
      <xs:choice minOccurs="0" maxOccurs="unbounded">
        <xs:element name="Vendors">
          <xs:complexType>
            <xs:sequence>
              <xs:element name="VendorID" msdata:ReadOnly="true"
              msdata:AutoIncrement="true" type="xs:int" />
              <xs:element name="Name">
                <xs:simpleType>
                  <xs:restriction base="xs:string">
                    <xs:maxLength value="50" />
                  </xs:restriction>
                </xs:simpleType>
              </xs:element>
            </xs:sequence>
            ...
          </xs:complexType>
        </xs:element>
      </xs:choice>
    </xs:complexType>
    <xs:unique name="Constraint1" msdata:PrimaryKey="true">
      <xs:selector xpath=".//mstns:Vendors" />
      <xs:field xpath="mstns:VendorID" />
    </xs:unique>
  </xs:element>
</xs:schema>
```

XML Schema Definition language elements

Element	Description
Schema	The parent element for the schema.
Element	Declares elements that can occur in the document.
Choice	Declares a list of elements, only one of which can occur in the document.
ComplexType	Declares a type that can contain attributes and other elements.
Sequence	Declares a sequence of items that must occur in the specified order.
SimpleType	Declares constraints and other information for elements that can't contain attributes or other elements.
Unique	Declares that the value of an attribute or element must be unique.

Description

- ADO.NET is designed to work with the *XML Schema Definition* (XSD) language. This language uses the elements listed above, as well as other elements, to define the structure of an XML document.

Figure 15-4 An introduction to the XML Schema Definition language

How to work with the XML Editor

Visual Studio includes an XML Editor that you can use to create or edit an XML document. The XML Editor is similar to the Code Editor that you use for working with Visual Basic code, but it includes features that make it easier to work with XML. Figure 15-5 shows how to use this editor.

Of course, since an XML file is just a text file with XML tags, you don't need to use the XML Editor to edit it. Instead, you can open or create an XML file in any text editor. Also, since XML is a standard format that's used on the web, you can use a web browser to open and view an XML document. For editing, though, you're going to want to take advantage of the improved layout, syntax checking, and Intellisense of Visual Studio's XML Editor.

How to add a new XML file to a project

To create a new XML file and add it to your project, you can use the Project→Add New Item command. This adds the file to your project, adds the XML declaration to the top of the file, and opens the file in the XML Editor. By default, the XML declaration will include both the XML version attribute and the encoding attribute that indicates which character set the document uses.

How to open an existing XML file

To open an existing XML file without adding the file to your project, you can use the File→Open command. Then, if the file has a common XML extension (such as xml, xsl, or config), it is opened in the XML Editor. In contrast, text files that contain XML content but don't have one of these file extensions will be opened in the text editor of Visual Studio.

To open an existing XML file that is contained in the Solution Explorer, right-click on the file, select the Open With command, and select XML (Text) Editor from the resulting dialog box.

How to edit an XML file

When you use the XML Editor, the task of editing XML files is simplified. For example, tags, content, attributes, values, and comments are color-coded so you can easily tell them apart. Also, when you type a start tag, the XML Editor automatically adds the end tag and positions the cursor between the start and end tags. To make it easy for you to view XML data, the XML Editor automatically indents child elements, and it provides for expanding and collapsing elements. If you experiment with this editor, you'll quickly see how easy it is to use.

An XML document in the XML Editor

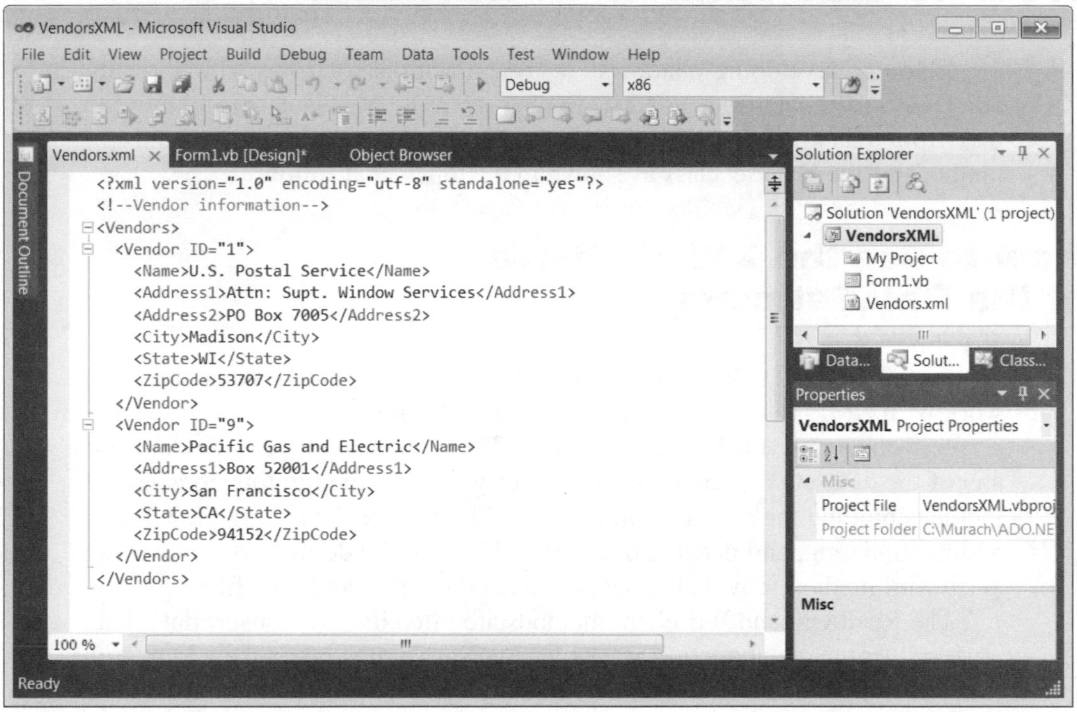

How to add a new XML file to a project

- Choose the Project→Add New Item command. In the Add New Item dialog box, select XML File in the Templates box, type a name for the XML file in the Name text box, and click Add. This adds an XML file to your project, adds the XML declaration for the document, and opens the document in the XML Editor.

How to open an existing XML file

- To open an existing XML file without adding the file to your project, use the File→Open command.
- To open an existing XML file that's stored in the project, double-click on the file in the Solution Explorer.

How to edit an XML file

- When you type a start tag, the XML Editor automatically adds an end tag for the element and positions the insertion point between the start and end tags so you can type the element's content.
- When you type an attribute, the XML Editor automatically adds a pair of quotation marks and positions the insertion point between them so you can type the attribute value.

How to use XML with datasets

If you're developing Windows Forms applications, one way to work with XML is to read data from an XML file into an ADO.NET dataset and to write data from a dataset to an XML file. To do that, you use the properties and methods of the DataSet class as shown in the topics that follow.

How to use the XML methods of the DataSet class

Figure 15-6 presents the methods of the DataSet class that you can use to work with XML data. To read data from an XML file into a dataset, for example, you can use the ReadXml method. Then, you can process the data using any of the dataset programming techniques you've learned in this book. That includes binding the data to form controls, filtering the data using views, and adding, updating, and deleting data rows. When you're done, you can use the WriteXml method to write the data from the dataset to an XML file.

The ReadXml and WriteXml methods are often used to convert data that's retrieved from a database to XML or vice versa. To illustrate, take a look at the first example in this figure. The first statement in this example uses the Fill method of a data adapter to load data from a database into a dataset. Then, the second statement uses the WriteXml method to write the data in XML format.

If you use the WriteXml method as shown in this example, the resulting XML file won't include schema information. But if you want to include an XML Schema Definition in the XML file, you code the XmlWriteMode.WriteSchema argument on the WriteXml method as shown in the second example. When you use the WriteXml method in this way, the XML file includes both the schema and the data. In that case, the schema appears as a separate element immediately after the root element, but before any data elements. If you want the file to include just the schema, you use the WriteXmlSchema method.

The third example shows how to read the contents of an XML file into a dataset. Here, a file named Payables.xml is read into a dataset named payablesDataSet. Note that you can use this method whether or not the XML file includes schema information. If it does include schema information, the ReadXml method uses this information to create the schema for the dataset. Otherwise, the ReadXml method creates the schema based on the XML data it finds in the file.

You can also use the GetXml method to retrieve XML data from a dataset as a string value. And you can use the GetXmlSchema method to retrieve the XML schema from a dataset as a string value. These methods are useful if you want to view the XML while you're testing an application.

Methods of the DataSet class for working with XML data

Method	Description
GetXml	Gets a string that contains the XML data for a dataset.
GetXmlSchema	Gets a string that contains the XML schema for a dataset.
ReadXml	Reads XML data from a file or stream into a dataset. The schema is inferred from the data if it isn't included in the file or stream.
ReadXmlSchema	Reads an XML schema from a file or stream into a dataset.
WriteXml	Writes XML data from a dataset to a stream or file.
WriteXmlSchema	Writes an XML schema from a dataset to a stream or file.

XmlWriteMode enumeration members

Member	Description
WriteSchema	Includes the XML schema in the output.
IgnoreSchema	Doesn't include the XML schema in the output. This is the default.
DiffGram	Includes the original and current versions of the rows in the output.

Code that fills a dataset and then writes the data to an XML file

```
vendorsTableAdapter.Fill(payablesDataSet.Vendors)
payablesDataSet.WriteXml("C:\Temp\Payables.xml")
```

Code that writes XML data and schema information to a file

```
vendorsTableAdapter.Fill(payablesDataSet.Vendors)
payablesDataSet.WriteXml("C:\Temp\Payables.xml", XmlWriteMode.WriteSchema)
```

Code that loads a dataset from an XML file

```
payablesDataSet.ReadXml("C:\Temp\Payables.xml")
```

Description

- The DataSet class includes methods that let you work with XML data. You can use these methods to save the contents of a dataset in XML format or to load a dataset from an XML file rather than from a database.
- The GetXml and GetXmlSchema methods are useful if you want to view the XML for a dataset. If you want to save the XML for a dataset to a file, use the WriteXml and WriteXmlSchema methods.
- The WriteXml, WriteXmlSchema, ReadXml, and ReadXmlSchema methods are overloaded to provide different ways of specifying the file to be written or read. You can specify the file name and path as a string, or you can specify a Stream, a TextWriter, or an XmlWriter object.
- You can specify one of the three values of the XmlWriteMode enumeration as a second argument on the WriteXml method to indicate what's included in the output. See figure 15-9 for more information on the DiffGram option.

Figure 15-6 How to use the XML methods of the DataSet class

How to control the format of XML output with column mappings

When you use one of the Write or Get methods in figure 15-6, ADO.NET generates the XML based on the data in the dataset and the information in the dataset class. By default, each row of each table is written as a separate element, and each column is represented as a child element. The dataset name, table names, and column names are used for the names of the elements.

If you're writing the dataset to an XML file so you can read it back into a dataset later on, this default XML format is fine. However, if the XML file will be processed by another application, you may need to alter the XML output based on the format that the application expects. For example, the application may expect different element names than the defaults, and it may expect some of the columns to be represented as attributes rather than elements.

Figure 15-7 presents some properties you can use to control the XML that's generated. To control the names of the elements that are generated, you use the DataSetName, TableName, and ColumnName properties of the appropriate object. To indicate whether the data in a child table is nested within the data in its parent table, you use the Nested property of the DataRelation object that defines the relationship between the two tables. You'll learn more about how this works in the next topic.

The ColumnMapping property lets you control how a column is rendered in the XML output. To set this property, you use the members of the MappingType enumeration shown in this figure. To see how this property works, look at the coding example. This example uses a dataset named payablesDataSet that contains a table named Vendors. The query that's used for this dataset (not shown) returns just the row for the vendor whose VendorID is 122, and it limits the selected fields to the six you can see in the first screenshot.

In the example, the second statement uses the GetXml method to retrieve the XML for the one row, and the third statement displays the data for the row as shown in the first message box. Then, the statements within the With statement set the ColumnMapping properties of five of the columns. Here, the first statement sets the ColumnMapping property of the VendorID column so it's created as an attribute rather than as an element, and the other statements set the ColumnMapping properties of other columns so they're hidden. Then, the last two statements in this example retrieve and display the XML again, as shown in the second message box. This illustrates how *column mappings* can be used to get the XML data that you want in the format that you want.

Properties that affect the XML that's generated for a dataset

Class	Property	Description
DataSet	DataSetName	Provides the name of the root element.
DataTable	TableName	Provides the name of the element for the table.
DataColumn	ColumnName	Provides the name of the element or attribute for the column.
DataColumn	ColumnMapping	Specifies how the column should be rendered in the XML output.
DataRelation	Nested	Specifies whether the data in a child table should be nested within the data in the parent table. See figure 15-8 for more information.

Common MappingType enumeration members

Member	Description
Attribute	Maps the column to an XML attribute.
Element	Maps the column to an XML element.
Hidden	Hides the column so it doesn't appear in the XML output.

Code that displays two variations of the XML for a dataset

```
Dim xmlData As String
xmlData = payablesDataSet.GetXml
MessageBox.Show(xmlData, "Vendor with elements")
With payablesDataSet.Vendors
    .VendorIDColumn.ColumnMapping = MappingType.Attribute
    .Address1Column.ColumnMapping = MappingType.Hidden
    .Address2Column.ColumnMapping = MappingType.Hidden
    .StateColumn.ColumnMapping = MappingType.Hidden
    .ZipCodeColumn.ColumnMapping = MappingType.Hidden
End With
xmlData = payablesDataSet.GetXml
MessageBox.Show(xmlData, "Vendor with an attribute and hidden columns")
```

The resulting message boxes

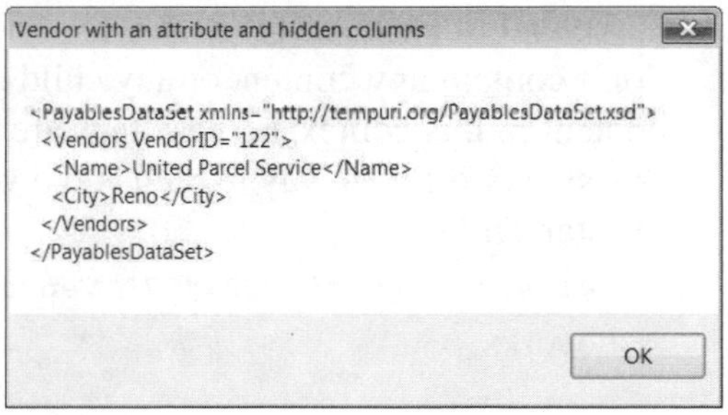

Description

- You can use the properties shown above to influence how the XML is generated when you use the GetXml, GetXmlSchema, WriteXml, or WriteXmlSchema methods.
- These properties don't affect the schema of the dataset within the application.

Figure 15-7 How to control the format of XML output with column mappings

How to nest data in XML output

The Nested property of the DataRelation class lets you control how the XML data for parent and child rows is generated. The examples in figure 15-8 should help you understand how this works. These examples show nested and unnested XML for a dataset that has two tables named Invoice and LineItem. In these examples, two invoices are shown for the Invoice table. The invoice with ID 77 has one line item, and the invoice with ID 78 has two line items.

If you nest the XML output, the LineItem elements appear nested within their corresponding Invoice elements as illustrated by the first XML example. To generate nested XML like this, you set the Nested property of the DataRelation object to True. Of course, for this to work properly you first have to define a data relation between the two tables. The example at the top of this figure shows how to set this property on a DataRelation named InvoicesLineItems in the payablesDataSet.

If you don't define a data relation between two related tables or you leave the Nested property of the data relation at its default setting of False, the data in the tables isn't nested. Then, the result will be as shown in the second XML example. Here, all the Invoice elements are listed first, and all of the LineItem elements follow.

The technique that you use depends on what the XML data will be used for. If it will be read back into a dataset, you'll usually create unnested XML. That way, the XML file will more closely correspond to the dataset's relational tables. On the other hand, if the XML data will be processed by an XML application, you'll usually create nested XML. That's because XML applications typically expect the data to be organized hierarchically, with child elements nested within their parent elements.

By the way, as you look at the unnested XML, you will see that the two Invoice elements don't have separate start and end tags. Instead, there is a slash at the end of each start tag. This is allowed in XML in cases where the elements don't contain any content or any child elements. (Attributes don't count as content in this context). These tags are usually referred to as *empty tags*, and this syntax offers a way to reduce the verbosity of the code. Note, however, that the standard syntax

```
<Invoice InvoiceID="77" VendorID="121"></Invoice>
```

also works.

Code that sets the Nested property

```
payablesDataSet.Relations("InvoicesLineItems").Nested = True
```

Nested XML

```
<Invoices xmlns="http://tempuri.org/PayablesDataSet.xsd">
  ...
  <Invoice InvoiceID="77" VendorID="121">
    <LineItem InvoiceSequence="1">
      <Amount>904.1400</Amount>
      <Description>Cover design</Description>
    </LineItem>
  </Invoice>
  <Invoice InvoiceID="78" VendorID="121">
    <LineItem InvoiceSequence="1">
      <Amount>1197.0000</Amount>
      <Description>Cover design</Description>
    </LineItem>
    <LineItem InvoiceSequence="2">
      <Amount>765.1300</Amount>
      <Description>Catalog design</Description>
    </LineItem>
  </Invoice>
  ...
</Invoices>
```

Unnested XML

```
<Invoices xmlns="http://tempuri.org/PayablesDataSet.xsd">
  ...
  <Invoice InvoiceID="77" VendorID="121" />
  <Invoice InvoiceID="78" VendorID="121" />
  ...
  <LineItem InvoiceID="77" InvoiceSequence="1">
    <Amount>904.1400</Amount>
    <Description>Cover design</Description>
  </LineItem>
  <LineItem InvoiceID="78" InvoiceSequence="1">
    <Amount>1197.0000</Amount>
    <Description>Cover design</Description>
  </LineItem>
  <LineItem InvoiceID="78" InvoiceSequence="2">
    <Amount>765.1300</Amount>
    <Description>Catalog design</Description>
  </LineItem>
  ...
</Invoices>
```

Description

- You can use the Nested property of the DataRelation class to nest child data within its parent data when you use the GetXml or WriteXml method. By default, the data isn't nested.
- Before you can set the Nested property, you must define a data relation between the two tables involved in the relationship.

Figure 15-8 How to nest data in XML output

How to use DiffGrams

Because the data in an application is likely to change, ADO.NET maintains one or more versions of each row in a data table. Rows that existed when the table was loaded have both an original version and a current version. If the row hasn't been changed, these versions are identical. If the row has been changed, the current version contains the modified data and the original version contains the original data. In addition, a row that's been added to the table has a current version but no original version. And a row that's been deleted has an original version but no current version.

Normally, the WriteXml method writes only the current version of each row to the XML file. However, you can write both versions by specifying XmlWriteMode.DiffGram on the WriteXml method as shown in figure 15-9. An XML file like this one, which contains both current and original row versions, is called a *DiffGram*.

If you study the XML output in this figure, you can see the two versions of the vendor row. Here, the difference between the current and original versions is the value of the Name column. In the current version, it's UPS. In the original version, it's United Parcel Service.

In most cases, you won't need to use a DiffGram. Instead, after you update the data in the database, you'll write the current version of each row to an XML file if you need to save it in that format. If you think you may need to recreate the dataset with both versions later on, though, you can save it as a DiffGram before you update the database. Sometimes, you may also need to save a dataset as a DiffGram to send it to another application for processing.

A DiffGram for a table that contains a single row

```
<?xml version="1.0" standalone="yes"?>
<diffgr:diffgram xmlns:msdata="urn:schemas-microsoft-com:xml-msdata"
xmlns:diffgr="urn:schemas-microsoft-com:xml-diffgram-v1">
  <PayablesDataSet xmlns="http://tempuri.org/PayablesDataSet.xsd">
    <Vendors diffgr:id="Vendors1" msdata:rowOrder="0"
        diffgr:hasChanges="modified">
      <VendorID>122</VendorID>
      <Name>UPS</Name>
      <Address1>P.O. Box 505820</Address1>
      <City>Reno</City>
      <State>NV</State>
      <ZipCode>88905</ZipCode>
    </Vendors>
  </PayablesDataSet>
  <diffgr:before>
    <Vendors diffgr:id="Vendors1" msdata:rowOrder="0"
        xmlns="http://tempuri.org/PayablesDataSet.xsd">
      <VendorID>122</VendorID>
      <Name>United Parcel Service</Name>
      <Address1>P.O. Box 505820</Address1>
      <City>Reno</City>
      <State>NV</State>
      <ZipCode>88905</ZipCode>
    </Vendors>
  </diffgr:before>
</diffgr:diffgram>
```

Current Vendor data

Original Vendor data

Code that writes an XML file in DiffGram format

```
payablesDataSet.WriteXml("C:\PayablesDiff.xml", XmlWriteMode.DiffGram)
```

Description

- A *DiffGram* is an XML document that contains both the current and original versions of the rows in a dataset. To create a DiffGram, specify XmlWriteMode.DiffGram as the second argument on a WriteXml method.
- You should save a dataset to a DiffGram before you execute the Update method of the dataset. Otherwise, the values in the current and original versions will be identical.
- When you use the ReadXml method to load a dataset from an XML file in DiffGram format, the appropriate row versions are created automatically.

Figure 15-9 How to use DiffGrams

How to use XML with web applications

If you're developing web applications, you can use the XML data source control to quickly and easily bind a control to an XML file so it displays the data in that file. In the topics that follow, you'll first learn how to create an XML data source. Then, you'll learn the basic skills for using an XML data source with a GridView control.

How to create an XML data source

Figure 15-10 shows the dialog box that's displayed when you drag the XmlDataSource component from the Toolbox to a form and select Configure Data Source from the smart tag menu. The only entry that's required in this dialog box is the location and name of the XML file that will be used as the source of data for the control, and you can use the first Browse button to locate this file. In this example, the file is located in the App_Data folder of the application.

In the Configure Data Source dialog box, you can also specify a transform file if you need to restructure the data in the XML file. To bind a GridView control to an XML data source, for example, the data you want to display in the control must be coded as attributes in the XML file. Then, if the data is coded as elements, you can use a transform file to change the elements to attributes. You'll see how this works in figure 15-14.

The third option is to specify an XPath expression that will be used to filter the data that's returned from the XML file. *XPath* is another query language, and you'll see how it works in figure 15-12.

The dialog box for creating an XML data source

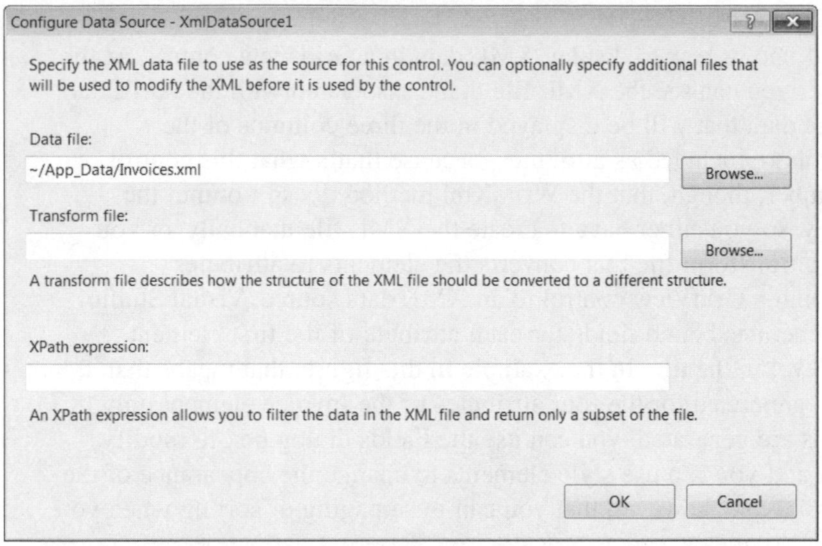

The code for the XML data source

```
<asp:XmlDataSource ID="XmlDataSource1" runat="server"
    DataFile="~/App_Data/Invoices.xml">
</asp:XmlDataSource>
```

Basic XML data source control attributes

Attribute	Description
ID	The ID for the XML data source control.
Runat	Must specify "server."
DataFile	The name and location of the XML file that's used as the data source.
TransformFile	The name and location of an XSL file that's used to transform the data.
XPath	An XPath query that's used to filter the data in the XML file.

Description

- To create an XML data source control, drag the XmlDataSource component from the Toolbox. Then, complete the Configure Data Source dialog box.
- You can also create an XML data source control by starting a new data source from a bindable control. This displays the Data Source Configuration Wizard dialog box you saw in figure 11-13 of chapter 11. Then, you can select the XML File option and click the OK button to display the dialog box shown above.
- To restructure the data in the XML file, you can enter the name and location of a transform file (see figure 15-14).
- To filter the data in the XML file, you can enter an XPath expression (see figure 15-12).
- The file you specify in the Data File text box is assigned to the DataFile property of the XML data source, and the XPath query you specify in the XPath Expression box is assigned to the XPath property.

Figure 15-10 How to create an XML data source

How to display XML data in a GridView control

Figure 15-11 shows how to display XML data in a GridView control. At the top of this figure, you can see the XML file that's associated with the XML data source. Here, the data that will be displayed in the three columns of the GridView control are included as attributes, because that's what this control requires. Remember, though, that the WriteXml method doesn't output the XML in this way, so you either have to create the XML file manually, or you need to specify a transform file that converts the elements to attributes.

When you bind a GridView control to an XML data source, Visual Studio automatically generates bound fields for each attribute of the first element below the root level in the file. In the example in this figure, that means that bound fields are generated for the four attributes of the Invoice element only. Once these fields are generated, you can use the Fields dialog box to modify their properties, and you can use style elements to change the appearance of the GridView control. Note, however, that you can't use paging or sorting when you use an XML data source.

Although this figure shows only how to display XML data in a GridView control, you should know that you can also use an XML data source to maintain XML data. To do that, however, you must use custom code to work with the XML data source. Because of that, the XML data source control is typically used only to display data in a bound control.

An XML file with invoice and line item data

```
<?xml version="1.0" standalone="yes"?>
<Invoices>
  <Invoice InvoiceID="77" InvoiceNumber="97/553"
           InvoiceDate="10/25/2010" InvoiceTotal="904.14" >
    <LineItem InvoiceSequence="1" Amount="904.14"
              Description="Cover design" >
    </LineItem>
  </Invoice>
  <Invoice InvoiceID="78" InvoiceNumber="97/522"
           InvoiceDate="10/28/2010" InvoiceTotal="1962.13">
    <LineItem InvoiceSequence="1" Amount="1197"
              Description="Cover design" >
    </LineItem>
    <LineItem InvoiceSequence="2" Amount="765.13"
              Description="Catalog design" >
    </LineItem>
  </Invoice>
</Invoices>
```

A GridView control that displays invoice data from the XML file

Invoice Number	Invoice Date	Invoice Total
97/553	10/25/2010	904.14
97/522	10/28/2010	1962.13

The aspx code for the GridView and XML data source controls

```
<asp:GridView ID="grdInvoices" runat="server"
    AutoGenerateColumns="False" DataSourceID="XmlDataSource1"
    CellPadding="4" ForeColor="#333333" GridLines="None">
    <AlternatingRowStyle BackColor="White" />
    <Columns>
        <asp:BoundField DataField="InvoiceID" HeaderText="InvoiceID"
            Visible="false" />
        <asp:BoundField DataField="InvoiceNumber"
            HeaderText="Invoice Number">
            <HeaderStyle HorizontalAlign="Left" />
            <ItemStyle Width="125px" />
        </asp:BoundField>
        ...
    </Columns>
    ...
</asp:GridView>
<asp:XmlDataSource ID="XmlDataSource1" runat="server"
    DataFile="~/App_Data/Invoices.xml"></asp:XmlDataSource>
```

Description

- The GridView control requires that all data that's displayed from an XML file must be represented as attributes. In addition, all attribute values must be enclosed in quotes.
- The GridView control can bind to only one level of data in an XML file. By default, it binds to the first level below the root level.

Figure 15-11 How to display XML data in a GridView control

How to filter XML data with an XPath query

In the previous figure, the GridView control displayed the attributes of the Invoice element, since this element is the first element below the root element. If you want to display attributes at a different level, however, you can specify an *XPath query* for the XML data source. Figure 15-12 illustrates how this works.

At the top of this figure, you can see the GridView control from the previous figure with a Select command field added. When the user clicks the Select button for a specific invoice, a second GridView control is displayed with the line items for that invoice. To accomplish that, this GridView control is bound to the data source that's shown in this figure. As you can see, this data source specifies an XPath query that points to the LineItem element in the XML file that's shown in figure 15-11.

If you ran this application with just these two GridView controls and XML data sources, you'd see that no matter which invoice you selected, the line items for all invoices would be displayed. That's because the XPath query doesn't specify which invoice line items to display. To do that, you have to use Visual Basic code like the code shown in this figure to set the XPath property of the data source so it retrieves the appropriate line items.

Before I describe this code, you may be wondering why you specify the XPath query when you create the data source if you have to change it as the application executes. The answer is that you need to include the XPath query so the appropriate bound fields are generated for the GridView control. In this case, for example, bound fields are generated for the attributes of the LineItem element.

The Visual Basic code for this application is executed when the user clicks a Select button in the first GridView control. Then, the SelectedValue property of the grid is used to get the InvoiceID for the selected invoice. Note that for this to work, you have to set the DataKeyNames property of the first GridView control to the InvoiceID field, so its aspx code will look like this:

```
<asp:GridView ID="grdInvoices" runat="server"
    AutoGenerateColumns="False" DataSourceID="XmlDataSource1"
    DataKeyNames="InvoiceID">
```

Once it retrieves the invoice ID, the Visual Basic code uses the Format method of the String class to create the XPath query. This method returns the string specified by the first argument with the value specified by the second argument substituted for the format specification ({0} in this example). In this case, the string is a location path and the value is the invoice ID. Here, the invoice ID is used to get the Invoice element with an InvoiceID attribute that's equal to the invoice ID. Then, only the LineItem elements for that invoice are included in the results.

The last line of code sets the Visible property of the GridView control that displays the line items to True so it's displayed on the form. As you can see in the aspx code for this GridView control, this property is set to False initially. If it was set to True, the line items for all of the invoices would be displayed in the grid when the page was first displayed, which isn't what you want.

GridView controls that use an XPath query to display child elements

Invoice Number	Invoice Date	Invoice Total	
97/553	10/25/2010	904.14	Select
97/522	**10/28/2010**	**1962.13**	Select

Description	Amount
Cover design	1197
Catalog design	765.13

The aspx code for the second XML data source control

```
<asp:XmlDataSource ID="XmlDataSource2" runat="server"
    DataFile="~/App_Data/Invoices.xml"
    XPath="/Invoices/Invoice/LineItem">
</asp:XmlDataSource>
```

The aspx code for the second GridView control

```
<asp:GridView ID="grdLineItems" runat="server" Visible="False"
    AutoGenerateColumns="False" DataSourceID="XmlDataSource2" >
    <Columns>
        <asp:BoundField DataField="InvoiceSequence"
            HeaderText="InvoiceSequence" Visible="False" />
        <asp:BoundField DataField="Description" HeaderText="Description">
            <ItemStyle Width="200px"/>
            <HeaderStyle HorizontalAlign="Left" />
        </asp:BoundField>
        <asp:BoundField DataField="Amount" HeaderText="Amount">
            <ItemStyle HorizontalAlign="Right" Width="100px" />
            <HeaderStyle HorizontalAlign="Right" />
        </asp:BoundField>
    </Columns>
    ...
</asp:GridView>
```

VB code for the first GridView control that sets the XPath property

```
Protected Sub grdInvoices_SelectedIndexChanged(ByVal sender As Object,
       ByVal e As System.EventArgs) Handles
grdInvoices.SelectedIndexChanged
    Dim invoiceID As Integer = grdInvoices.SelectedValue
    XmlDataSource2.XPath =
       String.Format("/Invoices/Invoice[@InvoiceID='{0}']/LineItem",
           invoiceID)
    grdLineItems.Visible = True
End Sub
```

Description

- To display child elements from an XML file, you can specify a path location for the XPath property. To display selected child elements, include an expression that specifies the attribute values you want to include.
- To use the SelectedValue property of a GridView control, the DataKeyNames property of the master GridView control in a master/detail display must be set to the key field.

Figure 15-12 How to filter XML data with an XPath query

How to use XSLT to transform XML

XML documents describe the structure and content of the data, but they don't include any instructions on how the data should be formatted when it's displayed. In contrast, *Extensible Stylesheet Language,* or *XSL,* consists of three components that let you transform XML documents into formats that suit the requirements of your applications.

XSL Transformations, or *XSLT*, is the component that you use for transforming an XML file into another format. *XPath*, which you've already seen, is the component that you use to navigate to specific parts of an XML document. And *XSL Formatting Objects (XSL-FO)* is the component that you use to specify the visual formatting of XML data as output on a monitor, printer, or other device.

In the topics that follow, you'll learn how to use XSLT because that's the component that you'll use for doing the transformations that your applications require. Specifically, you'll see how XSLT can be used for three different types of applications.

An introduction to XSL style sheets

To transform the XML data into the required output format, you use an XSL style sheet, as diagramed in figure 15-13. Within that style sheet, XSLT is used to set the detailed instructions for transforming the XML to the required output format. To do this, XSLT uses XPath to search the XML source document for content that matches its template specifications.

An XSLT template is a set of rules that are applied when a match is found. The instructions in the template are used to transform the matching section of the source document into the required format. This transformation results in a new document, so the XML source document isn't changed

The table in this figure lists some of the commonly-used elements of XSL style sheets and XSLT templates. In the next three figures, you'll see how these elements are used for three different applications.

The XML transformation process using XSL

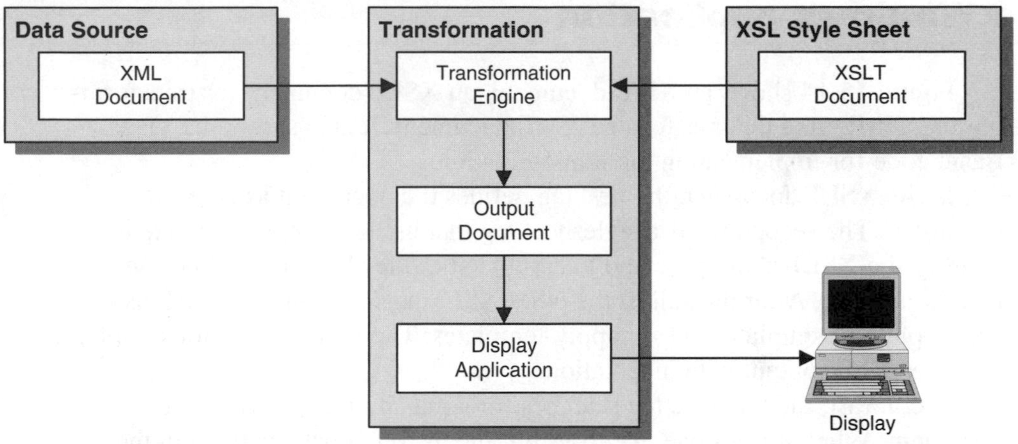

Common elements used in XSL Transformations

Element	Description
xsl:stylesheet	Defines the XSLT document and creates the xsl namespace.
xsl:output	Specifies the spacing and indenting used in the output.
xsl:template	Defines a series of statements to be executed when a matching element is found.
xsl:apply-templates	Applies a template to the current element or to its child elements.
xsl:value-of	Outputs a value specified by its select argument.
xsl:attribute	Creates an attribute in the output file.
xsl:choose	Evaluates a set of expressions and executes instructions when the expression is true.
xsl:for-each	Loops through a set of elements.
xsl:if	Performs an action if the specified condition is true.
xsl:preserve-space	Preserves the white space found in specified elements of the source document.
xsl:text	Adds text to the output document.

Description

- *Extensible Stylesheet Language* (XSL) consists of three components: XSL Transformations (XSLT), XPath, and XSL Formatting Objects (XSL-FO).
- An XSL style sheet can be applied to an XML source document to create an output document in a different format.
- XPath is used to find content in the source document that matches the templates in the XSL style sheet.
- When a match is found, the transformation described in the XSLT document is applied. Then, the transformed output is saved in a new file, which in some cases is a temporary file.

Figure 15-13 How to transform an XML file using XSL

How to transform an XML file for a Windows application

Figure 15-14 shows an XML document, an XSLT document for transforming that XML, and the transformed XML document. It also shows the Visual Basic code for implementing the transformation.

In the XSLT document, the first tag defines the document as an XML document. The second tag is a stylesheet tag that uses the xmlns attribute to identify the XSLT namespace and to assign xsl as the alias that will be used for that namespace. After that, all of the other XSLT tags can start with xsl: as in xsl:output, xsl:template, and xsl:apply-templates. The output tag, for example, specifies XML output with indentation.

In contrast, the template tag searches for a match in the XML source document. When it finds one, it carries out the instructions contained in the template. For instance, the first template tag searches for the root name Vendors, and it transforms this name to VendorsMin. Then, it uses the apply-templates tag to apply the second template tag within the VendorsMin tag.

This second template tag searches for an element named Vendor in the XML document. Then, it transforms this name to VendorName, sets the ID attribute for the VendorName tag to the ID value in the original document, and uses the value-of tag to take the content from the Name element of the original document and use it as the content for the VendorName tag. You can see the results in the transformed XML document.

To implement the transformation that's specified by the XSLT file, you use Visual Basic code, as shown in the last example in this figure. This code first creates a new XslCompiledTransform object named TransformVendors. Then, it uses the Load method of this object to load the transform file, and it uses the Transform method of this object to convert the original Vendors.xml file to a new file named VendorsMin.xml.

An XML document (Vendors.xml)

```
<?xml version="1.0" encoding="utf-8" standalone="yes"?>
<Vendors>
  <Vendor ID="1">
    <Name>U.S. Postal Service</Name>
    <Address>PO Box 7005</Address>
    <City>Madison</City>
    <State>WI</State>
  </Vendor>
  <Vendor ID="9">
    <Name>Pacific Gas and Electric</Name>
    <Address>Box 52001</Address>
    <City>San Francisco</City>
    <State>CA</State>
  </Vendor>
</Vendors>
```

An XSLT document (VendorsTransform.xsl)

```
<?xml version="1.0" encoding="UTF-8"?>
<xsl:stylesheet xmlns:xsl="http://www.w3.org/1999/XSL/Transform"
    version="1.0">
<xsl:output method="xml" indent="yes" />
  <xsl:template match="/Vendors">
    <VendorsMin>
      <xsl:apply-templates select="Vendor"/>
    </VendorsMin>
  </xsl:template>
  <xsl:template match="Vendor">
    <VendorName ID="{@ID}">
      <xsl:value-of select="Name" />
    </VendorName>
  </xsl:template>
</xsl:stylesheet>
```

The transformed XML document (VendorsMin.xml)

```
<?xml version="1.0" encoding="utf-8"?>
<VendorsMin>
  <VendorName ID="1">U.S. Postal Service</VendorName>
  <VendorName ID="9">Pacific Gas and Electric</VendorName>
</VendorsMin>
```

Visual Basic code that implements the transformation

```
Dim TransformVendors As New Xml.Xsl.XslCompiledTransform()
TransformVendors.Load("VendorsTransform.xsl")
TransformVendors.Transform("Vendors.xml", "VendorsMin.xml")
```

Description

- To transform an XML document as specified by an XSLT style sheet, you create a new XslCompiledTransform object. Then, you use its Load method to load the XSLT document, and its Transform method to transform the contents of the original XML file into a new XML file.
- In the xmlns attribute of the stylesheet tag for an XSLT document, you specify the namespace for XSLT as well as an alias like xls that is used to identify the XSLT tags.

Figure 15-14 How to transform an XML file for a Windows application

How to transform an XML file for a GridView control

Figure 15-15 shows how to create a transform file for a GridView control. Since a GridView control requires that all the data for a row be stored as attributes in an XML file, this transform file converts the elements for the required columns to attributes.

Here again, the stylesheet tag identifies the namespace of the XSLT language and assigns the alias xsl to the XSLT tags. This time, the output tag says that the XML declarations should be omitted and that the document should be a standalone document. This is consistent with the requirements of the GridView control.

Next, the template tag moves recursively through the XML source document and creates attributes for each of the targeted attributes and elements. First, a for-each tag goes through all of the Vendor elements in the Vendors root tag. Then, a second for-each tag goes through all of the fields within each Vendor tag. Within this second loop, the four fields shown in the GridView control are set to attributes. These are the ID attribute, and the Name, City, and State elements.

Note that in order to tell the processor that ID is an attribute in the source document, it is prefixed with an @ symbol. In contrast, if ID were an element instead of an attribute, you would code the expression "ID".

To do the transformation that's specified by this XSLT file, you specify the transform file when you configure the XML data source. This is shown by the text box in this figure, which is a part of the Configure Data Source dialog box shown in figure 15-10.

An XSLT document for a GridView control (Vendors.xsl)

```
<xsl:stylesheet version="1.0"
  xmlns:xsl="http://www.w3.org/1999/XSL/Transform">
  <xsl:output method="xml" omit-xml-declaration="yes"
      indent="yes" standalone="yes" />
  <xsl:template match="/">
    <xsl:for-each select="Vendors">
      <xsl:element name="Vendors">
        <xsl:for-each select="Vendor">
          <xsl:element name="Vendor">
            <xsl:attribute name="ID">
              <xsl:value-of select="@ID"/>
            </xsl:attribute>
            <xsl:attribute name="Name">
              <xsl:value-of select="Name"/>
            </xsl:attribute>
            <xsl:attribute name="City">
                <xsl:value-of select="City"/>
            </xsl:attribute>
            <xsl:attribute name="State">
              <xsl:value-of select="State"/>
            </xsl:attribute>
          </xsl:element>
        </xsl:for-each>
      </xsl:element>
    </xsl:for-each>
  </xsl:template>
```

The transform file specification in the Configure Data Source dialog box

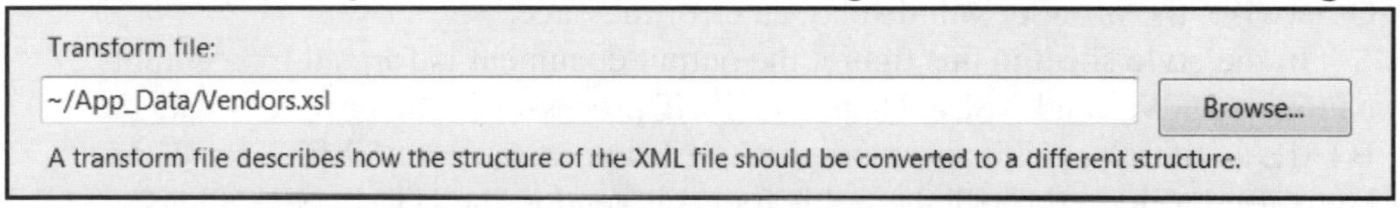

A GridView control that displays the transformed data

ID	Name	City	State
1	U.S. Postal Service	Madison	WI
9	Pacific Gas and Electric	San Francisco	CA

Description

- The XSL style sheet for a GridView control should read the XML source document and output all of the elements that are used by the GridView control as attributes.
- When you configure the XML data source for the GridView control, you enter the name of the XSLT file in the Transform file text box (see figure 15-10). Then, the transformed XML data is used to populate the columns of the GridView control.

How to transform an XML file when it's displayed in a browser

Figure 15-16 demonstrates another way in which an XML file can be transformed. This time, an XML document is linked to an XSLT style sheet. Then, when the XML document is opened by a browser, it is automatically transformed.

The first example in this figure shows the first three lines of another version of the XML file that's in figure 15-1. The only change to this document is the addition of the xml-stylesheet tag that identifies the XSLT file that will be used for the transformation. This tag must be placed at the start of the file, right after the XML declaration. This tag links the XML document to an XSLT style sheet named VendorsToHTML.xsl

The second example in this figure shows the VendorsToHTML.xsl document. This document contains the template tag that's used to transform the XML document when the document is opened in the browser. Because the XML file is being opened in a browser, the output is written to a temporary output tree, not to a new file.

This works because Internet Explorer and the other major browsers have built-in XSLT processors that enable them to read the XML document and the XSLT style sheet. Assuming that both documents conform to the standard syntax requirements of XML, all of the required transformations are done on the fly, and the results are displayed in the browser, as shown in this figure. Otherwise, the browser will display an error message.

In the style sheet in this figure, the output document is formed by a combination of HTML and XSLT. Then, the XSLT processor in the browser treats the HTML as literals, and it processes the XSLT. For instance, the XSLT for-each tag is used to loop through the fields for each Vendor, the HTML SPAN tags display the labels for the Name and City fields, and the XSLT value-of tags get the data for the Name and City fields.

A transformed XML file in a browser

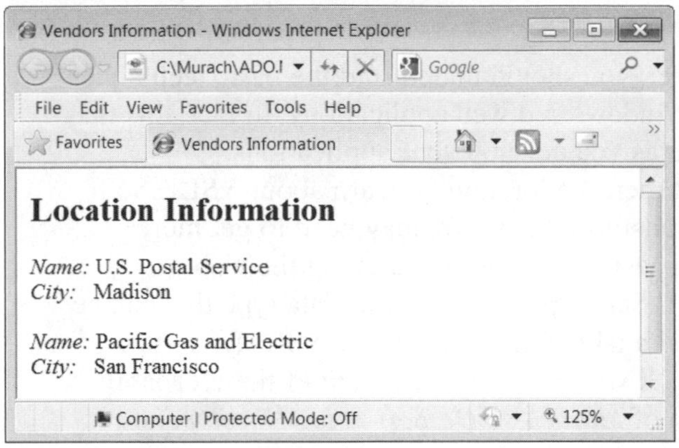

The start of the XML document in figure 15-1 with an xml-stylesheet tag

```
<?xml version="1.0" encoding="utf-8" standalone="yes"?>
<?xml-stylesheet type="text/xsl" href="VendorsToHTML.xsl"?>
<Vendors>
  ...
```

The XSLT document for the transformation (VendorsToHTML.xsl)

```
<xsl:stylesheet version="1.0"
    xmlns:xsl="http://www.w3.org/1999/XSL/Transform">
  <xsl:output method="xml" omit-xml-declaration="yes"
      indent="yes" standalone="yes"   />
  <xsl:template match="/">
    <HTML>
      <HEAD>
        <TITLE>Vendors Information</TITLE>
      </HEAD>
      <BODY>
      <H2>Location Information </H2>
        <xsl:for-each select="Vendors/Vendor">
          <SPAN STYLE="font-style:italic">Name: </SPAN>
            <xsl:value-of select="Name"/><BR/>
          <SPAN STYLE="font-style:italic">City:   </SPAN>
            <xsl:value-of select="City"/><BR/><BR/>
        </xsl:for-each>
      </BODY>
    </HTML>
  </xsl:template>
</xsl:stylesheet>
```

Description

- An XSLT style sheet can be linked to an XML document by coding the xml-stylesheet tag in the XML document. Then, the XML document is transformed when it is opened by a browser.
- The XSLT style sheet can include HTML tags and content, which are treated as literals, as well as XSLT tags.

Figure 15-16 How to transform an XML file when it's displayed in a browser

Perspective

Now that you've read this chapter, you should understand the basic techniques for working with XML from both Windows and web applications. In fact, this may be all you need to know about XML as you develop your applications.

You should realize, though, that there's a lot more to learn about XSLT. So if you need to do more complicated transformations, you may need to get more information about XSLT, which can easily be done by searching the web.

You should also realize that SQL Server provides an xml data type that can be used for storing XML in a column of a table. Then, you can use SELECT statements to retrieve and work with that XML. For a full treatment of these capabilities, please refer to the latest edition of *Murach's SQL Server for Developers.*

Terms

XML (Extensible Markup Language)
XML document
tag
XML declaration
comment
element
start tag
end tag
content
child element
parent element
root element
attribute
XML schema
valid XML document
schema language
Document Type Definition (DTD)
XML Schema Definition (XSD)
column mapping
empty tag
DiffGram
XPath query
Extensible Stylesheet Language (XSL)
XSL Transformations (XSLT)
XSL Formatting Objects (XSL-FO),

Exercise 15-1 Write XML files from a dataset

In this exercise, you'll use the methods of the DataSet class to write XML data and schema to files.

Use the WriteXml method of the DataSet class

1. Open the VendorsInformation project in your Chapter 15 folder. Then, open the code for Form1.
2. In the click event handler for the first button (btnXML) on the form, use the code in the first example in figure 15-6 to load the Payables dataset and write its data to an XML file named Vendors.xml in the Chapter 15 folder. To make this work, you'll have to adjust the path used in the WriteXML method and make sure that the path is valid.
3. Run the project, and click the Write XML button to write the XML file. Then, use the File→Open command to open the XML file in the XML text editor.

Use the WriteXmlSchema method of the DataSet class

4. In the click event handler for the second button (btnSchema), load the Payables dataset again. Then, use the WriteXmlSchema method shown in the table at the top of figure 15-6 to write the schema of the Payables dataset to an XML file named VendorsSchema.xml in the Chapter 15 folder.
5. Run the project, and click the Write Schema Only button. Then, use the File→Open command to view this file.

Write the XML data and schema to file

6. In the click event handler for the third button (btnXmlAndSchema), load the Payables dataset again. Then, use the WriteXml method shown in the second example in figure 15-6 to write both the XML and the schema of the Payables dataset to an XML file named VendorsWithSchema.xml in the Chapter 15 folder.
7. Run the project, and click the XML + Schema button. Then, view this file in the XML Editor.

Exercise 15-2 Use an XML data source with a GridView control

In this exercise, you'll create and configure an XmlDataSource control and use it to populate a GridView control in a web application. Then you'll edit the transform file that's used by the XML data source.

Use an XmlDataSource with a GridView

1. Use the File→Open Web Site command to open the VendorsGridView project in your Chapter 15 folder.

2. Right-click on the App_Data folder in the Solution Explorer and select the Add Existing Item menu command. Then, navigate to the Exercise Documents subfolder in the Chapter 15 folder, select the VendorsTopTen.xml and VendorsTransform.xsl files, and click on the Add button to add these files to the App_Data folder.
3. Open the xml and xsl files that you just added to the App_Data folder. Then, confirm that the xml file contains the data for just 10 vendors, and the xsl file transforms four of the elements in the xml file to attributes.
4. Double-click on the Default.aspx file in the Solution Explorer to open it. Then, drag an XmlDataSource control from the Toolbox onto it.
5. Configure the XmlDataSource control as shown in figure 15-10. Set the Data file to VendorsTopTen.xml and the Transform file to VendorsTransform.xsl.
6. Drag a GridView control from the Toolbox onto the Design pane of the Default.aspx page. Then, in the smart tag menu for this control, use the drop-down list for Choose Data Source to select the XML data source.
7. Build and run the application. Then, confirm that the data for 10 vendors is displayed in the GridView control. Also confirm that the columns for each vendor consist of the four elements that were converted to attributes by the transform file.

Edit the transform file

8. In the VendorsTransform.xsl file, add code that will convert the zip code element to an attribute so it can be displayed in the GridView control right after the state column. To do that, you insert code like this into the transform file:

```
<xsl:attribute name="ZipCode">
    <xsl:value-of select="ZipCode"/>
</xsl:attribute>
```

9. Click on the smart tag of the GridView control, and select Refresh Schema. Then, click Yes in answer to the question that's displayed in the message box. Note that the GridView control in the Design pane now shows the change.
10. Run the application, and confirm that the additional information for the vendors is displayed in the GridView control.

16

How to use the reporting features of Visual Studio

This chapter shows you how to use the Visual Studio features for preparing reports and for displaying those reports in both Windows and web applications. These are powerful features that are valuable for many types of applications.

Note, however, that these features aren't available with the Express Editions of either Visual Basic 2010 or Visual Web Developer 2010. So, if you're using an Express Edition, you won't be able to practice the skills of this chapter.

Introduction to the reporting features

The reporting features of Visual Studio are based on the technology used by Microsoft's *SQL Server Reporting Services (SSRS)*. SSRS offers a wide range of tools that can be used to create, manage, display, and deliver reports from SQL Server.

In contrast, Visual Studio offers a Report Wizard and a Report Designer that you can use to design reports. It also offers a ReportViewer control that you can use to display and print your reports in both Windows and web applications. This control lets you display *local reports* that are stored on the client computer, as well as remote reports that are stored on a report server. In this chapter, you will learn how to create and display local reports.

The five types of reports

The table in figure 16-1 shows the five types of reports that you can create with Visual Studio. When you're using the Report Designer, each of these report types is called a *data region.* For instance, a table data region displays a table report, and a list data region displays a list report. If necessary, you can combine two or more data regions in a single report.

A *table* displays data in tabular form and can include totals for each group in the data. For instance, a table can list all of the invoices for each vendor, display an invoice total for each vendor, and display a grand total for all of the invoices. In contrast, a *list* is free form display that can be used for name badges, menus, customer information, and so on.

A *matrix* is also known as a crosstab or pivot table report. In a matrix, both the rows and columns can be expanded to reveal further levels of data.

A *chart* can be used to display data in a variety of graphical presentations. For instance, pie charts and bar charts are commonly used to present business data.

A *gauge* also presents data graphically, but in two different ways. A radial gauge is similar to a vehicle speedometer. A linear gauge is similar to a progress bar.

Five types of reports that you can prepare with Visual Studio

Data Region	Layout style
Table	Columns and rows in a tabular format, as in figure 16-16.
List	Free form, as in the example below.
Matrix	Columns and rows in a tabular format, as in figure 16-18.
Chart	Graph or chart, as in figure 16-20.
Gauge	Graphical representation of data with an indicator to highlight a value.

A list report displayed in a ReportViewer control

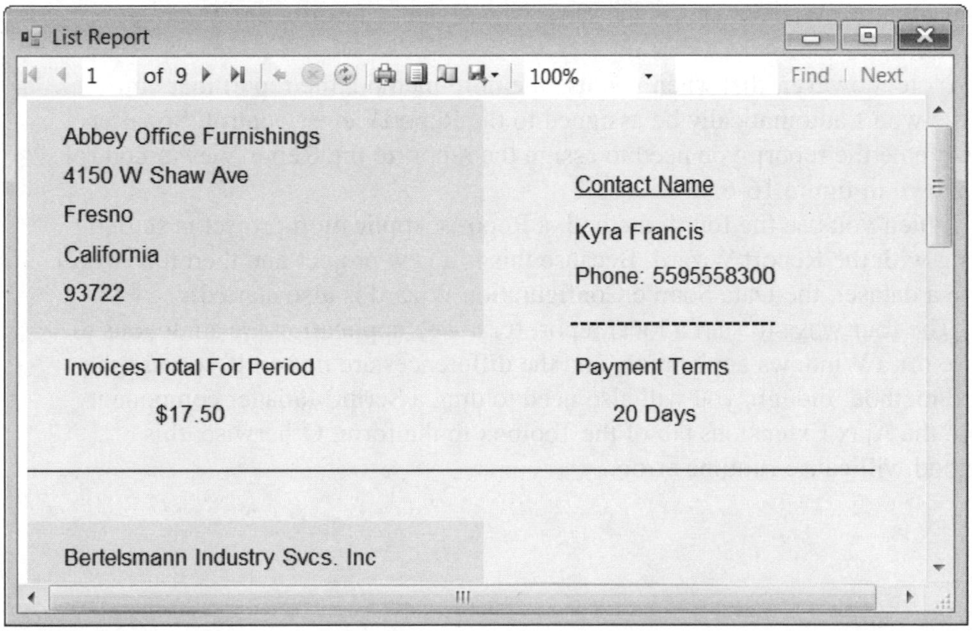

Description

- To help you prepare reports from a dataset, Visual Studio provides a Report Wizard and a Report Designer.
- To display a report in a Windows or web application, you add a ReportViewer control to a form.
- A *local report* is a report that is stored with the application on a client computer. A remote report is a report that is stored on a report server.
- When you design local reports with the Report Designer, each of the report types is known as a *data region*.
- A single report may contain more than one data region.

Figure 16-1 Introduction to the reporting features of Visual Studio

Four ways to start a local report for a Windows or web application

When you use Visual Studio, you can start a report in four different ways, as summarized in figure 16-2. When you use the first method for a Windows application, an empty report will be added to the project and displayed in the Report Designer. You can then use the Report Designer to build the report.

When you use the second or third method, the Report Wizard will start. Then, if the project doesn't already contain a dataset that can be used as the data source for the report, the Wizard will automatically start the Data Source Configuration Wizard. This is the same wizard that's described in figure 3-2 of chapter 3.

Note, however, that when you use the third method, the report that you create won't automatically be assigned to the ReportViewer control. So, after you create the report, you need to assign the report to the ReportViewer control as shown in figure 16-6.

When you use the fourth method, a Reports Application project is started along with the Report Wizard. Because this is a new project and therefore won't have a dataset, the Data Source Configuration Wizard is also started.

The four ways to start a local report for a web application are analogous to those for a Windows application, and the differences are minor. If you use the third method, though, you will also need to drag a ScriptManager component from the Ajax Extensions tab of the Toolbox to the form. Otherwise, this method will cause runtime errors.

The Add New Item dialog box for creating reports

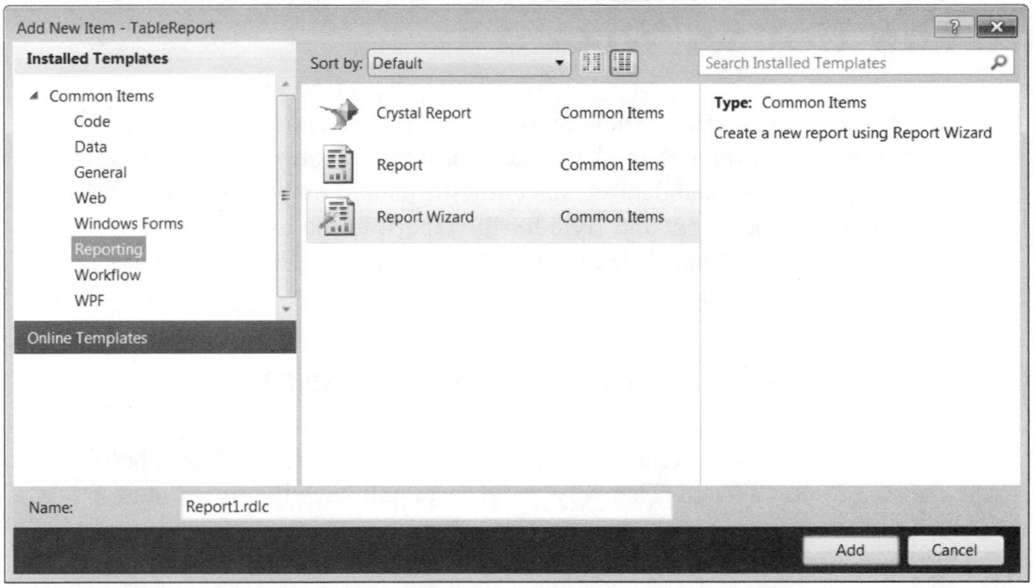

Four ways to create a local report in a Windows application

- Select the Project→Add New Item command, and select Reporting from the Common Items list in the dialog box that appears. Then, select Report from the list in the center pane.
- Select the Project→Add New Item command, and select Reporting from the Common Items list in the dialog box that appears. Then, select Report Wizard from the list in the center pane.
- Drag the ReportViewer control from the Reporting tab of the Toolbox to a form. Then, select the Design a New Report item from its smart tag menu.
- Create a new project. In the New Project dialog box, select Reporting from the list under the Installed Templates heading. Then, select Reports Application from the list in the center pane.

Four ways to create a local report in a web application

- Select the Website→Add New Item command. Then, select Report from the list in the center pane of the dialog box that appears.
- Select the Website→Add New Item command. Then, select Report Wizard from the list in the center pane of the dialog box that appears.
- Drag the ReportViewer control from the Reporting tab of the Toolbox to a form. Then, select the Design a New Report item from the smart tag menu. Last, drag a ScriptManager component from the Ajax Extensions tab of the Toolbox to the form. Otherwise, this method will cause runtime errors.
- Create a new web site. In the New Web Site dialog box, select ASP.NET Reports Web Site from the list in the center pane.

Figure 16-2 Four ways to start a local report for a Windows or web application

How to create a report with the Report Wizard

The easiest way to create a new report is to use the Report Wizard. This wizard will walk you through the basic steps of report creation. That includes setting up a data source and dataset, selecting the data to display and summarize, and choosing the layout and style for the report. In the example that follows, I've used the Report Wizard for a Windows application, but the steps are the same for a web application.

How to select a data source and dataset

In general, it's best to create the data source and dataset for a report before you start the Report Wizard. That way, the dataset will have the right data for the report that you're creating, including data from two or more tables if that's needed. In contrast, if you create a new report within the Report Wizard, you can only use the data from a single database table in your report.

With that as background, figure 16-3 shows how to use the Dataset Properties dialog box of the Report Wizard, assuming that the data source and dataset for the report are already available. You use this dialog box to define the dataset that will be used as the *report dataset*. To start, you can give this report dataset a meaningful name by entering it in the Name text box. In this example, I've changed the default name to VendorInvoices.

Next, you select the data source that you want to use for the report from the Data Source list. Then, you can select the dataset that you want to use from the Available Datasets list, which lists all of the datasets that are in the data source. In this example, I selected VendorInvoicesDataSet as the data source, and VendorInvoicesDataTable as the dataset. Once I did that, all of the fields in that dataset were displayed in the Fields pane of this dialog box.

When you complete this dialog box by clicking on the Next button, you've created the report dataset that will only be used for building the report. In contrast, the data source and the datasets that it contains are available throughout the project.

The DataSet Properties dialog box of the Report Wizard

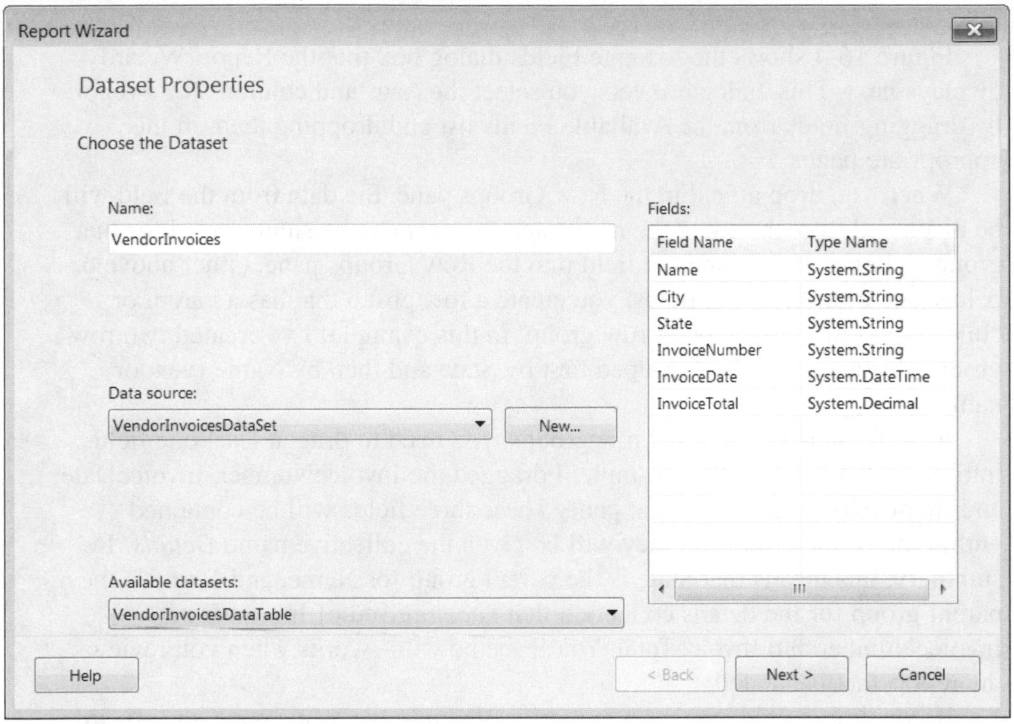

Description

- The dataset you create in this step is referred to as the *report dataset*. In the Name text box, you can enter a name for this report dataset. This is different from the dataset that the report dataset is going to be derived from.
- If the project already contains one or more datasets, you can select one of them from the Data Source list. This is the dataset that the report dataset will be derived from.
- If you don't want to use an existing dataset as the data source, you can create a new data source by clicking the New button. Then, if the project doesn't contain any datasets, the Data Source Configuration Wizard will be displayed, and you can follow the steps in figures 3-2 to 3-6 to create a new dataset.
- After you select a data source, you can select a dataset from the Available Datasets list. Then, the fields for this dataset are shown in the Fields pane.

Figure 16-3 How to select a data source and dataset for a report

How to select the rows and columns

Figure 16-4 shows the Arrange Fields dialog box that the Report Wizard displays next. This dialog box lets you select the rows and columns for a report by dragging fields from the Available Fields list and dropping them in the appropriate panes.

When you drop a field in the Row Groups pane, the data from the field will be displayed in each row of the report and the data can be summarized for that group. When you drag another field into the Row Groups pane, either above or below one of the existing fields, you create a row group that has a parent or child relationship to the other row group. In this example, I've created two row groups so the data will be grouped first by State and then by Name (vendor name).

In addition to creating the row groups, you need to drag at least one field into the Value pane. In this example, I dragged the InvoiceNumber, InvoiceDate, and InvoiceTotal fields into that pane. These three fields will be contained within the Name group and they will be given the collective name *Details.* In summary, this means that State is the parent group for Name, and Name is the parent group for the details collection that is comprised of InvoiceDate, InvoiceNumber and InvoiceTotal. You'll see how this works when you review the report that is created.

If you drag a field that has a numeric value into the Value pane, the wizard will automatically apply an aggregate function to it. In this example, the Sum function has been applied to the InvoiceTotal field because the type of this field is System.Decimal. As a result, the invoice totals will be summed for each of the row groups that you've created.

If you don't want to use the function that's automatically applied, you can click on the down arrow to the right of the field name and select a different function. For more information on the functions, you can refer back to figure 5-3 in chapter 5.

If you're creating a matrix report, you can also drag fields to the Column Groups pane. You'll see how this works in figure 16-18.

To reorder the items in the pane, you can just drag and drop them into new locations. To remove a field that you've added to a pane, you can drag it back into the Available Fields list or drop it in the space outside the panes.

The Arrange fields dialog box of the Report Wizard

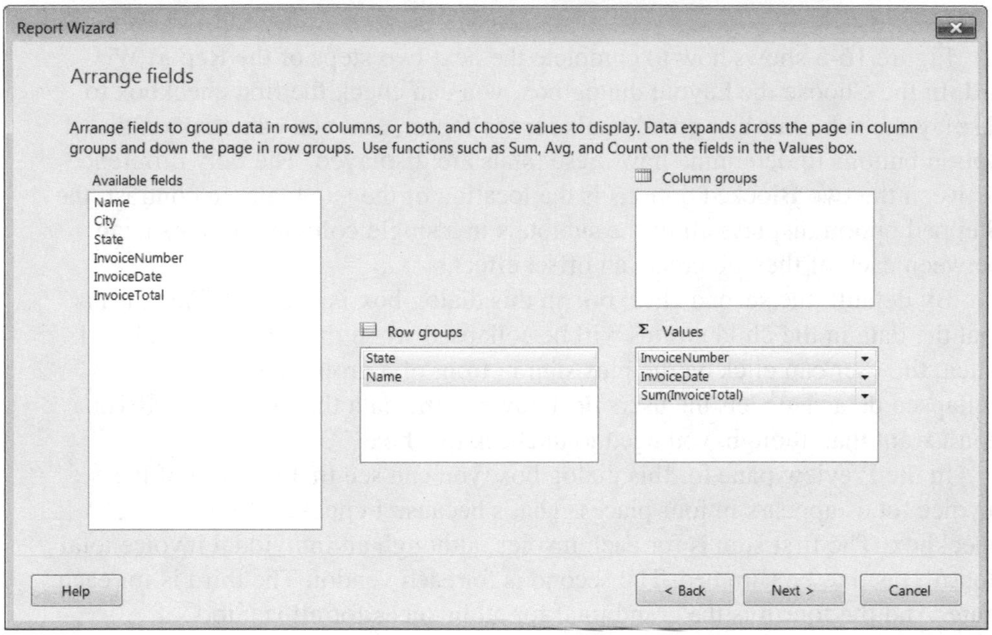

Description

- To create a row for a table, drag a field from the Available Fields list to the Row Groups pane. Data from this field will be used to populate each row of the table.
- If you drag more than one field into the Row Groups pane, the data from each field will be grouped under the field that appears above it in the list.
- Before you can go on to the next step, you must drag one or more fields from the Available Fields list into the Values pane. The fields in this pane, which are the lowest level of the group hierarchy, are referred to as the *Details* group.
- If the wizard doesn't automatically supply an aggregate function to a numeric field that you have added to the Values pane or if it supplies an inappropriate function, click on the down arrow to the right of the field and select a function.
- For a matrix report, you also drag fields into the Column Groups pane. Otherwise, this wizard creates a table report.
- To reorder the fields in the panes, you can drag them from one location to another. If you want to remove a field from a pane, you can drag it back to the Available Fields pane or drop it outside the panes.

Figure 16-4 How to select the rows and columns for a table

How to choose a layout

Figure 16-5 shows how to complete the next two steps of the Report Wizard. In the Choose the Layout dialog box, you can check the first checkbox to display the subtotals and grand totals for the report, and you can click on the option buttons to determine how these totals are displayed. The only difference between the two Blocked options is the location of the subtotals. In contrast, the Stepped option displays all of the subtotals in a single column, but puts a tab between each of them to create an offset effect.

By default, the second checkbox in this dialog box is checked. This means that the data in the child groups will be collapsed when the report is displayed. Then, the user can click on the plus sign in front of a group to expand its collapsed data. This lets the users drill down to the data that they want. If you don't want that, though, you need to uncheck this box.

In the Preview pane for this dialog box, you can see that the sum of the invoice totals appears in four places. That's because I checked the first checkbox. The first sum is for each invoice, although an individual invoice total doesn't need to be summed. The second is for each vendor. The third is for each state. And the fourth is the grand total for all invoices for all vendors.

How to choose a style

In the Choose a Style dialog box, you can select one of the six styles for a report. By default, the style is Ocean. Except for the Generic style, each style applies colors to the rows in the report. After you complete the wizard, you can use the Report Designer to change the background colors for specific cells, rows, and columns. When you click the Finish button in this dialog box, the report is displayed in the designer.

Layout and style options in the Report Wizard

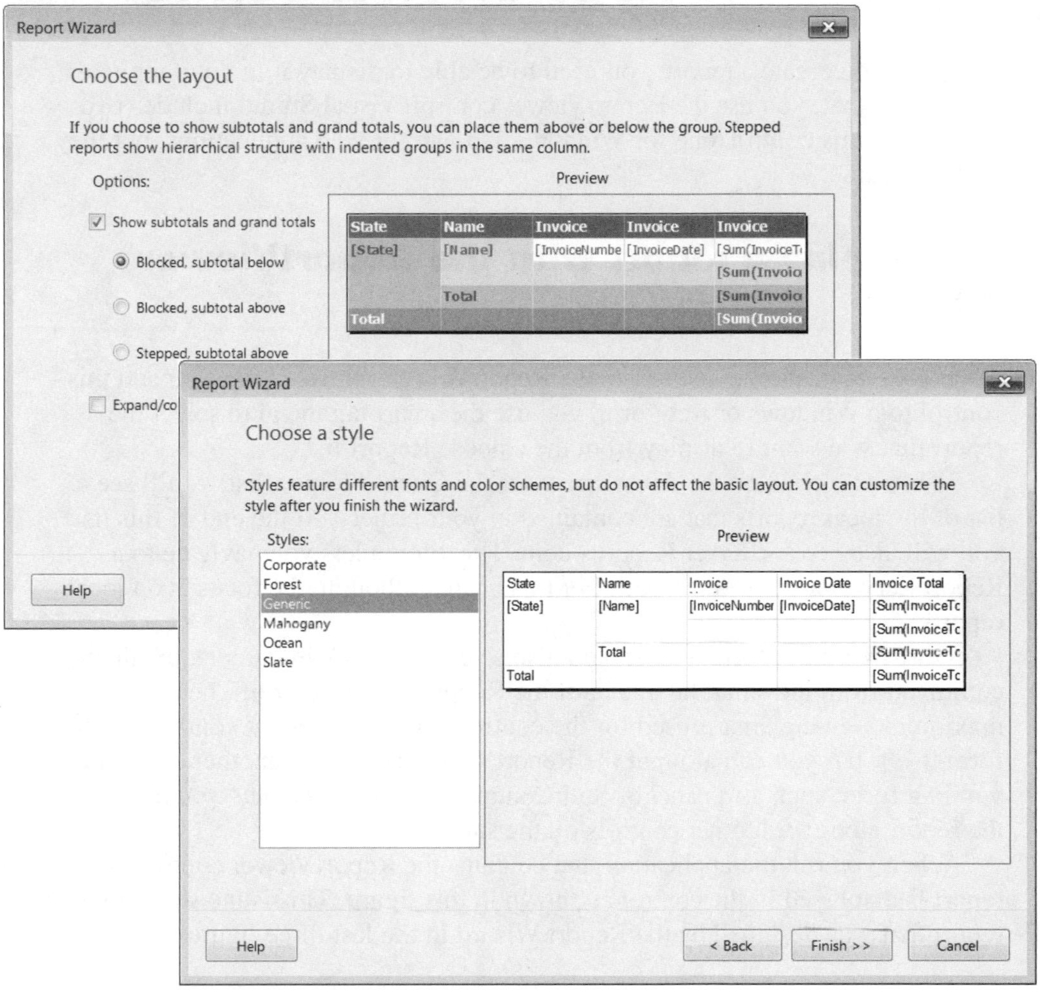

How to choose the layout

- In the Choose the Layout dialog box, you can check the Show Subtotals and Grand Totals checkbox if you want to have these totals created. Then, you can click one of the option buttons to specify how you want the subtotals and totals displayed.
- By default, the Expand/Collapse Groups box is checked. Then, the groups are collapsed when the report is first displayed, and the user clicks on plus signs to expand the data for a group. If you don't want that, you can uncheck that checkbox.

How to choose a style

- In the Choose a Style dialog box, you can select one of the six styles from the Styles list. By default, the Ocean style is selected.
- With the exception of the Generic style, each style applies background and foreground colors to the column and row headings and to the totals row.

Figure 16-5 How to choose a layout and style for a report

How to use the ReportViewer control

After you create a report, you need to be able to display it in your application. To do that, you use the ReportViewer control. Visual Studio includes two versions of this control, one for Windows and one for web applications, but they work the same.

How to display a report with the ReportViewer control

Figure 16-6 shows how to use the ReportViewer control. After you add this control to a Windows or web form, you use the smart tag menu to select the report that you want to display from the Choose Report list.

When you click on the down arrow for the Choose Report list, you'll see a list of the local reports that are contained in your project. At the end of this list, you will also see a <Server Report> item. This option lets you navigate to a Report Server and select a report. For this chapter, though, the focus is on local reports.

For a Windows form, you should also select the Dock in Parent Container command from the smart tag menu of the ReportViewer control. Then, the maximum viewing area is used for the control. Often, the parent container is the form itself, but you can also put the ReportViewer control in another container within a form, such as a panel or SplitContainer control. That lets you display the report along with other controls on the same form.

When you run the application that contains the ReportViewer control, the report is displayed in the control as shown in this figure. This is the start of the report that was designed by the Report Wizard in the last three figures.

A ReportViewer control in a Windows form

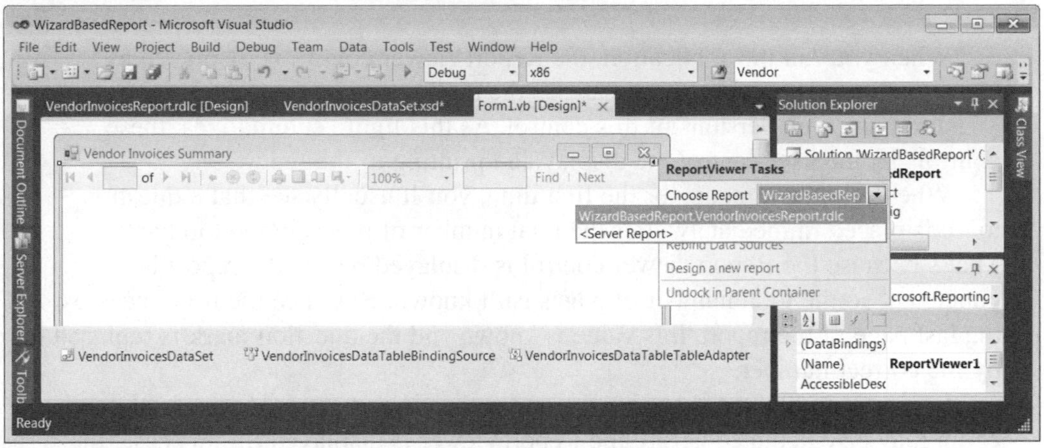

The report displayed in the ReportViewer control

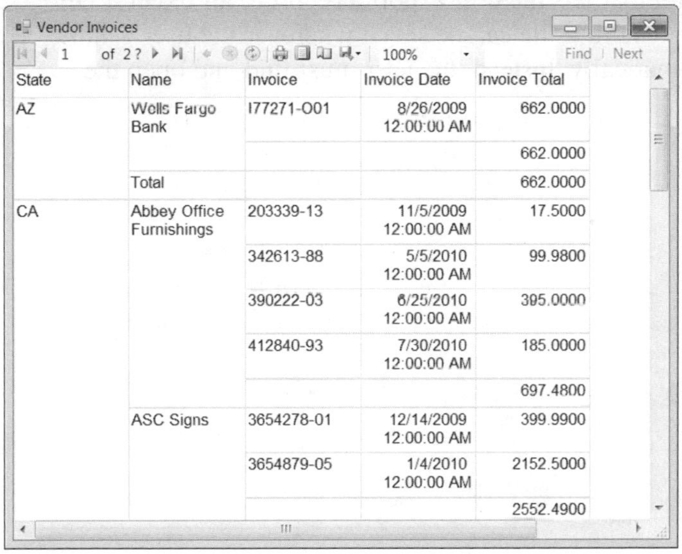

Description

- To add a ReportViewer control to a Windows Form or a web application, select it from the Reporting tab in the Toolbox and drag it to the form.
- To assign a report to the control, click on its smart tag, and then choose a report from the Choose Report list.
- If necessary, you can select the options that let you choose or rebind a data source.
- If there are no reports available or if you want to create a new report, select the Design a New Report option.
- In a Windows application, select the Dock in Parent Container item to ensure that the maximum viewing area is used to display the report. Often, the container for a ReportViewer control is the form, but it can also be another control like a panel.

Figure 16-6 How to display a report with the ReportViewer control

How to work with the ReportViewer toolbar

When you run the application, the ReportViewer control is displayed as shown in figure 16-7. Here, you can see the toolbars that are used for the Windows and web versions of this control. As this figure summarizes, these controls let the user control the display and printing of the report.

When you run a report for the first time, you'll usually see that a question mark is placed immediately after the total number of pages in the toolbar. That's because the ReportViewer control is displayed before the report is generated, so the total number of pages isn't known. But once the user accesses the last page of the report, this value is known and the question mark is replaced by the correct number.

In more complex reports, like the one shown in figure 16-16, the total page count may be calculated before the ReportViewer is displayed. In this case, the correct total will be displayed from the start without a question mark.

The Exports list in the toolbar lets the user export a report to an Excel, PDF, or Microsoft Word file. The resulting file can be saved wherever the user wants, but it won't be opened automatically. Instead, the user must find and open the file separately.

The ReportViewer toolbar in a Windows application

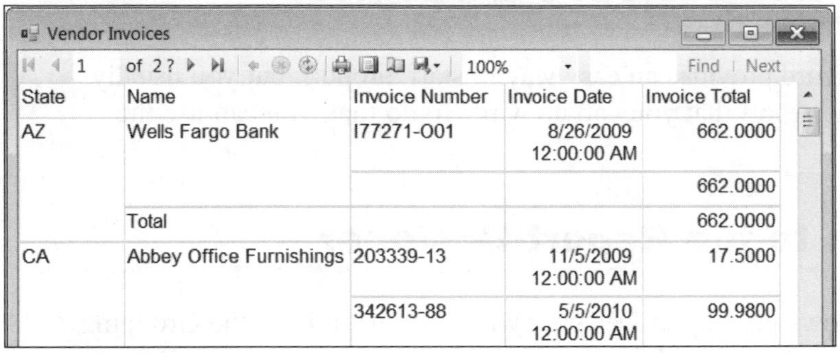

The ReportViewer toolbar in a web application

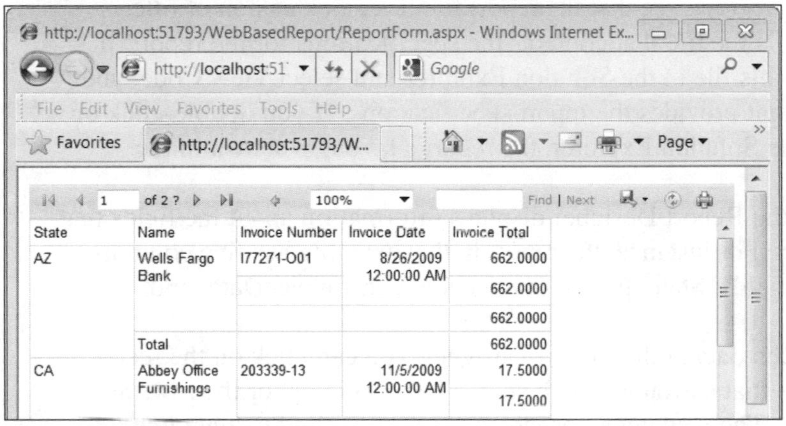

The controls in the Windows toolbar (from left to right)

- The navigation buttons let the user move between pages in a multi-page report.
- The Back to Parent Report button (the first disabled button) lets the user display a parent report, if one exists.
- The Stop Rendering button (also disabled) is used to stop the report from being rendered. This is useful if the rendering process is taking too long, but this button isn't available in the toolbar for a web application.
- The Refresh button fetches the most recent data that's available for the report and rebuilds the report using that data.
- The Print, Print Layout, and Print Setup buttons let the user print the report, preview the layout, and set the print options. (In a web application, only the Print button is available.)
- The Export list lets the user save the current report to Excel, PDF, or Microsoft Word format.
- The Zoom list lets the user change the display size.
- The Find button searches for the characters that are entered in the text box to the left of the button. The Next button finds the next occurrence of the characters.

Figure 16-7 How to work with the ReportViewer toolbar

How to use the Report Designer

The Report Wizard provides an easy way to start a report, but you usually want to enhance the report that you end up with. To do that, you can use the Report Designer.

An introduction to the Report Designer

Figure 16-8 shows the Report Designer with a report in it. In the Grouping pane, you can see the fields that have been used for row groups. In the Report Data pane, you can see the fields that are available in the report dataset. In the Solution Explorer, you can see that the report file has an extension of rdlc.

The report file is the file that contains the specifications for the report. If you right-click on this file in the Solution Explorer and select View Code, you can see the XML that provides the report specifications. If you double-click on the report file in the Solution Explorer, the report's layout is shown in the Report Designer.

The layout in the Report Designer displays information about the fields that are used in a report. For instance, the report in this example has five columns that contain these fields: State, Name, InvoiceNumber, InvoiceDate, and InvoiceTotal.

To work with the data in the Report Designer, you can click on the rectangles in the frame that surrounds the layout. The rectangles for the rows are called *row handles*. The rectangles for the columns are called *column handles*. And the rectangle in the upper left corner of the frame is called a *corner handle*. You can click on the row and column handles to select rows and columns. You can click on the corner handle to hide the handles. And you can click in any cell to display the handles again.

If you click on the corner handle to select the report, the Properties window will show that the selected item is a *tablix*. This is a template that is used for displaying the data in a *tab*le, *l*ist, or matr*ix*.

As you work with the layout in the Report Designer, remember that the data in each cell is actually stored in a text box. This means that you can set the properties for each text box so the data is displayed the way you want it. You'll learn more about this later.

The Report Designer

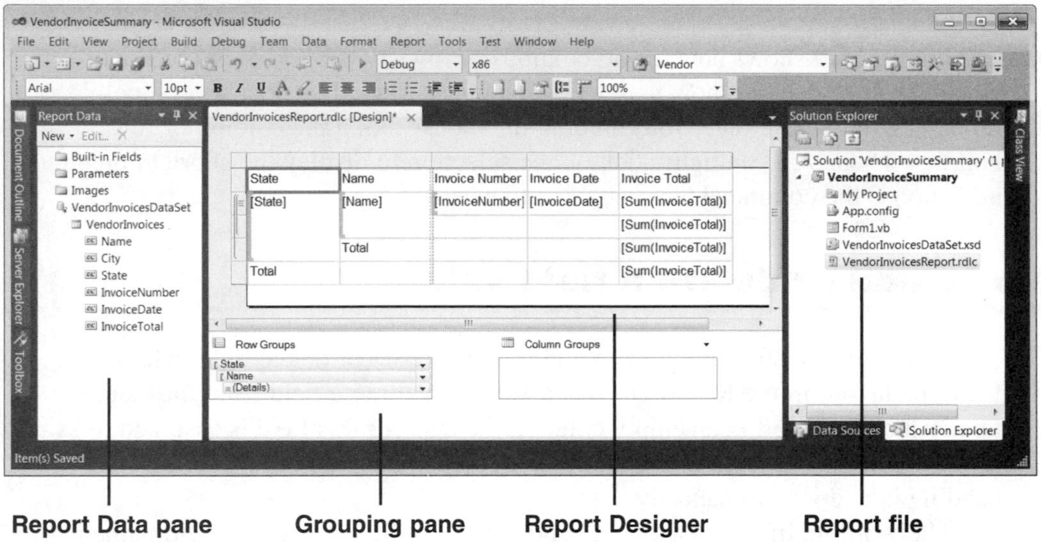

Description

- The Report Data pane displays the folders and items that can be used to build a report. These include built-in fields, parameters, images, and datasets.
- The Grouping pane shows the row groups and column groups.
- The report file in the Solution Explorer contains the design details for the report in XML format.
- The rectangle to the left of each row in the Report Designer is a *row handle*. The rectangle above each column is a *column handle*. To select a column or row, you can click on the column or row handle.
- The rectangle above and to the left of the table is a *corner handle*. To hide all of the handles, you can click the corner handle. To display all of the handles, you can click anywhere in the table.
- If you click on the corner handle, the Properties window is displayed. There, you can see that the selected item is a *tablix*, which is a template for a table, list, or matrix. This tablix is within the report.

Figure 16-8 An introduction to the Report Designer

How to add or delete a column or row

Figure 16-9 shows how to add columns or rows to the layout in the Report Designer. It also shows how to delete columns or rows. To select several columns or rows at one time, you can drag the mouse along the column or row handles. Then, you can right-click on the selection to display the shortcut menu, and choose the command that you want to execute.

How to add or delete a field value

Figure 16-9 also shows how to add field values to or delete field values from the layout in the Report Designer. When you drag a field from the Report Data pane into a cell in an empty column, the data for this field is assigned to the text box for that cell. If this is the first entry in the column, a column heading is added automatically.

The wording of this heading depends on the field name. If the field name is a single word, that word is used as the column heading. If the field name consists of several words, the Designer will attempt to insert spaces between known words. In the case of the InvoiceDate field, for example, the header is set to Invoice Date.

You can also use the Field Selector list to add a field value to a cell. If the cell is empty, the field will be added to the cell. If the cell isn't empty, the field will overwrite the existing content. When you use the Field Selector list, though, a column heading isn't automatically created.

The shortcut menu for a column

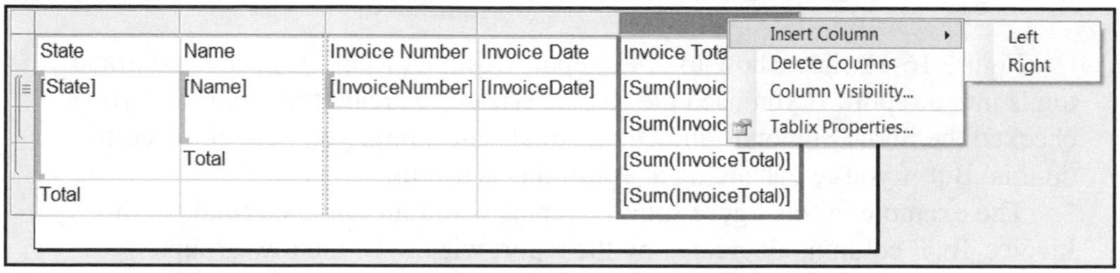

The Field Selector menu for a cell

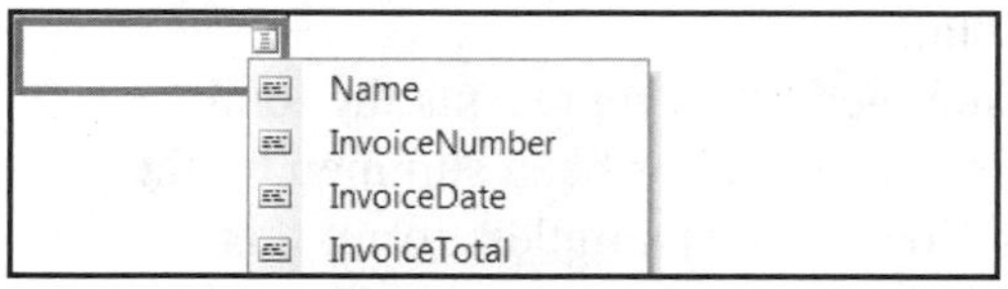

How to add or delete a column in a table

- To display a shortcut menu, right-click on a column handle or inside any cell.
- To add a new column, select the Insert Column command from the shortcut menu, then select Left or Right to add the column.
- To delete a column, select the Delete Columns command from the shortcut menu.
- Another way to add a column is to drag a field from the list of fields in the Report Data pane and drop it in a column that already has some content. A new column will automatically be added to the table and the field you just dropped will be inserted into the column.

How to add or delete a row in a table

- To display a shortcut menu, right-click on a row handle or inside any cell.
- To add a new row, select the Insert Row command from the shortcut menu. Then, select either Above or Below to add the row.
- To delete a row, select the Delete Rows command from the shortcut menu. If the row contains a row group, click OK to confirm the row and row group deletion.

How to add a field value to a table

- Drag one of the fields from the Report Data pane and drop it in the cell where you want the value of that field to appear.
- If the cell already has a field value assigned to it, a new column will be created.
- Another way to add a field value is to click the Field Selector that appears when you hover the mouse over a cell. Then, you can choose a field from the list that appears.

How to delete a field value from a table

- Right-click in the cell that contains the field, then select Delete from the shortcut menu.

Figure 16-9 How to add or delete a column, row, or field value

How to insert group and grand totals

Figure 16-10 shows how use the Report Designer to insert group and grand totals into a report. If you used the Report Wizard to create the report and you checked the Show Subtotals and Grand Totals checkbox, you may not need to do this. But if you're enhancing a report, this is useful.

The example in this figure shows a report with four summed totals in the Invoice Total column, all created by the report wizard. In the row groups portion of this example, you can see that three row groups were created by the wizard: State, Name, and Details. In this case, the Details group consists of invoice number, invoice date and invoice total.

In the designer layout, the first of the summed totals represents the total value of a single invoice. In this case, the invoice total has been summed by the wizard. However, since the invoice total is already in its simplest form, that isn't necessary. As a result, you can remove the sum function, as you'll see in figure 16-12.

The next summed total in the designer layout is the vendor total, which is the sum of all the invoice totals for each vendor. To get that subtotal, each of the invoice totals within that vendor group are added together. If you use the second method in this figure to add a subtotal like that to the report, you right-click on the second row of the Invoice Total column, and select Add Total from the shortcut menu. That will cause the sum to be inserted in the row below the cell you selected.

The third summed total in the designer layout is the state total, which is the sum of all the invoice totals for all the vendors in the state. Then, the last summed total is the grand total, which is the sum of all of the invoice totals.

If you need to add a grand total after you've finished the wizard, you can use the third method in this figure. Then, if necessary, the Report Designer will add a new row to the table to accommodate this total.

In most cases, when you add a subtotal or a grand total, either with the Report Wizard or with the Report Designer, the word *Total* is added to a cell to the left of the total. Then, you can edit or delete it. To edit it, you just click in the cell and enter the change. In this example, I edited the cells that contained Total so they now contain Vendor Total, State Total, and Grand Total.

The second example in this figure shows the final page of the report when it's run and displayed in a ReportViewer control. Here, you can see the cascading subtotals for the groups, together with a grand total at the end of the report.

A tablix with vendor, state, and grand totals

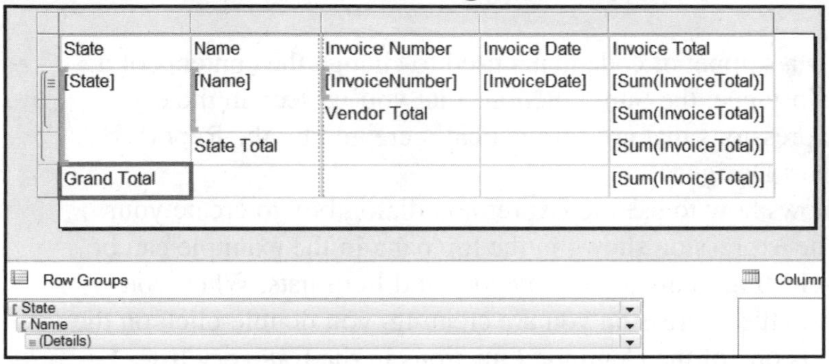

The vendor, state, and grand totals in a ReportViewer control

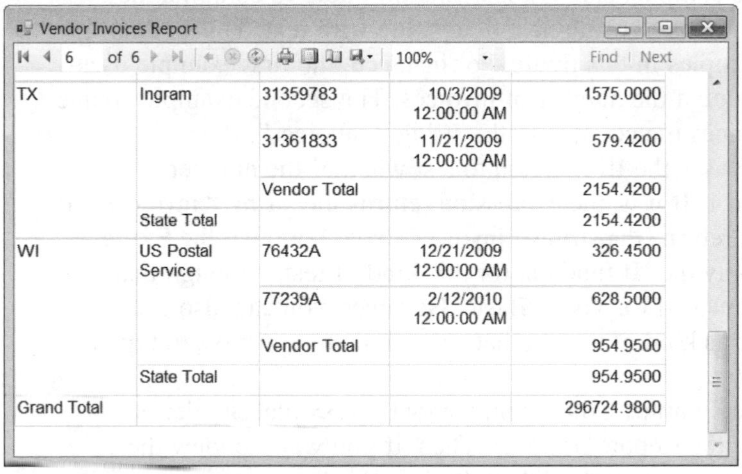

How to insert a group total

- To add a group total, select a group in the Grouping pane.
- Click on the down arrow to the right of the group name, and select the Add Total command from the menu that appears.
- Select the Before option to have the total displayed in the row above this group or the After option to have the total displayed in the row below this group.

Another way to insert a group total

- Right-click in the cell that contains the group you want to total, and select the Add Total command from the shortcut menu that appears. Then, the sum function will be inserted into the cell in the row below.

How to insert a grand total at the end of a report

- To insert a grand total at the end of the report, right-click in the cell that contains the field for the parent group. Then, select the Add Total command from the menu that appears.

Figure 16-10 How to insert group and grand totals

How to create an expression

An expression is a snippet of code that's used to change the contents of a cell in a report. For instance, the Sum functions that you've seen in the examples so far are expressions that are automatically created by the Report Wizard and the Report Designer.

Figure 16-11 shows how to use the Expression dialog box to create your own expressions. The expression shown in the top pane in the example can be created simply by selecting items in the Category and Item lists. When you want to add an item to the expression you are creating, you double-click on the item. If your choice is one of the Common Functions in the Category list, Intellisense will be activated to help you complete the function.

As you build more complex expressions, you are likely to combine the values of two or more fields or combine a field value with text. This is illustrated by the three examples in this figure. For instance, the first example uses the Count function to count the number of invoices. The second example counts the invoices and combines the count with the string " invoices".

The third example uses the IIf function to test whether the number of invoices is greater than 1. If it is, the expression returns the string " invoices". If it isn't, the expression returns the string " invoice". Note here that the Expression dialog box lists only the IIf function for this kind of test, although that function has been deprecated for Visual Basic. However, you can also use the newer If function for this kind of test. In that case, though, you have to type in the complete expression.

When you create a complex expression, the <<Expr>> placeholder is displayed in the cell in the Report Designer. Then, if you want to view the expression, you can right-click in the cell and select Expression from the shortcut menu.

The Expression dialog box

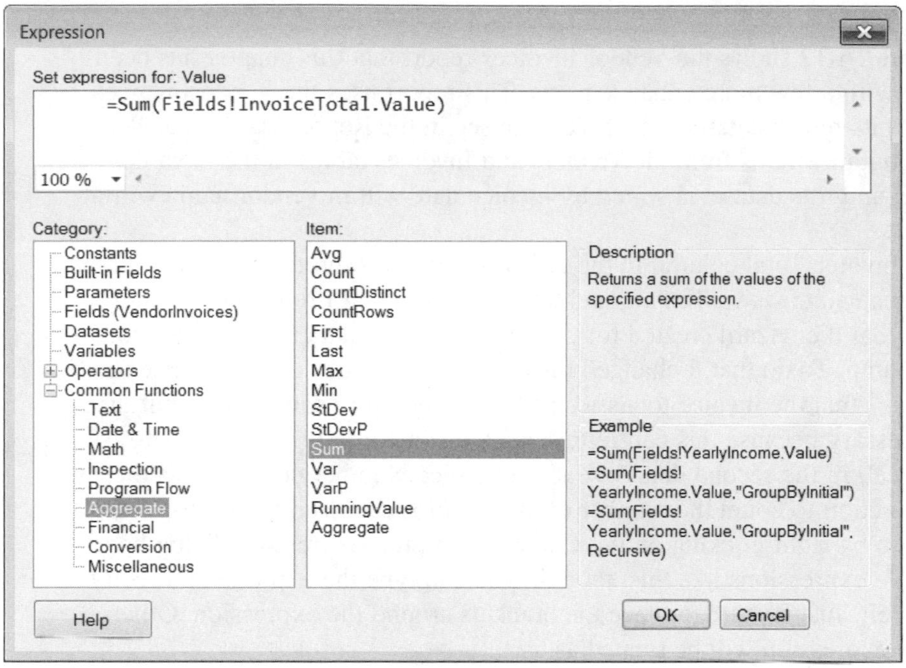

How to create an expression

- Right-click in the cell where you want to place the expression, then select Expression from the menu that appears. This displays the Expression dialog box.
- Double-click a category in the Category list to select it.
- Double-click an item in the Item list to display it in the pane at the top of the Expression dialog box. Then, select more items or type in the details of the expression that you want to create.
- Click the OK button to close the dialog box and insert the expression into the current cell.

An expression that uses an aggregate function

```
=Count(Fields!InvoiceNumber.Value)
```

An expression that combines text and data

```
=Count(Fields!InvoiceNumber.Value) & " invoices"
```

An expression that uses a program flow function

```
=IIf(Count(Fields!InvoiceTotal.Value) > 1, " invoices", " invoice")
```

Description

- You can use combinations of strings, data, and functions to form complex expressions in the Expression dialog box.

Figure 16-11 How to create an expression for a report

The Vendor Invoices report

Figure 16-12 shows the Vendor Invoices report that this chapter has been building with a few more enhancements. This report uses the VendorInvoices dataset as its report dataset, which you can see in the Report Data pane. This dataset contains fields from the Vendors and Invoices tables in the Payables database, and this dataset is sorted by invoice date within vendor name within state code.

The Invoice Total column in the tablix includes a subtotal for each vendor and for each state, as well as a grand total. But note that I removed the sum function that the wizard created for the cell in the first data row of the Invoice Total column. To do that, I changed the expression in this cell to [InvoiceTotal]. This means that the invoice totals won't be summed for each invoice, but that isn't necessary because this cell represents the value of a just one invoice.

The cell in the second data row of the Invoice Number column uses the Count function to count the number of invoices for each vendor. I created this expression by right-clicking on the cell and using the Expression dialog box. For simple expressions like this, though, you can type the expression directly into the cell. Just be sure to place the brackets around the expression. Otherwise, the expression will be treated as text.

The cell in the second data row of the Invoice Date column contains a complex expression, as indicated by the <<Expr>> placeholder. This expression is the same as the one in the third example in the previous figure.

The Average Invoice column for this report shows the average invoice value for each vendor and for the entire report. These averages are calculated by dividing the count for the vendor or entire report into the sum of the invoice totals for the vendor or entire report. In the tablix, these expressions are represented by the <<Expr>> placeholder.

At this point, the report has the structure and data that I want, but the data needs formatting. For instance, the dates show a time of 12:00:00 AM, which should be removed, and the invoice totals have more than two decimal places. It would also be nice if the report had a title. These are the skills that you'll learn next.

The Vendor Invoices report in the Report Designer

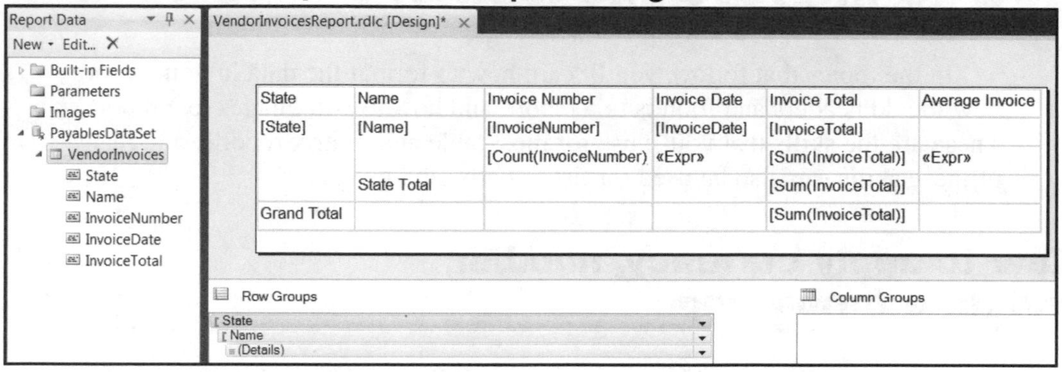

The report in a ReportViewer control

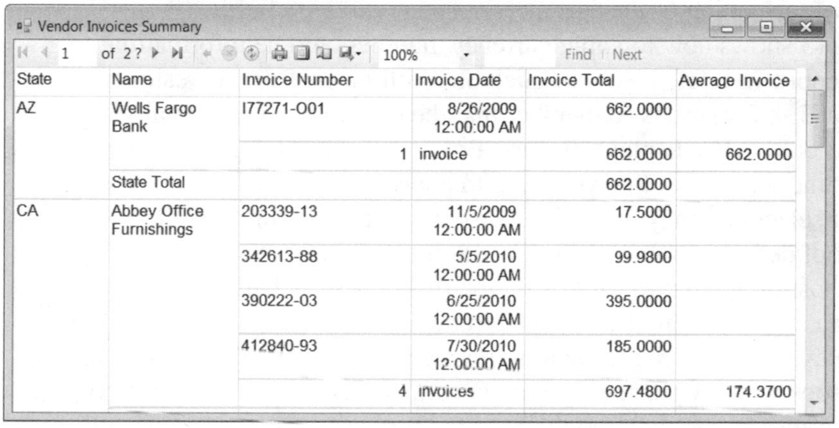

Report highlights

- The data rows are grouped by state, and then by vendor name.
- Totals are displayed for vendors and states, with a grand total of all invoice totals at the end of the report.
- Expressions are used to count the number of invoices for each vendor and to display either the word *invoice* or *invoices* in the cell to the right of the count.
- An expression is used to calculate the average invoice total for each vendor.

Figure 16-12 The Vendor Invoices report

How to improve the look of a report

In the topics that follow, you'll learn how to format the data in your reports, how to add headers and footers to a report, and how to add images to a report. These are the skills that you'll use for most table and matrix reports, and many of these skills can also be used for lists, charts, and gauges.

How to apply currency, number, and date formatting

When you create a table or matrix report, all field data and expressions are displayed with the default format. Usually, this means that you will want to apply your own formatting to the currency, number, and date fields.

Figure 16-13 shows how to apply currency, number, and date formatting to the data in a report. In brief, you right-click on a cell in the Report Designer, and select Text Box Properties (remember that the data in a cell is actually stored in a text box). This displays the Text Box Properties dialog box. Then, you can select the formatting that you want to apply.

When you select currency in the Text Box Properties dialog box, the currency symbol defaults to the correct one for the regional settings on the system that's hosting the report. In this figure, this default is United States dollars, but you can select an alternative currency symbol from the Symbol list.

Another way to change the formatting for a cell is to select the cell and then use the Properties window to type the correct format into the Format property. This is also useful if you want to apply the same format to more than one cell. Then, you can select all of the cells before you type the correct format into the Format property in the Properties window.

If you don't know the correct format, you can first select a single cell and set its format using the procedure in this figure. Then, you can see the format that's been assigned to the Format property of the cell in the Properties window. Last, you can copy this value, select all the other text boxes to which you want to apply this format, and paste the format into the Format property in the Properties window.

When you create local reports, you won't see your formatting changes in the Report Designer. It's also hard to tell what the formatting for a cell is by looking at the Format property in the Properties window. So, to make sure you have all the formatting right, you need to run the application.

The Text Box Properties dialog box

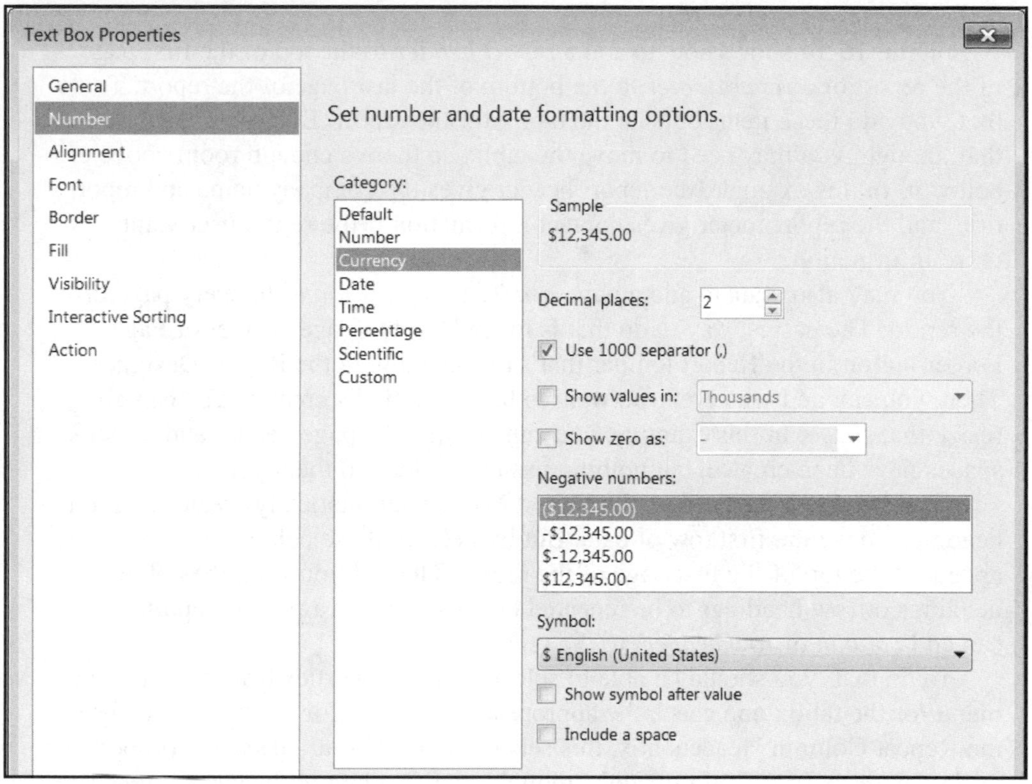

How to apply currency formatting to a text box

- Right-click on the text box, and select Text Box Properties from the shortcut menu. Then, select Number from the list at the left of the dialog box that appears, and select Currency from the Category list.
- The display at the right shows the default settings for your locale. Then, you can accept these default settings or select other settings.

How to apply other numeric formats to text boxes

- In the Text Box Properties dialog box, select Number, Percentage, Scientific, or Custom from the Category list. You can then select the settings that you want.

How to apply date formatting to a text box

- Right-click on the text box, and select Text Box Properties from the shortcut menu. Then, select Number from the list at the left of the dialog box that appears, and select Date from the Category list.
- The display at the right shows the available choices for date formatting. Then, you can select your preference.

Figure 16-13 How to apply currency, number, and date formatting

How to add headers and footers

Figure 16-14 shows how to add a *report header* to the top of the first page of the report or a *report footer* to the bottom of the last page of the report. To do that, you add these items outside the tablix for the report. Before you can do that, though, you may need to move the tablix so there's enough room above or below it. In this example, the report header gives the company name and report title, and the report footer gives contact information if the report user wants more information.

You may also want to add a *page header* or a *page footer* to every page of the report. The easiest way to do that is to click on the Page Header or Page Footer button in the Report toolbar that's displayed with the Report Designer. Then, you can add whatever you want to the space that's created. You can also resize that space. In this example, you can see that the page header and footer spaces have been created, but nothing has been added to them yet.

As you have already seen, the Report Wizard automatically creates column headings above the first row of data. But by default, these column headings only appear at the top of the first page of the report. Then, if you want the column headings or row headings to be repeated on each page of a printed report, you can add *column* or *row headers* to the report.

To do that, you should be able to select Tablix Properties from the shortcut menu for the tablix and check the appropriate boxes. If, for example, you check the Repeat Column Headers box, this sets the RepeatColumnHeaders property of the tablix to True. Unfortunately, though, there's a bug in the current release of the Report Designer, so this doesn't work for table reports although it usually works for matrix reports.

Until this bug gets fixed, you can get around it by first clicking on the small arrow at the side of the Column Groups list in the Grouping pane and selecting Advanced Mode. Then, you will see additional items in the Row Groups and Column Groups lists that contain the word Static. Next, click on the first Static member at the top of the Row Groups list to display the properties of that member in the Properties window.

The next step is to set the RepeatOnNewPage property to True, and set the KeepWithGroup property to After. Now, when you run this report the column headers will be displayed at the top of each page, both in the ReportViewer control and also if you print the report. If you also want the column headers to stay in view when you scroll down a report, set the FixedData property of the Tablix Member to True.

A report that contains a report header and footer

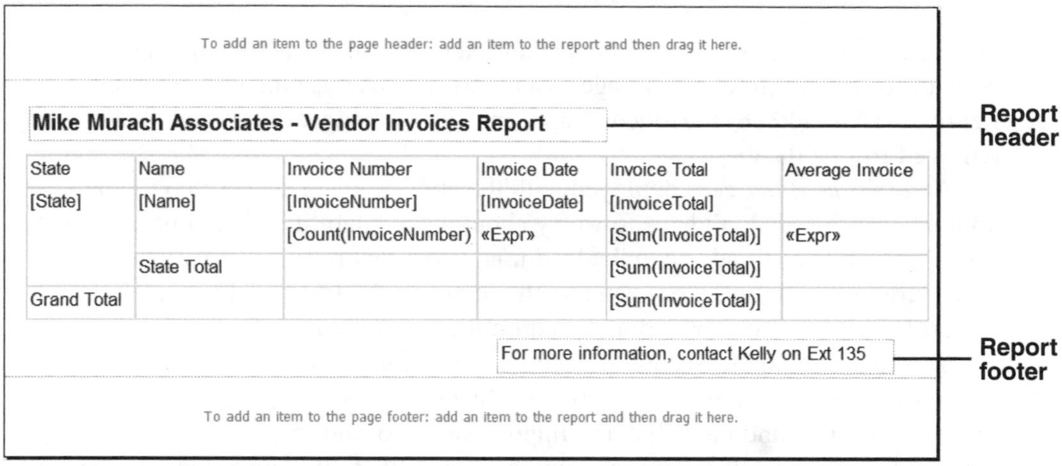

How to add a report header or footer

- To add a report header, drag items from the Toolbox into the whitespace above the tablix.
- To add a report footer, drag items from the Toolbox into the whitespace below the tablix.
- After you've dragged the items, you can edit their contents.

How to add a page header or footer

- Click the Page Header or Page Footer button in the Report toolbar of the Report Designer to add a page header or footer to a report.
- To resize the height of a page header or footer, hover the mouse over the dotted line that divides the header or footer from the main report. Then, when the double-headed arrow appears, click and drag it.
- Drag items from the Toolbox into the area of the page header or footer. Then, edit the content of these items.

How to add column or row headers to each page of the report

- Right-click on the corner handle of the tablix, and select Tablix Properties. Then, in the dialog box that's displayed, check any of these boxes: Repeat Row Headers on each Page, Repeat Column Headers on each Page, or Keep Header Visible While Scrolling. *Warning: this doesn't work for table reports in the current release (see text for more).*

Description

- A *report header* appears only at the top of the first page of the report, and a *report footer* appears only at the bottom of the last page of the report.
- A *page header* appears at the top of each page of the report, and a *page footer* appears at the bottom of each page of the report.
- A *column header* repeats the column headings on each page of the report. A *row header* repeats the row headings on each page of the report.

Figure 16-14 How to add headers and footers to a report

How to add an image to a report

Images are often used in headers and footers, but they can also be in the body of the report. To add an image to a report, you can use the procedures in figure 16-15 to add an embedded image, an external image, or a image that's retrieved from a database.

An *embedded image* is deployed with the application. This is often the best option because you don't have to worry about the availability of the image on a server or web site. To add an embedded image to a report, you can use the first procedure in this figure. First, you add the image to the Image folder in the Report Data pane. Then, you drag and drop the image on the report.

You can also use the second procedure in this figure to add an embedded image to a report. In the Image Properties dialog box, you select Embedded as the image source, and then click the Import button to find the image file that you want to embed. When you're done, the image file will be inserted into the report at the location you selected and the file name will be added to the Images folder in the Report Data pane. Once an image has been added to the Images folder, it will be in the Use this Image list of the Image Properties dialog box whenever the embedded option is selected.

If you select External as the image source in the Image Properties dialog box, you have to type or paste in the URL of the image into the Use this Image list. This syntax for doing that is illustrated by the code in the first example in this figure. The first URL is for an image file that is stored on a local machine. The second one is for an image file on a web site. When you click the OK button for an external image, you may see an error message that says the object reference isn't set to an instance of an object. This is a software bug, so you can safely ignore this message.

Before you deploy or run an application that contains an external image in a report, you must set the EnableExternalImages property of the ReportViewer control to True. If you don't do that, you'll get a runtime error and the report won't be displayed. You can set this property by navigating to the Local Report – EnableExternalImages property in the properties pane or by using the code that's shown in the second example in this figure.

Images that are used in the main body of the report usually come from the database that's being used as the data source for the report, although you can also use embedded or external images in the body of a report. To use a database image, you select the Database option in the Image Properties dialog box, and then select the field that holds the image from the Use this Field list that appears. You also have to select a MIME type, like jpeg, from the next list that appears.

The Image Properties dialog box

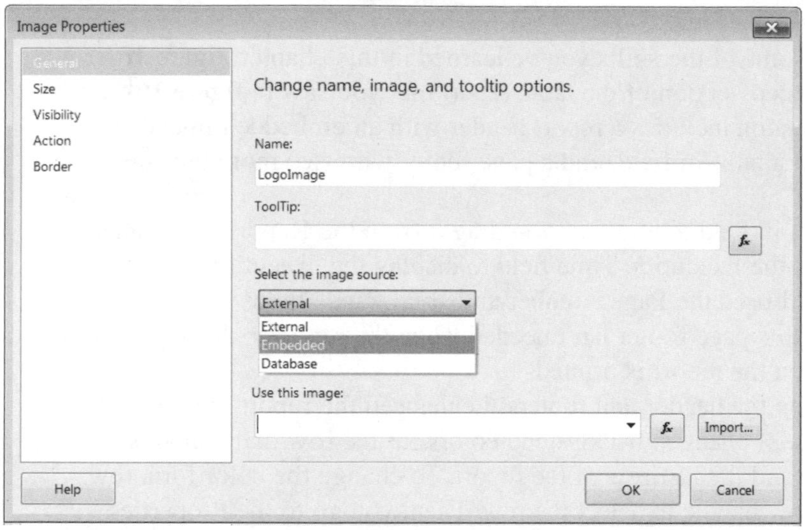

Examples of the code for selecting an external image file

```
file://C:\Images\MurachLogo2.png
http://www.mysite.com/MurachLogo2.png
```

Code that enables external images to be used in a ReportViewer control

```
Me.ReportViewer1.LocalReport.EnableExternalImages = True
```

How to use the Images folder of the Report Data pane to add an image

- To store an image file in the Images folder, you can use the New→Image command in the menu bar of the Report Data pane. You can also right-click on the Images folder, and select Add Image.
- To add an image in the Images folder to a report, just drag and drop it.

How to use the Image Properties dialog box to add an image

- To insert an image into a report, drag an Image report item from the Toolbox and drop it on the report. This will display the Image Properties dialog box. Then, select the source of the image from the Select the Image Source list: Embedded, External, or Database.
- To embed an image, either select a file from the Use this Image list or click on the Import button and navigate to the image file that you want to embed. Alternatively, you can click on the expression button (fx) and create an expression that selects the required file.
- To use an external file, enter the URL of the target image in the Use this Image list. For this to work, you must also set the EnableExternalImages property of the ReportViewer control to True, either by using the Properties window or Visual Basic code.
- To use images that are stored in the database, select the field that contains the image from the Use this Field list that appears when you select Database as the image source, and then select the appropriate MIME type.

Figure 16-15 How to add an image to a report

An enhanced Vendor Invoices report

To illustrate some of the skills you've learned in this chapter, figure 16-16 presents an enhanced version of the table report that you saw in figure 16-12. This enhanced version includes a report header with an embedded image, a report footer with a built-in field, and a page footer with two more built-in fields.

To add a built-in field to a report, you drag it from the Report Data pane. In this report, I used the Execution Time field to display the execution time in the report footer, and I used the Page Number and Total Pages fields in the page footer. Although this page footer isn't needed when the report is displayed, it can be useful when the report is printed.

Besides adding the header and footers, I enhanced the report in a few other ways. For instance, I changed background colors for the row that contains the column headings and the last row of the report. To change the color for a row, you click on its row handle to select the row. Then, you go to the Properties window, select the Background Color property, and select a color.

I also changed the font and alignment of some of the cells. To do that for a single cell, you display the Text Box Properties dialog box as shown in figure 16-13, click Alignment or Font in the left pane, and then select the options that you want. To do that for a complete row, you can click on its row handle and then change the settings in the Properties window. In this example, I centered the cells in the column header by changing the TextAlign property for the top row to Center.

Next, in the Average Invoice column that already contains one expression, I used a second expression for the Color property of the text box that holds the average invoice value. This expression sets the color of the font to Gray if the vendor has only a single invoice and to Black if the vendor has more than one invoice.

To review the expression for the average invoice total, you can right-click in the cell and select Expression to display that dialog box. To review the expression that changes the color, you can right-click in the cell and select Text Box Properties to display that dialog box. Then, if you click on Font in the left pane and click on the fx button for Color, you'll see the expression.

This should give you some ideas for expanding upon the skills that you've learned so far. If you experiment, you'll see that it's relatively easy to get a report looking just the way you want it.

An enhanced Vendor Invoices report in the Report Designer

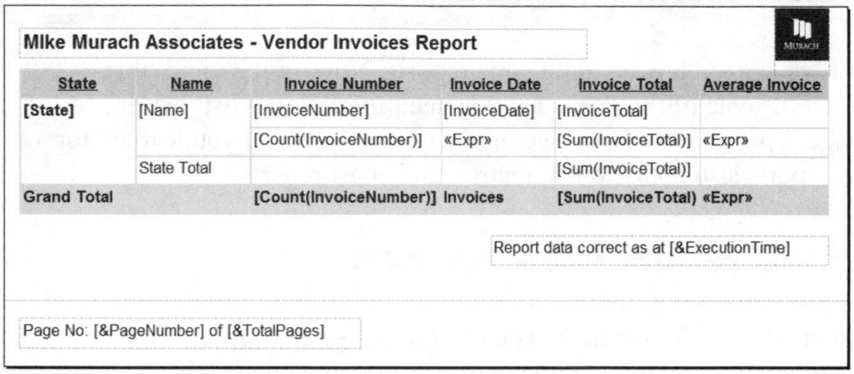

The enhanced Vendor Invoices report in a ReportViewer control

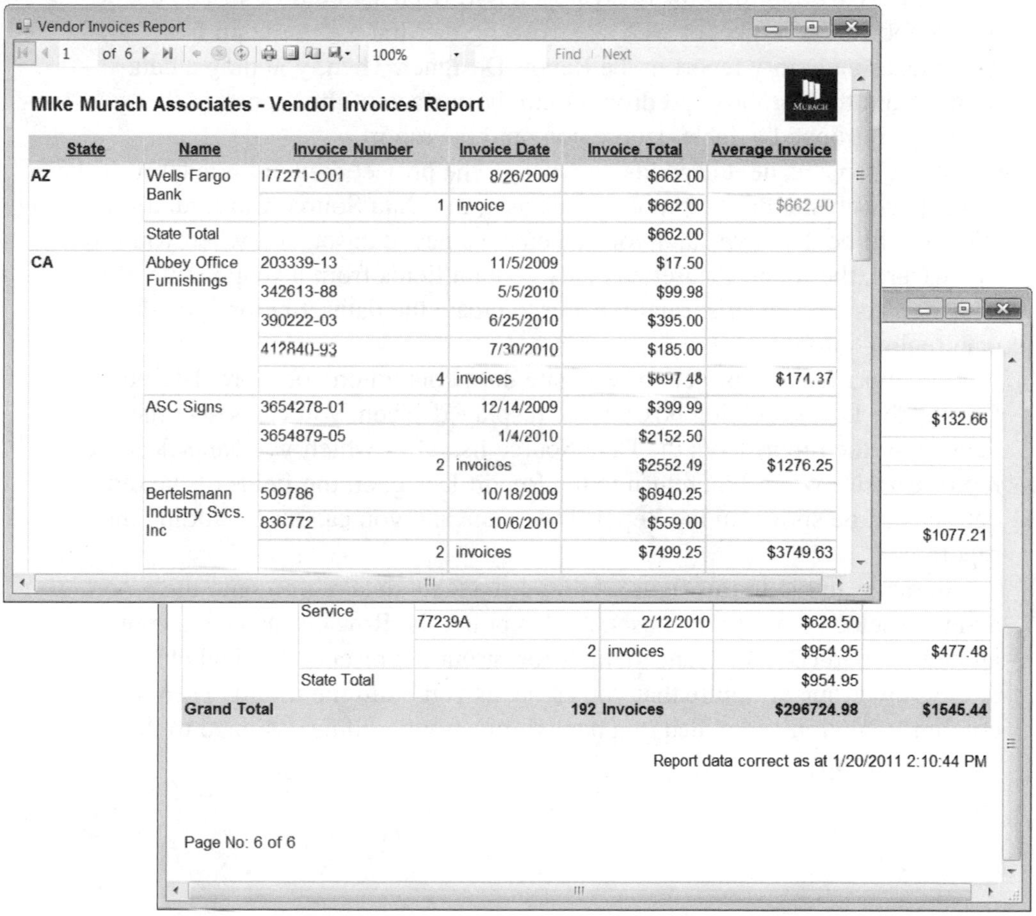

Description

- The report in this figure demonstrates many of the techniques described in this chapter.

How to build other types of reports

So far, you've learned how to build table reports. Now, in the topics that follow, you'll learn some of the skills that you need for creating list, matrix, chart, and gauge reports. As you will see, many of the skills that you learned for building table reports also apply to list, matrix, and chart reports.

How to create a report from scratch

When you create a table or matrix, you can either use the Report Wizard or you can start the report from scratch. In contrast, when you create a list, chart, or gauge, you have to start the report from scratch.

Figure 16-17 shows how to create a report from scratch. First, you add a new report to the project or web site by using the first technique in figure 16-2. This places an empty report in the Report Designer. Then, you drag a data region from the Toolbox and drop it onto the surface of the report. In this example, I dropped a Table data region onto the report.

What happens next depends on whether the project contains a dataset. If the project or web site doesn't contain a dataset, the Data Source Configuration Wizard will be displayed and you can create a new dataset. But when you use this wizard, the report dataset can only contain fields from a single table of the database. As a result, it's usually better to create the dataset before you drag the data region onto the report.

In contrast, if the project or web site does contain one or more datasets, the Choose the Dataset dialog box will be displayed. Then, you can select the dataset for the report from the Data Source list, after which you can select the report dataset. When you return to the Report Designer, the fields of the report dataset will be shown in the Report Data pane and you can start building the report.

In the example in this figure, I dragged a table data region onto the report and then selected a report dataset. At this point, the Row Groups pane contains an item named (Details). This default row group represents the final child group of any row group structure that you create as you build the report. Then, any columns that aren't included in a named row group will be assigned to the (Details) group.

The start of a report in the Report Designer

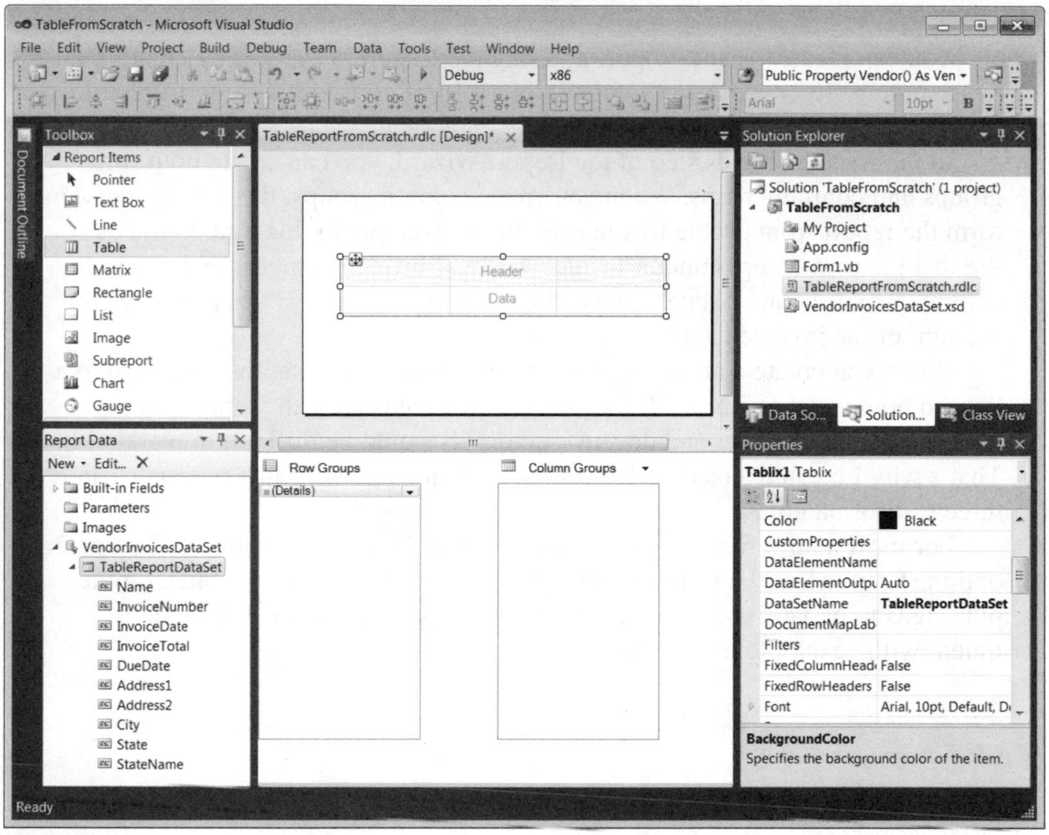

Procedure

- Use the first procedure in figure 16-2 to add a new report to a project or web site, so an empty report is shown in the Report Designer. Then, drag a report data region from the Toolbox onto the Designer. This region will be placed inside a Tablix template.
- If the project already contains a dataset, the Choose the Dataset dialog box will be displayed. Then, you can choose an existing dataset from the Data Source list.
- If the project doesn't contain a dataset, the Data Source Configuration Wizard will be displayed so you can create a new dataset that contains the data from a single table in the database.
- The fields for the dataset that you select or create will be displayed in the Report Data pane.
- At this point, you can use the techniques that you've already learned to change the layout, assign fields, create groups, and display totals.

Figure 16-17 How to create a report from scratch

How to create a matrix report

You can create a matrix report by using the Report Wizard or by creating it from scratch. To create the example in figure 16-18, I used the Report Wizard. Then, I added some formatting to improve the look of the report.

In the Arrange Fields step of the Report Wizard, you can create both row groups and column groups. When you create column groups, the wizard transform the report from a table to a matrix. In the example in this figure, you can see that the row groups contain InvoiceDate and InvoiceNumber fields; the column groups contain StateName and City fields; and the Values pane contains the sum of the invoice totals.

When you create a matrix report, you should use a dataset that will lead to a limited number of columns. If, for example, the dataset for the report in this figure included 40 states and dozens of cities, it would be difficult to work with. That's why I created a dataset for this matrix that consists of just two states and three California cities.

For most matrix reports, you should also use the Expand/Collapse Groups option. Then, when the matrix is displayed in a form, the user can click on the plus signs to expand data and the minus signs to collapse data. This is illustrated by the example in this figure.

The row and column groups for a matrix report in the Report Wizard

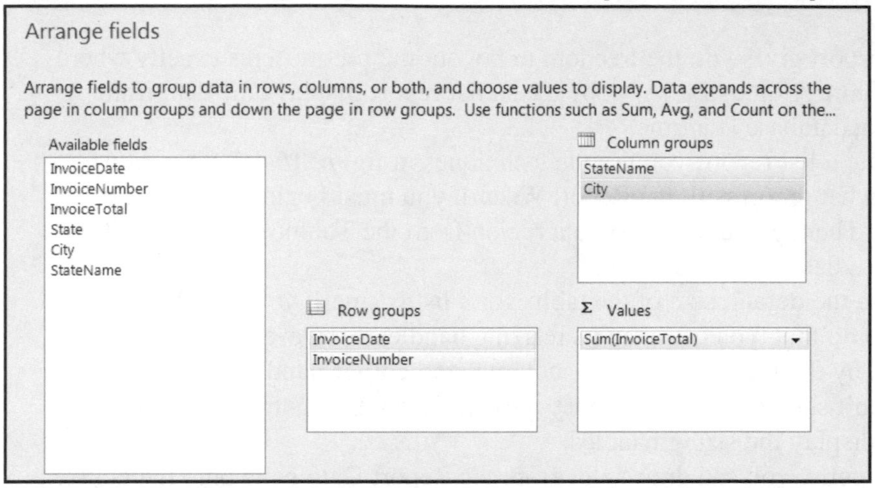

A matrix report in a ReportViewer control

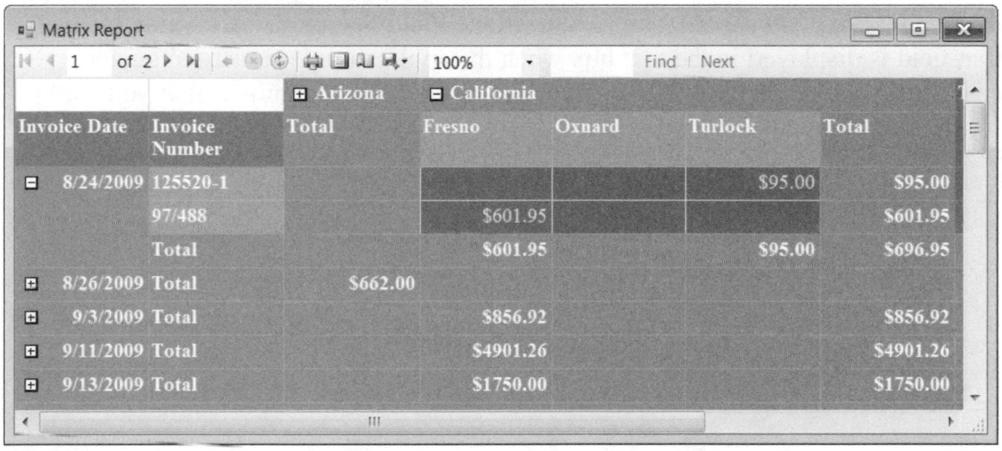

Description

- You can create a matrix report by using the Report Wizard or by building it from scratch.
- When you use the Report Wizard, select a dataset, as described in figure 16-3. Then, drag fields into the Row Groups, Column Groups, and Values panes, as shown above.
- After that, you can select the layout and style options, as described in figure 16-5.
- To build a matrix report from scratch, drag a matrix data region from the Toolbox onto the Report Designer, add the fields to the rows and columns, and create row and column groups.
- When you create a matrix report, you usually use the Expand/Collapse Groups option. You usually also use a dataset that will lead to a limited number of matrix columns in order to restrict the total width of the report.

Figure 16-18 How to create a matrix report

How to create a list report

A list report gives you the freedom to lay out the report items exactly where you want them. Although it isn't obvious, a list report displays the data from one row in a database at a time.

To create a list report, you use the techniques in figure 16-19. Since you can't start a list report with the Report Wizard, you must begin by creating a new report. Then, you drag a List data region from the Toolbox to the report, and choose a dataset for the report.

Because the default size of the tablix for a list is small, you usually need to resize it. To do that, you can drag its resizing handles. However, if the list is surrounded by the frame for the row, column, and corner handles, the sizing handles aren't shown. Then, you must click in the corner handle to remove the frame and display the sizing handles.

At this point, you can drag fields from the Report Data pane onto the tablix. You can also drag text boxes from the Toolbox onto the tablix. Then, you can enter string values or expressions into the text boxes. Or, if you hover the mouse over a text box, you can select a field from the Field Selector so the value of that field is displayed in the text box when the application is run. To align and size the text boxes in a list report, you can use the same techniques that you use for the text boxes in a Windows form.

A list report in the Report Designer

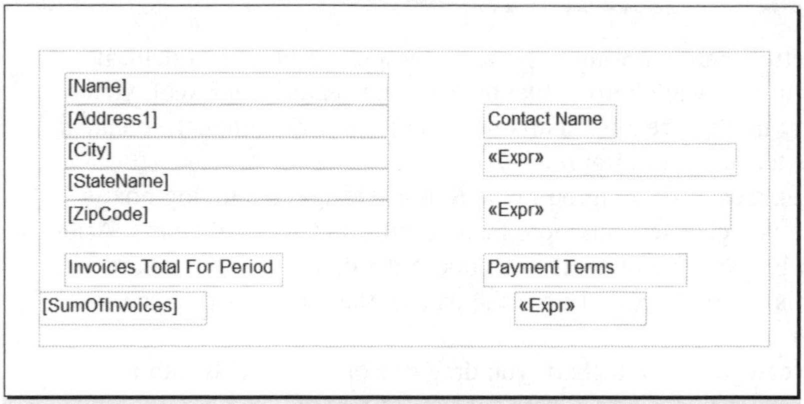

The list report in a ReportViewer control

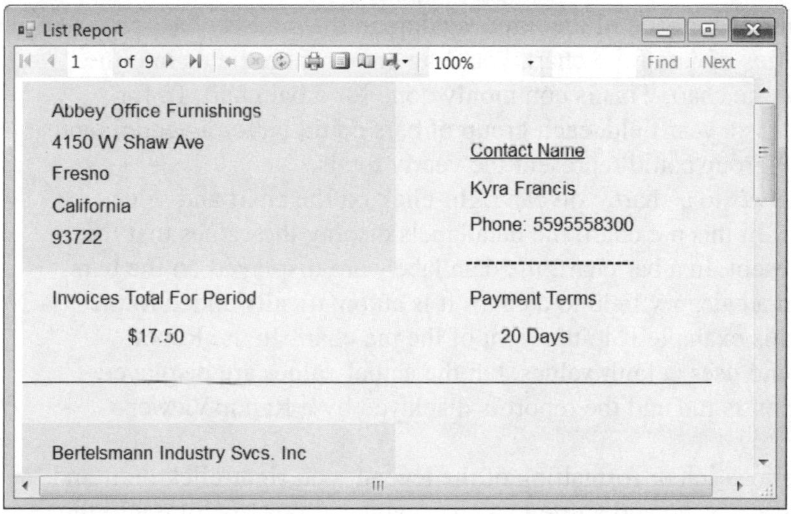

Description

- Since you can't create a list report by using the Report Wizard, you must first create a new report. Then, you can drag a list data region from the Toolbox to the report.
- When the Dataset Properties dialog box appears, use the procedure in figure 16-3 to choose or create the dataset for the list.
- To create labels for the fields that will be displayed, drag text boxes from the Toolbox onto the report. Then, enter text into the text boxes.
- To add fields to the report, drag fields onto the report. A text box will be used for displaying each field.
- When necessary, create expressions in the text boxes.
- To resize the area of the list, select the list and drag one of its handles.
- To align and format the text boxes and their data, use normal Windows techniques.

Figure 16-19 How to create a list report

How to create a chart report

A chart is useful when you want to present a graphical display of data. If you've used charting software before, like the charting features in Excel, you shouldn't have any trouble creating charts with the Report Designer. To create a chart, you use the techniques in figure 16-20.

When you drag a chart data region to the Report Designer, a dialog box is displayed that lets you choose from more than 50 different types of charts. After that, a dialog box is displayed that lets you choose the dataset for the report. For the pie chart in this figure, I created a special dataset that contains the data for just three vendors.

To define the categories for a chart, you drag one or more fields into the area below the chart. In this example, this consists of just the Name field. To define the data that will be used for the chart, you drag fields into the area above the chart. In this example, this consists of just the InvoiceTotal field, which will be summed for each of the three vendors in the dataset.

To define a series of data for a chart, you drag one or more fields into the area to the right of the chart. This is commonly done for a bar chart. If, for example, the series is a year field, each group of bars could be for a vendor, and the bars within the group could represent the yearly totals.

To add *data labels* to a chart, you can right-click on the chart and select Show Data Labels. In this pie chart, the data labels display the values that the pie segments represent. In a bar chart, the data labels are displayed on the bars.

When you add a category field to a chart, it is automatically added to the *legend*, which in this example is to the right of the pie chart. In the Report Designer, this legend uses default values, but the actual values are displayed when the application is run and the report is displayed by a ReportViewer control.

To modify the location or formatting of the legend, you right-click on it and select Legend Properties. To add a title to a chart, you can type the title into the chart area. To format the title, you can right-click on it and select Title Properties. That's how easy it is to create and format charts when you use the Report Designer. To get good at it, all you need to do is experiment.

How to create a gauge report

To create a gauge report, you use the same techniques that you use for creating a chart report. However, because gauges are more limited, you have fewer options. Here again, if you experiment, you should be able to create and format the gauges that your applications require.

A pie chart report at design time and run time

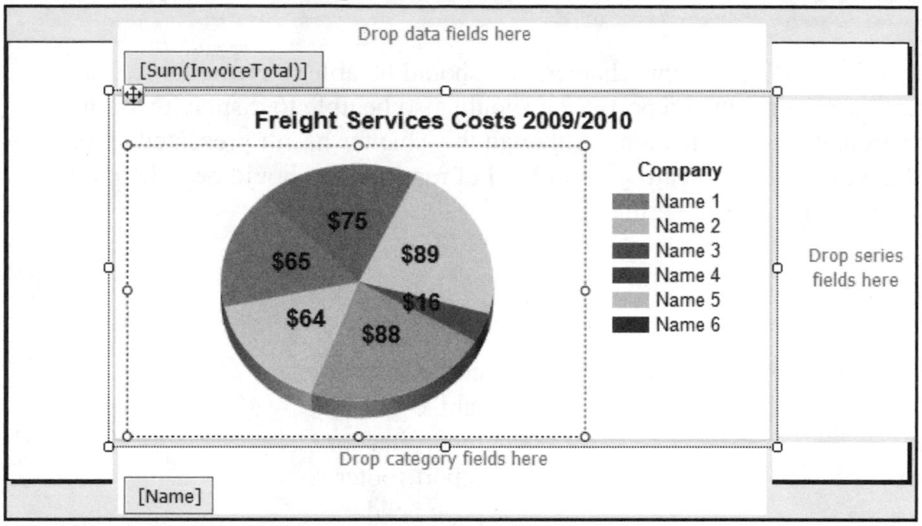

The pie chart in a ReportViewer control

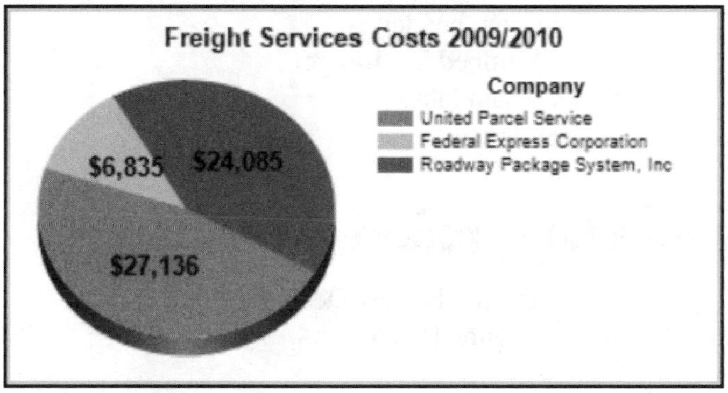

Description

- To start a chart, create a new report from scratch and drag a chart data region from the Toolbox to the report. Then, in the first dialog box that's displayed, choose the type of chart. In the second dialog box, choose the dataset for the chart.
- To group data in a chart, drag one or more fields to the area below the chart ("Drop category fields here"). These fields are automatically added to the *legend* for the chart.
- To display data in the chart, drag one or more fields to the area above the chart ("Drop data fields here").
- To add series fields to the chart, drag one or more fields to the area to the right of the chart ("Drop series fields here").
- To add *data labels* to the chart, right-click on the chart and select Show Data Labels.
- To change the formatting of a component like the title or legend, right-click on it and select the appropriate option like Title Properties or Legend Properties.

Figure 16-20 How to create a chart report

Perspective

Now that you've finished this chapter, you should be able to create table, list, matrix, chart, and even gauge reports. You should also be able to display them in both Windows and web applications. Although this chapter hasn't presented all of the skills that you need for creating every kind of report, you should be able build on what you've learned by experimenting.

Terms

SQL Server Reporting Services (SSRS)
local report
data region
table
list
matrix
chart
gauge
report dataset
row handle
column handle
corner handle
tablix
report header
report footer
page header
page footer
column header
row header
embedded image
data label
legend

Exercise 16-1 Create a table report

In this exercise, you'll use the Report Wizard and the Report Designer to create a table report that's similar to the one in figure 16-16.

Review the dataset for the report

1. Open the VendorInvoicesReport project that's in your Chapter 16 directory.
2. In the Solution Explorer, notice that this project contains a dataset named VendorInvoicesDataSet. Then, double-click on this file to view its diagram in the Dataset Designer.
3. To view the SQL statement for this dataset, right-click on the table adapter in the diagram and select Configure from the shortcut menu. Note that this statement joins the Vendors and Invoices tables and gets some data from each one.

Use the Report Wizard to create the initial report

4. Use the second method in figure 16-2 to start the Report Wizard. Then, enter VendorInvoicesReport in the Name text box and click the Add button.
5. In the Dataset Properties dialog box, change the name of the report dataset to VendorInvoices. Next, select the VendorInvoicesDataSet from the Data Source list, and note that the VendorInvoicesDataTable is automatically selected in the Available Datasets list. Then, click the Next button.

6. Use the methods in figure 16-4 to add the State and Name fields to the Row Groups pane. Next, add the InvoiceNumber, InvoiceDate, and InvoiceTotal fields to the Values pane. Note that the Sum function has been applied to the InvoiceTotal field, but not to the InvoiceNumber and InvoiceDate fields. Then, click the Next button.
7. Use the methods in figure 16-5 to choose the layout. Check the box for showing subtotals and grand totals, leave the first option button the way it is, and uncheck the box for expanding and collapsing groups. Then, click the Next button.
8. In the Choose a Style dialog box, leave the style set to Ocean. Then, click the Finish button.

Display the report in a ReportViewer control

9. Use the procedure in figure 16-6 to add a ReportViewer control to Form1. Then, use its smart tag menu to choose the VendorInvoicesReport that you just created. Also, select the Dock in Parent Container option from this menu.
10. Test the application to make sure the report is displayed properly in the ReportViewer control.

Enhance the report

11. In the Report Designer, increase the widths of the columns where necessary to ensure that all the column header text is visible.
12. In the empty, second row of the Invoice Number column, insert an aggregate expression that displays the Count of the number of invoices for each vendor. If necessary, refer to figure 16-11.
13. In the empty, second row of the Invoice Date column, use the procedure in figure 16-11 to add an expression to the cell that displays either "invoices" or "invoice", depending on the number of invoices in the group.
14. Test the application to make sure that the enhancements of the last two steps are working properly.
15. In the Report Designer, use the technique in figure 16-13 to change the formatting of the cell that contains the invoice date so that the time element isn't shown.
16. In each of the cells that contain currency values, change the formatting to your local currency format.
17. Add a report header that reads "Vendor Invoices Report". Then, set its font size to 14pt and font weight to Bold.
18. Insert an embedded image named murachlogo.jpg into the report header. This image is in your Chapter 16 folder.
19. In the State column, change the word Total to Grand Total. Then, in the Name column, change the word Total to Total for State'.
20. Test the application again to make sure that all of the enhancements are working properly. Then, experiment with other enhancements on your own. That's a great way to learn.

Exercise 16-2 Create a bar chart

In this exercise, you'll create a bar chart report. When you run the application, the bar chart should look like this.

Review the dataset for the report

1. Open the BarChartReport project that's in your Chapter 16 directory.
2. In the Solution Explorer, note that this project contains a dataset named FreightTotalsDataTable. Then, double-click on this file to view its diagram in the Dataset Designer.
3. To view the SQL statement for this dataset, right-click on the table adapter and select Configure from the shortcut menu. Note that this statement joins the InvoiceLineItems, Invoices, and Vendors tables. Note also that its WHERE clause only gets the invoices for the first six months of 2010 and only gets those invoices that have "Freight" as the description in one or more line items. The result is that the invoices for just three vendors are retrieved.

Create a new report and a report data set

4. Use the first method in figure 16-2 to create a new report from scratch. Then, name this report FreightCostsReport.
5. In the Report Designer, drag a Chart data region from the Toolbox to the designer. Then, select the first icon in the Column chart options to set the chart type to vertical bars. (Vertical bars are called "columns" in this designer).
6. In the Dataset Properties dialog box that appears next, change the name of the report dataset to FreightReportDataSet. Then, select FreightCostsDataSet from the Data source list and note that FreightTotalsDataTable is automatically selected in the Available datasets list. Next, click the OK button.

Define the data for the chart

7. Define the category by dragging the Month field from the Report Data pane and into the area marked "Drop category fields here". If you can't see this area in the Report Designer, double-click inside the chart to display it.
8. Define the data for the chart by dragging the InvoiceTotal field from the Report Data pane and dropping it in the area marked "Drop data fields here". If the data fields still include an item named (empty), right-click on that item and select Delete Series from the shortcut menu to remove it.
9. Define the series for the chart by dragging the Name field from the Report Data pane into the area marked "Drop series fields here".

Display the report in the ReportViewer control

10. Use the procedure in figure 16-6 to add a ReportViewer control to Form1. Then, use its smart tag menu to choose the FreightCostsReport that you just created. Also, select the Dock in Parent Container option from this menu.
11. Test the application. At this stage, the months will be shown as numbers from 1 to 6 and the chart may be smaller than you want, but you should see the names of three companies and values from 0 to 3000.

Enhance the report

12. In the Report Designer, increase the size of the report boundaries and then increase the size of the chart. Then, run the application again and continue to make adjustments until you are satisfied with how the report looks.
13. Double-click on the Chart Title, delete the default text, and replace it with:

    ```
    Freight Costs Jan - Jun 2010.
    ```
14. Drag and drop the chart legend so it is located underneath the Chart Title. Note that this changes the legend layout from vertical to horizontal.
15. Double-click on the Axis Title at the left of the chart and replace the default text with the word Cost. Then, double-click on the Axis Title at the bottom of the chart and replace the default text with the word Month.
16. To add currency symbols to the values on the Cost axis, right-click on the axis labels (which currently display the values from 0 to 100), then select Axis Properties from the shortcut menu. In the Value Axis Properties dialog box, choose the options that you want for formatting the data.
17. To replace the numbers on the Month axis with the names of months, right-click on the field that's assigned to the category (which currently shows [Month]), and then select Category Group Properties from the shortcut menu. In the dialog box that appears, click on the fx button at the side of the Label text box. Then, in the Expression dialog box, enter this expression:

    ```
    =MonthName(Fields!Month.Value)
    ```
18. Test the application to make sure that all of the enhancements are working properly. Then, experiment on your own by adding enhancements such as changing the font of the legend, adding a legend title, changing the fill style of the columns, or adding data labels to the bars.

17

How to use LINQ

LINQ is a feature of Visual Basic that lets you query five different types of data sources using the same query language. One of the most useful applications of LINQ is called LINQ to SQL, which lets you use LINQ instead of SQL queries to query a database. In this chapter, you'll learn how to use LINQ to Objects and LINQ to SQL, which will help you appreciate the benefits of using LINQ.

An introduction to LINQ

As its name implies, *LINQ*, or *Language-Integrated Query,* lets you query a data source using the Visual Basic language. In practice, this means you can query five different types of data sources with the same language, and you don't have to use a special query language like Transact-SQL.

To make that possible, Visual Basic includes the *LINQ providers* that are listed in figure 17-1. These providers translate LINQ queries into a form that each data source can understand. They also convert the returned data to the objects defined by the queries, and they convert the objects to data when the queries update a data source.

For instance, the *LINQ to Objects* provider lets you use LINQ to query an in-memory data structure like a list, *LINQ to DataSet* lets you query an ADO.NET dataset, and *LINQ to SQL* lets you query a SQL Server database. Because LINQ to DataSet, LINQ to SQL, and *LINQ to Entities* all work with ADO.NET objects, they are sometimes referred to as *LINQ to ADO.NET*.

In this chapter, you'll learn how to use the LINQ to SQL provider, and in the next chapter, you'll learn how to use the LINQ to Entities provider. As you will see, those are the providers that are most useful when you develop ADO.NET applications.

LINQ is implemented as a set of *extension methods* that are defined by the Enumerable and Queryable classes. These methods are referred to as *query operators*. Although you can call the query operators directly by coding a *method-based query*, you're more likely to use the clauses that Visual Basic provides. When you use Visual Basic clauses to code a LINQ query, the result is called a *query expression*.

When you use query expressions, Visual Studio's IntelliSense helps you code the queries correctly, and the syntax checker helps you catch errors at compile time. Visual Studio also provides debugging support. When compared to writing SQL queries as strings, these are major improvements.

Common LINQ query operators

Figure 17-1 presents the query operators that are commonly used in a query expression. As you'll see, the syntax looks similar to a SQL query, so you shouldn't have any trouble understanding what most of these clauses do. For example, you use the From clause to identify the data source for the query, the Where clause to filter the data that's returned by the query, and the Select clause to identify the fields you want to be returned by the query.

Some of the Visual Basic clauses for working with LINQ

Clause	Description
From	Identifies the source of data for the query.
Where	Provides a condition that specifies which elements are retrieved from the data source.
Order By	Indicates how the elements that are returned by the query are sorted.
Select	Specifies the content of the returned elements.
Let	Performs a calculation and assigns an alias to the result that can be used within the query.
Join	Combines data from two data sources.
Aggregate	Lets you include aggregate functions, such as Sum, Average, and Count, in a query.
Group By	Groups the returned elements and, optionally, applies aggregate functions to each group.

The LINQ providers that are included with Visual Basic

Provider	Description
LINQ to Objects	Lets you query in-memory data structures such as generic lists and arrays.
LINQ to DataSet	Lets you query the data in a dataset.
LINQ to SQL	Lets you query and update the data in a SQL Server database.
LINQ to XML	Lets you query and modify in-memory XML or the XML stored in a file.
LINQ to Entities	Lets you query and update the data in any relational database.

The benefits of using LINQ

- IntelliSense, compile-time syntax checking, and debugging support make it easier to code a LINQ query.
- Using the same syntax makes it easier to query different types of data sources.
- The designer tools let you create object-relational mappings that make it easier to work with relational data sources.

Description

- *Language-Integrated Query* (*LINQ*) lets you query different kinds of data sources using the same Visual Basic syntax.
- LINQ provides a set of *query operators* that are implemented using *extension methods*. These methods are static members of the Enumerable and Queryable classes.
- A query that calls the extension methods is a *method-based query*. A query that uses Visual Basic clauses is a *query expression*. You use either a method-based query or a query expression to identify the data you want to retrieve from a data source.
- To use LINQ with a data source, the data source must implement the IEnumerable(Of T) interface or another interface that implements IEnumerable(Of T) such as IQueryable(Of T). A data source that implements one of these interfaces is called an *enumerable type*.
- *LINQ providers* perform three main functions: (1) Translate queries into commands that the data source can execute; (2) Convert the data that's returned from a data source to the objects defined by the query; and (3) Convert objects to data when updating a data source.

Figure 17-1 An introduction to LINQ

The three stages of a query operation

Figure 17-2 presents the three stages of a query operation and illustrates these stages using a generic list. This example uses LINQ to Objects, but you use the same techniques with other LINQ providers.

The first stage is to get the data source. How you do that depends on the type of data source you're working with. For a generic list, getting the data source means declaring a variable to hold the list and then calling a method that returns a List(Of Invoice) objects. In this example, the GetInvoices method in the InvoiceDB class is used to return the objects.

The second stage is to define the query expression. This expression identifies the data source and the data to be retrieved from that data source. For instance, the query expression in this figure retrieves all the invoices with an invoice total greater than 22,000. It also sorts those invoices by invoice total in descending sequence.

Notice here that the query expression is stored in a *query variable* named invoices. That's necessary because this query isn't executed when it's defined. Also notice that the query variable isn't declared with a type. Instead, it's given a type implicitly based on the type of elements returned by the query. This is one of the features of Visual Basic that supports LINQ. In this case, because the query returns Invoice objects, the query variable is given the type IEnumerable(Of Invoice).

For this to work, the data source must be an *enumerable type*, which means that it implements the IEnumerable(Of T) interface. Alternatively, the data source could implement the IQueryable(Of T) interface, since this interface implements IEnumerable(Of T). In case you aren't familiar with interfaces, they consist of a set of declarations for one or more properties, methods, and events, but they don't provide implementation for those properties, methods, and events. For the example in this figure, all you need to know is that the List() class implements the IEnumerable(Of T) interface.

The third stage of a query operation is to execute the query. To do that, you typically use a For Each statement like the one in this figure. Here, each element that's returned by the query expression is added to a string variable. Then, after all the elements have been processed, the string is displayed in a message box. As you can see, this message box lists the invoice numbers and invoice totals for all invoices with totals greater than 22,000.

When a query is defined and executed separately as shown here, the process is referred to as *deferred execution*. In contrast, queries that are executed when they're defined use *immediate execution*. Immediate execution typically occurs when a method that requires access to the individual elements returned by the query is executed on the query expression. For example, to get a count of the number of elements returned by a query, you can execute the Count method on the query expression. Then, the query will be executed immediately so the count can be calculated. You'll learn some of the methods for returning these types of values later in this chapter.

The three stages of a query operation

1. Get the data source.
2. Define the query expression.
3. Execute the query to return the results.

A LINQ query that retrieves data from a generic list of invoices

A statement that declares and populates the list

```
Dim invoiceList As List(Of Invoice) = InvoiceDB.GetInvoices
```

A statement that defines the query expression

```
Dim invoices = From invoice In invoiceList
    Where invoice.InvoiceTotal > 22000
    Order By invoice.InvoiceTotal Descending
    Select invoice
```

Code that executes the query

```
Dim displayResult As String = "Invoice No." & vbTab & "Invoice Total" & vbCrLf
For Each invoice In invoices
    displayResult &= invoice.InvoiceNumber & vbTab & vbTab &
                FormatCurrency(invoice.InvoiceTotal) & vbCrLf
Next
MessageBox.Show(displayResult, "Invoices Over $22,000")
```

The resulting message box

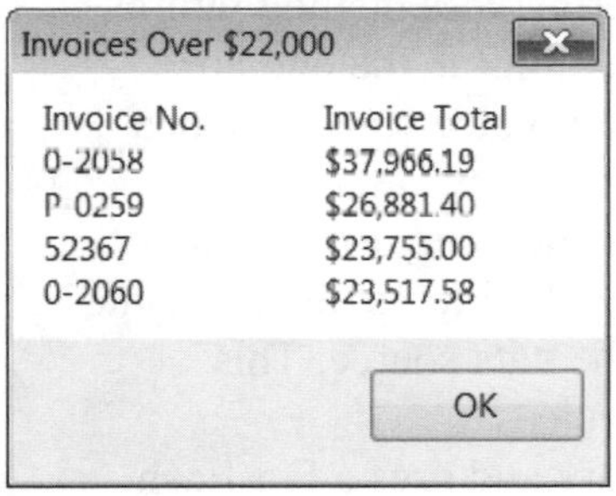

Description

- The process above is called *deferred execution* because the query isn't executed when it's defined. Instead, it's executed when the application tries to access the individual elements returned by the query, such as when the query is used in a For Each statement.
- If a query isn't executed when it's defined, it's stored in a *query variable*. In that case, the query variable is implicitly typed as IEnumerable(Of T) where T is the type of each element. In the example above, the invoices variable is assigned the type IEnumerable(Of Invoice), since the invoice list contains Invoice objects.
- If a query requires access to the individual elements identified by the query expression, such as when an aggregate value is requested, *immediate execution* occurs. In that case, the query expression isn't saved in a query variable.

Figure 17-2 The three stages of a query operation

How to code query expressions

Now that you have a basic understanding of what a LINQ query is, you need to learn the syntax for coding query expressions. Although the examples in the topics that follow use LINQ to Objects, LINQ is essentially the same no matter what type of data source you're using.

How to identify the data source for a query

To identify the source of data for a query, you use the From clause shown in figure 17-3. As you can see, this clause declares a *range variable* that will be used to represent each element of the data source, and it names the data source, which must be an enumerable type. Note that because the result of a query is an enumerable type, the data source can be a previously declared query variable. The From clause can also declare a type for the range variable, although the type is usually omitted. If it is omitted, the type is determined by the type of elements in the data source.

The example in this figure shows how to use the From clause with a generic list of invoices. Here, the first statement creates a list that's based on the Invoice class and loads invoices into it using the GetInvoices method of the InvoiceDB class. At this stage, all you need to know is that the GetInvoices method returns a List(Of Invoice) object, and that the Invoice class is similar to the one in figure 6-7 of chapter 6. The list object that contains the Invoice objects is then assigned to a variable named invoiceList.

Then, the second statement in this example defines the query expression, which consists of just the From clause. This clause uses the invoice as the name for the range variable, and it identifies invoiceList as the data source. This expression is then stored in a query variable named invoices.

Finally, the third set of statements executes the query and uses a For Each statement to loop through the invoices and calculate the sum of the InvoiceTotal fields for each invoice.

You may have noticed in this example that I used the same variable name (invoice) in the query expression and in the For Each loop. That makes sense because they both refer to an element in the data source, although they are of course two separate variables. When you code more sophisticated query expressions, you'll often want to use different variable names to indicate the differences between the elements they refer to. That'll make more sense when you see the Group By clause later in this chapter.

Incidentally, you wouldn't actually use a query expression that consists of just a From clause like the one in this example. That's because you could just as easily use the For Each statement on the list itself. So keep in mind that this example is just to help you get started with query expressions. With few exceptions, you'll usually code other clauses along with the From clause.

The syntax of the From clause

```
From elementName1 [As type1] In collectionName1
  [, elementName2 [As type2] In collectionName2]...
```

A LINQ query that includes only a From clause

A statement that declares and populates a generic list of invoices

```
Dim invoiceList As List(Of Invoice) = InvoiceDB.GetInvoices
```

A statement that defines the query expression

```
Dim invoices = From invoice In invoiceList
```

Code that executes the query

```
Dim sum As Decimal = 0
For Each invoice In invoices
    sum += invoice.InvoiceTotal
Next
MessageBox.Show(FormatCurrency(sum), "Sum of Invoices")
```

The resulting message box

Description

- The From clause identifies the source of data for a query and declares a *range variable* that's used to iterate through the elements of the data source.
- If the range variable you use in a query expression and the range variable you use in the For Each statement that executes the query refer to the same type of elements, you should give them the same name for clarity. Otherwise, you should give them different names to indicate the type of elements they refer to.
- The From clause can identify two or more data sources, each with its own range variable. In that case, data from the two sources is joined based on the condition you specify in the Where clause. See figure 17-7 for more information on joining data.
- The From clause is required in a query expression unless the Aggregate clause is coded (see figure 17-8). If the From clause is coded with other clauses, it must be the first clause in the expression.

Figure 17-3 How to identify the data source for a query

How to filter and sort the results of a query

To filter the results of a query, you use the Where clause that's illustrated by the first example in figure 17-4. On this clause, you specify a condition that an element must meet to be returned by the query. The condition is coded as a Boolean expression. The first example in this figure illustrates how this works.

In this example, the Where clause specifies that a calculated value (InvoiceTotal – PaymentTotal – CreditTotal) must be greater than zero. This clause also specifies that the due date must be less than 15 days from the current date. Notice here that the range variable that's declared in the From clause (invoice) is used in the Where clause to refer to each Invoice object.

To sort the results of a query, you use the Order By clause that's illustrated by the second example in this figure. Here, the query expression includes an Order By clause that sorts the invoices by vendor ID in ascending sequence (the default), followed by a calculated value in descending sequence. To do that, it uses the range variable that's declared by the From clause to refer to each Invoice object just like the Where clause does.

The third example in this figure shows how to execute these queries. Here, a For Each statement concatenates the VendorID, InvoiceNumber, InvoiceTotal, PaymentTotal, and CreditTotal properties of each Invoice object that's returned by the query to a string. When the For Each statement ends, this string is displayed in a message box.

If you compare the results of this query with the results shown in the first example, you'll see how the sequence has changed. In the second message box, the vendor IDs are listed from smallest to largest. Then, within each vendor ID, the invoices are listed from those with the largest balances due to those with the smallest balances due. For example, the first invoice for vendor ID 122 has a balance due of $328.05, and the second invoice for that vendor ID has a balance due of $98.50.

Incidentally, the third example uses an If function to vary the spacing in the message box based on the length of the invoice number. This function works like the IIf function, but the IIf function has been deprecated. As a result, If functions are used in the examples in this chapter instead of IIf functions.

The results of the filter and sort queries

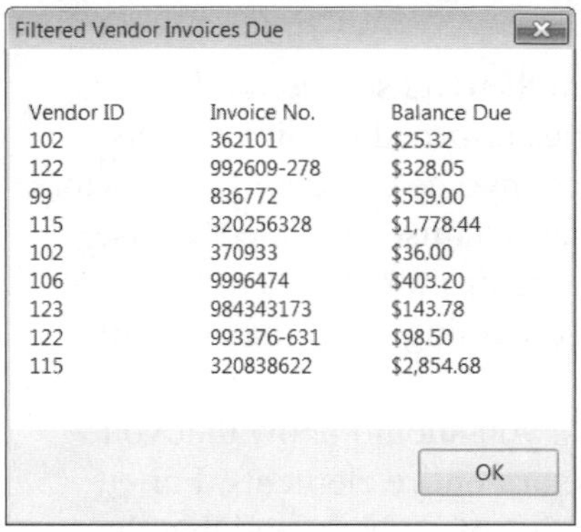

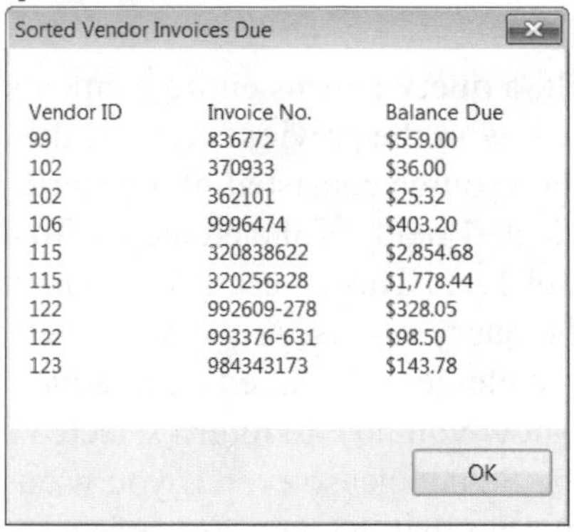

A LINQ query that filters the generic list of invoices

```
Dim invoices = From invoice In invoiceList
    Where invoice.InvoiceTotal - invoice.PaymentTotal -
          invoice.CreditTotal > 0 And
            invoice.DueDate < DateTime.Today.AddDays(15)
```

A LINQ query that filters and sorts the generic list of invoices

```
Dim invoices = From invoice In invoiceList
    Where invoice.InvoiceTotal - invoice.PaymentTotal -
          invoice.CreditTotal > 0 And
            invoice.DueDate < DateTime.Today.AddDays(15)
    Order By invoice.VendorID,
        invoice.InvoiceTotal - invoice.PaymentTotal - invoice.CreditTotal
        Descending
```

Code that executes the queries

```
Dim displayResult As String =
    "Vendor ID" & vbTab & "Invoice No." & vbTab & "Balance Due" & vbCrLf
For Each invoice In invoices
    displayResult &= invoice.VendorID & vbTab & vbTab &
        invoice.InvoiceNumber & vbTab &
        If(invoice.InvoiceNumber.Length < 8, vbTab, "").ToString &
        FormatCurrency(invoice.InvoiceTotal -
                       invoice.PaymentTotal -
                       invoice.CreditTotal) & vbCrLf
Next
MessageBox.Show(displayResult, "Sorted Vendor Invoices Due")
```

Description

- The Where clause lets you filter the data in a data source by specifying a condition that the elements of the data source must meet to be returned by the query.
- The condition is coded as a Boolean expression that can contain one or more relational and logical operators.
- The Order By clause lets you specify how the results of the query are sorted. You can specify one or more expressions on this clause, and each expression can be sorted in ascending or descending sequence.

Figure 17-4 How to filter and sort the results of a query

How to select fields from a query

By default, a query returns entire elements from the data source. In the examples you saw in the previous figures, the queries returned Invoice objects because the data source consisted of a generic list of Invoice objects. But you can also return selected fields of the elements. To do that, you use the Select clause shown in figure 17-5. This clause lets you identify one or more fields to be included in the query results. A query that returns something other than an entire range of source elements is called a *projection*.

Before I show you how to return selected fields, you should know that you can include the Select clause even if you want to return entire elements. For example, assuming that the data source is a generic list of invoices and that the range variable in the From clause is named invoice, you could use the first Select clause in this figure to return Invoice objects. That means that the results of the queries in the previous figures would be the same whether or not this Select clause was included. Although the Select clause isn't required when you want to return entire elements from the data source, it's often included for completeness.

The second Select clause in this figure returns a single field of each element. In this case, it returns the InvoiceTotal property of an Invoice object. Note that because the InvoiceTotal property is defined as a Decimal type, the query variable is declared implicitly as an IEnumerable(Of Decimal) type.

The third example shows a query expression that returns selected properties from the Invoice objects. Specifically, it returns the VendorID, InvoiceNumber, InvoiceTotal, PaymentTotal, and CreditTotal properties. If you look back at the examples in the previous figure, you'll see that these are the only properties that are used when the query is executed. Because of that, these are the only properties that need to be retrieved.

As I mentioned earlier, if a query returns a single field, the type of the query variable is determined by the type of the field. But what if the query returns more than one field? In that case, the query variable is declared as an *anonymous type*. This type is defined with properties that are based on the selected fields. In the third example, then, the anonymous type would be defined with the five properties named in the Select clause. Note that an anonymous type doesn't have a usable name, so you can't refer to it from your code.

The last example in this figure shows how you can assign an *alias* to a column in the query results. Here, the alias Number is assigned to the InvoiceNumber column, and the alias BalanceDue is assigned to the expression that calculates the balance due. These aliases are then used as the names of the properties in the anonymous type that's created, and you can refer to them when you execute the query. In this case, the output result is the same as in figure 17-4.

The syntax of the Select clause

```
Select [alias1 =] columnExpression1
    [, [alias2 =] columnExpression2]...
```

A Select clause that returns Invoice objects

```
Select invoice
```

A Select clause that returns a single field

```
Select invoice.InvoiceTotal
```

A Select clause that creates an anonymous type

```
Select invoice.VendorID, invoice.InvoiceNumber, invoice.InvoiceTotal,
       invoice.PaymentTotal, invoice.CreditTotal
```

A LINQ query that uses aliases in the Select clause

A query expression that assigns aliases to a column and a calculated value

```
Dim invoices = From invoice In invoiceList
    Where invoice.InvoiceTotal - invoice.PaymentTotal -
          invoice.CreditTotal > 0 And
            invoice.DueDate < DateTime.Today.AddDays(15)
    Order By invoice.VendorID,
        invoice.InvoiceTotal - invoice.PaymentTotal - invoice.CreditTotal
        Descending
    Select invoice.VendorID,
        Number = invoice.InvoiceNumber,
        BalanceDue = invoice.InvoiceTotal - invoice.PaymentTotal -
            invoice.CreditTotal
```

Code that executes the query

```
Dim displayResult As String =
    "Vendor ID" & vbTab & "Invoice No." & vbTab & "Balance Due" & vbCrLf
For Each invoice In invoices
    displayResult &= invoice.VendorID & vbTab & vbTab &
        invoice.Number & vbTab &
        If(invoice.Number.Length < 8, vbTab, "").ToString &
        FormatCurrency(invoice.BalanceDue) & vbCrLf
Next
MessageBox.Show(displayResult, "Sorted Vendor Invoices Due")
```

Description

- The Select clause identifies the data you want to return from each element of the query results.
- A query that returns anything other than entire source elements is called a *projection*. The second, third, and fourth examples above illustrate projections.
- If a projection returns two or more fields, an *anonymous type* that contains those fields as its properties is created. This is illustrated by the third and fourth examples above.
- You can assign an *alias* to a field by coding the alias name, followed by an equals sign, followed by a column expression. You can assign an alias to an existing column in the data source or to a calculated column as shown in the fourth example above.

Figure 17-5 How to select fields from a query

How to assign an alias to the result of a calculation

In the last figure, you saw one way to assign an alias to the result of a calculation. If you look back at the example in that figure, however, you'll see that the same calculation is performed in the Where, Order By, and Select clauses. To avoid that, you can use the Let clause shown in figure 17-6.

As you can see, you can use the Let clause to assign aliases to one or more expressions. In the query expression in this figure, the Let clause calculates the balance due for each invoice and assigns the alias BalanceDue to the result of that calculation. Then, the Where, Order By, and Select clauses that follow all refer to this alias.

If you look at the code that executes this query, you'll see that it's identical to the code in the previous figure. That's possible because both queries return an anonymous type with VendorID, Number, and BalanceDue properties. However, the query expression in this figure is easier to read and much simpler because the balance due is calculated only once.

The syntax of the Let clause

```
Let alias1 = expression1 [, alias2 = expression2]...
```

A LINQ query that assigns the result of a calculation to a variable

A query expression that calculates the balance due

```
Dim invoices = From invoice In invoiceList
    Let BalanceDue =
        invoice.InvoiceTotal - invoice.PaymentTotal - invoice.CreditTotal
    Where BalanceDue > 0 And
        invoice.DueDate < DateTime.Today.AddDays(15)
    Order By invoice.VendorID, BalanceDue Descending
    Select invoice.VendorID, Number = invoice.InvoiceNumber, BalanceDue
```

Code that executes the query

```
Dim displayResult As String =
    "Vendor ID" & vbTab & "Invoice No." & vbTab & "Balance Due" & vbCrLf
For Each invoice In invoices
    displayResult &= invoice.VendorID & vbTab & vbTab &
        invoice.Number & vbTab &
        If(invoice.Number.Length < 8, vbTab, "").ToString &
            FormatCurrency(invoice.BalanceDue) & vbCrLf
Next
MessageBox.Show(displayResult, "Sorted Vendor Invoices Due")
```

The resulting message box

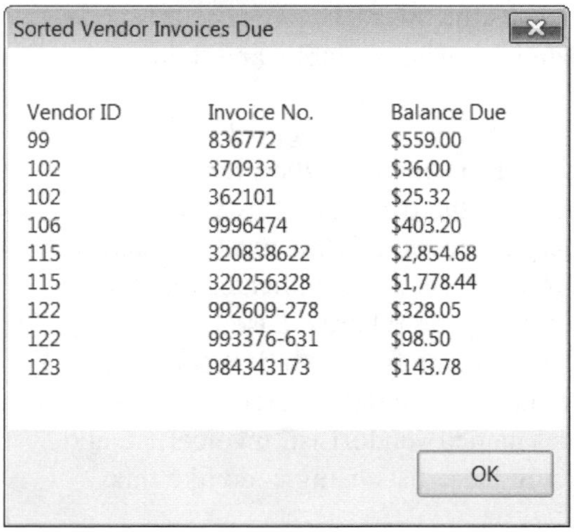

Description

- The Let clause lets you assign an alias to a calculation that you perform within a query. Then, you can use that alias in other clauses of the query that follow the Let clause.
- The Let clause can simplify a query expression because it eliminates the need to include a calculation two or more times in the same query.

Figure 17-6 How to assign an alias to the result of a calculation

How to join data from two or more data sources

Figure 17-7 shows how you can include data from two or more data sources in a query. One way to do that is to use the Join clause shown at the top of this figure. To start, this clause declares a range variable and names a data source just like the From clause does. Then, it indicates how the two data sources are related.

To illustrate, the first example in this figure joins data from the list of Invoice objects you've seen in the previous figures with a list of Vendor objects. To do that, it names the invoice list on the From clause, and it names the vendor list on the Join clause. Then, the On condition indicates that only vendors in the vendor list with vendor IDs that match vendor IDs in the invoice list should be included in the results.

Because both the invoice and vendor lists are included as data sources in this query expression, the rest of the query can refer to properties of both Invoice and Vendor objects. For example, the Order By clause in this query expression sorts the results first by the Name property of the Vendor objects and then by the InvoiceTotal of the Invoice objects. Similarly, the Select clause selects the Name property from the Vendor objects and the InvoiceTotal and InvoiceNumber properties from the Invoice objects. In this case, the InvoiceNumber property has been assigned an alias of Number.

The second example in this figure executes the query. Here again, this code uses a For Each loop to store the query data in a string variable, and then displays the variable in a message box.

The last example in this figure shows that you can also join data without using the Join clause. To do that, you list the data sources in the From clause. Then, you code the condition that indicates how the two data sources are related on the Where clause. For instance, the query expression in this example names both the invoice and vendor lists on the From clause, and it indicates that the VendorID fields in the two lists must be equal on the Where clause.

Although this figure only shows how to join data from two data sources, you can extend this syntax to join data from additional data sources. For example, suppose you have three data sources named vendorList, invoiceList, and lineItemList. Then, you could join the data in these lists using code like this:

```
From vendor In vendorList
Join invoice In invoiceList
  On vendor.vendorID Equals invoice.vendorID
Join lineItem In lineItemList
  On invoice.invoiceID Equals lineItem.invoiceID...
```

You could also perform this join by naming all three lists in the From clause and then coding both join conditions in the Where clause. In either case, you could then refer to properties from any of the three lists in the query expression.

The basic syntax of the Join clause

```
Join elementName In collectionName On keyName1 Equals keyName2
```

A LINQ query that joins data from two data sources

A query expression that joins data from generic lists of invoices and vendors

```
Dim invoiceList As List(Of Invoice) = InvoiceDB.GetInvoices
Dim vendorList As List(Of Vendor) = VendorDB.GetVendors

Dim invoices = From invoice In invoiceList
    Join vendor In vendorList
        On invoice.VendorID Equals vendor.VendorID
    Where invoice.InvoiceTotal > 22000
    Order By vendor.Name, invoice.InvoiceTotal Descending
    Select vendor.Name, invoice.InvoiceTotal,
           Number = invoice.InvoiceNumber
```

Code that executes the query

```
Dim displayResult As String = "Vendor Name" & Space(38) &
    "Invoice No." & Space(20) & "Total" & vbCrLf
For Each invoice In invoices
    displayResult &= invoice.Name & vbTab & vbTab &
        If(invoice.Name.Length < 10, vbTab, "").ToString &
        If(invoice.Name.Length < 20, vbTab, "").ToString &
            invoice.Number & vbTab &
        If(invoice.Number.Length < 8, vbTab, "").ToString &
            FormatCurrency(invoice.InvoiceTotal) & vbCrLf
Next
MessageBox.Show(displayResult, "Joined Vendor and Invoice Data")
```

The resulting message box

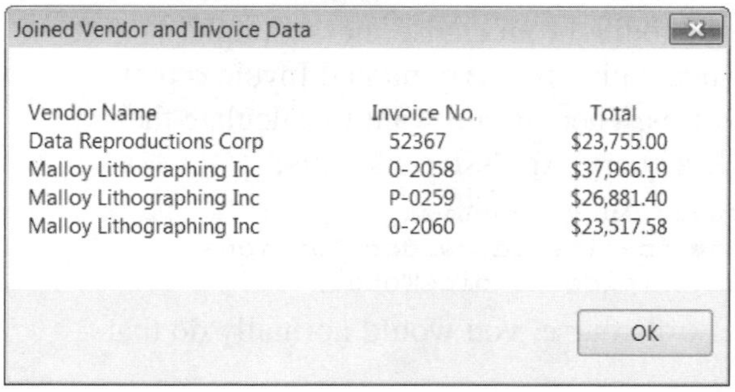

Another way to join the data in the two data sources

```
Dim invoices = From invoice In invoiceList, vendor In vendorList
    Where invoice.VendorID = vendor.VendorID...
```

Description

- The Join clause lets you combine data from two or more data sources based on matching key values. The query results will include only those elements that meet the condition specified by the Equals operator.
- You can also join data without using the Join clause by coding the join condition as illustrated by the last example above.

Figure 17-7 How to join data from two or more data sources

How to use aggregate functions

If you want to summarize the data returned by a query, you can use the Aggregate clause shown in figure 17-8. On this clause, you name a range variable and a data source just as you do on a From clause. In fact, you'll frequently code the Aggregate clause in place of a From clause.

To identify the summary calculations you want to perform, you code the Into keyword followed by one or more expressions. Each expression must use one of the *aggregate functions* listed in this figure. These functions perform an operation on a set of selected elements.

The query expression in this figure includes an Aggregate clause that uses two aggregate functions. The Average function calculates an average of the invoice totals in a list of generic invoices, and the Sum function calculates the total of all the invoices. The result is a single instance of an anonymous type that includes properties named Average and Sum. You can see how these properties are used in the code that displays the results of the query. If you want to use different names for these properties, you can assign aliases to the aggregate functions.

Note that the Into clause doesn't have to be coded immediately after the Aggregate clause. In this query expression, for example, a Where clause is coded between the Aggregate and Into clauses. Also note that a query expression that includes the Aggregate clause is executed immediately. That's because the aggregate functions require access to the individual elements of the query result.

Although you'll typically code the Aggregate clause in place of the From clause, you can also code it in addition to the From clause. For example, suppose that the Vendor class is defined with a property named Invoices that provides access to all a vendor's invoices. Then, if you want to calculate the total of all the invoices, you can code a query expression like this:

```
Dim invoiceTotal = From vendor In vendorList
                   Aggregate invoice In vendor.Invoices
                   Into Sum(invoice.InvoiceTotal)
```

If you can access the invoices directly, of course, you would normally do that instead because it's more efficient.

The syntax of the Aggregate clause

```
Aggregate elementName1 [As type1] In collectionName1
    [, elementName2 [As type2] In collectionName2]...
    [queryClause]...
  Into [alias1 = ] aggregateFunction1
    [, [alias2 = ] aggregateFunction2]...
```

Aggregate functions

Function	Description
All	Returns a Boolean value that specifies if all the elements of a collection satisfy a condition.
Any	Returns a Boolean value that specifies if any elements of a collection satisfy a condition.
Average	Calculates the average of a given field or expression.
Count	Counts the total number of elements in a collection or the number of elements that satisfy a condition.
LongCount	Same as Count, but returns the count as a Long type.
Max	Calculates the maximum value of a given field or expression.
Min	Calculates the minimum value of a given field or expression.
Sum	Calculates the sum of a given field or expression.

A LINQ query that includes aggregates

A query expression that calculates the average and sum of invoice totals

```
Dim invoiceSummary = Aggregate invoice In invoiceList
    Where invoice.InvoiceDate > #1/1/2010#
    Into Average(invoice.InvoiceTotal), Sum(invoice.InvoiceTotal)
```

Code that displays the query results

```
Dim displayResult As String = String.Empty
displayResult &= "Average invoice total:" & vbTab &
               FormatCurrency(invoiceSummary.Average) & vbCrLf &
           "Total invoices:" & vbTab & vbTab &
               FormatCurrency(invoiceSummary.Sum)
MessageBox.Show(displayResult, "Invoice Total Summary")
```

The resulting message box

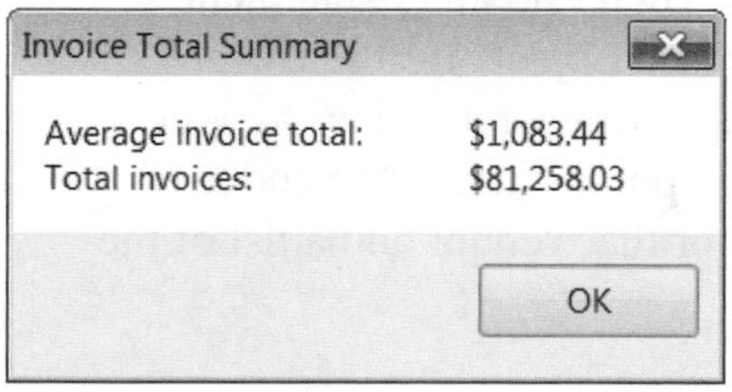

Description

- The Aggregate clause lets you include *aggregate functions* in a query. It can be used in place of the From clause or as an additional clause in a query.
- The use of the Aggregate clause causes the query to be executed immediately.

Figure 17-8 How to use aggregate functions

How to group query results

If you want to group the elements returned by a query, you can use the Group By clause presented in figure 17-9. To start, you can list the fields or elements you want to use after the Group keyword. In the query expression in this figure, I used invoice as the range variable for the query, which represents an Invoice object. That way, I can use any of the properties of the Invoice object in the Group By clause. Since this is the default, however, I could have omitted this variable.

Next, you code the By keyword followed by one or more expressions that identify the fields you want to use to group the elements. In this example, the invoices will be grouped by vendor ID. You can also assign an alias to an expression. In most cases, you'll only do that if the expression is a calculated value.

Finally, you code the Into keyword followed by one or more aggregate expressions. Each aggregate expression can use one of the aggregate functions you learned about in the previous figure. For example, the first aggregate expression uses the Count() function, which returns a count of the items returned by the query.

By default, an aggregate expression is given the same name as the aggregate function it uses. If that's not what you want, you can assign an alias to the expression. In this example, I assigned the alias InvoiceCount to the Count function.

Instead of an aggregate function, one of the aggregate expressions in a Group By clause can use the Group keyword. This keyword refers to the elements that are being grouped. In this case, the Group keyword refers to Invoice objects. Because of that, I assigned an alias of Invoices to the group. Notice that I also included the Invoices alias in the Select clause. That way, the query results are defined as an anonymous type that includes the Invoice objects as well as the vendor ID and Count.

You can see how this works in the code that executes this query. This code uses nested For Each statements to retrieve the query results. The outer statement uses a variable named vendor to refer to each vendor so the vendor ID and count of invoices can be retrieved for that vendor. Then, the inner statement uses the Invoices property, which refers to the invoice objects for the current vendor. This property is used to get the invoice total for each invoice. As you can see in the message box that's displayed, the output includes the vendor ID for each vendor, followed by a count of invoices for that vendor and a list of the invoice totals.

The syntax of the Group By clause

```
Group [listField1 [, listField2]...]
   By [alias1 = ] keyExpression1
   [, [alias2 = ] keyExpression2]...
 Into [alias3 = ] {Group|aggregateExpression1}
   [, [alias4 = ] aggregateExpression2]...
```

A LINQ query that groups data by vendor

A query expression that calculates the balance due for each vendor

```
Dim vendorsDue = From invoice In invoiceList
    Where invoice.InvoiceTotal > 22000
    Group invoice By invoice.VendorID
        Into InvoiceCount = Count(), Invoices = Group
    Order By VendorID
    Select VendorID, InvoiceCount, Invoices
```

Code that executes the query

```
Dim displayResult As String = "Vendor ID (Invoices)" & vbTab &
                              "Invoice Total" & vbCrLf
For Each vendor In vendorsDue
    displayResult &= String.Format("{0} ({1}){2}", vendor.VendorID,
                vendor.InvoiceCount, vbCrLf)
    For Each invoice In vendor.Invoices
        displayResult &= Space(50) &
                   FormatCurrency(invoice.InvoiceTotal) & vbCrLf
    Next
Next
MessageBox.Show(displayResult, "Invoices Due By Vendor")
```

The resulting message box

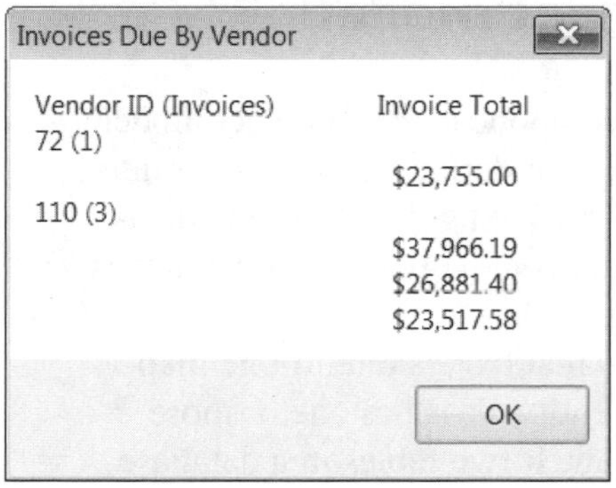

Description

- The Group By clause lets you group the elements returned by a query. It's typically used to calculate aggregate values for the grouped elements.
- You can use the Group keyword in the Into clause to refer to the element that's being grouped. Then, when you execute the query, you can use the Group keyword or the alias that's assigned to it to refer to individual elements within the group.

Figure 17-9 How to group query results

How to use LINQ to SQL

When you use LINQ to SQL, you can retrieve data from a database without using SQL. Instead, you use LINQ as the query language along with an object model as shown by the diagram in figure 17-10. Note, however, that you can only use LINQ to SQL with a SQL Server database.

As this figure shows, LINQ to SQL consists of two main components: an *object model* and the LINQ to SQL runtime. You can think of the object model as a set of business classes that define business objects that are directly related to the tables or views in a database. Before you can use LINQ to SQL, you must create this object model.

To retrieve data from a database, you code a LINQ query expression that queries the objects that are created from the classes defined by the object model. Then, when the query is executed, the LINQ to SQL runtime translates it into a SQL Select statement and sends it to ADO.NET, which sends it on to SQL Server for processing. When the requested data is returned, the LINQ to SQL runtime translates it back to the objects used by the application..

You can also use LINQ to SQL to change the data in a database. To do that, you first change the objects defined by the object model. Then, when you submit the changes, the LINQ to SQL runtime generates the required Insert, Update, and Delete statements and passes them on for processing. LINQ to SQL also detects concurrency errors so you can handle them in your applications.

The basic components of an object model

The table in this figure describes the basic components of an object model. To start, an object model contains a *data context* that defines the connection to the database. The data context also provides for retrieving data from the database. If the application changes that data, the data context tracks those changes and submits them to the database when requested.

An object model also contains *entity classes* that have a one-to-one mapping with tables or views in the database. Each entity class has one or more members that map to columns in the table or view. If two tables in a database are related by a foreign key, an *association* defines the relationship in the object model.

In addition to entity classes, an object model can include data context methods. These methods are mapped to stored procedures or functions in the database. You can use stored procedures and functions to retrieve data from a database. You can also use stored procedures to update the data in a database.

How LINQ to SQL works

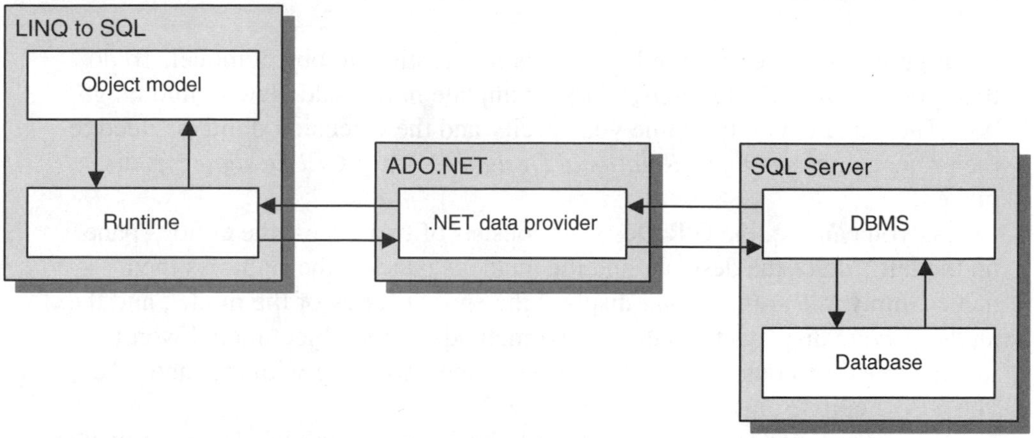

Basic components of an object model

Component	Description
Data context	Defines the connection to the database and provides for retrieving data from the database, tracking changes made to the data, and submitting the changes to the database.
Entity class	Maps to a table or view in the database.
Class member	Maps to a column in a table or view.
Association	Defines a relationship between two tables in the object model.
Method	Maps to a stored procedure or function in the database.

Description

- To use LINQ to SQL, you create an *object model* that represents the objects used by your applications and maps them to objects in a database.
- When you execute a query against an object model, the *LINQ to SQL runtime* translates the query into a SQL Select statement and sends it to the .NET data provider for execution. The .NET data provider sends the statement on to the DBMS for processing. When the results are returned from the DBMS through the .NET data provider, the LINQ to SQL runtime translates them back to the objects defined by the object model.
- When you submit changes to the database based on changes made to the objects defined by the object model, the LINQ to SQL runtime generates the required Insert, Update, and Delete statements and passes them to ADO.NET for processing.
- An object model consists of a *data context class* that manages the flow of data to and from the database and *entity classes* that map to tables and views in the database.
- Each entity class can define one or more class members that represent columns in the table or view.
- If two tables in a database are related by a foreign key, an *association* is created between the two tables in the object model.

Figure 17-10 An introduction to LINQ to SQL

How to start a new object model

Figure 17-11 presents the basic skills for creating an object model. To do that, you use the LINQ to SQL Classes template in the Add New Item dialog box. Then, a file with the name you specify and the extension dbml is added to the project, and the *Object Relational Designer*, or just *O/R Designer*, is displayed.

As you can see, the O/R Designer consists of two panes: the entities pane on the left side of the designer and the methods pane on the right. As their names imply, the *entities pane* displays the entity classes of the model, and the *methods pane* displays the data context methods. If the object model won't include any data context methods or if you aren't working with the methods, you can of course close the methods pane.

When the O/R Designer is displayed, the Toolbox contains components that you can use to work with an object model. However, because it's easier to drag elements from the Server Explorer, you usually won't use these tools.

How to create entity classes

An easy way to create an entity class is to drag a table or view from the Server Explorer to the entities pane of the O/R Designer. In this figure, I dragged two entity classes that represent the Vendors and Invoices tables in the Payables database. Note that when the name of the table or view in the database is plural, the O/R Designer gives the entity class a singular name. This makes sense because the class will be used to create objects that represent a single item in the table or view. For example, an object created from the Vendor class represents a single vendor.

When you create an entity class using the O/R Designer, the designer generates Visual Basic code that defines the class. That code includes properties that you can use to refer to each column in the table or view. By default, these properties have the same names as the columns. The designer also adds a property to the data context class that you can use to refer to the table in code. When I created the Vendor class, for example, the O/R Designer generated a property named Vendors.

If you create entity classes for two tables that are related by a foreign key, the O/R Designer creates an association between the two classes. In this figure, for example, the arrow represents the association between the Vendor and Invoice classes. This association is based on the VendorID column in the Invoices table, which is a foreign key to the VendorID column in the Vendors table. Because the association between the Vendor and Invoice classes represents a one-to-many relationship, the Invoice class will include a property named Vendor that you can use in a query to refer to columns in the Vendors table. Similarly, the Vendor class will include a property named Invoices that you can use to refer to the collection of invoices for a vendor.

The Object Relational Designer with two entity classes

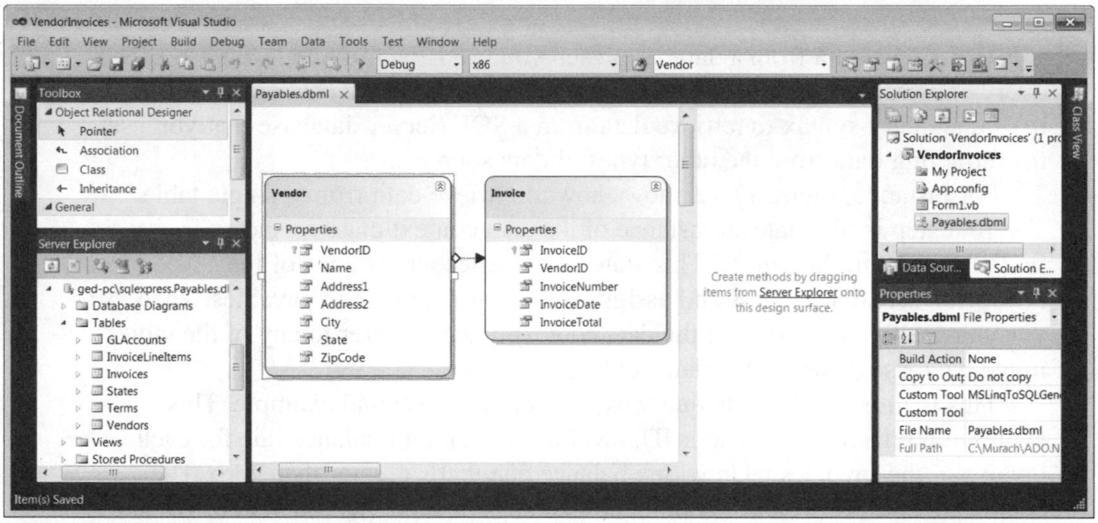

Description

- To create an object model, display the Add New Item dialog box, select the LINQ to SQL Classes template from the Data category, and enter a name for the dbml file that will define the object model.
- After you create an object model, the *Object Relational Designer* (*O/R Designer*) is displayed. You can use this designer to create entity classes or to create data context *methods* that map to stored procedures or functions.
- The O/R Designer consists of two panes. The *entities pane* on the left is where the entity classes you create are displayed, and the *methods pane* on the right is where the data context methods you create are displayed.
- To create an entity class, drag a table or view or columns of a table or view from the Server Explorer to the O/R Designer. The first time you do that, the connection for the data context is set to the database that contains the table or view.
- Each time you add an entity class, a property is added to the data context that you can use to refer to the table that the class is mapped to. In addition, a property is added to the entity class for each column in the table or view that the class is created from.
- If two tables that you add to an object model are related by a foreign key, the O/R Designer defines an association between the entity classes based on that relationship. An association is defined by properties in the entity classes, and you can use these properties to refer to one class from the other class.
- By default, if the name of a table or view in the database is plural, the O/R Designer creates a class with a singular name. If that's not what you want, display the Options dialog box (Tools→Options), expand the Database Tools node, select O/R Designer, and select False from the Enabled drop-down list in the Pluralization of Names group.

Figure 17-11 How to start a new object model and create entity classes

How to retrieve data from a single table

To retrieve data from a database when you use LINQ to SQL, you use LINQ query expressions. This is one of the key benefits of LINQ. That is, you can use the same query syntax to retrieve data from a SQL Server database that you use for retrieving data from the other types of data sources.

For instance, figure 17-12 shows how to retrieve data from a single table. The first step is to create an instance of the data context class as shown in the first statement in this figure. This statement creates an instance of the PayablesDataContext class and assigns it to a variable named payables. Then, you can use the properties of the data context object to refer to any of the tables in the database to which the data context is mapped.

This is illustrated by the query expression in the second example. This expression retrieves the vendor ID, invoice number, and balance due for each invoice in the Invoices table with a balance due that's greater than zero. The results are sorted by balance due in descending sequence within vendor ID.

The only difference between this example and the earlier ones is that the data source for the query is the Invoices table in the Payables database. To refer to this table, the query expression uses the Invoices property of the payables variable that contains a reference to the data context object.

This query expression also uses several of the properties defined by the Invoice class within the object model. For example, the Let clause refers to the InvoiceTotal, PaymentTotal, and CreditTotal properties. This works because the range variable in this query represents a single Invoice object.

The code that executes the query is similar to the code you've seen earlier. Here, a For Each loop is used to concatenate the data in a string. Then, the string is displayed in a message box.

A LINQ query that retrieves data from the Invoices table

A statement that creates an instance of the data context

```
Dim payables As New PayablesDataContext
```

A query expression that gets invoice balances due

```
Dim invoicesDue =
    From invoice In payables.Invoices
    Let BalanceDue =
      invoice.InvoiceTotal - invoice.PaymentTotal - invoice.CreditTotal
    Where (BalanceDue > 0)
    Order By invoice.VendorID, BalanceDue Descending
    Select invoice.VendorID, Number = invoice.InvoiceNumber, BalanceDue
```

Code that executes the query

```
Dim displayResult As String =
     "Vendor ID" & vbTab & "Invoice No." & vbTab & "Balance Due" & vbCrLf
For Each invoice In invoicesDue
    displayResult &= invoice.VendorID & vbTab & vbTab &
        invoice.Number & vbTab &
        If(invoice.Number.Length < 8, vbTab, "").ToString &
            FormatCurrency(invoice.BalanceDue) & vbCrLf
Next
MessageBox.Show(displayResult, "Sorted Vendor Invoices Due")
```

The resulting message box

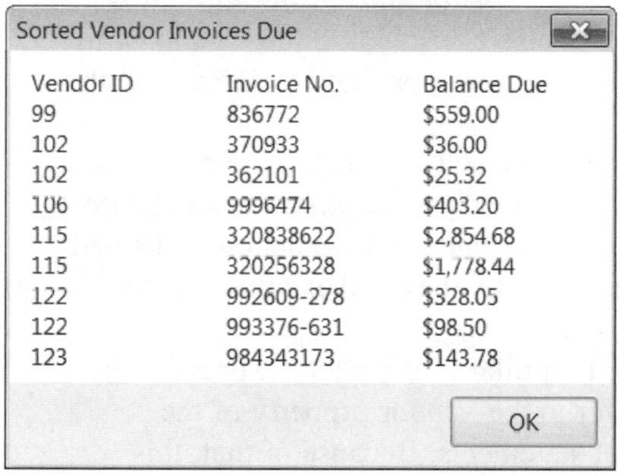

Description

- Before you can work with the entity classes in an object model, you have to create an instance of the data context for the model.
- To refer to a database table in a query expression, you use the property of the data context class that returns data from the table as a collection of entity objects.
- To refer to a member of an entity object, you use the property that defines the member. In a LINQ query, you refer to that member through the range variable.

Figure 17-12 How to retrieve data from a single table

How to query across relationships

To query data from a database across relationships, you use the properties of the entity classes that provide access to the relationships. These properties reflect the primary and foreign key relationships between the tables in the underlying database. In figure 17-13, you can see how LINQ query expressions can use these relationships. These examples use the one-to-many relationship between the Vendor and Invoice classes.

The first query expression in this figure gets information for a vendor through the Invoice objects. To do that, it uses the Vendor property of the Invoice class. In this case, the Vendor property is used to get the Name property of the Vendor object. This Vendor property is automatically included in the query results because of the relationship between the Invoice and Vendor tables.

After this query expression, you can see a For Each loop that will execute the query and display the results in the console window. Here, the variable named vendor is an anonymous type that's created by the query. This anonymous type has three properties, Name, InvoiceNumber and BalanceDue, which are created due to the Select clause in the LINQ query.

The second query expression in this figure gets invoice information through the Vendor objects. To do that, it uses the Invoices property of the Vendor class. In this expression, the relationship between the Vendor and Invoice classes is shown in the From clause. Although you can also use standard join syntax with LINQ to SQL, it's more common to use the relationships that are defined by the object model, as shown in this example.

When you work with relationships, you can also use a technique called *deferred loading*, which is sometimes referred to as *lazy loading*. In some cases, this can make your applications more efficient because related data isn't loaded into memory until it's needed. This is illustrated by the third example in this figure.

The query expression in this example is similar to the query expression in the first example except that it doesn't refer to the Vendor property of the Invoice objects in the Order By and Select statements. Because of that, this query doesn't retrieve the related vendor data. Instead, the vendor data isn't retrieved until the query is executed as illustrated by the code that follows the query expression in this example.

When you use this technique, the query expression must not return a projection. That's why the query expression in this example returns entire invoice rows, which are stored in Invoice objects. That's required because the Vendor property is available only from an Invoice object. It isn't available from anonymous types like the ones returned by the first two query expressions.

A query expression that gets vendor data through the Invoice objects

```
Dim payables As New PayablesDataContext

Dim invoicesDue =
    From invoice In payables.Invoices
    Let BalanceDue =
        invoice.InvoiceTotal - invoice.PaymentTotal - invoice.CreditTotal
    Where (BalanceDue > 0)
    Order By invoice.Vendor.Name, BalanceDue Descending
    Select invoice.Vendor.Name, invoice.InvoiceNumber, BalanceDue

For Each vendor In invoicesDue
    Console.WriteLine("{0} {1} : ${2}",
        vendor.Name, vendor.InvoiceNumber, vendor.BalanceDue)
Next
```

A query expression that gets invoice data through the Vendor objects

```
Dim invoicesDue =
     From vendor In payables.Vendors,
          invoice In vendor.Invoices
     Let BalanceDue =
         invoice.InvoiceTotal - invoice.PaymentTotal - invoice.CreditTotal
     Where BalanceDue > 0
     Order By vendor.Name, BalanceDue Descending
     Select vendor.Name, invoice.InvoiceNumber, vendor.Invoices,
         BalanceDue, invoice.InvoiceTotal
```

A query expression that defers the loading of vendor data

```
Dim invoicesDue =
    From invoice In payables.Invoices
    Let BalanceDue =
        invoice.InvoiceTotal - invoice.PaymentTotal - invoice.CreditTotal
    Where BalanceDue > 0
    Order By BalanceDue Descending
    Select invoice

For Each invoice In invoicesDue
    Dim vendor As Vendor = invoice.Vendor
    Console.WriteLine("{0} {1} : ${2}",
        vendor.Name, invoice.InvoiceNumber, invoice.InvoiceTotal)
Next
```

Description

- Instead of using joins in LINQ to SQL queries, you typically use the associations defined by the object model that identify the relationships between the classes. To refer to an association, you use the property of an entity class that defines the association.
- You can simplify the reference to objects on the many side of a relationship by including the association in the From clause as shown in the second example above.
- You can defer the loading of related objects by omitting references to those objects from the query expression. Then, the objects aren't loaded until you refer to them from the query results. For this to work, the query must not return a projection.

Figure 17-13 How to query across relationships

How to use bound controls with LINQ to SQL

When you use LINQ to SQL, you can bind controls to an entity collection, to the results of a query, and to an object data source that's created from an entity class. You'll learn about these binding techniques in the next two topics.

How to create an object data source from an entity class

In chapter 9, you learned how to create an object data source from a business class that you develop. In a similar way, you can also create an object data source from an entity class in an object model. Figure 17-14 shows you how to do that.

As you can see, you use the Data Source Configuration Wizard just as you do for any other data source. In the first step, though, you select the Object option. Then, in the second step, you select the entity type you want to use as the source of data. In this figure, for example, I selected the Vendor entity. Of course, for this to work you must first create the entity class as described in figure 17-11. When you click the Finish button, the Vendor data source appears in the Data Sources window.

After you create an object data source, you can use it to create bound controls as described in chapter 9. Then, you can work with the bound controls using techniques that are similar to those presented in that chapter. However, instead of using database classes to access the data in a database, you can use LINQ to SQL as shown in the next figure.

The first step of the Data Source Configuration Wizard

The second step of the Data Source Configuration Wizard

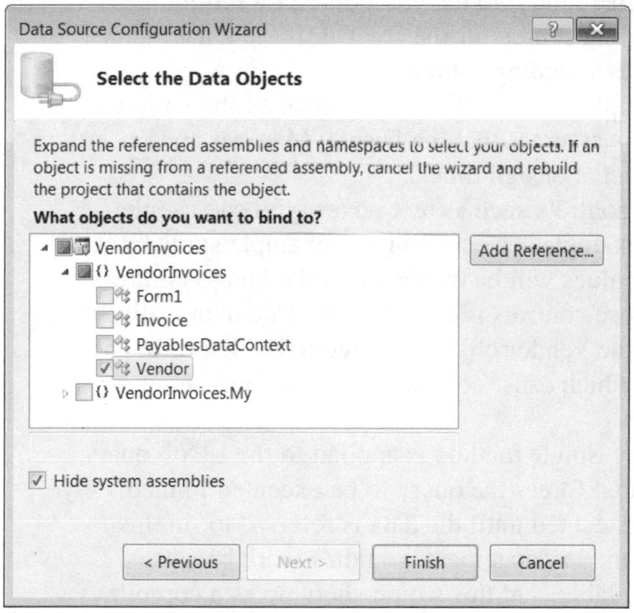

Description

- To create an object data source from an entity class, select the Object option from the first step of the Data Source Configuration Wizard. Then, select the entity type you want to use from the list that's displayed in the second step.

Figure 17-14 How to create an object data source from an entity class

How to bind controls

Figure 17-15 shows five techniques you can use to bind a control when you use LINQ to SQL. To start, you can complex-bind a control to an entity collection as shown in the first example in this figure. Here, the first statement sets the DataSource property of a combo box to the entity collection, in this case, the Vendors collection in the payables data context. Then, the second statement sets the DisplayMember property of the combo box so the Name property of the entity will be displayed in the combo box list. Finally, the third statement sets the ValueMember property of the combo box so the VendorID property of the entity will be stored in the combo box list.

When you bind a control to an entity collection, all the rows and columns that the entity is mapped to in the database are retrieved into the data context. This may result in large amounts of unwanted data being fetched, so if that's not what you want, you can bind the control to the results of a query instead. You can see this illustrated in the second example in this figure. In this example, only the VendorID and Name columns are retrieved from the database, since these are the only two columns that are used by the combo box.

In the first two examples, the combo box is bound directly to the data source through its DataSource property. If a control is created from an object data source, however, you can also bind it to the data source by setting the DataSource property of the binding source for the control. If the DataSource property of a combo box is set to a binding source named VendorBindingSource, for example, you can bind the control as shown in the third example in this figure. This assumes that the DisplayMember and ValueMember properties were set at design time.

If you want to simple-bind controls such as text boxes, you can use the technique shown in the fourth example. The code in this example starts by getting a Vendor object whose values will be displayed in the bound controls. Then, the binding source for those controls is cleared so that no data is displayed in the controls. Finally, the Vendor object is added to the list of bound objects for the binding source, which causes the properties of the Vendor object to be displayed in the text boxes.

Note in this example that the Single method is applied to the LINQ query. Single is an extension method that forces the query to be executed immediately. Otherwise, the query won't be executed until the data is referred to. In this example, that would mean that the last statement wouldn't work because selectedVendor wouldn't be available, and this would show up as a compile-time error.

The last example in this figure shows how to bind a control to a collection of entity objects related to another entity object. To do that, you set the DataSource property of the control or binding source to the association property that provides access to the entity collection. In this example, the DataSource property of an Invoice binding source is set to the Invoices association property for a vendor. When this statement is executed, the invoices for the vendor are loaded automatically if necessary.

Code that binds a combo box to an entity collection

```
cboVendors.DataSource = payables.Vendors
cboVendors.DisplayMember = "Name"
cboVendors.ValueMember = "VendorID"
```

Code that binds a combo box to the results of a query

```
Dim vendors = From vendor In payables.Vendors
              Order By vendor.Name
              Select vendor.VendorID, vendor.Name

cboVendors.DataSource = vendors
cboVendors.DisplayMember = "Name"
cboVendors.ValueMember = "VendorID"
```

A statement that binds a combo box using its binding source

```
VendorBindingSource.DataSource = vendors
```

Code that binds text boxes to an entity object

```
Dim vendorID As Integer = CInt(NameComboBox.SelectedValue)
Dim selectedVendor =
    (From vendor In payables.Vendors
     Where vendor.VendorID = vendorID).Single

VendorBindingSource.Clear()
VendorBindingSource.Add(selectedVendor)
```

A statement that binds a DataGridView control to related objects

```
InvoiceBindingSource.DataSource = selectedVendor.Invoices
```

Description

- You can complex-bind a control such as a combo box or a DataGridView control to an entity collection or to the results of a query by setting the DataSource property of the control or the binding source associated with the control to the collection or results.
- You can simple-bind controls such as text boxes that are created from an object data source to the properties of an entity object by clearing the binding source for the controls and then adding the object to the list of bound objects for the binding source.
- If an object has a one-to-many relationship with other objects, you can complex-bind a control to the objects on the many side by setting the DataSource property of the control or the binding source associated with the control to the association property of the object on the one side. If the objects on the many side haven't already been loaded, they're loaded automatically.
- To execute a query immediately, you can use the Single extension method, as shown in the fourth example. If this method wasn't used, selectedVendor wouldn't be available in the last statement because the query wouldn't be executed yet.
- You can use bound controls to display, add, modify, and delete data.

Figure 17-15 How to bind controls

A Vendor Invoices application

Now that you've learned the basics of using LINQ to SQL, you're ready to see how you can use LINQ to SQL in an application. That will help you decide whether you are interested in using LINQ in your own applications.

The user interface

Figure 17-16 presents the user interface for a Vendor Invoices application. As you can see, the Vendor Invoices form includes a combo box that lets the user select a vendor. Then, the address information for that vendor is displayed in the text boxes on the form, and the invoices for that vendor are displayed in the DataGridView control.

The object model

Figure 17-16 also presents the object model for this application. It includes just Vendor and Invoice entity classes. These classes only include the columns needed by the application. To remove columns from an entity class, you can select the columns in the O/R Designer, right-click on the selection, and click Delete.

Although you can't tell it from this figure, this application uses two object data sources for the Vendor and Invoice objects. First, I used the Vendor object from the data source to generate the combo box and text boxes. When I dragged the fields from the Data Sources pane onto the form, that automatically created a Vendor binding source. Similarly, I used the Invoice object to generate the DataGridView control, and that created the Invoice binding source.

The next step was to set the DisplayMember and ValueMember properties of the combo box. To do that, I used the options in the smart tag menu of the combo box.

Finally, I selected the combo box, and expanded the DataBindings collection in the Properties window. Then, I set the Text property of the combo box to a value of None. If you don't do this when you bind a combo box this way, the combo box won't work correctly.

The Vendor Invoices form

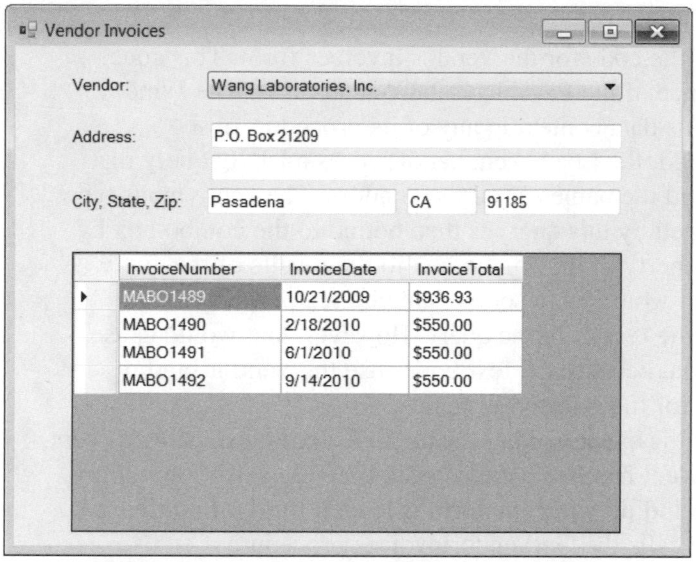

The object model

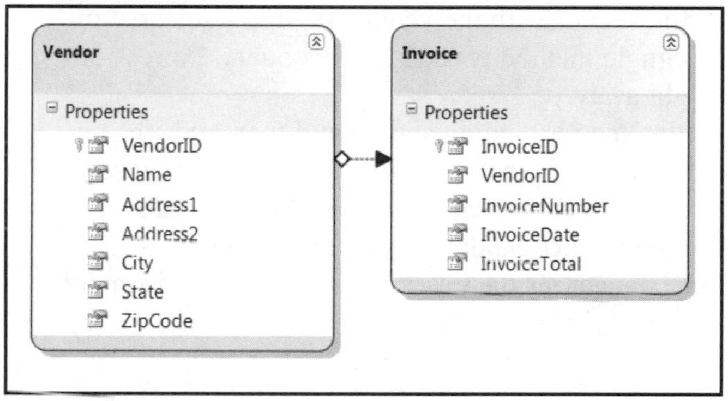

Description

- When the user selects a vendor from the combo box, the vendor address is displayed in the text boxes and the invoices for the vendor are displayed in the DataGridView control.
- The object model for this application consists of just the Vendor and Invoice classes. These classes have a one-to-one correspondence with the Vendors and Invoices tables in the Payables database. Only the columns that are used by this application are included in the object model, however.
- A one-to-many association is defined between the Vendor and Invoice classes based on the foreign key defined between the Vendors and Invoices tables in the database.
- This application uses two object data sources that were created from the Vendor and Invoice classes. The Vendor object is used to generate the combo box and text boxes on the form, and the Invoice object is used to generate the DataGridView control.

Figure 17-16 The user interface and object model for the Vendor Invoices application

The code for the Vendor Invoices form

Figure 17-17 presents the code for the Vendor Invoices form. This code starts by creating an instance of the PayablesDataContext class. The Windows Form class can then use this data context in any of its procedures.

When the form is loaded, the Load event handler uses a LINQ query that retrieves the vendor IDs and the names of all the vendors. The anonymous type named vendors that's created by this query is then bound to the combo box by setting the DataSource property of the combo box to the results of the query.

Another way to do that would be to set the DataSource property of the Vendor binding source to the results of the query. However, that would cause problems in this application, because the text boxes use the Vendor binding source to display the data for the selected vendor.

The next procedure is the event handler for the SelectedIndexChanged event for the combo box. This event handler is called each time the selection in the combo box is changed, including when the form is loaded for the first time. This event handler simply calls the GetVendorInvoices procedure.

The task of the GetVendorInvoices procedure is to display the address and invoices for the vendor that's selected in the combo box. It starts by declaring a query expression that retrieves the vendor with the vendor ID that's selected in the combo box. Notice that the Single method is used for this query expression so the expression is executed right away.

Next, this procedure clears the Vendor binding source and then adds the vendor that's retrieved by the current query to the binding source. That causes the details of the vendor's address to be displayed in the text boxes. Finally, it sets the DataSource property of the Invoice binding source to the Invoices property of the selected vendor. That causes the invoices for the selected vendor to be loaded and displayed in the DataGridView control.

The code for the Vendor Invoices form

```
Public Class Form1
    Dim payables As New PayablesDataContext

    Private Sub Form1_Load(ByVal sender As Object,
        ByVal e As System.EventArgs) Handles Me.Load

        Dim vendors = From vendor In payables.Vendors
                      Order By vendor.Name
                      Select vendor.VendorID, vendor.Name

        NameComboBox.DataSource = vendors

    End Sub

    Private Sub NameComboBox_SelectedIndexChanged(ByVal sender As Object,
      ByVal e As System.EventArgs) Handles NameComboBox.SelectedIndexChanged

        GetVendorInvoices()

    End Sub

    Private Sub GetVendorInvoices()
        Dim selectedVendor =
            (From vendor In payables.Vendors
             Where (vendor.VendorID = CInt(NameComboBox.SelectedValue))
             Select vendor).Single

        VendorBindingSource.Clear()
        VendorBindingSource.Add(selectedVendor)

        InvoiceBindingSource.DataSource = selectedVendor.Invoices

    End Sub

End Class
```

Notes

- The DisplayMember and ValueMember properties of the combo box are set at design time.
- This application uses deferred loading to load the invoices for a selected vendor.

Figure 17-17 The code for the Vendor Invoices form

Perspective

Now that you've completed this chapter, you should know how to code LINQ queries, and you should be able to develop simple LINQ to SQL applications. You should also appreciate the benefits of using LINQ to SQL. In particular, you don't have to code the business classes or write the SQL code for accessing data from a SQL Server database. Instead, the business classes are generated when you use the O/R Designer, and the SQL code is generated when a LINQ query is executed.

Of course, there's a lot more to learn about LINQ to SQL, including how to use LINQ to SQL to update a database. But the goal here is to get you started with LINQ and to help you decide whether you like the idea of using LINQ in your own applications. In the next chapter, you'll learn how to use LINQ with the Entity Framework in a complete maintenance application.

Terms

Language-Integrated Query (LINQ)
LINQ provider
LINQ to Objects
LINQ to DataSet
LINQ to SQL
LINQ to Entities
LINQ to ADO.NET
extension method
query operator
method-based query
query expression
query variable
enumerable type
deferred execution
immediate execution
range variable
projection
anonymous type
alias
aggregate function
object model
data context class
entity class
association
O/R (Object Relational) Designer
entities pane
methods pane
deferred loading
lazy loading

Exercise 17-1 The Vendor Invoices application

In this exercise, you'll develop the Vendor Invoices application that was presented at the end of this chapter. This will show you how to build a simple application that uses LINQ to SQL to retrieve data.

Create the object model for the application

1. Start a new application named VendorInvoices in your Chapter 17 folder.
2. Start a new object model named Payables as described in figure 17-11. Then, use the Server Explorer to create entity classes from the Vendors and Invoices tables in the Payables database. Include just the columns needed by the application, which will be the ones shown in figure 17-16.

Create and use the object data sources for the application

3. Rebuild the project, then use the Data Source Configuration Wizard as shown in figure 17-15 to create object data sources for the Vendor and Invoice entities in the object model you just created.
4. With the form selected in design view, select the Vendor object in the Data Sources window. Change the default control setting for the Vendor object to Details, and then change the default control for the Name property to a combo box. Next, drag the vendor object onto the form and delete the navigation toolbar that's generated.
5. Set the binding properties for the combo box so the value of the Name property is used as the Display Member, and the value of the VendorID property is used as the Value Member. In addition, set the DropDownStyle property of the control to DropDownList, and remove the binding from the Text property of the control.
6. Drag the Invoice object from the Data Sources window to the form to generate a DataGridView control and automatically create the InvoiceBindingSource.
7. Make the necessary adjustments to the form and its controls so the form looks like the one in figure 17-16.

Code and test the application

If you need help with any of the coding steps that follow, please refer to figure 17-17.

8. Create an instance of the Payables data context and store it in a variable that's declared at the class level.
9. In the event handler for the Load event of the form, code a query expression that will retrieve the VendorID and Name columns from the Vendors table and sort the results by the Name column. Assign the results to the DataSource property of the combo box.
10. Run the application. At this point, the combo box list should include all the vendor names. However, the address and invoices for the selected vendor won't be displayed.

11. Add an event handler for the SelectedIndexChanged event of the combo box. This handler should just call a procedure named GetVendorInvoices.
12. Add the GetVendorInvoices procedure that uses a query to get the vendor that's selected in the combo box. This procedure should include code that binds the selected vendor to the text boxes on the form and binds the invoices for the vendor to the DataGridView control.
13. Run the application again. This time, the address information should be displayed for the first vendor, Abbey Office Furnishings. In addition, the invoices should be displayed in the DataGridView control.
14. Select a different vendor, such as Bertelsmann Industry Svcs. Inc, to be sure that the display of invoices changes when a new selection is made. When you're sure this is working correctly, close the project.

18

How to use the Entity Framework

The Entity Framework is a component of ADO.NET that uses an Entity Data Model to map the objects of an application to a database. Once the model is created and the objects are mapped to the database, the developer can work with the objects instead of the database. In this chapter, you'll learn how to use the Entity Framework with LINQ to Entities in a complete maintenance application.

How to create an Entity Data Model

In the topics that follow, you'll learn how to create an Entity Data Model. But first, you need to know how the Entity Framework works and where the Entity Data Model fits into that framework.

How the Entity Framework works

The *Entity Framework* provides another way to work with the data in a database. Its goal is to address the mismatch that often exists between the tabular structure of a relational database and the objects used in an application. To resolve this problem, the Entity Framework uses an *Entity Data Model* that maps the conceptual model of the objects used by the application to the relational model of the database.

Figure 18-1 shows the basic components of the Entity Framework. As you can see, the two key components are *Object Services* and the *EntityClient data provider*. These components work together to manage the transfer of data to and from the ADO.NET data provider, which accesses the database.

When you use the Entity Framework, you use queries to retrieve data from a database. However, these queries are executed against a *conceptual model* that is part of an Entity Data Model. This conceptual model defines the objects, or *entities*, used by the application and the relationships between those entities. The Entity Data Model also includes a *storage model* that describes the structure of the objects in the database. Finally, the Entity Data Model defines the *mappings* between the conceptual model and the storage model.

The Entity Data Model sits between the application and the database. It translates queries into a form that the database understands, and it translates the data that's returned from the database into the objects that are used by the application. It also tracks any changes that are made to those objects and provides for submitting those changes to the database.

Once a conceptual model has been created, you can query the data in several ways. First, you can use LINQ to Entities. Second, you can use Entity SQL, which works by using a dialect of SQL that's not specific to the database. Third, you can use query builder methods. These queries are like the method-based queries you use with LINQ, but they use Entity SQL. In this chapter, you'll learn how to use LINQ to Entities.

It's important to understand that because the Entity Framework has abstracted away the details of the underlying data source, you query the objects in the conceptual model, not the database itself. In fact, once the mappings have been set up, you don't need to consider how the underlying data source is configured. Instead, you work with the objects and properties that represent the tables and columns of the database.

How the Entity Framework works

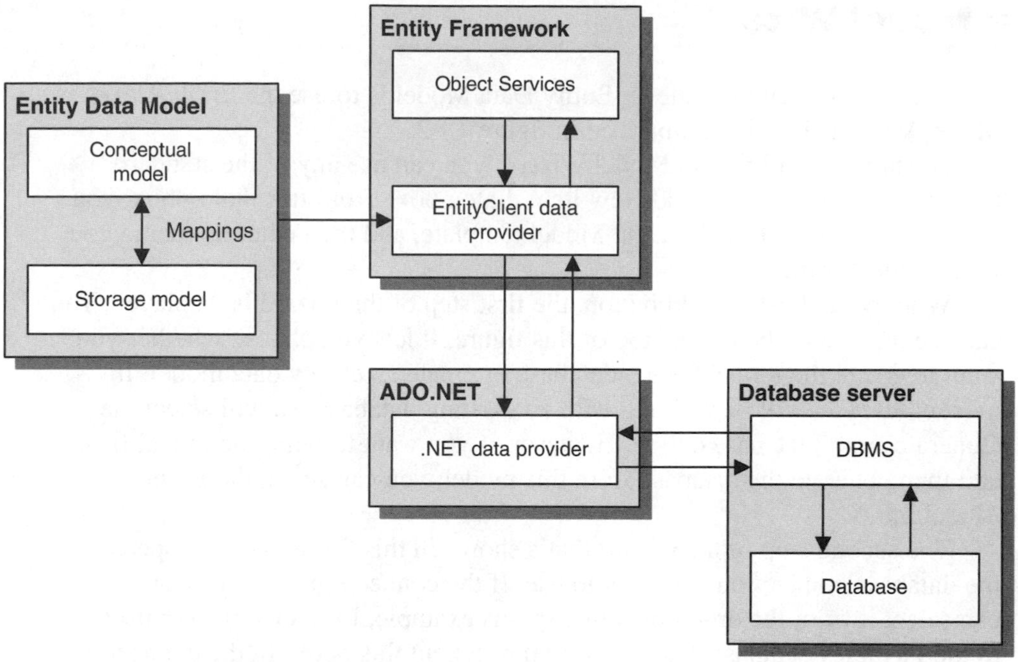

Three ways to query a conceptual model

Technique	Description
LINQ to Entities	LINQ that's designed for working with a conceptual model.
Entity SQL	An independent dialect of SQL that can be used to work with entities.
Query builder methods	LINQ-style queries that use Entity SQL.

Description

- The *Entity Framework* provides a layer between the database used by an application and the objects used by an application. The purpose of this layer is to provide an interface that allows the data in the database to be presented to the application as objects.
- To provide the interface between objects and database, the Entity Framework uses an *Entity Data Model* that defines a *conceptual model*, a *storage model*, and *mappings* between the two models.
- The conceptual model defines the entities and relationships used by the application. The storage model defines the structure of the database that's being used by the application. And the mappings define how the conceptual and storage model are related.
- When you execute a query against a conceptual model, *Object Services* works with the EntityClient data provider and the Entity Data Model to translate the query into one that can be executed by the database. When the results are returned from the database, Object Services translates them back to the objects defined by the conceptual model.
- The Entity Framework also provides for tracking changes to the objects created from the conceptual model and for submitting those changes to the database.

Figure 18-1 An introduction to the Entity Framework

How to start an Entity Data Model with the Entity Data Model Wizard

The easiest way to create an Entity Data Model is to use the Entity Data Model Wizard. This is summarized in figure 18-2.

To start the Entity Data Model Wizard, you can use any of the standard techniques to display the Add New Item dialog box. From this dialog box, you select the ADO.NET Entity Data Model template, and then enter the name you want to use for the model.

When you click the Add button, the first step of the wizard is displayed. You can see this dialog box at the top of this figure. It lets you choose whether you want to create the model from a database or create an empty data model. In most cases, you will be working with an existing database, so will select the Generate from Database option. However, if you want to build the model first and then generate the database from this model, you can select the Empty Model option.

The second step of the wizard that's shown in this figure lets you specify the database connection you want to use. If the connection already exists, you can select it from the drop-down list. In this example, I selected the connection to the Payables database that I've used throughout this book. In the connection string that was generated, you can see that the string includes the names of the conceptual model, the storage model, and the mappings, as well as information about the provider and the database to be accessed.

If the connection you need doesn't already exist, you can click the New Connection button and then use the Connection Properties dialog box that's displayed. This dialog box is identical to the dialog box that's displayed when you create a new connection from the Data Source Configuration Wizard, which you've used in previous chapters.

The first two steps of the Entity Data Model Wizard

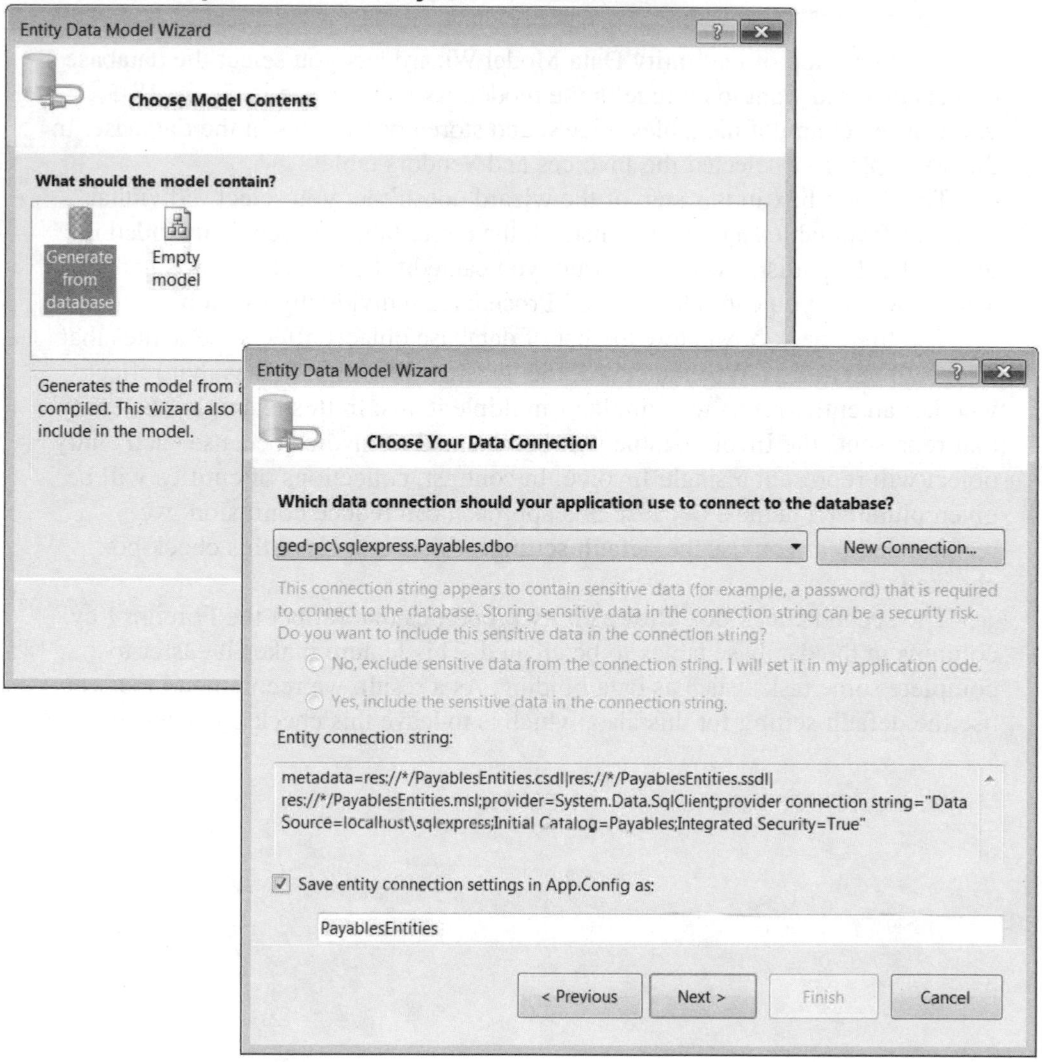

Description

- To start the Entity Data Model Wizard, display the Add New Item dialog box, select the ADO.NET Entity Data Model template, and enter a name for the model.
- In the first step, Choose Model Contents, you choose whether you want to create the model from an existing database or create it from scratch.
- In the second step, Choose Your Data Connection, you either choose the database connection you want to use or create a new connection. You can also decide whether the connection settings should be saved in the App.Config file.
- The Choose Your Data Connection dialog box also lets you enter a name for the connection string. The default is the name of the database you've connected to appended with the word "Entities".

Figure 18-2 How to start an Entity Data Model with the Entity Data Model Wizard

How to choose the database objects in the wizard

The third step of the Entity Data Model Wizard lets you select the database objects that you want to include in the model. As you can see in figure 18-3, you can select any of the tables, views, and stored procedures in the database. In this example, I've selected the Invoices and Vendors tables.

The dialog box in this step of the wizard doesn't let you select individual columns from tables and views. Instead, the entire table or view is included in the model. If that isn't what you want, you can edit the model after it's generated. However, you can select Stored Procedures individually by name.

The first check box below the list of database objects affects the names that are given to entities. When checked, the wizard will assign names that reflect whether an entity refers to a single or multiple items. In this example, the entity that represents the Invoices table will be renamed to Invoice because each entity object will represent a single Invoice. In contrast, collections of entities will be given pluralized names. Because this approach can reduce confusion, we recommend that you use the default setting, which is to leave this check box checked.

The second check box allows entity properties that reflect the Foreign Key columns in the database tables to be created. This feature makes it easier to complete some tasks, such as data binding. As a result, we recommend that you use the default setting for this also, which is to leave this check box checked.

The third step of the Entity Data Model Wizard

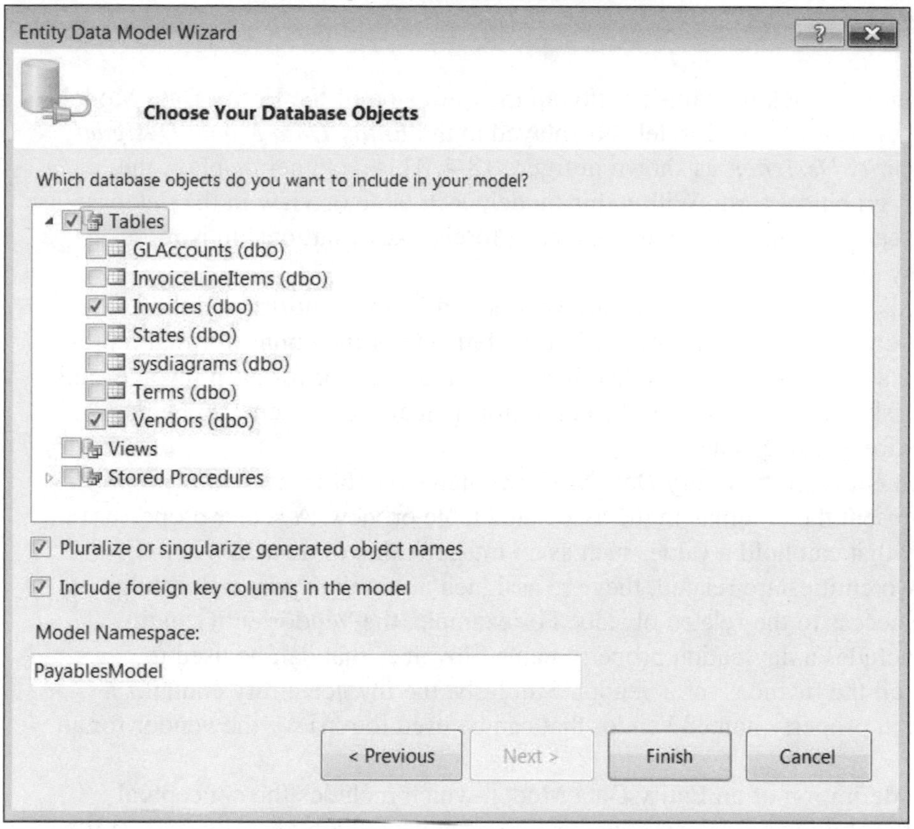

Description

- The Choose Your Database Objects step of the wizard lets you choose the tables, views, and stored procedures you want to include in the Entity Data Model.
- To include an object, expand the node that contains that object and click in its check box.
- To change the name that's used for the model's namespace, enter a new name in the Model Namespace text box. By default, this is the name of the database that you've connected to appended with the word "Model".
- To select all objects in a group, such as all the tables in the database, check the box for that node.
- To disable the renaming of object names in the Entity Data Model, uncheck the Pluralize or Singularize Generated Object Names check box.
- To disable the generation of Foreign Key properties for entities, uncheck the Include Foreign Key Columns in the Model check box.

Figure 18-3 How to choose the database objects for an object model

The Entity Data Model in the Entity Data Model Designer

When you click the Finish button in the third step of the Entity Data Model Wizard, the Entity Data Model is displayed in the *Entity Data Model Designer*, or just *Entity Designer*, as shown in figure 18-4. This designer displays the model in graphical form. Within this model, each table or view in the database is represented by an *entity class*, and each foreign key relationship is represented by an *association*.

In this example, you can see the Vendor and Invoice entities and the association between the two. Here, the 1 at the left side of the connector that represents the association indicates that there is a single vendor for each invoice, and the asterisk at the right side of the connector indicates that there can be many invoices for a single vendor.

Each entity in the Entity Data Model contains one or more *scalar properties* that represent the columns in the associated table or view. A scalar property is a property that can hold a value, such as an integer value or a string.

If two entities are related, they are assigned *navigation properties* that provide access to the related objects. For example, the Vendor entity in this figure includes a navigation property named Invoices that can be used to retrieve all the invoices for a vendor. Similarly, the Invoice entity contains a navigation property named Vendor that can be used to retrieve the vendor for an invoice.

The definition of an Entity Data Model, which includes the conceptual model, the storage model, and the mappings between the two, is stored in a file with the .edmx extension. You can see this file in the Solution Explorer in this figure. The graphical view of this file is what you see in the pane for the Entity Data Model Designer.

Subordinate to the edmx file is a file with the Designer.vb extension. This file contains the Visual Basic code that's generated from the conceptual model in the edmx file. It contains the generated classes that you'll use to work with the Entity Data Model from within your application.

To update the Entity Data Model, you can use the Update Wizard. This lets you change the entity data model so it reflects any changes that have been made to the structure of the database after you first created the model. You can also use this wizard to create entities based on tables that you didn't select when you first created the model, and you can select stored procedures or views that you didn't select initially. To display this wizard, you can use the technique in the last bulleted item in this figure.

The Entity Data Model in the Entity Data Model Designer

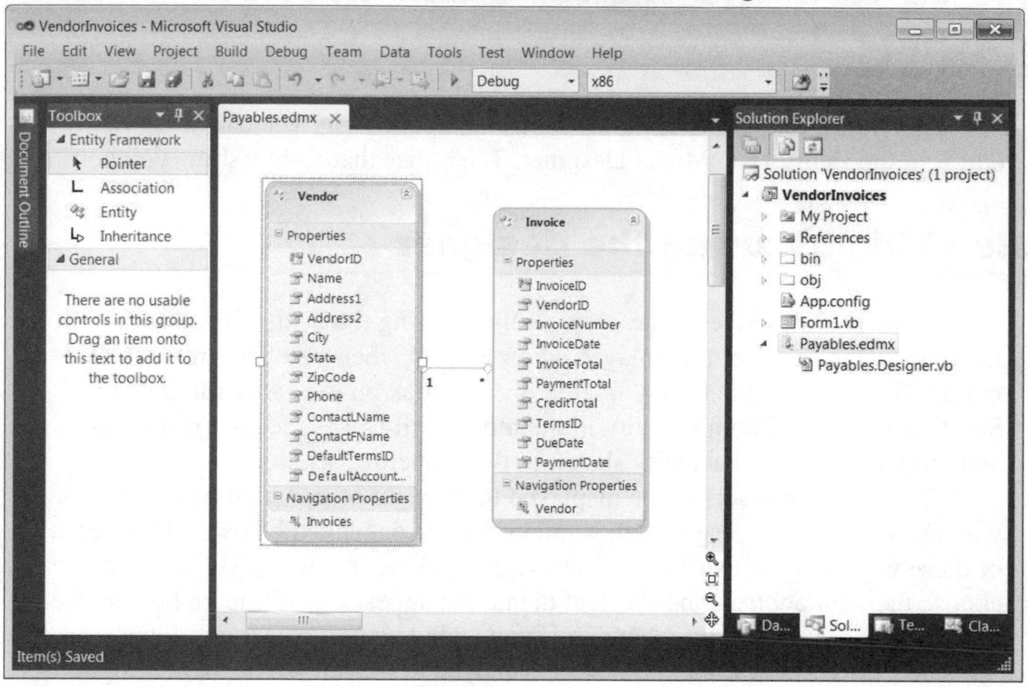

Description

- When you use the Entity Data Model Wizard to create an Entity Data Model, Visual Studio generates a file with the extension edmx that defines the model. This file encapsulates the storage model, the conceptual model, and the mappings between the two.
- Visual Studio also generates Visual Basic code that defines the classes that you use in your application to work with the model. This code is stored in the file with the Designer.vb extension that's subordinate to the edmx file.
- If the project doesn't already contain an App.config file, this file is also generated. The connection string that you saw in the Entity Data Model Wizard in figure 18-2 is stored in this file.
- Each table or view that you add to an Entity Data Model is defined by an *entity class*. Each entity class contains *scalar properties* that map to the columns in the table or view.
- If any two tables that you add to an Entity Data Model are related by a foreign key, an *association* is defined between the entity classes based on that relationship. An association is represented in the model by a line between the two tables with a diamond at each end and an indication of the type of relationship.
- An association is defined by *navigation properties* in the entity classes. These properties let you refer to one class from the other class.
- To update the Entity Data Model, you can use the Update Wizard. To display this wizard, right-click on the edmx file in the Solution Explorer or right-click anywhere in the Designer. Then, select Update Model from Database.

Figure 18-4 The Entity Data Model

How to use the Entity Data Model Designer

After you create Entity Data Model for an application, you can access and edit it in the Entity Data Model Designer. The topics that follow show you how.

Basic skills for using the designer

Figure 18-5 describes some basic skills for using the Entity Data Model Designer. This designer is displayed automatically when you first create the model. If you need to redisplay it later, double-click on the edmx file in the Solution Explorer. The first entity in the model will be selected automatically and the properties of that entity shown in the Properties window.

The Model Browser will be displayed to the right of the main designer window, and the Mapping Details window will be displayed below it. If either of these windows isn't visible, you can right-click on the design surface and choose the window from the shortcut menu that appears. You'll learn how to use the Model Browser and the Mapping Details window in the next two figures.

The Entity Framework Toolbox is displayed to the left of the main designer window. You can use the components in this Toolbox to create new entities and associations and to implement inheritance. Often, though, you'll find it easier to right-click on the designer and use the dialog boxes that appear to create the entities, associations, and inheritance that you need.

In general, the skills for using the designer are straightforward, so you can use normal Visual Studio techniques to work with it. But note that if you change the Name property of an entity, Visual Studio automatically changes the Entity Set Name property so it's the same as the Name property appended with the letter "s".

The Entity Data Model Designer

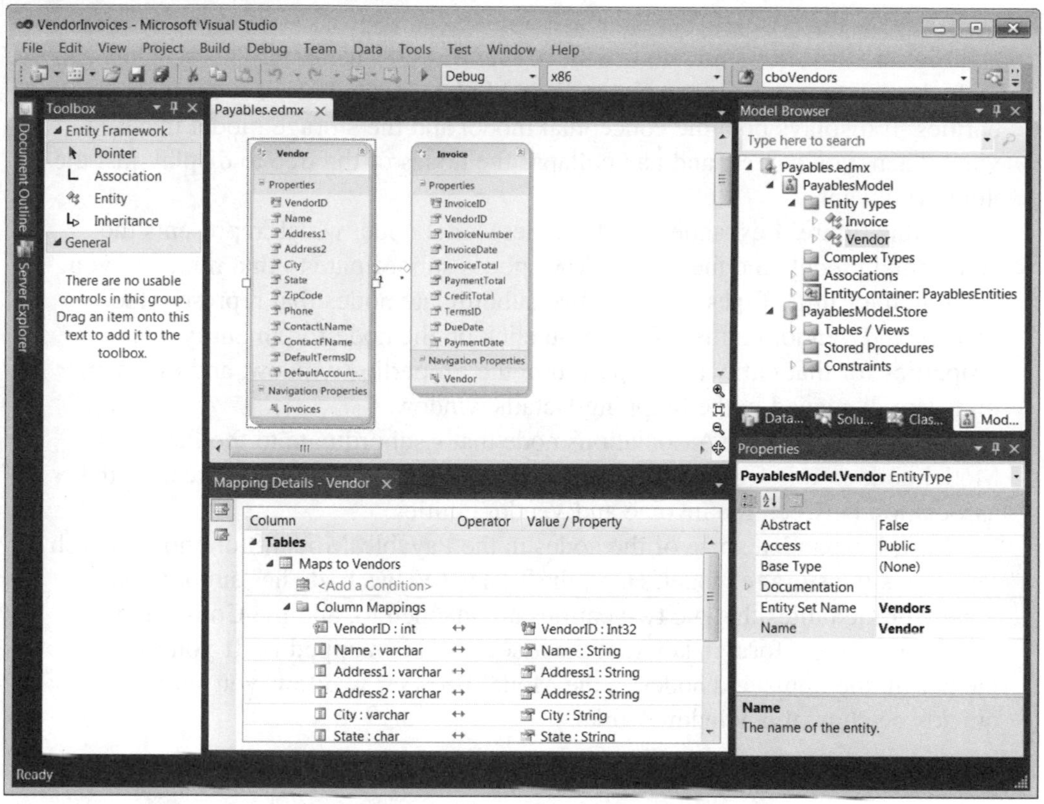

Description

- To display the Entity *Data Model Designer* for an Entity Data Model, double-click the edmx file in the Solution Explorer.
- To change the properties of an entity or any of its individual properties, click the entity or property to display its settings in the Properties window.
- To delete an entity, property, inheritance link, or association, click on it and then press the Delete key.
- To add an entity, right-click on the designer, select AddàEntity, and then complete the Add Entity dialog box that appears.
- To add a property to an entity, right-click on the entity and select the Add option for the type of property you want to add.
- To add an association, right-click on the design surface and select the Add option for the element you want to add.
- To add a Function Import, right-click on the designer, select AddàFunction Import, and then complete the Add Function Import dialog box (see figure 18-8).

Figure 18-5 Basic skills for using the Entity Data Model Designer

How to use the Model Browser window

Figure 18-6 shows how to use the *Model Browser window*. This window can make it easy to work with an Entity Data Model, particularly if it contains many entities. It displays both the conceptual model and the storage model in a tree view. Then, you can expand and collapse the nodes of the tree to display just the items you want.

In this figure, I expanded the PayablesModel node, which represents the conceptual model, and the Entity Types nodes subordinate to that node. As you can see, the Entity Types node has two subordinate nodes that represent the Invoice and Vendor entities. When you click on the node for an entity, the properties for that entity are displayed in the Properties window, and the mappings are displayed in the Mapping Details window.

I also expanded the Associations node that's subordinate to the Payables Model node in this figure. This node contains a single item that represents the association between the Invoice and Vendor entities.

Last, I expanded some of the nodes in the PayablesModel.Store node, which represents the storage model. Here, the Tables / Views node has subordinate nodes for the tables that the two entities are mapped to, and the Constraints node contains the foreign key that the association is mapped to. If you experiment with the items and nodes in the Model Browser window, you should quickly see how this window works.

The Model Browser window with some of its nodes expanded

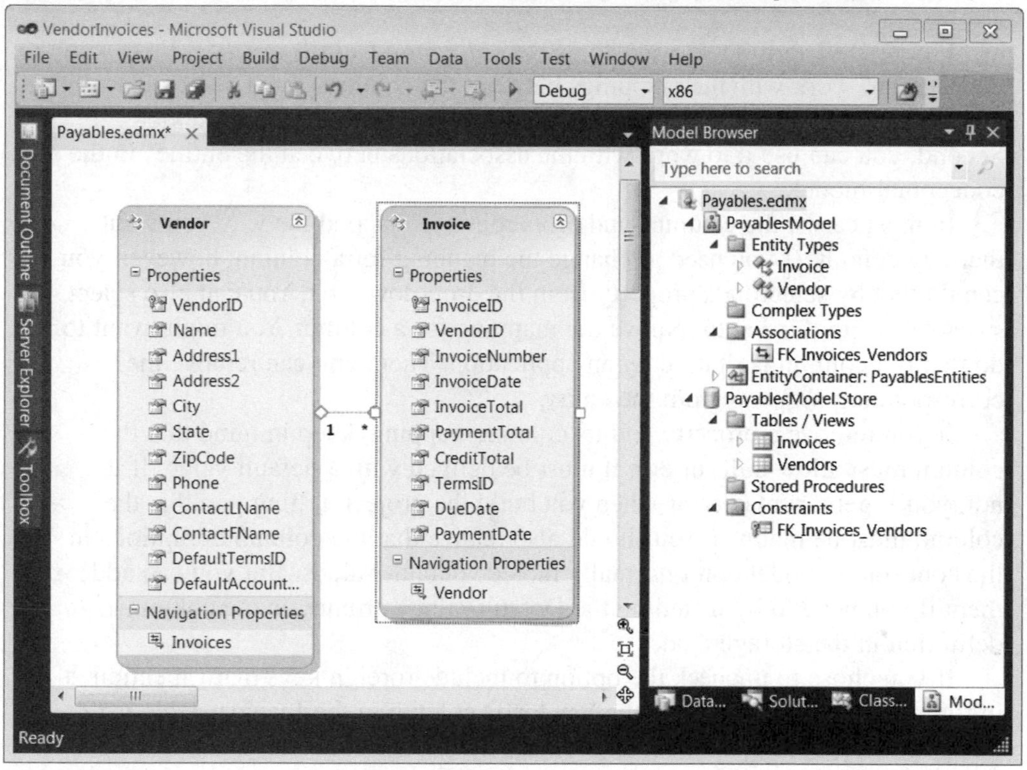

Description

- The *Model Browser window* displays the Entity Data Model in a tree view. The tree is divided into two nodes that represent the conceptual model and the storage model.
- You can expand the child nodes for the conceptual model to display the entity types and associations in the model. You can expand the child nodes for the storage model to display the tables, views, stored procedures, and constraints the conceptual model is mapped to.
- If you click an entity type, a property for an entity type, or an association in the Model Browser, the properties for that object are displayed in the Properties window so you can view or modify them.
- If you click an entity type or a property for an entity type in the Model Browser, the mappings for that entity are displayed in the Mapping Details window. If you click an association, the mappings for that association are displayed in the Mapping Details window. Then, you can use that window to work with the mappings.
- To locate an entity on the design surface, right-click the entity name in the Model Browser and select Show in Designer.
- You can also use the Model Browser to import a stored procedure (see figure 18-8).

How to use the Mapping Details window

Figure 18-7 shows two ways to use the *Mapping Details window*. First, you can use it to work with the mappings between the columns in a table or view in the storage model and the properties of an entity in the conceptual model. Second, you can use it to work with the associations between the entities in the conceptual model.

In most cases, the columns and properties are mapped the way you want them by default. If you need to change the mapping for a column, however, you can do that by selecting a property from the drop-down list. You can also select <Delete> from this list to remove the mapping for a column. You might want to do that if a column isn't used by an application. Then, you can remove the corresponding property from the entity.

If you remove a property and its column mapping, keep in mind that the column must allow nulls or else it must be defined with a default value. If it's not, you'll get a syntax error when you build the project, telling you that the column must be mapped. You should also realize that the column definitions in the conceptual model don't normally include default values. But you can add them if you need to by including the DefaultValue attribute on the column definition in the storage model.

If you chose to uncheck the option to include foreign keys that I mentioned in figure 18-3, you'll find that the VendorID column in the Invoices table isn't mapped to a property in the Invoice entity. That's because with that construct the Invoice entity doesn't include a VendorID property. Instead, it contains only a navigation property that provides access to the vendor for an invoice.

One useful feature of the Mapping Details windows is that it lets you map an entity to selected rows in a table or view. To do that, you specify one or more conditions for the rows you want to include. For example, suppose the Vendors table contains both U.S. and foreign vendors. In addition, suppose it contains a Boolean column that indicates whether a vendor is foreign. Then, if you want to work with just foreign vendors, you can specify a condition so only the rows for foreign vendors are retrieved.

Note that if you include a condition in the mappings for a table, you must delete the entity property that corresponds with the column that's used in the mapping. If you don't, you'll get an error when you build the project.

Another useful feature of the Mapping Details window is that it lets you map a single entity to two or more tables. For example, suppose the Vendors table has a one-to-one relationship with a table named VendorsSummary that contains summary information for each vendor. Then, you could create an Entity Data Model with a single entity that maps to both of these tables. This is just one way that you can provide a layer of abstraction between the conceptual model used by an application and the storage model used by a database.

The mappings for an association show the properties that define the relationship between the entities and the columns they map to in the database. Like the mappings for an entity, the mappings for an association are usually set the way you want them by default. You can only view these mappings if you've unchecked the option to include foreign keys.

A Mapping Details window with the mappings for the Invoice entity

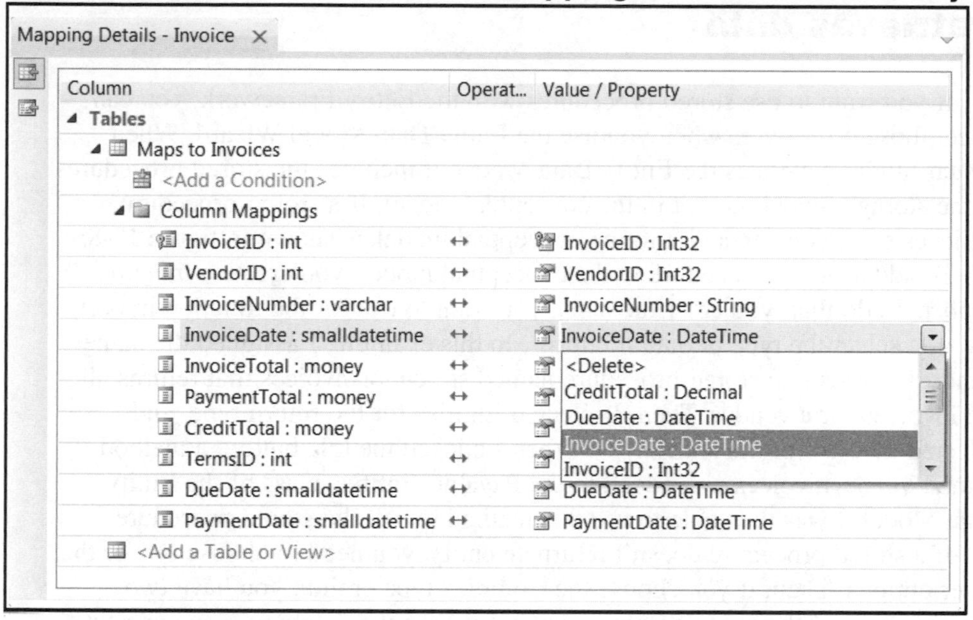

Description

- To display the mappings for an entity, click on the name of the entity in the Model Browser window or on the design surface to display the mappings in the *Mapping Details window*.
- The mappings for an entity show the columns in the underlying table or view and the properties in the entity that they map to.
- If a column isn't mapped to a property, it typically means that the column is a foreign key and that you didn't uncheck the option to include foreign keys when you created the model.
- To change the mapping for a column, use the drop-down list for the property. To delete a mapping, select <Delete> from the drop-down list.
- You can map an entity to selected rows in a table or view by entering one or more conditions. To do that, select <Add a Condition>, select the column you want the condition based on, select an operator (= or Is), and enter or select a value. You must also delete the entity property that the condition is based on. If the value of a condition is a string, you don't need to place it in quotes.
- To delete a condition, select <Delete> from the drop-down list for the column.
- If you want to map an entity to more than one table or view, you can click <Add a Table or View> and then select a table or view from the drop-down list that's displayed.

How to add a stored procedure that retrieves data

If you want to use stored procedures with the Entity Framework, you can select those procedures when you use the Entity Data Model Wizard. When Visual Studio generates the Entity Data Model, it includes the stored procedures in the storage model but not in the conceptual model. If a stored procedure retrieves data, you can add it to the conceptual model as shown in figure 18-8.

To add a stored procedure to the conceptual model, you create a *function import*. To do that, you enter the name you want to use for the function import, and you select the type of data it returns. In this example, I assigned the name VendorInvoices to a stored procedure named spVendorInvoices that returns all the invoices for a vendor. Then, I selected Entities for the return type, and I selected Invoice for the entity type. When I clicked the OK button, a method named VendorInvoices was added to the PayablesEntities class of the Entity Data Model. I was then able to use this method to call the stored procedure.

If a stored procedure doesn't return an entity, you need to choose one of the other options. Then, if you choose the Complex type option, you have two choices. First, if the complex type already exists in the database, you can select it from the drop-down list.

The other alternative is to create a new complex type. To do that, you click on the Get Column Information button, followed by the Create New Complex Type button. Then, all the columns used by the stored procedure are automatically added to the complex type.

After you add a stored procedure to a model, it is displayed in the Model Browser. In the example that I've been using, this would be under the PayablesModel→EntityContainer: PayablesEntities→FunctionImports node.

The dialog box for adding a function import

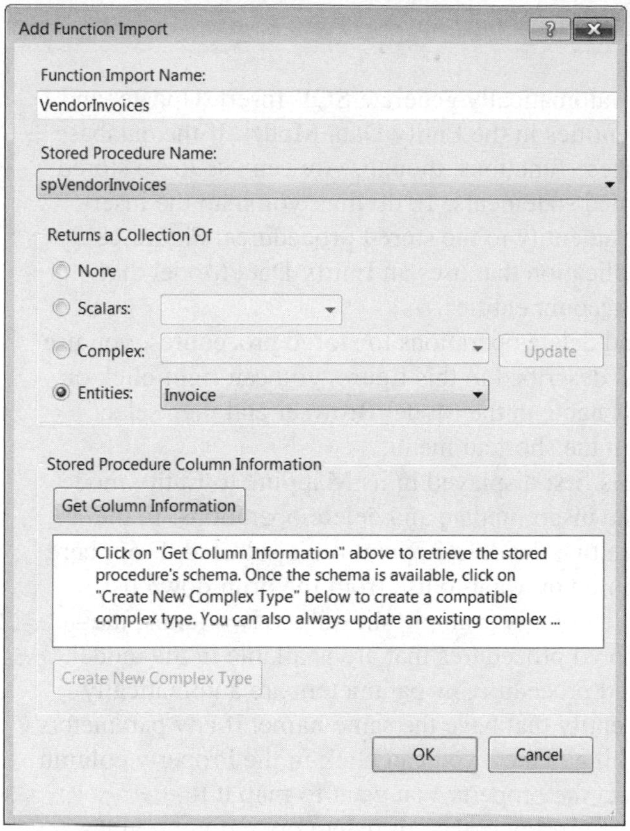

Description

- If you select any stored procedures when you use the Entity Data Model Wizard, you must import those stored procedures before you can use them in your application.
- A stored procedure that's imported into an Entity Data Model is called a *function import*. To create a function import, you use the Add Function Import dialog box.
- To display the Add Function Import dialog box, right-click on the stored procedure in the storage model node of the Model Browser and select Add Function Import option. Then, you can select the procedure that you want to import.
- By default, the function import name is the same as the name of the stored procedure, but you can change this name if you want to.
- After you select a procedure, you need to use the Returns a Collection Of controls to identify the type of data that's returned by the procedure.
- If you select the Complex option, you can either select a complex type that already exists in the model or you can create a new one. To create a new one, click on the Get Column Information button and then click the Create New Complex Type button.
- When you create a function import, it's displayed within the Entity Data Model in the Model Browser. Then, you can use that procedure to call the stored procedure.

Figure 18-8 How to add a stored procedure that retrieves data

How to map stored procedures that insert, update, and delete data

The Entity Framework will automatically generate SQL Insert, Update, and Delete statements based on the entities in the Entity Data Model. If the database provides stored procedures for these functions, though, you can use these stored procedures instead of the generated statements. To do that, you map the insert, update, and delete operations of an entity to the stored procedures. Figure 18-9 shows how this works for an application that uses an Entity Data Model that includes Vendor, State, and GLAccount entities.

To map the insert, update and delete operations to stored procedures, you use the Mapping Details window. As described in this figure, you can right-click on an entity in the designer or on its name in the Model Browser and then select Stored Procedure Mappings from the shortcut menu.

When the mapping window is first displayed in its Mapping to Entity mode, it includes an item for each of the insert, update and delete operations. In the example shown here, you can see that the delete operation is selected. From here you can select the stored procedure you want to use from the drop-down list. Although the stored procedures list in this example shows just two items, the scrollbar lets you view all the stored procedures that are available in the model.

Once you've selected a stored procedure, its parameters are automatically mapped to the properties of the entity that have the same name. If any parameters don't have properties with matching names, you can click in the Property column for each parameter and then select the property you want to map it to.

If a stored procedure that performs an update or delete operation provides parameters for optimistic concurrency, you need to map them to the appropriate properties too. You can see how this works for the update operation shown in this figure. Here, the parameters used for optimistic concurrency have the same names as the properties in the entity, preceded by "original_". Then, these parameters are mapped to the appropriate properties, and the Use Original Value option for each of these parameters is checked. That way, when this operation is performed, the current values of the properties will be assigned to the parameters with the same names as the properties, and the original values of the properties will be assigned to the parameters whose names start with "original_".

You should also notice here the State, DefaultAccountNo, original_State, and original_DefaultAccountNo are mapped. Because the Entity Data Model includes State and GLAccount entities as well as a Vendor entity, the State and DefaultAccountNo columns that are included in the Vendors table aren't included in the Vendor entity. So the parameters that refer to these columns must be mapped to properties of the State and GLAccount entities, which are accessed through navigation properties of the Vendor entity.

You can also provide for stored procedures that return values that are generated by the database, such as an identity value for an insert operation. For example, the stored procedure that inserts a vendor returns the value of the VendorID column for the new row. To update the vendor object with this value, you can create a column binding by using the <Add Result Binding> option.

The Mapping Details window for mapping stored procedures

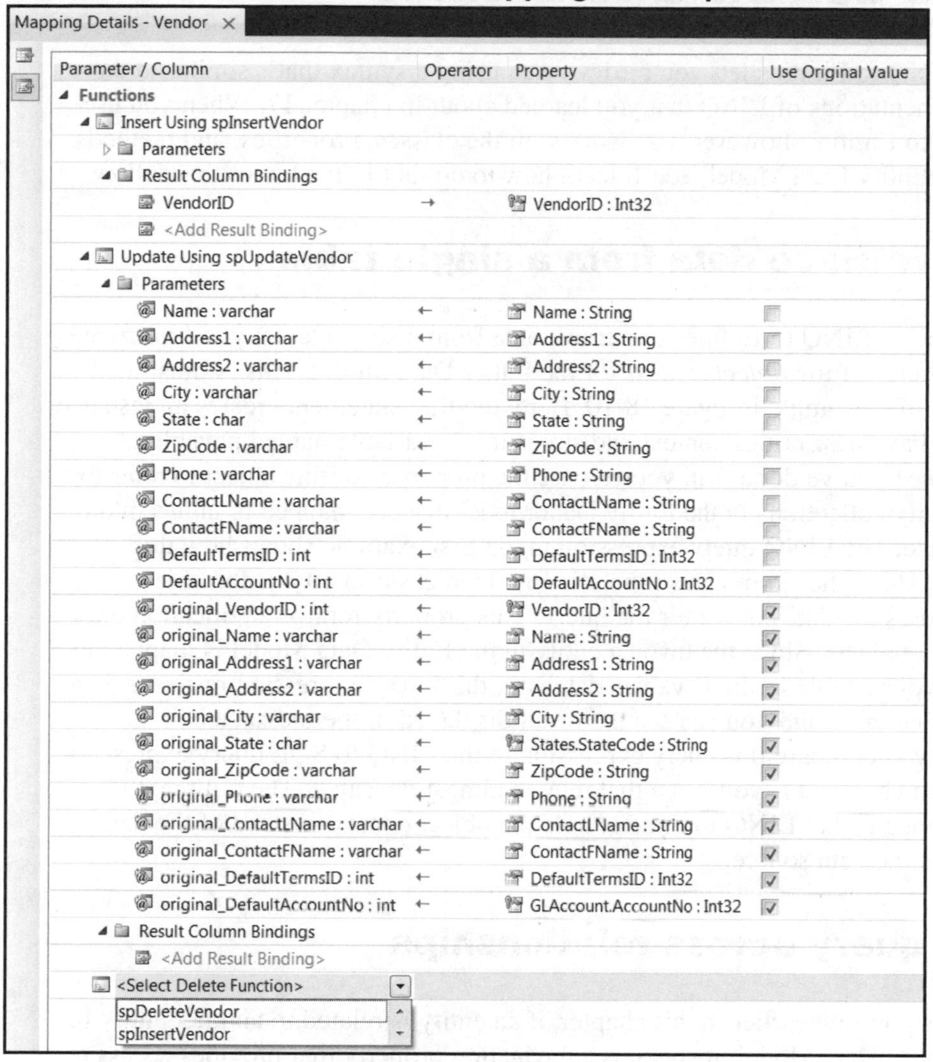

How to map an insert, update, or delete operation to a stored procedure

- Right-click the entity and select Stored Procedure Mappings to display the Map to Entity Functions pane of the Mapping Details window.
- Click <Select Insert Function>, <Select Update Function>, or <Select Delete Function>, and select the stored procedure from the drop-down list. The parameters required by the stored procedure are then mapped to entity properties with the same name.
- Review the mappings and make any necessary changes or additions. If a stored procedure uses parameters for optimistic concurrency, select properties to map them to and then check the Use Original Value check box.
- If a stored procedure returns a value such as an identity value, click <Add Result Binding>. Then, enter the name of the column in the result set and map it to an entity property.

Figure 18-9 How to map stored procedures that insert, update, and delete data

How to use LINQ to Entities

LINQ to Entities lets you retrieve data using a syntax that's similar to the implementations of LINQ that you learned about in chapter 17. When you use LINQ to Entities, however, you work with the classes, properties, and methods of the Entity Data Model. You'll learn how to do that in the topics that follow.

How to retrieve data from a single table

To use LINQ to Entities to retrieve data from a single table, you first create an instance of the *object context* for the Entity Data Model. This is illustrated by the first example in figure 18-10. Here, the first statement creates an instance of the PayablesEntities context and stores it in a variable named payables.

Once you've done that, you can use the properties of this object to refer to the entity collections in the Entity Data Model that are mapped to tables in the database. The LINQ query expression in the first example shows how this works. Here, the From clause specifies the Invoices property of the object context as the data source for the query. This property returns a collection of Invoice objects. Since the Invoice entity in the Entity Data Model is mapped to the Invoices table in the Payables database, this query expression retrieves data from that table and you can see the result displayed in the message box.

If you compare this query expression to the LINQ to SQL query expressions in chapter 17, you'll see that they're almost the same. The only real difference is that LINQ to Entities uses the object context instead of the database as the data source.

How to query across relationships

As you saw earlier in this chapter, if an entity is related to another entity in the Entity Data Model, it contains a navigation property that provides access to the related entity objects. Then, you can use these properties to query across relationships.

This is illustrated by the last example in this figure. Here, the query expression gets data from Invoice objects through the navigation property in the Vendor object. To do that, it includes the navigation property as a data source in the From clause. Then, it refers to properties of the Invoice object in the Order By and Select clauses.

A LINQ query that retrieves data from the Invoices table

A statement that creates an instance of the object context

```
Dim payables As New PayablesEntities
```

A query expression that retrieves invoices over $22,000

```
Dim highInvoices =
    From invoice In payables.Invoices
    Where invoice.InvoiceTotal > 22000
    Order By invoice.InvoiceTotal Descending
    Select invoice.InvoiceNumber, invoice.InvoiceTotal,
           invoice.InvoiceDate
```

Code that executes the query

```
Dim displayResult As String = "Invoice No." & vbTab &
                        "Invoice Total" & vbCrLf
For Each invoice In highInvoices
    displayResult &= invoice.InvoiceNumber & vbTab & vbTab &
              FormatCurrency(invoice.InvoiceTotal) & vbCrLf
Next
MessageBox.Show(displayResult, "Invoices Over $22,000")
```

The resulting message box

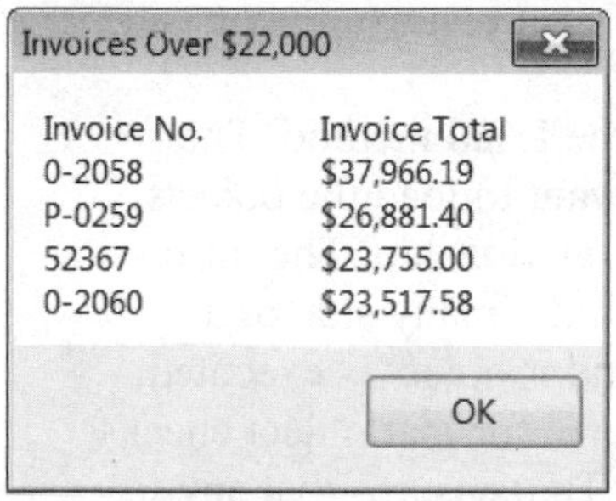

A LINQ query that gets invoice data through the Vendor object

```
Dim invoicesList = From vendor In payables.Vendors,
                   invoice In vendor.Invoices
Order By invoice.Vendor.Name, invoice.InvoiceDate
Select vendor.Name, invoice.InvoiceNumber, invoice.InvoiceTotal
```

Description

- To work with the entities in an Entity Data Model, you create an instance of the object context for the model.
- You can then use LINQ to Entity to query the entities in the Entity Data Model. This version of LINQ has essentially the same syntax that you learned in chapter 17.
- When querying across relationships, you can include a navigation property in the From clause, as shown in the last example above.

Figure 18-10 How to use LINQ to Entities to retrieve data

How to load related objects

In addition to using relationships to refer to properties of a related object, you can use them to load related objects. For example, suppose an application lets the user retrieve the data for a selected vendor and then displays the vendor data along with the invoices for that vendor. To do that, the application must load the invoice data as well as the vendor data. Figure 18-11 shows three ways you can do that.

The first example in this figure includes the invoices for a vendor in the query results. To do that, it includes the Invoices navigation property on the Select clause. Notice here that the First method is used to execute the query. This is done to create a more efficient query, because you know that only a single vendor will be returned.

The second example shows how to use the Include method to load related objects. As you can see, you code this method on the data source for the query, and you code a *query path* as an argument. In most cases, the query path is the name of the navigation property that identifies the related objects to be loaded. Note that when you use this technique, the related objects aren't included in the query results. Instead, they're simply loaded into the object context so you can access them later.

You can also load related objects explicitly using the Load method. The technique you use to do that depends on whether you want to load the objects on the one side of a relationship or the many side of a relationship. The third example in this figure shows how to load the objects on the many side of a relationship. Here, after the query that retrieves the Vendor object is executed, the IsLoaded property of the Invoices navigation property for that object checks that the invoices for that vendor aren't already loaded. This ensures that any existing data isn't overwritten, and it improves the efficiency of the application. If the invoices haven't been loaded, the Load method of the Invoices navigation property is then used to load them.

The fourth example in this figure shows how to use the Load method to load the related object on the one side of a relationship. In this example, the Vendor object for an Invoice object is being loaded. To do that, you don't use the navigation property of the Invoice object. Instead, you use the association property, in this case, VendorReference.

A query expression that uses a navigation property to load related objects

```
Dim vendorInvoices = (From vendor In payables.Vendors
                      Where vendor.VendorID = CInt(txtVendorID.Text)
                      Select vendor.Name, vendor.Invoices).First
```

A query expression that uses the Include method to load related objects

```
Dim selectedVendor = (From vendor In payables.Vendors.Include("Invoices")
                      Where vendor.VendorID = CInt(txtVendorID.Text)
                      Select vendor).First
```

Code that explicitly loads the objects on the many side of a relationship

```
Dim selectedVendor = (From vendor In payables.Vendors
                      Where vendor.VendorID = CInt(txtVendorID.Text)
                      Select vendor).First

If Not selectedVendor.Invoices.IsLoaded Then
    selectedVendor.Invoices.Load()
End If
```

Code that explicitly loads the object on the one side of a relationship

```
Dim invoiceID As Integer = CInt(cboInvoices.SelectedValue)
Dim selectedInvoice = (From invoice In payables.Invoices
                       Where invoice.InvoiceID = invoiceID
                       Select invoice).First

If Not selectedInvoice.VendorReference.IsLoaded Then
    selectedInvoice.VendorReference.Load()
End If
```

Description

- By default, only the entity objects that are specifically requested in a query are loaded into the object context. Related entity objects aren't automatically loaded.
- To load related objects, you can include the navigation property for the relationship in the query results, you can use the Include method with a *query path* that specifies the related objects to include in the query results, or you can use the Load method to load the related objects explicitly.
- To load the related objects on the many side of a relationship using the Load method, you use the navigation property for the object on the one side of the relationship. To load the related object on the one side of a relationship, you use the association property for the object on the many side of the relationship.
- Before you load related objects explicitly, you should use the IsLoaded property to check that the objects aren't already loaded. Otherwise, the current data will be overwritten, which may not be what you want.
- To use the Include or Load method, the query must return an entity type.

Figure 18-11 How to load related objects

How to insert, update, and delete data

Besides using the Entity Framework to retrieve data, you can use it to insert, update, and delete data. You'll learn how to do that in the next three topics.

How to update an existing row

To modify the data in an existing row of a database, you use the techniques shown in figure 18-12. To start, you must retrieve the row you want to modify. For example, the LINQ query at the top of this figure retrieves the vendor with the specified VendorID.

After you retrieve the row, you can modify the data in the entity object, as shown in the second example in this figure. This code simply assigns new values taken from text boxes to the Name and City properties of the Vendor object. Then, when the SaveChanges method of the context object is called, as in the last example in this figure, the changes are saved to the database.

If you need to, you can also change the parent of a child object. For instance, if you need to assign an invoice to a different vendor, you can use code like that in the third example. But here again, the changes won't be applied until the SaveChanges method is called.

How to delete an existing row

Figure 18-12 also shows how to delete an existing row from a database. To start, you retrieve the row you want to delete, just as you do when you modify a row. In the fourth example in this figure, the invoice with the specified ID is retrieved.

After you retrieve the object you want to delete, you call the DeleteObject method of the object context and pass that object as an argument, as in the fifth example. Here, the Invoice object that's retrieved by the query is marked for deletion. Finally, you call the SaveChanges method of the object context to actually delete the row.

In most cases, when you delete a row that has a one-to-many relationship with other rows in the database, you'll want to delete the related rows as well. If a foreign key relationship in the database provides for cascading deletes, this is done automatically.

But even if the database doesn't provide for cascading deletes, you can still delete the related rows. One way to do that is to use the Include method, as shown in the fourth example, where I've included the InvoiceLineItems for the selected invoice. This code is similar to the Include example you saw in the previous figure. Once those line items are loaded into the object context, they will be deleted along with the parent object when you call the SaveChanges method.

Code that retrieves a vendor row from the Payables database

```
Dim selectedVendor = (From vendor In payables.Vendors
                      Where vendor.VendorID = CInt(txtVendorID.Text)
                      Select vendor).First
```

Code that modifies the data in the vendor row

```
selectedVendor.Name = txtName.Text
selectedVendor.City = txtCity.Text
```

Code that assigns an invoice to a different vendor

```
Dim invoiceID As Integer = CInt(txtInvoiceID.Text)
Dim selectedInvoice = (From invoice In payables.Invoices
                       Where invoice.InvoiceID = invoiceID).First
selectedInvoice.Vendor = selectedVendor
```

Code that retrieves an invoice row and its related line item rows

```
Dim selectedInvoice =
      (From invoice In payables.Invoices.Include("InvoiceLineItems")
       Where invoice.InvoiceID = CInt(txtInvoiceID.Text)
       Select invoice).First
```

A statement that marks the Invoice object for deletion

```
payables.DeleteObject(selectedInvoice)
```

A statement that saves the changes to the database

```
payables.SaveChanges()
```

Description

- To modify a row in the database, you retrieve the row and store it in an object created from a class in the Entity Data Model. Then, you assign new values to the properties of the object. Finally, you execute the SaveChanges method of the object context.
- To delete a row from a database, you retrieve the row and store it in an object created from a class in the Entity Data Model. Then, you execute the DeleteObject method of the object context to mark the object for deletion. Finally, you execute the SaveChanges method of the object context to confirm the deletion.
- If you want to delete the child objects along with its parent object, you can do that by loading the child objects. Then, when the SaveChanges method is executed, the objects and the related rows in the database are deleted.
- If a foreign key relationship in a database provides for cascading deletes, you don't need to load the child objects to delete the related rows in the database.
- When you execute the SaveChanges method, the Entity Framework generates the appropriate SQL Update or Delete statement for each object to be updated or deleted, and then passes those statements to the database for processing.

Figure 18-12 How to update and delete rows

How to add a new row

When you create an Entity Data Model, the generated code includes methods that let you create a new entity object and add it to the collection of objects for that entity. These methods use the naming convention of Create*ObjectName*, and figure 18-13 shows examples of how to use these methods. But note that you can still create an entity object from an entity class using standard techniques.

The first example in this figure shows how to use the CreateInvoice method to create an Invoice object. On this method, you specify a value for each non-nullable column in the database. Visual Studio's Intellisense makes this easy, because it only includes non-nullable items in its list of arguments. In this case, the PaymentDate column is nullable, so it's omitted from the list of arguments. If you want to set its value, though, you can do it after you create the invoice.

When you use the Create*ObjectName* method, you must specify a value for each non-nullable column, even if the value is generated by the database. In this example, that applies to the InvoiceID column, which is an identity column. You can specify any value for this column, as long as an invoice with that value doesn't already exist in the object context. Then, when the SaveChanges method is executed, the database automatically changes your value and assigns the correct value. The object context is also updated with this amended value.

Another requirement of this create method is that you have to specify values for columns that have default values, such as the PaymentTotal and CreditTotal columns. In this example, I specified 0 for both of these columns.

After you create a new object, you need to add it to the collection of objects in the object context. To do that, you use the AddTo*EntitySetName* method of the object context. On this method, you name the object you want to add. In this example, the AddToInvoices method is used to add the Invoice object to the Invoices collection. Then, you call the SaveChanges method to update the database.

The second example in this figure shows how to add objects on the many side of a one-to-many relationship. Here, line items are added for the invoice created in the first example. In this case, the parent invoice has already been added to the invoices collection of the object context, so you can refer to it by its InvoiceID. This is illustrated by the first parameter of the CreateInvoiceLineItem method.

Next, a query is used to get the GLAccount object for the line item, and the GLAccount navigation property of the InvoiceLineItem object is set to the GLAccount object.

Last, the AddToInvoiceLineItems method is used to add the line item to the collection of line items in the object context. Then, when the SaveChanges method is called, the line item is added to the database.

Code that creates a new Invoice object

```
Dim newInvoice As Invoice = Invoice.CreateInvoice(999, 4,
    "JT 0001", Today, 123.45, 0, 0, 3, (Today.AddDays(30)))
```

Code that adds the object to the Invoices collection and updates the database

```
payables.AddToInvoices(newInvoice)
payables.SaveChanges()
```

Code that creates a new InvoiceLineItem object

```
Dim newLineItem As InvoiceLineItem =
    InvoiceLineItem.CreateInvoiceLineItem (newInvoice.InvoiceID,
        1, 589, 123.45, "Office Services")
Dim accountNo As Integer = 589

Dim selectedAccount = (From account In payables.GLAccounts
                       Where account.AccountNo = accountNo).First
newLineItem.GLAccount = selectedAccount
```

Code that adds the object to the InvoiceLineItems collection and updates the database

```
payables.AddToInvoiceLineItems(newLineItem)
payables.SaveChanges()
```

Description

- To add a row to the database, you can use the Create*ObjectName* method of an entity class to create a new instance of that class and assign values to its properties. Then, you can use the AddTo*EntitySetName* method to add the object to the collection of objects in the object context. Finally, you execute the SaveChanges method of the object context to save the changes to the database.
- If the value of a column is generated by the database, you can specify any value for that column on the Create*ObjectName* method as long as it's unique.
- The Create*ObjectName* methods only provide for setting properties that can't be null. You can set the values of nullable properties after you create the object.
- You can also create a new entity object by creating an instance of the entity class and then setting the values of its properties.
- To insert a new object and add child objects that are related to the parent object, you can create the parent object first, and then use the SaveChanges method. The object context will then be aware of this new object and you can create and insert new child objects that are related to the new parent.
- When you execute the SaveChanges method, the Entity Framework generates a SQL Insert statement for each object that was added to an object collection and then passes those statements to the database for processing.

Figure 18-13 How to add a new row

How to provide for concurrency

By default, optimistic concurrency isn't used when you modify or delete a row from a database when you use the Entity Framework. However, Object Services maintains the original values in the rows that you retrieve from the database so you can use optimistic concurrency if you need to. Figure 18-14 shows how to provide for concurrency.

To start, you need to identify the columns that you want to check for concurrency. To do that, you can use the Entity Designer to change the Concurrency Mode property for those columns from None to Fixed. Then, you code the SaveChanges method within the Try block of a Try…Catch statement, and you use the OptimisticConcurrencyException class to catch any concurrency exceptions that occur. Finally, you use the Refresh method of the object context to refresh the data if a concurrency exception does occur. On this method, you specify a refresh mode and the name of the object or object collection you want to refresh. The refresh mode indicates whether or not changes that have been made to the object or object collection are replaced with the current values in the database.

In some cases, you'll need to know whether a concurrency exception occurred due to the row being deleted or updated. To do that, you can check the EntityState property of the object after it has been refreshed. If the row was deleted, the value of this property will be EntityState.Detached. This state indicates that the object has been removed from the object context. You'll see how this works in the Vendor Maintenance application in this chapter.

If you use stored procedures to perform insert, update, and delete operations, you don't have to set the Concurrency Mode property for the columns whose values you want to check. Instead, the stored procedures should include code that checks the column values. In addition, the stored procedures must return a value that indicates the number of rows that were affected by the operation. Then, if this value is zero, it indicates that a concurrency exception has occurred.

A Try…Catch statement that catches concurrency exceptions

```
Try
    payables.SaveChanges()
Catch ex As OptimisticConcurrencyException
    payables.Refresh(RefreshMode.StoreWins, selectedVendor)
    ...
End Try
```

Code that checks if a concurrency exception occurred due to the row being deleted

```
If selectedVendor.EntityState = EntityState.Detached Then ...
```

Members of the RefreshMode enumeration

Member	Description
ClientWins	Changes made to the objects in the object context are not replaced by the current values in the database.
StoreWins	Changes made to the objects in the object context are replaced by the current values in the database.

Description

- By default, Object Services saves changes made to objects in the object context to the database without checking for concurrency.
- If you want to check columns for concurrency, you can use the Entity Data Model Designer to set the Concurrency Mode property for those columns to Fixed. Then, the original values of the columns will be checked against the current database values to determine if the row has been changed or deleted.
- If you use stored procedures for insert, update, and delete operations, you don't have to set the Concurrency Mode property. Instead, you include parameters in the update and delete stored procedures that check the original values against the current values in the database. In addition, the stored procedures must return a count of the rows that were affected by the operation.
- If an update or delete operation isn't performed because of a concurrency conflict, an OptimisticConcurrencyException is thrown. To handle this exception, you code the SaveChanges method within the Try block of a Try…Catch statement, and you include a Catch block that catches the OptimisticConcurrencyException.
- If a concurrency exception occurs, you can use the Refresh method of the object context to refresh the object or collection of objects that were being updated. On this method, you specify a member of the RefreshMode enumeration.
- To check whether a concurrency exception occurred due to the row being updated or the row being deleted, you can check the EntityState property of the object after it's re-freshed. If the row was deleted, the value of this property will be Detached.
- The Refresh method and the RefreshMode enumeration are members of the System.Data.Objects namespace.

Figure 18-14 How to provide for concurrency

How to use bound controls with entities

When you use the Entity Framework, you can bind controls to an entity collection, to the results of a query, and to an object data source that's created from an entity class. That's what you'll learn next.

How to create an object data source

If you want to bind controls to an object data source that's created from an entity class in an Entity Data Model, you start by creating the object data source. Figure 18-15 shows you how to do that.

First, you start the Data Source Configuration Wizard. To do that, you can right-click in the Data Sources window and select Add New Data Source. Then, you select Object in the first step. Next, you select the entity type you want to use as the data source in the second step o the wizard, shown at the top of this figure. In this example, I've selected the Vendor entity. When you click the Finish button, the Vendor data source will be shown in the Data Sources window. After you create an object data source, you can use it to create bound controls.

How to bind controls

This figure also shows how to bind controls when you use the Entity Framework. To start, you can complex-bind a control to an entity collection as shown in the first example. Here, the first statement sets the DataSource property of a combo box to the entity collection, which is the Vendors collection in the payables object context. Then, the second statement sets the DisplayMember property of the combo box so the Name property of the entity will be displayed in the combo box list. Finally, the third statement sets the ValueMember property of the combo box so the value of the VendorID property of the entity will be used when a name is selected.

When you bind a control to an entity collection, all the rows and columns that the entity is mapped to in the database are retrieved into the object context. If that's not what you want, you can bind the control to the results of a query instead as illustrated in the second example in this figure. Here, only the VendorID and Name columns are retrieved from the database since these are the only two columns that are used by the combo box.

In the first two examples, the combo box is bound directly to the data source through its DataSource property. If a control is created from an object data source, however, you can bind it to the data source by setting the DataSource property of the binding source for the control. If, for example, the DataSource property of a combo box is set to a binding source named VendorBindingSource, you can bind the control as shown in the third example.

The second step of the Data Source Configuration Wizard

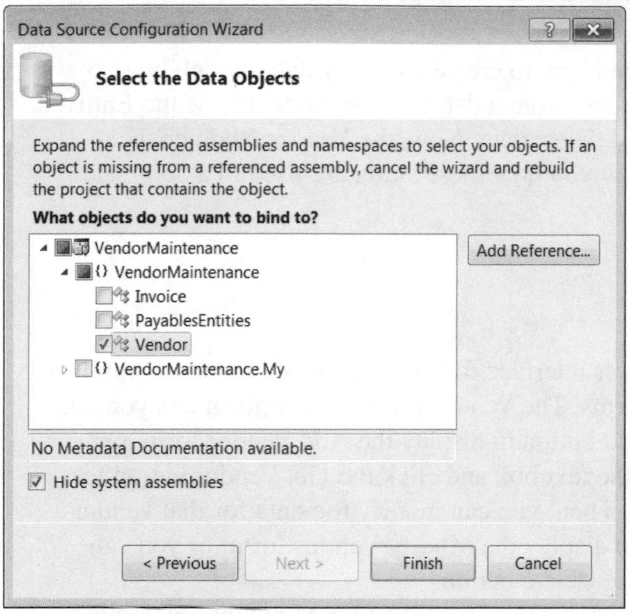

Code that binds a combo box to an entity collection

```
cboVendors.DataSource = payables.Vendors
cboVendors.DisplayMember = "Name"
cboVendors.ValueMember = "VendorID"
```

Code that binds a combo box to the results of a query

```
Dim vendors = From vendor In payables.Vendors
              Order By vendor.Name
              Select vendor.VendorID, vendor.Name

cboVendors.DataSource = vendors
cboVendors.DisplayMember = "Name"
cboVendors.ValueMember = "VendorID"
```

A statement that binds a combo box using its binding source

```
VendorBindingSource.DataSource = vendors
```

Description

- To create an object data source from an Entity Data Model, select the Object option from the first step of the Data Source Configuration Wizard. Then, select the entity type you want to use from the list that's displayed in the second step.
- You can complex-bind a control such as a combo box or a DataGridView control to an entity collection or to the results of a query by setting the DataSource property of the control or the binding source associated with the control to the collection or results.
- You can use bound controls to display, add, modify, and delete data. Then, you can use the SaveChanges method of the object context to save the changes to the database.

Figure 18-15 How to use bound controls with entities

A Vendor Maintenance application

In this chapter, you've learned how to create an entity data model, how to use LINQ to Entities to retrieve data from a database, and how to use the Entity Framework to insert, update, and delete data. Now, the Vendor Maintenance application that follows will show you how these skills are used in a complete application.

The user interface

Figure 18-16 displays the user interface for the Vendor Maintenance application, which consists of two forms. The Vendor Maintenance form lets you add a new vendor by clicking the Add button to display the Add Vendor form. Or, you can enter a vendor ID into the text box and click the Get Vendor button to retrieve the data for that vendor. Then, you can modify the data for that vendor by clicking the Modify button to display the Modify Vendor form, or you can delete that vendor by clicking the Delete button.

This user interface is similar to the one in the Vendor Maintenance application that you saw in chapter 7. But one difference of note is that the form in this application displays the state name rather than the state code. That's possible because of the relationship that's defined between the Vendor and State entities in the Entity Data Model. You'll see this model in the next figure, and you'll see how the relationship between the Vendor and State entities is used in the code for the Vendor Maintenance form.

The Vendor Maintenance Form

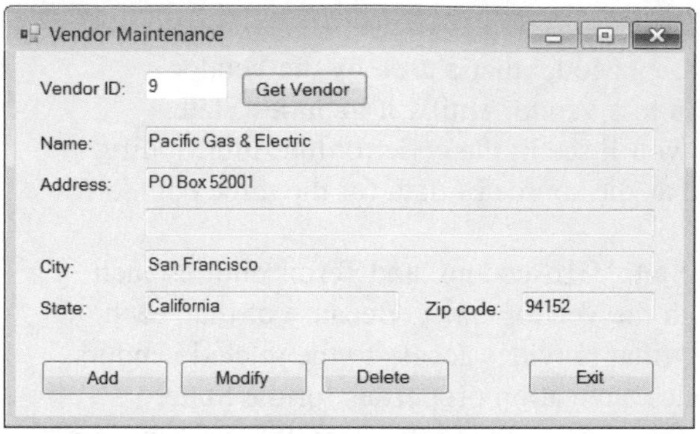

The Add/Modify Vendor form

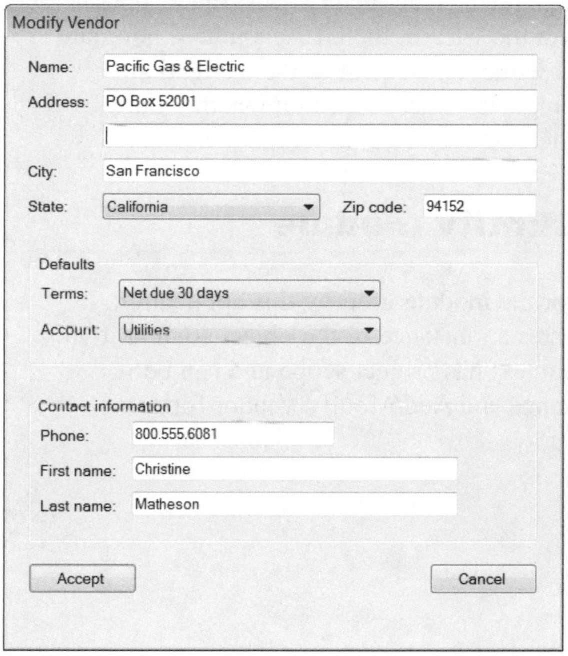

Description

- To add a new vendor, the user clicks the Add button on the Vendor Maintenance form to display a blank Add Vendor form. Then, the user enters the data for the new vendor and clicks the Accept button to return to the Vendor Maintenance form.
- To modify the data for an existing vendor, the user enters the vendor ID and clicks the Get Vendor button to display the basic information for that vendor. Then, the user clicks the Modify button to display the Modify Vendor form, makes the appropriate modifications, and clicks the Accept button to return to the Vendor Maintenance form.
- To delete an existing vendor, the user enters the vendor ID, clicks the Get Vendor button, and then clicks the Delete button.

Figure 18-16 The user interface for the Vendor Maintenance application

The Entity Data Model

Figure 18-17 shows the Entity Data Model that's used by the Vendor Maintenance application. In addition to a Vendor entity, it includes State, GLAccount, and Terms entities. As you'll see in the code for the Add/Modify Vendor form, these entities are used as the source of data for the three combo boxes on the form.

As this the diagram shows, the State, GLAccount, and Terms entities each have a one-to-many relationship with the Vendor entity. Because of that, each entity includes a navigation property that provides access to the related vendors. In addition, the Vendor entity includes navigation properties for the State, GLAccount, and Terms entities that provide access to the state, GL account, and terms for the vendor.

Because I left the Pluralize or Singularize Generated Object Names option checked when I created this model with the wizard, the GLAccount, Vendor and State entities have been given singular names Also, each of the navigation properties have been given plural or singular names, based on whether they refer to a single instance or a collection.

The code for the PayablesEntity module

This figure also shows the code for the module used by this application. It consists of a single statement that creates an instance of the object context. I've used a module for this so the object context has project scope and can be accessed by both the Vendor Maintenance and Add/Modify Vendor forms.

The Entity Data Model for the Vendor Maintenance application

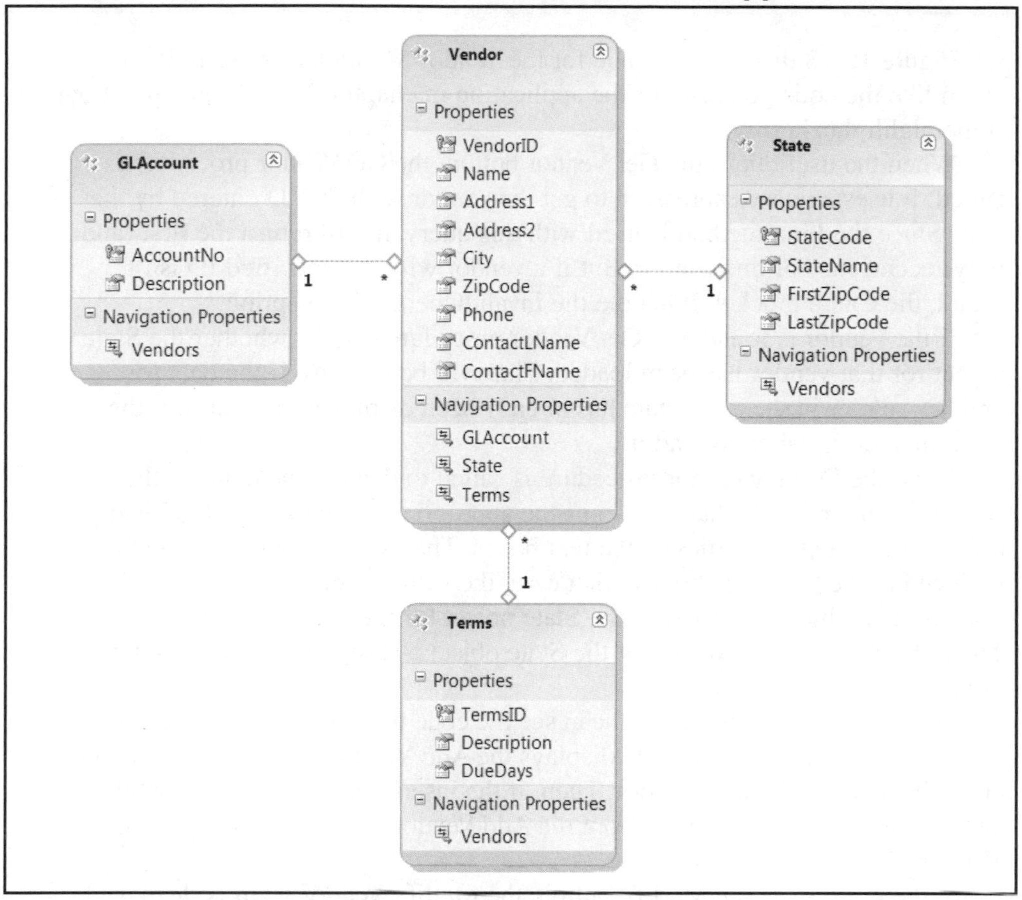

The code for the PayablesEntity module

```
Module PayablesEntity
    Public payables As New PayablesEntities
End Module
```

Description

- The Entity Data Model contains the entity classes that define the entities used by the Vendor Maintenance application. These classes correspond with tables in the Payables database.
- Associations are defined between the Vendor class and the State, GLAccount, and Terms classes based on the foreign keys defined between the related tables in the database.
- The entity and navigation property names have been modified to reflect their singular or plural status.
- The object context that's used by this application is created in the PayablesEntity module so it's available to both the Vendor Maintenance and the Add/Modify Vendor forms.

Figure 18-17 The Entity Data Model and the code for the PayablesEntity module

The code for the Vendor Maintenance form

Figure 18-18 displays the code for the Vendor Maintenance form. It works much like the code you saw for the application in chapter 7, so I'll just point out some highlights here.

When the user clicks the Get Vendor button, the GetVendor procedure is called. It uses a query expression to get the vendor with the ID entered by the user. Since the First method is used with this query, it will return the first (and only) occurrence of this vendor. But if a vendor with the specified ID isn't found, the Catch block will handle the InvalidOperationException.

If the vendor is found, the Get Vendor procedure checks whether the State object for that vendor has been loaded. That will be the case if the data for another vendor in the same state has already been displayed. If it hasn't, the Load method is called to load it.

Next, the DisplayVendor procedure is called to display the data for the selected vendor. To do that, it assigns the appropriate properties of the Vendor object to the Text properties of the text boxes. The exception is the value that's assigned to the State text box. In that case, the value is retrieved from the related State object. That's why the State object for the vendor had to be loaded. Then, the StateName property of the State object is assigned to the State text box.

On page 2 of this listing, you can see the code that's executed if the user clicks the Add button. This code displays the Add Vendor form so the user can enter the data for the new vendor. Then, if the insert operation is successful, the new Vendor object is retrieved from the Add Vendor form and displayed on the Vendor Maintenance form.

If the user clicks the Modify button, the Modify Vendor form is displayed. Then, the processing is determined by the result of that form. If the result is OK, it indicates that the update operation was successful. If it's Retry, it indicates that a concurrency error occurred because the data for the vendor changed. As you'll see in a minute, the Vendor object is refreshed when a concurrency error occurs. Then, the updated or refreshed Vendor object is retrieved from the Modify Vendor form and displayed on the Vendor Maintenance form.

If the result of the Modify Vendor form is Abort, it indicates that a concurrency error occurred because the vendor was deleted. In that case, all the controls on the Vendor Maintenance form are cleared.

On page 3, you can see the code that's executed if the user clicks the Delete button. This code starts by confirming the operation. If it is confirmed, the DeleteObject method of the object context is executed to mark the selected vendor for deletion. Then, the SaveChanges method is executed to delete the vendor from the database, and the controls on the form are cleared.

If a concurrency error occurs, the Vendor object is refreshed with the data in the database. Then, the state of the object is checked to determine if the vendor was updated or deleted. If it was deleted, the state of the object is Detached. In that case, a message is displayed and the controls on the form are cleared. If the object was updated, a message is displayed and the current values are displayed on the form.

The code for the Vendor Maintenance form — Page 1

```
Imports System.Data.Objects

Class frmVendorMaintenance

    Private selectedVendor As Vendor

    Private Sub btnGetVendor_Click(ByVal sender As System.Object,
            ByVal e As System.EventArgs) Handles btnGetVendor.Click
        If Validator.IsPresent(txtVendorID) AndAlso
           Validator.IsInt32(txtVendorID) Then
               Dim vendorID As Integer = CInt(txtVendorID.Text)
               Me.GetVendor(vendorID)
        End If
    End Sub

    Private Sub GetVendor(ByVal vendorID As Integer)
        Try
            selectedVendor = (From vendor In payables.Vendors
                              Where vendor.VendorID = vendorID
                              Select vendor).First
            If Not selectedVendor.StateReference.IsLoaded Then
                selectedVendor.StateReference.Load()
            End If
            Me.DisplayVendor()
        Catch ex As InvalidOperationException
            MessageBox.Show("No vendor found with this ID. " &
                "Please try again.", "Vendor Not Found")
            Me.ClearControls()
            txtVendorID.Select()
        Catch ex As Exception
            MessageBox.Show(ex.Message, ex.GetType.ToString)
        End Try
    End Sub

    Private Sub DisplayVendor()
        txtName.Text = selectedVendor.Name
        txtAddress1.Text = selectedVendor.Address1
        txtAddress2.Text = selectedVendor.Address2
        txtCity.Text = selectedVendor.City
        txtState.Text = selectedVendor.State.StateName
        txtZipCode.Text = selectedVendor.ZipCode
        btnModify.Enabled = True
        btnDelete.Enabled = True
    End Sub
```

Figure 18-18 The code for the Vendor Maintenance form (part 1 of 3)

The code for the Vendor Maintenance form **Page 2**

```
Private Sub ClearControls()
    txtName.Text = ""
    txtAddress1.Text = ""
    txtAddress2.Text = ""
    txtCity.Text = ""
    txtState.Text = ""
    txtZipCode.Text = ""
    btnModify.Enabled = False
    btnDelete.Enabled = False
End Sub

Private Sub btnAdd_Click(ByVal sender As System.Object,
        ByVal e As System.EventArgs) Handles btnAdd.Click
    Dim addModifyVendorForm As New frmAddModifyVendor
    addModifyVendorForm.addVendor = True
    Dim result As DialogResult = addModifyVendorForm.ShowDialog()
    If result = DialogResult.OK Then
        selectedVendor = addModifyVendorForm.vendor
        txtVendorID.Text = selectedVendor.VendorID.ToString
        Me.DisplayVendor()
    End If
End Sub

Private Sub btnModify_Click(ByVal sender As System.Object,
        ByVal e As System.EventArgs) Handles btnModify.Click
    Dim addModifyVendorForm As New frmAddModifyVendor
    addModifyVendorForm.addVendor = False
    addModifyVendorForm.vendor = selectedVendor
    Dim result As DialogResult = addModifyVendorForm.ShowDialog()
    If result = DialogResult.OK OrElse
            result = DialogResult.Retry Then
        selectedVendor = addModifyVendorForm.vendor
        Me.DisplayVendor()
    ElseIf result = DialogResult.Abort Then
        txtVendorID.Text = ""
        Me.ClearControls()
    End If
End Sub
```

Figure 18-18 The code for the Vendor Maintenance form (part 2 of 3)

The code for the Vendor Maintenance form **Page 3**

```
    Private Sub btnDelete_Click(ByVal sender As System.Object,
            ByVal e As System.EventArgs) Handles btnDelete.Click
        Dim result As DialogResult =
            MessageBox.Show("Delete " & selectedVendor.Name & "?",
                "Confirm Delete", MessageBoxButtons.YesNo,
                MessageBoxIcon.Question)
        If result = DialogResult.Yes Then
            Try
                payables.DeleteObject(selectedVendor)
                payables.SaveChanges()
                txtVendorID.Text = ""
                Me.ClearControls()
            Catch ex As OptimisticConcurrencyException
                payables.Refresh(RefreshMode.StoreWins, selectedVendor)
                If selectedVendor.EntityState = EntityState.Detached Then
                    MessageBox.Show("Another user has deleted that vendor.",
                                    "Concurrency Error")
                    txtVendorID.Text = ""
                    Me.ClearControls()
                Else
                    MessageBox.Show("Another user has updated that vendor.",
                                    "Concurrency Error")
                    Me.DisplayVendor()
                End If
            Catch ex As Exception
                MessageBox.Show(ex.Message, ex.GetType.ToString)
            End Try
        End If
    End Sub

    Private Sub btnExit_Click(ByVal sender As System.Object,
            ByVal e As System.EventArgs) Handles btnExit.Click
        Me.Close()
    End Sub

End Class
```

Figure 18-18 The code for the Vendor Maintenance form (part 3 of 3)

The code for the Add/Modify Vendor form

Figure 18-19 shows the code used in the Add/Modify Vendor form. When this form is first loaded, the LoadComboBoxes procedure is called to get the data for the State, Terms, and Account combo boxes. To do that, this procedure uses query expressions that retrieve and sort the required data. Then, the combo boxes are bound to the query results.

If a vendor is being modified, the DisplayVendorData procedure is called to display the data for that vendor. This procedure is similar to the DisplayVendor procedure of the Vendor Maintenance form. It assigns properties of the Vendor object to the Text properties of the text boxes on the form. It also assigns properties of the State, Terms, and GLAccount objects that are accessed through navigation properties of the Vendor object to the SelectedValue properties of the combo boxes on the form.

On page 2 of this listing, you can see the code that's executed if the user clicks the Accept button. This code starts by calling the IsValidData procedure to determine if the data on the form is valid. If the data is valid and a vendor is being added, a new Vendor object is created, the PutVendorData procedure is called to set its property values, and the AddToVendors method of the object context is called to add the Vendor object to the Vendors collection. Finally, the SaveChanges method is executed to add the vendor to the database, and the DialogResult property of the form is set to DialogResult.OK.

If the vendor is being modified, the PutVendorData procedure is called to update the properties of the Vendor object. Then, the SaveChanges method is executed to update the database. If this method is successful, the DialogResult property of the form is set to DialogResult.OK. If a concurrency error occurs, however, the Vendor object is refreshed with the data in the database. Then, the state of the object is checked to determine if the vendor was updated or deleted, an appropriate message is displayed, and the DialogResult property of the form is set accordingly.

On page 3 of this listing, you can see the IsValidData procedure. Here, you should notice the statement that follows the last call to the IsPresent method. This statement retrieves the State object for the vendor from the State combo box using its SelectedItem property. Then, it uses the FirstZipCode and LastZipCode properties of that object to check that the zip code the user entered is valid for the state.

The PutVendorData procedure also uses this technique to get the State, Terms, and GLAccount objects for the vendor. Then, it sets the State, Terms, and GLAccount navigation properties of the Vendor object to these objects. That way, the appropriate values will be saved in the State, DefaultTermsID, and DefaultAccountNo columns of the row in the Vendors table.

The code for the Add/Modify Vendor form — Page 1

```
Imports System.Data.Objects

Public Class frmAddModifyVendor

    Public addVendor As Boolean
    Public vendor As Vendor

    Private Sub frmAddModifyVendor_Load(ByVal sender As System.Object,
            ByVal e As System.EventArgs) Handles MyBase.Load

        Me.LoadComboBoxes()

        If addVendor Then
            Me.Text = "Add Vendor"
            cboStates.SelectedIndex = -1
            cboTerms.SelectedIndex = -1
            cboAccounts.SelectedIndex = -1
        Else
            Me.Text = "Modify Vendor"
            Me.DisplayVendorData()
        End If
    End Sub

    Private Sub LoadComboBoxes()
        Try
            Dim states = From state In payables.States
                         Order By state.StateName
            cboStates.DataSource = states
            cboStates.DisplayMember = "StateName"
            cboStates.ValueMember = "StateCode"

            Dim terms = From term In payables.Terms
                        Order By term.Description
            cboTerms.DataSource = terms
            cboTerms.DisplayMember = "Description"
            cboTerms.ValueMember = "TermsID"

            Dim accounts = From account In payables.GLAccounts
                           Order By account.Description
            cboAccounts.DataSource = accounts
            cboAccounts.DisplayMember = "Description"
            cboAccounts.ValueMember = "AccountNo"
        Catch ex As Exception
            MessageBox.Show(ex.Message, ex.GetType.ToString)
        End Try
    End Sub

    Private Sub DisplayVendorData()
        txtName.Text = vendor.Name
        txtAddress1.Text = vendor.Address1
        txtAddress2.Text = vendor.Address2
        txtCity.Text = vendor.City
```

Figure 18-19 The code for the Add/Modify Vendor form (part 1 of 3)

The code for the Add/Modify Vendor form **Page 2**

```
        cboStates.SelectedValue = vendor.State.StateCode
        txtZipCode.Text = vendor.ZipCode
        cboTerms.SelectedValue = vendor.Terms.TermsID
        cboAccounts.SelectedValue = vendor.GLAccount.AccountNo
        If vendor.Phone = "" Then
            txtPhone.Text = ""
        Else
            txtPhone.Text = FormattedPhoneNumber(vendor.Phone)
        End If
        txtFirstName.Text = vendor.ContactFName
        txtLastName.Text = vendor.ContactLName
    End Sub

    Private Function FormattedPhoneNumber(ByVal phone As String) As String
        Return phone.Substring(0, 3) & "." &
               phone.Substring(3, 3) & "." &
               phone.Substring(6, 4)
    End Function

    Private Sub btnAccept_Click(ByVal sender As System.Object,
            ByVal e As System.EventArgs) Handles btnAccept.Click
        If IsValidData() Then
            If addVendor Then
                vendor = New Vendor
                Me.PutVendorData(vendor)
                payables.AddToVendors(vendor)
                Try
                    payables.SaveChanges()
                    Me.DialogResult = DialogResult.OK
                Catch ex As Exception
                    MessageBox.Show(ex.Message, ex.GetType.ToString)
                End Try
            Else
                Me.PutVendorData(vendor)
                Try
                    payables.SaveChanges()
                    Me.DialogResult = DialogResult.OK
                Catch ex As OptimisticConcurrencyException
                    payables.Refresh(RefreshMode.StoreWins, vendor)
                    If vendor.EntityState = EntityState.Detached Then
                        MessageBox.Show("Another user has deleted " &
                                        "that vendor.", "Concurrency Error")
                        Me.DialogResult = DialogResult.Abort
                    Else
                        MessageBox.Show("Another user has updated " &
                                        "that vendor.", "Concurrency Error")
                        Me.DialogResult = DialogResult.Retry
                    End If
                Catch ex As Exception
                    MessageBox.Show(ex.Message, ex.GetType.ToString)
                End Try
            End If
        End If
    End Sub
```

Figure 18-19 The code for the Add/Modify Vendor form (part 2 of 3)

The code for the Add/Modify Vendor form Page 3

```
    Private Function IsValidData() As Boolean
        If Validator.IsPresent(txtName) AndAlso
           Validator.IsPresent(txtAddress1) AndAlso
           Validator.IsPresent(txtCity) AndAlso
           Validator.IsPresent(cboStates) AndAlso
           Validator.IsPresent(txtZipCode) AndAlso
           Validator.IsInt32(txtZipCode) AndAlso
           Validator.IsPresent(cboTerms) AndAlso
           Validator.IsPresent(cboAccounts) Then
            Dim state As State = CType(cboStates.SelectedItem, State)
            If Validator.IsStateZipCode(txtZipCode, state.FirstZipCode,
                                        state.LastZipCode) Then
                If txtPhone.Text <> "" Then
                    If Validator.IsPhoneNumber(txtPhone) Then
                        Return True
                    Else
                        Return False
                    End If
                Else
                    Return True
                End If
            Else
                Return False
            End If
        Else
            Return False
        End If
    End Function

    Private Sub PutVendorData(ByVal vendor As Vendor)
        vendor.Name = txtName.Text
        vendor.Address1 = txtAddress1.Text
        vendor.Address2 = txtAddress2.Text
        vendor.City = txtCity.Text
        Dim state As State = CType(cboStates.SelectedItem, State)
        vendor.State = state
        vendor.ZipCode = txtZipCode.Text
        Dim terms As Terms = CType(cboTerms.SelectedItem, Terms)
        vendor.Terms = terms
        Dim account As GLAccount = CType(cboAccounts.SelectedItem, GLAccount)
        vendor.GLAccount = account
        vendor.Phone = txtPhone.Text.Replace(".", "")
        vendor.ContactFName = txtFirstName.Text
        vendor.ContactLName = txtLastName.Text
    End Sub

End Class
```

Figure 18-19 The code for the Add/Modify Vendor form (part 3 of 3)

Perspective

Now that you've completed this chapter, you should be able to develop simple applications that use the Entity Framework along with LINQ to Entities. You should also appreciate the benefits of using the Entity Framework.

In particular, when you create an Entity Data Model, the framework generates all of the properties and methods that you need for working with the entities. This means that you can work directly with the entities so you don't have to use SQL to work with the database. This also means that you write a minimum of code so you can develop applications faster.

Of course, there's a lot more to learn about the Entity Framework, including how to use Entity SQL and query builder methods. But the goal here is to get you started with the Entity Framework and to help you decide whether you like the idea of using it for developing your own applications.

Terms

Entity Framework
Entity Data Model
Object Services
EntityClient
conceptual model
storage model
entity
mappings
Entity Data Model Designer
Entity Designer
entity class
association
scalar property
navigation property
Model Browser window
Mapping Details window
function import
object context

Exercise 18-1 Create an Entity Data Model

In this exercise, you'll create an Entity Data Model. Then, you'll use the Model Browser and Mapping Details windows to view the model and the mappings.

Create the Entity Data Model

1. Start a new project named InvoiceDataModel in your chapter 18 directory. Then, use the Entity Data Model Wizard as described in figures 18-2 and 18-3 to create an Entity Data Model named payables that includes the Invoices, InvoiceLineItems, GLAccounts, and Terms tables plus the spGetInvoicesDue stored procedure from the Payables database.
2. Review the entities in the Entity Data Model Designer. In particular, notice the navigation properties that are defined for each table and the associations between the tables.

Use the Mapping Details window

3. Display the Mapping Details window. Then, select the Invoice entity in the Entity Data Model, and review its mappings.
4. Click on <Add a Condition> and then on the drop-down arrow that's displayed. Select the PaymentDate column, select Is for the operator, and select Null for the condition to restrict the invoices that are retrieved to only those for which payments haven't been received.
5. Rebuild the Solution and notice the error that's displayed. Then, delete the mapping between the PaymentDate column and the Value/Property from the Invoice entity. Rebuild the solution and check the project Error List to see if any error conditions remain.
6. If you left the box for Include Foreign Key Columns in the Model checked when you used the wizard (as recommended), you will see a further error. In the Entity Designer, select the PaymentDate property of the Invoice entity and delete it. Rebuild the solution and check that the error condition has been fixed.

Use the Model Browser window

7. Display the Model Browser window, and expand the Entity Types folder in the node for the conceptual model. Then, click on any entity to see that its mappings are displayed in the Mapping Details window.
8. Expand the Stored Procedures folder in the node for the storage model so you can see the stored procedure that you selected in step 1. Then, create a function import for the stored procedure as described in figure 18-8. Set the return type of the function import to the Invoice entity.
9. Open the EntityContainer node and then the Function Import folder in the node for the conceptual model to see that the stored procedure is now included in this model.
10. Close the Entity Designer, then close the solution.

Exercise 18-2 Develop the Vendor Maintenance application

In this exercise, you'll write code that uses an Entity Data Model in a Vendor Maintenance application to retrieve, insert, update, and delete data from the Vendors table. Because I want you to focus on the skills presented in this chapter, the Entity Data Model, the user interface, and much of the surrounding code has been written for you. To help you identify where you need to add code, the starter project has been marked to show where the code for each step needs to be added.

Review the application and add a module

1. Open the project that's in the Chapter 18\VendorMaintenance directory. This project contains the Entity Data Model, forms, and starting code for the Vendor Maintenance application.

2. Review the Entity Data Model and notice the names it uses for the entities and navigation properties.
3. Add a module named PayablesEntity to the project. Declare a public variable named payables within this class and assign an instance of the object context class to it.
4. Save the changes and then close the module.

Add the code to retrieve a vendor

5. Display the code for the Vendor Maintenance form.
6. Add a query to the GetVendor method that retrieves the data for the vendor with the ID that's entered in the Vendor ID text box, and assign the result to the selectedVendor class variable.
7. Add code to the GetVendor method that checks if the State object has been loaded and that loads it if it hasn't.
8. Run the application, enter 9 for the vendor ID, and click the Get Vendor button. If you coded the query correctly, the information for that vendor will be displayed on the form as shown at the top of figure 18-16.

Add the code to load the combo boxes on the Add/Modify Vendor form

9. Display the code for the Add/Modify Vendor form.
10. Add a query to the LoadComboBoxes procedure that retrieves the required data from the States table and sorts the results by state name. Do the same for the Terms and GLAccounts tables, but sort the results by description. Then, bind the three combo boxes on the form to the results of the appropriate query.
11. Run the application, retrieve the data for vendor ID 9, and then click the Modify button to display the Modify Vendor form. Then, display the lists for the three combo boxes to be sure they were loaded correctly.

Add the code to add a new vendor

12. Add code to the event handler for the Click event of the Accept button that adds a new vendor to the Vendors collection of the object context and then updates the database.
13. Run the application and click the Add button on the Vendor Maintenance form to display the Add Vendor form.
14. Enter the data for a new vendor and then click the Accept button to return to the Vendor Maintenance form. Make a note of the ID for the new vendor and then end the application.

Add the code to modify a vendor

15. Add a statement to the event handler for the Click event of the Accept button that updates the database when changes are made to a vendor.
16. Run the application, enter the ID for the vendor you added in step 14, and click the Get Vendor button.
17. Click the Modify button to display the Modify Vendor form. Make one or more changes to the vendor's address, accept the changes, and make sure the changes are reflected on the Vendor Maintenance form.

Add the code to delete a vendor

18. Return to the code for the Vendor Maintenance form. Then, add code to the event handler for the Click event of the Delete button to mark the selected vendor for deletion and to delete the vendor from the database.
19. Run the application, enter the ID for the vendor you added in step 14 and modified in step 17, and click the Get Vendor button.
20. Click the Delete button and then click Yes when you're asked to confirm the operation. The data for the vendor should be cleared from the form.
21. Enter the same vendor ID and click the Get Vendor button to confirm that the vendor has been deleted.

Add the code to handle concurrency conflicts

22. At this point, the application can perform the basic retrieval, insert, update, and delete operations. Now, you just need to add code for handling concurrency conflicts to the event handler for the click event of the Accept button in the Add/Modify Vendor form and to the event handler for the click event of the Delete button in the Vendor Maintenance form.
23. When you've added the concurrency handling code, test the application again. When you're done, close the solution.

Appendix A

How to install and use the software and files for this book

To develop the Windows Forms applications presented in this book, you need to have Visual Studio 2010 or Visual Basic 2010 Express Edition installed on your system. To develop the web applications presented in this book, you need to have Visual Studio 2010 or Visual Web Developer 2010 Express Edition installed on your system. If you're going to install the database for this book on your own PC rather than on a remote server, you also need to install SQL Server or SQL Server Express on your PC.

This appendix shows you how to install Visual Studio 2010 or the Express Editions. It also shows how to install SQL Server 2008 R2 Express and how to use it with our database. But first, it shows you how to download, install, and use the files for this book.

How to download, install, and use the files for this book

Figure A-1 shows you how to download the files for this book from our web site. These files are in a single download that installs four subdirectories within this directory: C:\Murach\ADO.NET 4 VB.

The Book Applications directory contains all of the applications that are presented in this book. To open these applications, you can use the techniques in this figure. Then, you can view the source code for these applications, and you can run them to see how they work. Note that all of the web applications were developed as file-system applications, so you don't need IIS to run them. You should also note that before you can run a web application, you must set the start page for the application.

The Exercise Starts directory contains the starting applications for the exercises in this book. After the setup file installs the download, it copies the subdirectories in the Exercise Starts directory to a new directory named C:\ADO.NET 4 VB. This directory contains one subdirectory for each chapter that has one or more exercises, and the starting applications are stored in the chapter subdirectories. Then, if you want to restore one of the starting applications, you can copy it from the Exercise Starts directory to the appropriate chapter subdirectory in the C:\ADO.NET 4 VB directory.

The Exercise Solutions directory contains the solutions for the exercises in the book. That way, you can check your solutions against the book solutions. You can also refer to a solution if you can't figure out how to do some aspect of an exercise.

The Database directory contains the files that create and install the Payables database that's used throughout this book. It also contains a PDF named Troubleshooting Tips that you can refer to if you have any problems when you install the database. Figure A-4 describes how to use these files.

What the downloadable files for this book contain

- All of the applications that are presented in this book including the source code.
- The starting applications for all of the exercises, which we call "Exercise starts."
- The solutions to the exercises.
- The files for creating the Payables database that's used by the book applications and exercises, plus a PDF named "Troubleshooting Tips" that will help you if you have any problems installing the database.

How to download and install the files for this book

- Go to www.murach.com, and go to the page for *Murach's ADO.NET 4 with VB 2010.*
- Click the link for "FREE download of the book applications." Then, select the "All book files" link and respond to the resulting dialog boxes. This will download a setup file named d4vb_allfiles.exe onto your hard drive.
- Use the Windows Explorer to find the setup file on your hard drive. Then, double-click this file and respond to the dialog boxes that follow.
- This installs the subdirectories and files in C:\Murach\ADO.NET 4 VB. The subdirectories are Book Applications, Exercise Starts, Exercise Solutions, and Database.

How your system is prepared for doing the exercises

- After the setup file installs the files in the download, it runs a batch file named exercise_starts_setup.bat that copies the applications for the exercise starts from C:\Murach\ADO.NET 4 VB\Exercise Starts to C:\ADO.NET 4 VB directory. Then, you can open and work with these applications, which are stored in subdirectories that range from Chapter 03 to Chapter 18.

How to view the source code for the book applications

- The source code for the book applications is in C:\Murach\ADO.NET 4 VB\Book Applications.
- To open a Windows Forms application like those for chapters 3-10 and 15-18, you use the File→Open Project command.
- To open a web application like those for chapters 11-14, you use the File→Open Web Site command.

How to prepare your system for using the database

- To use the database that comes with this book on your PC, you need to make sure that SQL Server 2008, SQL Server 2008 R2, SQL Server 2008 Express, or SQL Server 2008 R2 Express is installed as described in figure A-3.
- Then, you need to run the batch file in the Database subdirectory to create the database and attach it to SQL Server Express as described in figure A-4.

Figure A-1 How to download, install, and use the files for this book

How to install Visual Studio 2010 or the Express Editions

If you've installed Windows applications before, you shouldn't have any trouble installing Visual Studio 2010. You simply insert the DVD or the first CD and the setup program starts automatically. The setup program will lead you through the steps for installing Visual Studio as summarized in figure A-2.

When you click the Install Microsoft Visual Studio 2010 link, the setup program starts loading the installation components it needs. Then, after you click the Next button and accept the license terms, the program lets you select the type of installation. In most cases, you'll perform a full installation so all the available features are installed, including the .NET Framework, Visual Studio, Visual Basic, and SQL Server Express 2008.

When the installation is complete, you will have the opportunity to install the documentation for Visual Studio on your local system. If you don't do that, the default will be to use the documentation that's available online. However, you can change this default later by using the Help Library Manager from within Visual Studio.

The final setup step is to apply any updates that have become available since Visual Studio 2010 was released. However, if you don't do this step, you can check for updates from within Visual Studio by using the Help→Check for Updates command. In fact, you should do this periodically to be sure that Visual Studio is up-to-date.

If you're going to use the Visual Basic 2010 Express Edition, you can download it for free from Microsoft's site as summarized in this figure. After you've installed Visual Basic 2010 Express, the Microsoft web page will invite you to download both SQL Server 2008 R 2 Express, which you will need throughout this book, and Visual Web Developer 2010 Express, which you can use for the web projects in section 4 of this book. If you don't already have SQL Server 2008 installed on your machine, even if you have SQL Server 2005 or an earlier edition, I recommend that you accept this option and download the new version.

The Visual Studio 2010 setup program

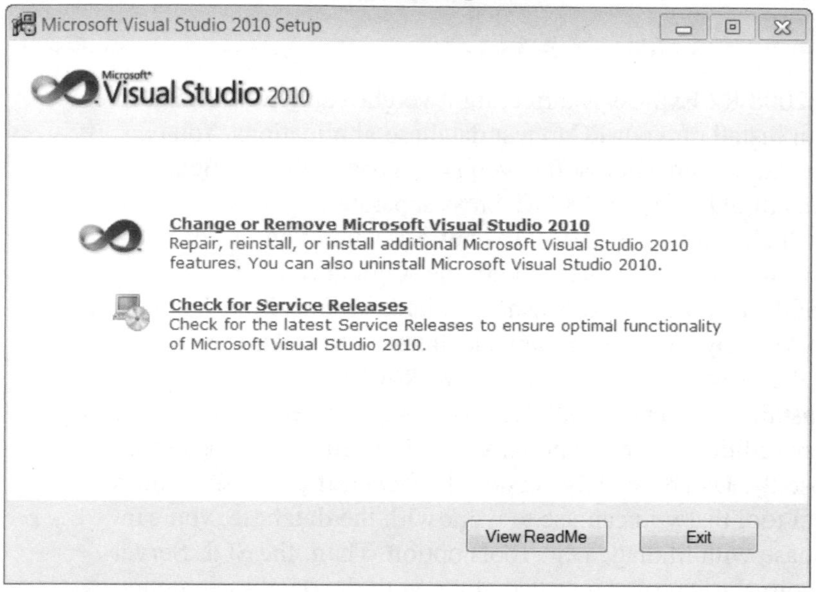

How to install Visual Studio 2010

- Insert the installation DVD or Disc 1 of the installation CDs. The setup program will start automatically.
- Click the Install Microsoft Visual Studio 2010 link and follow the instructions. When the Options page is displayed, you can accept the Full option unless you have special requirements. When the Finish page is displayed, you can click the Install Documentation button to install the Visual Studio documentation on your local system.
- To install any updates that are available, click the Check for Service Releases link.

How to install the Express Editions of Visual Basic and Web Developer

1. Go to the page on Microsoft's web site for the download of Visual Basic 2010 Express or Visual Web Developer 2010 Express and follow the directions to install the programs.
2. They work similarly to the setup program for Visual Studio 2010, but Visual Basic 2010 Express has fewer installation options, and Visual Web Developer uses Microsoft's Web Platform for the installation process.

Description

- The Visual Studio 2010 Setup program installs not only Visual Studio, but also the .NET Framework 4, the development web server, and SQL Server 2008 Express.
- The setup program for Microsoft Visual Basic 2010 Express offers the option of installing SQL Server 2008 R2 Express and Visual Web Developer 2010 Express at the end of the installation process.

Figure A-2 How to install Visual Studio 2010 or the Express Editions

How to install and use SQL Server 2008 R2 Express

SQL Server 2008 R2 Express is a free, lightweight version of SQL Server 2008 that you can install on your PC to test database applications. You can download and install it from Microsoft's web site, as described in figure A-3.

When you install SQL Server 2008 Express separately, you will get the newest release, which is Release 2 (R2). In contrast, when you install SQL Server 2008 Express as part of Visual Studio, the original release is installed. That's because SQL Server 2008 R2 wasn't available when Visual Studio 2010 was released. Fortunately, you use the same techniques to work with both releases, and all the projects in this book will work with either release.

When you install SQL Server 2008 R2 Express separately, you can choose from four different editions. For this book, you only need the database engine, so you can choose the Database Only version. However, if you also want to install a graphical tool that you can use to work with the database, you can choose the Database with Management Tools option. Then, the SQL Server Management Studio Basic tool is installed along with the database engine. Note, however, that the use of this tool isn't covered in this book, although it can be helpful when troubleshooting database installations.

You may also be able to upgrade an instance of SQL Server 2000 or 2005 to 2008 R2. To do that, select the "Upgrade from SQL Server 2000 or 2005" option from the SQL Server Installation Center dialog box. If you do this, though, any existing databases will run as if they're still running under SQL Server 2000 or 2005.

If you install SQL Server 2008 R2 alongside another instance of SQL Server, each instance must have a different name. So if you have a 2005 instance named SQLEXPRESS, you'll need to give the 2008 instance another name like SQLEXPRESS2008. In that case, you'll need to modify the applications in this book to use that name since they assume you're using an instance named SQLEXPRESS.

After you install SQL Server Express, you can use the SQL Server Configuration Manager shown at the top of this figure to work with the server. In particular, you can use it to start, continue, pause, or stop the SQL Server engine. By default, SQL Server is started each time you start your PC. If that's not what you want, you can display the Properties dialog box for the server, click the Service tab, click on the Start Mode option, and select Manual from the drop-down list in the right column. Then, you can start SQL Server whenever you need it by using the Configuration Manager.

The SQL Server Configuration Manager

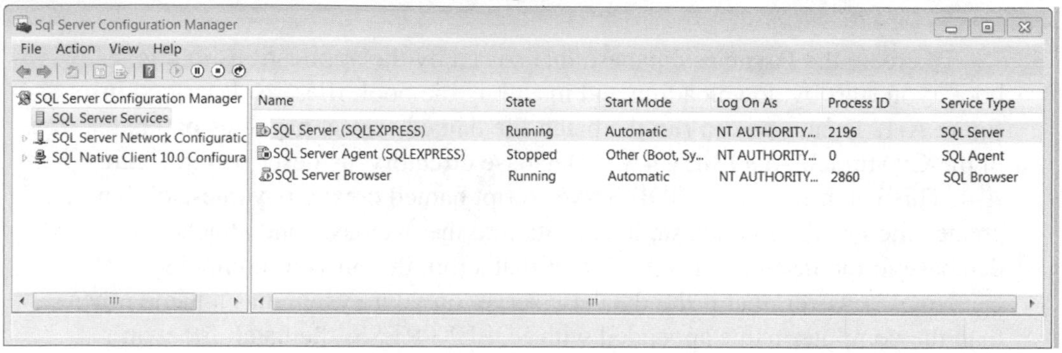

How to install SQL Server 2008 R2 Express

- If you choose not to install SQL Server 2008 when you install one of the retail versions of Visual Studio, you can download the setup file for SQL Server 2008 R2 Express from Microsoft's web site for free. To install just the database engine, download the SQL Server 2008 R2 Express (Database only) option. To install the database engine and SQL Server Management Studio Express, download the Database with Management Tools option.
- When the download has finished, run the setup program. Then, when the SQL Server Installation Center dialog box is displayed, select the Installation option, select the "New installation or add feature to an existing installation" option to start the SQL Server 2008 R2 Setup wizard, and respond to the resulting dialog boxes.
- At the Feature Selection step, select all available features.
- At the Instance Configuration step, create a named instance with SQLEXPRESS as the name.
- At the Server Configuration step, select NT AUTHORITY\SYSTEM as the account name for the SQL Server Database Engine service to run SQL Server on your computer.
- At the Database Engine Configuration step, you can accept the default setting of Windows Authentication Mode. You can also click the Add Current User button to add the current user as a SQL Server administrator.

How to use SQL Server 2008 R2 Express

- After you install SQL Server 2008 R2 Express, it will start each time you start your PC. To start or stop this service or change its start mode, start the SQL Server Configuration Manager: Start→All Programs→Microsoft SQL Server 2008 R2→Configuration Tools→SQL Server Configuration Manager. Then, select the server in the right pane, and use the toolbar buttons.
- The setup program creates a copy of SQL Server with a name that consists of your computer name followed by a backslash and the name you enter in the Instance Configuration step of the wizard. You can use this name to define connections to the databases that you use with this server.

Figure A-3 How to install and use SQL Server 2008 R2 Express

How to create the Payables database for this book

To create the Payables database that's used by the applications in this book, you start by downloading and installing the book files, as described in figure A-1. Then, you can run the batch file named create_payables.bat that's in the C:\Murach\ADO.NET 4 VB\Database directory, as described in figure A-4. This batch file runs a SQL Server script named create_payables.sql that creates the Payables database, loads data into the database, and attaches the database to the instance of SQL Server that's running on your computer.

Note, however, that if the database server on your system has a name other than the computer name appended with SQLEXPRESS, the batch file won't work. However, you can easily change it so it will work. To do that, just open the file in a text editor such as Notepad. When you do, you'll see a single command with this server specification:

```
sqlcmd -S localhost\SQLExpress -E /i create_PayablesDatabase.sql
```

Then, you just change this specification to the name of your server.

As the batch file runs, it displays the details of its progress in a Command Prompt window, as shown in this figure. If any errors occur, details of these errors will be displayed in the window. Then, you can resolve the problems and run the batch file again. If you need help resolving the problems, you can refer to the Troubleshooting Tips PDF that's in the Database directory for the downloaded files.

Although you don't need to know the details of the SQL Server script that creates the Payables database, you should realize that it uses SQL statements to create the tables of the database and to insert data into the rows of these tables. You should also know that this script starts by deleting the Payables database if it already exists. That's why you can recreate the Payables database and restore its original data by running the batch file again.

The output for a successful installation in the Command Prompt window

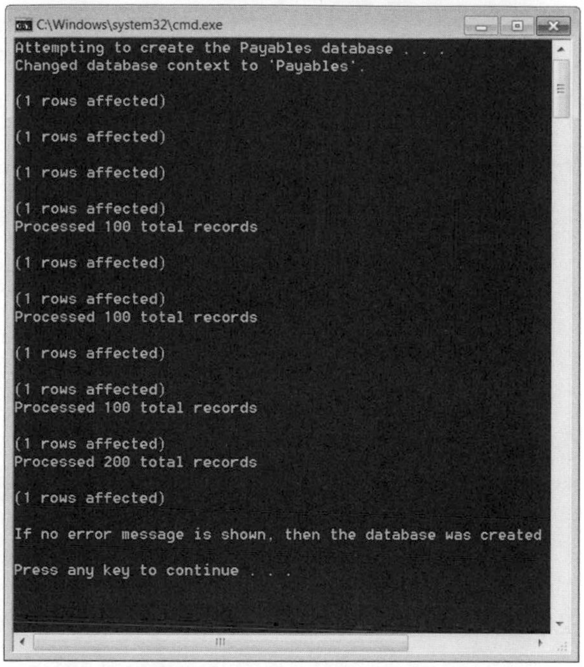

How to create the Payables database

- In Windows Explorer, navigate to the C:\Murach\ADO.NET 4 VB\Database directory and double-click on the create_payables.bat file. As this file runs, the Command Window displays progress and the details of any errors it encounters.
- The batch file runs the create_payables.sql file that creates the database and inserts the data into the tables.
- The .sql file creates two database files named Payables.mdf and Payables_log.ldf and stores them in the default data directory for your instance of SQL Server. For SQL Server 2008 R2 Express, that directory will typically be:

  `C:\Program files\Microsoft SQL Server\MSSQL10.SQLEXPRESS\MSSQL\DATA`
- If no error message is displayed in the Command Prompt window, the database has been successfully created.

How to recreate the Payables database and restore the original data

- Redo the procedure for creating the Payables database.

How to get help if something goes wrong

- Read the PDF named Troubleshooting Tips that's stored in the Database directory.

Description

- The .sql file starts by deleting the Payables database if it already exists. Then, it creates the Payables database. That's why you can use the batch file to both create and restore the database.

Figure A-4 How to create the Payables database for this book

Index

B

C

D

E

F

G

H

I

J

K

L

M

N

O

P

Q

R

S

T

U

V

W

XYZ